D0027888

Received On:

APR 16 2019

Ballard Branch

NO LONGER PROPERTY OF
SEATTLE PUBLIC LIBRARY

USA'S BEST TRIPS

51 AMAZING ROAD TRIPS

Simon Richmond, Kate Armstrong, Carolyn Bain, Amy C Balfour, Ray Bartlett, Loren Bell, Sara Benson, Celeste Brash, Gregor Clark, Michael Grosberg, Ashley Harrell, Mark Johanson, Adam Karlin, Brian Kluepfel, Stephen Lioy, Carolyn McCarthy, Hugh McNaughtan, Becky Ohlsen, Christopher Pitts, Kevin Raub, Brendan Sainsbury, Regis St Louis, Ryan Ver Berkmoes, Mara Vorhees, Benedict Walker, Karla Zimmerman

SYMBOLS IN THIS BOOK

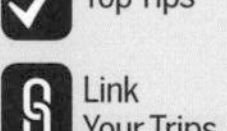

- Top Tips
- History & Culture
- Essential Photo
- Link Your Trips
- Family
- Walking Tour
- Tips from Locals
- Food & Drink
- Eating
- Trip Detour
- Outdoors
- Sleeping

- Telephone Number
- Opening Hours
- Parking
- Nonsmoking
- Air-Conditioning
- Internet Access
- Wi-Fi Access
- Vegetarian Selection
- Swimming Pool
- English-Language Menu
- Family-Friendly
- Pet-Friendly

MAP LEGEND

Routes
- Trip Route
- Trip Detour
- Linked Trip
- Walk Route
- Tollway
- Freeway
- Primary
- Secondary
- Tertiary
- Lane
- Unsealed Road
- Plaza/Mall
- Steps
- Tunnel
- Pedestrian Overpass
- Walk Track/Path

Boundaries
- International
- State/Province
- Cliff

Hydrography
- River/Creek
- Intermittent River
- Swamp/Mangrove
- Canal
- Water
- Dry/Salt/Intermittent Lake
- Glacier

Route Markers
- 97 US National Hwy
- 5 US Interstate Hwy
- 44 State Hwy

Trips
- 1 Trip Numbers
- 9 Trip Stop
- Walking tour
- Trip Detour

Population
- Capital (National)
- Capital (State/Province)
- City/Large Town
- Town/Village

Areas
- Beach
- Cemetery (Christian)
- Cemetery (Other)
- Park
- Forest
- Reservation
- Urban Area
- Sportsground

Transport
- Airport
- BART station
- Boston T station
- Cable Car/Funicular
- Metro/Muni station
- Parking
- Subway station
- Train/Railway
- Tram
- Underground station

Note: Not all symbols displayed above appear on the maps in this book

PLAN YOUR TRIP

ON THE ROAD

CONTENTS

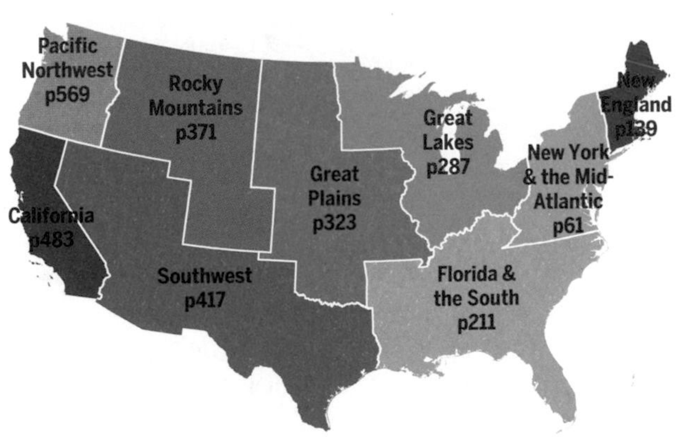

Pacific Northwest p569
Rocky Mountains p371
New England p139
Great Lakes p287
New York & the Mid-Atlantic p61
Great Plains p323
California p483
Southwest p417
Florida & the South p211

Contents cont.

ROAD TRIP ESSENTIALS

Classic Trips

Look out for the Classic Trips stamp on our favorite routes in this book.

WELCOME TO THE USA

Fill up the gas tank and buckle up – the USA is an unforgettably crazy trip. And there's no better way to get to know this enormous, energetic and engaging country than by hitting the road, Jack.

With this book as your travel companion, you can drive up, down, across or straight through every state on the continental map. If you're on the hunt for that perfect California seafood shack, Texas hill-country swimming hole or New England ivy-clad college town, we've got you covered.

Whether you want to dive into the wildest terrain or connect the dots between the USA's brightest, most buzzing cities, you'll find a trip designed just for you in this book. And if you've only got time for one journey, pick from our 15 Classic Trips, which take you on a tour of the very best of the USA. Turn the page for more.

Bixby Creek Bridge, Monterey, CA
PHITHA TANPAIROJ / SHUTTERSTOCK ©

THE USA HIGHLIGHTS

Classic Trip 46

Cascade Drive Wild West towns, Bavarian villages and moody mountains. **4–5 DAYS**

Classic Trip 29

Grand Teton to Yellowstone Outstanding wildlife, gushing geysers and alpine scenery. **7 DAYS**

Classic Trip 49

Highway 101 Oregon Coast Diversions include whale-watching, lighthouses and seafood. **7 DAYS**

Classic Trip 40

Pacific Coast Highways The ultimate coastal road trip takes in beaches, redwood forests and more. **7–10 DAYS**

Classic Trip 2

Four Corners Cruise Loop past the Southwest's biggest and boldest parks and sights. **10 DAYS**

Classic Trip 33

Fantastic Canyon Voyage Cowboy up in Wickenburg, then applaud the Grand Canyon. **4–5 DAYS**

Classic Trip 39

California's Greatest Hits & Las Vegas Epic trip from the Golden State to Las Vegas. **12–15 DAYS**

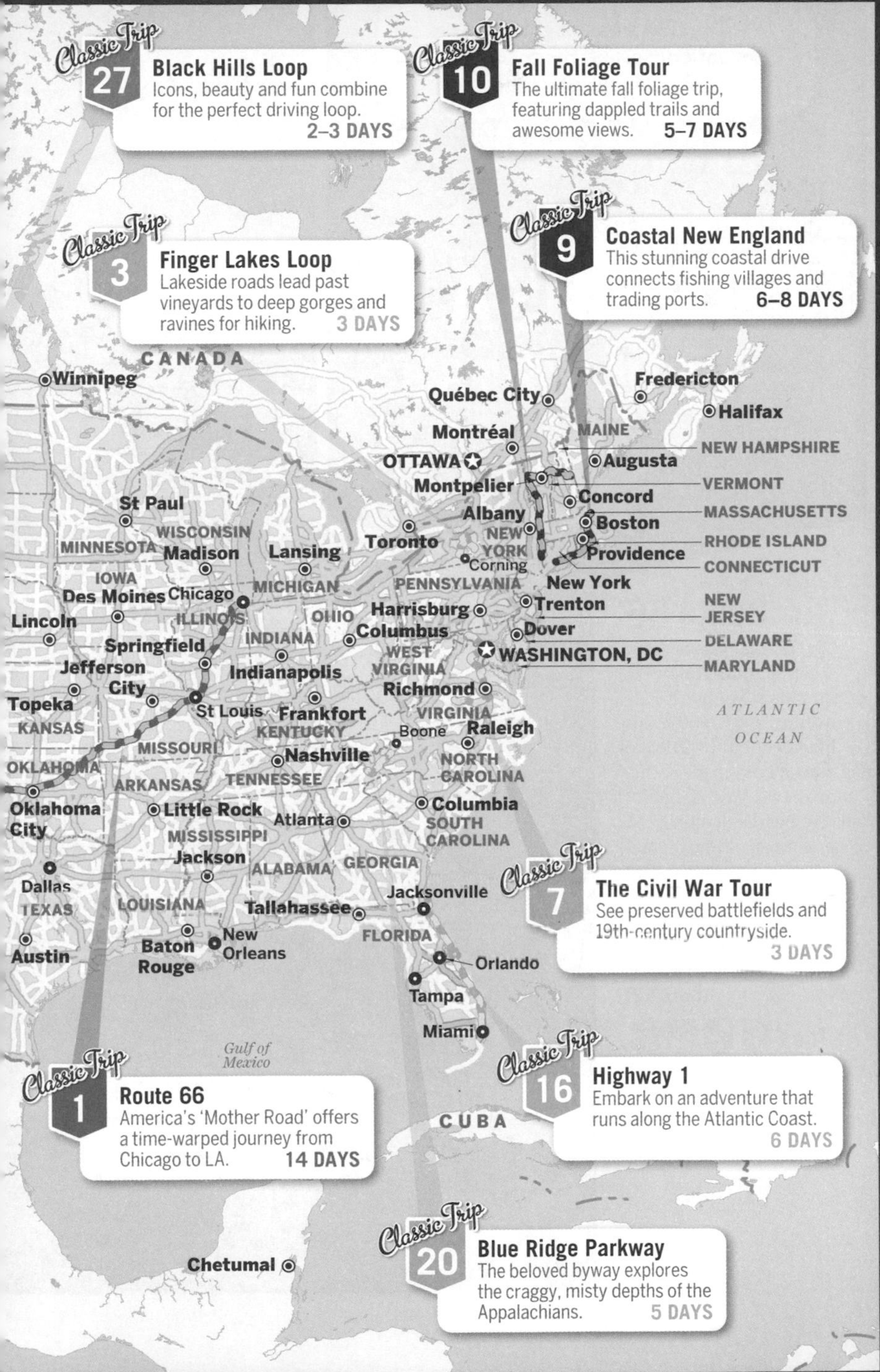

Classic Trip

27 **Black Hills Loop**
Icons, beauty and fun combine for the perfect driving loop.
2–3 DAYS

Classic Trip

10 **Fall Foliage Tour**
The ultimate fall foliage trip, featuring dappled trails and awesome views. **5–7 DAYS**

Classic Trip

3 **Finger Lakes Loop**
Lakeside roads lead past vineyards to deep gorges and ravines for hiking. **3 DAYS**

Classic Trip

9 **Coastal New England**
This stunning coastal drive connects fishing villages and trading ports. **6–8 DAYS**

CANADA
Winnipeg
Québec City
Fredericton
Halifax
Montréal
MAINE
NEW HAMPSHIRE
OTTAWA
Augusta
Montpelier
VERMONT
Concord
St Paul
Albany
MASSACHUSETTS
Boston
WISCONSIN
NEW YORK
RHODE ISLAND
MINNESOTA
Madison
Lansing
Toronto
Corning
Providence
CONNECTICUT
IOWA
MICHIGAN
PENNSYLVANIA
New York
Des Moines
Chicago
Harrisburg
Trenton
NEW JERSEY
Lincoln
ILLINOIS
OHIO
Columbus
Dover
INDIANA
DELAWARE
Springfield
WEST VIRGINIA
WASHINGTON, DC
MARYLAND
Jefferson City
Indianapolis
Richmond
Topeka
St Louis
Frankfort
VIRGINIA
KANSAS
KENTUCKY
Boone
Raleigh
ATLANTIC OCEAN
MISSOURI
OKLAHOMA
Nashville
NORTH CAROLINA
ARKANSAS
TENNESSEE
Oklahoma City
Little Rock
Columbia
Atlanta
SOUTH CAROLINA
MISSISSIPPI
Jackson
ALABAMA
GEORGIA
Dallas
TEXAS
LOUISIANA
Tallahassee
Jacksonville
FLORIDA
Austin
Baton Rouge
New Orleans
Orlando
Tampa
Miami
Gulf of Mexico
CUBA
Chetumal

Classic Trip

7 **The Civil War Tour**
See preserved battlefields and 19th-century countryside.
3 DAYS

Classic Trip

16 **Highway 1**
Embark on an adventure that runs along the Atlantic Coast.
6 DAYS

Classic Trip

1 **Route 66**
America's 'Mother Road' offers a time-warped journey from Chicago to LA. **14 DAYS**

Classic Trip

20 **Blue Ridge Parkway**
The beloved byway explores the craggy, misty depths of the Appalachians. **5 DAYS**

The USA's best sights and experiences, and the road trips that will take you there.

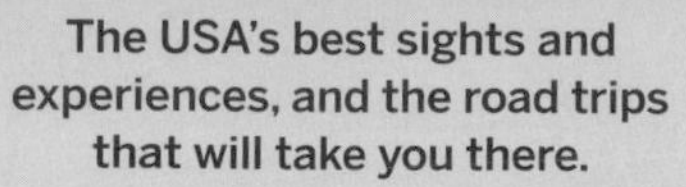

THE USA HIGHLIGHTS

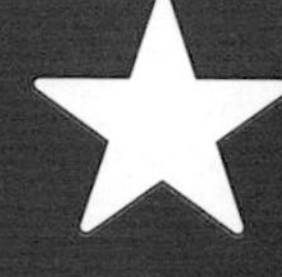

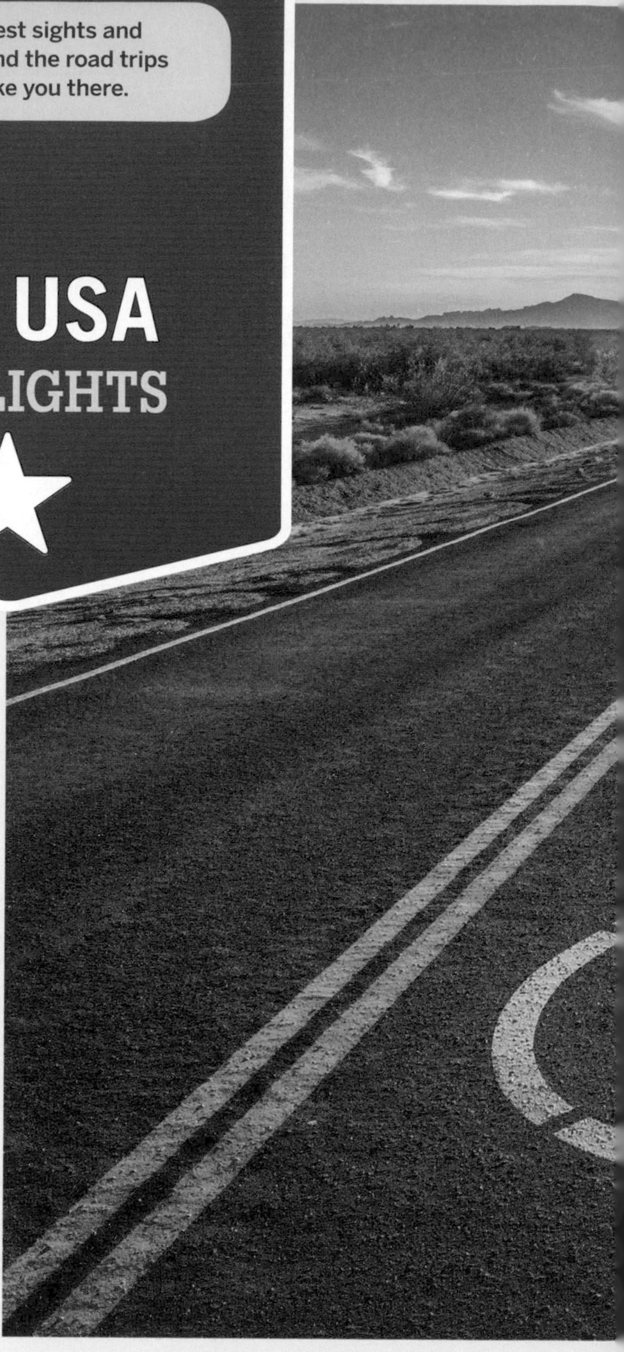

Route 66

No US road trip is more classic than Route 66, America's 'Mother Road'. Running over 2400 miles between windy Chicago and sunny Los Angeles, this mostly two-lane ribbon of concrete passes neon-signed motor courts, old-fashioned diners dishing up pie, and drive-in theaters under the stars. Meet genuinely friendly, small-town Americans on **Trip 1: Route 66**.

Trips 1 2 23 25 28 33 40

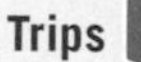

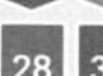

AARON MORGAN / AJMORGAN591 / 500PX ©

Route 66 America's classic road trip

HIGHLIGHTS ★

Grand Canyon North Rim, AZ Spectacular colors at sunset

Grand Canyon

Protected by a national park and Native American tribal lands, this canyon cut by the Colorado River is an eye-popping spectacle of colorful rock strata. Its spiring buttes, sculpted cliffs and waterfall springs make up an ever-changing landscape that shifts moods with the weather and seasons. Be awed by Mother Nature's showstopper on **Trip 33: Fantastic Canyon Voyage**.

Trips 2 33

Pacific Coast Highways

Stretching from Mexico to Canada, the West Coast's ocean-view highways snake past dizzying beach cliffs and dozens of beach towns, all with their own idiosyncratic personalities. On **Trip 40: Pacific Coast Highways** you'll uncover hidden strands, ancient redwood forests, seafood shacks grilling up the catch of the day and creaky old wooden piers for watching glorious sunsets.

Trips   

National Mall

Kick off **Trip 7: The Civil War Tour** in Washington DC, the USA's capital. Along the National Mall stand iconic monuments styled like ancient Greek and Roman temples, moving memorials to wars and civic heroes, and the Smithsonian Institution's immense museums. There's no better place to take the country's pulse than on the long, grassy lawn, where Americans gather in protest and celebration.

Trips 6 7

PEERASITH PATRICK TRIRATPADOONGPHOL / SHUTTERSTOCK ©

KAMIRA / SHUTTERSTOCK ©

National Mall, Washington, DC A summer day by the Lincoln Memorial

BEST ROADS FOR DRIVING

US 101 Panoramic views from the West Coast. **Trips** 40 47 49

Blue Ridge Parkway Roll alongside Appalachian hills. **Trips** 8 20 21

Going-to-the-Sun Road Glimpse glaciers before they vanish. **Trip** 30

Route 66 A nostalgic journey back in time. **Trip** 1

Route 100 Wind through Vermont's green mountains. **Trip** 13

Great Smokies

Welcoming more visitors annually than any other US national park, this 800-sq-mile pocket of southern Appalachian woodland is ribbed by forested ridges where black bears, white-tailed deer, wild turkeys and over 1600 different kinds of wildflowers all find refuge. Take an unforgettable trip amid gold, orange and flame-colored autumn foliage on **Trip 21: The Great Smokies**.

Trip 21

Miami Beach, FL Bright blue water and sparkling sand

STBAUS7 / GETTY IMAGES ©

Florida's Beaches

Blessed with almost year-round sunshine, Florida is a beautiful, sexy, semitropical peninsula edged with bone-white sand, lapped by aquamarine waters and drenched in lurid, neon sunsets. Florida's beaches are its calling card: you could hit a different one every day for a year. Track down some of the very best on **Trip 16: Florida's Highway 1.**

Trip 16

BEST ODDBALL ROADSIDE ATTRACTIONS

Gemini Giant Ready to rocket down Route 66. **Trip** 1

Wall Drug The USA's most shameless tourist trap. **Trip** 27

Tunnel Log Drive through a fallen giant sequoia tree. **Trip** 41

Marfa Lights Watch for otherworldly apparitions in West Texas. **Trip** 37

Salvation Mountain A folk-art monument to religious fervor. **Trip** 43

F11PHOTO / SHUTTERSTOCK ©

HIGHLIGHTS

Acadia National Park, ME Idyllic scenery

MARIE-LOUISE MANDL / EYEEM / GETTY IMAGES ©

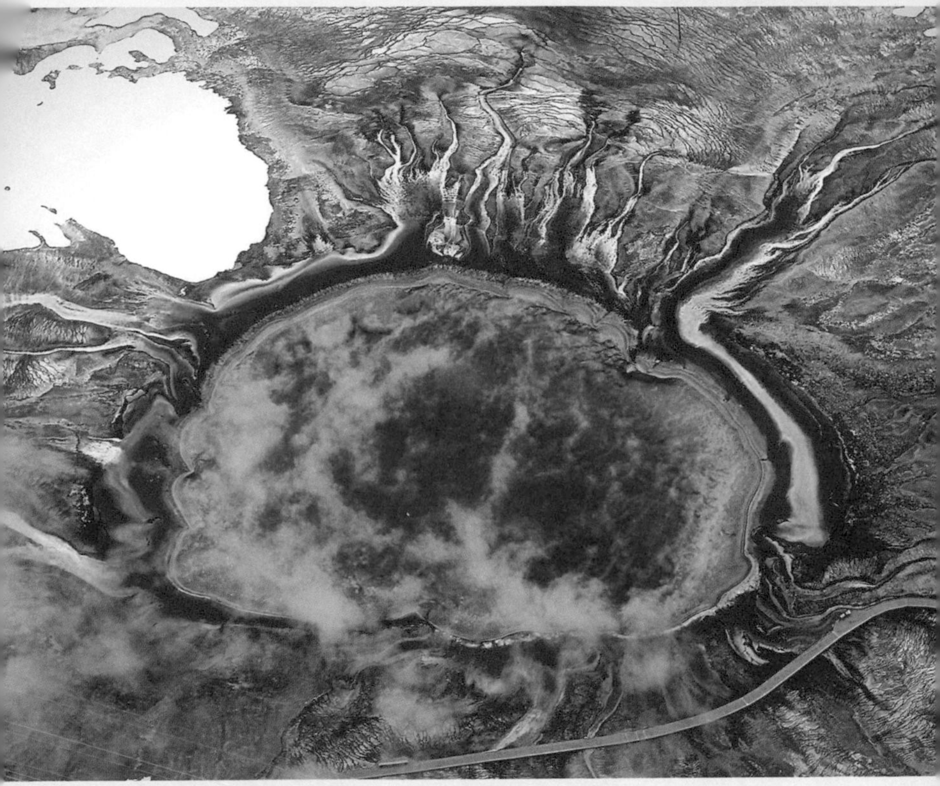

Yellowstone National Park, WY Grand Prismatic Spring

Yellowstone National Park

The country's oldest national park never fails to amaze with its spouting geysers, rainbow-colored hot springs and heart-stopping megafauna – grizzly bears, bison, elk, wolves, moose and more – that range across North America's largest intact ecosystem. Trek into some of the West's wildest wonderlands on **Trip 29: Grand Teton to Yellowstone**.

Trip 29

Great Lakes

Like huge inland seas, the gorgeous Great Lakes are freckled with beaches, sand dunes and lighthouses on rocky shores, as you'll discover while basking in the sun on **Trip 22: Michigan's Gold Coast**. Ready for a bigger adventure? Meander south down by the Mississippi River, motor west along retro Route 66 or make your way north up to the Canadian border.

Trips  1  22  23 24

Acadia National Park

It's a weather-beaten New England tradition to witness the first sunrise of the year from atop Cadillac Mountain, the highest peak on the USA's eastern seaboard. But if a winter sojourn sounds too chilly, then show up during summer instead to explore these end-of-the-world islands tossed along rocky North Atlantic shores on **Trip 15: Acadia Byway**.

Trip 15

Cajun Country

Down by the bayou in the swamplands of southern Louisiana, delve into a gumbo mix of Creole, French Canadian, Native American and African American folk culture. Step inside ramshackle roadside taverns, where fresh crawfish boil in big pots and zydeco musicians jam all night long. *Allons danser* ('Let's dance!') on **Trip 17: Cajun Country**.

Trip 17

Blue Ridge Parkway

Traversing rural Appalachia from Shenandoah National Park to the Great Smoky Mountains, the Blue Ridge Pkwy is the nation's most popular scenic drive, statistics say. Each year more than 15 million people drive over its rolling hills and through pastoral valleys, touring historic battlegrounds and listening to bluegrass music. Join the parade on **Trip 20: Blue Ridge Parkway**.

Trips   

WELCOMIA / SHUTTERSTOCK ©

(left) **Rocky Mountains, CO** Elks rest in a meadow
(below) **Crawfish boil** An essential Cajun tradition

BRUCE YUANYUE BI / GETTY IMAGES ©

Rocky Mountains

Wildflower-strewn meadows, saw-toothed peaks and placid lakes along the jagged spine of the Continental Divide, call to outdoor adventurers. Equally rich in wildlife, pioneer history and Native American traditions, the Rocky Mountains embody the American frontier spirit. Be haunted by Old West ghost towns on **Trip 31: Top of the Rockies**.

Trips    32

BEST NATIVE AMERICAN PLACES

Monument Valley Preserved inside the Navajo Nation. **Trip** 35

Mesa Verde Visit Ancestral Puebloan cliff dwellings. **Trips** 2 35

Grand Canyon Sacred to tribes across the Southwest. **Trips** 2 33

Natchez Trace Pkwy Follow the footsteps of indigenous peoples. **Trip** 19

Anadarko A Great Plains tribal center. **Trip** 25

Apple pie As American as...

Outdoor Adventures

Towering forests, deep canyons, alpine lakes, chiseled peaks, alien-looking deserts and unspoiled beaches – there's no shortage of spectacular landscapes unscrolling before your windshield in the USA. Hop out of the car for an afternoon hike, morning paddle or all-day communion with nature.

2 Four Corners Cruise See the Southwest's canyon country from rim to rim.

10 Fall Foliage Tour Breathe in New England's natural beauty during its showiest season.

29 Grand Teton to Yellowstone Quintessential Western national parks in the Rocky Mountains.

41 Yosemite, Sequoia & Kings Canyon National Parks Drive across the Sierra Nevada's highlands.

History

Start on the East Coast, home of America's revolutionary 13 colonies. Go west, following scouts' trails across the Great Plains and over the Continental Divide to Pacific shores. Dig up the country's Spanish colonial roots mixed with indigenous traditions across the Southwest.

7 The Civil War Tour Follow in the wake of men and women who fought the USA's bloodiest conflict.

26 On the Pioneer Trails Where homesteaders once rolled their 'prairie schooners' and daring Pony Express riders galloped.

48 On the Trail of Lewis & Clark America's original cross-country trip.

Family Travel

Coast to coast, there's endless fun for anyone traveling with kids, including eye-popping theme parks, hands-on science museums, zoos and aquariums. Or focus your road trip on the great outdoors: beaches and national parks rank among the most popular destinations for families.

15 Acadia Byway An island idyll in New England, most bewitching in summer.

21 The Great Smokies Wildlife-spotting, historical train rides, waterfall hikes and kitschy Dollywood.

27 Black Hills Loop A summer-vacation rite of passage for uncountable American kids.

42 Disneyland & Orange County Beaches Mickey's 'Magic Kingdom' is a short drive from SoCal's cinematic coast.

SEAN PAVONE / SHUTTERSTOCK ©

Fall foliage Rural Vermont's autumnal colors

Beaches

With 5000-plus miles of coastline along two oceans and the Gulf of Mexico, there's enough sand to satisfy all kinds of beach lovers here, from the rugged and wild shores of New England to the sunny, surfable strands of Florida and Southern California.

4 **The Jersey Shore** It's a nonstop party with Atlantic boardwalks, carnival fun and funnel cake.

16 **Highway 1** Spring-break beaches and peaceful islands and inlets down in the Sunshine State.

40 **Pacific Coast Highways** Kick back in quirky beach towns on California's coast, equal parts sunshine and rainbow mist.

49 **Highway 101 Oregon Coast** For lighthouses, rocky bluffs, jewel-like beaches and Pacific horizons.

Urban Exploration

In the USA's biggest, most diverse cities, high and low culture collide in a heady blow-up of sights, sounds and tastes: from star chefs' kitchens to food trucks, symphony halls to underground punk clubs, museums to graffiti-art murals, and much more.

1 **Route 66** Link the skyscrapers of Chicago and glamorous Los Angeles with a chain of other great American cities.

9 **Coastal New England** Bop through Boston on this seaboard drive – it's not too much of a detour from NYC either.

40 **Pacific Coast Highways** Cruise up the West Coast from San Diego to Los Angeles, San Francisco and beyond, where Portland and Seattle await.

Regional Food

Down-home cooking is the cherry on top of any classic American road trip. Make a mess at a Maine lobster shack, plow through BBQ in Texas, order 'Christmas-style' enchiladas at a New Mexico diner or find farm-to-table goodness in the Midwest. What's for dessert? Pie, oh my.

5 **Pennsylvania Dutch Country** Amish bakeries, all-you-can-eat suppers and pretzel and chocolate factories.

13 **Vermont's Spine: Route 100** Roadside apple orchards, dairy cows and microbreweries.

17 **Cajun Country** Where rustic Cajun spice mixes with sophisticated Creole cooking.

NEED TO KNOW

CELL PHONES

The only foreign phones that work in the USA are GSM tri- or quad-band models. Buy pay-as-you-go cell phones from electronics stores or rent them at major airports.

INTERNET ACCESS

Free wi-fi is found in hotels, cafes and several fast-food chains, though the smaller the town, the harder it is to find.

FUEL

Gas stations are everywhere, except in some remote desert and mountain areas and national parks. Average cost per gallon is $3.55.

RENTAL CARS

Alamo (www.alamo.com)

Enterprise (www.enterprise.com)

Rent-a-Wreck (www.rentawreck.com)

IMPORTANT NUMBERS

AAA (800-222-4357) Roadside assistance for auto-club members.

Emergency (911)

Directory Assistance (411)

Operator (0)

Climate

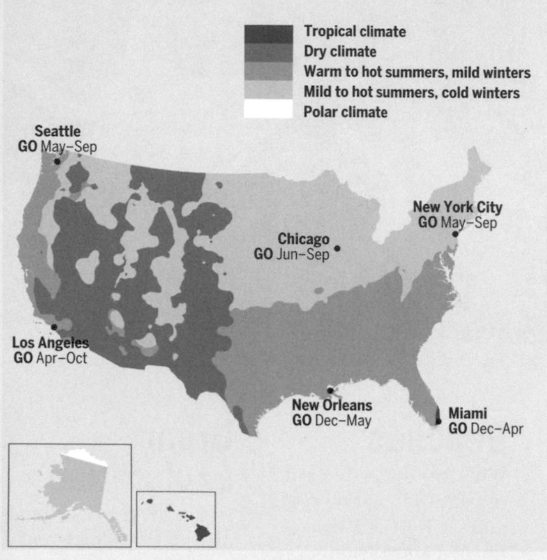

When to Go

High Season (Jun–Aug)

» Warm days nationwide, with generally high temperatures.

» Busy travel season brings huge crowds and higher prices.

» Tourism slows in hot deserts; very humid in southeastern US.

Shoulder Seasons (Apr–May & Sep–Oct)

» Milder temperatures; hurricane season peaks (Aug–Nov) on Gulf and Atlantic coasts.

» Fewer crowds, discounted accommodations and airfares.

» Spring wildflowers (April–May) and autumn foliage (Sep–Oct) in many areas.

Low Season (Nov–Mar)

» Colder wintry days, with snowfall and heavy rainstorms in many regions.

» Lowest prices on lodgings, except at ski resorts and in warm, sunny destinations, such as Florida.

Daily Costs

Budget: Less than $150

» Camping or hostel: $20–50; cheap motel room: $60–100

» Roadside diner or take-out meal: $10–15

Midrange: $150–300

» Two-star hotel room: $90–200

» Casual sit-down restaurant meal: $25–40

Top End: Over $300

» Resort hotel room: from $200

» Three-course meal in top restaurant: $75–100

Eating

Diners, drive-ins & cafes Cheap, simple and occasionally homemade food.

Seafood shacks Casual waterfront kitchens for fresh catch.

Brewpubs & gastropubs Regional craft beers and wines, 'pub grub' from hearty to high-end cuisine.

Vegetarians & other diets Food restrictions and allergies can often be catered for, especially in cities.

Eating price indicators represent the cost of a main course:

$	less than $10
$$	$10–20
$$$	more than $20

Sleeping

Camping Ranging from amenity-rich RV parks to primitive wilderness sites.

Motels Everywhere along highways, around cities and in heavily touristed spots.

Hotels & hostels Common in metro areas and popular tourist destinations.

B&Bs Smaller, often historic and romantic, but pricey.

Sleeping price indicators represent the cost of a room with private bathroom, excluding taxes:

$	less than $100
$$	$100–200
$$$	more than $200

Arriving in the USA

Major US airports offer free inter-terminal transportation and car-rental shuttles.

Los Angeles International Airport (LAX)

Taxis $30–55; 30 to 60 minutes.

Door-to-door shuttles Around $17–28.

Public transportation Shuttle C (free) to LAX City Bus Center or Shuttle G (free) to Metrorail's Aviation Station; LAX FlyAway Bus to downtown LA's Union Station ($9.75, 30 to 50 minutes).

John F Kennedy International Airport (JFK; New York)

Taxis To Manhattan: $52 plus tolls and tip.

Subway AirTrain to Jamaica Station ($5) for the LIRR into Penn Station or to Howard Beach for A train ($7.50 to $10.25) into city.

Shuttles From $18.

Money

ATMs are practically everywhere. Credit cards are almost universally accepted, and usually required for making reservations.

Tipping

Tipping is expected, not optional: 15% to 20% at restaurants, 10% to 15% for taxi drivers, and $2 per bag for porters.

Opening Hours

Opening hours may be shorter in winter (November to March).

Banks 8:30am to 4:30pm Monday to Thursday, to 5:30pm or 6pm Friday (and possibly 9am to noon Saturday)

Businesses & government offices 9am to 5pm Monday to Friday

Restaurants 7am to 10:30am, 11:30am to 2:30pm & 5pm to 9pm daily, some later Friday and Saturday

Shops 10am to 6pm Monday to Saturday, noon to 5pm Sunday (malls close later)

Useful Websites

Lonely Planet (www.lonelyplanet.com/usa) Destination information, hotel and hostel bookings, traveler forums and more.

Festivals.com (www.festivals.com) Fun celebrations of music, food, drink and dance.

Roadside America (www.roadsideamerica.com) For everything weird and wacky.

For more, see the USA Driving Guide (p637).

NEW YORK CITY

Loud, fast and pulsing with energy, New York City is symphonic, exhausting and constantly reinventing itself. Fashion, theater, food, music, publishing and the arts all thrive here and almost every country in the world has its own enclave somewhere in the five boroughs.

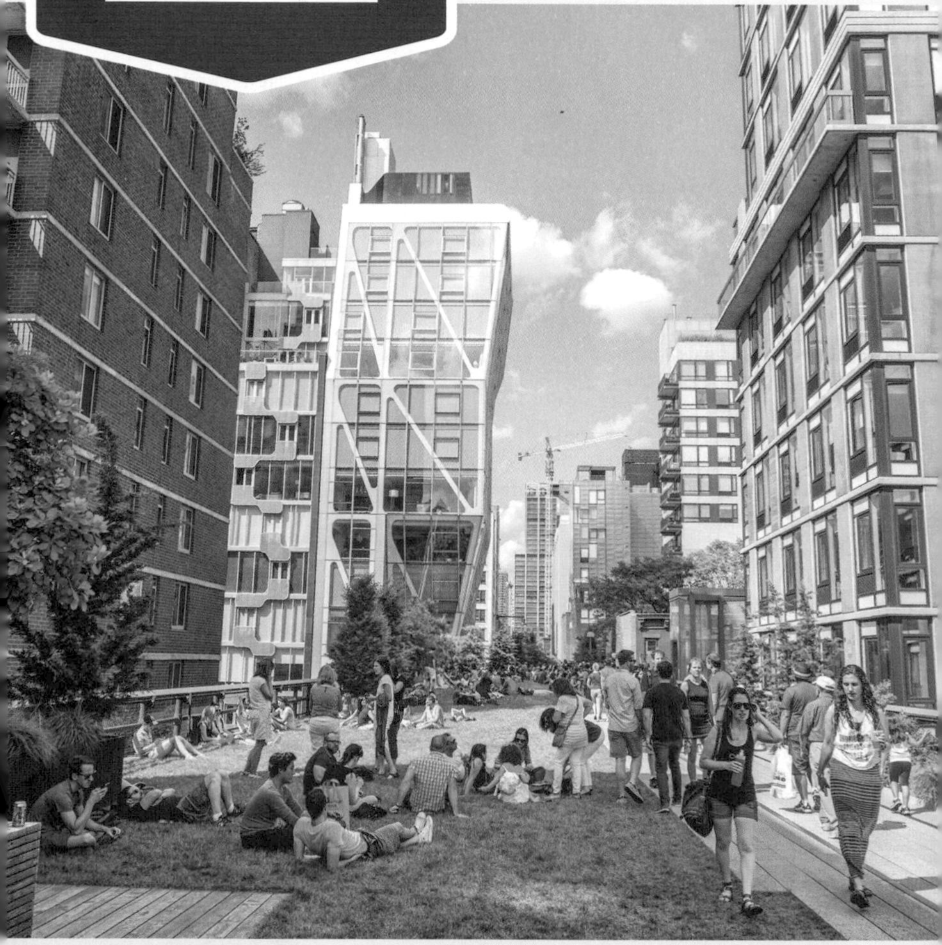

The High Line A green space 30ft above street level

Getting Around

With a comprehensive subway, bus, train and bike-sharing system, there's little need to drive yourself in NYC. For drivers, turning right on red is illegal except where posted.

Parking

It's cheaper and easier to park near an outer borough subway stop or at a suburban train station, then ride into the city.

Where to Eat

NYC's neighborhoods, from Chinatown to Tribeca, offer up a global buffet of ethnic tastes. Uncover break-out restaurants in Brooklyn (hello, Williamsburg, Park Slope and Red Hook).

GAGLIARDIIMAGES / SHUTTERSTOCK ©

Where to Stay

In Manhattan, Midtown's high-rise hotels are convenient for sightseeing, while stylish boutique and luxury properties lie further south, including in SoHo and Chelsea, and north around Central Park on the Upper West and East Sides.

Useful Websites

NYC: The Official Guide (www.nycgo.com) New York City's official tourism portal.

New York Magazine (www.nymag.com) News, culture and latest happenings.

Lonely Planet (www.lonelyplanet.com/usa) Tips, videos, accommodations and traveler forums.

For trips around New York City, see New York & the Mid-Atlantic Trips (p61), and for a NYC walking tour, see p132.

For more, check out our city and country guides. www.lonelyplanet.com

TOP EXPERIENCES

➡ Head up the Empire State Building

The striking art-deco skyscraper may no longer be New York's tallest building, but it remains one of its recognizable icons.

➡ Be dazzled by world art and culture at the Met

The Metropolitan Museum of Art's collection numbers over 2 million objects. Head up to the rooftop for a sweeping view over Central Park.

➡ Sail out to the Statue of Liberty & Ellis Island

Lady Liberty overlooks Ellis Island, home to one of the city's most moving museums, paying tribute to generations of courageous immigrants.

➡ Stroll across Brooklyn Bridge

This Gothic Revival masterpiece has inspired poetry, music and art. It is also the most scenic way to cross from Manhattan into Brooklyn.

➡ See a show and the lights on Broadway

Between Sixth and Eighth Aves, Broadway is NYC's dream factory, with bright, blinding Times Square the district's undisputed star.

➡ Chill out on the High Line

The elevated train track that once snaked between slaughterhouses has morphed into an emerald necklace of calming park space.

➡ Pay your respects at Ground Zero

The National September 11 Memorial & Museum is a beautiful, dignified response to the city's darkest chapter.

F11PHOTO / SHUTTERSTOCK ©

Navy Pier Cool breezes and city views

CHICAGO

The Windy City will blow you away with its cloud-scraping architecture and lakefront beaches. High and low culture comfortably coexist without any hint of pretension. Take in world-class museums and landmark theater stages, or drop by divey blues clubs and graffiti-scrawled pizzerias – they're all equally beloved in 'Chi-town.'

Getting Around

Driving Chicago's well laid-out street grid is slow, but not too difficult, except around the Loop. If you're exploring downtown and other neighborhoods served by 'L' lines, ditch your car for the day and get around on foot and by train (or bus) instead.

Parking

Overnight hotel parking and city parking garages are expensive. Metered on-street parking is easier to find in outlying neighborhoods than around downtown, but it's not necessarily cheap (occasionally it's free in residential areas).

Where to Eat

Essential eats include Chicago-style hot dogs, Italian beef sandwiches and deep-dish pizza. Star chefs run restaurants in the West Loop and on the North Side. For an eclectic mix of cafes, bistros, gastropubs and more, nose around Wicker Park, Bucktown and Andersonville.

Where to Stay

Base yourself in the Loop for convenient 'L' train stops, seek luxury on the Gold Coast or look for deals at the Near North's boutique and high-rise hotels. For more personalized stays, book a B&B in a trendy neighborhood like Wicker Park.

Useful Websites

Choose Chicago (www.choosechicago.com) Official tourist information site.

CTA (www.transitchicago.com) Bus and train maps, schedules and fares.

Chicago Reader (www.chicagoreader.com) Alternative weekly, covering events, arts and entertainment.

For trips around Chicago, see the Great Lakes Trips (p287), and for a Chicago walking tour, see p320.

Hollywood Boulevard Visitors and performers on the Walk of Fame

LOS ANGELES

If you think you've already got LA figured out – celebrity culture, smog, traffic and bikini babes – think again. Dozens of independent mini cities, where over 90 languages are spoken, comprise the West's biggest, most provocative metropolis, home of Hollywood stars, boundary-breaking artists and musicians, and other cultural icons.

Getting Around

Most people get around by car, despite jammed freeways and slow surface streets. Metro rail lines and a network of local buses connect many of the neighborhoods that are popular with visitors.

Parking

Valet parking is widely available at hotels, restaurants, nightspots etc; fees vary (a tip is expected). Metered on-street parking is limited but inexpensive. In downtown LA, parking lots and garages are plentiful but pricey – the cheapest are in Chinatown.

Where to Eat

LA's creative culinary scene embraces TV chefs, food trucks and farmers markets. With some 140 nationalities living here, there's an abundance of immigrant neighborhoods with good eats including downtown's Little Tokyo, Thai Town near Hollywood and East LA for Mexican flavors.

Where to Stay

For seaside life, book a motel or hotel in Santa Monica, Venice or Long Beach. Cool-hunters and party people will be happy at boutique and luxury hotels in Hollywood, West Hollywood and Beverly Hills. Culture vultures descend on downtown LA's high-rise hotels.

Useful Websites

Discover Los Angeles (www.discoverlosangeles.com) Official tourist information site.

Metro (www.metro.net) Bus and rail maps, schedules and fares.

LA Weekly (www.laweekly.com) Alternative tabloid covering food, film, music, nightlife and more.

For trips around Los Angeles, see California Trips (p483), and for a LA walking tour, see p564.

WASHINGTON DC

No stranger to the world's gaze, the nation's capital is complicated and controversial, a place of politics and protests. Yet it's also a proud city of grand boulevards, illustrious monuments and postcard vistas over the Potomac River. Walk colonial cobblestone streets past unmissable museums, theaters and more.

Getting Around

Driving around Washington DC can be a headache. It's better to leave your car parked for the day, then plan on walking between sights, riding Metrorail trains and taking Metrobus and DC Circulator buses.

Parking

Metered (occasionally free) on-street parking is limited, especially by the National Mall. Public garages and lots are expensive in the city, but more affordable at suburban train stations. Hotels charge steeply for overnight parking.

EASTVILLAGE IMAGES / SHUTTERSTOCK ©

Lincoln Memorial Home to the iconic statue

TOP EXPERIENCES

➡ Lincoln Memorial at Sunset
No other monument on the National Mall evokes the heritage and ideals of the USA more than this one. Snap a photo as the white marble of this Greek-style temple lights up for nighttime.

➡ Size up the Smithsonian
Be astonished by the renowned collections housed inside 19 different museums and galleries, plus the national zoo.

➡ Stroll Tidal Basin in Spring
Around this picturesque reservoir, capture panoramic views of famous DC landmarks, best when framed by delicate pink cherry blossoms.

➡ Tour the White House
Request permission many months in advance to visit the most famous address in the country, only a short walk from Capitol Hill.

Where to Eat

Make a beeline for Capitol Hill's Eastern Market, then check out rave-reviewed restaurants along the 14th St corridor and downtown's Penn Quarter. For a big array of dining and drinking options, wander U St, Dupont Circle, Adams Morgan, the West End or Georgetown.

Where to Stay

Downtown claims the bulk of DC's historic and high-rise hotels. Conveniently located, busy Dupont Circle has historical inns, B&Bs and boutique and luxury hotels. Save money at hotels just across the river in Arlington, VA.

Useful Websites

Destination DC (www.washington.org) Official tourism site packed with sightseeing and event info.

Cultural Tourism DC (www.culturaltourismdc.org) Neighborhood-oriented events and tours.

Washingtonian (www.washingtonian.com) Covers all elements of DC's cultural scene.

For trips around Washington, DC, see New York & the Mid-Atlantic Trips (p61), and for a Washington, DC walking tour, see p134.

Road-tripping is the ultimate way to see the USA, from coastal highways to mountain roads. Here's your guide to what each region has to offer and the best road trips to experience it for yourself.

Rocky Mountains (p371)

Gasp at postcard views from high-country byways, then drive around pristine lakes, natural geysers, celebrity ski resorts and wild national parks.

Climb to ancient cliff dwellings on Trip 32

Pacific Northwest (p569)

Lose yourself amid snow-topped volcanoes, bubbling hot springs, wind-whipped beaches and deep coastal rainforest, or trace pioneer trails beside the Columbia River.

Go whale-watching on Trip 49

California (p483)

Cruise by surf-tossed strands on the famous Pacific Coast Hwy, reach for the sky in the Sierra Nevada and recharge at cool desert oases.

Take in beaches, redwood forests and more on Trip 40

The Southwest (p417)

Gaze out at boundless horizons from the Grand Canyon, between Monument Valley's buttes or on the banks of the Rio Grande.

Savor tasty chile on Trip 

Great Plains (p323)

Tales of Wild West outlaws and cowboys, Native American tribal traditions and endless miles of golden prairie unroll through America's heartland.

Go where buffalo still roam on Trip 27

Great Lakes (p287)

Motor from Chicago's skyscrapers down Route 66, America's 'Mother Road,' then wind beside the mighty Mississippi River or past lakefront beaches and lighthouses.

Spy moose on Trip 

New England (p139)

Craggy coastlines strung with fishing villages, ivy-covered colleges and brilliant fall foliage along country roads beckon drivers to this landed literary landscape.

Eat lobster on Trip 9

New York & the Mid-Atlantic (p61)

Americana abounds, from Amish farms and Civil War battlefields to Maryland's historic roads. Spot waterfalls on Skyline Dr and around the Finger Lakes.

Party on the Jersey Shore on Trip 4

Florida & the South (p211)

Natural beauty is always nearby, whether you're lazing on the breezy Gulf and Atlantic coasts or rolling inland through rural Appalachia and Cajun country.

Sing the blues on Trip 

THE USA Classic Trips

DAVIDHOFFMANN PHOTOGRAPHY / SHUTTERSTOCK ©

RIRF STOCK / SHUTTERSTOCK ©

What is a Classic Trip?

All the trips in this book show you the best of the USA, but we've chosen 15 as our all-time favorites. These are our Classic Trips – the ones that lead you to the best of the iconic sights, the top activities and the unique USA experiences. Turn the page to see our cross-regional Classic Trips, and look out for more Classic Trips throughout the book.

Above: Oxbow Bend, Grand Teton National Park
Left: General Sherman Tree, Sequoia National Park

STAGECOACH
66
MOTEL
NORWEGIAN OWNED
WI-FI HBO PETS

VACANCY

Classic Trip

Route 66

America's 'Mother Road' offers a time-warped journey from Chicago to LA past neon-lit diners, drive-in movie theaters and roadside attractions that beg for a photo.

TRIP HIGHLIGHTS

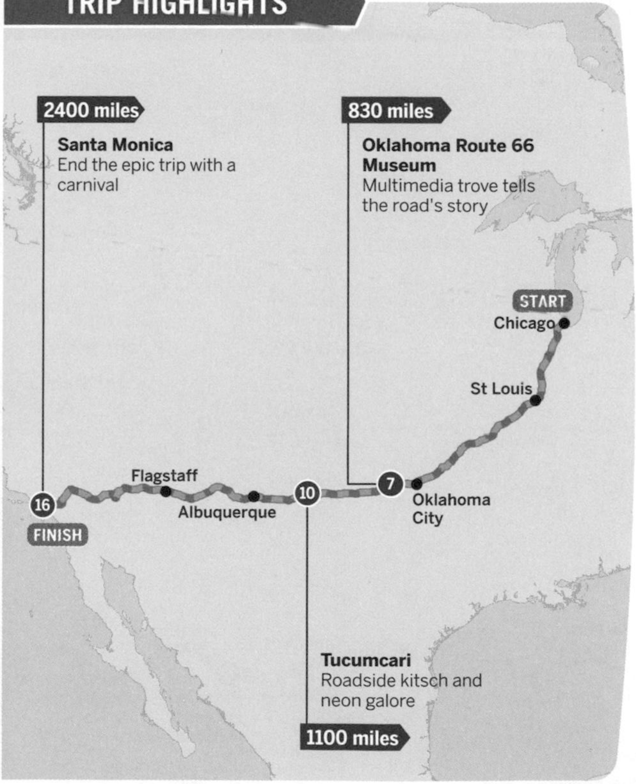

2400 miles
Santa Monica
End the epic trip with a carnival

830 miles
Oklahoma Route 66 Museum
Multimedia trove tells the road's story

START
Chicago
St Louis
Oklahoma City
Flagstaff
Albuquerque
16
FINISH
10
7

Tucumcari
Roadside kitsch and neon galore
1100 miles

14 DAYS
2400 MILES / 3862KM

GREAT FOR...

BEST TIME TO GO

May to September for extended opening hours at attractions.

ESSENTIAL PHOTO

The Gemini Giant, a fiberglass spaceman, in Wilmington, IL.

BEST TWO DAYS

California's stretch of road offers tumbleweed landscapes and malted milkshakes.

Seligman An eye-catching motel sign

Classic Trip

1 Route 66

It's a lonely road – a ghost road really – that appears for a stretch then disappears, gobbled up by the interstate. You know you've found it again when a 20ft lumberjack holding a hot dog rises up from the roadside, or a sign points you to the 'World's Largest Covered Wagon,' driven by a giant Abe Lincoln. And that's just Illinois – the first of eight states on the nostalgic, kitschy, slowpoke drive west.

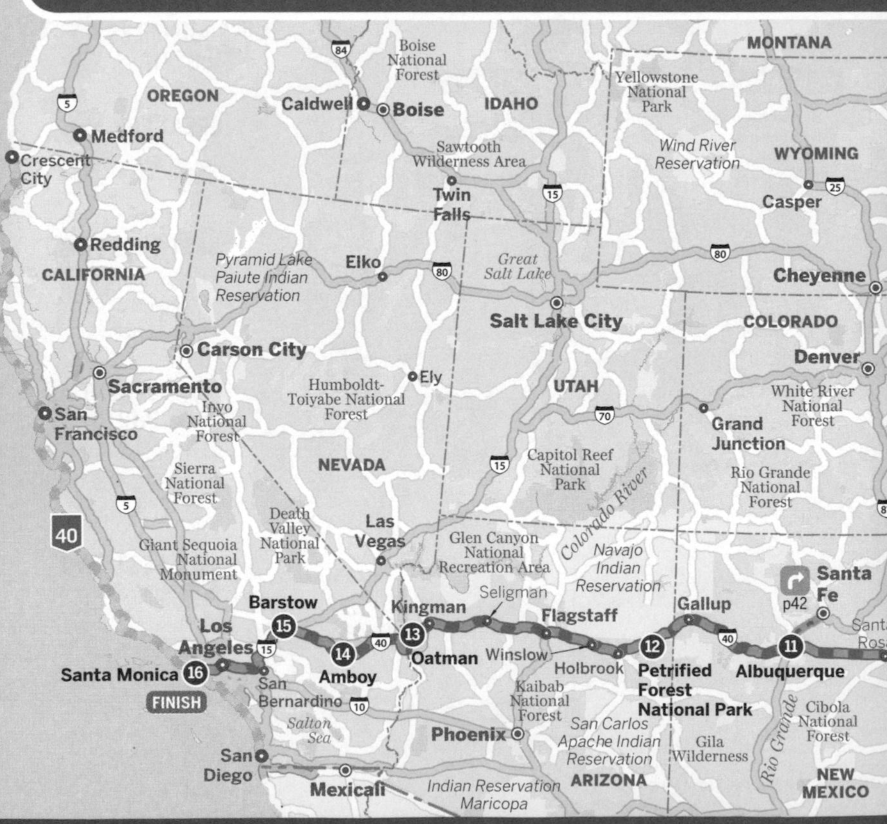

1 Chicago

Route 66 kicks off in downtown Chicago on Adams St just west of Michigan Ave. Before you snap the obligatory photo with the 'Route 66 Begin' sign (on the south side of Adams, FYI), spend some time exploring the Windy City. Wander through the **Art Institute** (☎312-443-3600; www.artic.edu; 111 S Michigan Ave; adult/child $25/free; ⏲10:30am-5pm Fri-Wed, to 8pm Thu; 👪; Ⓜ Brown, Orange, Green, Purple, Pink Line to Adams) – literally steps from the Mother Road's launching point – and browse Edward Hopper's *Nighthawks* (a diner scene) and Grant Wood's *American Gothic* (a farmer portrait) to set the scene for what you'll see en route. Nearby **Millennium Park** (☎312-742-1168; www.millenniumpark.org; 201 E Randolph St; ⏲6am-11pm; 👪; Ⓜ Brown, Orange, Green, Purple, Pink Line to Washington/Wabash)

LINK YOUR TRIP

Along the Great River Road

The epic roadway (actually a series of roads) traces the meanderings of the Mississippi River. Pick it up in St Louis.

Pacific Coast Highways

This route along the edge of the continent cruises along an equally iconic numbered route: Hwy 1. When you finish Route 66, follow Hwy 1 north or south.

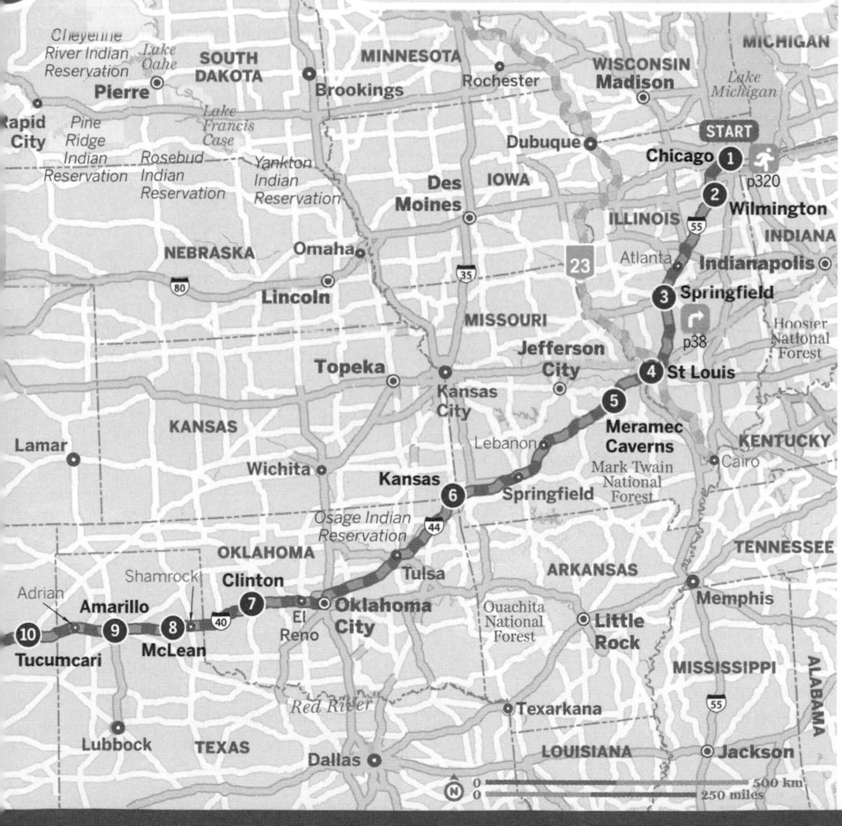

is just plain cool, with mod public artworks and concerts at lunchtime and many evenings June through August.

p46

The Drive » Stay on Adams St for 1.5 miles until you come to Ogden Ave. Go left, and continue through the suburbs of Cicero and Berwyn. At Harlem Ave, turn left (south) and stay on it briefly until you jump onto Joliet Rd. Soon Joliet Rd joins southbound I-55 (at exit 277), and you're funneled onto the interstate.

❷ Gemini Giant

Our first stop rises from the cornfields 60 miles south of Chicago. Leave I-55 at exit 241, and follow Hwy 44 south a short distance to Hwy 53, which rolls into the town of Wilmington. Here the **Gemini Giant** (810 E Baltimore St, Wilmington) – a 28ft fiberglass spaceman – stands guard outside the Launching Pad Drive-In. The restaurant is now shuttered, but the humongous green rocket-holding statue remains a quintessential photo op.

The Drive » Get back on I-55. Take exit 154 for Funks Grove, a 19th-century maple-sirup farm (yes, that's sirup with an 'i'). Get on Old Route 66 (a frontage road that parallels the interstate), and in 10 miles you'll reach Atlanta and its pie-filled cafe (p46). Springfield is 50 miles southwest.

❸ Springfield

Illinois is the Land of Lincoln, according to local license plates, and the best place to get your Honest Abe fix is Springfield, the state capital. Fans of the 16th president get weak-kneed at the holy trio of sights: **Lincoln's Tomb** (217-782-2717; www.lincolntomb.org; 1441 Monument Ave; 9am-5pm), the **Lincoln Presidential Library & Museum** (217-558-8844; www.illinois.gov/alplm; 212 N 6th St; adult/child $15/6; 9am-5pm;) and the **Lincoln Home** (217-492-4150; www.nps.gov/liho; 426 S 7th St; 8:30am-5pm), all in or near downtown. Oh, Springfield's Route 66 claim to fame? It's the birthplace of the corn dog (a cornmeal-battered, fried hot dog on a stick).

p46

The Drive » Return to I-55, which supersedes Route 66 here as in most of the state. The Route 66 Association of Illinois (www.il66assoc.org) tells you where to veer off for restored gas stations, vintage cafes and giant Lincoln statues. Near Edwardsville get on I-270, on which you'll swoop over the Mississippi River and enter Missouri.

❹ St Louis

Just over the border is St Louis, a can-do city that has launched westbound travelers for centuries. To ogle the city's most iconic attraction, exit I-270 onto Riverview Dr and point your car south toward the 630ft-tall **Gateway Arch** (314-655-1700; www.gatewayarch.com; tram ride adult/child $13/10; 8am-10pm Jun-Aug, 9am-6pm Sep-May, last tram 1hr before closing;), a graceful reminder of the city's role in westward expansion. For up-close views of the stainless-steel span and the Jefferson National

DETOUR: OLD CHAIN OF ROCKS BRIDGE

Start: ❸ Springfield

Before driving into Missouri, detour off I-270 at exit 3. Follow Hwy 3 (aka Lewis and Clark Blvd) south, turn right at the first stoplight and drive west to the 1929 **Old Chain of Rocks Bridge** (Old Chain of Rocks Rd; 9am-sunset). Open only to pedestrians and cyclists these days, the mile-long span over the Mississippi River has a 22-degree angled bend (the cause of many a crash, hence the ban on cars). Hide your valuables and lock your car if you leave it to go exploring.

Expansion Memorial surrounding it, turn left onto Washington Ave from Tucker Blvd (12th St). St Louis is also a great place to stretch those muscles, with a massive park to explore (p368).

p46, p367

The Drive » From St Louis, I-44 closely tracks – and often covers – chunks of original Mother Road. Take the interstate southwest to Stanton, then follow the signs to Meramec Caverns.

5 Meramec Caverns

Admit it: you're curious. Kitschy billboards have been touting **Meramec Caverns** (☎573-468-3166; www.americascave.com; I-44 exit 230, Stanton; adult/child $21/11; ⌚8:30am-7:30pm Jun-Aug, reduced hours Sep-May) for miles. The family-mobbed attraction and campground has lured road-trippers with its offbeat ads since 1933. From gold panning to riverboat rides, you'll find a day's worth of distractions, but don't miss the historically and geologically engaging cave tour. Note to kitsch seekers: the restaurant and gift store are actually inside the mouth of the cave.

The Drive » Continue on I-44; Lebanon makes a good pit stop (p46). Ditch the interstate west of Springfield, taking Hwy 96 to Civil War–era Carthage with its historic town square and 66 Drive-In Theatre. From Joplin, follow Hwy 66 to Old Route 66 then hold tight: Kansas is on the horizon.

6 Kansas

The tornado-prone state holds a mere 13 miles of Mother Road (less than 1% of the total) but there's still a lot to see. First you'll pass through mine-scarred **Galena**, where a rusty old tow truck inspired animators from Pixar to create the character Mater in *Cars*. A few miles later, stop at the red-brick **Nelson's Old Riverton Store** (☎620-848-3330; www.eislerbros.com; 7109 SE Hwy 66, Riverton; ⌚7:30am-8pm Mon-Sat, noon-7pm Sun) and stock up on batteries, turkey sandwiches and Route 66 memorabilia. The 1925 property looks much like it did when first built – note the pressed-tin ceiling and the outhouse – and it's on the National Register of Historic Places.

Cross Hwy 400 and continue to the **1923 Marsh Arch Bridge**, from where it's 3 miles south to **Baxter Springs**, site of a Civil War massacre and numerous bank robberies.

The Drive » Enter Oklahoma. From Afton, Route 66 parallels I-44 (now a tollway) through Vinita, home to a famed chicken-fried-steak cafe (p46). Tulsa to Oklahoma City offers one of the longest (and almost continuous) stretches of Mother Road (110 miles). From here it joins Business I-40 for 20 miles to El Reno and its distinctive onion burgers (p46), and then parallels I-40 to Clinton.

TRIP HIGHLIGHT

7 Oklahoma Route 66 Museum

Flags from all eight Mother Road states fly high beside the memorabilia-filled **Oklahoma Route 66 Museum** (☎580-323-7866; www.route66.org; 2229 W Gary Blvd; adult/child $7/4; ⌚9am-7pm Mon-Sat, 1-6pm Sun May-Aug, reduced hours Sep-Apr) in Clinton. This fun-loving treasure trove, run by the Oklahoma Historical Society, isn't your typical mishmash of photos, clippings and knick-knacks (though there is an artifact-filled Cabinet of Curios). Instead, it uses music and videos to dramatize six decades of Route 66 history. Last exhibit? A faux-but-fun drive-in theater.

The Drive » Continue west 70 miles to the Texas border. From here old Route 66 runs immediately south of I-40 through barely changed towns such as Shamrock, with its restored 1930s buildings, including the Tower Station and U-Drop Inn, and minuscule McLean.

8 Devil's Rope Museum

The sprawling grasslands of Texas and other western cattle states were once open range, where steers and cowboys could wander where they darn well pleased. That all changed in the 1880s

Classic Trip

GIMAS / SHUTTERSTOCK ©

DAVID LITMAN / SHUTTERSTOCK ©

WHY THIS IS A CLASSIC TRIP

MARK JOHANSON, WRITER

There is no other journey that allows you to scratch beneath the surface and get to the heart of the American experience quite like Route 66. It may start and end in two of the country's biggest cities, but the vast majority of the Mother Road rambles through the nation's most forgotten corners on a rollicking and unforgettable trip down memory lane.

Top: Old Chain of Rocks Bridge
Left: Santa Monica Pier
Right: Big Texan Steak Ranch sign

STEPHEN SAKS / GETTY IMAGES ©

when the devil's rope – more commonly known as barbed wire – began dividing up the land into private parcels. This **museum** (www.barbwire museum.com; 100 Kingsley St, McLean; ⌚9am-4pm Mon-Sat Mar-Nov) in the battered town of McLean has vast barbed-wire displays and a small but homey and idiosyncratic room devoted to Route 66. The detailed map of the road in Texas is a must.

The Drive » I-40 west of McLean glides over low-rolling hills. The landscape flattens at Groom, home of the tilting water tower and a 19-story cross at exit 112. Take exit 96 for Conway to snap a photo of the forlorn VW Beetle Ranch, aka the Slug Bug Ranch, on the south side of I-40. For the Big Texan, take exit 74.

---

9 Amarillo

This cowboy town holds a plethora of Route 66 sites: the Big Texan Steak Ranch (p46; you've seen the billboards), the historic livestock auction and the San Jacinto District, which still has original Route 66 businesses.

As for the Big Texan, this hokey but classic attraction opened on Route 66 in 1960. It moved to its current location when I-40 opened in 1971 and has never looked back. The attention-grabbing gimmick here is the 'free 72oz steak' offer – you have to eat this massive portion of cow plus a range of sides in under one hour, or you pay for the entire meal ($72). Contestants sit at a raised table to 'entertain' the other diners. Less than 20% pass the challenge.

 p46

The Drive » Continue west on I-40. To see the Cadillac Ranch, an art installation of spray-painted cars, take exit 60 then backtrack on the southern frontage road from the Love's gas station. From there, follow I-40 west through Adrian and past the Midpoint Cafe (p46) to the New Mexico border. Tucumcari is 40 miles west.

TRIP HIGHLIGHT

10 Tucumcari

A ranching and farming town sandwiched between the mesas and the plains, Tucumcari is home to one of the best preserved sections of Route 66 in the country. It's a great place to drive through at night, when dozens of neon signs – relics of the town's Route 66 heyday – cast a crazy rainbow-colored glow. Tucumcari's Route 66 motoring legacy and other regional highlights are recorded on 35 murals in the downtown and surrounding area. Pick up a map for the murals at the **chamber of commerce** (☎575-461-1694; www.tucumcarinm.com; 404 W Route 66; ⏲8:30am-5pm Mon-Fri).

The engaging **Mesalands Dinosaur Museum** (☎575-461-3466; www.mesalands.edu/community/dinosaur-museum; 222 E Laughlin St; adult/child $6.50/4; ⏲10am-6pm Tue-Sat Mar-Aug, noon-5pm Tue-Sat Sep-Feb; 👪) showcases real dinosaur bones and has hands-on exhibits for kids. Casts of dinosaur bones are done in bronze (not the usual plaster of paris), which shows fine detail.

 p47

The Drive » West on I-40, dry and windy plains spread into the distance, the horizon interrupted by flat-topped mesas. To stretch your legs, take exit 277 from Route 66/I-40 to downtown Santa Rosa and the Route 66 Auto Museum, which has upwards of 35 cars from the 1920s through the 1960s, all in beautiful condition.

---

11 Albuquerque

After 1936, Route 66 was realigned from its original path, which linked north through Santa Fe, to a direct line west into Albuquerque. Today, the city's Central Ave follows the post-1937 route. It passes through Nob Hill, the university, downtown and Old Town.

The patioed **Kelly's Brewery** (www.kellysbrewpub.com; 3222 Central Ave SE; ⏲8am-10:30pm Sun-Thu, to midnight Fri & Sat), in today's trendy Nob Hill, was an art moderne gas station on the route, commissioned in 1939. West of I-25, look for the spectacular tile-and-wood artistry of the **KiMo Theatre** (☎505-768-3544; www.cabq.gov/kimo; 423 Central Ave NW), across from the old trading post. This 1927 icon of pueblo deco architecture blends Native American culture with art deco design. It also screens classic movies. For prehistoric designs,

DETOUR: SANTA FE

Start: 11 Albuquerque

New Mexico's capital city is an oasis of art and culture lifted 7000ft above sea level, against the backdrop of the Sangre de Christo Mountains. It was on Route 66 until 1937, when a realignment left it by the wayside. It's well worth the detour to see the Georgia O'Keeffe Museum, to fork into uberhot green chile dishes in the superb restaurants, and to stroll past the town's churches and galleries (p480). Route 66 follows the Old Pecos Trail (NM466) into town.

take exit 154 off I-40, just west of downtown, and drive north 3 miles to **Petroglyph National Monument** (☎505-899-0205; www.nps.gov/petr; 6001 Unser Blvd NW; ⏰visitor center 8am-5pm), which has more than 20,000 rock etchings.

✖ p47, p59

The Drive » Route 66 dips from I-40 into Gallup, becoming the main drag past beautifully renovated buildings, including the 1928 Spanish Colonial El Morro Theater. Cool murals also adorn many buildings. From Gallup, it's 21 miles to Arizona. In Arizona, take exit 311 to enter Petrified Forest National Park.

⓬ Petrified Forest National Park

The 'trees' of the **Petrified Forest** (☎928-524-6228; www.nps.gov/pefo; vehicle $20, walk-in/bicycle/motorcycle $10; ⏰7am-7pm Mar-Sep, shorter hours Oct-Feb) are fragmented, fossilized 225-million-year-old logs; in essence, wood that has turned to stone, scattered over a vast area of semidesert grassland. Many are huge – up to 6ft in diameter.

The scenic drive has about 15 pullouts with interpretive signs and some short trails. Two trails near the southern entrance provide the best access for close-ups of the petrified logs: the 1.6-mile Long Logs Trail, which has the largest concentration, and the 0.4-mile Giant Logs Trail, which is entered through the Rainbow Forest Museum and sports the park's largest log.

North of the I-40 enjoy sweeping views of the Painted Desert, where nature presents a hauntingly beautiful palette, especially at sunset.

The park, which straddles I-40, has an entrance at exit 311 in the north and another off Hwy 180 in the south. A 28-mile paved scenic road links the two. To avoid backtracking, westbound travelers should start in the north, eastbound travelers in the south.

The Drive » Take I-40 west 25 miles to Holbrook, a former Wild West town now home to the photo-ready Wigwam Motel. Motor on through lonesome Winslow, which has an elegant hotel (p47), and college-y Flagstaff. At Seligman grab a burger (p47) before the Mother Road arcs northwest away from I-40 through scrub-covered desert, then rejoins the interstate at quiet Kingman. From here you corkscrew through the Black Mountains and Sitgreaves Pass to Oatman.

⓭ Oatman

Since the veins of ore ran dry in 1942, crusty Oatman has reinvented itself as a movie set and Wild West tourist trap, complete with staged gun fights (daily at 1:30pm and 3:30pm) and gift stores named Fast Fanny's Place and the Classy Ass.

Speaking of asses, there are plenty of them (the four-legged kind, that is) roaming the streets. Stupid and endearing, they're descendants from pack animals left by the early miners. These burros may beg for food, but do not feed them carrots. Instead, buy healthier hay cubes for $1 per bag at nearby stores.

Squeezed among the shops is the 1902 Oatman Hotel, a surprisingly modest shack (no longer renting rooms) where Clark Gable and Carole Lombard spent their wedding night in 1939. On July 4 the town holds a sidewalk egg-frying contest. Now that's hot!

The Drive » From here, Route 66 twists down to Golden Shores and I-40. Soon you'll enter California at Needles. About 40 miles later, the road dips south and joins with the National Old Trails Rd. This is some of the coolest stretch of road, with huge skies and vintage signs rusting in the sun.

⓮ Amboy

Potholed and crumbling in a romantic way, the USA's original transnational highway was established in 1912, more than a decade before Route 66 first ran through here. The rutted highway races through tiny towns, sparsely scattered across the Mojave. Only a few landmarks interrupt the horizon, including **Roy's Motel &**

Cafe (www.rt66roys.com; National Old Trails Hwy; ⏲7am-8pm, seasonal variations; Ⓟ), a landmark Route 66 watering hole. If you'll believe the lore, Roy once cooked his famous Route 66 double cheeseburger on the hood of a '63 Mercury. Although the motel is abandoned, the gas station and cafe are occasionally open. It's east of **Amboy Crater** (☎760-326-7000; www.blm.gov/ca; ⏲sunrise-sunset; Ⓟ), an almost perfectly symmetrical volcanic cinder cone. You can hike to the top, but it's best to avoid the midday sun – the 1.5-mile hike doesn't have a stitch of shade.

The Drive » Stay on the National Old Trails Rd to Ludlow. Turn right onto Crucero Rd and pass under I-40, then take the north frontage road west and turn left at Lavic Rd. Keep heading west on the National Old Trails Rd through windswept Daggett. Join I-40 at Nebo St. Drive for about 15 minutes before taking the exit for Barstow Rd.

15 Barstow

Exit the interstate onto Main St, which runs through Barstow, a railroad settlement and historic crossroads, where murals adorn empty buildings downtown. Follow 1st St north across the Mojave River over a trestle bridge to the 1911 Harvey House, nicknamed 'Casa del Desierto,' designed by Western architect Mary Colter. Next to a small railroad museum is the **Route 66 'Mother Road' Museum** (☎760-255-1890; www.route66museum.org; 681 N 1st St; ⏲10am-4pm Fri & Sat, 11am-4pm Sun, or by appointment; Ⓟ 👪), displaying black-and-white historical photographs and odds and ends of everyday life in the early 20th century. Back in the day, it was also a Harvey House.

p47

The Drive » Rejoin the National Old Trails Rd. At Victorville take I-15 out of town, heading south to San Bernardino, home to an iconic Route 66 motor court. From there follow Foothill Blvd/Route 66 west through retro-suburban Pasadena and check out the diner (p47). Finally, for your Hollywood ending, take Arroyo Seco Pkwy to LA, where Sunset Blvd connects to Santa Monica Blvd.

EDUARDO FREDERIKSEN / 500PX ©

TRIP HIGHLIGHT

16 Santa Monica

This is the end of the line: Route 66 reaches its

TOP TIP: NAVIGATING ROUTE 66

Because Route 66 is no longer an official road, it doesn't appear on most maps. We've provided high-level directions, but you'll fare best using one of these additional resources: free turn-by-turn directions at www.historic66.com, or maps from the National Historic Route 66 Federation (www.national66.org).

Santa Monica Pier Extends nearly a quarter-mile over the Pacific

finish, over 2400 miles from its starting point in Chicago, on an ocean bluff in **Palisades Park**, where a Will Rogers Hwy memorial plaque marks the official end of the Mother Road. Celebrate on **Santa Monica Pier** (☎310-458-8901; www.santamonicapier.org; 👪), where you can ride a 1920s carousel featured in *The Sting,* gently touch tide-pool critters at the **Santa Monica Pier Aquarium** (☎310-393-6149; www.healthebay.org; 1600 Ocean Front Walk; adult/child $5/free; ⏲2-6pm Tue-Fri, 12:30-6pm Sat & Sun; 👪; Ⓜ Expo Line to Downtown Santa Monica), and soak up a sunset atop the solar-powered Ferris wheel at **Pacific Park** (☎310-260-8744; www.pacpark.com; 380 Santa Monica Pier; per ride $5-10, all-day pass adult/child under 8yr $32/18; ⏲daily, seasonal hours vary; 👪; Ⓜ Expo Line to Downtown Santa Monica). Year-round carnival rides include the West Coast's only oceanfront steel roller coaster – a thrilling ride to end this classic trip.

🛏 p47

Classic Trip

Eating & Sleeping

Chicago 1

Lou Mitchell's Breakfast $

(312-939-3111; www.loumitchellsrestaurant.com; 565 W Jackson Blvd; mains $9-14; 5:30am-3pm Mon, to 4pm Tue-Fri, 7am-4pm Sat, to 3pm Sun; ; M Blue Line to Clinton) A relic of Route 66, Lou's brings in elbow-to-elbow locals and tourists for breakfast. The old-school waitresses deliver fluffy omelets that hang off the plate and thick-cut French toast with a jug of syrup.

Atlanta

Palms Grill Cafe Diner $

(217-648-2233; www.thepalmsgrillcafe.com; 110 SW Arch St; mains $6-10; 10am-4pm Sun-Wed, to 8pm Thu-Sat) Thick slabs of gooseberry, chocolate cream and other retro pies tempt from the glass case. Then walk across the street to snap a photo with Tall Paul, a sky-high statue of Paul Bunyan clutching a hot dog.

Springfield 3

Cozy Dog Drive In American $

(217-525-1992; www.cozydogdrivein.com; 2935 S 6th St; mains $2-5; 8am-8pm Mon-Sat) This Route 66 legend – the reputed birthplace of the corn dog! – has memorabilia and souvenirs in addition to the deeply fried main course on a stick.

St Louis 4

Ted Drewes Sweets $

(314-481-2652; www.teddrewes.com; 6726 Chippewa St; cones $2-6; 11am-11pm Feb-Dec) Don't dare leave town without licking yourself silly on this super-creamy ice-cream-like treat at historic Ted Drewes, west of the city center. There's a smaller summer-only branch south of the city center at 4224 S Grand Blvd.

Lebanon

Munger Moss Motel Motel $

(417-532-3111; www.mungermoss.com; 1336 E Rte 66; r from $60;) Ready for a snooze? Head to this 1940s motel. It's got a monster of a neon sign and Mother Road–loving owners.

Vinita

Clanton's American $

(918-256-9053; www.clantonscafe.com; 319 E Illinois Ave; mains $4-12; 6am-8pm Mon-Fri, to 2pm Sat & Sun) Clanton's dates back to 1927 and is the place for chicken fried steak and calf fries (don't ask).

El Reno

Sid's Diner Burgers $

(405-262-7757; 300 S Choctaw Ave; mains from $4; 7am-8pm Mon-Sat) The most heralded of El Reno's onion burgers with lines out the door to prove it. Sit at the counter to watch the burger-making magic.

Amarillo 9

Big Texan Steak Ranch Steak $$

(www.bigtexan.com; 7701 I-40 E, exit 75; mains $10-40; 7am-10:30pm;) A classic, hokey Route 66 roadside attraction. The legendary come-on: the 'free 72oz steak' – you have to eat this enormous portion of cow plus a multitude of sides in under one hour, or you pay for the meal ($72).

Adrian

Midpoint Cafe Cafe $

(806-538-6379; http://route66midpointcafe.com; 305 W Historic Route 66; mains $5-10; 8am-4pm, days vary) Vibrant vinyl chairs and 1950s-esque knickknacks form the backdrop here. The food is familiar (barbecue and burgers), but aims higher with added touches: it's not just potato salad, it's deviled-egg potato salad.

Tucumcari ⑩

Kix on 66 — Diner $

(☎575-461-1966; www.kixon66.com; 1102 E Tucumcari Blvd; mains $5-10; 6am-2pm; wifi) Very popular morning hangout serving breakfast in all shapes and sizes, from *huevos rancheros* to biscuits and gravy, plus espresso coffees, doughnuts and lunch sandwiches.

Blue Swallow Motel — Motel $

(☎575-461-9849; www.blueswallowmotel.com; 815 E Tucumcari Blvd; r from $75; ac, wifi) Spend the night in this beautifully restored Route 66 motel and feel the decades melt away. Friendly owners and vintage, uniquely decorated rooms.

Albuquerque ⑪

Artichoke Cafe — Modern American $$$

(☎505-243-0200; www.artichokecafe.com; 424 Central Ave SE; lunch mains $12-19, dinner mains $16-39; 11am-2:30pm & 5-9pm Mon-Fri, 5-10pm Sat) This popular bistro prepares creative gourmet cuisine with panache.

Marble Brewery — Brewery $

(☎505-243-2739; www.marblebrewery.com; 111 Marble Ave NW; noon-midnight Mon-Sat, to 10:30pm Sun) Popular downtown brewpub, with a snug interior for winter nights and a beer garden where local bands play gigs in summer.

Winslow

La Posada — Historic Hotel $$

(☎928-289-4366; www.laposada.org; 303 E 2nd St; d/deluxe $139/169; ac, wifi, pets) An impressively restored 1930 hacienda designed by star architect Mary Jane Colter. Elaborate tilework, glass-and-tin chandeliers, Navajo rugs and other details accent its Western-style elegance.

Seligman

Delgadillo's Snow Cap Drive-In — Burgers $

(☎928-422-3291; 301 Rte 66; mains $5-6.50; 10am-6pm Mar-Nov) A Route 66 institution – the crazy decor is only the beginning. Beware the fake mustard bottle!

Barstow ⑮

Idle Spurs Steakhouse — Steak $$

(☎760-256-8888; www.thespurs.us; 690 Old Hwy 58; mains lunch $9-24, dinner $12-45; 11am-9pm Tue-Fri, from 4pm Sat & Sun; P, family) In the saddle since 1950, this Western-themed spot is a fave with locals and travelers. Surrender to your inner carnivore with slow-roasted prime rib, hand-cut steaks and succulent lobster tail.

San Bernardino

Wigwam Motel — Motel $

(☎909-875-3005; www.wigwammotel.com; 2728 W Foothill Blvd; r $73-110; P, ac, wifi, pool, pets) Get your kitsch on Route 66: stay snug in one of 19 concrete, 30ft-tall tipis. Built in 1949, they're equipped with nice furniture and have motel-type mod cons.

Pasadena

Fair Oaks Pharmacy — Diner $

(☎626-799-1414; www.fairoakspharmacy.net; 1526 Mission St, South Pasadena; mains $6-11; 9am-9pm Mon-Sat, 10am-7pm Sun; family) Get your kicks at this original 1915 soda fountain right on Route 66. Slurp an old-fashioned 'phosphate' (flavored syrup, soda water and 'secret potion') or stock up on classic candy in the gift shops.

Saga Motor Hotel — Motel $$

(☎800-793-7242, 626-795-0431; www.thesagamotorhotel.com; 1633 E Colorado Blvd; r from $105; P, ac, @, wifi, pool, pets) This peach-tinted 70-room motel isn't fancy or as cool as its vintage 1950s sign makes it look. But even if some of the decor could use a refresh, rates include simple continental breakfast and rooms are clean.

Santa Monica ⑯

Sea Shore Motel — Motel $$

(☎310-392-2787; www.seashoremotel.com; 2637 Main St; r $125-175, ste $200-300; P, ac, wifi) The friendly, family-run lodgings at this comfy but basic 25-unit motel put you just a Frisbee toss from the beach on happening Main St. Families can stretch out in the suites a few doors down.

Classic Trip

Four Corners Cruise

Everything about this trip demands superlatives – from the Grand Canyon to Vegas, Zion and beyond, it's a procession of some of the biggest, boldest items on many a bucket list.

TRIP HIGHLIGHTS

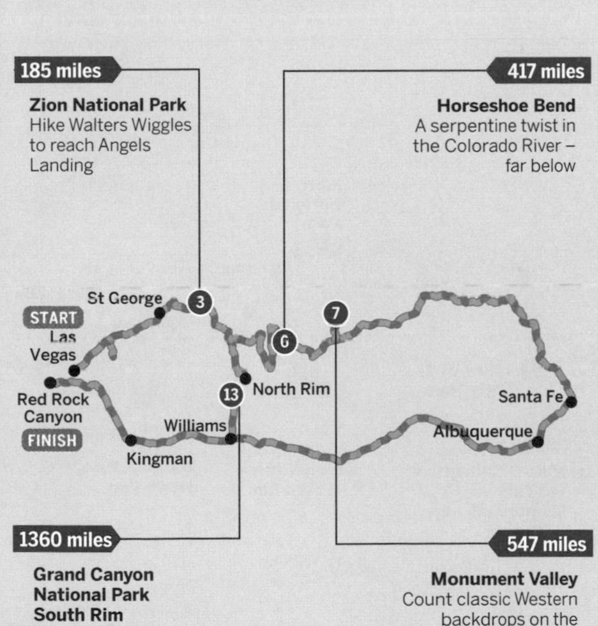

10 DAYS
1593 MILES / 2564KM

GREAT FOR...

BEST TIME TO GO

Spring and fall for thinner crowds and pleasant temperatures.

ESSENTIAL PHOTO

The glory of the Grand Canyon from the Rim Trail.

BEST FOR OUTDOORS

Angels Landing Trail in Zion National Park.

Zion National Park The path to Angels Landing

Classic Trip

2 Four Corners Cruise

From a distance, the rugged buttes and mesas of Monument Valley resemble the remains of a prehistoric fortress, red-gold ramparts protecting ancient secrets. Up close, you'll find these rocks mesmerizing, an alluring mix of the familiar and otherworldly. Yes, they're recognizable from multitudes of Westerns, but the big screen doesn't capture the changing light patterns, imposing height or sense of fathomless antiquity. It's a captivating spell – but by no means the only one cast along this Four Corners Cruise.

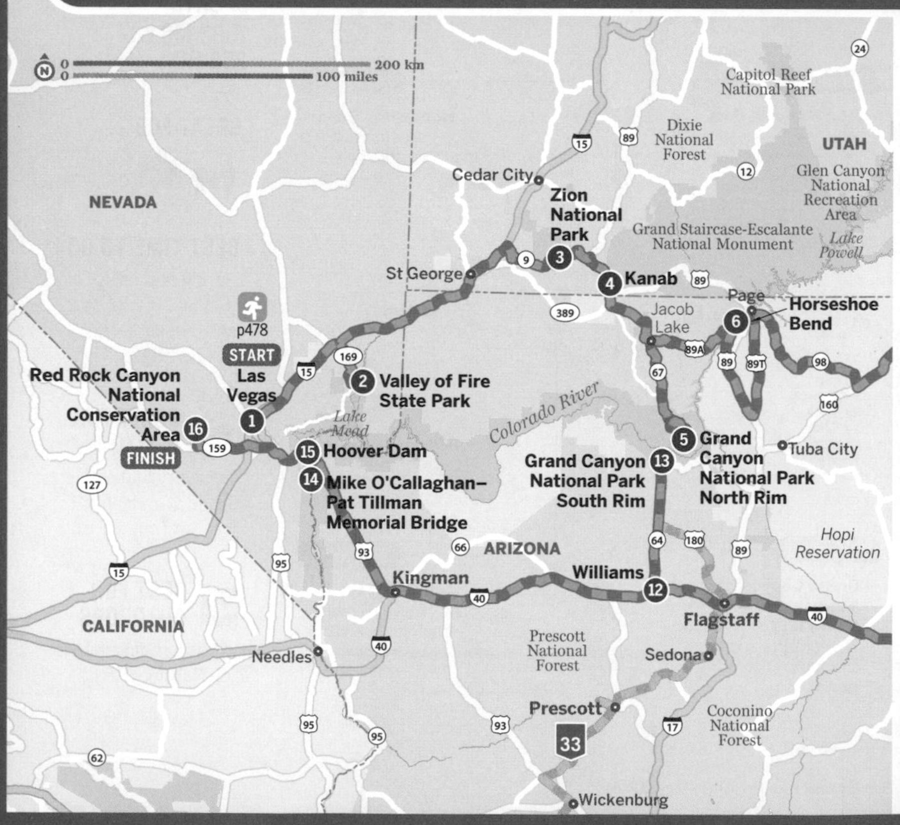

❶ Las Vegas

Take in Sin City's synthetic charms on a morning walk past the iconic casinos and hotels of the **Strip** (p478), then spend the afternoon downtown at the **Mob Museum** (☎702-229-2734; www.themobmuseum.org; 300 Stewart Ave; adult/child $24/14; ⏲9am-9pm; P; 🚌Deuce), a three-story collection examining organized crime in America and its connection to Las Vegas. One block south, zip-line over **Fremont St** from the 11th-story launchpad of **Slotzilla** (www.vegasexperience.com/slotzilla-zip-line; Fremont St Mall, Fremont Street Experience; lower line $25, upper line $45; ⏲1pm-1am Sun-Thu, to 2am Fri & Sat; 👪; 🚌Deuce, SDX), then end the night with an illuminated stroll at the **Neon Museum** (☎702-387-6366; www.neonmuseum.org; 770 N Las Vegas Blvd; 1hr tour adult/child $19/15, after dark $26/22; ⏲tours daily, schedules vary; 🚌113).

The giant pink stiletto in the lobby of Vegas' **Cosmopolitan**

LINK YOUR TRIP

33 Fantastic Canyon Voyage

For red rocks and mining history swing south from Flagstaff on I-17 to Hwy 89A.

36 High & Low Roads to Taos

Take the high or the low road between Santa Fe and Taos, with fine craftwork, historic churches and mountain scenery.

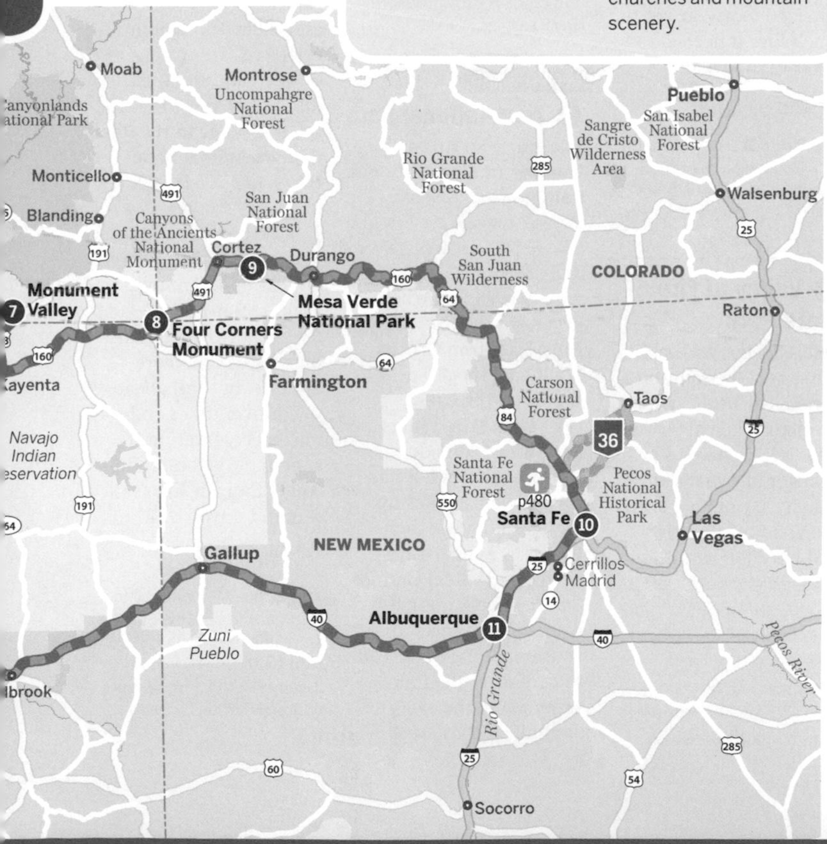

(☎702-698-7000; www.cosmopolitanlasvegas.com; 3708 S Las Vegas Blvd; ⌚24hr; P) is an eye-catcher. Designed by Roark Gourley, the 9ft-tall shoe was supposed to be treated with the reverence due a piece of art, but its protective ropes were soon pushed aside by partygoers seeking 'unique' selfies. In response, the Cosmopolitan removed the ropes and in 16 months the outsized footwear got so much love it needed to be sent out for repairs.

p59, 499

The Drive » Follow I-15 north for 34 miles then take exit 75. From here, Hwy 169/Valley of Fire Hwy travels 18 miles to the park.

2 Valley of Fire State Park

Before losing yourself in the sandstone sculpture-gardens of Utah, swing through this masterwork of desert scenery to prime yourself for what's ahead. It's an easy detour, with the Valley of Fire Hwy and Hwy 169 running through the **park** (☎702-397-2088; www.parks.nv.gov/parks/valley-of-fire; 29450 Valley of Fire Hwy, Overton; per vehicle $10; ⌚visitor center 8:30am-4:30pm, park 7am-7pm) and passing close to the psychedelically shaped red rock formations. From the visitor center, take the winding, scenic side road out to **White Domes**, an 11-mile round-trip. En route you'll pass **Rainbow Vista**, followed by the turn-off to **Fire Canyon** and **Silica Dome** (where Captain Kirk perished in *Star Trek: Generations*).

Spring and fall are the best times to visit; avoid summer when temperatures typically exceed 100°F (37°C).

The Drive » Return to I-15 north, cruising through Arizona and into Utah. Leave the highway at exit 16 and follow Hwy 9 east for 32 miles.

TRIP HIGHLIGHT

3 Zion National Park

The climb up **Angels Landing** in **Zion National Park** (www.nps.gov/zion; Hwy 9; 7-day pass per vehicle $30; ⌚24hr, visitor center 8am-7:30pm Jun-Aug, closes earlier Sep-May) may be the best day hike in North America. From **Grotto Trailhead**, the 5.4-mile round-trip crosses the Virgin River, hugs a towering cliffside, squeezes through a narrow canyon, snakes up Walters Wiggles, then traverses a razor-thin ridge where steel chains and the encouraging words of strangers are your only safety net. Your reward after the final scramble to the 5790ft summit? A bird's-eye view of Zion Canyon. The hike reflects what's best about the park: beauty, adventure and the shared community of people who love the outdoors.

The Drive » Twist out of the park on Hwy 9 east, driving almost 25 miles to Hwy 89. Follow Hwy 89 south to the vast open-air movie set that is Kanab.

4 Kanab

Sitting between Zion, Grand Staircase–Escalante and the Grand Canyon North Rim, Kanab is a good spot for a base camp. Hundreds of Western movies were filmed here – John Wayne and other gunslingin' celebs really put the town on the map. Today, animal lovers know that the town is home to the **Best Friends Animal Sanctuary** (☎435-644-2001; www.bestfriends.org; Hwy 89, Angel Canyon; ⌚9:30am-5:30pm; 👪), the country's largest no-kill animal shelter. Tours of the facility – home to dogs, cats, pigs, birds and more – are free, but call ahead to confirm times and to make a reservation. The sanctuary is located in Angel Canyon, also called Kanab Canyon by locals.

p59

The Drive » Continue into Arizona – now on Hwy 89A – and climb the Kaibab Plateau. Turn south onto Hwy 67 at Jacob Lake and drive 44 miles to Grand Canyon Lodge.

❺ Grand Canyon National Park North Rim

While driving through the ponderosa forest that opens onto rolling meadows in Kaibab National Forest, keep an eye out for mule deer as you approach the entrance to the **park** (www.nps.gov/grca; per vehicle $30, per motorcycle $25, per bicycle, pedestrian or shuttle-bus passenger $15; ⌚mid-May–mid-Oct). Stop by the **North Rim Visitor Center** (☎928-638-7888; www.nps.gov/grca; ⌚8am-6pm mid-May–mid-Oct), beside Grand Canyon Lodge (both closed during the snows of October to May), for information and to join ranger-led nature walks and nighttime programs. If it's five o'clock somewhere, enjoy a cocktail from the lodge terrace of the **Rough Rider Saloon** (www.grandcanyonforever.com; Grand Canyon Lodge; ⌚5:30-10:30am & 11:30am-10:30pm) while soaking up the view.

For an easy but scenic half-day hike, follow the 4-mile **Cape Final Trail** (round-trip) through ponderosa pine forests with great canyon views. The steep and difficult 14-mile **North Kaibab Trail** is the only maintained rim-to-river trail and connects with trails to the South Rim near Phantom Ranch. The trailhead is 2 miles north of Grand Canyon Lodge. For a taste of inner-canyon hiking, walk 0.75 miles down to **Coconino Overlook** or 2 miles to the **Supai Tunnel**.

TOP TIP: NO BOTTLED WATER

As a conservation measure, Grand Canyon National Park no longer sells bottled water. Instead, fill your thermos at water filling stations along the rim or at Canyon View Marketplace. Water bottles had constituted 20% of the waste generated in the park.

The Drive » Track back to Jacob Lake, then head east on Hwy 89A, down the Kaibab Plateau, past blink-and-miss-it Marble Canyon and to the junction with Hwy 89. Turn left and drive 26 miles north to Page.

TRIP HIGHLIGHT

❻ Horseshoe Bend

The clifftop view at Horseshoe Bend will sear itself onto your memory. One thousand feet below, the **Colorado River** carves a perfect U through a colossal thickness of Navajo sandstone. It's simultaneously beautiful and terrifying. There are no railings – it's just you, a sheer drop and dozens of people you don't know, taking selfies on the treacherous rim. Free-range toddlers are not a good idea. From the parking lot it's a 0.75-mile one-way hike to the rim. There's a moderate hill along the way, and the trail is unshaded, so the walk can be a little strenuous in summer – but it's worth it. The trailhead is on Hwy 89, south of Page and just south of mile marker 541.

The Drive » Rejoin Hwy 89 and drive north a short distance to Hwy 98. Turn right and follow 98 southeast to Hwy 160. Turn left and drive 34 miles north, passing the entrance to Navajo National Monument. In Kayenta, turn left onto Hwy 163 North and drive almost 22 miles to Monument Valley, on the Arizona–Utah border.

TRIP HIGHLIGHT

❼ Monument Valley

'May I walk in beauty' is the final line of a famous Navajo prayer. Beauty comes in countless forms on this vast reservation, but Monument Valley's majestic array of rugged buttes and wind-worn mesas must be its most sensational. For up-close views of the formations, drive into the **Monument Valley Navajo Tribal Park** (☎435-727-5870; www.navajonationparks.org; per 4-person vehicle $20; ⌚drive 6am-7pm Apr-Sep, 8am-4:30pm Oct-Mar, visitor center 6am-8pm Apr-Sep, 8am-5pm Oct-Mar; Ⓟ) and follow the unpaved 17-mile scenic loop that

WHY THIS IS A CLASSIC TRIP

HUGH MCNAUGHTAN, WRITER

Epic, grandiose and utterly beguiling, this trip is nothing less than a crash course in the glories of America's Southwest. While Vegas is a global byword for sin and frivolity, there are plenty of opportunities to make peace with your soul in the wilds of the Grand Canyon's North Rim, in the peerless splendor of Zion National Park's canyons and in the sacred places of the vast Navajo Reservation.

Above left: Grand Canyon National Park
Above right: Riding the South Kaibab Trail

passes some of the most dramatic formations, such as the **East and West Mitten Buttes** and the **Three Sisters**. For a guided tour (1½/2½ hours $65/85), which will take you into areas where private vehicles cannot go, stop by one of the kiosks in the parking lot beside the View Hotel.

p59, p449

CANADASTOCK / SHUTTERSTOCK ©

ROMAN KHOMLYAK / SHUTTERSTOCK ©

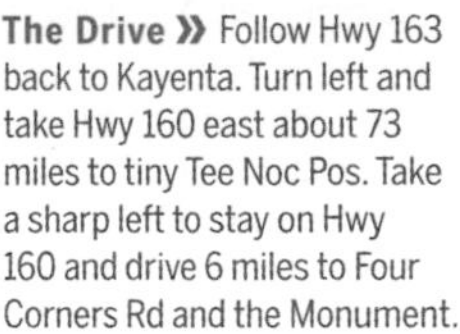

The Drive » Follow Hwy 163 back to Kayenta. Turn left and take Hwy 160 east about 73 miles to tiny Tee Noc Pos. Take a sharp left to stay on Hwy 160 and drive 6 miles to Four Corners Rd and the Monument.

8 Four Corners Monument

It's seriously remote, but you can't skip the **Four Corners Monument** (☎928-871-6647; www.navajonationparks.org; $5; ⏰8am-7pm May-Sep, to 5pm Oct-Apr) on a road trip through the epicenter of the Southwest! Once you arrive, don't be shy: put a foot into Arizona and plant the other in New Mexico. Slap a hand in Utah and place the other in Colorado. Smile for the camera. It makes a good photo, even if it's not 100% accurate – government surveyors have admitted that the marker is almost 2000ft east of where it should be (although it remains a legally recognized border point). Half the fun here is watching the contortions performed by happy-snappers determined to straddle all four states.

The Drive » Return to Hwy 160 and turn left. It's a 50-mile drive across the northwestern

tip of New Mexico and through Colorado to Mesa Verde. Hwy 160 becomes Hwy 491 for around 20 miles of this journey.

9 Mesa Verde National Park

Ancestral Puebloan sites are found throughout the canyons and mesas of **Mesa Verde** (970 529 4465; www.nps.gov/meve; 7-day car/motorcycle pass Jun-Aug $20/10, Sep-May $15/7; P), perched on a high plateau south of Cortez and Mancos. According to the experts, the Ancestral Puebloans didn't 'disappear' 700 years ago, they simply migrated south, developing into the American Indian tribes that live in the Southwest to this day. If you only have time for a short visit, check out the **Chapin Mesa Museum** and walk through the **Spruce Tree House**, where you can climb down a wooden ladder into a kiva.

Mesa Verde rewards travelers who set aside a day or more to take the ranger-led tours of **Cliff Palace** and **Balcony House**, explore **Wetherill Mesa** (the quieter side of canyon), linger around the museum, or participate in one of the campfire programs at **Morefield Campground** (970-529-4465; www.visitmesaverde.com; Mile 4; tent/RV site $30/40; May-early Oct;). The park also provides plenty of hiking, skiing, snowshoeing and mountain-biking options. Visitors can camp out or stay in luxury at the lodge.

The Drive » Hop back onto US 160, following it 36 miles east to Durango and then another 61 miles to join US 84 south for the 151-mile run to Santa Fe. You'll pass through Abiquiú, home of artist Georgia O'Keeffe from 1949 until her death in 1986. Continue toward Santa Fe, exiting onto N Guadalupe St to head toward the Plaza.

10 Santa Fe

This 400-year-old city is pretty darn inviting. You've got the juxtaposition of art and landscape, with cow skulls hanging from sky-blue walls and slender crosses topping centuries-old missions. And then there's the comfortable mingling of American Indian, Hispanic and Anglo cultures, with ancient pueblos, 300-year-old haciendas and stylish modern buildings standing in easy proximity.

The beauty of the region was captured by New Mexico's most famous artist, Georgia O'Keeffe. Possessing the world's largest collection of her work, the **Georgia O'Keeffe Museum** (505-946-1000; www.okeeffemuseum.org; 217 Johnson St; adult/child $12/free; 10am-5pm Sat-Thu, to 7pm Fri) showcases the thick brushwork and luminous colors that don't always come through on the ubiquitous posters. Take your time to relish them here firsthand. The museum is housed in a former Spanish Baptist church with adobe walls that has been renovated to form 10 skylit galleries.

The city is anchored by the Plaza, which was the end of the Santa Fe Trail between 1822 and 1880.

p59, p459

The Drive » The historic route to Albuquerque is the Turquoise Trail, which follows Hwy 14 south for 50 miles through Los Cerrillos and Madrid. If you're in a hurry, take I-25 south.

11 Albuquerque

Most of Albuquerque's top sites are concentrated in **Old Town**, which is a straight shot west on Central Ave from Nob Hill and the University of New Mexico (UNM).

The most extravagant route to the top of 10,378ft Sandia Crest is via the **Sandia Peak Tramway** (505-856-7325; www.sandiapeak.com; 30 Tramway Rd NE; adult/youth 13-20yr/child $25/20/15, parking $2; 9am-9pm Jun-Aug, 9am-8pm Wed-Mon, from 5pm Tue Sep-May). The 2.7-mile tram ride starts in the desert realm of cholla cactus and soars to the pine-topped summit. For exercise, take the beautiful 8-mile (one-way) **La Luz Trail** (www.laluztrail.com; FR 444; parking $3) back down, connecting with the 2-mile **Tramway Trail** to return to your car. The La Luz Trail passes a small waterfall, pine forests and spectacular views. It gets hot, so start early. Take Tramway Blvd east from I-25 to get to the tramway.

✕ p47, p59

The Drive » From Albuquerque to Williams, in Arizona, I-40 overlaps or parallels Route 66. It's 359 miles to Williams.

⓬ Williams

Train buffs, Route 66 enthusiasts and Grand Canyon–bound vacationers all cross paths in Williams, an inviting small town with all the charm and authenticity of 'Main Street America.' If you only have time for a day visit to the park, the **Grand Canyon Railway** (☎reservations 800-843-8724; www.thetrain.com; 233 N Grand Canyon Bvd, Railway Depot; round-trip adult/child from $79/47) is a fun and hassle-free way to get there and back. After a **Wild West show** beside the tracks, the train departs for its 2½-hour ride to the South Rim, where you can explore by foot or shuttle. Late March through October passengers can ride in reconditioned open-air Pullman cabooses.

On Route 66 the divey **World Famous Sultana Bar** (☎928-635-2021; 301 W Route 66; ⏲10am-2am, shorter hours in winter), which once housed a speakeasy, is a great place to sink some suds beneath a menagerie of stuffed wildlife.

TRIP HIGHLIGHT

⓭ Grand Canyon National Park South Rim

A walk along the **Rim Trail** (www.nps.gov/grca; 👪; 🚌Hermits Rest, 🚌Village, 🚌Kaibab/Rim) in **Grand Canyon Village** brings stunning views of the iconic canyon, as well as historic buildings, American Indian crafts and geological displays.

Starting from the plaza at **Bright Angel Trail**, walk east on the Rim Trail to **Kolb Studio** (☎928-638-2771; www.nps.gov/grca; National Historic Landmark District; ⏲8am-7pm Mar-May & Sep-Nov, to 6pm Dec-Feb, to 8pm Jun-Aug; 🚌Village), which holds a small bookstore and an art gallery. Next door is **Lookout Studio** (www.nps.gov/grca; ⏲8am-sunset mid-May–Aug, 9am-5pm Sep–mid-May; 🚌Village), designed by noted architect Mary Jane Colter to look like the stone dwellings of the Southwest's Puebloans.

Step into the 1905 El Tovar hotel (p431) to see its replica Remington bronzes, stained glass, stuffed mounts and exposed beams, or to admire the canyon views from its porches.

Next door, the **Hopi House** (www.nps.gov/grca; Grand Canyon Village; ⏲8am-8pm mid-May–Aug, 9am-6pm Sep–mid-Oct, 9am-5pm mid-Oct–mid-May; 🚌Village), another Colter-designed structure, has sold high-quality American Indian jewelry and other crafts

PHOTO FINISH: KOLB STUDIO

Before digital photography, brothers Ellsworth and Emery Kolb were shooting souvenir photos of mule-riding Grand Canyon visitors as they began their descent down the Bright Angel Trail. The brothers would sell finished prints to the tourists returning to the rim at the end of the day. But in the early 1900s there was no running water on the South Rim – so how did they process their prints?

After snapping photos from their studio window that overlooked a bend in the trail, one of the brothers would run 4.6 miles down to the waters of Indian Garden with the negatives, print the photos in their lab there and then run, or perhaps hike briskly, back up the Bright Angel to meet visitors with their prints.

since 1904. Just east, the **Trail of Time** (www.nps.gov/grca; Grand Canyon Village; [icon]; [icon]Village) interpretative display traces the history of the canyon's formation. End with the intriguing exhibits and gorgeous views of the **Yavapai Geology Museum** ([icon]928-638-7890; www.nps.gov/grca; Grand Canyon Village; [icon]8am-7pm Mar-May & Sep-Nov, to 6pm Dec-Feb, to 8pm Jun-Aug; [icon]; [icon]Kaibab/Rim).

The Drive » Having returned to Williams, take the I-40 113 miles west to Kingman, then join US 93 north. Head north for 75 miles, crossing into Nevada, where exit 2 leads on to Hwy 172 and Hoover Dam.

14 Mike O'Callaghan–Pat Tillman Memorial Bridge

This graceful span, dedicated in 2010, was named for Mike O'Callaghan, governor of Nevada from 1971 to 1979, and for NFL star Pat Tillman, who was a safety for the Arizona Cardinals when he enlisted as a US Army Ranger after September 11. Tillman was killed by friendly fire during a battle in Afghanistan in 2004.

Open to pedestrians along a walkway separated from traffic on Hwy 93, the bridge sits 900ft above the Colorado River. It's the second-highest bridge in the US, and provides a bird's-eye eye view of Hoover Dam and Lake Mead behind it.

The Drive » Turn right onto the access road and drive a short distance down to Hoover Dam.

15 Hoover Dam

A statue of bronze winged figures stands atop **Hoover Dam** ([icon]702-494-2517; www.usbr.gov/lc/hooverdam; off Hwy 93; admission visitor center incl parking $10; [icon]9am-6pm Apr-Oct, to 5pm Nov-Mar; [icon]), memorializing those who built the massive 726ft concrete structure, one of the world's tallest dams. This New Deal public works project, completed ahead of schedule and under budget in 1936, was the first major dam of the **Colorado River**. Thousands of men and their families, eager for work in the height of the Depression, came to Black Canyon and worked in excruciating conditions – dangling hundreds of feet above the canyon in desert heat of up to 120°F (49°C). Over 100 lost their lives.

Today, guided tours begin at the visitor center, where a video screening features original footage of the construction. After the movie take an elevator ride 50 stories below to view the dam's massive power generators, each of which alone could power a city of 100,000 people.

The Drive » Return to US 93, following it west then north as it joins I-515. Take exit 61 for I-215 north. After 11 miles I-215 becomes Clark County 215. Follow it just over 13 miles to Charleston Blvd/Hwy 159 at exit 26 and follow it west.

16 Red Rock Canyon National Conservation Area

The evidence of awesome natural forces in this **national conservation area** ([icon]702-515-5350; www.redrockcanyonlv.org; 1000 Scenic Loop Dr; car/bicycle $7/3; [icon]scenic loop 6am-8pm Apr-Sep, to 7pm Mar & Oct, to 5pm Nov-Feb; [icon]) can't be exaggerated. Created about 65 million years ago, the canyon is more like a valley, with a steep, rugged red rock escarpment rising 3000ft on its western edge, dramatic evidence of tectonic-plate collisions.

The 13-mile, one-way scenic drive passes some of the canyon's most striking features, where you can access hiking trails and rock-climbing routes. The 2.5-mile round-trip hike to **Calico Tanks** climbs through the sandstone and ends atop rocks offering a grand view of the desert and mountains, with Vegas thrown in for sizzle.

National park passes are accepted for admission.

Eating & Sleeping

Las Vegas 1

✕ Joël Robuchon — French $$$

(☎702-891-7925; www.joel-robuchon.com; MGM Grand, 3799 S Las Vegas Blvd; tasting menus $120-425; ⏲5-10pm) The acclaimed 'Chef of the Century' leads the pack in the French culinary invasion of the Strip. Adjacent to the MGM Grand's high-rollers' gaming area, Robuchon's plush dining rooms, done up in leather and velvet, feel like a dinner party at a 1930s Paris mansion. Complex seasonal tasting menus promise the meal of a lifetime – and they often deliver.

W Las Vegas — Boutique Hotel $$

(☎702-761-8700; www.wlasvegas.com; 2535 S Las Vegas Blvd; r from $109; P ❄ 📶 🏊 🐾) At the time of writing, the new-in-2017 W Las Vegas, occupying what was one of two towers belonging to sister property **SLS** (☎702-761-7000; www.slslasvegas.com; 2535 S Las Vegas Blvd; d from $79; P ❄ 📶 🏊), was the hottest ticket on the north Strip, offering excellent rates for a stylish brand-new-room product by this exciting world-recognized brand. If you like design and a cooler crowd, head north and hang here.

Kanab 4

✕ Sego Restaurant — Modern American $$

(☎435-644-5680; 190 N 300 W, Canyons Boutique Hotel; mains $14-23; ⏲5-9pm Tue-Sat) If Kanab is aspiring to be the next Sedona, this boutique hotel-restaurant will fast track things. Gorgeous eats range from foraged mushrooms with goat's cheese to noodles with red-crab curry and a decadent flourless torte for dessert. There are also craft cocktails and local beers. Hours may be expanding. Reserve ahead: there are few tables.

Canyons Lodge — Motel $$

(☎435-644-3069; www.canyonslodge.com; 236 N 300 W; r $169-179; ❄ @ 📶 🏊 🐾) A renovated motel with an art-house Western feel. There's a warm welcome, free cruiser bikes and good traveler assistance. In summer, guests enjoy twice-weekly live music and wine and cheese by the fire pit. Rooms feature original artwork and whimsical touches. Recycles soaps and containers.

Monument Valley 7

View Hotel — Hotel $$$

(☎435-727-5555; www.monumentvalleyview.com; Indian Rte 42; r/ste from $247/349; ❄ @ 📶) You'll never turn on the TV during the day at this aptly named hotel. Spread over three floors, the 95 Southwestern-themed rooms are pleasant, but nothing compared to the show from the balconies. Rooms that end in numbers higher than 15 (eg 216) have unobstructed panoramas of the valley below; the best, on the 3rd floor, cost $20 more.

Santa Fe 10

✕ Cafe Pasqual's — New Mexican $$$

(☎505-983-9340; www.pasquals.com; 121 Don Gaspar Ave; breakfast & lunch $14-19, dinner $15-39; ⏲8am-3pm & 5:30-10pm; 🌿 👪) Whatever time you visit this exuberantly colorful, utterly unpretentious place, the food, most of which has a definite south-of-the-border flavor, is worth every penny of the high prices. The breakfast menu is famous for dishes such as *huevos motuleños*, made with sautéed bananas, feta cheese and more; later on, the meat and fish mains are superb. Reservations taken for dinner only.

Albuquerque 11

✕ Pop Fizz — Mexican $

(☎505-508-1082; www.pop-fizz.net; 1701 4th St SW, National Hispanic Cultural Center; mains $5-8; ⏲11am-8pm; 📶 👪) These all-natural *paletas* (popsicles) straight up rock: cool off with flavors such as cucumber chile lime, mango or pineapple habanero – or perhaps you'd rather splurge on a cinnamon-churro ice-cream taco? Not to be outdone by the desserts, the kitchen also whips up all sorts of messy goodness, including carne asada fries, Sonoran dogs and Frito pies.

New York & the Mid-Atlantic

ALONG THE EAST COAST, SANDWICHED BETWEEN THE PICTURESQUE HAMLETS of New England and the gracious plantations of the South, you'll find the Northeast Corridor. Stretching from Washington DC to Boston, this scenic strip includes America's most dynamic, cosmopolitan metropolis: New York. But there is so much more to be discovered in this beautiful and remarkably diverse area.

After 48 unforgettable hours in Manhattan, seek out the Jersey Shore or Pennsylvania's backroads. Further south, Appalachian landscapes await on Virginia's Skyline Drive, while waterfalls and vineyards provide food for the soul around the Finger Lakes. No matter where you find yourself, you're guaranteed to find something unexpected and delightful.

Robert H Treman State Park Lucifer Falls
COLIN D. YOUNG / SHUTTERSTOCK ©

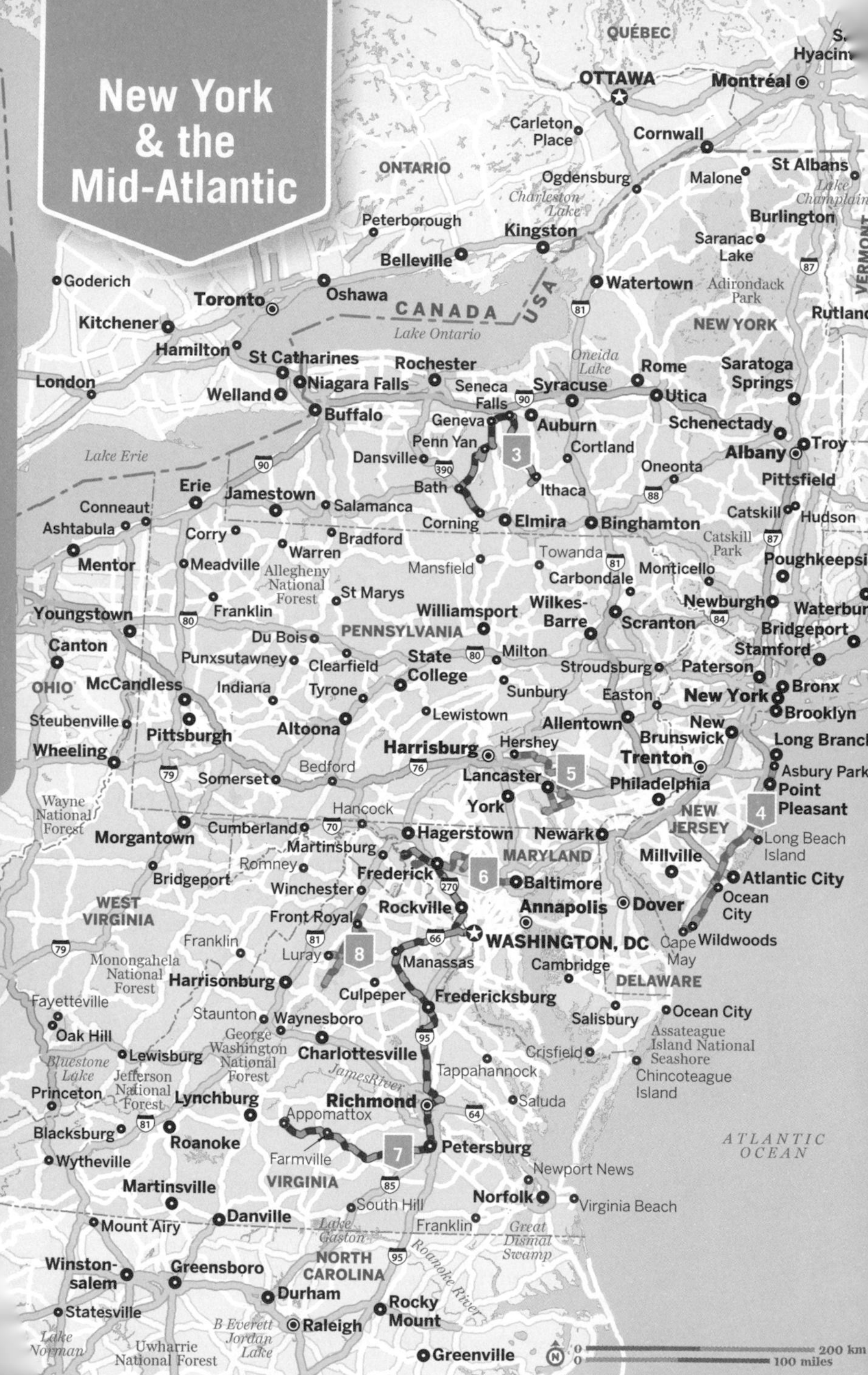
New York & the Mid-Atlantic
QUÉBEC
OTTAWA
Montréal
Carleton Place
Cornwall
ONTARIO
Ogdensburg
Malone
St Albans
Charleston Lake
Lake Champlain
Peterborough
Kingston
Burlington
Saranac Lake
VERMONT
Belleville
Goderich
Oshawa
Watertown
Adirondack Park
Toronto
CANADA
USA
Kitchener
NEW YORK
Rutland
Lake Ontario
Hamilton
St Catharines
Rochester
Oneida Lake
Rome
Saratoga Springs
London
Niagara Falls
Seneca Falls
Syracuse
Utica
Welland
Buffalo
Geneva
Auburn
Schenectady
Penn Yan
Cortland
Troy
Albany
Lake Erie
Dansville
Oneonta
Pittsfield
Erie
Jamestown
Bath
Ithaca
Conneaut
Salamanca
Catskill
Hudson
Ashtabula
Corning
Elmira
Binghamton
Corry
Bradford
Catskill Park
Mentor
Warren
Towanda
Poughkeepsie
Meadville
Allegheny National Forest
Mansfield
Monticello
Carbondale
St Marys
Newburgh
Waterbury
Youngstown
Franklin
Williamsport
Wilkes-Barre
Scranton
PENNSYLVANIA
Bridgeport
Du Bois
Canton
Milton
Stamford
Punxsutawney
Clearfield
State College
Stroudsburg
Paterson
OHIO
McCandless
Indiana
Tyrone
Sunbury
Easton
New York
Bronx
Steubenville
Lewistown
Brooklyn
Pittsburgh
Altoona
Allentown
New Brunswick
Hershey
Long Branch
Wheeling
Harrisburg
Trenton
Bedford
Asbury Park
Somerset
Lancaster
Philadelphia
Point Pleasant
Wayne National Forest
York
NEW JERSEY
Hancock
Morgantown
Cumberland
Hagerstown
Newark
Long Beach Island
Martinsburg
MARYLAND
Millville
Romney
Frederick
Baltimore
Atlantic City
Bridgeport
Winchester
Ocean City
WEST VIRGINIA
Rockville
Annapolis
Dover
Front Royal
WASHINGTON, DC
Cape May
Wildwoods
Franklin
Luray
Manassas
Cambridge
Monongahela National Forest
Harrisonburg
DELAWARE
Culpeper
Fredericksburg
Fayetteville
Staunton
Waynesboro
Ocean City
Oak Hill
Salisbury
George Washington National Forest
Charlottesville
Assateague Island National Seashore
Lewisburg
Crisfield
Bluestone Lake
James River
Tappahannock
Jefferson National Forest
Chincoteague Island
Princeton
Lynchburg
Richmond
Saluda
Appomattox
Blacksburg
Roanoke
Petersburg
ATLANTIC OCEAN
Wytheville
Farmville
Newport News
VIRGINIA
Martinsville
Norfolk
South Hill
Virginia Beach
Danville
Mount Airy
Lake Gaston
Franklin
Great Dismal Swamp
NORTH CAROLINA
Winston-salem
Greensboro
Roanoke River
Durham
Statesville
Rocky Mount
B Everett Jordan Lake
Raleigh
Lake Norman
Uwharrie National Forest
Greenville
0
200 km
0
100 miles

3 Finger Lakes Loop 3 Days

Lakeside roads lead past dozens of vineyards to deep gorges and ravines for hiking. (p65)

4 The Jersey Shore 3–7 Days

Boardwalks and beaches galore line the Atlantic for classic summertime fun. (p75)

5 Pennsylvania Dutch Country 3–4 Days

Back roads snake their way past farmers markets through Amish countryside. (p87)

6 Maryland's National Historic Road 2 Days

Drive from Baltimore's docks to the tiny villages of the Catoctin Mountains. (p99)

Classic Trip

7 The Civil War Tour 3 Days

See preserved battlefields, 19th-century countryside, museums aplenty and Southern small towns. (p109)

8 Skyline Drive 3 Days

Cross the Commonwealth's high-altitude spine in the green Shenandoah Valley. (p121)

DON'T MISS

The Music Man

Vaudeville-style performances at an ice-cream theatre encapsulate the Jersey Shore culture. Stop by for a taste on Trip 4

Urban Exploration

Cities like Baltimore and Frederick are steeped in history, good eats and hot nightlife. See them on Trip 6

Trail Trekking

Many trails arc along Skyline Drive, plunging past forests, white waterfalls and lonely mountains. Get your boots on for Trip 8

Strasburg Railroad

Board a beautifully restored steam-driven locomotive for a slow roll through the lush Amish countryside. Ride the rails on Trip 5

Taughannock Falls State Park

A short hike takes you to this narrow cascade, higher than Niagara and in a majestic amphitheater-like setting. Hike to the falls on Trip 3

Classic Trip

Finger Lakes Loop

'Ithaca is Gorges' T-shirts don't lie: Cornell's Ivy League campus has stunning canyons, and there are dozens more in the area, as well as lakeside vineyards producing top-flight wines.

TRIP HIGHLIGHTS

92 miles

Rte 54, Keuka Lake
Picturesque vineyards on bluffs overlooking the lake

1 mile

Ithaca
Dramatic gorges run through and around this college town

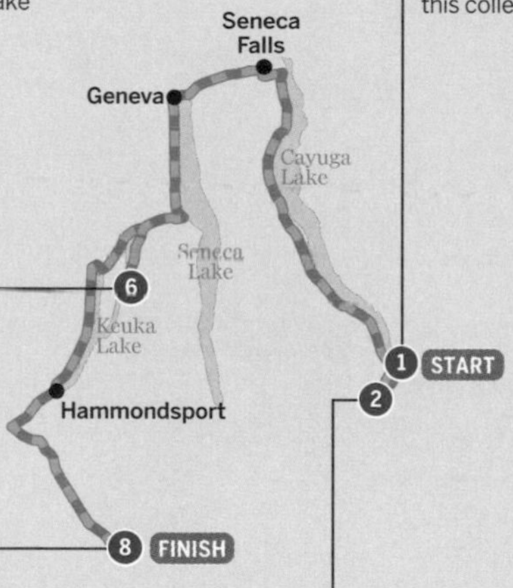

Seneca Falls
Geneva
Cayuga Lake
Seneca Lake
6
Keuka Lake
1 START
2
Hammondsport
8 FINISH

Corning
One of the world's finest collections of glass

144 miles

Buttermilk Falls & Robert H Treman State Parks
A dazzling variety of falls and swimming holes

5 miles

3 DAYS
144 MILES / 231KM

GREAT FOR...

BEST TIME TO GO

May to October for farmers markets and glorious sunny vistas.

The full height of Taughannock Falls.

With more than 120 vineyards, a designated driver is needed.

Taughannock Falls Higher than Niagara Falls

Classic Trip

3 Finger Lakes Loop

A bird's-eye view of this region of rolling hills and 11 long, narrow lakes – the eponymous fingers – reveals an outdoor paradise stretching all the way from Albany to far-western New York. Of course, there's boating, fishing, cycling, hiking and cross-country skiing, but this is also the state's premier wine-growing region, with enough variety for the most discerning oenophile and palate-cleansing whites and reds available just about every few miles.

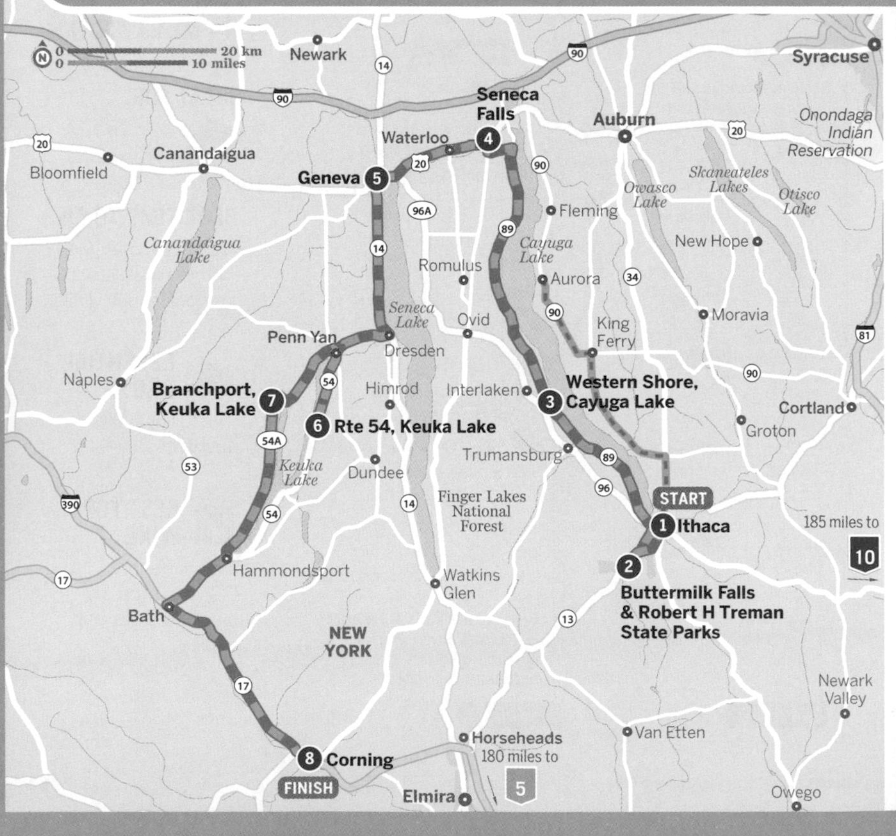

TRIP HIGHLIGHT

1 Ithaca

Ithaca, perched above Cayuga Lake, is an idyllic home for college students and for older generations of hippies who cherish elements of the traditional collegiate lifestyle – laid-back vibes, cafe poetry readings, art-house cinemas, green quads and good eats.

Founded in 1865, Cornell University boasts a lovely campus, mixing traditional and contemporary architecture, and sits high on a hill overlooking the picturesque town below. The modern **Herbert F Johnson Museum of Art** (607-255-6464; www.museum.cornell.edu; 114 Central Ave; 10am-5pm Tue-Sun), in a brutalist building designed by IM Pei, has a major Asian collection, plus pre-Columbian, American and European exhibits. Just east of the center of the campus is **Cornell Botanical Gardens** (607-255-2400; www.cornellbotanicgardens.org; 124 Comstock Knoll Dr; grounds dawn-dusk, visitor center 10am-4pm), an expertly curated herb and flower garden and arboretum. Kids can go interactive-wild at the extremely hands-on **Sciencenter** (607-272-0600; www.sciencenter.org; 601 1st St; adult/child $8/6; 10am-5pm Tue-Sat, noon-5pm Sun).

The area around Ithaca is known for its waterfalls, gorges and gorgeous parks.

p72

The Drive » It's only 2 miles south on Rte 13 to Buttermilk Falls State Park.

LINK YOUR TRIP

5 Pennsylvania Dutch Country

Journey south through Scranton and Allentown to southern PA to reach these tranquil country roads.

10 Fall Foliage Tour

Make your way east from Ithaca through Albany to the Berkshires to experience legendary New England colors.

TRIP HIGHLIGHT

2 Buttermilk Falls & Robert H Treman State Parks

A sprawling swath of wilderness, **Buttermilk Falls State Park** (607-273-5761; www.parks.ny.gov; 112 E Buttermilk Falls Rd; per car Apr-Oct $8) has something for everyone – a beach, cabins, fishing, hiking, recreational fields and camping. The big draw, however, is the waterfalls. There are more than 10, with some sending water tumbling as far as 500ft below into clear pools. Hikers like the raggedy Gorge Trail that brings them up to all the best cliffs. It parallels Buttermilk Creek, winding up about 500ft. On the other side of the falls is the equally popular Rim Trail, a loop of about 1.5 miles around the waterfalls from a different vantage point. Both feed into Bear Trail, which will take you to neighboring Treman Falls.

It's a trek of about 3 miles to Treman, or you can pop back in the car after exploring Buttermilk and drive the 3 miles south to **Robert H Treman State Park** (607-273-3440; www.parks.ny.gov; 105 Enfield Falls Rd; per car Apr-Oct $8), still on bucolic Rte 13. Also renowned for cascading falls, Treman's gorge trail passes a stunning 12 waterfalls in under 3 miles. The two biggies you don't want to miss are Devil's Kitchen and Lucifer Falls, a multi-tiered wonder that spills Enfield Creek over rocks for about 100ft. At the bottom of yet another watery gorge – Lower Falls – there's a natural swimming hole.

The Drive » Take Rte 13 back into Ithaca to connect with Rte 89 that hugs Cayuga Lake shore for 10 miles. The entrance to Taughannock Falls State Park is just after crossing the river gorge.

3 Western Shore, Cayuga Lake

Trumansburg, a one-street town about 15 miles north of Ithaca, is the gateway to **Taughannock Falls State Park** (607-387-6739; www.parks.ny.gov; 1740 Taughannock Blvd, Trumansburg; per car Apr-Oct $8; dawn-dusk). At 215ft, the falls of the same name are 30ft higher than Niagara Falls and the highest cascade east of the Rockies. There are five miles of hiking trails, most of which wind their way around the slippery parts to bring you safely to the lookout spots at the top.

A little further along on Rte 89, near the village of Interlaken, is **Lucas Vineyards** (607-532-4825; www.lucasvineyards.com; 3862 County Hwy 150, Interlaken; 10:30am-6pm Jun-Aug, to 5:30pm Sep-May), one of the pioneers of Cayuga wineries. A little further north again, down by the lake shore and a small community of modest but charming summer homes, is **Sheldrake Point Winery** (607-532-9401; www.sheldrakepoint.com; 7448 County Hwy 153, Ovid; 10am-5:30pm Apr-Oct, 11am-5pm Nov-Mar), which has stunning views and award-winning whites.

p72

The Drive » Rte 89 continues along the lake shore and passes Cayuga Lake State Park, which has beach access and picnic tables. Continue north until you hit the junction with E Bayard St; turn left here to reach downtown Seneca Falls.

4 Seneca Falls

This small, sleepy town is where the country's organized women's rights movement was born. After being excluded from an anti-slavery meeting, Elizabeth Cady Stanton and her friends drafted an 1848 declaration asserting that 'all men and women are created equal.' The inspirational **Women's Rights National Historical Park** (315-568-0024; www.nps.gov/wori; 136 Fall St; 9am-5pm Fri-Sun) has a small but impressive museum, with an informative film available for viewing, plus a visitor center offering tours of Cady Stanton's house. The tiny **National Women's Hall of Fame** (315-568-8060; www.womenofthehall.org; 76 Fall St; adult/child $4/free; noon-4pm Wed-Fri, 10am-4pm Sat) honors inspiring American women. Learn about some of the 256 inductees, including first lady Abigail Adams, American Red Cross founder Clara Barton and civil-rights activist Rosa Parks.

p72

The Drive » The 10 miles on I-20 west to Geneva passes through strip mall-lined Waterloo; Mac's Drive In, a classic 1961-vintage burger joint, is worth a stop. As you drive into town you pass Seneca Lake State Park which is a good spot for a picnic.

DETOUR: AURORA

Start: 1 Ithaca

Around 28 miles north of Ithaca on the east side of Cayuga Lake is the picturesque village of Aurora. Established in 1795, the village has over 50 buildings on the National Register of Historic Places, including parts of the campus of Wells College, founded in 1868 for the higher education of women (it's now co-ed). The **Inns of Aurora** (315-364-8888; www.innsofaurora.com; 391 Main St; r $200-400; P), which is composed of four grand properties – the Aurora Inn (1833), EB Morgan House (1858), Rowland House (1903) and Wallcourt Hall (1909) – is a wonderful place to stay. Stop by the Aurora Inn's lovely dining room for a meal with lakeside views and pick up a copy of the self-guided walking tour of the village.

5 Geneva

Geneva, one of the larger towns on this route, has interesting, historic architecture and a lively vibe, with both Hobart and William Smith colleges calling it home. South Main St is lined with an impressive number of turn-of-the-century Italianate, Federal and Greek Revival homes in immaculate condition. The restored 1894 **Smith Opera House** (☎315-781-5483; www.thesmith.org; 82 Seneca St) is the place to go for theater, concerts and performing arts in the area. Stop by **Microclimate** (☎315-787-0077; www.facebook.com/microclimatewinebar; 38 Linden St; ⌚5-10pm Mon, 4:30pm-midnight Wed-Fri, to 1am Sat, 10am-1pm Sun), a cool little wine bar offering wine flights.

✕ 🛏 p73

The Drive » On your way south on Rte 14 you pass – what else? – a winery worth visiting. This one is Red Tail Ridge Winery, a certified gold Leadership in Energy & Environmental Design (LEED) little place on Seneca Lake. Then turn right on Rte 54 to Penn Yan.

TRIP HIGHLIGHT

6 Route 54, Keuka Lake

Y-shaped Keuka is about 20 miles long and in some parts up to 2 miles wide, its lush vegetation uninterrupted except for neat patches of vineyards. If you have a trail bike you could get a workout on the **Keuka Lake Outlet Trail**, a 7.5-mile route following the old Crooked Lake Canal between Penn Yan and Dresden on Seneca Lake.

Just south of Penn Yan, the largest village on Keuka Lake's shores, you come to **Keuka Spring Vineyards** (☎315-536-3147; www.keukaspringwinery.com; 243 E Lake Rd/Rte 54, Penn Yan; ⌚10am-5pm Apr-Nov, 10am-5pm Fri-Sun Dec-Mar) and then **Rooster Hill Vineyards** (☎315-536-4773; www.roosterhill.com; 489 Rte 54, Penn Yan; tastings $5; ⌚10am-5pm Mon-Sat, 11am-5pm Sun Jun-Oct, 11am-5pm Fri-Sun Nov-May) – two local favorites that offer tastings and tours in pastoral settings. A few miles further south along Rte 54 brings you to **Barrington Cellars** (☎315-531-8923; www.barringtoncellars.com; 2794 Gray Rd, Penn Yan; ⌚10:30am-5pm Mon-Sat, noon-5pm Sun Jun-Oct, reduced hours Nov-May), 500ft off the lake and flush with Labrusca and Vinifera wines made from local grapes.

On Saturdays in summer everyone flocks to the **Windmill Farm & Craft Market** (www.thewindmill.com; 3900 Rte 14A, Penn Yan; ⌚8am-4:30pm Sat May–mid-Dec), just outside Penn Yan. Check out Amish and Mennonite goods, ranging from hand-carved wooden rockers to homegrown veggies and flowers.

The Drive » After about 5.5 miles on Rte 54A take a detour south onto Skyline Dr, which runs down the middle of 800ft Bluff Point, for outstanding views. Backtrack to Rte 54A and Branchport is only a few miles further along.

7 Branchport, Keuka Lake

As you pass through the tiny village of Branchport at the tip of Keuka's left fork in its Y, keep an eye out for **Hunt Country Vineyards** (☎315-595-2812; www.huntwines.com; 4021 Italy Hill Rd; tastings $2; ⌚10am-6pm Mon-Sat, 11am-6pm Sun Jun-Oct, reduced hours Nov-May) and **Stever Hill Vineyards** (☎315-595-2230; www.steverhillvineyards.com; 3962 Stever Hill Rd; tastings $5; ⌚10am-5pm May-Nov, reduced hours Dec-Apr), the latter of which has its tasting room in a restored old barn. Both wineries are family run and edging into their sixth generation. On top of tastings there are tours of the grape-growing facilities and snacks from the vineyards' own kitchens.

The Drive » Rte 54A along the west branch of Keuka passes by several other wineries as well as the Taylor Wine Museum just north of Hammondsport (p73), a quaint town with a charming square. Carry on through to Bath where you connect with I-86 east/Rte 17 east for another 19 miles to Corning.

Classic Trip

DENNIS MACDONALD / GETTY IMAGES ©

DENNIS MACDONALD / GETTY IMAGES ©

WINE & DINE

SIMON RICHMOND, WRITER

Where you find good wine – and the Finger Lakes region produces some of the country's best bottles – it's a sure bet you'll also find great food. Relax, as gourmet isn't stuffy and white-tablecloth here, but friendly and communal, such as at Geneva's FLX Table. Also not to be missed is Hazelnut Kitchen near Ithaca, where you'll also find a stellar farmers market.

Above: Wine casks
Left: Wine tasting at a cellar door
Right: Fruit for sale

DENNIS MACDONALD / GETTY IMAGES ©

TRIP HIGHLIGHT

8 Corning

The massive **Corning Museum of Glass** (☎800-732-6845; www.cmog.org; 1 Museum Way; adult/child $19.50/free; ⏲9am-8pm Jun-Aug, to 5pm Sep-May) complex is home to fascinating exhibits on glassmaking arts, complete with demonstrations and interactive items. It's possibly the world's finest collection, both in terms of its historic breadth – which span 35 centuries of craftsmanship – as well as its sculptural pieces. Stop by **Vitrix Hot Glass Studio** (☎607-936-8707; www.vitrixhotglass.com; 77 W Market St; ⏲10am-8pm Mon-Sat, noon-5pm Sun) in the charming Market Street district to take a gander at museum-quality glass pieces ranging from functional bowls to organic-shaped sculptures.

Housed in the former City Hall, a Romanesque Revival building c 1893, the **Rockwell Museum of Western Art** (☎607-937-5386; www.rockwellmuseum.org; 111 Cedar St; adult/child $11/free; ⏲9am-8pm Jun-Aug, to 5pm Sep-May) has a wide-ranging collection of art of the American West, including great works by Albert Bierstadt, Charles M Russell and Frederic Remington.

✕ p73

Eating & Sleeping

Ithaca 1

Glenwood Pines — Burgers $

(607-273-3709; www.glenwoodpines.com; 1213 Taughannock Blvd/Rte 89; burgers $7; 11am-10pm) If you work up an appetite hiking at Taughannock Falls, stop by this roadside restaurant for burgers and fish fry that have been voted the best in Ithaca.

Moosewood Restaurant — Vegetarian $$

(607-273-9610; www.moosewoodcooks.com; 215 N Cayuga St; mains $8-18; 11:30am-8:30pm;) Established in 1973, this near-legendary veggie restaurant is run by a collective. It has a slightly upscale feel, with a full bar and global menu.

Watershed — Bar $

(607-345-0691; www.thewatershedithaca.com; 121 Martin Luther King Jr St; 4pm-1am) This appealing new bar, with distressed plaster and brick walls, prides itself on providing a conversational, family-friendly atmosphere, with its policy of no music or dance parties. Alongside a full bar, there are plenty of soft and hot drinks as well as light bites.

Inn on Columbia — Inn $$

(607-272-0204; www.columbiabb.com; 228 Columbia St; r from $175;) This inn is spread across several homes clustered in a quiet residential area a short walk from downtown. The slick interior design is refreshingly contemporary.

William Henry Miller Inn — B&B $$

(877-256-4553; www.millerinn.com; 303 N Aurora St; r from $195;) Gracious and grand, and only a few steps from the Commons, this is a historic home with luxurious rooms (two with whirlpool tubs and two in a separate carriage house), gourmet breakfast and a dessert buffet.

Cayuga Lake 3

Hazelnut Kitchen — American $$

(607-387-4433; 53 East Main St, Trumansburg; mains $16-26, tasting menu $40; 5-9:30pm Thu-Mon) The chefs at this cozy place, 11 miles northwest of Ithaca, source quality produce from local farmers to create dishes that have made this arguably the finest restaurant in the region. It's well worth opting for the four-course tasting menu, where the chefs will personally present each seasonally inspired dish.

Knapp Winery & Restaurant — Winery $$

(607-930-3495; www.knappwine.com; 2770 Ernsberger Rd, Romulus; tastings $5; 10am-5:30pm Apr-Nov, reduced hours Dec-Mar) This winery, 12 miles south of Seneca Falls, has a wide lawn surrounded by gnarly roots and rioting wildflowers; you can look out over the trellis-covered vineyards while sampling the wines, grappas and limoncellos. The winery restaurant is open 11am to 5pm Wednesday to Sunday in April; daily May to October; and Friday to Sunday in November.

Seneca Falls 4

Gould Hotel — Boutique Hotel $$

(877-788-4010; www.thegouldhotel.com; 108 Fall St; r $169;) Originally a 1920s-era hotel, the downtown building has undergone a stylish renovation with a nod to the past – the mahogany bar comes from an old Seneca Falls saloon. The standard rooms are small, but the decor, in metallic purple and gray, is quite flash. The hotel's upscale restaurant and tavern serves local food, wine and beer. Around Christmas there's a projection of Frank Capra's film *It's a Wonderful Life* on the lobby wall; Seneca Falls was Capra's inspiration for the small American town in the movie.

Geneva 5

FLX Table American $$$

(www.flxtable.com; 22 Linden St; 5 courses $49; 5:45pm & 8:15pm Thu-Mon) Book online well ahead for one of the 12 spots at two sittings around this communal table for a dinner-party style, five-course gourmet feast. Dishes are crafted from seasonal local produce and beautifully presented. Wine pairings are available.

Belhurst Castle Heritage Hotel $$

(315-781-0201; www.belhurst.com; 4069 West Lake Rd; r $105-435; P) This 1880s lakefront folly, listed on the National Register of Historic Places, is worth a stop just to see its ornate interior and the gorgeous view. The best rooms in the main mansion have stained glass, heavy antique furniture and fireplaces. Inquire about availability well ahead as it's a popular wedding venue.

Hammondsport

Switzerland Inn Seafood $

(607-292-6927; www.theswitz.com; 14109 Keuka Village Rd; mains $8-16; 4-10pm Wed & Thu, noon-10pm Fri-Sun) A rowdy, outdoorsy burger joint, 9 miles northeast of Hammondsport, that also serves up all-you-can-eat crab legs and a weekend fish fry. On hot days you can dive off the dock into the lake.

Village Tavern Restaurant & Inn American $$

(607-569-2528; www.villagetaverninn.com; 30 Mechanic St; mains $14-32; 11:30am-8:30pm May-Oct) Located next to the attractive village square and specializing in fresh fish and seafood, this popular restaurant is known for its award-winning wine list, which covers a wide selection of Finger Lakes vineyards. Four rooms above the restaurant and several more in handsome wooden houses around the town are also available (from $119).

Gone with the Wind B&B B&B $$

(607-868-4603; www.gonewiththewindonkeukalake.com; 14905 W Lake Rd/Rte 54A, Pulteney; r $110-200;) This lakeside B&B, 10 miles north of Hammondsport, isn't exactly Tara, but it is pleasant and has a sweeping deck with great views. There are two accommodation choices – the original stone mansion and a log lodge annex – though both have generally homey furnishings.

Corning 8

Gaffer Grille & Tap Room Steak $$

(www.gaffergrilleandtaproom.com; 58 W Market St; mains $13-33; restaurant 11:30am-9pm Mon-Fri, 4:30-9pm Sat & Sun, bar to 10:30pm) An old-school steakhouse with a contemporary dedication to sourcing meat only from local organic farms. Also on the menu are brisket sandwiches and pasta, fish and chicken dishes. Above the restaurant there are four spacious and comfortable guest rooms ($139 to $149), making this also a good place to stay in downtown Corning.

Hand & Foot International $$

(607-973-2547; www.handandfoot.co; 69 W Market St; mains $10-21; 11:30am-midnight) The globally footloose menu here jets between banh mi sandwiches and pierogi to Korean rice cakes and sausage platters. Drinks-wise, the bar menu is equally wide-ranging with a strong showing of regional ales. The overall vibe is hipster-chic.

FISH HAWK

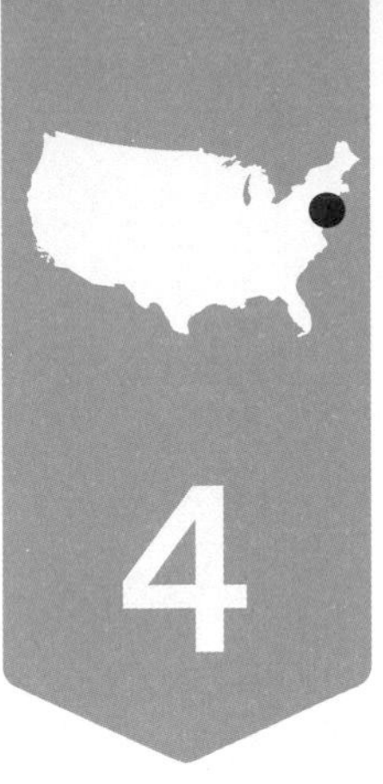

The Jersey Shore

Jersey girls in bikinis, tatted-up guidos, mile-long boardwalks, clanging arcades, neon-lit Ferris wheels and 127 miles of sandy Atlantic Ocean coast. Pack the car and hit the shore.

TRIP HIGHLIGHTS

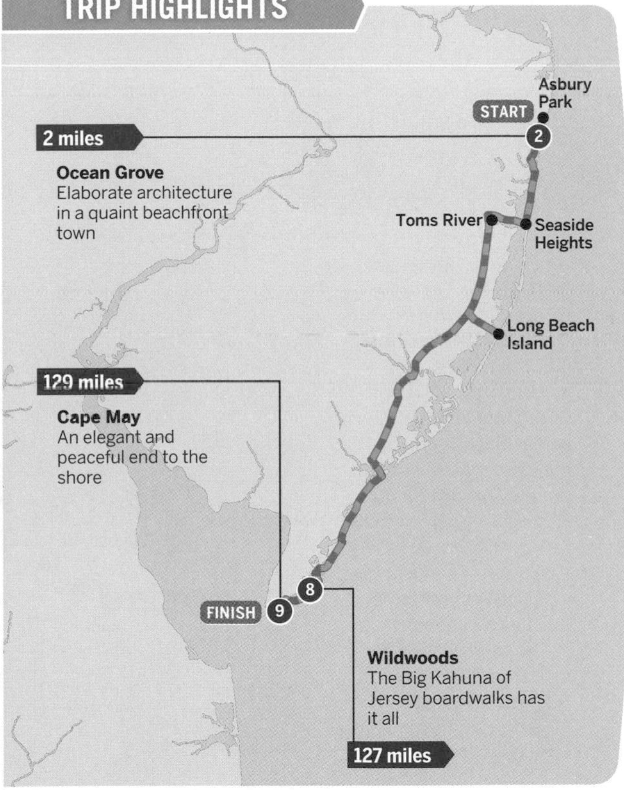

3–7 DAYS
129 MILES / 207KM

GREAT FOR...

BEST TIME TO GO

Midweek in June – crowds are smaller and rooms cheaper than in the high season. End of September – Indian summer temps and cheaper, too.

ESSENTIAL PHOTO

Cape May sunset.

BEST TWO DAYS

Polar opposites, Wildwood and Cape May: both classics.

Cape May The oldest seashore resort in the United States

4 The Jersey Shore

The New Jersey coastline is studded with resort towns from classy to tacky that fulfill the Platonic ideal of how a long summer day should be spent. Super-sized raucous boardwalks where singles more than mingle are a short drive from old-fashioned intergenerational family retreats. When the temperature rises, the entire state tips eastward and rushes to the beach to create memories that they'll view later with nostalgia and perhaps some regret.

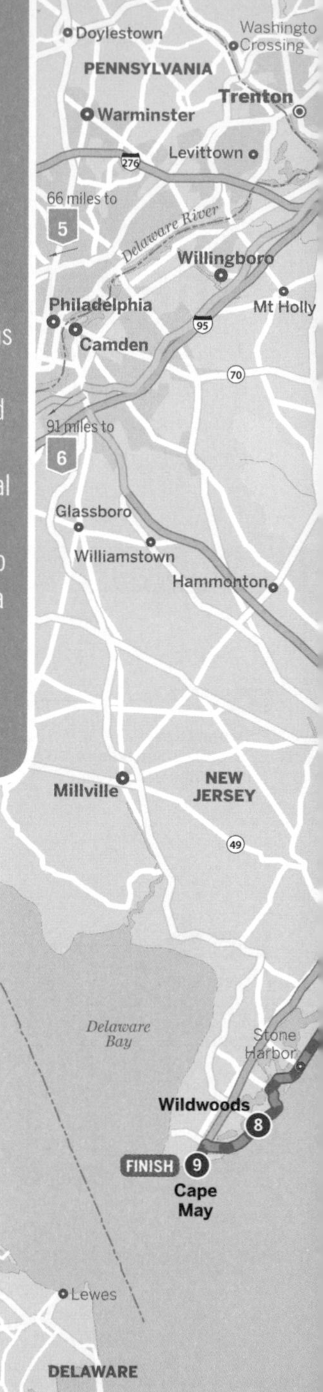

❶ Asbury Park

Let's start with the town that Bruce Springsteen, the most famous of a group of musicians who developed the Asbury Sound in the 1970s, immortalized in song. Several of these musicians – such as Steve Van Zandt, Garry Tallent, and the late Danny Federici and Clarence Clemons – formed Springsteen's supporting E Street Band. The main venues to check out are the still-grungy, seen-it-all clubs **Stone Pony** (☎732-502-0600; www.stoneponyonline.com; 913 Ocean Ave; ⏲box office noon-5pm Wed-Mon & during shows) and **Wonder Bar** (☎732-502-8886; www.wonderbarasburypark.com; 1213 Ocean Ave); the latter is across the street from the majestic red-brick **Paramount Theatre** (☎732-897-6500; www.apboardwalk.com/portfolio/convention-hall; 1300 Ocean Ave) where big acts perform and free movies are shown.

Led by wealthy gay men from NYC who snapped up blocks of forgotten Victorian homes and storefronts to refur-

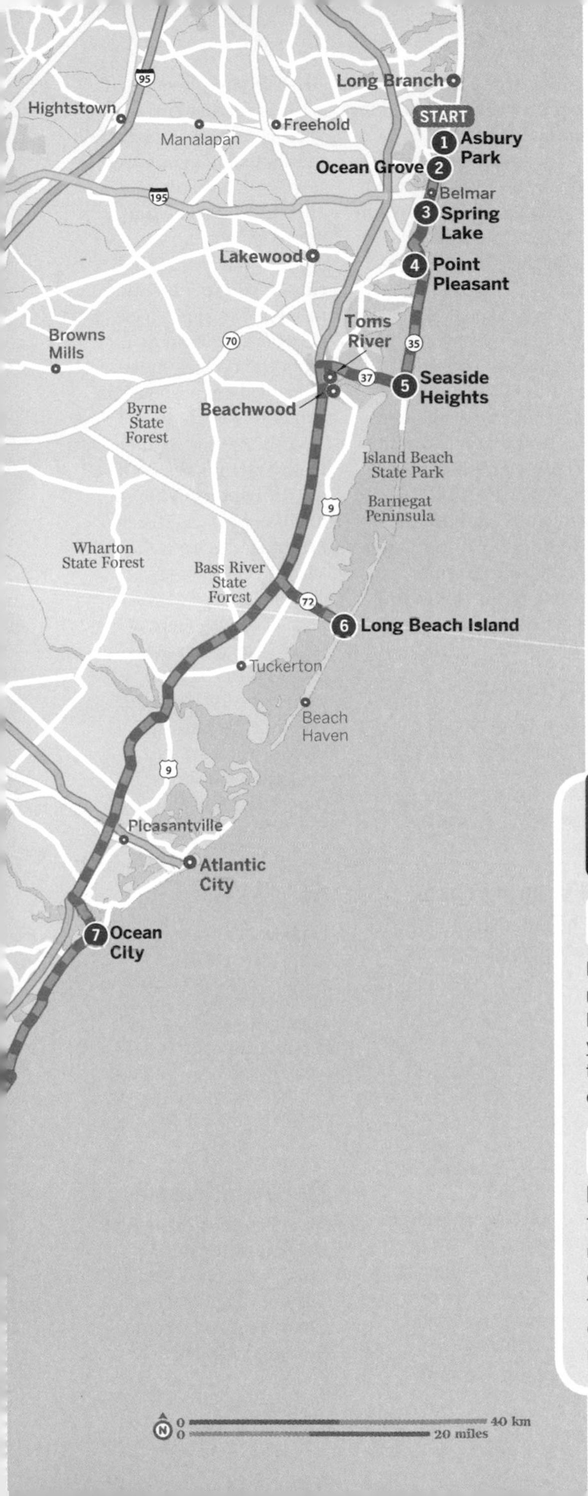

Long Branch
START
1 Asbury Park
2 Ocean Grove
Belmar
3 Spring Lake
4 Point Pleasant
5 Seaside Heights
6 Long Beach Island
7 Ocean City
Hightstown
Manalapan
Freehold
Lakewood
Browns Mills
Toms River
Beachwood
Byrne State Forest
Island Beach State Park
Barnegat Peninsula
Wharton State Forest
Bass River State Forest
Tuckerton
Beach Haven
Pleasantville
Atlantic City
95
195
70
35
37
9
72
0 40 km
0 20 miles

bish, the **downtown** area includes several blocks of Cookman and Bangs Aves, lined with charming shops, bars, cafes, restaurants and a restored art-house cinema.

The **boardwalk** itself is short and unspectacular by Jersey standards: at one end is the gorgeous but empty shell of a 1920s-era carousel and casino building, the Paramount Theatre is near the other end, and there's an attractive, well-cared-for stretch of sand in front. Asbury Park's amusements tend to be more for adults than children: its clubs and bars rock late, it has decent surf, and the shore's liveliest gay scene.

p84

LINK YOUR TRIP

5 Pennsylvania Dutch Country

From Atlantic City, head northwest through Philadelphia and make your way west to US-30 for the rural byways of Amish country.

6 Maryland's National Historic Road

Take the Alantic City Expwy north toward Camden and connect with I-95 south to Baltimore to take in the diversity of this bay-to-mountains trip.

The Drive ›› There's no beachfront road to Ocean Grove – the two towns are separated by narrow Wesley Lake. Take the generically commercial Main St/Rte 71 and turn left on Ocean Grove's own Main Ave. It might be worthwhile, however, to first head north on Rte 71 for a few miles to take a gander at the impressively grand homes in the community of Deal.

TRIP HIGHLIGHT

2 Ocean Grove

Next to Asbury Park is Ocean Grove, one of the cutest Victorian seaside towns anywhere, with a boardwalk boasting not a single business to disturb the peace and quiet. Known as 'God's Square Mile at the Jersey Shore,' Ocean Grove is perfectly coiffed, sober, conservative and quaint – it used to shut down entirely on Sundays. Founded by Methodists in the 19th century, the place retains what's left of a post–Civil War **Tent City** revival camp – now a historic site with 114 cottagelike canvas tents clustered together that are used for summer homes.

Towering over the tents, the 1894 mustard-yellow **Great Auditorium** (☎732-775-0035, tickets 800-965-9324; www.ocean-grove.org; 21 Pilgrim Pathway; recitals free, concerts $13; ⌚recitals 7:30pm Wed, noon Sat Jul & Aug) shouldn't be missed: its vaulted interior, amazing acoustics and historic organ recall Utah's Mormon Tabernacle. Make sure to catch a recital or concert (Wednesday or Saturday during the summer) or one of the open-air services held in the boardwalk pavilion.

✕ 🛏 p84

The Drive ›› Follow Rte 71 south through a string of relatively sleepy towns (Bradley Beach, Belmar) for just over 5 miles to reach Spring Lake.

3 Spring Lake

The quiet streets of this prosperous community, once known as the 'Irish Riviera,' are lined with grand oceanfront Victorian houses set in meticulously manicured lawns. As a result of Hurricane Sandy, the gorgeous beach is extremely narrow at high tide. If you're interested in a low-key quiet base, a stay here is about as far from the typical shore boardwalk experience as you can get.

Only 5 miles inland from Spring Lake is the quirky **Historic Village at Allaire** (☎732-919-3500; www.allairevillage.org; 4263 Atlantic Ave, Farmingdale; parking May-Sep $7; ⌚bakery 10am-4pm Mon-Fri, historic village 11am-5pm Sat & Sun), the remains of what was a thriving 19th-century village called Howell Works. You can still visit various 'shops' in this living museum, all run by folks in period costume.

🛏 p84

The Drive ›› For a slow but pleasant drive, take Ocean Ave south – at Wreck Pond turn inland before heading south again. At Crescent Park in the town of Sea Girt, Washington Ave connects back to Union Ave/Rte 71, which leads into Rte 35 and over the Manasquan Inlet.

4 Point Pleasant

Point Pleasant is the first of five quintessential bumper-car-and-Skee-Ball boardwalks. On a July weekend, Point Pleasant's long beach

TOP TIP: PLAN AHEAD

We love the shore but let's be honest, in summer months, the traffic's a nightmare, parking's impossible and the beaches are overflowing. Pack the car the night before, leave at dawn and, if at all possible, come midweek. And if you want something besides a run-down, sun-bleached, three-blocks-from-the-water flea box to stay in, make reservations six months to a year in advance.

is jam-packed: squint, cover up all that nearly naked flesh with striped unitards, and it could be the 1920s, with umbrellas shading every inch of sand and the surf clogged with bodies and bobbing heads.

Families with young kids love Point Pleasant, as the boardwalk is big but not overwhelming, and the squeaky-clean amusement rides, fun house and small aquarium – all run by **Jenkinson's** (☎732-295-4334; www.jenkinsons.com; 300 Ocean Ave, Point Pleasant Beach; aquarium adult/child $12/7; ⏰ rides noon-11pm, aquarium 10am-10pm Jul & Aug, hours vary Sep-Jun) – are geared to the height and delight of the 10-and-under set. That's not to say Point Pleasant is only for little ones. **Martell's Tiki Bar** (☎732-892-0131; www.tikibar.com; 308 Boardwalk, Point Pleasant Beach; ⏰11am-11pm Sun-Thu, to 12:30am Fri & Sat), a place margarita pitchers go to die, makes sure of that: look for the neon-orange palm trees and listen for the live bands.

The Drive » Head south on Rte 35 past several residential communities laid out on a long barrier island only a block or two wide in parts – Seaside Heights is where it's at its widest on this 11-mile trip.

WE'RE HAVIN' A PARTY

Yes, in summer, every day is a party at the Jersey Shore. But here are some events not to miss:

Gay Pride Parade (www.gayasburypark.com) Asbury Park, early June.

Polka Spree by the Sea (www.northwild.com/events.asp) Wildwood, late June.

New Jersey Sandcastle Contest (www.njsandcastle.com) Belmar, July.

New Jersey State Barbecue Championship (www.njbbq.com) Wildwood, mid-July.

Ocean City Baby Parade (www.ocnj.us/babyparade) Ocean City, early August.

Asbury Park Zombie Walk (www.asburyparkzombiewalk.com) Asbury Park, October.

5 Seaside Heights

Coming from the north, Seaside Heights has the first of the truly overwhelming boardwalks: a sky ride and two rollicking amusement piers with double corridors of arcade games and adult-size, adrenaline-pumping rides, roller coasters and various iterations of the vomit-inducing 10-story drop.

During the day, it's as family-friendly as Point Pleasant, but once darkness falls Seaside Heights becomes a scene of such hedonistic mating rituals that an evangelical church has felt the need for a permanent booth on the pier. Packs of young men – caps askew, tatts gleaming – check out packs of young women in shimmering spaghetti-strap microdresses as everyone rotates among the string of loud bars, with live bands growling out Eagles tunes. It's pure Jersey.

Detour south on Rte 35 to the 10-mile-long **Island Beach State Park** (☎732-793-0506; www.islandbeachnj.org; Seaside Park; weekday/weekend May-Sep $12/20, Oct-Apr $5/10; ⏰8am-8pm Mon-Fri, 7am-8pm Sat & Sun May-Sep, 8am-dusk Oct-Apr), a completely undeveloped barrier island backed by dunes and tall grasses separating the bay from the ocean.

✕ p84

The Drive » To reach the mainland, take Rte 37 from Seaside Heights; you cross a long bridge over Barnegat Bay before reaching the strip-mall-filled sprawl of Toms River. Hop on the Garden State Pkwy south, then Rte 72 and the bridge over Manahawkin Bay.

CREATIVE FAMILY / SHUTTERSTOCK ©

Above: Wildwood amusement park
Below: Asbury Park
Right: Barnegat Lighthouse

LITTLENY / SHUTTERSTOCK ©

EILEEN_10 / SHUTTERSTOCK ©

6 Long Beach Island

Only a very narrow inlet separates this long sliver of an island, with its beautiful beaches and impressive summer homes, from the very southern tip of Island Beach State Park and the northern shore towns. Within throwing distance of the park is the landmark **Barnegat Lighthouse** (609-494-2016; www.state.nj.us/dep/parksandforests/parks/barnlig.html; off Long Beach Blvd; lighthouse adult/child $3/1; state park 8am-6pm, lighthouse 10am-4:30pm), which offers panoramic views from the top. Fishers cast off from a jetty extending 2000ft along the Atlantic Ocean, and a short nature trail begins just in front of a visitor center with small history and photography displays.

Nearly every morning practically half the island is jogging, walking, blading or biking on Beach Ave, the 7.5-mile stretch of asphalt that stretches from Ship Bottom to Beach Haven (south of the bridge); it's a great time to exercise, enjoy the sun and people-watch. Tucked down a residential street is **Hudson House** (609-492-9616; 19 E 13th St, Beach Haven; noon-2am Jul & Aug, 8pm-2am Fri & Sat Apr-Jun & Sep-Dec), a nearly locals-only dive bar about as worn and comfortable as an old pair of flip-flops. Don't be intimidated by the fact that it looks like a crumbling biker bar – it is.

The Drive » Head back over the bridge, then take the Garden State Pkwy south past the marshy pinelands area and Atlantic City. Take exit 30 for Somers Point; Laurel Dr turns into MacArthur Blvd/Rte 52 and then a long causeway crosses Great Egg Harbor Bay. This is a 48-mile drive. When you cross the causeway, turn left for peace and quiet, right for the action.

7 Ocean City

An almost heavenly amalgam of Ocean Grove and Point Pleasant, Ocean City is a dry town with a roomy boardwalk packed with genuine family fun and facing an exceedingly pretty beach. There's a small water park, and **Gillian's Wonderland** has a heart-thumpingly tall Ferris wheel, a beautifully restored merry-go-round and kiddie rides galore – and no microphoned teens hawking carnie games. The mood is light and friendly (a lack of alcohol will do that).

Mini-golf aficionados: dingdingdingding! You hit the jackpot. Pint-size duffers can play through on a three-masted schooner, around great white sharks and giant octopuses, under reggae monkeys piloting a helicopter and even in black light. If you haven't already, beat the heat with a delicious Kohr's soft-serve frozen custard, plain or dipped. While saltwater taffy is offered in many places, **Shriver's Taffy** (☎609-399-0100; www.shrivers.com; cnr E 9th St & Boardwalk; taffy per pound $9-10; ⏰9am-midnight Jun-Sep, to 5pm Oct-May) is, in our humble opinion, the best: watch machines stretch and wrap it, and then fill a bag with two dozen or more flavors.

🛏 p85

The Drive » If time isn't a factor, cruise down local streets and over several small bridges ($1.50 toll on two of the four in each direction; coins only) through the beachfront communities of Strathmere, Sea Isle City, Avalon and Stone Harbor. Otherwise, head back to the Garden State Pkwy and get off at one of two exits for the Wildwoods on a 30-mile drive.

TRIP HIGHLIGHT

8 Wildwoods

A party town popular with teens, 20-somethings and the young, primarily Eastern Europeans who staff the restaurants and shops, Wildwood is the main social focus here. Access to all three beaches is free, and the width of the beach – more than 1000ft in parts, making it the widest in NJ – means there's never a lack of space. Several massive piers are host to water parks and amusement parks – easily the rival of any Six Flags Great Adventure – with roller coasters and rides best suited to aspiring astronauts anchoring the 2-mile-long Grand Daddy of Jersey Shore boardwalks. Glow-in-the-dark 3D mini-golf is a good example of the Wildwood boardwalk ethos – take it far, then one step further. Maybe the best ride of all is the tram running the length of the boardwalk from Wildwood Crest to North Wildwood. There's always a line for a table at Jersey Shore staple pizzeria **Mack & Manco's** on the boardwalk (it also has other shore boardwalk locations).

Wildwood Crest is an archaeological find, a kitschy slice of 1950s Americana – white-washed motels with flashing neon signs. Check out eye-catching motel signs like the **Lollipop** at 23rd and Atlantic Aves.

🍴 🛏 p85

The Drive » Take local roads: south on Pacific Ave to Ocean Dr, which passes over a toll bridge over an estuary area separating Jarvis Sound from Cape May Harbor. Then left on Rte 109 over the Cape May harbor. You can turn left anywhere from here, depending on whether you want to head to town or the beach.

TRIP HIGHLIGHT

9 Cape May

Founded in 1620, Cape May – the only place in New Jersey where

ANEESE / SHUTTERSTOCK ©

Ocean City Ferris wheel at Gillian's Wonderland

the sun both rises and sets over the water – is on the state's southern tip and is the country's oldest seashore resort. Its sweeping beaches get crowded in summer, but the stunning Victorian architecture is attractive year-round. In addition to 600 gingerbread-style houses, the city boasts antique shops and places for dolphin-, whale- (May to December) and bird-watching, and is just outside the **Cape May Point State Park** (www.state.nj.us/dep/parksandforests/parks/capemay.html; 707 E Lake Dr; ⌚8am-4pm) and its 157ft **Cape May Lighthouse** (☎609-884-5404; www.capemaymac.org; 215 Lighthouse Ave; adult/child $8/5; ⌚10am-5pm May-Sep, 11am-3pm Mar & Apr, 11am-3pm Sat Feb & Oct-Dec), with 199 steps to the observation deck at the top; there's an excellent visitor center and museum with exhibits on wildlife in the area, as well as trails to ponds, dunes and marshes. A mile-long loop of the nearby **Cape May Bird Observatory** (☎609-884-2736; www.birdcapemay.org; 701 E Lake Dr; ⌚9am-4:30pm Apr-Oct, Wed-Mon Nov-Mar) is a pleasant stroll through preserved wetlands. The wide sandy beach at the park (free) or the one in town is the main attraction in summer months. **Aqua Trails** (☎609-884-5600; www.aquatrails.com; 1600 Delaware Ave; rental per hour single/double $25/35, tours single/double from $45/75) offers kayak tours of the coastal wetlands.

✕ 🛏 p85

Eating & Sleeping

Asbury Park 1

Sunset Landing — Cafe $

(☎732-776-9732; www.sunsetlandingap.com; 1215 Sunset Ave; mains $5-8; ⏰7am-2pm Tue-Sun) On Deal Lake, about 10 blocks from the beach, Sunset Landing is like a Hawaiian surf shack transported to a suburban Asbury lakeside. Vintage long-boards crowd the wooden rafters, cheesy omelets are super-fresh, and delicious specialty pancakes come with cranberries, cinnamon, coconut, macadamia nuts and other island flavors. Cash only.

Asbury Hotel — Boutique Hotel $$

(☎732-774-7100; www.theasburyhotel.com; 210 5th Ave; r $125-275; P ❄ 📶 🏊) Wow. From the performance space/lobby stocked with LP records, old books and a solarium to the rooftop bar, this new hotel oozes cool. A 2016 addition to the AP scene, two blocks from Convention Hall and the boardwalk, you could stay inside all day, playing pool or lounging by the rooftop one. Weeknights are a better deal.

Ocean Grove 2

Moonstruck — Italian $$$

(☎732-988-0123; www.moonstrucknj.com; 517 Lake Ave; mains $22-38; ⏰5-10pm Wed, Thu & Sun, to 11pm Fri & Sat) With views of Wesley Lake dividing Asbury and Ocean Grove, and an extensive martini menu, it's hard to find fault. The menu is eclectic, though it leans toward Italian with a good selection of pastas; the meat and fish dishes have varied ethnic influences.

Starving Artist — Cafe $

(☎732-988-1007; 47 Olin St; mains $3-9; ⏰8am-3pm Mon, Tue & Thu-Sat, to 2pm Sun; 👪) The menu at this adorable eatery with a large outdoor patio highlights breakfast, the grill and fried seafood; tasty ice cream is served at the adjacent shop. Stuffed French toast and 'loaded' potatoes are a morning must; bust out the crayons while you wait for your meal.

Quaker Inn — Inn $$

(☎732-775-7525; www.quakerinn.com; 39 Main Ave; r $90-200; ❄ 📶) A great old creaky Victorian with 28 rooms, some of which open onto wraparound porches or balconies. There's a nice common area/library to linger over your coffee, and the owners reflect the town's overall charm and hospitality.

Spring Lake 3

Grand Victorian at Spring Lake — Inn $$

(☎732-449-5237; www.grandvictorianspringlake.com; 1505 Ocean Ave; r with shared/private bath $239/309; ❄ 📶) Fifteen minutes south of Asbury Park, a stay at this bright and airy Victorian directly across the street from the beach is about as far from the TV version of a shore break as you can get. Rooms are simple and tastefully done and a wraparound porch and excellent attached restaurant add to the general air of oceanfront elegance.

Seaside Heights 5

Music Man — Ice Cream $

(☎732-854-2779; www.themusicman.com; 2305 Grand Central Ave, Lavallette; ice cream $3-8; ⏰11am-midnight) Have a little razzle-dazzle with your ice-cream sundae – the waitstaff belt out Broadway show tunes all night (from 5:30pm Friday to Sunday in June and daily in July and August). Cash only.

Shut Up and Eat! — Breakfast $

(☎732-349-4544; www.shutupandeat-tr.com; 804 Main St, Toms River; mains $9; ⏰6:30am-3:30pm) About 6 miles west of Seaside Heights, tucked away in the Kmart shopping plaza in Toms River, this sarcastically named place could be the silliest breakfast joint ever: waitresses in pajamas (wear yours for a 13% discount), snappy repartee, mismatched furniture and a cornucopia of kitsch. Even better: the French toast with real maple syrup, plus top-quality omelets, pancakes and more.

Ocean City 7

Flanders Hotel Hotel **$$**

(609-399-1000; www.theflandershotel.com; 719 E 11th St; r $199-445; P wifi pool) Shake off those sandy motel blues at Ocean City's Flanders Hotel: every room is a modern, immaculate 650-sq-ft (or larger) suite, with kitchenette or full kitchen. The blue-and-yellow decor evokes a pleasantly low-key seaside feel.

Wildwoods 8

Key West Cafe Breakfast **$**

(609-522-5006; 4701 Pacific Ave; mains $8-10; 7am-2pm) Basically every permutation of pancakes and eggs imaginable, all freshly prepared – oh, and lunch, too. Bonus: it's open year-round.

Starlux Boutique Hotel **$$**

(609-522-7412; www.thestarlux.com; 305 E Rio Grande Ave; r from $205, trailer $240; P wifi pool) The sea-green-and-white Starlux has the soaring profile, the lava lamps, the boomerang-decorated bedspreads and the sailboat shaped mirrors, plus it's clean as a whistle. Even more authentically retro are its two chrome-sided Airstream trailers. Rooms in a house behind the hotel are discounted.

Summer Nites B&B B&B **$$**

(609-846-1955; www.summernites.com; 2110 Atlantic Ave, North Wildwood; r $155-280; P air-con) North of the noise and lights, in an unassuming white house, is the coolest vintage experience of all: real jukeboxes play 45s; the breakfast room is a perfectly recreated diner; and the eight themed rooms are dominated by wall-size murals and framed, signed memorabilia. Treat yourself like a King: stay in the Elvis Suite.

Cape May 9

Lobster House Seafood **$$**

(609-884-8296; www.thelobsterhouse.com; 906 Schellengers Landing Rd; mains $14-30; 11:30am-3pm & 4:30-10pm Apr-Dec, to 9pm Jan-Mar) This clubby-feeling classic on the wharf serves local oysters and scallops. No reservations means very long waits – go early or late, or have a drink on the boat-bar, the *Schooner American*, docked next to the restaurant.

Mad Batter American **$**

(609-884-5970; www.madbatter.com; Carroll Villa Hotel, 19 Jackson St; brunch $8-11; 8am-9pm May-Aug, hours vary Sep-Apr) Tucked in a white Victorian B&B, this restaurant is locally beloved for brunch – including fluffy oat pancakes and rich clam chowder. Dinner is fine, but pricier, with mains around $30. The Chesapeake Bay Benedict, stuffed with crab, is to die for.

Congress Hall Hotel **$$$**

(609-884-8421; www.caperesorts.com; 200 Congress Pl; r from $259; air-con wifi pool) Opened in 1816, the enormous Congress Hall is a local landmark, now suitably modernized without wringing out all the history. The same company manages several other excellent hotels in the area.

Pennsylvania Dutch Country

On this fairly compact trip, discover Amish farmers markets and roadside stalls offering homemade goods, and traditions and history preserved in everyday life.

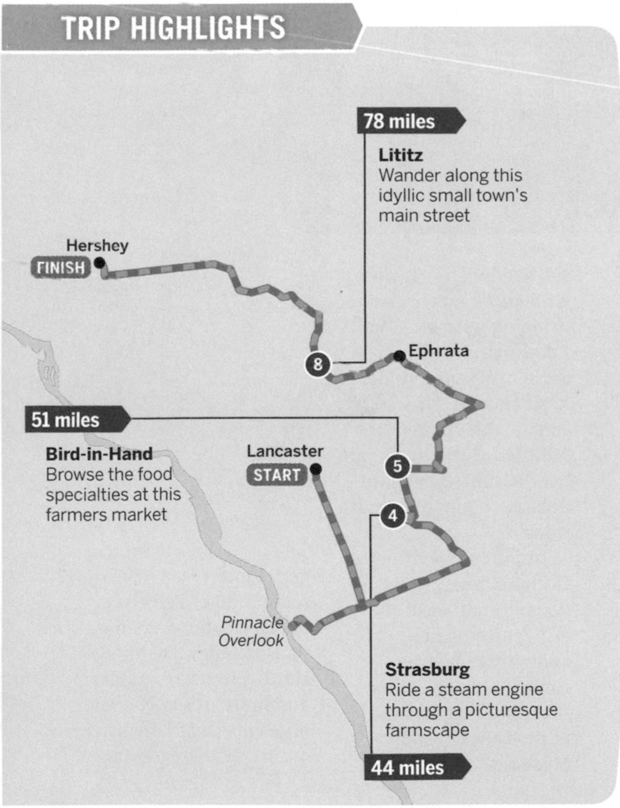

TRIP HIGHLIGHTS

78 miles
Lititz
Wander along this idyllic small town's main street

Hershey
FINISH

Ephrata

51 miles
Bird-in-Hand
Browse the food specialties at this farmers market

Lancaster
START

Pinnacle Overlook

Strasburg
Ride a steam engine through a picturesque farmscape
44 miles

3–4 DAYS
102 MILES / 164KM

GREAT FOR...

BEST TIME TO GO

Less crowded in early Spring or September.

ESSENTIAL PHOTO

A windmill or grain silo with a horse-drawn plow in the foreground.

BEST FOR FOODIES

Almost everything here comes in a buffet.

Lancaster County Riders in an Amish buggy

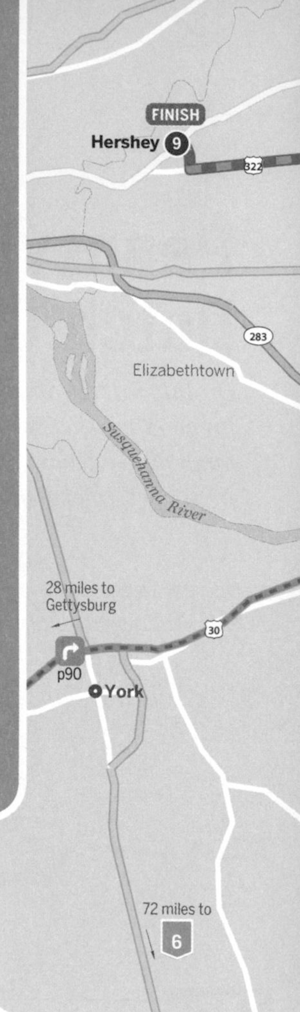

5 Pennsylvania Dutch Country

The Amish really do drive buggies and plow their fields by hand. In Dutch Country, the pace is slower, and it's no costumed reenactment. For the most evocative Dutch Country experience, go driving along the winding, narrow lanes between the thruways – past rolling green fields of alfalfa, asparagus and corn, past pungent working barnyards and manicured lawns, waving to Amish families in buggies and straw-hatted teens on scooters.

1 Lancaster

A good place to start is the walkable, red-brick historic district of Lancaster (LANK-uh-stir), just off Penn Sq. The Romanesque-revival-style **Central Market** (717-735-6890; www.centralmarketlancaster.com; 23 N Market St; snacks from $2; 6am-4pm Tue & Fri, to 2pm Sat), which is like a smaller version of Philadelphia's Reading Terminal Market, has all the regional gastronomic delicacies – fresh horseradish, whoopie pies, soft pretzels, and sub sandwiches stuffed with cured meats and dripping with oil. You'll find surprises, too, such as Spanish and Middle Eastern food. Plus, of course, the market is crowded with handicraft booths staffed by plain-dressed, bonneted Amish women.

In the 18th century, German immigrants flooded southeastern Pennsylvania, and only some were Amish. Most lived like the costumed docents at the **Landis Valley Museum** (717-569-0401; www.landisvalleymuseum.org; 2451 Kissel Hill Rd; adult/child $12/8; 9am-5pm Tue-Sat, noon-5pm Sun Mar-Dec, reduced hours Jan & Feb), a recreation of Pennsylvania German village life that includes a working smithy, weavers, stables and more. It's only a few miles north of Lancaster off Rte 272/Oregon Pike.

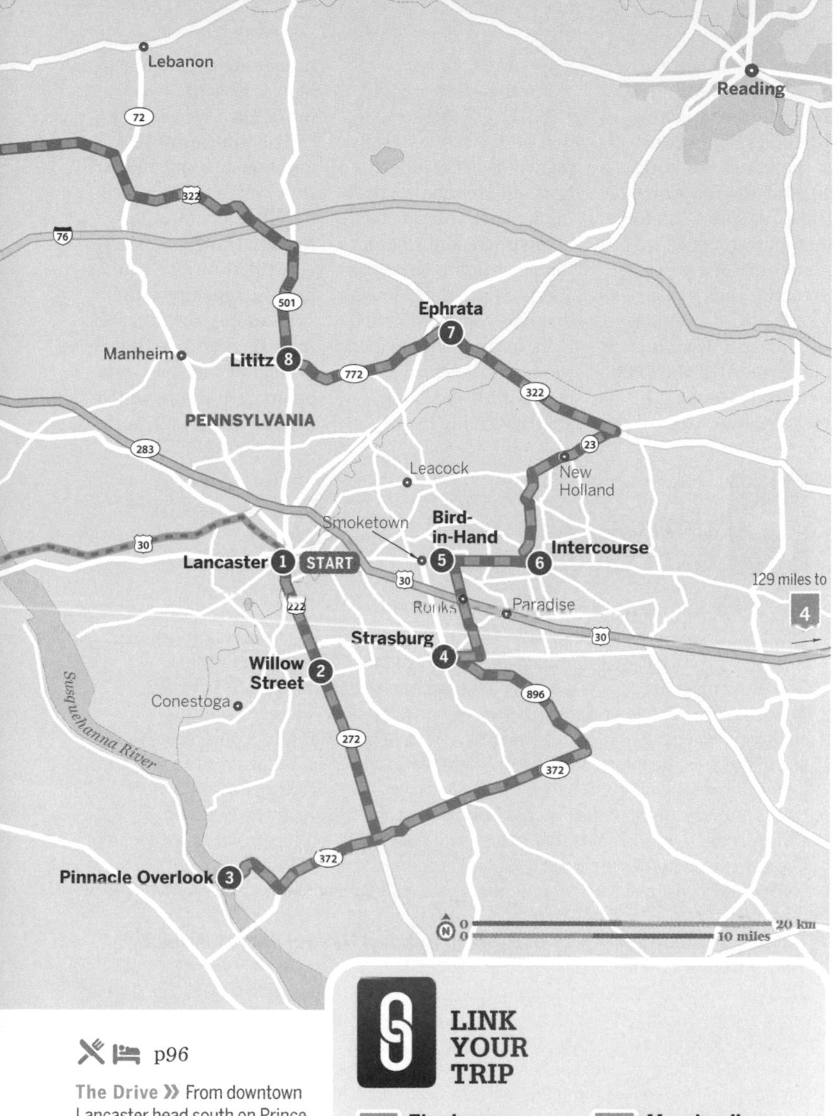

p96

The Drive » From downtown Lancaster head south on Prince St, which turns into Rte 222 and then Rte 272 all the way to Willow Street.

❷ Willow Street

Before the arrival of European emigres, Coney, Lenape, Mohawk,

LINK YOUR TRIP

4 The Jersey Shore

Head east to Philadelphia where you can connect to a number of routes that will transport you to the boardwalks of Jersey Shore towns.

6 Maryland's National Historic Road

Continue on US 30 west to York and then head south to Baltimore for a journey through this state's defining small towns.

Seneca and other Native Americans lived in the area. However, Pennsylvania remains one of the few states with no officially recognized tribal reserves – or, for that matter, tribes. In something of a gesture to rectify their erasure from history, a replica longhouse now stands on the property of the **1719 Hans Herr House** (717-464-4438; www.hansherr.org; 1849 Hans Herr Dr, Willow St; combined guided tour adult/child $15/7; 9am-4pm Mon-Sat Apr-Nov), generally regarded as the oldest original Mennonite meeting house in the western hemisphere and where the Herr family settled. Today, Hans Herr House displays colonial-era artifacts in period furnished rooms; there's also a blacksmith shop and a barn. 'Living history interpreters' provide an idea of how life was lived in the 18th century.

The interior of the longhouse, a typical narrow, single room multifamily home built only from natural materials, is divided into pre- and post-European contact sides and decorated and furnished with artifacts typical of each era. The primary mission, which is done quite well, is to

DETOUR: GETTYSBURG

Start: 1 Lancaster

Take US 30 west (also referred to as Lincoln Hwy) for 55 miles right into downtown Gettysburg. This tranquil, compact and memorial-laden town saw one of the Civil War's most decisive and bloody battles for three days in July, 1863. It's also where, four months later, Lincoln delivered his Gettysburg Address, consecrating, eulogizing and declaring the mission unfinished. At only 200-plus words, surely it's one of the most defining and effective rhetorical examples in US history. Much of the ground where Robert E Lee's Army of Northern Virginia and Major General Joseph Hooker's Union Army of the Potomac skirmished and fought can be explored – either on your own, on a bus tour or on a two-hour guide-led tour in your own car. The latter is recommended, but if you're short on time it's still worth driving the narrow lanes past fields with monuments marking significant sites and moments in the battle.

Don't miss the massive new **Gettysburg National Military Park Museum & Visitor Center** (717-334-1124; www.nps.gov/gett; 1195 Baltimore Pike; museum adult/child $15/10, bus tour $35/21, licensed guide per vehicle $75; museum 8am-6pm Apr-Oct, 9am-5pm Nov-Mar, grounds 6am-10pm Apr-Oct, to 7pm Nov-Mar) several miles south of town, which houses a fairly incredible museum filled with artifacts and displays exploring every nuance of the battle; a film explaining Gettysburg's context and why it's considered a turning point in the war; and Paul Philippoteaux's 377ft cyclorama painting of Pickett's Charge. The aforementioned bus tours and ranger-led tours are booked here. While overwhelming, in the very least, it's a foundation for understanding the Civil War's primacy and lingering impact in the nation's evolution.

The annual Civil War Heritage Days festival, taking place from the last weekend of June through the first weekend of July, features living history encampments, battle reenactments, a lecture series and book fair that draws war reenactment aficionados from near and wide. You can find reenactments at other times throughout the year as well.

teach visitors about the history of Native American life in Lancaster County from around 1570 to 1770 when, for all intents and purposes, they ceased to exist as distinctive groups in the area. And this includes the infamous Conestoga Massacre of 1763 when vigilante colonists from Paxton (given the curiously anodyne epithet the 'Paxton Boys') murdered 20 Native American men, women and children from the settlement of Conestoga. A guided tour of both the Hans Herr House and the longhouse makes for an interesting juxtaposition of historical perspectives.

The Drive » The simplest route is Rte 272 south to Rte 372 west. If you have time, however, head west on W Penn Grant Rd and then left on New Danville Pike, which turns into Main St in Conestoga. From there, follow Main St to a T-junction and turn left on River Rd, a backcountry road with lots of turns, passing Tucquan Glen Nature Preserve on the way.

❸ Pinnacle Overlook

High over Lake Aldred, a wide portion of the Susquehanna River just up from a large dam, is this overlook (8am to 9pm) with beautiful views, and eagles and other raptors soaring overhead. This and the adjoining Holtwood Environmental Preserve are parts of a large swath of riverfront property maintained by the Pennsylvania Power & Light Co (PPL). But electrical plant infrastructure and accompanying truck traffic is largely kept at bay, making this a popular spot for locals, non-Amish, that is (it's too far to travel by horse and buggy). The 4-mile-long Fire Line Trail to the adjoining Kelly's Run Natural Area is challenging and steep in parts and the rugged Conestoga Trail follows the east side of the lake for 15 miles. It's worth coming out this way if only to see more rough-hewn landscape and the rural byways that reveal another facet to Lancaster County's character, which most visitors bypass.

The Drive » You could retrace your route back to Willow Street and then head on to Strasburg, but to make a scenic loop, take Rte 372 east, passing some agrarian scenes as well as suburban housing, to the small hamlet of Georgetown. Make a left onto Rte 896 – vistas open up on either side of the road.

TRIP HIGHLIGHT

❹ Strasburg

The main attraction in Strasburg is trains – the old-fashioned, steam-driven kind. Since 1832 the **Strasburg Railroad** (☎866-725-9666; www.strasburgrailroad.com; 301 Gap Rd, Ronks; coach class adult/child $15/8; ⏱times vary; 👪) has run the same route (and speed) to Paradise and back that it does today, and wooden train cars are gorgeously restored with stained glass, shiny brass lamps and plush burgundy seats. Several classes of seats are offered, including the private President's Car; there's also a wine-and-cheese option.

The **Railroad Museum of Pennsylvania** (☎717-687-8628; www.rrmuseumpa.org; 300 Gap Rd, Ronks; adult/child $10/8; ⏱9am-5pm Mon-Sat, noon-5pm Sun Apr-Oct, closed Mon Nov-Mar; 👪) has 100 gigantic mechanical marvels to climb around and admire, but even more delightful is the HO-scale **National Toy Train Museum** (☎717-687-8976; www.nttmuseum.org; 300 Paradise Lane, Ronks; adult/child $7/4; ⏱10am-5pm May-Oct, hours vary Nov-Apr; 👪). The push-button interactive dioramas are so up-to-date and clever (such as a 'drive-in movie' that's a live video of kids working the trains), and the walls are packed with so many gleaming railcars, that you can't help but feel a bit of that childlike Christmas-morning wonder. Stop at the Red Caboose Motel (p97) next to the museum – you can climb the silo in back for wonderful views (50c), and kids can enjoy a petting zoo.

GEORGE SHELDON / SHUTTERSTOCK ©

Above: Amish buggies in Lancaster County
Below: Pushing a scooter bicycle
Right: Dolls for sale, Intercourse

LEE SNIDER PHOTO IMAGES / SHUTTERSTOCK ©

PETER PTSCHELINZEW / GETTY IMAGES ©

The Drive » Continue north on S Ronks Rd past Ronks' bucolic farmland scenery, cross busy Rte 30 (Miller's Smorgasbord restaurant is at this intersection; p97) and carry on for another 2 miles to Bird-in-Hand. Still hungry? Smoketown's Good 'N Plenty Restaurant (p96) is a mile west of Bird-in-Hand on Rte 340/ Old Philadelphia Pike at the intersection with Rte 896.

TRIP HIGHLIGHT

5 Bird-in-Hand

The primary reason to make your way to this delightfully named Amish town is the **Bird-in-Hand Farmers Market** (717-393-9674; www.birdinhandfarmersmarket.com; 2710 Old Philadelphia Pike; lunches $6-8; 8:30am-5:30pm Fri & Sat, also Wed Apr-Nov & Thu Jul-Oct), which is pretty much a one-stop shop of Dutch Country highlights. There's fudge, quilts and crafts, and you can buy scrapple (pork scraps mixed with cornmeal and wheat flour, shaped into a loaf and fried), homemade jam and shoofly pie (a pie made of molasses or brown sugar sprinkled with a crumbly mix of brown sugar, flour and butter). Two lunch counters sell sandwiches, pretzels and juices and smoothies: stock up for the onward drive.

The Drive » It's less than 4 miles east on Old Philadelphia Pike/Rte 340, but traffic can back up, in part because it's a popular route for horse-and-buggy rides.

6 Intercourse

Named for the crossroads, not the act, Intercourse is a little more amenable to walking than Bird-in-Hand. The **horse-drawn buggy rides** (717-768-8828; www.amishbuggyrides.com; 3121 Old Philadelphia Pike, Bird-in-Hand; tours adult/child from $10/6; 9am-6pm Mon-Sat Apr-Oct, 10am-4:30pm Mon-Sat Nov-Mar;) on offer can also be fun. How much fun depends largely on your driver: some Amish are strict, some liberal, and Mennonites are different again. All drivers strive to present Amish culture to the 'English' (the Amish term for non-Amish, whether English or not), but some are more openly personal than others.

Kitchen Kettle Village, essentially an open-air mall for tourists with stores selling smoked meats, jams, pretzels, gifts and tchotchkes, feels like a Disneyfied version of the Bird-in-the-Hand Farmers Market. It's a one-stop shop for the commercialized 'PA Dutch Country experience,' which means your perception of it will depend on your attitude toward a parking lot jammed with tour buses.

The Drive » Head north on Rte 772 and make your first right onto Centerville Rd (which becomes S Shirk Rd), a country lane that takes you to Rte 23. Turn right here and it's a few miles to Blue Ball (try not to giggle that you're so close to Intercourse) – and then left on the busier Rte 322 all the way to Ephrata.

7 Ephrata

One of the country's earliest religious communities was founded in 1732 by Conrad Beissel, an emigre escaping religious persecution in his native Germany. Beissel, like others throughout human history dissatisfied with worldly ways and distractions (difficult to imagine what these were in his pre-pre-pre-digital age), sought a mystical, personal relationship with God. At its peak there were close to 300 members, including two celibate orders of brothers and sisters, known collectively as 'the Solitary,' who patterned their dress after Roman Catholic monks (the last of these passed away in 1813), as well as married 'households' who were less all-in, if you will.

THE AMISH

The Amish (ah-mish), Mennonite and Brethren religious communities are collectively known as the 'Plain People.' All are Anabaptist sects (only those who choose the faith are baptized) who were persecuted in their native Switzerland, and from the early 1700s settled in tolerant Pennsylvania. Speaking German dialects, they became known as 'Dutch' (from 'Deutsch'). Most Pennsylvania Dutch live on farms and their beliefs vary from sect to sect. Many do not use electricity, and most opt for horse-drawn buggies – a delightful sight, and sound, in the area. The strictest believers, the Old Order Amish who make up nearly 90% of Lancaster County's Amish, wear dark, plain clothing (no zippers, only buttons, snaps and safety pins) and live a simple, Bible-centered life – but have, ironically, become a major tourist attraction, thus bringing busloads of gawkers and the requisite strip malls, chain restaurants and hotels that lend this entire area an oxymoronic quality, to say the least. Because there is so much commercial development continually encroaching on multigenerational family farms, it takes some doing to appreciate the unique nature of the area.

Today, the collection of austere, almost medieval-style buildings of the **Ephrata Cloister** (717-733-6600; www.ephratacloister.org; 632 W Main St; adult/child $10/6; 9am-5pm Mon-Sat, noon-5pm Sun Mar-Dec, reduced hours Jan & Feb) have been preserved and are open to visitors; guided tours are offered or take an audio cell phone tour on your own. There's a small museum and a short film in the visitor center that very earnestly and efficiently tells the story of Ephrata's founding and demise – if the narrator's tone and rather somber mise-en-scène are any indication, not to mention the extremely spartan sleeping quarters, it was a demanding existence. No doubt Beissel would disapprove of today's Ephrata, the commercial Main St of which is anchored by a Walmart.

If you're around on a Friday, be sure to check out the **Green Dragon Farmers Market** (717-738-1117; www.greendragonmarket.com; 955 N State St; 9am-9pm Fri).

The Drive » This is a simple 8.5-mile drive; for the most part, Rte 772/Rothsville Rd between Ephrata and Lititz is an ordinary commercial strip.

8 Lititz

Like other towns in Pennsylvania Dutch Country, Lititz was founded by a religious community from Europe, in this case Moravians who settled here in the 1740s. However, unlike Ephrata, Lititz was more outward looking and integrated with the world beyond its historic center. Many of its original handsome stone and wood buildings still line its streets today. Take a stroll down E Main from the **Sturgis Pretzel House** (717-626-4354; www.juliussturgis.com; 219 E Main St; adult/child $3.50/2.50; 9am-5pm Mon-Sat, tours to 4:30pm mid-Mar–Dec, 10am-4pm Mon-Sat, tours to 3:30pm mid-Jan–mid-Mar;), the first pretzel factory in the country – you can try your hand at rolling and twisting the dough.

Across the street is the Moravian Church (c 1787); then head to the intersection with S Broad. Rather than feeling sealed in amber, the small shops, which do seem to relish their small-town quality, are nonetheless the type that sophisticated urbanites cherish. There's an unusual effortlessness to this vibe, from the Bulls Head Public House, a traditional English-style pub with an expertly curated beer menu, to Greco's Italian Ices, a little ground-floor hole-in-the-wall where local teenagers and families head on weekend nights for delicious homemade ice cream.

p97

The Drive » It's an easy 27 miles on Rte 501 to US 322. Both pass through a combination of farmland and suburban areas, though the latter is generally a fast-moving highway.

9 Hershey

Hershey is home to a collection of attractions that detail, hype and, of course, hawk the many trappings of Milton Hershey's chocolate empire. The pièce de résistance is **Hershey Park** (717-534-3900; www.hersheypark.com; 100 W Hersheypark Dr; adult/child $65/42; 10am-10pm Jun-Aug, reduced hours Sep-May), an amusement park with more than 60 thrill rides, a zoo and a water park. Don a hairnet and apron and punch in a few choices on a computer screen and then voilà, watch your very own chocolate bar roll down a conveyor belt at the Create Your Own Candy Bar attraction ($15), part of Hershey's Chocolate World, a mock factory and massive candy store with overstimulating features such as singing characters and free chocolate galore.

For a more low-key informative visit, try the Hershey Story, The Museum on Chocolate Avenue, which explores the life and fascinating legacy of Mr Hershey through interactive history exhibits; try molding your own candy in the hands-on Chocolate Lab.

Eating & Sleeping

Lancaster 1

✕ Bube's Brewery — Brewery

(☎717-653-2056; www.bubesbrewery.com; 102 N Market St, Mt Joy; mains $12-20; ⏲11am-10pm Mon-Thu, 11am-11pm Fri-Sat, noon-10pm Sun) This well-preserved 19th-century German brewery-cum-restaurant complex contains several atmospheric bars and four separate dining rooms (one underground), hosts costumed 'feasts' and, naturally, brews its own beer. There's also a murder-mystery-themed dining event and an outdoor *biergarten*.

✕ Lancaster Brewing Co — Pub Food $$

(☎717-391-6258; www.lancasterbrewing.com; 302 N Plum St; mains $16-24; ⏲11:30am-9:30pm; 👪) This brewery, established in 1995, is a local favorite. The restaurant serves hearty but sophisticated food – lamb chops with tzatziki, say – and housemade sausages at tables with copper-clad tops and great views of the brewing tanks. You can't beat specials such as $5 all-you-can-eat wings and $6 beer-tasting flights.

✕ Maison — European $$$

(☎717-293-5060; www.maisonlancaster.com; 230 N Prince St; mains $26-30; ⏲5-11pm Wed-Sat; ✍) A husband-and-wife team run this homey but meticulous place downtown, giving local farm products a rustic Italian-French treatment: pork braised in milk, housemade rabbit sausage, fried squash blossoms or handmade gnocchi, depending on the season.

🛏 Cork Factory — Boutique Hotel $$

(☎717-735-2075; www.corkfactoryhotel.com; 480 New Holland Ave, Suite 3000; r from $190; P ⊖ ❄ 📶) An abandoned brick behemoth now houses this stylish hotel, with 93 posh rooms. It's a short drive from downtown.

🛏 Lancaster Arts Hotel — Hotel $$

(☎717-299-3000; www.lancasterartshotel.com; 300 Harrisburg Ave; r from $230; P ❄ 📶) For a refreshingly hip and urban experience, make a beeline to the snazzy Lancaster Arts Hotel, a member of the Historic Hotels of America, housed in an old brick tobacco warehouse and featuring a groovy boutique-hotel ambience. Room prices include complementary passes to a nearby pool and fitness club.

🛏 Landis Farm Guest House — Guesthouse $$

(☎717-283-7648; www.landisfarm.com; 2048 Gochlan Rd, Manheim; d $160; P ❄ 📶) A slightly upscale and modern homestay farm experience (complete with satellite TV and wi-fi) can be had at this 200-year-old stone home with pinewood floors. Farm animals include miniature horses, cattle, and calves (at the right time of year).

Smoketown

✕ Good 'N Plenty Restaurant — American $$

(☎717-394-7111; www.goodnplenty.com; 150 Eastbrook Rd/Rte 896; mains $9-12; ⏲11:30am-8pm Mon-Sat Feb-Dec; 👪) Sure, you'll be dining with busloads of tourists and your cardiologist might not approve, but hunkering down at one of the picnic tables for a full family-style meal ($23) is a lot of fun. Besides the main dining room, which is nearly the size of a football field, there are smaller rooms where you can order from an à la carte menu.

Fulton Steamboat Inn Hotel $$

(717-299-9999; www.fultonsteamboatinn.com; 1 Hartman Bridge Rd; r $95-160;) Even if you know the inventor of the steamboat was born in this area, this nautical-themed hotel is gimmicky. But the brass fixtures and flowery wallpaper are all well kept, the rooms are comfortable, and there's even an indoor pool. Add $20 for a 3rd-floor suite.

Ronks

Miller's Smorgasbord Buffet $

(717-687-6621; www.millerssmorgasbord.com; 2811 Lincoln Hwy; mains $10-14, buffet $24; 11:30am-8pm Mon-Fri, 7:30-10:30am & 11:30am-8pm Sat & Sun;) To smorgasbord or not to smorgasbord – there's no question. Otherwise, the alternative menu of diner-style dishes is fairly ordinary. The anchor of a touristy complex of shops, this pavilion-size restaurant draws crowds for the buffet featuring Amish-style mains and desserts.

Quiet Haven Motel $

(717-397-6231; www.quiethavenmotel.com; 2556 Siegrist Rd; r from $94;) If your vision of a PA Dutch getaway is sitting in a rocking chair and gazing out over farmland, book in at this family-owned motel, surrounded by green fields. Most of the 15 rooms still have a hint of 1960s flair, such as 'hi-fi' switches that once went to 8-track and console radios.

Red Caboose Motel Motel $$

(717-687-5000; www.redcaboosemotel.com; 312 Paradise Lane; s/d from $95/130;) A novelty hotel, but completely fun: these are fairly standard motel rooms, TV and mini-fridge included, wedged in the narrow confines of a collection of caboose cars of every shape and color, apparently purchased for a song just before they were heading to the scrap heap. The surroundings – all farmland – are lovely, too, and the silo (50¢ per person) is well worth ascending for a look around.

Lititz 8

Tomato Pie Cafe Cafe $

(717-627-1762; www.tomatopiecafe.net; 23 N Broad St; mains $7-12; 7am-9pm Mon-Sat, 8am-5pm Sun;) The creative, fresh food and the complex coffee drinks wouldn't be out of place in a city, but the atmosphere is pure friendly small town. Tomato pie is their signature dish, a rich, soft, cheesy mix that's unique and worth a try. Espresso here is excellent, well worth the detour for.

General Sutter Inn Inn $$

(717-626-2115; www.generalsutterinn.com; 14 E Main St; s/d/ste from $100/160/260;) At this 18th-century inn, 12 rooms are furnished with tasteful antiques, and on the incongruous top floor, six suites have a loose rock-and-roll theme. Downstairs is the popular Bulls Head Pub, for Scotch eggs and cask ales. Guests can use a nearby rec center for fitness and the pool.

GEORGE WASHINGTON

Maryland's National Historic Road

From Baltimore's salty docks to the forested foothills around old Frederick, delve into the past of one of the most diverse states in the country.

TRIP HIGHLIGHTS

26 miles
Sykesville
Old rail town on a bucolic hill

Gathland State Park
FINISH
7
New Market
Mount Airy
3
Baltimore
2
START

Frederick
Picture-perfect town center framed by a lively arts district
73 miles

Patapsco Valley
Green nature hikes by a rushing river
13 miles

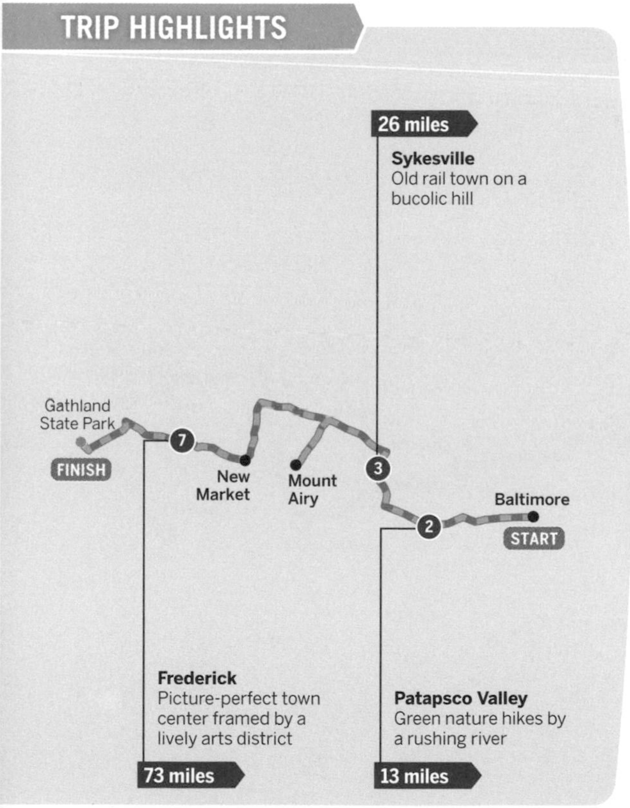

2 DAYS
92 MILES / 150KM

GREAT FOR...

BEST TIME TO GO
April to June to soak up late spring's sunniness and warmth.

ESSENTIAL PHOTO
The historic buildings lining New Market, MD.

BEST FOR OUTDOORS
Hiking along the bottom of Patapsco Valley.

6 Maryland's National Historic Road

For such a small state, Maryland has a staggering array of landscapes and citizens, and this trip engages both of these elements of the Old Line State. Move from Chesapeake Bay and Baltimore, a port that mixes bohemians with blue collar workers, through the picturesque small towns of the Maryland hill country, into the stately cities that mark the lower slopes of the looming Catoctin Mountains.

1 Baltimore

Maryland's largest city is one of the most important ports in the country, a center for the arts and culture and an melting pot of immigrants from Greece, El Salvador, East Africa, the Caribbean and elsewhere. These streams combine into an idiosyncratic culture that, in many ways, encapsulates Maryland's depth of history and prominent diversity – not just of race, but creed and socioeconomic status.

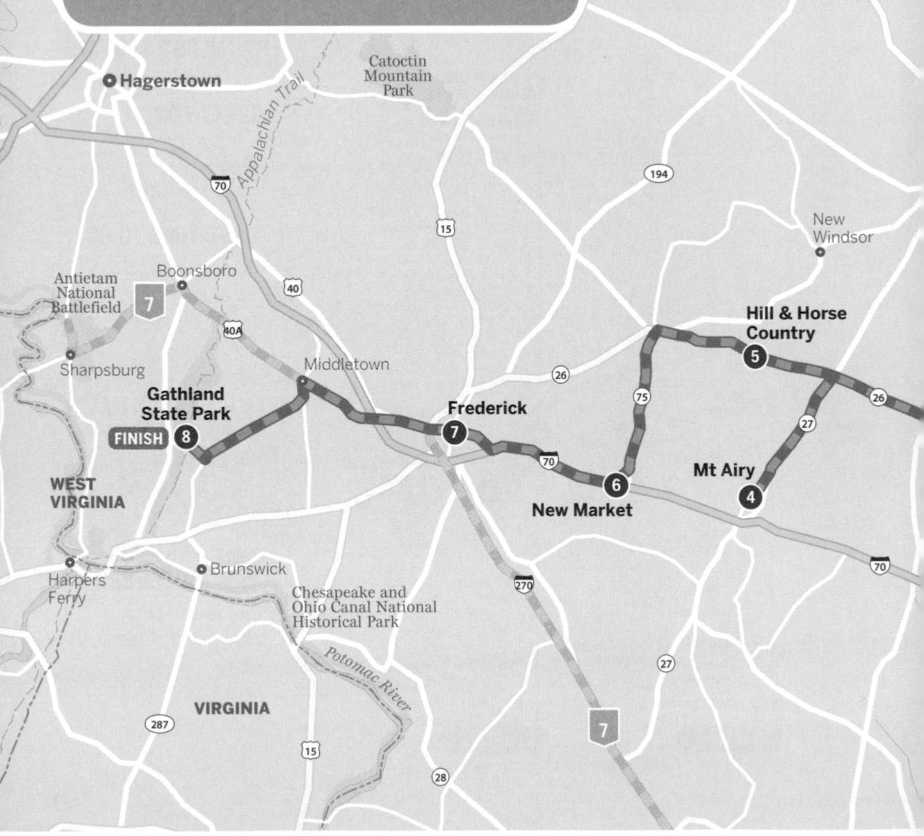

Baltimore was a notable holdout against the British military during the War of 1812, even after Washington, DC, fell. The morning after an intense shelling, staring 'through the rockets' red glare,' local lawyer Francis Scott Key saw that 'our flag was still there' and wrote The Star-Spangled Banner. The history of that battle and the national anthem are explored at **Fort McHenry** (☎410-962-4290; www.nps.gov/fomc; 2400 E Fort Ave; adult/child under 16yr $10/free; ⏲9am-5pm), located in South Baltimore.

Have a wander through nearby **Federal Hill Park**, a 70-acre hill that rises above the city, and admire the view out over the harbor.

p107

The Drive » Get on US 40 (Baltimore National Pike – and the basis of the National Historic Road this trip is named for) westbound in Baltimore. The easiest place to access it is at Charles and Franklin St. Franklin becomes US 40/the Pike as you head west out of downtown Baltimore, into the woods that mark the edges of the Patapsco Valley. The whole drive takes about 30 minutes in traffic.

TRIP HIGHLIGHT

2 Patapsco Valley

The Patapsco river and river valley are the defining geographic features of the region, running through Central Maryland to Chesapeake Bay. To explore the area, head to **Patapsco Valley State Park** (☎410-461-5005; http://dnr2.maryland.gov/publiclands; 8020 Baltimore National Pike, Ellicott City; per car Mon-Fri $4, per person Sat & Sun $5; ⏲9am-sunset), an enormous protected area – one of the oldest in the state – that runs for 32 miles along a whopping 170 miles of trails. The main visitor center provides insight into the settled history of the area, from Native Americans

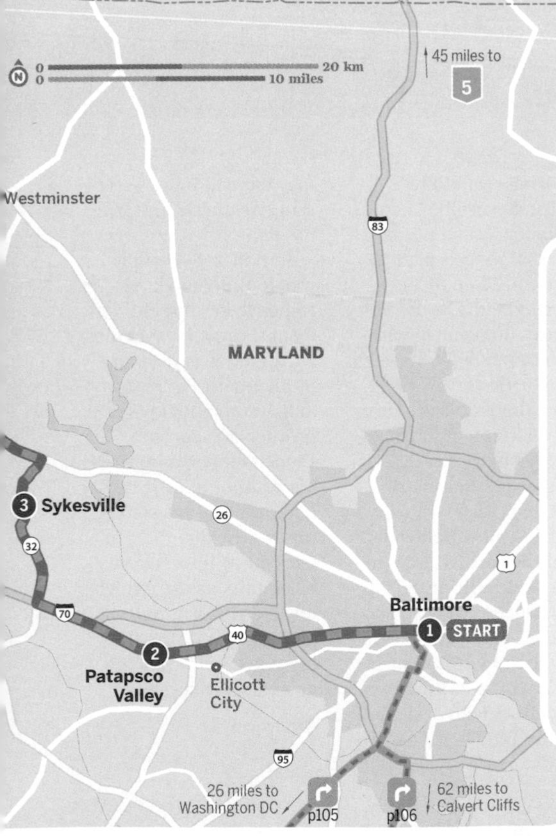

LINK YOUR TRIP

5 Pennsylvania Dutch Country

Take I-95 north from Baltimore and then MD-222 towards Lancaster to begin exploring this patch of bucolic farmland.

7 The Civil War Tour

In Gathland State Park, head 10 miles west to Antietam to begin exploring America's seminal internal conflict.

DRNADIG / GETTY IMAGES ©

to the present, and is housed in a 19th-century stone cottage that looks as though it were plucked from a CS Lewis bedtime story.

The Drive » Get back on US 40/the Pike westbound until you see signs to merge onto I-70W, which is the main connecting road between Baltimore and central and western Maryland. Get on 70, then take exit 80 to get onto MD 32 (Sykesville Rd). Follow for about 5 miles into Sykesville proper.

TRIP HIGHLIGHT

3 Sykesville

Like many of the towns in the central Maryland hill country between Baltimore and Frederick, Sykesville has a historic center that looks and feels picture perfect. Main St, between Springfield Ave and Sandosky Rd, is filled with structures built between the 1850s and 1930s, and almost looks like an advertisement for small-town America.

The old Baltimore & Ohio (B&O) train station, now **Baldwin's Restaurant** (7618 Main St), was built in 1883 in the Queen Anne style. The station was the brainchild of E Francis Baldwin, a Baltimore architect who designed many B&O stations, giving that rail line a satisfying aesthetic uniformity along its extent.

Fun fact: Sykesville was founded on land James Sykes bought from George Patterson. Patterson was the son of Elizabeth Patterson and Jerome Bonaparte, brother of Napoleon. The French emperor insisted his brother marry royalty and never let his sister-in-law (the daughter of a merchant) into France; her family estate (which formed the original parcel of land that the town grew from) is the grounds of Sykesville.

p107

Baltimore Federal Hill Park

The Drive » Although this trip is largely based on US 40 – the actual National Historic Road – detour up to Liberty Rd (MD-26) and take that west 8 miles to Ridge Rd (MD-27). Take Ridge Rd/27 south for 5.5 miles to reach Mt Airy.

4 Mt Airy

Mt Airy is the next major (we use that term with a grain of salt) town along the B&O railroad and US 40/the National Historic Road. Like Sykesville, it's a handsome town, with a stately center that benefited from the commerce the railway brought westward from Baltimore. When the railway was replaced by the highway, Mt Airy, unlike other towns, still retained much of its prosperity thanks to the proximity of jobs in cities like DC and Baltimore.

Today the town centers on a historic district of 19th- and early-20th-century buildings, many of which can be found around Main St. The posher historical homes near 'downtown' Mt Airy were built in the Second Empire, Queen Anne and Colonial Revival styles, while most 'regular' homes are two-story, center-gable 'I-houses,' once one of the most common housing styles in rural America in the 19th-century, but now largely displaced in this region by modern split-levels.

The Drive » Take Ridge Rd/MD-27 back to Liberty Rd/MD-26. Turn left and proceed for 10 miles to reach Elk Run.

5 Hill & Horse Country

Much of Frederick, Carroll, Baltimore and Hartford counties consist of trimmed, rolling hills intersected by copses of pine and broadleaf woods and tangled hedgerows; it's the sort of landscape that could put you in mind of the bocage country of northern France or rural England. A mix of working farmers and wealthy city folks live out here, and horse breeding and raising is a big industry.

It can be pretty enchanting just driving around and getting lost on some of the local back roads, but if you want a solid destination, it's tough to go wrong with **Elk Run Vineyards** (☎410-775-2513; www.elkrun.com; 15113 Liberty Rd, Mt Airy; tastings from $6, tours free; ⏰10am-6pm Tue, Wed & Sat, to 9pm Fri & 1-5pm Sun May-Sep, 10am-5pm Wed-Sat & noon-5pm Sun Oct-Apr), almost exactly halfway between Mt Airy and New Market. Free tours are offered at 1pm and 3pm, and tastings can be arranged without reservations for at least two people.

The Drive » Continue west on Liberty Rd/MD-26 for 6 miles, then turn left (southbound) onto MD-75/Green Valley Rd. After about 7 miles, take a right onto Old New Market Rd to reach New Market's Main St.

6 New Market

Pretty New Market is the smallest and best preserved of the historical towns that sit between Baltimore and Frederick. Main St, full of antique shops, is lined with Federal and Greek Revival houses. More than 90% of the structures are of brick or frame construction, as opposed to modern vinyl, sheet rock and/or dry wall; the National Register of Historical Places deems central New Market 'in appearance, the quintessence of the c[irca] 1800 small town in western central Maryland.'

The Drive » Frederick is about 7 miles west of New Market via I-70. Take exit 56 for MD-144 to reach the city center.

SOME MORE OF BALTIMORE'S BEST

Everyone knows DC is chock-a-block replete with museums, but the capital's scruffier, funkier neighbor to the northeast gives Washington a run for its money in the museum department.

Out by the Baltimore waterfront is a strange building, seemingly half enormous warehouse, half explosion of intense artsy angles, multicolored windmills and rainbow-reflecting murals, like someone had bent the illustrations of a Dr Seuss book through a funky mirror. This is quite possibly the coolest art museum in the country: the **American Visionary Art Museum** (AVAM; ☎410-244-1900; www.avam.org; 800 Key Hwy; adult/child $16/10; ⏰10am-6pm Tue-Sun). It's a showcase for self-taught (or 'outsider' art), which is to say art made by people who aren't formally trained artists. It's a celebration of unbridled creativity utterly free of arts-scene pretension. Some of the works come from asylums, others are created by self-inspired visionaries, but it's all rather captivating and well worth a long afternoon.

The Baltimore & Ohio railway was (arguably) the first passenger train in America, and the **B&O Railroad Museum** (☎410-752-2490; www.borail.org; 901 W Pratt St; adult/child 2-12yr $18/12; ⏰10am-4pm Mon-Sat, 11am-4pm Sun; 👪) is a loving testament to both that line and American railroading in general. Train spotters will be in heaven among more than 150 different locomotives. Train rides cost an extra $3; call for the schedule.

If you're traveling with a family, or if you just love science and science education, come by the **Maryland Science Center** (☎410-685-2370; www.mdsci.org; 601 Light St; adult/child 3-12yr $25/19; ⏰10am-5pm Mon-Fri, to 6pm Sat, 11am-5pm Sun, longer hours in summer). This awesome center features a three-story atrium, tons of interactive exhibits on dinosaurs, outer space and the human body, and the requisite IMAX theater.

DETOUR: WASHINGTON, DC

Start: 1 Baltimore

A natural complement to your historical tour is the nation's capital, just 40 miles south of Baltimore on the BWI Pkwy. The **National Mall** has been the site of some of the nation's most iconic protests, from Martin Luther King's March on Washington to recent rallies for the legalization of gay marriage.

The east end of the mall is filled with the (free!) museums of the **Smithsonian Institution**. All are worth your time. We could easily get lost amid the silk screens, Japanese prints and sculpture of the often-bypassed **Freer-Sackler Museums of Asian Art** (202-633-1000; www.asia.si.edu; cnr Independence Ave & 12th St SW; 10am-5:30pm; Circulator, M Orange, Silver, Blue Lines to Smithsonian). On the other side of the mall is a cluster of memorials and monuments. The most famous is the back of the penny: the **Lincoln Memorial** (www.nps.gov/linc; 2 Lincoln Memorial Circle NW; 24hr; Circulator, M Orange, Silver, Blue Lines to Foggy Bottom-GWU). The view over the reflecting pool to the Washington Monument is as spectacular as you've imagined. The **Roosevelt Memorial** (www.nps.gov/frde; 400 W Basin Dr SW; 24hr; Circulator, M Orange, Silver, Blue Lines to Smithsonian) is notable for its layout, which explores the entire term of America's longest-serving president.

On the north flank of the Lincoln Memorial (left if you're facing the pool) is the immensely powerful **Vietnam Veterans Memorial** (www.nps.gov/vive; 5 Henry Bacon Dr NW; 24hr; Circulator, M Orange, Silver, Blue Lines to Foggy Bottom-GWU), a black granite 'V' cut into the soil inscribed with names of the American war dead of that conflict. Search for the nearby but rarely visited **Constitution Gardens** (Constitution Ave NW; 24hr; Circulator, M Orange, Silver, Blue Lines to Foggy Bottom-GWU), featuring a tranquil, landscaped pond and artificial island inscribed with the names of the signers of the Constitution.

TRIP HIGHLIGHT

7 Frederick

Frederick boasts a historically preserved center, but unlike the previously listed small towns, this is a mid-sized city, an important commuter base for thousands of federal government employees and a biotechnology hub in its own right.

Central Frederick is, well, perfect. For a city of its size (around 65,000), what more could you want? A historic, pedestrian-friendly center of redbrick row houses with a large, diverse array of restaurants usually found in a larger town; an engaged, cultured arts community anchored by the excellent events calendar at the **Weinberg Center for the Arts** (301-600-2828; www.weinbergcenter.org; 20 W Patrick St); and the meandering Carroll Creek running through the center of it all. Walking around downtown is immensely enjoyable.

The creek is crossed by a lovely bit of community art: the mural on **Frederick Bridge**, at S Carroll St between E Patrick & E All Saints. The trompe l'oeil–style art essentially transforms a drab concrete span into an old, ivy-covered stone bridge from Tuscany.

p107

The Drive » Head west on old National Pike (US 40A) and then, after about 6.5 miles, get on MD-17 southbound/Burkittsville Rd. Turn right on Gapland Rd after 6 miles

DETOUR: CALVERT CLIFFS

Start: 1 Baltimore

In aouthern Maryland, 75 miles south of Baltimore via US 301 and MD-4, skinny Calvert County scratches at Chesapeake Bay and the Patuxent River. This is a gentle landscape ('user-friendly' as a local ranger puts it) of low-lying forests, estuarine marshes and placid waters, but there is one rugged feature: the Calvert cliffs. These burnt-umber pillars stretch along the coast for some 24 miles, and form the seminal landscape feature of **Calvert Cliffs State Park** (☎301-743-7613; www.dnr.maryland.gov/publiclands; 9500 HG Trueman Rd, Lusby; per vehicle $5; ⏲sunrise-sunset; P), where they front the water and a pebbly, honey-sand beach scattered with driftwood and drying beds of kelp.

Back in the day (10 to 20 million years ago), this area sat submerged under a warm sea. Eventually, that sea receded and left the fossilized remains of thousands of prehistoric creatures embedded in the cliffs. Fast forward to the 21st-century, and one of the favorite activities of southern Maryland families is coming to this park, strolling across the sand and plucking out fossils and sharks' teeth from the pebbly debris at the base of the cliffs. Over 600 species of fossils have been identified at the park. In addition, a full 1079 acres and 13 miles of the park are set aside for trails and hiking and biking.

While this spot is pet- and family-friendly, fair warning: it's a 1.8-mile walk from the parking lot to the open beach and the cliffs, so this may not be the best spot to go fossil hunting with very small children unless they can handle the walk. Also: don't climb the cliffs, as erosion makes this an unstable and unsafe prospect.

and follow it for 1.5 miles to Gathland.

8 Gathland State Park

This tiny **park** (☎301-791-4767; http://dnr2.maryland.gov/publiclands; 900 Arnoldstown Rd; ⏲8am-sunset) is a fascinating tribute to a profession that doesn't lend itself to many memorials: war correspondents. Civil War correspondent and man of letters George Alfred Townsend fell in love with these mountains and built an impressive arch decorated with classical Greek mythological features and quotes that emphasize the needed qualities of a good war correspondent.

Eating & Sleeping

Baltimore 1

Papermoon Diner Diner $

(www.papermoondiner24.com; 227 W 29th St, Harwood; mains $10-18; 7am-9pm Sun, Mon, Wed & Thu, to 10pm Fri & Sat) This brightly colored, quintessential Baltimore diner is decorated with thousands of old toys, creepy mannequins and other quirky knickknacks. The real draw here is the anytime breakfast – fluffy buttermilk pancakes, crispy bacon, and crab-and-artichoke heart omelets. Wash it down with a caramel and sea salt milkshake.

Chaps Barbecue $

(410-483-2379; www.chapspitbeef.com; 5801 Pulaski Hwy; mains $7-19; 10:30am-10pm) This is the go-to stop for pit beef, Baltimore's take on barbecue – thinly sliced top round grilled over charcoal. Park and follow your nose to smoky mouthwatering goodness, and get that beef like a local: shaved onto a kaiser roll with a raw onion slice on top, smothered in Tiger Sauce (a creamy blend of horseradish and mayonnaise).

Dukem Ethiopian $$

(410-385-0318; www.dukemrestaurant.com; 1100 Maryland Ave, Mt Vernon; mains $12-34; 11am-10pm) Dukem is a standout among Baltimore's many Ethiopian places. Delicious mains, including spicy chicken, lamb and vegetarian dishes, all sopped up with spongy flatbread.

Inn at 2920 B&B $$

(410-342-4450; www.theinnat2920.com; 2920 Elliott St, Canton; r $195-235;) Housed in a former bordello, this boutique B&B offers five individual rooms; high-thread-count sheets; sleek, avant-garde decor; and the nightlife-charged neighborhood of Canton right outside your door. The Jacuzzi bathtubs and green sensibility of the owners add a nice touch.

Sykesville 3

E.W. Beck's Pub Food $

(410-795-1001; www.ewbecks.com; 7565 Main St; mains $10-22; 11:30am-10pm, bar to 1am) In the middle of Sykesville's historic district, Beck's feels like a traditional pub, with wooden furnishings, soused regulars and serviceable pub grub mains.

Frederick 7

Brewer's Alley Pub Food $$

(301-631-0089; www.brewers-alley.com; 124 N Market St; mains $9-22; noon-11:30pm;) This bouncy brewpub is one of our favorite places in Frederick for several reasons. First, the beer: house-brewed, plenty of variety, delicious. Second, the burgers: enormous, half-pound monstrosities of staggeringly yummy proportions. Third, the rest of the menu: excellent Chesapeake seafood (including a wood-fired pizza topped with crab) and Frederick County farm produce and meats. The small patio is pleasant on sunny days.

Cacique Latin American $$

(301-695-2756; www.caciquefrederick.com; 26 N Market St; mains $12-29; 11:30am-10pm Sun-Thu, to 1:30pm Fri & Sat) This interesting spot mixes up a menu of Spanish favorites like paella and tapas with Latin American gut busters like enchiladas ceviche. That said, the focus and the expertise seem bent more toward the Iberian side of the menu; the shrimp sautéed in garlic and olive oil is wonderful.

Hollerstown Hill B&B B&B $$

(301-228-3630; www.hollerstownhill.com; 4 Clarke Pl; r $149; P) The elegant, friendly Hollerstown has four pattern-heavy rooms, two resident terriers and an elegant billiards room. This lovely Victorian sits right in the middle of the historic downtown area of Frederick, so you're within easy walking distance of all the goodness. No kids under 16.

Classic Trip

The Civil War Tour

Virginia and Maryland pack many of the seminal sites of America's bloodiest war into a space that includes some of the Eastern seaboard's most attractive countryside.

TRIP HIGHLIGHTS

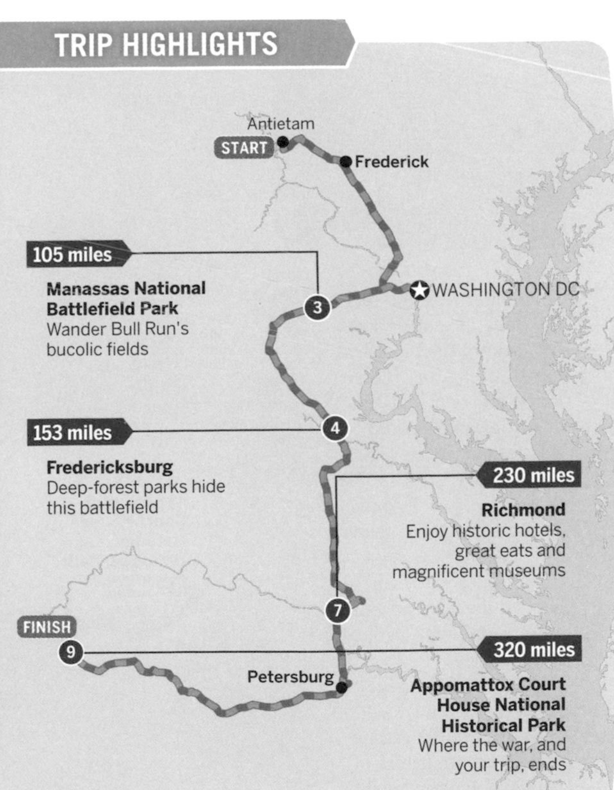

3 DAYS
320 MILES / 515KM

GREAT FOR...

BEST TIME TO GO

September to November; the brisk air still comes with sunny skies and autumnal color shows at preserved battlefields.

ESSENTIAL PHOTO

The fences and fields of Antietam at sunset.

BEST FOR FOODIES

Lamb burgers at Richmond's Burger Bach.

Antietam National Battlefield National Cemetery

Classic Trip

7 The Civil War Tour

The Civil War was fought from 1861–65 in the nation's backyards, and many of those backyards are between Washington, DC and Richmond. On this trip you will cross battlefields where more than 100,000 Americans perished and are buried, foe next to foe. Amid rolling farmlands, sunny hills and deep forests, you'll discover a jarring juxtaposition of bloody legacy and bucolic scenery, and along the way, the places where America forged its identity.

❶ Antietam

While the majority of this trip takes place in Virginia, there is Civil War ground to be covered in neighboring Maryland, a border state officially allied with the Union yet close enough to the South to possess Southern sympathies. Confederate General Robert E Lee, hoping to capitalize on a friendly populace, tried to invade Maryland early in the conflict.

The subsequent Battle of Antietam, fought in Sharpsburg, MD, on September 17, 1862, has the dubious distinction of marking the bloodiest day in US history. The battle site is preserved at **Antietam National Battlefield** (☎301-432-5124; www.nps.gov/anti; 5831 Dunker Church Rd, Sharpsburg; 3-day pass per person/vehicle $5/10; ⏲grounds sunrise-sunset, visitor center 9am-5pm) in the corn-and-hill country of north-central Maryland.

As befits an engagement that claimed 22,000 casualties in the course of a single, nightmarish day, even the local geographic nomenclature became violent. An area known as the Sunken Rd turned into 'Bloody Lane' after bodies were stacked there. In the park's cemetery, many of the Union gravestones bear the names of Irish and German immigrants who died in a country they had only recently adopted.

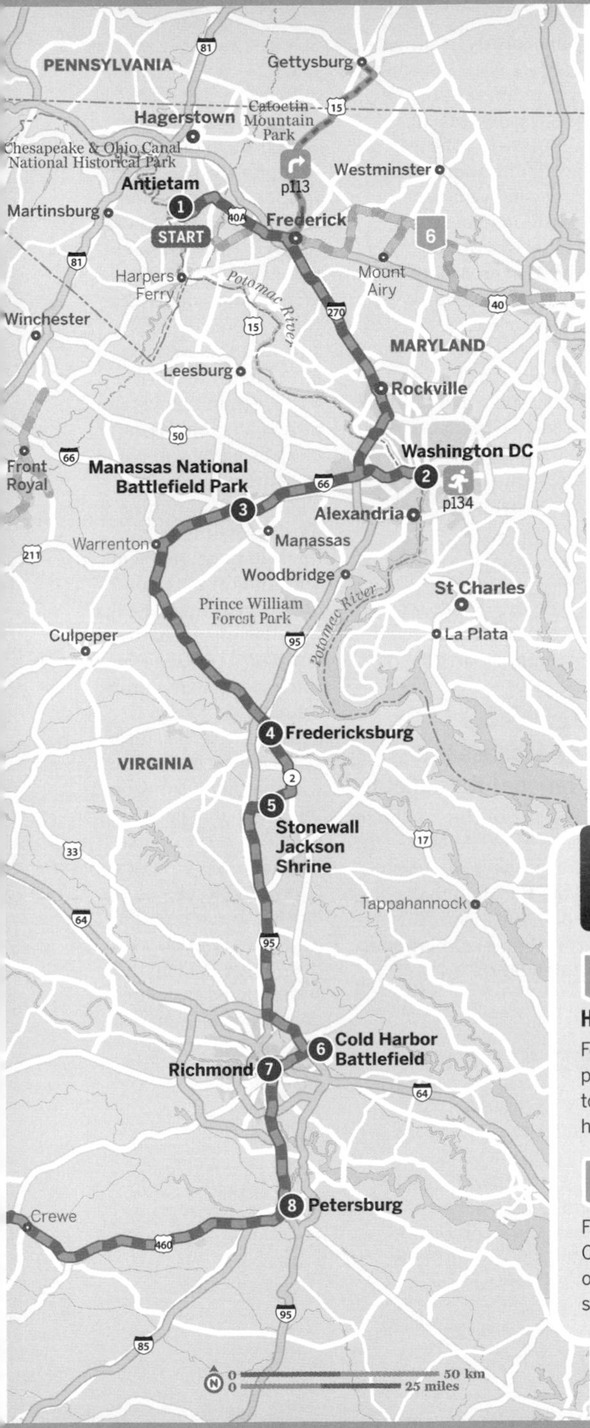

The Drive » Take MD-65 south out of Antietam to the town of Sharpsburg. From here, take MD-34 east for 6 miles, then turn right onto US 40A (eastbound). Take US 40A for 11 miles, then merge onto US 70 south, followed 3 miles later by US 270 (bypassing Frederick). Take 270 south to the Beltway (I-495); access exit 45B to get to I-66 east, which will eventually lead you to the National Mall, where the next stops are located.

LINK YOUR TRIP

6 Maryland's National Historic Road

For another look into the past, go east from Antietam to the picturesque and historic Frederick.

8 Skyline Drive

Travel west from Fredericksburg through Culpeper to this trip along one of the nation's most scenic roadways.

2 Washington, DC

Washington, DC, was the capital of the Union during the Civil War, just as it is the capital of the country today. While the city was never invaded by the Confederacy, thousands of Union soldiers passed through, trained and drilled inside of the city; indeed, the official name of the North's main fighting force was the Army of the Potomac.

The **National Museum of American History** (202-663-1000; www.americanhistory.si.edu; cnr 14th St & Constitution Ave NW; 10am-5:30pm, to 7:30pm some days; ; Circulator, M Orange, Silver, Blue cLines to Smithsonian or Federal Triangle), located directly on the National Mall, has good permanent exhibitions on the Civil War. Perhaps more importantly, it provides visitors with the context for understanding why the war happened.

Following the war, a grateful nation erected many monuments to Union generals. A statue worth visiting is the **African American Civil War Memorial** (www.afroamcivilwar.org; cnr U St & Vermont Ave NW; M Green, Yellow Lines to U St), next to the eastern exit of the U St metro, inscribed with the names of soldiers of color who served in the Union army.

The Drive » From Washington, DC, it takes about an hour along I-66W through the tangled knots of suburban sprawl that blanket Northern Virginia to reach Manassas.

TRIP HIGHLIGHT

3 Manassas National Battlefield

The site of the first major pitched battle of the Civil War is mere minutes from the strip malls of northern Virginia. NPS-run **Manassas National Battlefield Park** (703-361-1339; www.nps.gov/mana; 12521 Lee Hwy; park dawn-dusk, visitor center 8:30am-5pm, tours 11:15am, 12:15pm & 2:15pm Jun-Aug) occupies the site where, in 1861, 35,000 Union soldiers and 32,500 Confederates saw the view you have today: a stretch of gorgeous countryside that has miraculously survived the predations of the Army of Northern Virginia real-estate developers. This is as close as many will come to 19th-century rural America; distant hills, dark, brooding treelines, low curving fields and the soft hump of overgrown trench works.

Following the battle, both sides realized a long war was at hand. Europe watched nervously; in a matter of weeks, the largest army in the world was the Union Army of the Potomac. The second biggest was the Confederate States of America Army. A year later, at the Battle of Shiloh, 24,000 men were listed as casualties – more than all the accumulated casualties of every previous American war combined.

p118

The Drive » In Manassas, take US 29N for 13 miles and then turn left onto US 17S (Marsh Rd). Follow 17/Marsh Rd south for about 35 miles to get to downtown Fredericksburg.

WHAT'S IN A NAME, PART 1?

Although the Civil War is the widely accepted label for the conflict covered in this trip, you'll still hear die-hard Southern boosters refer to the period as the 'War Between the States.' What's the difference? Well, a Civil War implies an armed insurrection against a ruling power that never lost its privilege to govern, whereas the name 'War Between the States' suggests said states always had (and still have) a right to secession from the Republic.

DETOUR: GETTYSBURG NATIONAL MILITARY PARK

Start: Frederick

The Battle of Gettysburg, fought in Gettysburg, PA, in July of 1863, marked the turning point of the war and the high water mark of the Confederacy's attempted rebellion. Lee never made a gambit as bold as this invasion of the North, and his army (arguably) never recovered from the defeat it suffered here.

Gettysburg National Military Park (717-334-1124; www.nps.gov/gett; 1195 Baltimore Pike; museum adult/child $15/10, bus tour $35/21, licensed guide per vehicle $75; museum 8am-6pm Apr-Oct, 9am-5pm Nov-Mar, grounds 6am-10pm Apr-Oct, to 7pm Nov-Mar), one hour and 40 minutes north of DC, does an excellent job of explaining the course and context of the combat. Look for Little Round Top hill, where a Union unit checked a Southern flanking maneuver, and the field of Pickett's Charge, where the Confederacy suffered its most crushing defeat up to that point. Following the battle, Abraham Lincoln gave his Gettysburg Address here to mark the victory and the 'new birth of the nation' on the country's birthday: July 4.

You can easily lose a day here just soaking up the scenery – a gorgeous swath of rolling hills and lush forest. To get here, jump on US 15 northbound in Frederick, MD. Follow US 15 north for about 35 miles to Gettysburg.

TRIP HIGHLIGHT

4 Fredericksburg

If battlefields preserve rural, agricultural America, Fredericksburg is an example of what the nation's main streets once looked like: orderly grids, touches of green and friendly storefronts. But for all its cuteness, this is the site of one of the worst blunders in American military history. In 1862, when the Northern Army attempted a massed charge against an entrenched Confederate position, a Southern artilleryman looked at the bare slope Union forces had to cross and told a commanding officer, 'A chicken could not live on that field when we open on it.' Sixteen charges resulted in an estimated 6000 to 8000 Union casualties.

Fredericksburg & Spotsylvania National Military Park (540-693-3200; www.nps.gov/frsp; 1013 Lafayette Blvd; Fredericksburg & Chancellorsville visitor centers 9am-5pm, hours vary at other exhibit areas) is not as immediately compelling as Manassas because of the thick forest that still covers the battlefields, but the woods themselves are a sylvan wonder. Again, the pretty nature of... well, nature, grows over graves; the nearby Battle of the Wilderness was named for these thick woods, which caught fire and killed hundreds of wounded soldiers after the shooting was finished.

p118

The Drive » From Fredericksburg, take US 17 south for 5 miles, after which 7 becomes VA-2 (also known as Sandy Lane Dr and Fredericksburg Turnpike). Follow this road for 5 more miles, then turn right onto Stonewall Jackson Rd (State Rd 606).

5 Stonewall Jackson Shrine

In Chancellorsville, Robert E Lee, outnumbered two to one, split his forces and attacked both flanks of the Union army. The audacity of the move caused the Northern force to crumble and flee

Classic Trip

VISIONSOFMAINE / GETTY IMAGES ©

VISIONSOFMAINE / GETTY IMAGES ©

WHY THIS IS A CLASSIC TRIP

AMY C BALFOUR, WRITER

Some of the prettiest countryside on the Eastern seaboard remains hallowed ground, where whispers of brutal battles and unfinished stories drift between the remote farmhouses, dark forests, grassy earthworks and rolling fields, where thousands lost their lives. This tour explores the formative spaces of the nation, much of it unchanged since those deadly clashes of the 1860s.

Above: Appomattox Court House National Historical Park
Left: Manassas National Battlefield Park
Right: Gettysburg National Military Park

DELMAS LEHMAN / SHUTTERSTOCK ©

across the Potomac, but the victory was a costly one; in the course of the fighting, Lee's ablest general, Stonewall Jackson, had his arm shot off by a nervous Confederate sentry. The arm is buried at nearby Ellwood Manor. Ask a ranger for directions. The wound was patched, but Jackson went on to contract a fatal dose of pneumonia. He was taken to what is now the next stop on this tour: the **Stonewall Jackson Shrine** (☎804-633-6076; www.nps.gov/frsp; 12019 Stonewall Jackson Rd, Woodford; ⏲grounds sunrise-sunset; building 9am-5pm) in nearby Guinea Station. In a small white cabin set against attractive Virginia horse-country, overrun with sprays of purple flowers and daisy fields, Jackson uttered a series of prolonged ramblings. Then he fell silent, whispered, 'Let us cross over the river and rest in the shade of the trees,' and died.

The Drive ›› You can get here via I-95, which you take to I-295S (then take exit 34A), which takes 50 minutes. Or, for a back road experience (one hour, 10 minutes), take VA-2S south for 35 miles until it connects to VA-643/Rural Point Rd. Stay on VA-643 until it becomes VA-156/Cold Harbor Rd, which leads to the battlefield.

6 Cold Harbor Battlefield

By 1864, Union General Ulysses Grant was ready

to take the battle into Virginia. His subsequent invasion, dubbed the Overland (or Wilderness) Campaign, was one of the bloodiest of the war. It reached a violent climax at Cold Harbor, just north of Richmond.

At the site now known as **Cold Harbor Battlefield** (804-226-1981; www.nps.gov/rich; 5515 Anderson-Wright Dr, Mechanicsville; sunrise-sunset, visitor center 9am-4:30pm), Grant threw his men into a full frontal assault; the resultant casualties were horrendous, and a precursor to WWI trench warfare. The area has now reverted to a forest and field checkerboard overseen by the NPS. Ask a local ranger to direct you to the Third Turnout, a series of Union earthworks from where you can look out at the most preserved section of the fight: the long, low field Northern soldiers charged across.

The Drive » From Cold Harbor, head north on VA-156/Cold Harbor Rd for about 3 miles until it intersects Creighton Rd. Turn left and follow it for 6 miles into downtown Richmond.

TRIP HIGHLIGHT

7 Richmond

There are two Civil War museums in the former capital of the Confederacy, and they make for

LOCAL KNOWLEDGE: CIVIL WAR BATTLEFIELDS

What is the appeal of Civil War battlefields?

Civil War battlefields are the touchstone of the not-too-distant past. They are the physical manifestation of the great eruptive moments in American history that defined America for the last 150 years. Large events on a large landscape compel us to think in big terms about big issues.

The Civil War battlefields appeal to visitors because they allow us to walk in the virtual footsteps of great men and women who lived and died fighting for their convictions. Their actions transformed nondescript places into hallmarks of history. The Civil War converted sleepy towns and villages into national shrines based on a moment of intense belief and action. The battlefields literally focus our understanding of the American character. I linger longest on the battlefields that are best preserved, like Antietam and Gettysburg, because they paint the best context for revealing why things happened the way they did, where they did. Walking where they walked, and seeing the ground they saw, makes these battlefields the ultimate outdoor classrooms in the world!

Why is Virginia such a hotbed for Civil War tourism?

Virginia paid a terrible price during the Civil War. Hosting the capital of the Confederacy only 100 miles from the capital of the United States made sure that the ground between and around the two opposing capitals would be a relentless nightmare of fighting and bloodshed. People can visit individual, isolated battlefields all across America – but people come to Virginia to visit several, many, if not all of them. Unlike anywhere else, Virginia offers a Civil War immersion. It gives visitors a sense of how pervasive the Civil War was – it touched every place and everyone. Around the country, people may seek out the Civil War; but in Virginia, it finds you.

– Frank O'Reilly, Historian and Interpretive Ranger with the National Park Service

an interesting study in contrasts. Both are now managed by the American Civil War Center. The first is the **Museum of the Confederacy** (MOC; ☎804-649-1861; www.acwm.org; 1201 E Clay St; museum adult/child 6-17yr $10/5, incl White House of Confederacy $18/9; ⏰10am-5pm Mon-Sat), which was once a shrine to the Southern 'Lost Cause'. But the MOC has also graduated into a respected educational institution, and its collection of Confederate artifacts is probably the best in the country. The optional tour of the Confederate White House is recommended for its quirky insights.

The second museum, inside the old **Tredegar** (☎804-649-1861; www.acwm.org; 500 Tredegar St; adult/child 6-17yr $10/5; ⏰9am-5pm) ironworks, makes an admirable, ultimately successful, effort to present the war from three perspectives: Northern, Southern and African American. The permanent exhibits are well-presented, the rotating exhibits insightful. The effect is clearly powerful and occasionally divisive.

p118

The Drive » Take Rte 95 southbound for about 23 miles and get on exit 52. Turn onto 301 (Wythe St) and follow it until it becomes Washington St, and eventually VA-35/Oaklawn Dr. Look for signs to the battlefield park from here.

WHAT'S IN A NAME, PART 2?

One of the more annoying naming conventions of the war goes thus: while the North preferred to name battles for defining geographic terms (Bull Run, Antietam), Southern officers named them for nearby towns (Manassas, Sharpsburg). Although most Americans refer to battles by their Northern names, in some areas folks know Manassas as the Battle of, not as the strip mall with a good Waffle House.

8 Petersburg

Petersburg, just south of Richmond, is the blue-collar sibling city to the Virginia capital, its center gutted by white flight following desegregation. **Petersburg National Battlefield Park** (☎804-732-3531; www.nps.gov/pete; 5001 Siege Rd, Eastern Front Visitor Center; ⏰visitor center 9am-5pm, grounds from 8am) marks the spot where Northern and Southern soldiers spent almost a quarter of the war in a protracted, trench-induced standoff. The Battle of the Crater, made well-known in Charles Frazier's *Cold Mountain*, was an attempt by Union soldiers to break this stalemate by tunneling under the Confederate lines and blowing up their fortifications.

The Drive » Drive south of Petersburg, then west through a skein of back roads to follow Lee's last retreat. There's an excellent map available at www.civilwartraveler.com; we prefer taking VA-460 west from Petersburg, then connecting to VA-635, which leads to Appomattox via VA-24.

TRIP HIGHLIGHT

9 Appomattox Court House National Historical Park

About 92 miles west of Petersburg is **Appomattox Court House National Historical Park** (☎434-352-8987; www.nps.gov/apco; 111 National Park Dr; ⏰9am-5pm), where the Confederacy finally surrendered. There are several marker stones dedicated to the surrendering Confederates, and the most touching one marks the spot where Robert E Lee rode back from Appomattox after surrendering to Union General Ulysses Grant. Lee's soldiers stood on either side of the field waiting for the return of their commander. When Lee rode into sight, he doffed his hat; the troops surged toward him, some saying goodbye while others, too overcome with emotion to speak, passed their hands over the white flanks of Lee's horse, Traveller.

p119

Eating & Sleeping

Manassas 3

Tandoori Village — Indian $$

(703-369-6526; www.tandoorivillage.net; 7607 Centreville Rd; mains $8-22; 11am-2:30pm & 5-10pm Mon-Fri, 11am-10pm Sat & Sun) Tandoori Village serves up solid Punjabi cuisine, offering a welcome dash of spice and flavor complexity to an area that's pretty rife with fast-food chains. No menu shockers here, but all the standards, like butter chicken, dal and paneer, are executed with competence.

Fredericksburg 4

Sammy T's — American $

(540-371-2008; www.sammyts.com; 801 Caroline St; 11:30am-9pm Mon, Wed & Thu, 1:30am-10pm Fri & Sat, 9:30am-7pm Sun;) Located in a circa 1805 building in the heart of historic Fredericksburg, Sammy T's serves soups and sandwiches and pub-y fare, with an admirable mix of vegetarian options including a local take on lasagna and black-bean quesadillas.

Foode — American $$

(540-479-1370; www.facebook.com/foodeonline; 900 Princess Anne St; lunch mains $10-12, dinner mains $15-26; 11am-9pm Tue-Thu, 11am-10pm Fri, 9am-10pm Sat, 9am-3pm Sun;) Foode serves up tasty farm-to-table fare in a rustic but artsy setting. Lots of intriguing small plates for sharing at dinner. Attentive service, too.

Bistro Bethem — American $$$

(540-371-9999; www.bistrobethem.com; 309 William St; lunch mains $9-22, dinner mains $17-32; 11:30am-2:30pm & 5-10pm Tue-Sat, to 9pm Sun) The New American menu, seasonal ingredients and down-to-earth but dedicated foodie vibe here all equal gastronomic bliss. On any given day duck confit and quinoa may share the table with a roasted beet salad and local clams.

Richard Johnston Inn — B&B $$

(540-899-7606; www.therichardjohnstoninn.com; 711 Caroline St; r $165-300; P) In an 18th-century brick mansion, this cozy B&B scores points for its downtown location, comfort and friendliness. The cookies offered in the afternoon are delicious.

Richmond 7

Burger Bach — Pub Food $

(804-359-1305; www.theburgerbach.com; 10 S Thompson St; mains $9-13; 11am-10pm Sun-Thu, to 11pm Fri & Sat;) We give Burger Bach credit for being the only restaurant found in the area that self-classifies as a New Zealand–inspired burger joint. And that said, why yes, they do serve excellent lamb burgers here, although the locally sourced beef (and vegetarian) options are awesome as well. You should really go crazy with the 14 different sauces available for the thick-cut fries.

Sidewalk Cafe — American, Greek $

(804-358-0645; www.sidewalkinthefan.com; 2101 W Main St; mains $9-18; 11am-2am Mon-Fri, from 9:30am Sat & Sun) A much-loved local haunt, Sidewalk Cafe feels like a dive bar (year-round Christmas lights, wood-paneled walls, kitschy artwork), but the food is first-rate. There's outdoor seating on the sidewalk, daily specials (eg Taco Tuesdays) and legendary weekend brunches.

Croaker's Spot — Seafood $$

(804-269-0464; www.croakersspot.com; 1020 Hull St; mains $10-26; 11am-9pm Mon-Wed, to 10pm Thu, to 11pm Fri, noon-11pm Sat, noon-9pm Sun; P) Croaker's is an institution in these parts, a backbone of the African American dining scene. Richmond's most famous rendition of refined soul food is comforting, delicious and sits in your stomach like a brick. Beware the intimidating Fish Boat: fried catfish, cornbread and mac 'n' cheese.

Millie's Diner Modern American **$$**
(804-643-5512; www.milliesdiner.com; 2603 E Main St; lunch mains $9-14, dinner mains $16-29; 11am-2:30pm & 5:30-10:30pm Tue-Fri, 9am-3pm & 5:30-10:30pm Sat & Sun) Lunch, dinner or weekend brunch – Richmond icon Millie's does it all, and does it well. It's a small, but handsomely designed space with creative seasonal fare. The Devil's Mess – an open-faced omelet with spicy sausage, curry, veg, cheese and avocado – is legendary.

L'Opossum American, French **$$$**
(804-918-6028; www.lopossum.com; 626 China St; mains $18-32; 5pm-midnight Tue-Sat) We're not exactly sure what's going on here, but it works. The name of the place is terrible. Statues of Michelangelo's *David* pose here and there. And dishes come with names that are almost too hip, like the Darth Grouper Held at Bay by a Rebellious Coalition. What ties it together? The culinary prowess of award-winning chef David Shannon and his attentive and talented staff. Make a reservation or get to there early to snag a seat at the bar.

Linden Row Inn Boutique Hotel **$$**
(804-783-7000; www.lindenrowinn.com; 100 E Franklin St; r from $139, ste $289; P) This antebellum gem has 70 attractive rooms (with period Victorian furnishings) spread among neighboring Greek Revival town houses in an excellent downtown location. Friendly southern hospitality, reasonable prices and thoughtful extras (free passes to the YMCA, free around-town shuttle service, included breakfast) sweeten the deal.

Jefferson Hotel Luxury Hotel **$$$**
(804-649-4750; www.jeffersonhotel.com; 101 W Franklin St; r from $355; P) The Jefferson is Richmond's grandest hotel and one of the finest in America. The vision of tobacco tycoon and Confederate major Lewis Ginter, the beaux-arts–style hotel was completed in 1895. Rooms are plush but inviting – you will sleep well. According to rumor (probably untrue), the magnificent grand staircase in the lobby served as the model for the famed stairs in *Gone with the Wind*. Even if you don't stay here, it's worth having a peek inside. Pick up a hotel walking tour brochure at the concierge desk. A statue of the hotel's namesake, Thomas Jefferson, anchors the lobby. Afternoon tea is served beneath Tiffany stained glass in the Palm Court lobby (from 3pm Friday to Sunday), or have a drink at the grand Lemaire Bar. Self-parking is $12 per night. Valet is $20 per night. The pet fee is $50 per pet per night.

Quirk Hotel Boutique Hotel **$$$**
(804-340-6040; www.destinationhotels.com/quirk-hotel; 201 W Broad St; r from $259; P) From the moment you stroll into the big-windowed lobby, which pops with bright colors and sleek lines, this perky number impresses. The brainchild of the folks behind Quirk art gallery next door, this stylish boutique property fills its rooms and common areas with unique pieces of eye-catching art. Don't miss the city view from the popular rooftop bar.

Appomattox Court House National Historical Park 9

Longacre B&B **$$**
(434-352-9251; www.longacreva.com; 1670 Church St; r from $115; P) Longacre looks like it got lost somewhere in the English countryside and decided to set up shop in Virginia. Its elegant rooms are set with antiques, and lush grounds surround the sprawling Tudor house.

Skyline Drive

Skyline Dr is one of the USA's classic road trips. Befittingly, it comes studded like a leather belt with natural wonders and stunning scenery.

TRIP HIGHLIGHTS

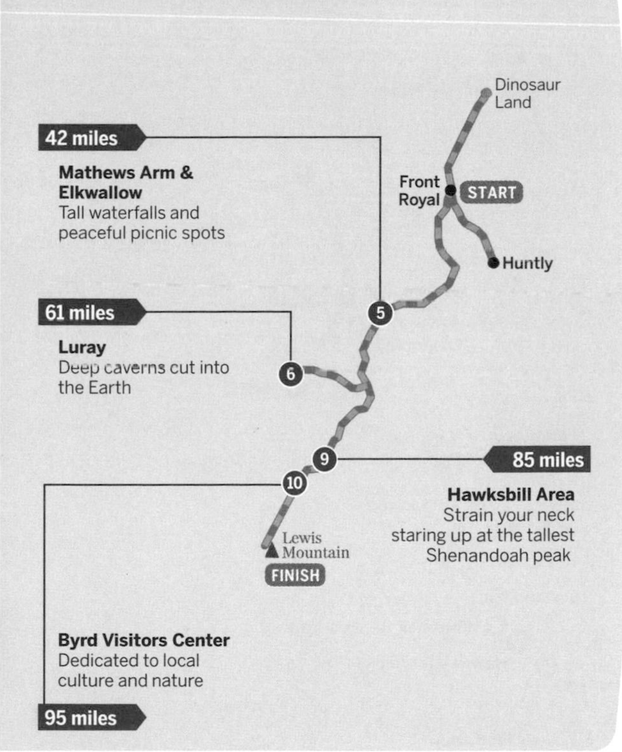

Dinosaur Land

Front Royal START

Huntly

42 miles

Mathews Arm & Elkwallow
Tall waterfalls and peaceful picnic spots

61 miles

Luray
Deep caverns cut into the Earth

85 miles

Hawksbill Area
Strain your neck staring up at the tallest Shenandoah peak

Lewis Mountain FINISH

Byrd Visitors Center
Dedicated to local culture and nature

95 miles

5 6 9 10

3 DAYS
150 MILES / 240 KM

GREAT FOR...

BEST TIME TO GO

From May to Nov for great weather, open facilities and views.

ESSENTIAL PHOTO

The fabulous 360-degree horizon at the top of Bearfence Rock Scramble.

BEST FOR CULTURE

Byrd Visitor Center offers an illuminating peek into Appalachian folkways.

8 Skyline Drive

The centerpiece of the ribbon-thin Shenandoah National Park is the jaw-dropping beauty of Skyline Dr, which runs for just over 100 miles atop the Blue Ridge Mountains. Unlike the massive acreage of western parks like Yellowstone or Yosemite, Shenandoah is at times only a mile wide. That may seem to narrow the park's scope, yet it makes it a perfect space for traversing and road-tripping goodness.

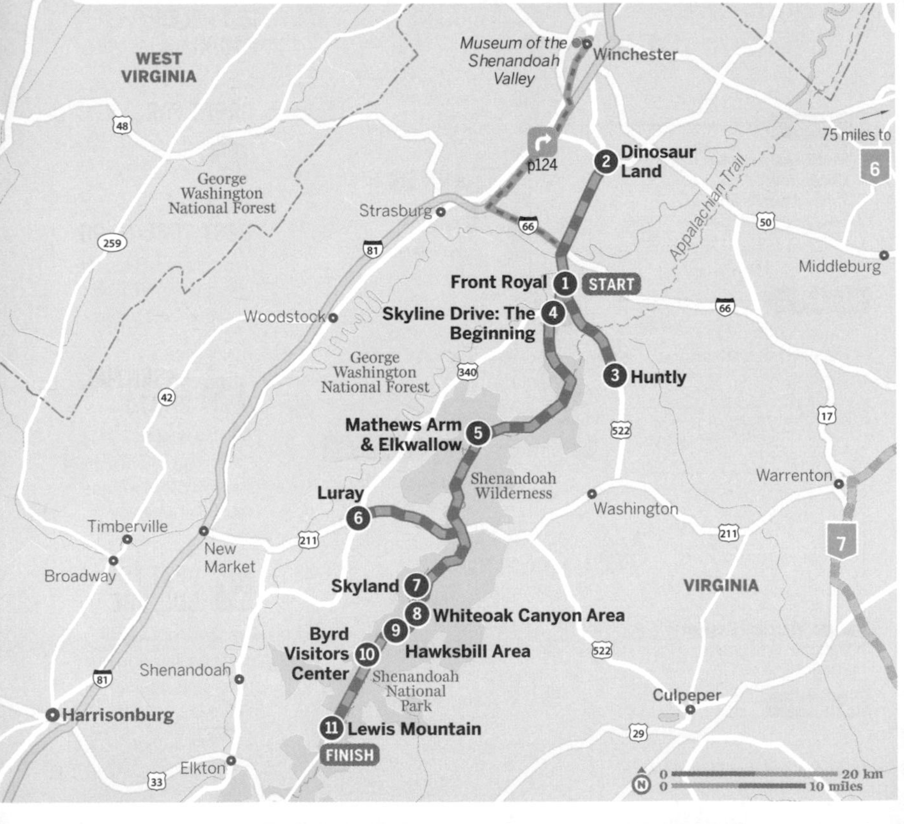

❶ Front Royal

Straddling the northern entrance to the park is the tiny city of Front Royal. Although it's not among Virginia's fanciest ports of call, this lush riverside town offers all the urban amenities one might need before a camping or hiking trip up in the mountains.

If you need to gather your bearings, an obvious place to start is the **Front Royal Visitor Center** (800-338-2576; https://frontroyalva.com/101/Visiting; 414 E Main St; 9am-5pm). Friendly staff are on hand to overwhelm you with information about what to do in the area.

p130

The Drive » Dinosaur Land is 10 miles north of Front Royal, toward Winchester, via US 340 (Stonewall Jackson Hwy).

❷ Dinosaur Land

Before you head into the national park and its stunning natural beauty, visit **Dinosaur Land** (540-869-2222; www.dinosaurland.com; 3848 Stonewall Jackson Hwy, White Post; adult/child $6/5; 9:30am-5:30pm Mar-May, to 6pm Jun-Aug, to 5pm Sep-Dec;) for some fantastic human-made tackiness. This spectacularly low-brow shrine to concrete sculpture is not to be missed. Although it's an 'educational prehistoric forest,' with more than 50 life-size dinosaurs (and a King Kong for good measure), you'd probably learn more about the tenants by fast-forwarding through *Jurassic Park 3*. But that's not why you've stopped here, so grab your camera and sidle up to the triceratops for memories that will last a millennium.

The Drive » Head back to Front Royal, then go south on US 522 (Remount Rd) for about 9 miles to reach Huntly.

❸ Huntly

Huntly is a small-ish town nestled in the green foothills of the Shenandoahs, lying just in the southern shadows of Front Royal. It's a good spot to refuel on some cosmopolitan culture and foodie deliciousness in the form of **Rappahannock Cellars** (540-635-9398; www.rappahannockcellars.com; 14437 Hume Rd; tasting $10; 11:30am-5pm Sun-Fri, to 6pm Sat), one of the nicer wineries of north-central Virginia, where vineyard-covered hills shadow the horizon, like some slice of northern Italian pastoral prettiness that got lost somewhere in the upcountry of the Old Dominion. Give the port a whirl (well, maybe not if you're driving).

The Drive » Head back to Front Royal, as you'll enter Skyline Dr from there. From the beginning of Skyline Dr, it's 5.5 miles to Dickey Ridge.

❹ Skyline Drive: The Beginning

Skyline Dr is the scenic drive to end all scenic drives. The 75 overlooks, with views into the Shenandoah Valley and the Piedmont, are all breathtaking. In spring and summer, endless variations on the color green are sure to enchant, just as the vibrant reds and yellows will amaze you in autumn. This might be your chance to finally hike a section of the Appalachian Trail, which crosses Skyline Dr at 32 places.

LINK YOUR TRIP

6
Maryland's National Historic Road

US-340 takes you north from Front Royal to historic Frederick, the gateway to a region of quintessential stately small towns.

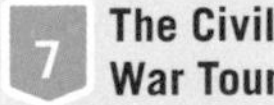

7
The Civil War Tour

From the Luray Caverns head southeast past the town of Culpeper to Fredericksburg to begin traversing the battlefields where the nation's identity was forged.

The logical first stop on an exploration of Skyline and Shenandoah National Park is the **Dickey Ridge Visitors Center** (☎540-635-3566; www.nps.gov/shen; Mile 4.6, Skyline Dr; ⏰9am-5pm mid-Apr–Nov). It's not just an informative leaping-off point; it's a building with a fascinating history all of its own. This spot originally operated as a 'wild' dining hall in 1908 (back then, that simply meant it had a terrace for dancing). However, it closed during WWII and didn't reopen until 1958, when it became a visitor center. Now it's one of the park's two main information centers and contains a little bit of everything you'll need to get started on your trip along Skyline Dr.

The Drive » It's a twisty 19 more miles along Skyline Dr to Mathews Arm.

TRIP HIGHLIGHT

❺ Mathews Arm & Elkwallow

Mathews Arm is the first major section of Shenandoah National Park you encounter after leaving Dickey Ridge. Before you get there, you can stop at a pullover at Mile 19.4 and embark on a 4.8 mile loop hike to **Little Devils Stairs**. Getting through this narrow gorge is as tough as the name suggests; expect hand-over-hand climbing for some portions.

At Mathews Arm there's a campground as well as an amphitheater, and some nice breezes; early on in your drive, you're already at a 2750ft altitude.

From the amphitheater, it's a 6½-mile moderately taxing hike to lovely **Overall Run Falls**, the tallest in the national park (93ft). There are plenty of rock ledges where you can enjoy the view and snap a picture, but be warned that the falls sometime dry out in the summer.

Elkwallow Wayside, which includes a nice picnic area and lookout, is at Mile 24, just past Mathews Arm.

The Drive » From Mathews Arm, proceed south along Skyline for about 10 miles, then take the US 211 ramp westbound for about 7 miles to reach Luray.

TRIP HIGHLIGHT

❻ Luray

Luray is a good spot to grab some grub and potentially rest your head if you're not into camping. It's also where you'll find the wonderful **Luray Caverns** (☎540-743-6551; www.luraycaverns.com; 970 US Hwy 211 W; adult/child 6-12yr $27/14; ⏰9am-7pm daily mid-Jun–Aug, to 6pm Sep-Nov

DETOUR: MUSEUM OF THE SHENANDOAH VALLEY

Start: ❶ Front Royal

Of all the places where you can begin your journey into Shenandoah National Park, none seem to make quite as much sense as the **Museum of the Shenandoah Valley** (☎540-662-1473, 888-556-5799; www.themsv.org; 901 Amherst St, Winchester; adult/student 13-18yr/child $10/8/free, Wed free; ⏰10am-5pm Tue-Sun Apr-Dec, 11am-4pm Jan-Mar), an institution dedicated to its namesake. Located in the town of Winchester, some 25 miles north of Front Royal, the museum is an exhaustive repository of information on the valley, Appalachian culture and its associated folkways, some of the most unique in the USA. Exhibits are divided into four galleries, accompanied by the restored Glen Burnie historical home and 6 acres of gardens.

To get here, take I-66 west from Front Royal to I-81 and head north for 25 miles. In Winchester, follow signs to the museum, which is located on the outskirts of town.

& Apr–mid-Jun, to 4pm Mon-Fri, to 5pm Sat & Sun Dec-Mar), one of the most extensive cavern systems on the East Coast.

Here you can take a one-hour, roughly 1-mile guided tour of the caves, opened to the public more than 100 years ago. The rock formations throughout are quite stunning, and Luray boasts what is surely a one-of-a-kind attraction – the Stalacpipe Organ – in the pit of its belly. This crazy contraption has been banging out melodies on the rock formations for decades. As the guide says, the caves are 400 million years old '*if* you believe in geological dating' (if the subtext is lost on you, understand this is a conservative part of the country where creationism is widely accepted, if hotly debated). No matter what you believe in, you'll be impressed by the fantastic underground expanses.

p131

The Drive » Take US 211 east for 10 miles to get back on Skyline Dr. Then proceed 10 miles south along Skyline to get to Skyland. Along the way you'll drive over the highest point of Skyline Dr (3680ft). At Mile 40.5, just before reaching Skyland, you can enjoy amazing views from the parking overlook at Thorofare Mountain (3595ft).

GARDEN MAZE ALERT

Next to the Luray Caverns is an excellent opportunity to let your inner Shelley Duvall or Scatman Crothers run wild. Go screaming *Shining*-style through the **Garden Maze**, but beware! This maze is harder than it looks and some could spend longer inside it than they anticipated. Paranormal and psychic abilities are permitted, but frowned upon, when solving the hedge maze. Redrum! Redrum!

7 Skyland

Horse-fanciers will want to book a trail ride through Shenandoah at **Skyland Stables** (877-847-1919; www.goshenandoah.com; Mile 42.5, Skyline Dr; guided group rides 1/2½hr $50/95; 9am-5pm May-Oct). Rides last up to 2½ hours and are a great way to see the wildlife and epic vistas. Pony rides are also available for the wee members of your party. This is a good spot to break up your trip if you're into hiking (and if you're on this trip, we're assuming you are).

There's great access to local trailheads around here, and the sunsets are fabulous. The accommodations are a little rustic, but in a charming way (the Trout Cabin was built in 1911, and it feels like it, but we mean this in the most complimentary way possible). The place positively oozes nostalgia, but if you're into amenities, you may find it a little dilapidated.

The Drive » It's only 1.5 miles south on Skyline Dr to get to the Whiteoak parking area.

8 Whiteoak Canyon Area

At Mile 42.6, Whiteoak Canyon is another area of Skyline Dr that offers unmatched hiking and exploration opportunities. There are several parking

TOP TIP

Handy stone mileposts (MP) are still the best means of figuring out just where you are on Skyline Dr. They begin at Mile 0 near Front Royal, and end at Mile 105 at the national park's southern entrance near Rockfish Gap.

CAMROCKER / GETTY IMAGES ©

Above: Scenic bends on Skyline Drive
Below: View from Hawksbill Mountain
Right: Stalagmites and stalagtites in Luray Caverns

JON BILOUS / SHUTTERSTOCK ©

JACOBH / GETTY IMAGES ©

areas that all provide different entry points to the various trails that snake through this ridge- and stream-scape.

Most hikers are attracted to Whiteoak Canyon for its **waterfalls** – there are six in total, with the tallest topping out at 86ft high. At the Whiteoak parking area, you can make a 4.6-mile round-trip hike to these cascades, but beware – it's a steep climb up and back to your car. To reach the next set of waterfalls, you'll have to add 2.7 miles to the round-trip and prepare yourself for a steep (1100ft) elevation shift.

The **Limberlost Trail** and parking area is just south of Whiteoak Canyon. This is a moderately difficult 1.3-mile trek into spruce upcountry thick with hawks, owls and other birds; the boggy ground is home to many salamanders.

The Drive » It's about 3 miles south of Whiteoak Canyon to the Hawksbill area via Skyline Dr.

TRIP HIGHLIGHT

9 Hawksbill Area

Once you reach Mile 45.6, you've reached **Hawksbill**, the name of both this part of Skyline Dr and the tallest peak in Shenandoah National Park. Numerous trails in this area skirt the summits of the mountain.

Pull into the parking area at Hawksbill Gap (Mile 45.6). You've got a few hiking options to pick from. The **Lower Hawksbill Trail** is a steep 1.7-mile round-trip that circles Hawksbill Mountain's lower slopes; that huff-inducing ascent yields a pretty great view over the park. Another great lookout lies at the end of the **Upper Hawksbill Trail**, a moderately difficult 2.1-mile trip. You can link up with the Appalachian Trail here via a spur called the Salamander Trail.

If you continue south for about 5 miles, you'll reach **Fishers Gap Overlook**. The attraction here is the **Rose River Loop**, a 4-mile, moderately strenuous trail that is positively Edenic. Along the way you'll pass by waterfalls, under thick forest canopy and over swift-running streams.

The Drive » From Fishers Gap, head about a mile south to the Byrd Visitor Center, technically located at Mile 51.

TRIP HIGHLIGHT

⑩ Byrd Visitors Center

The **Harry F Byrd Visitors Center** (☎540-999-3283; www.nps.gov/shen; Mile 51, Skyline Dr; ⏰9am-5pm late Mar-Nov) is the central visitor center of Shenandoah National Park, marking (roughly) a halfway point between the two ends of Skyline Dr. It's devoted to explaining the settlement and development of the Shenandoah Valley via a series of small but well-curated exhibitions; as such, it's a good place to stop and learn about the surrounding culture (and pick up backcountry camping permits). There's camping and ranger activities in the **Big Meadows** area, located across the road from the visitors center.

The **Story of the Forest** trail is an easy, paved, 1.8-mile loop that's quite pretty; the trailhead connects to the visitors center. You can also explore two nearby waterfalls. **Dark Hollow Falls**, which sounds (and looks) like something out of a Tolkien novel, is a 70ft high cascade located at the end of a quite steep 1.4-mile trail. **Lewis Falls**, accessed via Big Meadows, is on a moderately difficult 3.3-mile trail that intersects the Appalachian Trail; at one point you'll be scrabbling up a rocky slope.

The Drive » The Lewis Mountain area is about 5 miles south of the Byrd Visitors Center via Skyline Dr. Stop for good overlooks at Milam Gap and Naked Creek (both clearly signposted from the road).

⑪ Lewis Mountain

Lewis Mountain is both the name of one of the major camping areas of Shenandoah National Park and a nearby 3570ft mountain. The trail to the mountain is only about a mile long with a small elevation gain, and leads to a nice overlook. But the best view here is at the **Bearfence Rock Scramble**. That name is no joke; this 1.2-mile hike gets steep and rocky, and you don't want to attempt it during or after rainfall. The reward is one of the best panoramas of the Shenandoahs. After you leave, remember there's still about 50 miles of Skyline Dr between you and the park exit at Rockfish Gap.

Dinosaur Land Abundant photo opportunities with life-size dinosaur statues

Eating & Sleeping

Front Royal ❶

Jalisco's Mexican $

(☎540-635-7348; 1303 N Royal Ave; mains $5-14; 11am-10pm Mon-Thu, to 10:30pm Fri & Sat, to 9:30pm Sun) Jalisco's has pretty good Mexican food. It's definitely the sort of Mexican that derives flavor from refried beans and melted cheese, but that's not such a terrible thing (well, unless we're talking about your heart). The chili relleños go down a treat, as do the margaritas.

Main Street Mill & Tavern Cafe $

(☎540-636-3123; 500 E Main St; mains $8-20; 10:30am-9pm Sun-Thu, to 10pm Fri & Sat;) This folksy restaurant is located in a spacious renovated 1880s feed mill. There are no big surprises when it comes to the cuisine, which is of the soup, sandwich and salad school of cookery, but it is filling, satisfying and does the job.

Element Fusion $$

(☎540-636-9293; www.jsgourmet.com; 317 E Main St; lunch mains $8-10, dinner mains $14-28; 11am-3pm & 5-9pm Tue-Sat;) Element is a foodie favorite for quality bistro fare. The small dinner menu features changing specials such as roasted quail with Mexican corn salad and sweet potatoes; at lunch, come for gourmet sandwiches, soups and salads.

Woodward House on Manor Grade B&B $$

(☎540-635-7010, 800-635-7011; www.acountryhome.com; 413 S Royal Ave/US 320; r $110-155, cottage $225; P) Offers seven cheerful rooms and a separate cottage (with wood-burning fireplaces). Sip your coffee from the deck and don't let the busy street below distract from the Blue Ridge Mountains vista.

Shenandoah National Park

The following three accommodations options are all operated by the same concessionaire. There are also four **campgrounds** (☎877-444-6777; www.recreation.gov; Mile 51.3, Skyline Dr; campsite $20; late Mar–mid-Nov) in the park if you're so inclined.

Big Meadows Lodge Lodge $$

(☎540-999-2221; www.goshenandoah.com; Mile 51.2, Skyline Dr; r $122-185; mid-May–Oct; P) The historic Big Meadows Lodge has 29 cozy wood-paneled rooms and five rustic cabins. The on-site Spotswood Dining Room serves three hearty meals a day; reserve well in advance.

Lewis Mountain Cabins Cabin $

(☎540-999-2255; www.goshenandoah.com; Mile 57.6, Skyline Dr; cabins $130-135; mid-Mar–Nov; P) Lewis Mountain has several pleasantly furnished cabins complete with private bathrooms for a hot shower after a day's hiking. The complex also has a campground with a store, a laundry and showers. This is the most rustic accommodations option in the area short of camping. Bear in mind that many cabins are attached, although we've never heard our neighbors here.

Skyland Resort Resort $$

(☎540-999-2212; www.goshenandoah.com; Mile 41.7, Skyline Dr; r $141-227, cabins $117-120; Apr-Nov; P) Founded in 1888, this beautifully set resort has fantastic views over the countryside. You'll find simple, wood-finished rooms and rustic but comfy cabins, and a full-service dining room. You can also arrange horseback rides from here. Opens a month or so before Big Meadows in the spring.

Pollock Dining Room American $$

(www.visitshenandoah.com; Mile 41.7, Skyline Dr; lunch mains $9-20, dinner mains $12-28; 7:30-10:30am, noon-2:30pm & 5-9:30pm Apr-Nov) The food is solid, if not life altering, in Skyland's dining room. But the view of the leafy park through the big windows? Now that's a different story. Lunch means sandwiches and burgers, while dinner aims at being a little fancier – stick to classics like Rapidan Camp Trout and Roosevelt Chicken. The adjacent taproom (2pm to 10pm) serves cocktails, local beers and a limited menu of sandwiches and a few specialties.

Spottswood Dining Room American **$$**

(www.visitshenandoah.com; Mile 51.3, Skyline Dr; lunch mains $8-17, dinner mains $12-28; 7:30-10am, noon-2pm & 5:30-9pm May-Nov) Highlights from the wide-ranging menu at the dining room in Big Meadows include pan-seared trout, roasted turkey with mashed potatoes and grass-fed beef gourmet burger, with many locally sourced ingredients. Complement your food with Virginian wines and local microbrews, all enjoyed in an old-fashioned rustic lodge ambience. There's also a taproom (2pm to 11pm) with a limited menu and live entertainment.

Luray 6

Hawksbill Diner Diner **$**

(540-778-2006; www.facebook.com/TheHawksbillDiner; 1388 Hwy 340 Business, Stanley; breakfast & lunch mains $2-8, dinner mains $7-10; 6am-8pm Mon-Thu, to 9pm Fri & Sat) It may be off the beaten path, but this well-loved place is everything you want in a diner: gabbing locals who all seem to know each other, welcoming and efficient service and darn good Southern food, with dishes like country-fried steak with white gravy on the menu. We like it for an early breakfast – don't miss the hash browns. Six miles south of Luray.

Gathering Grounds Patisserie & Cafe Cafe

(540-743-1121; www.ggounds.com; 55 E Main St; baked goods under $5, mains $5-7; 7am-6pm Mon-Thu, to 8pm Fri, 8am-8pm Sat, 11am-3pm Sun;) If you need a bit of caffeine or an internet break, Gathering Grounds is the spot to stop by in Luray. The coffee is served strong, but what really sets this place apart is the interior, a refreshingly innovative, airy space that combines warm artsy hippie cafe chic with modern hip.

West Main Market Deli **$**

(540-743-1125; www.westmainmarket.com; 123 W Main St; sandwiches $6-7; 10am-3pm Sun & Mon, 10am-6pm Tue-Thu, to 7pm Fri & Sat; P) Exploring Skyline Dr lends itself to picnic lunches, and there are few better places to pick up said lunch than the salad and sandwich counter at West Main. The grilled turkey and avocado is wonderful, while the fresh garden salad kept us rolling all the way down Skyline Dr.

Yogi Bear's Jellystone Park Campsite Campground **$**

(540-743-4002; www.campluray.com; 2250 Hwy 211 E; campsites/cabins from $45/116) Miniature-golf courses, water slides and paddleboats all await inside this fanciful campus. Bargain-basement campsite and cabin prices don't reflect the possibility you might strike it rich while panning for gold at Old Faceful Mining Company. For those interested in passing by and peeking in, there are a few oversized figures of Yogi and Boo Boo that are ready-made photo-ops.

STRETCH YOUR LEGS NEW YORK CITY

Start/Finish: New Museum of Contemporary Art

Distance: 2.6 miles

Duration: Three hours

A stroll through these downtown neighborhoods, home to successive waves of immigrants and lively ethnic communities, is a microcosm of how the city blends the old and the new.

New Museum of Contemporary Art

Housed in an architecturally ambitious building, the **New Museum of Contemporary Art** (☎212-219-1222; www.newmuseum.org; 235 Bowery, btwn Stanton & Rivington Sts; adult/child $18/free, 7-9pm Thu by donation; 🕑11am-6pm Tue, Wed & Fri-Sun, to 9pm Thu; S R/W to Prince St; F to 2nd Ave; J/Z to Bowery; 6 to Spring St) towers over this formerly gritty, but now gentrified strip of the Lower East Side. Be sure to check out the rooftop viewing platform for a unique perspective on the neighborhood landscape.

The Walk » Head south on the relatively wide Bowery for a block until Spring St. Make a right and in three fashionable blocks you'll reach Mulberry St.

Mulberry Street

Although it feels more like a theme park than an authentic Italian strip, Mulberry St is still the heart of Little Italy. It's home to such landmarks as the old-time **Mulberry Street Bar** (☎212-226-9345; www.mulberrystreetbar.com; 176 Mulberry St, at Broome St; 🕑11am-3am Sun-Thu, to 4am Fri & Sat; S B/D to Grand St; J/Z to Bowery), one of Frank Sinatra's favorite haunts.

The Walk » Follow Mulberry St over the wide, traffic-clogged Canal St and continue south to Columbus Park.

Columbus Park

Mah-jongg and domino games take place at bridge tables in this popular park while tai chi practitioners move through lyrical, slow-motion poses under shady trees. Judo-sparring folks and relaxing families are also common sights.

The Walk » Near the southern end of the park is a small alley that leads up to Mott St. Follow Mott St back through ever-expanding Chinatown and make a right on Canal St – explore these blocks at your leisure.

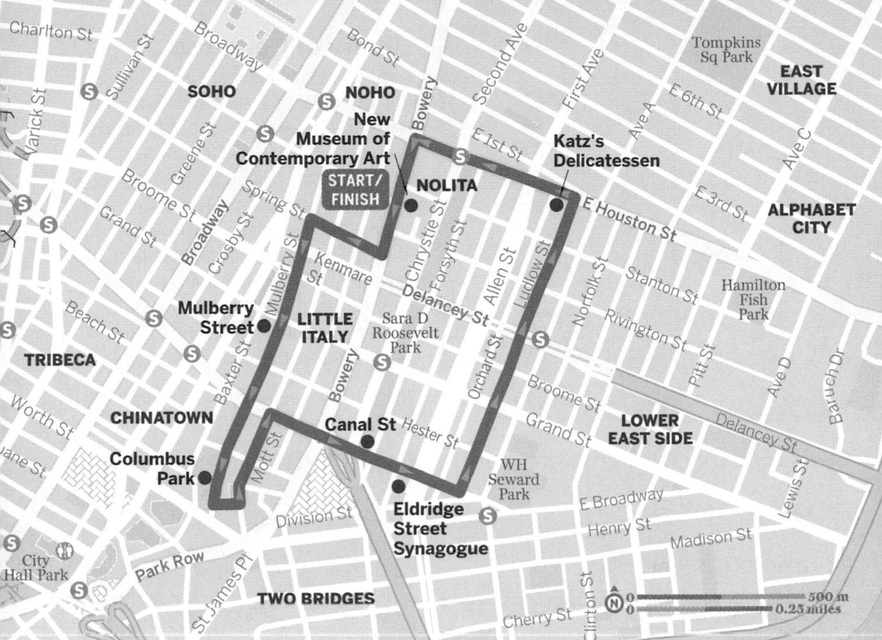

Canal Street

Along Chinatown's busy main artery duck into back alleys to scout for treasures from the Far East. You'll pass stinky seafood stalls hawking slippery fish; herb shops displaying a witch's cauldron's worth of roots and potions; restaurants with whole roasted ducks hanging by their skinny necks in the windows; and street vendors selling every iteration of knock-off designer goods.

The Walk » Walk east on Canal St and navigate the tricky intersection where the Manhattan Bridge on- and off-ramps converge. Continue for another two blocks before making a right on Eldridge St.

Eldridge Street Synagogue

Built in 1887 with Moorish and Romanesque ornamental work, this **synagogue** (212-219-0302; www.eldridgestreet.org; 12 Eldridge St, btwn Canal & Division Sts; adult/child $14/8, Mon free; 10am-5pm Sun-Thu, to 3pm Fri; S F to East Broadway), now a museum, has been beautifully restored. The interior is dominated by the massive circular stained-glass window above the ark (where torahs are kept).

The Walk » Take Orchard or Ludlow Sts, both lined with trendy cafes, boutiques and bars, north to Katz's.

Katz's Delicatessen

A remnant of the classic, old-world Jewish Lower East Side dining scene, **Katz's** (212-254-2246; www.katzsdelicatessen.com; 205 E Houston St, at Ludlow St; sandwiches $15-22; 8am-10.45pm Mon-Wed & Sun to 2:45am Thu, from 8am Fri, 24hr Sat; S F to 2nd Ave) is where Meg Ryan faked her famous orgasm in the movie *When Harry Met Sally*. If you love classic deli grub like massive pastrami, corned beef, brisket and tongue sandwiches, it might have the same effect on you. Go very early or late to avoid the worst of the crowds.

The Walk » Head west on East Houston St until you reach the Bowery; a left will take you back to the New Museum of Contemporary Art.

STRETCH YOUR LEGS WASHINGTON, DC

Start/Finish: Library of Congress

Distance: 3 miles

Duration: Three hours

Washington, DC, is more than monuments, museums and memorials, but it is still partly defined by these structures. All along the National Mall, you'll find symbols of the American dream, the physical representation of the nation's highest ideals and aspirations.

Take this walk on Trips

Library of Congress

To prove America was just as cultured as the Old World, second US president John Adams established the **Library of Congress** (☎202-707-8000; www.loc.gov; 1st St SE; ⌚8:30am-4:30pm Mon-Sat; Ⓜ Orange, Silver, Blue Lines to Capitol South), now the largest library in the world. Stunning in scope and design, the building's baroque interior and flourishes are set off by a Main Reading Room that looks like an ant colony constantly harvesting millions of books.

The Walk » Just head across the street to the underground Capitol Visitor Center.

Capitol Visitor Center

The US Capitol – that would be the big domed building that dominates the eastern end of the National Mall – is the seat of the legislative branch of government, otherwise known as Congress. The underground **Capitol Visitor Center** (☎202-226-8000; www.visitthecapitol.gov; 1st St NE & E Capitol St; ⌚8:30am-4:30pm Mon-Sat; Ⓜ Orange, Silver, Blue Lines to Capitol South) is an introduction to the history and architecture of this iconic structure. Use the center's website to book tours of the Capitol.

The Walk » Walk south on 1st St SE to Independence Ave SW and turn right. You'll pass a couple of blocks of Congressional office buildings before arriving at the Botanic Garden on your right. Follow the signs to the main entrance on Maryland Ave.

United States Botanic Garden

This overlooked **gem** (☎202-225-8333; www.usbg.gov; 100 Maryland Ave SW; ⌚10am-5pm; 👪; 🚌 Circulator, Ⓜ Orange, Silver, Blue Lines to Federal Center SW) provides a beautiful setting for displays of local and exotic plants including orchids, ferns and cacti.

The Walk » Continue on Maryland Ave for a little over 500ft; the National Museum of the American Indian is on your right-hand side.

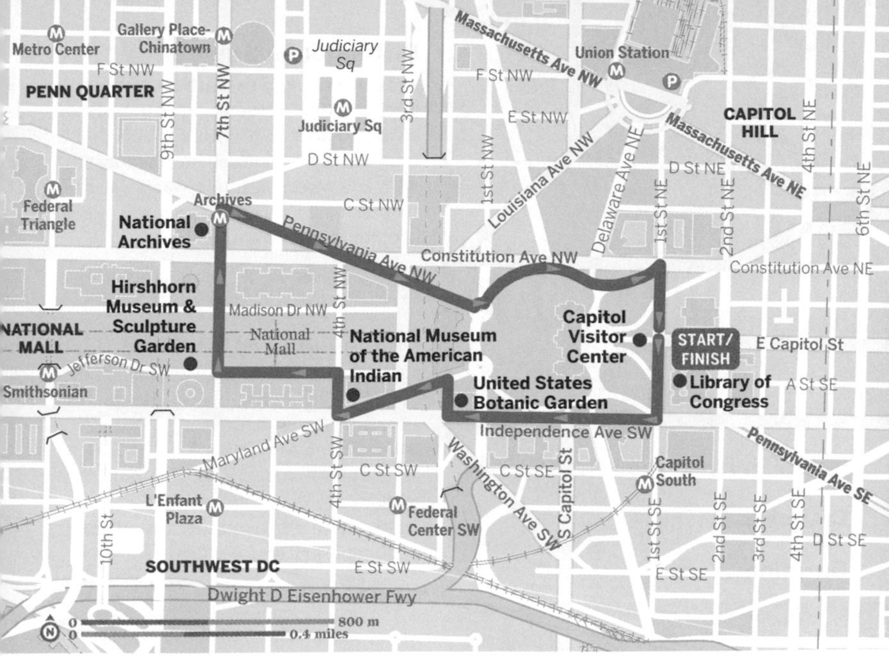

National Museum of the American Indian

This **museum** (☎202-663-1000; www.nmai.si.edu; cnr 4th St & Independence Ave SW; ⏰10am-5:30pm; 👪; 🚌Circulator, Ⓜ Orange, Silver, Blue, Green, Yellow Lines to L'Enfant Plaza) uses native communities' voices and their own interpretive exhibits to tell respective tribal sagas. The ground-floor **Mitsitam Native Foods Cafe** (www.mitsitamcafe.com) is one of the Mall's best dining options.

The Walk » Walk west across the Mall, following Jefferson Ave. After about 2000ft you'll reach the doughnut-shaped Hirshhorn Museum.

Hirshhorn Museum & Sculpture Garden

The **Hirshhorn Museum** (☎202-633-1000; www.hirshhorn.si.edu; cnr 7th St & Independence Ave SW; ⏰10am-5:30pm; 👪; 🚌Circulator, Ⓜ Orange, Silver, Blue, Green, Yellow Lines to L'Enfant Plaza) houses the Smithsonian's modern art collection. Just across Jefferson Dr, the sunken Sculpture Garden feels, on the right day, like a bouncy jaunt through a Lewis Carroll–style Wonderland.

The Walk » Head north up 7th Ave to reach the National Archives.

National Archives

It's hard not to feel a little in awe of the big documents in the **National Archives** (☎866-272-6272; www.archives.gov/museum; 700 Pennsylvania Ave NW; ⏰10am-5:30pm; Ⓜ Green, Yellow Lines to Archives). The Declaration of Independence, the Constitution and the Bill of Rights, plus one of four copies of the Magna Carta: viewed together, it becomes clear just how radical the American experiment was for its time.

The Walk » Head down Pennsylvania Ave toward the Capitol Building. Skirt the Capitol and you're back at the start.

STRETCH YOUR LEGS PHILADELPHIA

Start/Finish: Rittenhouse Sq

Distance: 2.8 miles

Duration: 2½ hours

Historic Philadelphia, so well known, lives side by side with contemporary skyscrapers and fashionable squares. This walk takes in the old and the new, which often means regal-looking spaces and structures from centuries past revitalized for a vibrant modern city.

Rittenhouse Square

This elegant square, with its wading pool and fine statues, marks the heart of the prosperous Center City neighborhood. Several excellent restaurants with sidewalk seating in warm weather line the east side of the square – a great spot for people-watching.

The Walk » It's only 10 steps or so from the southeast corner of the square to the next stop.

Philadelphia Art Alliance

Housed in a Gilded Age–era mansion, one of the few buildings on the square to escape the skyscraper age, is the **Philadelphia Art Alliance** (☎216-646-4302; www.philartalliance.org; 251 S 18th St; adult/child $5/3; ⏲noon-5pm Tue-Sun). It hosts interesting rotating exhibits of contemporary crafts.

The Walk » Walk back through the square and exit on the west side onto Locust St. Turn left on 21st before making a left on Delancey Pl.

Rosenbach Museum & Library

This **library** (☎215-732-1600; www.rosenbach.org; 2008 Delancey Pl; adult/child $10/5; ⏲noon-5pm Tue & Fri, to 8pm Wed & Thu, to 6pm Sat & Sun) is a bibliophile's dream and includes 30,000 rare books, drawings by William Blake, James Joyce's original manuscript for *Ulysses* and a recreation of the modernist poet Marianne Moore's Greenwich Village apartment.

The Walk » Head east on Delancey Pl for three blocks, then left on 17th St, then right on Spruce.

Avenue of the Arts

Tours of **Kimmel Center for the Performing Arts** (☎215-893-1999; www.kimmelcenter.org; 300 S Broad St), Philadelphia's most active center for fine music, are available at 1pm Tuesday through Saturday. When walking north on Broad St (aka 'the Avenue of the Arts'), look up. The facades of these early incarnations of skyscrapers have sig-

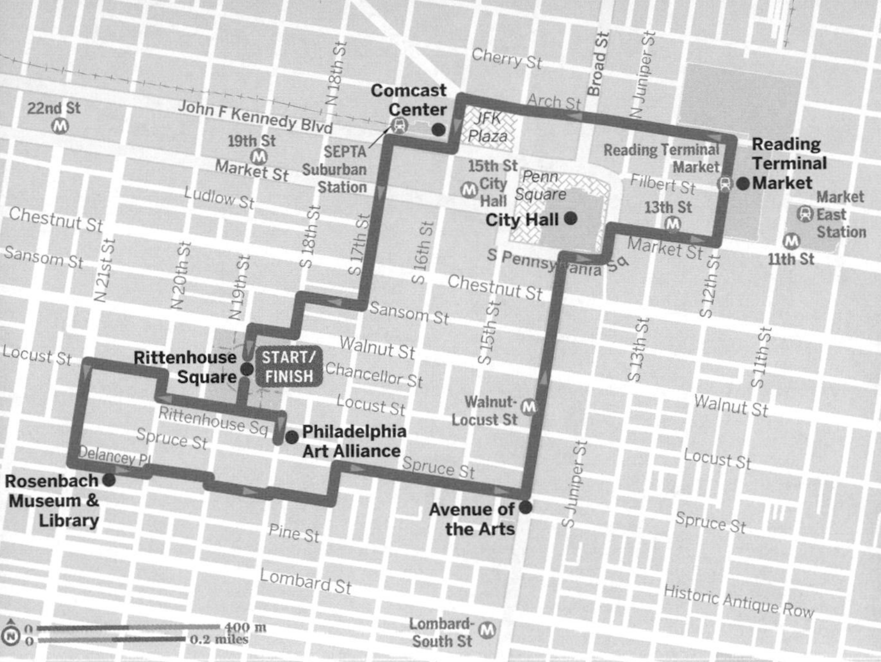

nature flourishes like terracotta roofs and elaborate filigree work highlighted even more when they're illuminated at night.

The Walk » City Hall is dead center down Broad St; it's visible the entire way. Entering from the south portal, keep an eye out for the keystone sculpture of Moses.

City Hall

The majestic 548ft-tall **City Hall** (☎215-686-2840; www.phlvisitorcenter.com; cnr Broad & Market Sts; tower $6, tour & tower $12; ⏲9am-5pm Mon-Fri, also 11am-4pm one Sat per month, tour at 12:30pm, tower closes at 4:15pm Mon-Fri) was the world's tallest occupied building until 1909 and the tallest in Philly until 1987. Check out the 250 sculptures including a 37ft-tall, 27-ton statue of William Penn on the top.

The Walk » Walk through the east side portal; look for the Benjamin Franklin keystone. Tower and building tours leave from here. The two-block stretch of Market St isn't the prettiest; turn left at 12th.

Reading Terminal Market

Housed in a renovated late-19th-century railroad terminal, this massive multiethnic food **market** (☎215-922-2317; www.readingterminalmarket.org; 51 N 12th St; ⏲8am-6pm Mon-Sat, 9am-5pm Sun) has everything: cheesesteaks, Amish crafts, regional specialties, ethnic eats, top-quality butchers, produce, cheese, flowers, bakeries and more.

The Walk » Head west on Arch until you reach JFK Plaza and Robert Indiana's LOVE sculpture. Good food trucks congregate here at lunchtime.

Comcast Center

This skyscraper, the tallest in the city, has a massive all-glass atrium. On the back wall is the world's largest 4mm LED screen displaying high-definition images 18 hours a day.

The Walk » Walking south on 17th you'll pass a Lichtenstein sculpture and several hotels. Go right on Sansom for a block of nice little boutiques and then left on 18th or 19th to return to Rittenhouse Sq.

New England

THIS REGION'S NAME HAS LONG DEPARTED FROM ITS LITERAL MEANING. Today, New England is synonymous with a memorable medley of sights, smells and sounds. Craggy coastlines dotted with lonely lighthouses. Fresh lobsters served on weathered picnic tables. The shimmering colors of the autumnal flag flanking a quiet country road. Old, ivy-clad colleges, the hallowed halls of which are filled with hot-blooded scholars.

This collection of trips covers the best of New England. They create a family of unique vignettes that swirl through the region revealing scores of inspiring superlatives. Perhaps you'll be moved to pick up a paintbrush, dust off your typewriters, maybe even get a PhD. Somehow, the country's northeast nook has that effect on folks.

New Hampshire A scenic drive during leaf-peeping season
SNEHIT / SHUTTERSTOCK ©

New England

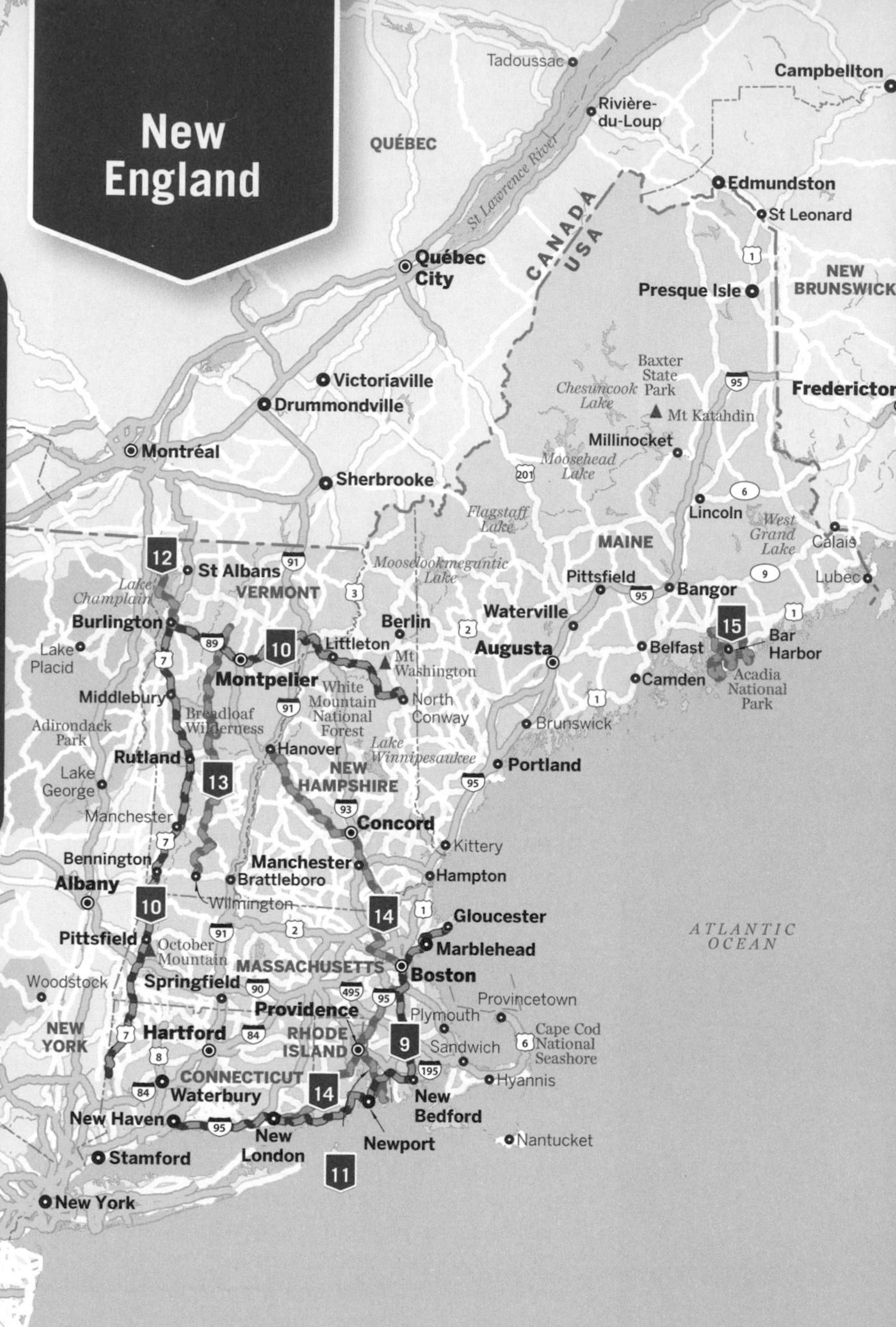

Tadoussac
Campbellton
Rivière-du-Loup
QUÉBEC
St Lawrence River
Edmundston
St Leonard
CANADA
USA
Québec City
NEW BRUNSWICK
Presque Isle
Baxter State Park
Chesuncook Lake
Mt Katahdin
Fredericton
Victoriaville
Drummondville
Millinocket
Montréal
Moosehead Lake
Sherbrooke
Lincoln
Flagstaff Lake
West Grand Lake
MAINE
Calais
St Albans
Lake Champlain
Mooselookmeguntic Lake
VERMONT
Pittsfield
Bangor
Lubec
Burlington
Berlin
Waterville
Littleton
Lake Placid
Augusta
Belfast
Bar Harbor
Mt Washington
Montpelier
Camden
Acadia National Park
White Mountain National Forest
Middlebury
North Conway
Breadloaf Wilderness
Adirondack Park
Brunswick
Hanover
Lake Winnipesaukee
Rutland
Portland
NEW HAMPSHIRE
Lake George
Manchester
Concord
Kittery
Bennington
Manchester
Brattleboro
Hampton
Albany
Wilmington
Gloucester
ATLANTIC OCEAN
Pittsfield
October Mountain
Marblehead
MASSACHUSETTS
Boston
Woodstock
Springfield
Provincetown
Providence
Plymouth
NEW YORK
Hartford
RHODE ISLAND
Cape Cod National Seashore
Sandwich
CONNECTICUT
Hyannis
Waterbury
New Bedford
New Haven
New London
Newport
Nantucket
Stamford
New York
0 200 km
0 100 miles

9 Coastal New England 6–8 Days
The ultimate coastal drive connects fishing villages, trading ports and naval centers. (p143)

10 Fall Foliage Tour 5–7 Days
The ultimate fall foliage trip, featuring dappled trails and awesome views. (p153)

11 Rhode Island: East Bay 3–4 Days
A historic drive exploring the founding days of America. (p163)

12 Lake Champlain Byway 1–2 Days
Discover the scenic road spanning the mainland to the Lake Champlain Islands. (p171)

13 Vermont's Spine: Route 100 3–4 Days
Cross the state from south to north along the Green Mountains. (p179)

14 Ivy League Tour 5 Days
History, architecture and traditions are highlights during tours of New England's Ivies. (p189)

15 Acadia Byway 3 Days
Swoop up Cadillac Mountain, and roll past cliffs on Mt Desert Island. (p199)

DON'T MISS

Stellwagen Bank
This National Marine Sanctuary is a rich feeding ground for humpback whales. See them on Trip 9

Polo
Enjoy polo in Portsmouth at the Glen Farm country estate on Trip 11

Ben & Jerry's Factory Tour
Find out how two high-school pals created America's most celebrated ice cream on Trip 13

Magic Hat Brewery
Take an 'Artifactory' tour at Vermont's most famous microbrewery. Taste your favorite on Trip 12

Heavenly Views
Lie on the sand and ponder the universe during the Stars over Sand Beach program at Acadia National Park. Enjoy it on Trip 15

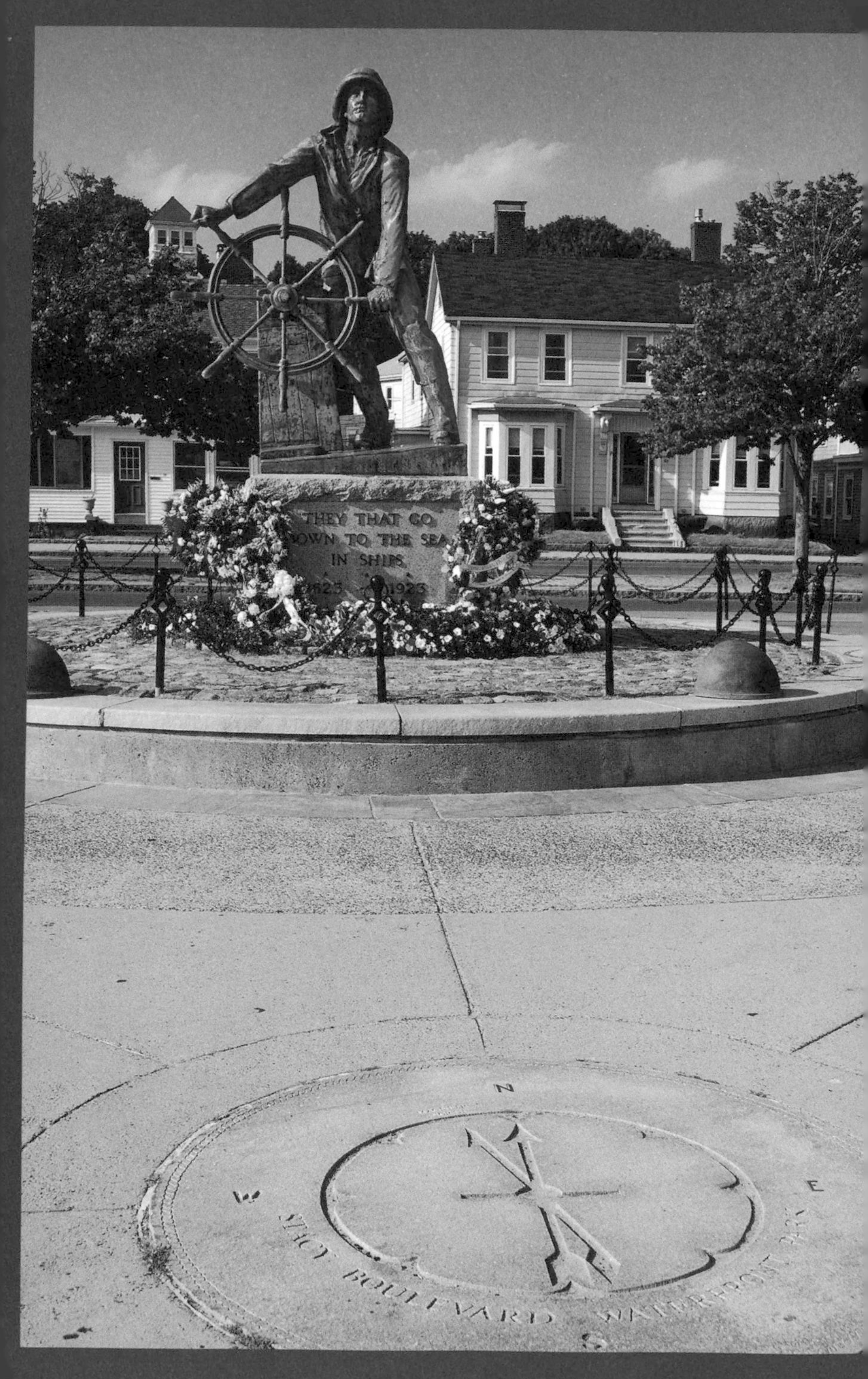
THEY THAT GO
TO THE SEA
IN SHIPS
N
W
E
BOULEVARD

Classic Trip

Coastal New England

This drive follows the southern New England coast. A week of whale-watching, maritime museums and sailboats will leave you feeling pleasantly waterlogged.

TRIP HIGHLIGHTS

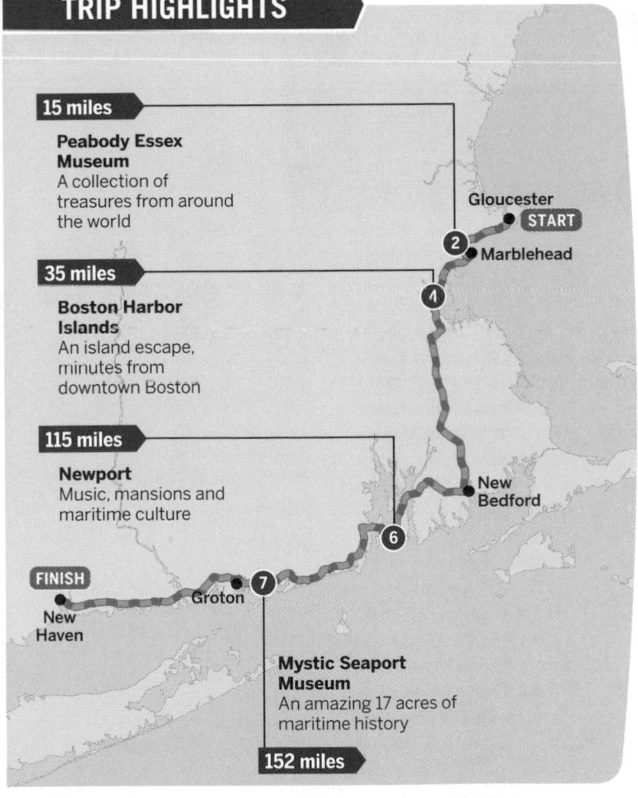

15 miles

Peabody Essex Museum
A collection of treasures from around the world

35 miles

Boston Harbor Islands
An island escape, minutes from downtown Boston

115 miles

Newport
Music, mansions and maritime culture

Mystic Seaport Museum
An amazing 17 acres of maritime history

152 miles

Gloucester START
2
Marblehead
4
New Bedford
6
7
Groton
FINISH
New Haven

6–8 DAYS
240 MILES / 386KM

GREAT FOR...

BEST TIME TO GO

Sites are open and weather is fine from May to September.

ESSENTIAL PHOTO

Pose for a snap alongside the *Gloucester Fisherman.*

BEST TWO DAYS

The first 35 miles (stops one to four) showcase coastal New England, past and present.

Gloucester, MA *Gloucester Fisherman's Memorial* by sculptor Leonard Craske

Classic Trip

9 Coastal New England

From a pirate's perspective, there was no better base in Colonial America than Newport, given the easy access to trade routes and friendly local merchants. Until 1723, that is, when the new governor ceremoniously hanged 26 sea bandits at Gravelly Point. This classic trip highlights the region's intrinsic connection to the sea, from upstart pirates to upper-crust merchants, from Gloucester fisherfolk to New Bedford whalers, from clipper ships to submarines.

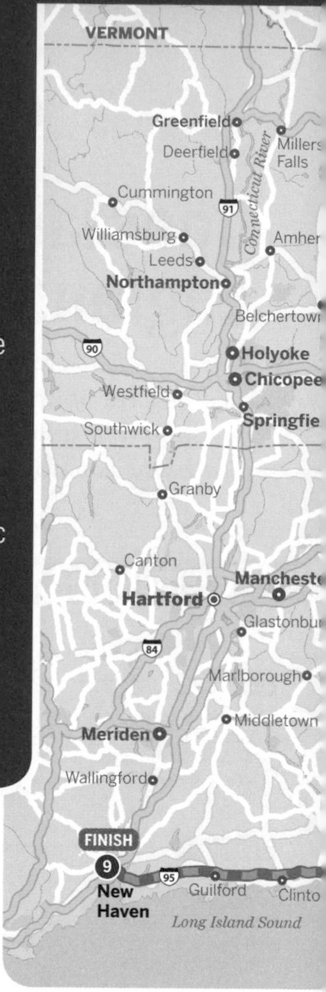

1 Gloucester

Founded in 1623 by English fisherfolk, Gloucester is among New England's oldest towns. This port on Cape Ann has made its living from fishing for almost 400 years, and has inspired works like Rudyard Kipling's *Captains Courageous* and Sebastian Junger's *The Perfect Storm*. Visit the **Maritime Gloucester museum** (☎978-281-0470; www.maritimegloucester.org; 23 Harbor Loop; adult/child $9/7; ⏲10am-5pm late May–early Oct; 👪) to see the working waterfront in action. There is plenty of hands-on educational fun, including an outdoor aquarium and an excellent exhibit, dedicated to Stellwagen Bank, the nearby **National Marine Sanctuary** (www.stellwagen.noaa.gov). **Capt Bill & Sons Whale Watch** (☎978-283-6995; www.captbillandsons.com; 24 Harbor Loop; adult/child $48/32; 👪) boats also depart from here.

Don't leave Gloucester before you pay your respects at the **Gloucester Fishermen's Memorial**, where Leonard Craske's famous *Gloucester Fisherman's Memorial* stands.

✂ p151

The Drive » Head out of town on Western Ave (MA 127), cruising past *The Gloucester Fisherman* and Stage Fort Park. This road follows the coastline south through swanky seaside towns like Manchester-by-the-Sea and Beverly Farms, with glimpses

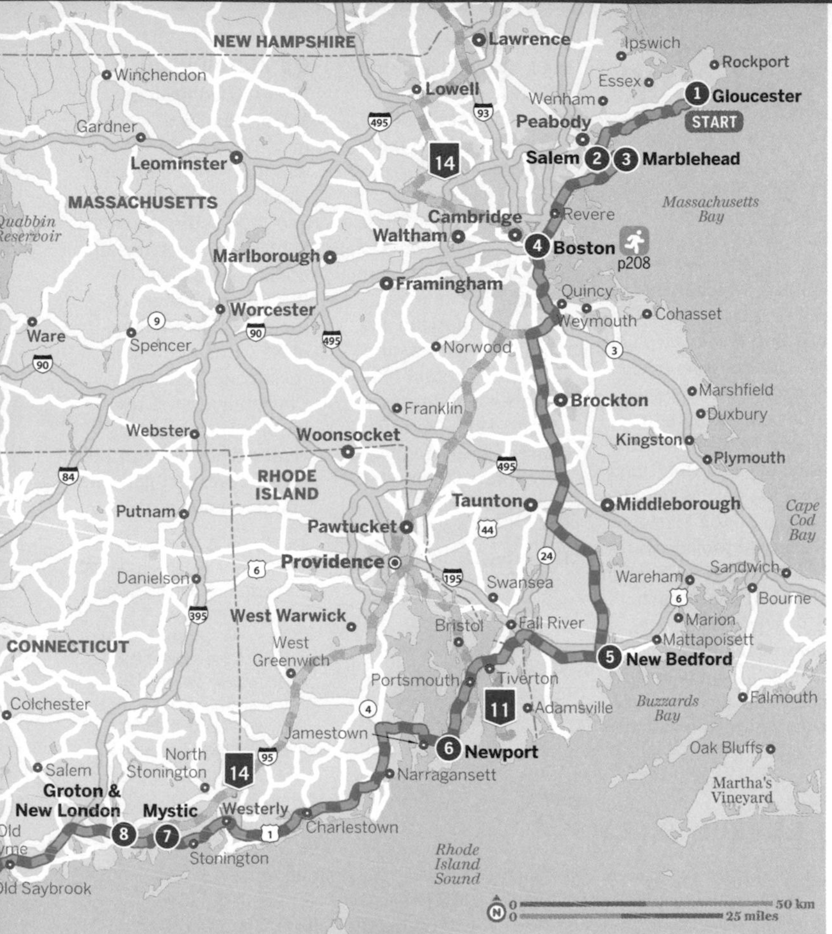

of the bay. After about 14 miles, cross Essex Bridge and continue south into Salem. For a quicker trip, take MA 128 S to MA 114.

LINK YOUR TRIP

11 Rhode Island: East Bay
Join at Newport, or head north on I-95 and south on RI 77 to start at Little Compton.

14 Ivy League Tour
Start in New Haven and do the Ivy League Tour in reverse.

TRIP HIGHLIGHT

2 Salem

Salem's glory dates to the 18th century, when it was a center for clipper-ship trade with the Far East, thanks to the enterprising efforts of merchant Elias Hasket Derby. His namesake Derby Wharf is now the center of the **Salem Maritime National**

Historic Site (☎978-740-1650; www.nps.gov/sama; 160 Derby St; ⌚9am-5pm daily May-Oct, 10am-5pm Wed-Sun Nov-Apr), which includes the 1871 lighthouse, the tall ship *Friendship* and the state custom house.

Many Salem vessels followed Derby's ship *Grand Turk* around the Cape of Good Hope, and soon the owners founded the East India Marine Society to provide warehousing services for their ships' logs and charts. The new company's charter required the establishment of 'a museum in which to house the natural and artificial curiosities' brought back by members' ships. The collection was the basis for what is now the world-class **Peabody Essex Museum** (☎978-745-9500; www.pem.org; 161 Essex St; adult/child $20/free; ⌚10am-5pm Tue-Sun; 👪). Still today, the museum contains an amazing collection of Asian art, among other treasures.

A stroll around town reveals some impressive architecture – grand houses that were once sea captains' homes.

🛏 p151

The Drive » Take Lafayette St (MA 114) south out of Salem center, driving past the campus of Salem State College. After crossing an inlet, the road bends east and becomes Pleasant St as it enters Marblehead center.

3 Marblehead

First settled in 1629, Marblehead is a maritime village with winding streets, brightly painted Colonial houses, and 1000 sailing yachts bobbing at moorings in the harbor. This is the Boston area's premier yachting port and one of New England's most prestigious addresses. Clustered around the harbor, Marblehead center is dotted with historic houses, art galleries and waterside parks.

The Drive » Drive south on MA 129, exiting Marblehead and continuing through the seaside town of Swampscott. At the traffic circle, take the first exit onto MA 1A, which continues south through Lynn and Revere. Take the VFW Pkwy (MA 1A) to the Revere Beach Pkwy (MA 16) to the Northeast Expwy (US 1),

REVERE BEACH

Cruising through Revere, MA 1A parallels the wide, sandy stretch of Revere Beach, which proudly proclaims itself America's first public beach, established in 1896. Scenic but soulless, the condo-fronted beach belies the history of this place, which was a raucous boardwalk and amusement park for most of the 20th century. Famous for roller coasters, dance halls and the Wonderland dog track, Revere Beach attracted hundreds of thousands of sunbathers and fun-seekers during summer months.

The area deteriorated in the 1970s due to crime and pollution. In 1978 a historic blizzard wiped out many of the remaining buildings and businesses, and the 'Coney Island of New England' was relegated to the annals of history.

Revere Beach benefited from a clean-up effort in the 1980s; nowadays, the beach itself is lovely to look at and a safe place to swim. Unfortunately, dominated by high-end condominium complexes, the area retains nothing of its former charm. Only one vestige of 'old' Revere Beach remains: the world-famous **Kelly's Roast Beef** (☎781-284-9129; www.kellysroastbeef.com; 410 Revere Beach Blvd, Revere; sandwiches $5-22, mains $13-25; ⌚10am-2:30am), which has been around since 1951 and still serves up the best roast-beef sandwiches and clam chowder in town. There's no indoor seating, so pull up some sand and enjoy the view. Beware of the seagulls: they're crazy for roast beef.

which goes over Tobin Bridge and into Boston.

TRIP HIGHLIGHT

4 Boston

Boston's seaside location has influenced every aspect of its history, but it's only in recent years that the waterfront has become an attractive and accessible destination for visitors. Now you can stroll along the **Rose Kennedy Greenway** (www.rosekennedygreenway.org; [family]; [T]Aquarium, Haymarket), with the sea on one side and the city on the other. The focal point of the waterfront is the excellent **New England Aquarium** (www.neaq.org; Central Wharf; adult/child $27/19; 9am-5pm Mon-Fri, to 6pm Sat & Sun, 1hr later Jul & Aug; [P] [family]; [T]Aquarium), home to seals, penguins, turtles and oodles of fish.

From Long Wharf, you can catch a ferry out to the **Boston Harbor Islands** (www.bostonharborislands.org; 9am-dusk mid-Apr–mid-Oct; [ferry] from Long Wharf) for berry picking, beachcombing and sunbathing. Harbor cruises and trolley tours also depart from these docks. If you prefer to keep your feet on dry land, take a walk (p208) to explore Boston's flower-filled parks and shop-lined streets.

 p151

The Drive » Drive south out of Boston on I-93. You'll recognize the urban 'hood of Dorchester by pretty Savin Hill Cove and the landmark Rainbow Swash painted on the gas tank. At exit 4, take MA 24 S toward Brockton, then MA 140 S toward New Bedford. Take I-195 E for 2 miles, exiting onto MA 18 for New Bedford.

PARKING IN BOSTON

Parking in downtown Boston is prohibitively expensive. For more affordable rates, cross the Fort Point Channel and park in the Seaport District. There are some (relatively) reasonable deals to be found in the lots on Northern Ave (near the Institute of Contemporary Art); alternatively, head for the Necco Street Garage (further south, off A St), which charges only $5 per day on weekends and $10 for overnight parking on weekdays.

5 New Bedford

During its heyday as a whaling port (1765–1860), New Bedford commanded some 400 whaling ships – a vast fleet that brought in hundreds of thousands of barrels of whale oil for lighting lamps. Novelist Herman Melville worked on one of these ships for four years, and thus set his celebrated novel *Moby-Dick* in New Bedford.

The excellent, hands-on **New Bedford Whaling Museum** (508-997-0046; www.whalingmuseum.org; 18 Johnny Cake Hill; adult/child $17/7; 9am-5pm Apr-Dec, 9am-4pm Tue-Sat, 11am-4pm Sun Jan-Mar) commemorates this history. A 66ft skeleton of a blue whale welcomes you at the entrance. Inside, you can tramp the decks of the *Lagoda,* a fully rigged, half-size replica of an actual whaling bark.

The Drive » Take I-195 W for about 10 miles. In Fall River, head south on MA 24, which becomes RI 24 as you cross into Rhode Island. Cross the bridge, with views of Mt Hope Bay to the north and Sakonnet River to the south, then merge onto RI 114, heading south into Newport.

TRIP HIGHLIGHT

6 Newport

Blessed with a deep-water harbor, Newport has been a shipbuilding base since 1646. Bowen's and Bannister's Wharf, once working wharves, now typify Newport's transformation from a working city by the sea to a resort town. Take a narrated cruise with **Classic Cruises of Newport** (401-847-0298; www.cruisenewport.com; 24 Bannister's Wharf; adult/child from $25/20; May–Oct) on *Rum Runner II,* a Prohibition-era bootlegging vessel, or *Madeleine,* a 72ft schooner.

IMAGE COURTESY OF NEW BEDFORD WHALING MUSEUM ©

TIM LAMAN / GETTY IMAGES ©

Classic Trip

WHY THIS IS A CLASSIC TRIP

MARA VORHEES, WRITER

Nothing evokes New England's salty air like driving along the old coastal roads. MA 127 winds through some of the state's prettiest seaside towns, giving glimpses of gracious mansions perched at the ocean's edge. Even better, I love cruising along MA 1A with the windows down, feeling the ocean breeze, hearing the seagulls' cries and recalling the glory days of Revere Beach.

Above: Boston's New England Aquarium
Left: New Bedford Whaling Museum
Right: Breakers mansion

Although its pirate days are over, Newport's harbor remains one of the most active yachting centers in the country, while its waterfront boasts a standout lineup of other attractions. Be sure to tour at least one of the city's magnificent mansions, such as the **Breakers** (☎401-847-1000; www.newportmansions.org; 44 Ochre Point Ave; adult/child $24/8; ⏰9am-5pm Apr–mid-Oct, hours vary mid-Oct–Mar; 🅿) or **Rosecliff** (☎401-847-1000; www.newportmansions.org; 548 Bellevue Ave; adult/child $17.50/8; ⏰9am-4pm Apr–mid-Oct, hours vary mid-Oct–Mar; 🅿), then stop in for a visit at **Fort Adams** (☎401-841-0707; www.fortadams.org; 90 Fort Adams Dr; tours adult/child $12/6; ⏰10am-4pm late May–Oct, reduced hours Nov & Dec), one of the largest seacoast fortifications in the US.

In summer it's the venue for the **Newport Jazz Festival** (www.newportjazz.org; Fort Adams State Park; tickets $65-89, 3 days $170; ⏰Jul/Aug) and the **Newport Folk Festival** (www.newportfolk.org; Fort Adams State Park; 1-/3-day passes $85/199, parking per day $15; ⏰late Jul).

✕ 🛏 p151, p169

The Drive » Head west out of Newport on RI 138, swooping over Newport Bridge onto Conanicut Island and then over Jamestown Bridge to pick up US 1 for the drive into Mystic. The views of the bay from both bridges are a highlight.

TRIP HIGHLIGHT

7 Mystic

Many of Mystic's clipper ships launched from George Greenman & Co Shipyard, now the site of the **Mystic Seaport Museum** (☎860-572-0711; www.mysticseaport.org; 75 Greenmanville Ave; adult/child $29/19; ⏰9am-5pm Apr-Oct, 10am-4pm Thu-Sun Nov-Mar; P 👪). Today the museum covers 17 acres and includes more than 60 historic buildings, four tall ships and almost 500 smaller vessels. Interpreters staffing all the buildings are glad to discuss their crafts and trades. Most illuminating are the demonstrations on such topics as ship rescue, oystering and whaleboat launching. The museum's exhibits also include a replica of the 77ft slave ship *Amistad*.

If the call of the sea beckons, set sail on the **Argia** (☎860-536-0416; www.argiamystic.com; 12 Steamboat Wharf; adult/child $50/40), a replica of a 19th-century schooner, which cruises down the Mystic River to Fishers' Island Sound.

🛏 p151

The Drive » The 7-mile drive from Mystic to Groton along US 1 S is through built-up suburbs and light industrial areas. To hop across the Thames River to New London, head north along North St to pick up I-95 S.

8 Groton & New London

Groton is home to the US Naval Submarine Base, the first and the largest in the country. It is off-limits to the public, but you can visit the **Historic Ship Nautilus & Submarine Force Museum** (☎800-343-0079; www.ussnautilus.org; 1 Crystal Lake Rd; ⏰9am-5pm Wed-Sun May-Oct, to 4pm Nov-Apr; P), which is home to *Nautilus,* the world's first nuclear-powered submarine and the first sub to transit the North Pole.

Across the river, New London has a similarly illustrious seafaring history, although these days it's built a reputation for itself as a budding creative center. Each summer it hosts **Sailfest** (www.sailfest.org; ⏰Jul), a three-day festival with free entertainment, topped off by the second-largest fireworks display in the Northeast. There's also a **Summer Concert Series**, organized by **Hygienic Art** (☎860-443-8001; www.hygienic.org; 79 Bank St; ⏰2-7pm Tue-Fri, 11am-7pm Sat, noon-4pm Sun).

✕ p151

The Drive » It's a 52-mile drive from Groton or New London to New Haven along I-95 S. The initial stages of the drive plow through the suburbs, but after that the interstate runs through old coastal towns such as Old Lyme, Old Saybrook and Guilford.

9 New Haven

Although most famous for its Ivy League university, Yale, New Haven also played an important role in the burgeoning antislavery movement when, in 1839, the trial of mutineering Mendi tribesmen was held in New Haven's District Court.

Following their illegal capture by Spanish slave traders, the tribesmen, led by Joseph Cinqué, seized the schooner *Amistad* and sailed to New Haven seeking refuge. Pending the successful outcome of the trial, the men were held in a jailhouse on the green, where a 14ft-high bronze memorial now stands. It was the first civil-rights case held in the country.

For a unique take on the New Haven shoreline, take the 3-mile round-trip on the **Shore Line Trolley** (☎203-467-6927; www.shorelinetrolley.org; 17 River St, East Haven; adult/child $10/7; ⏰10:30am-4:30pm daily Jul & Aug, Sat & Sun May, Jun, Sep & Oct; 👪), the oldest operating suburban trolley in the country, which takes you from East Haven to Short Beach in Branford. A wealth of art and architecture is packed into the streets of downtown New Haven.

✕ 🛏 p151 , p197

Eating & Sleeping

Gloucester ❶

Two Sisters Coffee Shop Diner **$**

(978-281-3378; www.facebook.com/TwoSistersCoffeeShop; 27 Washington St; mains $5-8; 6:30am-noon Mon-Fri, to 1pm Sat & Sun;) This local place is where the fisherfolk go for breakfast when they come in from their catch. They're early risers, so you may have to wait for a table. Corned-beef hash, eggs in a hole and pancakes all get rave reviews. Service is a little salty.

Salem ❷

The Daniels House B&B **$$**

(978-744-5709; http://thedanielshouse.com; 1 Daniels St; r $165-185; P) This must be Salem's oldest lodging, with parts dating from 1667. Two walk-in fireplaces grace the common area, and the rooms are filled with period antiques. It's appropriate in this spooky town that such an old house be haunted: rumor has it that a ghost cat roams the ancient halls, and it's even been known to jump into bed with guests.

Boston ❹

Barking Crab Seafood **$$**

(617-426-2722; http://barkingcrab.com; 88 Sleeper St; sandwiches $12-18, mains $18-32; 11:30am-10pm Sun-Wed, to 11pm Thu-Sat; SL1, SL2, T South Station) Big buckets of crabs, steamers (steamed clams) dripping in lemon and butter, paper plates piled high with all things fried, pitchers of ice-cold beer... Devour your feast at communal picnic tables overlooking the water. Service is slack, noise levels are high, but the atmosphere is jovial.

Newport ❻

White Horse Tavern American **$$$**

(401-849-3600; http://whitehorsenewport.com; 26 Marlborough St; mains lunch $12-29, dinner $24-42; 11am-9pm Sun-Thu, to 10pm Fri & Sat) If you'd like to eat at a tavern, opened by a 17th-century pirate, that once served as an annual meeting place for the Colonial Rhode Island General Assembly, try this historic, gambrel-roofed beauty. Menus for dinner (at which men should wear a jacket) might include baked escargot, truffle-crusted Atlantic halibut or beef Wellington. Service is hit or miss.

Mystic ❼

Whaler's Inn Inn **$$**

(860-536-1506; www.whalersinnmystic.com; 20 E Main St; d $159-299; P @) This hotel combines an 1865 Victorian house with a reconstructed luxury hotel from the same era (the original landmark 'Hoxie House' burned down in the 1970s) and a modern motel known as Stonington House. Seasonal packages available; these include the price of dinners and area attractions. Rates include continental breakfast, a small gym and complimentary bicycles.

New London ❽

Captain Scott's Lobster Dock Seafood **$$**

(860-439-1741; www.captscotts.com; 80 Hamilton St; mains $7-21; 11am-9pm May-Oct;) The Coast Guard knows a thing or two about the sea, and you'd be remiss if you didn't follow students of its academy to *the* place for seafood in the summer. The setting's just a series of picnic tables by the water, but you can feast on succulent lobster rolls, followed by steamers, fried whole-belly clams, scallops or lobsters.

New Haven ❾

Caseus Fromagerie & Bistro Bistro **$$**

(203-624-3373; http://caseusnewhaven.com; 93 Whitney Ave; mains $12-30; 11:30am-2:30pm Mon-Sat plus 5:30-9pm Wed-Sat;) With a boutique cheese counter piled with locally sourced labels and a concept menu devoted to *le grand fromage*, Caseus has hit upon a winning combination. After all, what's not to like about a perfectly executed mac 'n' cheese or the dangerously delicious poutine (*pommes frites*, cheese curds and velouté). There's also European-style pavement seating.

Classic Trip

Fall Foliage Tour

Touring New England in search of autumn's changing colors has become so popular that it has sprouted its own subculture of 'leaf-peepers.' Immerse yourself in the fall harvest spirit.

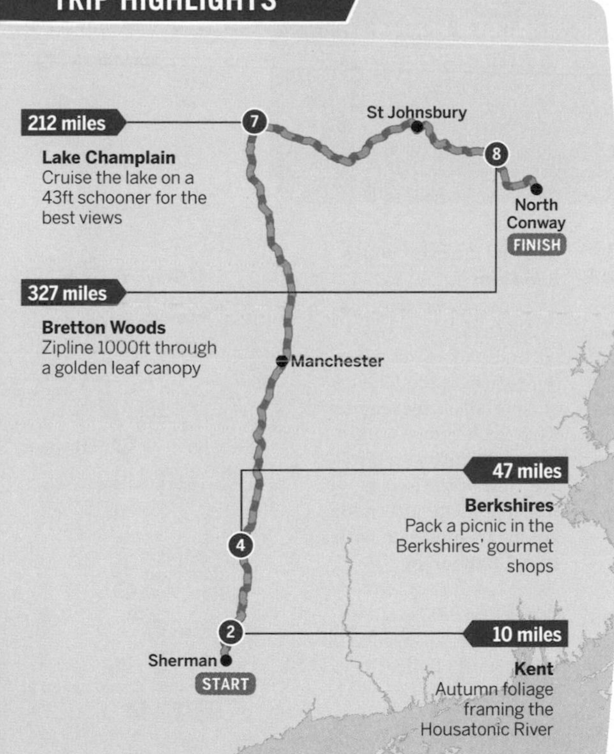

5–7 DAYS
424 MILES / 682KM

GREAT FOR...

BEST TIME TO GO

Mid-September to late October for the harvest and autumn leaves.

ESSENTIAL PHOTO

Kent Falls set against a backdrop of autumnal colors.

BEST FOR OUTDOORS

Ziplining through the tree canopy in Bretton Woods.

Kent Falls State Park, CT Easy hiking trails and impressive views

Classic Trip

10 Fall Foliage Tour

The brilliance of fall in New England is legendary. Scarlet and sugar maples, ash, birch, beech, dogwood, tulip tree, oak and sassafras all contribute to the carnival of autumn color. But this trip is about much more than just flora and fauna: the harvest spirit makes for family outings to seasonal fairs, leisurely walks along dappled trails and tables groaning beneath delicious seasonal produce.

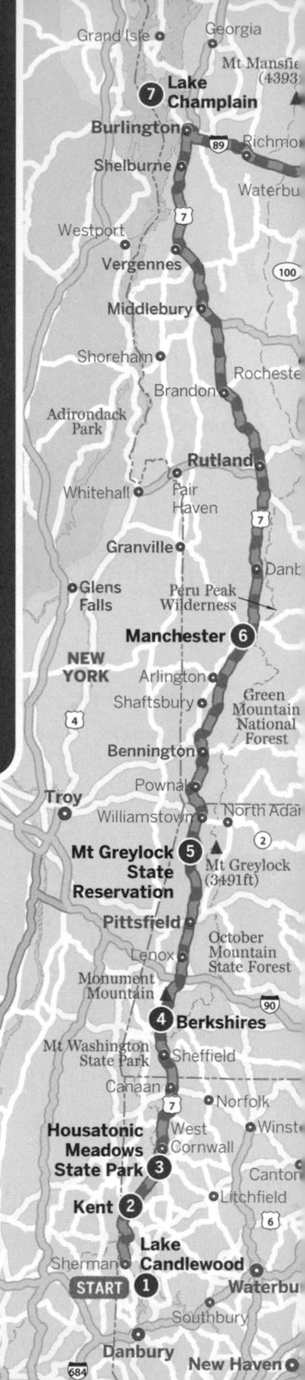

❶ Lake Candlewood

With a surface area of 8.4 sq miles, Candlewood is the largest lake in Connecticut. On the western shore, the **Squantz Pond State Park** (☎203-312-5023; www.ct.gov/deep/squantzpond; 178 Shortwoods Rd, New Fairfield; weekdays/weekends $15/22; ⏰8am-sunset; P 🐾) is popular with leaf-peepers, who come to amble the pretty shoreline. In Brookfield and Sherman, quiet vineyards with acres of gnarled grapevines line the hillsides. Visitors can tour the intimate **White Silo Farm** (☎860-355-0271; www.whitesilowinery.com; 32 CT 37, Sherman; tastings $8; ⏰11am-6pm Fri-Sun Apr-Dec; P 👪), where the focus is on specialty wines made from farm-grown fruit.

For the ultimate bird's-eye view of the foliage, consider a late-afternoon hot-air balloon ride with **GONE Ballooning** (☎203-262-6625; www.flygoneballooning.com; 88 Sylvan Crest Dr, Southbury; adult/under 13yr $250/125; 👪) in nearby Southbury.

🍴 p161

The Drive » From Danbury, at the southern tip of the lake, you have a choice of heading 28 miles north via US 7, taking in Brookfield and New Milford (or trailing the scenic eastern shoreline along Candlewood Lake Rd S); or heading 26 miles north along CT 37 and CT 39 via New Fairfield, Squantz Pond and Sherman, before reconnecting with US 7 to Kent.

TRIP HIGHLIGHT

2 Kent

Kent has previously been voted *the* spot in all of New England (yes, even beating Vermont) for fall foliage viewing. Situated prettily in the Litchfield Hills on the banks of the Housatonic River, it is surrounded by dense woodlands. For a sweeping view of them, hike up Cobble Mountain in **Macedonia Brook State Park** (860-927-3238; www.ct.gov/deep/macedoniabrook; 159 Macedonia Brook Rd; mid-Apr–Sep; P),

LINK YOUR TRIP

9 Coastal New England

From North Conway, take NH 16 south to I-95, then head east on MA 128 to Gloucester.

14 Ivy League Tour

Follow NH 16 and I-93 northwest into Vermont. Then follow I-91 south all the way to Hanover, NH.

a wooded oasis 2 miles north of town. The steep climb to the rocky ridge affords panoramic views of the foliage against a backdrop of the Taconic and Catskill mountain ranges.

The 2175-mile Georgia-to-Maine **Appalachian National Scenic Trail** (www.appalachiantrail.com) also runs through Kent and up to Salisbury on the Massachusetts border. Unlike much of the trail, the Kent section offers a mostly flat 5-mile river walk alongside the Housatonic, the longest river walk along the entire length of the trail. The trailhead is accessed on River Rd, off CT 341.

The Drive » The 15-mile drive from Kent to Housatonic Meadows State Park along US 7 is one of the most scenic drives in Connecticut. The single-lane road dips and weaves between thick stands of forest, past Kent Falls State Park with its tumbling waterfall (visible from the road), and through West Cornwall's picturesque covered bridge, which spans the Housatonic River.

❸ Housatonic Meadows State Park

During the spring thaw, the churning waters of the Housatonic challenge kayakers and canoeists. By summer the scenic waterway transforms into a lazy, flat river, perfect for fly-fishing. In **Housatonic Meadows State Park** (☎860-927-3238; www.ct.gov/deep/housatonicmeadows; 90 CT 7 North, Sharon; ⏰8am-sunset), campers vie for a spot on the banks of the river while hikers take to the hills on the Appalachian Trail. **Housatonic River Outfitters** (☎860-672-1010; www.dryflies.com; 24 Kent Rd, Cornwall Bridge; ⏰8am-5pm Sun-Thu, to 6pm Fri & Sat) runs guided fishing trips with gourmet picnics.

Popular with artists and photographers, one of the most photographed fall scenes is the **Cornwall Bridge** (West Cornwall), an antique covered bridge that stretches across the broad river, framed by vibrantly colored foliage.

On Labor Day weekend, in the nearby town of Goshen, you can visit the **Goshen Fair** (☎860-491-3655; www.goshenfair.org; Goshen; ⏰early Sep) – one of Connecticut's best old-fashioned fairs, with ox-pulling and wood-cutting contests.

The Drive » Continue north along US 7 toward the Massachusetts border and Great Barrington, 27 miles away. After a few miles you leave the forested slopes of the park behind and enter expansive rolling countryside dotted with large, red-and-white barns. Look out for hand-painted signs advertising farm produce and consider stopping overnight in Falls Village, which has an excellent inn (p161).

TRIP HIGHLIGHT

❹ Berkshires

Blanketing the westernmost part of Massachusetts, the rounded mountains of the Berkshires turn crimson and gold as early as mid-September. The effective capital of the Berkshires is **Great Barrington**, a formerly industrial town

LOCAL KNOWLEDGE: KENT FALLS

Kent is a great place to base yourself in the fall, with lots of accessible spots for viewing the leaves and good amenities in the pretty town center. The best hiking trail in season is the section that connects with the Appalachian Trail at Caleb's Peak, affording fantastic views. If you're less able to hike, the easiest way to get a beautiful vista is to head 5 miles south out of town on US 7 to **Kent Falls State Park**, which is unmissable on your right. The falls' wonderfully lazy cascade is right before you and there are lots of easy trails into the forest.

whose streets are now lined with art galleries and upscale restaurants. It's the perfect place to pack your picnic or rest your legs before or after a hike in nearby **Beartown State Forest** (☎413-528-0904; www.mass.gov/dcr; 69 Blue Hill Rd, Monterey; parking $15). Crisscrossing some 12,000 acres, **hiking trails** yield spectacular views of wooded hillsides and pretty Benedict Pond.

Further north, **October Mountain State Forest** (☎413-243-1778; www.mass.gov/dcr; 317 Woodland Rd; ⏲sunrise-sunset) is the state's largest tract of green space (16,127 acres), also interwoven with hiking trails. The name – attributed to Herman Melville – gives a good indication of when this park is at its loveliest, with its multicolored tapestry of hemlocks, birches and oaks.

p161

The Drive » Drive north on US 7, the spine of the Berkshires, cruising 11 miles through Great Barrington and Stockbridge. In Lee, the highway merges with scenic US 20, from where you can access October Mountain. Continue 16 miles north through Lenox and Pittsfield to Lanesborough. Turn right on N Main St and follow the signs to the Mt Greylock State Reservation entrance.

LOCAL KNOWLEDGE: NORTHERN BERKSHIRE FALL FOLIAGE PARADE

If your timing is right, you can stop in North Adams for the **Northern Berkshire Fall Foliage Parade** (www.1berkshire.com), held in late September or early October. Held for over 60 years, the event follows a changing theme, but it always features music, food and fun – and, of course, foliage.

5 Mt Greylock State Reservation

At 3491ft, Massachusetts' highest peak is perhaps not very high, but a climb up the 92ft **War Veterans Memorial Tower** rewards you with a panorama stretching up to 100 verdant miles, across the Taconic, Housatonic and Catskill ranges, and over five states. Even if the weather seems drab from the foot, driving up to the summit may well lift you above the gray blanket, and the view with a layer of cloud floating between tree line and sky is simply magical.

Mt Greylock State Reservation (☎413-499-4262; www.mass.gov/dcr; 30 Rockwell Rd, Lanesborough; ⏲9am-4:30pm Jun–early Oct, shorter hours rest of year) has some 45 miles of **hiking trails**, including a portion of the Appalachian Trail. Frequent trail pull-offs on the road up – including some that lead to waterfalls – make it easy to get at least a little hike in before reaching the top of Mt Greylock.

p161

The Drive » Return to US 7 and continue north through the quintessential college town of Williamstown. Cross the Vermont border and continue north through the historic village of Bennington. Just north of Bennington, turn left on VT 7A and continue north to Manchester (51 miles total).

6 Manchester

Stylish Manchester is known for its magnificent New England architecture. For fall foliage views, head south of the center and take the **Mt Equinox Skyline Drive** (☎802-362-1114; www.equinoxmountain.com; VT 7A, btwn Manchester & Arlington; car & driver $15, each additional passenger $5, under 13yr free; ⏲9am-4pm late May-Oct) to the summit of 3828ft Mt Equinox, the highest mountain accessible by car in the Taconic Range. Wind up the 5.2 miles – with gasp-inducing scenery at every hairpin turn – seemingly to the top of the world, where the 360-degree panorama unfolds, offering views of the Adirondacks, the lush Battenkill Valley and Montreal's Mt Royal.

If early snow makes Mt Equinox inaccessible, visit 412-acre **Hildene** (☎802-362-1788; www.hildene.org;

Classic Trip

ROB RUDESKI / SHUTTERSTOCK ©

JACOBS STOCK PHOTOGRAPHY / GETTY IMAGES ©

WHY THIS IS A CLASSIC TRIP

BENEDICT WALKER, WRITER

There's something truly magical about Mother Nature's autumnal palette. If she's on time and you're in sync, this classic leaf-peeping itinerary will show you the full spectrum of yellows, golds, oranges, crimsons and reds. The route takes enough time and heads far enough north to offer real variety. Throw in a lake cruise and a zipline above the forest canopy and we've got you covered!

Above: Lake Champlain
Left: North Conway
Right: Mount Washington Cog Railway

DANITA DELIMONT / GETTY IMAGES ©

1005 Hildene Rd/VT 7A; adult/child $20/5, guided tours $7.50/2; ⌚9:30am-4:30pm), a Georgian Revival mansion that was once home to the Lincoln family. It's filled with presidential memorabilia and sits nestled at the edge of the Green Mountains, with access to 8 miles of wooded **walking trails**.

🛏 p161

The Drive » Take VT 7 north, following the western slopes of the Green Mountains through Rutland and Middlebury to reach Burlington (100 miles) on the shores of Lake Champlain.

TRIP HIGHLIGHT

7 Lake Champlain

With a surface area of 490 sq miles straddling New York, Vermont and Quebec, Lake Champlain is the largest freshwater lake in the US after the Great Lakes. On its eastern side, **Burlington** is a gorgeous base for enjoying the lake. Explore it on foot, then scoot down to the wooden promenade, take a swing on the four-person rocking benches and consider a bike ride along the 7.5-mile lakeside bike path.

For the best offshore foliage views, we love the *Friend Ship* sailboat at **Whistling Man Schooner Company** (☎802-825-7245; www.whistlingman.com; Burlington Community Boathouse, 1 College St, at Lake Champlain; 2hr cruises adult/child $50/35; ⌚3-4 trips daily, late May–early Oct), a 43ft sloop that accommodates just 17 passengers. Next door, **Echo Leahy Center for Lake Champlain** (802-864-1848; www.echovermont.org; 1 College St; adult/child $16.50/13.50; 10am-5pm;) explores the history and ecosystem of the lake, including a famous snapshot of 'Champ,' Lake Champlain's mythical sea creature.

p161

The Drive » Take I-89 S to Montpelier, savoring gorgeous views of Vermont's iconic Mt Mansfield and Camel's Hump, then continue northeast on US 2 to St Johnsbury, where you can pick up I-93 S across the New Hampshire line to Littleton. Take the eastbound US 302 exit and continue toward Crawford Notch State Park and Bretton Woods. The drive is 115 miles.

TRIP HIGHLIGHT

8 Bretton Woods

Unbuckle your seat belts and step away from the car. You're not just peeping at leaves today, you're swooping past them on ziplines that drop 1000ft at 30mph. The four-season **Bretton Woods Canopy Tour** (603-278-4947; www.brettonwoods.com; US 302; per person $89-110; tours twice daily year-round, additional times during peak periods) includes a hike through the woods, a stroll over sky bridges and a swoosh down 10 cables to tree platforms.

If this leaves you craving even higher views, cross US 302 and drive 6 miles on Base Rd to the coal-burning, steam-powered **Mount Washington Cog Railway** (603-278-5404; www.thecog.com; 3168 Base Station Rd; adult $69-75, child $39; daily Jun-Oct, Sat & Sun late Apr, May & Nov) at the western base of Mt Washington, the highest peak in New England. This historic railway has been hauling sightseers to the mountain's 6288ft summit since 1869.

The Drive » Cross through Crawford Notch and continue 20 miles southeast on US 302, a gorgeous route through the White Mountains that parallels the Saco River and the Conway Scenic Railroad. At the junction of NH 16 and US 302, continue 5 miles on US 302 into North Conway.

9 North Conway

Many of the best restaurants, pubs and inns in North Conway come with expansive views of the nearby mountains, making it an ideal place to wrap up a fall-foliage road trip. If you're traveling with kids or you skipped the cog railway ride up Mt Washington, consider an excursion on the antique steam Valley Train with the **Conway Scenic Railroad** (603-356-5251; www.conwayscenic.com; 38 Norcross Circle; Notch Train coach/1st class/dome car $64/78/90; mid-Jun–Oct;); it's a short but sweet round-trip ride through the Mt Washington Valley from North Conway to Conway, 11 miles south, with the Moat Mountains and the Saco River as your scenic backdrop. First-class seats are usually in a restored Pullman observation car.

p161

DETOUR: KANCAMAGUS SCENIC BYWAY

Start: 9 North Conway

Just south of North Conway, the 34.5-mile Kancamagus Scenic Byway, otherwise known as NH 112, passes through the White Mountains from Conway to Lincoln, NH. You'll drive alongside the Saco River and enjoy sweeping views of the Presidential Range from Kancamagus Pass. Inviting trailheads and pull-offs line the road. From Lincoln at the highway's western end, a short drive north on I-93 leads to **Franconia Notch State Park** (603-745-8391; www.nhstateparks.org; I-93, exit 34A; 8.30am-5pm early May–late Oct), where the foliage in September and October is simply spectacular.

Eating & Sleeping

Lake Candlewood 1

American Pie Bakery $$

(860-350-0662; www.americanpiecompany.com; 29 Sherman Rd/CT 37, Sherman; mains $10-22; 7am-9pm Tue-Sun, to 3pm Mon) A local favorite serving up 20 varieties of homemade pie, including pumpkin and blueberry crumb, alongside burgers, steaks and salads.

Falls Village

Falls Village Inn Inn $$$

(860-824-0033; www.thefallsvillageinn.com; 33 Railroad St, Falls Village; d/ste $239/299; P) The heart and soul of one of the smallest villages in Connecticut, this inn originally served the Housatonic Railroad. Now the six rooms are styled by interior decorator Bunny Williams, and the Tap Room is a hangout for Lime Rock's racers.

Berkshires (Great Barrington) 4

Allium Modern American $$

(413-528-2118; www.alliumberkshires.com; 42 Railroad St; small plates $9-16, mains $16-28; 5-9:30pm) Allium subscribes to the slow-food movement, with a seasonal menu that relies on fresh organic produce, cheeses and meats. Go for cocktails and small plates in the lounge area, with a window facing the street, or a more formal meal in the dining room, with a view into the kitchen. This stylish restaurant combines rustic and modern design elements to great effect.

Mt Greylock State Reservation 5

Bascom Lodge Lodge $

(413-743-1591; www.bascomlodge.net; 1 Summit Rd; dm/d/tr/q without bath $40/125/170/190; Sat & Sun May–mid-Jun, daily mid-Jun–Oct, restaurant 8am-4:30pm, dinner from 7pm by reservation; P) High atop Mt Greylock, this truly rustic hostelry was built as a federal work project in the 1930s. In the lobby, inviting leather sofas are arranged around a stone fireplace. Room have shared bathrooms, comfortable beds and wonderful views. The meals – fresh, hot and individually prepared – are excellent and filling, providing perfect sustenance for hikers (mains $8 to $12).

Manchester 6

Barnstead Inn Inn $$

(802-362-1619, reservations 800-331-1619; www.barnsteadinn.com; 349 Bonnet St; r $129-195, ste $210-310;) Barely a half-mile from Manchester Center, this converted 1830s hay barn exudes charm and is in a good location. Rooms have refrigerators and homey braided rugs, while the porch has wicker rockers for watching the world pass by.

Lake Champlain 7

American Flatbread Pizza $$

(802-861-2999; www.americanflatbread.com; 115 St Paul St; flatbreads $14-23; 11:30am-3pm & 5-11:30pm Mon-Fri, 11:30am-11:30pm Sat & Sun) Central downtown location, bustling atmosphere, great beers on tap from the in-house Zero Gravity microbrewery, and superb flatbread (thin-crust pizza) with locally sourced ingredients are reason enough to make this one of your first lunch or dinner stops in Burlington. Throw in an outdoor terrace in the back alleyway in warm weather, and you've got one of Vermont's finest eateries.

North Conway 9

Red Elephant Inn Inn $$

(603-356-3548; www.redelephantinn.com; 28 Locust Lane; r $139-239;) Set on a quiet street behind the Red Jacket Mountain View Inn, this lovely Victorian is a hidden gem. The eight rooms are individually decorated in colorful, eclectic themes with telling names like the Hippie Room, Country Quilts and Neiman Marcus.

Rhode Island: East Bay

The East Bay is Rhode Island's historical heart. Tour the shoreline, and follow the trail from America's Colonial roots in Little Compton to the boomtowns of Newport and Providence.

TRIP HIGHLIGHTS

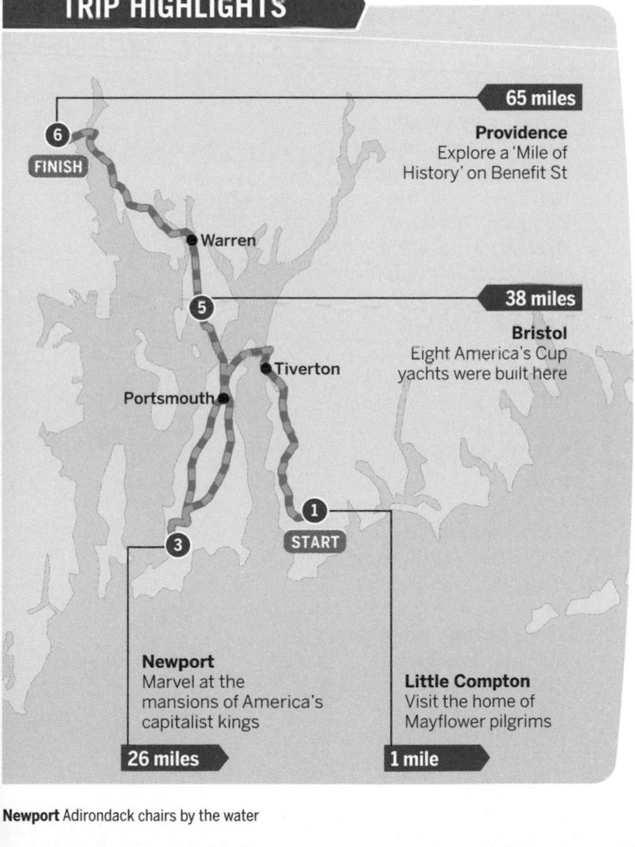

6 FINISH

Warren

5

Tiverton

Portsmouth

3

1 START

65 miles

Providence
Explore a 'Mile of History' on Benefit St

38 miles

Bristol
Eight America's Cup yachts were built here

Newport
Marvel at the mansions of America's capitalist kings

26 miles

Little Compton
Visit the home of Mayflower pilgrims

1 mile

3–4 DAYS
65 MILES / 106KM

GREAT FOR...

BEST TIME TO GO

May to October for good weather and farm food.

ESSENTIAL PHOTO

Capture the mansions and sheer cliffs along Cliff Walk.

BEST FOR HISTORY

Find modern America's beginnings in Little Compton.

Newport Adirondack chairs by the water

11 Rhode Island: East Bay

Rhode Island's jagged East Bay tells the American story in microcosm. Start in Little Compton with the grave of Elizabeth Pabodie (1623–1717), the first European settler born in New England. Then meander through historic Tiverton and Bristol, where slave dealers and merchants grew rich. Prosperous as they were, their modest homes barely hold a candle to the mansions, museums and libraries of Newport's capitalist kings and Providence's intelligentsia.

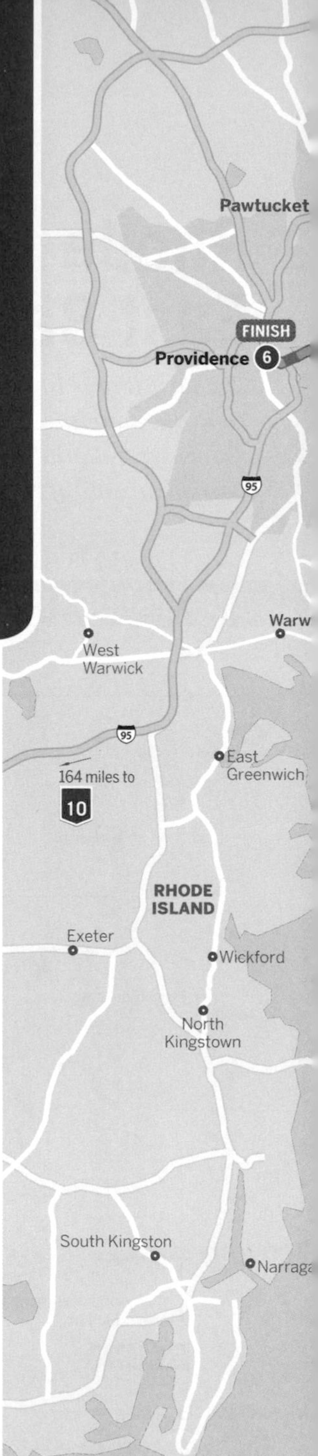

TRIP HIGHLIGHT

1 Little Compton

No doubt tiring of the big-city bustle of 17th-century Portsmouth, early settler Samuel Wilbor crossed the Sakonnet River to Little Compton. His plain family home, **Wilbor House** (☎401-635-4035; www.littlecompton.org; 548 West Main Rd; adult/child $6/3; ⏰1-5pm Thu-Sun Apr-Oct, 9am-3pm Tue-Fri Nov-Mar), built in 1690, still stands on a manicured lawn behind a traditional five-bar gate and tells the story of eight generations of Wilbors who lived here.

The rest of Little Compton, from the hand-hewn clapboard houses to the white-steepled **United Congregational Church**, overlooking the **Old Commons Burial Ground**, is one of the oldest and most quaint villages in all of New England. Elizabeth Pabodie, daughter of Mayflower pilgrims Priscilla and John Alden and the first settler born in New England, is buried here.

Lovely, ocean-facing **Goosewing Beach** (⏰dawn-dusk) is the only good public beach. Parking costs $10 at **South Shore Beach**, from where you can walk across a small tidal inlet.

🛏 p169

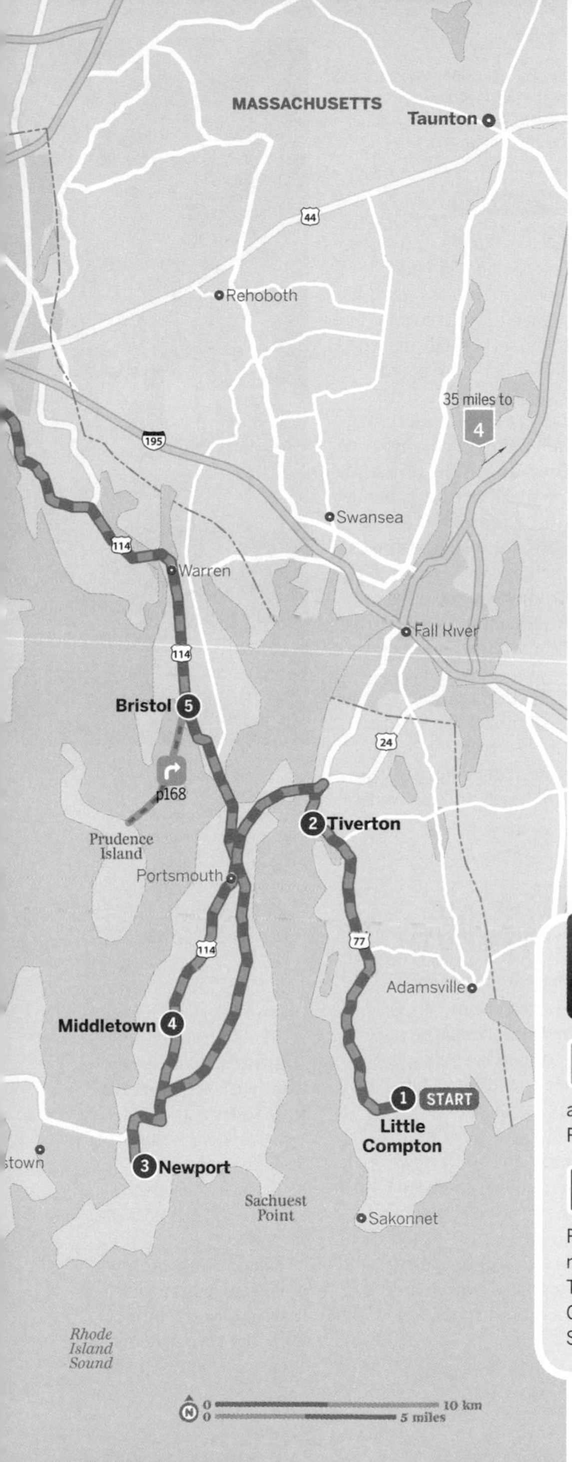

The Drive ›› Head north along RI 77 at a leisurely pace, enjoying the peaceful country scenery of rambling stone walls and clapboard farmhouses. As you approach Tiverton, look out to your left and you'll occasionally get glimpses out to the water.

❷ Tiverton

En route to Tiverton's historic Four Corners, stop in at **Carolyn's Sakonnet Vineyard** (☎401-635-8486; www.sakonnetwine.com; 162 West Main Rd; ⏲11am-6pm Sun-Thu, to 8pm Fri & Sat late May–mid-Oct, 11am-5pm daily rest of year; P) for free daily wine tastings and guided tours. This will set you up nicely for the gourmet treats that await in Tiverton: **Gray's Ice Cream** (☎401-624-4500; www.graysicecream.com; 16 East Rd; scoops from $3; ⏲6:30am-9pm), where over 40 flavors are made on-site daily; artisanal cheeses from the **Milk &**

LINK YOUR TRIP

4 The Jersey Shore Drive south on I-95 and take the Garden State Pkwy to Asbury Park.

10 Fall Foliage Tour Take I-95 south from Providence to CT 9 heading northwest across the state. Take I-84 west to the border. CT 37 and CT 39 lead to Sherman.

Honey Bazaar (☎401-624-1974; www.milkandhoneyri.com; 3838 Main Rd; ⏲10am-5pm Tue-Sat, noon-5pm Sun); and the gourmet deli bar at **Provender Fine Foods** (☎401-624-8084; www.provenderfinefoods.com; 3883 Main Rd; items $4-18; ⏲9am-5pm Tue-Sun), where you can munch on giant cookies or forage for picnic fare.

Tiverton is an artists colony so it also offers some of the best shopping in the state, including handwoven Shaker-style rugs from **Amy C Lund** (☎401-816-0000; www.aclhandweaver.com; 3964 Main Rd; ⏲10am-5pm Wed-Sat, noon-5pm Sun) and museum-quality art from **Gallery 4** (☎401-816-0999; www.gallery4tiverton.com; 3848 Main Rd; ⏲11am-4:30pm Thu-Sat, noon-4:30pm Sun).

The Drive » Head north up Main St, leaving Tiverton and its green fields behind you, and merge onto the westbound RI 138/RI 24 S, which leads you directly into Newport.

TRIP HIGHLIGHT

3 Newport

Established by religious moderates fleeing persecution from Massachusetts Puritans, the 'new port' flourished to become the fourth-richest city in the newly independent colony. Downtown, the Colonial-era architecture is beautifully preserved along with notable landmarks, such as Washington Sq's **Colony House**, where Rhode Island's declaration of independence was read in May 1776.

Just off the square, the gaslights of the White Horse Tavern (p151), America's oldest tavern, still burn, and on Touro St, America's first synagogue, **Touro Synagogue** (☎401-847-4794; www.tourosynagogue.org; 85 Touro St; adult/child $12/free; ⏲10:30am-2:30pm Sun-Fri May & Jun, 9:30am-4:30pm Sun-Fri Jul & Aug, 9:30am-2:30pm Sun-Fri Sep & Oct, 11:30am-2:30pm Sun Nov-Apr), still stands. Tour the past on a guided walk with **Newport History Tours** (☎401-841-8770; www.newporthistorytours.org; Brick Market Museum & Shop, 127 Thames St; tours adult $15-20, child $5; ⏲tour times vary; 👪).

Fascinating as Newport's early history is, it struggles to compete with the town's latter-day success, when wealthy

THORNTON COHEN / ALAMY STOCK PHOTO ©

LOCAL KNOWLEDGE: POLO IN PORTSMOUTH

Drab though the urban environs of Portsmouth may seem, in-the-know locals rate Portsmouth as a family-friendly destination. Not least because the polo matches hosted at Glen Farm make for a great family day out. Home to the **Newport Polo Club** (☎401-846-0200; www.nptpolo.com; 250 Linden Lane, Portsmouth; lawn seats adult/child $12/free; ⏲gates open 1pm), the 700-acre 'farm' was assembled by New York businessman Henry Taylor, who sought to create a gentleman's country seat in the grand English tradition.

In summer, the farm is host to the club's polo matches (check the website for dates), which are a perfect way to enjoy the property and get an authentic taste of Newport high life.

Middletown Nostalgic souvenirs decorate Flo's clam shack

industrialists made Newport their summer vacation spot and built country 'cottages' down lantern-lined Bellevue Ave, modeled on Italianate palazzos, French chateaux and Elizabethan manor houses. Tour the most outstanding with the **Preservation Society of Newport County** (☎401-847-1000; www.newportmansions.org; 424 Bellevue Ave; 5-site tickets adult/child $35/12).

✕ 🛏 p151, p169

The Drive » Leave Newport by way of 10-mile Ocean Dr, which starts just south of Fort Adams and curls around the southern shore, and up Bellevue Ave before intersecting with Memorial Blvd. Turn right here for a straight shot into Middletown.

4 Middletown

Flo's (☎401 847-8141; www.flosclamshacks.com; 4 Wave Ave; mains $11-22; ⏰11am-9pm Sun-Thu, to 10pm Fri & Sat mid-May–mid-Sep, reduced hours mid-Sep–mid-May) jaunty red-and-white clam shack would be enough reason to visit Middletown, which now merges seamlessly with Newport. But the best fried clams in town taste better after a day on **Sachuest Beach** (Second Beach; ☎401-846-6273; http://parks.middletownri.com; Sachuest Point Rd), the largest and most beautiful beach on Aquidneck Island. Curving around Sachuest Bay, it is backed by the 450-acre **Norman Bird Sanctuary** (☎401-846-2577; www.normanbirdsanctuary.org; 583 Third Beach Rd; adult/child $7/3; ⏰9am-5pm).

The Drive » Leave Aquidneck Island via East Main Rd, which takes you north through the suburbs of Middletown and Portsmouth. After 6.5 miles, pick up the RI 114 and cross the bay via the scenic Mt Hope suspension bridge. From here it's a short 3-mile drive into Bristol.

TRIP HIGHLIGHT

5 Bristol

One-fifth of all slaves transported to America were brought in Bristol ships and by the 18th century the town was one of the country's major commercial ports. The world-class **Herreshoff Marine Museum** (401-253-5000; www.herreshoff.org; 1 Burnside St; adult/child $12/5; 10am-5pm May-Oct;) showcases some of America's finest yachts.

Local resident Augustus Van Wickle bought a 72ft Herreshoff yacht for his wife Bessie in 1895, but having nowhere suitable to moor it, he then had to build **Blithewold Mansion** (401-253-2707; www.blithewold.org; 101 Ferry Rd; adult/child $14/5; 10am-4pm Tue-Sat, to 3pm Sun Apr–mid-Oct; P). The arts-and-crafts mansion sits in a peerless position on Narragansett Bay and is particularly lovely in spring. Other local magnates included slave trader General George DeWolf, who built **Linden Place** (401-253-0390; www.lindenplace.org; 500 Hope St; adult/child $8/6; 10am-4pm Tue-Sat, noon-4pm Sun May-Oct & Dec, by appointment Nov & Jan-Apr; P), famous as a film location for *The Great Gatsby*.

Bristol's **Colt State Park** (401-253-7482; www.riparks.com; RI 114; sunrise-sunset; P) is Rhode Island's most scenic park, with its entire western border fronting Narragansett Bay.

p169

The Drive » From Bristol it's a straight drive north along RI 114, through the suburbs of Warren and Barrington, to Providence. After 17 miles, merge onto I-195 W, which takes you the remaining 18 miles into the center of town.

DETOUR: PRUDENCE ISLAND

Start: 5 Bristol

Idyllic **Prudence Island** (401-683-0430; www.prudencebayislandstransport.com; ferries 5:45am-6pm Mon-Fri, 7:30am-6pm Sat & Sun) sits in the middle of Narragansett Bay, an easy 25-minute ferry ride from Bristol. Originally used for farming and later as a summer vacation spot for families from Providence and New York, who traveled here on the Fall River Line Steamer, the island now has only 88 inhabitants. There are some fine Victorian and beaux-arts houses near Stone Wharf, a lighthouse and a small store, but otherwise it's wild and unspoiled. Perfect for mountain biking, barbecues, fishing and paddling.

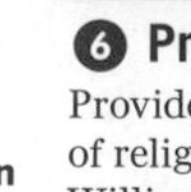

TRIP HIGHLIGHT

6 Providence

Providence, the first town of religious liberal Roger Williams' new Rhode Island and Providence Plantation colony, was established so that 'no man should be molested for his conscience sake.' **Benefit Street's 'Mile of History'** gives a quick lesson in the city's architectural legacy with over 100 Colonial, Federal and Revival houses. Amid them you'll find William Strickland's 1838 **Providence Athenaeum** (401-421-6970; www.providenceathenaeum.org; 251 Benefit St; 10am-6pm Mon-Thu, 9am-5pm Fri, 10am-2pm Sat). Atop the hill sits **Brown University** (401-863-1000; www.brown.edu), with its Gothic and beaux-arts buildings arranged around the College Green. Nearby is **John Brown House** (ext 362 401-331-8575; www.rihs.org; 52 Power St; adult/child $10/6; tours 1:30pm & 3pm Tue-Fri, 10:30am, noon, 1:30pm & 3pm Sat Apr-Nov), which President John Quincy Adams thought to be 'the most magnificent and elegant mansion...on this continent.'

End the tour with a nod toward the bronze statue of *Independent Man,* which graces the **Rhode Island State House** (401-222-3983; www.sos.ri.gov; 82 Smith St; self-guided tours 8:30am-4:30pm Mon-Fri, guided tours 9am, 10am, 11am, 1pm & 2pm Mon-Fri).

p169, p197

Eating & Sleeping

Little Compton ❶

Stone House Inn Historic Hotel $$$

(☎401-635-2222; www.newportexperience.com/stonehouse; 122 Sakonnet Point Rd; d $229-544; P 📶) When this unashamedly upmarket inn opened its doors in 2016, Little Compton's notoriously private elite feared it meant the out-of-towners were coming. With only 13 rooms (lavish as they may be), it's hardly cause for an invasion. If you have cash and the inclination, this is your chance to take a peek at how the other half lives.

Newport ❸

Fluke Wine Bar Seafood $$$

(☎401-849-7778; www.flukenewport.com; 41 Bowens Wharf; mains $26-36; ⏲5-11pm daily May-Oct, Wed-Sat Nov-Apr) Fluke's Scandinavian-inspired dining room, with its blond wood and picture windows, offers an accomplished seafood menu featuring roasted monkfish, seasonal striped sea bass and plump scallops. Upstairs, the bar serves a rock-and-roll cocktail list.

Attwater Boutique Hotel $$$

(☎401-846-7444; www.theattwater.com; 22 Liberty St; r $259-599; P ❄ 📶) Newport's newest hotel has the bold attire of a midsummer beach party with turquoise, lime green and coral prints, ikat headboards and snazzily patterned geometric rugs. Picture windows and porches capture the summer light and rooms come furnished with thoughtful luxuries, like iPads, Apple TV and beach bags.

Bristol ❺

Governor Bradford Inn Inn $$

(☎401-254-1745; www.mounthopefarm.org/the-inn; 250 Metacom Ave; r $150-299; P ❄) Administered by the Mount Hope Trust, the Governor Bradford offers four individually styled rooms in a 300-year-old Georgian farmhouse. Once owned by the Haffenreffer family, of beer-brewing fortune, the house sits on 200 acres of pristine farmland.

Providence ❻

Loie Fullers Modern American $$

(☎401-273-4375; www.loiefullers.com; 1455 Westminster St; mains $15-21; ⏲5-11pm Mon-Sat, 10am-2pm & 5-11pm Sun) This wonderfully original, atmospheric little bistro on the outskirts of the Federal Hill neighborhood is an oasis of fun and deliciousness on an otherwise drab trunk road. Inside, candles, ornate polished woods, frescoes and art-nouveau elements transport you to another time, another place. On the French-inspired Modern American menu, comfort is king. Somebody had to let the cat outta the bag...

Local 121 Modern American $$

(☎401-274-2121; www.local121.com; 121 Washington St; mains $17-30; ⏲5-10pm Wed & Thu, 5-11pm Fri, 10am-3pm & 5-11pm Sat, 10am-3pm & 5-9pm Sun) Locavore mania comes to Providence with this opulent, old-school restaurant with contemporary aspirations. Housed in the old Dreyfus hotel (built in the 1890s), a building owned by the arts organization AS220, Local 121 has an easy, unpretentious grandeur – and some damn fine food. The menu is seasonal, but recent options include a perfect (local) scallop po'boy and (local) duck-ham pizza.

The Dean Hotel Boutique Hotel $$

(☎401-455-3326; http://thedeanhotel.com; 122 Fountain St; d from $109) New kid on the block, The Dean epitomizes all that is design in Providence. A one-stop shop with beer hall, karaoke bar, cocktail den and beer hall downstairs, upstairs it has eight quirky, personalized design-themed rooms that will be your stylish urban oasis from the fun and frivolity downstairs and beyond. One for the hipsters and the funsters.

Lake Champlain Byway

Vermont's 'Great Lake' offers delights not found elsewhere in the state, from the semi-urban sophistication of Burlington to the tranquil Champlain Islands, stretching like stepping stones to the Canadian border.

TRIP HIGHLIGHTS

53 miles

Isle La Motte
A pristine island, home to the world's largest fossil reef

FINISH 7

South Alburg

Winooski

13 miles

3

Burlington
Vermont's biggest city boasts one of New England's best chocolatiers

1 START

0 miles

Shelburne
Visit an open-air museum that speaks volumes about Vermont history

1–2 DAYS
53 MILES / 85KM

GREAT FOR...

BEST TIME TO GO

June to October for long, summery days and abundant leaf-peeping opportunities.

Grab a shot at water's edge on Isle La Motte.

Sample the state's most famous beer export and indulge in Burlington's vibrant restaurant scene.

Burlington Church St Marketplace

12 Lake Champlain Byway

Tucked between the Green Mountains and the Adirondacks of New York, Lake Champlain is the defining feature of northwest Vermont's landscape. Survey the lake from the museum in Shelburne and the pedestrian-friendly waterfront in Burlington, then set off to discover the Champlain Islands, a 27-mile ribbon of isles where simpler pleasures prevail: swimming, boating, apple-picking, wine-tasting, or rambling along farm roads and inter-island causeways.

TRIP HIGHLIGHT

1 Shelburne

Feast your eyes on the stunning array of 17th- to 20th-century American artifacts – folk art, textiles, toys, tools, carriages and furniture – spread over the 45-acre grounds and gardens at **Shelburne Museum** (802-985-3346; www.shelburnemuseum.org; 6000 Shelburne Rd/US 7, Shelburne; adult/child/teen $24/12/14; 10am-5pm daily May-Dec, Wed-Sun Jan-Apr;). This remarkable place is set up as a mock village, with 150,000 objects housed in 39 buildings. Highlights include a full-size covered bridge, a classic round barn, an 1871 lighthouse, a one-room schoolhouse, a railway station with a locomotive and a working blacksmith's forge.

The collection's sheer size lets you tailor your visit. Families are drawn to the carousel, the Owl Cottage children's center and the *Ticonderoga* steamship, while aficionados of quilts or, say, duck decoys can spend hours investigating their personal passion. Indeed, the buildings themselves are exhibits. Many were moved here from other parts of New England to ensure their preservation.

p177

The Drive » Head north on US 7 for 4 miles until you reach South Burlington.

2 South Burlington

One of the pioneers – and among the most famous – of Vermont's microbreweries is **Magic Hat Brewery** (802-658-2739; www.magichat.net; 5 Bartlett Bay Rd, South Burlington; 11am-7pm Mon-Sat, noon-5pm Sun), which started brewing in 1995. The 'Artifactory' exudes an infectious creative energy, with over 20 varieties flowing from four dozen taps.

Guided 30-minute tours take you through the history of Vermont breweries and Magic Hat's role, how it makes its beer and keeps the environmental impact as low as possible, and its involvement in the community (such as the annual Magic Hat Mardi Gras and its support of the performing arts). Guides will happily answer any question you have, such as who writes the sayings on the inside of each bottle cap. You can enjoy free tastes both before and after the tour. Must-tries are the trademark No 9 (pale ale with a hint of apricot), Circus Boy (lemongrass-infused Hefeweizen) and the whimsically changing lineup of seasonal brews and 'Reclusive Rarities.' (There's also a self-guided tour in case you miss one of the guided ones.)

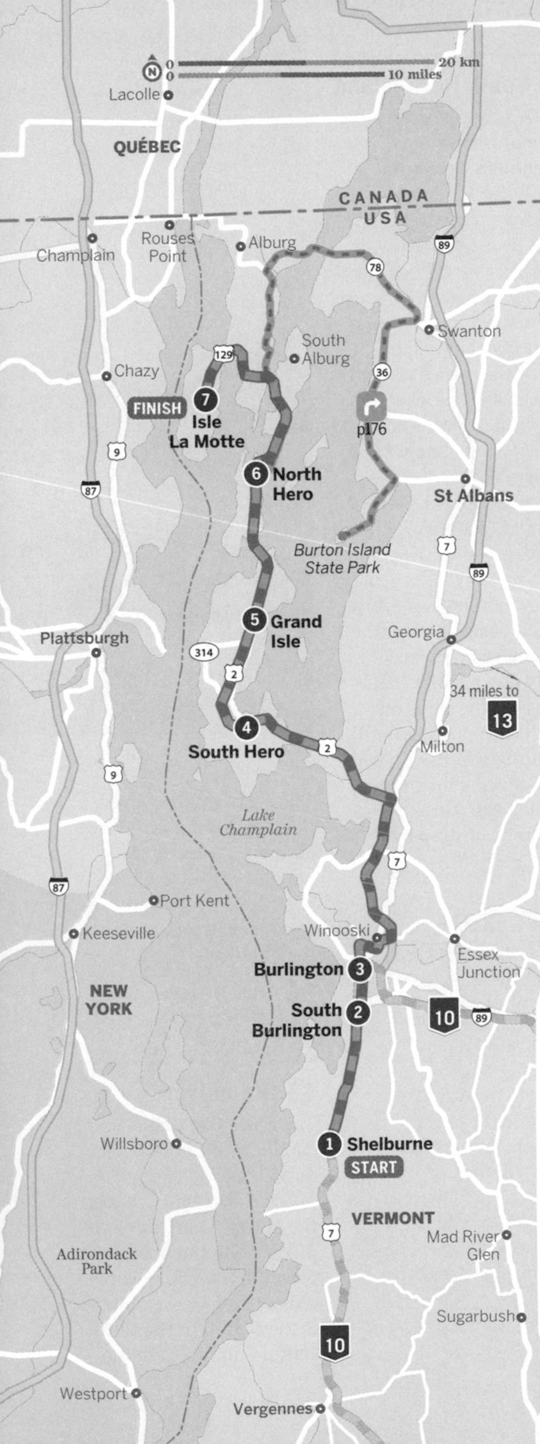

The Drive » Continue north on US 7 for 4 miles to Burlington.

TRIP HIGHLIGHT

❸ Burlington

Perched above glistening Lake Champlain, Vermont's largest city would be a small city in most other states. Yet Burlington's diminutive size is one of its charms, with an easily walkable downtown and a gorgeous, accessible lakefront. With the University of Vermont (UVM) swelling the city (by 13,000 students) and a vibrant cultural and social life, Burlington has a spirited, youthful character. And when it comes to nightlife, this is Vermont's epicenter.

Just before you reach the city center, a chocolate stop is in order. The aroma of rich melted cocoa is intoxicating as you enter the gift shop next to the glass wall overlooking the small factory at **Lake**

LINK YOUR TRIP

10 Fall Foliage Tour
Intersect with the Fall Foliage tour in Burlington.

13 Vermont's Spine: Route 100
Drive south on I-89 to hook up with VT 100 at Waterbury.

Champlain Chocolates (☎802-864-1807; www.lakechamplainchocolates.com; 750 Pine St; ⏰9am-6pm Mon-Sat, 11am-5pm Sun). Take the tour to get the history of the chocolatier and ample samples to taste-test the gooey goodness. Oh, and this shop is the only one with factory-seconds shelves containing stacks of chocolate at a discount. It tastes the same as the pretty stuff but for cosmetic reasons can't be sold at regular price. The cafe serves coffee drinks and its own luscious ice cream.

p177

The Drive » Cast off for the Champlain Islands, cruising 10 miles north of Burlington on I-89 to exit 17, then west on US 2 for 9 miles. After Sand Bar State Park – a great picnic and swimming spot – cross the causeway and look for the photo-perfect parking island halfway across.

4 South Hero Island

Settle into the slower pace of island life at **Allenholm Orchards** (☎802-372-5566; www.allenholm.com; 111 South St, South Hero; ⏰9am-5pm late May–Christmas Eve; 👪), just outside the town of South Hero; grab a creemee (that's Vermont-speak for soft-serve ice cream) or pick a few apples for the road ahead. About 3 miles west is **Snow Farm Winery** (☎802-372-9463; www.snowfarm.com; 190 W Shore Rd, South Hero; ⏰11am-5pm daily May-Dec, 5-9pm Fri, 11am-4pm Sat & Sun Jan-Apr), Vermont's first vineyard, which boasts a sweet tasting room tucked away down a dirt road (look for the signs off US 2). Sample its award-winning whites or have a sip of ice wine in the rustic barn (three tastes are free), or drop by on a Thursday summer evening at 6:30pm for the free **concert series** on the lawn next to the vines – you can expect anything from jazz to folk to light rock and roll.

JIAWANGKUN / SHUTTERSTOCK ©

The Drive » Continue north on US 2 for 8 miles.

5 Grand Isle

The **Hyde Log Cabin** (☎802-372-8339; US 2; adult/child $3/free; ⏰11am-5pm Fri-Sun late May–mid-Oct; 🐾), the oldest (1783) log cabin in Vermont and one of the oldest in the US, is worth a short stop to see how settlers lived in the 18th century and to examine

LOCAL KNOWLEDGE: CHAMPLAIN'S LOVABLE LAKE MONSTER

Dinosaur relic or Ice Age proto-whale? Tree trunk? Really, really big fish? Lake Champlain's legendary lake monster – nicknamed 'Champ' – has long fascinated local residents. Known to the Abenaki as Tatoskok, Champ was even sighted by French explorer Samuel de Champlain back in the early 17th century. Indulge your curiosity at the Champ display in the Echo Leahy Center for Lake Champlain (p160). For a more dependable sighting, attend a Vermont Lake Monsters baseball game, where a lovable green-costumed Champ mascot dances on the dugout roof between innings.

Shelburne Lighthouse at the Shelburne Museum

traditional household artifacts from Vermont.

🛏 p177

The Drive » Continue north on US 2 for another 8 miles.

6 North Hero Island

Boaters for miles around cast anchor at popular general store **Hero's Welcome** (☎802-372-4161; www.heroswelcome.com; 3537 US 2, North Hero; ⏲6:30am-8pm Mon-Fri, 7am-7pm Sat & Sun mid-Jun–early Sep, shorter hours rest of year). The store's amusing wall display of 'World Time Zones' – four clocks showing identical hours for Lake Champlain's North Hero, South Hero, Grand Isle and Isle La Motte – reflects the prevailing island-centric attitude. Pick up a souvenir, grab a sandwich or coffee and snap some pics on the outdoor terrace overlooking the boat landing.

🛏 p177

The Drive » From US 2, head west 4 miles on VT 129 to historic Isle La Motte.

TRIP HIGHLIGHT

7 Isle La Motte

Pristine Isle La Motte is one of the most historic of the Champlain Islands. Signs along its western shore signal its traditional importance as a crossroads for Native Americans; French explorer Samuel de Champlain landed here in 1609.

Tool around the loop road hugging the coast, stopping at **St Anne's Shrine** (☎802-928-3362; www.saintannesshrine.org; 92 St Anne's Rd, Isle La Motte; ⏲shrine late May–mid-Oct, grounds year-round) on the site of Fort St Anne, Vermont's oldest settlement. (Though it is welcoming to all, this is a religious place, so be respectful of those who come to

DETOUR: BURTON ISLAND

Start: 6 North Hero Island

For a deeper immersion in Lake Champlain's natural beauty, spend a night or two camping at **Burton Island State Park** (802-524-6353; www.vtstateparks.com; 2714 Hathaway Point Rd, St Albans; late May–early Sep;), in the middle of the lake. Between Memorial Day and Labor Day, the *Island Runner* ferry (10 minutes) shuttles campers and their gear across a narrow channel from the mainland near St Albans to this pristine, traffic-free island with over two dozen lakefront lean-tos and campsites. Park facilities include boat rentals, a nature center with daily kids' activities and a store selling breakfast, lunch and groceries; the sign outside ('No shoes, no shirt, no problem!') epitomizes the island's laid-back vibe.

It's an easy 45-minute loop around the lake from North Hero to the ferry dock at Kill Kare State Park. Head 10 miles north on US 2 and then 10 miles east on VT 78 to get to Swanton; from there drive 10 miles south on VT 36 and turn right onto Hathaway Point Rd for the final 2.5 miles.

pray.) The site features a striking granite statue of Samuel de Champlain, and its waterfront has spectacular views and a large picnic area.

Isle La Motte is also home to the 20-acre **Fisk Quarry Preserve** (www.ilmpt.org; W Shore Rd, Isle La Motte; dawn-dusk), the world's largest fossil reef, 4 miles south of St Anne's Shrine. Half a million years old, the reef once provided limestone for Radio City Music Hall and Washington's National Gallery. Interpretive trails explain the history of the quarry.

Eating & Sleeping

Shelburne 1

🛏 Inn at Shelburne Farms — Inn $$$

(📞802-985-8498; www.shelburnefarms.org/staydine; 1611 Harbor Rd, Shelburne; r $270-525, without bath $160-230, cottages & houses $270-850; ⏰early May–late Oct; 📶) One of New England's top 10 places to stay, this inn, 7 miles south of Burlington off US 7, was once the summer mansion of the wealthy Webb family. It now welcomes guests, with rooms in the gracious, welcoming country manor house by the lakefront, as well as four independent, kitchen-equipped cottages and guesthouses scattered across the property.

Burlington 3

✕ Penny Cluse Cafe — Cafe $

(📞802-651-8834; www.pennycluse.com; 169 Cherry St; mains $6-14; ⏰6:45am-3pm Mon-Fri, 8am-3pm Sat & Sun) In the heart of downtown, one of Burlington's most popular breakfast spots serves pancakes, biscuits and gravy, breakfast burritos, omelets and tofu scrambles, along with sandwiches, fish tacos, salads and the best chile relleno you'll find east of the Mississippi. Expect an hour's wait on weekends – best bet is to put your name down, grab a coffee and take a pre-meal wander.

✕ Citizen Cider — Microbrewery $

(📞802-497-1987; www.citizencider.com; 316 Pine St; ⏰11am-10pm Mon-Sat, to 7pm Sun) Tucked into an industrial-chic building with painted concrete floors and long wooden tables, this animated cidery is a homegrown success story, using only Vermont apples to make its ever-growing line of hard ciders. Taste-test a flight of five for $7, including perennial favorites such as the crisp, classic Unified Press, or the Dirty Mayor, infused with ginger and lemon peel.

✕ Revolution Kitchen — Vegan, Vegetarian $$

(📞802-448-3657; http://revolutionkitchen.com; 9 Center St; mains $14-18; ⏰5-10pm Tue-Sat; 🌱) Vegetarian fine dining? And romantic atmosphere to boot? Yep, they all come together at this cozy brick-walled restaurant that makes ample and creative use of Vermont's abundant organic produce. Asian, Mediterranean and Latin American influences abound in house favorites like Revolution Tacos, crispy seitan piccata and the Laksa Noodle Pot. Most items are (or can be adapted to be) vegan.

🛏 Willard Street Inn — Inn $$

(📞802-651-8710; www.willardstreetinn.com; 349 S Willard St; r $169-269; 📶) Perched on a hill within easy walking distance of UVM and the Church St Marketplace, this mansion, fusing Queen Anne and Georgian Revival styles, was built in the late 1880s. It has a fine-wood and cut-glass elegance, yet radiates a welcoming warmth. Many of the guest rooms overlook Lake Champlain.

Grand Isle 5

🛏 Grand Isle State Park — Campground $

(📞802-372-4300; www.vtstateparks.com; 36 E Shore South, Grand Isle; tent & RV sites $20-22, lean-tos $27-29, cabins $50; ⏰mid-May–mid-Oct) Vermont's most popular state park campground straddles a pretty stretch of Lake Champlain waterfront, with 117 tent and RV sites, 36 lean-tos and four cabins.

North Hero Island 6

🛏 North Hero House — Inn $$

(📞888-525-3644, 802-372-4732; www.northherohouse.com; 3643 US 2, North Hero; r $125-250, ste $295-350; 📶) This country inn sits right across from the water, with quilt-filled rooms, many with a private porch and four-poster bed. Eating options include a cozy restaurant serving New American cuisine, Oscar's Oasis pub and the fantastic outdoor Steamship Pier Bar & Grill, where you can enjoy kabobs, burgers, lobster rolls and cocktails smack on the pier, the water glistening beside you.

THE VERMONT
COUNTRY STORE
MAIL ORDER DELIVERY

Vermont's Spine: Route 100

Idyllic green landscapes, charming villages and scoops of America's most famous ice cream make this one of New England's most iconic road trips.

TRIP HIGHLIGHTS

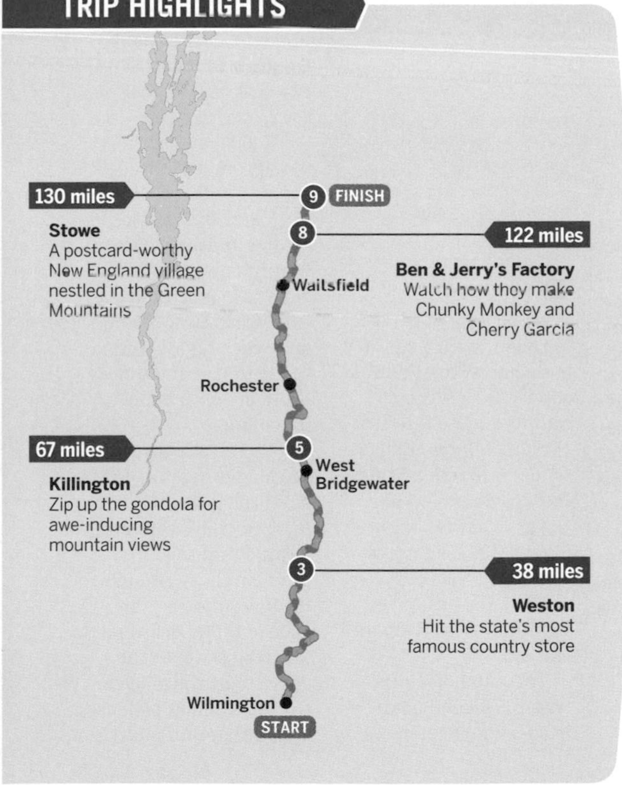

130 miles
9 FINISH
Stowe
A postcard-worthy New England village nestled in the Green Mountains

8
122 miles
Ben & Jerry's Factory
Watch how they make Chunky Monkey and Cherry Garcia

Waitsfield

Rochester

67 miles
5
Killington
Zip up the gondola for awe-inducing mountain views

West Bridgewater

3
38 miles
Weston
Hit the state's most famous country store

Wilmington
START

3–4 DAYS
130 MILES / 209KM

GREAT FOR...

BEST TIME TO GO

May to October for snow-free roads and sun-filled days.

ESSENTIAL PHOTO

The 360-degree views from the K1 Gondola above Killington.

BEST FOR FAMILIES

Poking around the Weston country store and taking a Ben & Jerry's Factory tour.

Weston Vermont Country Store

13

Vermont's Spine: Route 100

Spanning the state from bottom to top, Vermont's revered Route 100 winds past the Northeast's most legendary ski resorts and through some of New England's prettiest scenery, with the verdant Green Mountains always close at hand. This drive takes you on a slow meander through the state, though you might speed up in anticipation of the Ben & Jerry's Factory tour beckoning on the final stretch of road.

1 Wilmington

Chartered in 1751, Wilmington is the winter and summer gateway to Mt Snow, one of New England's best ski resorts and an excellent summertime mountain-biking and golfing spot. There are no main sights per se but the **Historic District** on W Main St is a prime example of 18th- and 19th-century architecture and is chock-full of restaurants and boutiques; the bulk of the village is on the National Register of Historic Places. This is an excellent base where you can stay overnight and grab a bite before your journey up north.

✕ p187

The Drive » Ski country (look for Mt Snow on your left) gives way to sleepy hamlets as you drive 26 miles north on VT 100 to the village of Jamaica.

2 Jamaica

A prime dose of rural Vermont, with a country store and several antique shops, this artsy community tucked into the evergreen forest is also home to **Jamaica State Park** (☎802-874-4600; www.vtstateparks.com; 48 Salmon Hole Lane, Jamaica; adult/child $4/2; ⏲mid-May–mid-Oct), the best place in Vermont for riverside camping.

The annual Whitewater Weekend held here in late September draws kayaking enthusiasts from all over New England to pit their skills against the rampaging West River. There's good swimming right in the heart of the campground, and walkers can also head 3 miles upstream along a 19th-century railway bed to **Hamilton Falls**, a 50ft ribbon of water cascading into a natural swimming hole.

The Drive » Continue north 17 miles on VT 100 to Weston.

TRIP HIGHLIGHT

3 Weston

Picturesque Weston is home to the **Vermont Country Store** (☎802-824-3184; www.vermontcountrystore.com; 657 Main St/VT 100; ⏲8:30am-7pm late May–mid-Oct, 9am-6pm rest of year), founded in 1946 and still going strong under the Orton family's ownership, four generations later. It's a time warp from a simpler era, when goods were made to last and quirky products with appeal had a home.

The eclectic mix filling the shelves today ranges from the genuinely useful (cozy old-fashioned flannel nighties) to the nostalgic (vintage tiddlywinks and the classic 1960s board game Mystery Date) to the downright weird (electronic yodeling pickles, anyone?). For a midtrip

pick-me-up, don't miss prowling through the vast array of traditional penny-candy jars and cases of Vermont cheese.

The Drive » Continue north on VT 100. At Plymouth Union, veer off to the right onto VT 100A for about a mile until you reach Plymouth Center. The total drive is 22 miles.

❹ Plymouth

Gazing across the high pastures of Plymouth, you feel a bit like Rip Van Winkle – only it's the past you've woken up to. President Calvin Coolidge's boyhood home looks much as it did a century ago, with houses, barns, a church, a one-room schoolhouse and a general store gracefully arrayed among old maples on a bucolic hillside. At Plymouth's heart is the preserved **President Calvin Coolidge State Historic Site** (☎802-672-3773;

LINK YOUR TRIP

3 Finger Lakes Loop
From Wilmington, drive west across the border into New York, then pick up I-88 to Ithaca.

10 Fall Foliage Tour
Drive west from Rte 100 to pick up the Fall Foliage Tour at Manchester or Lake Champlain.

http://historicsites.vermont.gov; 3780 Rte 100A, Plymouth Notch; adult/child $9/2; ⌚9:30am-5pm late May–mid-Oct). The village's streets are sleepy today, but the museum tells a tale of an earlier America filled with elbow grease and perseverance. Tools for blacksmithing, woodworking, butter making and hand laundering are indicative of the hard work and grit it took to wrest a living from Vermont's stony pastures. As a boy, Calvin hayed with his grandfather and kept the wood box filled.

Originally cofounded by Coolidge's father, the **Plymouth Artisan Cheese company** (☎802-672-3650; www.plymouthartisancheese.com; 106 Messer Hill Rd, Plymouth; ⌚10am-5pm Jun-Oct, to 4pm Nov-May) still produces a classic farmhouse cheddar known as granular curd cheese. Its distinctively sharp tang and grainy texture are reminiscent of the wheel cheese traditionally found at general stores throughout Vermont. Panels downstairs tell the history of local cheese making, while a museum upstairs displays cheese-making equipment from another era.

The Drive » Drive back along VT 100A and turn right to return to VT 100 N. The drive is 13 miles.

TRIP HIGHLIGHT

5 Killington

The largest ski resort in the east, Killington spans seven mountains,

KYLE SPARKS / GETTY IMAGES ©

DETOUR: MIDDLEBURY & LINCOLN GAPS

Start: 6 Rochester

The 'gap roads' that run east–west over the Green Mountains offer some of the most picturesque views of the region. Ready to explore? Four miles north of Rochester, in Hancock, scenic VT 125 splits west off of VT 100 and climbs over **Middlebury Gap**. Stops to look out for as you make the 15-mile crossing from Hancock to East Middlebury include beautiful **Texas Falls** (3 miles from Hancock), Middlebury Gap (6 miles), and the **Robert Frost Interpretive Trail**, an easygoing loop trail enlivened by plaques featuring Frost's poetry (10 miles).

For a scenic loop back to the main route, continue west on VT 125 to East Middlebury, then take VT 116 north. Soon after crossing through the pretty village of **Bristol**, turn right on Lincoln Gap Rd and follow it 14 miles east to rejoin the main route at Warren.

The return trip also offers some nice stops. As you turn onto Lincoln Gap Rd, look for the parked cars at **Bartlett Falls**, where the New Haven River's raging waters cascade into one of Vermont's most pristine swimming holes. Later, after a crazy-steep climb (partly unpaved) to **Lincoln Gap**, stop at the 2428ft summit for lovely views and some nice trails, including the 5-mile round trip to the 4000ft summit of **Mt Abraham**.

Killington Snowboarding down a glade

highlighted by 4241ft **Killington Peak**, the second highest in Vermont. It operates the largest snow-making system in North America and its numerous outdoor activities – from skiing and snowboarding in winter to mountain biking and hiking in summer – are all centrally located on the mountain. **Killington Resort** (☎info 800-734-9435, reservations 800-621-6867; www.killington.com; 4763 Killington Rd; lift tickets adult/teen/senior $105/89/81), the East Coast's answer to Vail, runs the efficient **K1-Express Gondola**, which in winter transports up to 3000 skiers per hour in heated cars along a 2.5-mile cable – it's the highest lift in Vermont. In summer and fall it whisks you to impeccable vantage points above the mountains: leaf-peeping atop the cascading rainbow of copper, red and gold in foliage season is truly magical.

The Drive » Enter the idyllic valley of the White River as you drive 24 miles north on VT 100 to Rochester.

6 Rochester

This unassuming blink-and-you'll-miss-it town, with a vast village green lined by well-maintained, historic New England homes, is worth a stop to experience rural Vermont life minus the masses of tourists in other towns along VT 100.

Stop in at **Sandy's Books & Bakery** (☎802-767-4258; www.seasonedbooks.com; 30 North Main St; baked goods & light meals $3-10; ⏰7:30am-6pm Mon-Sat, to 2pm Sun; 📶), a cafe, bookstore and popular local hangout. With homemade everything – granola, bagels, whole-wheat bread – Sandy's serves up mean dishes such as spinach-and-egg-filled biscuits, spanakopita, salads and soups. Tables are scattered between bookshelves, so it's a great spot for a java break and a browse of the new and used books (or the locally made Vermont soap). We dare you to resist the cookies.

p187

The Drive » Continue on VT 100 N. Roughly 10 miles past Rochester, the road enters a narrow and wild corridor of protected land. A little pullout on the left provides viewing access to pretty Moss Glen Falls. A mile or so later, the small ponds of Granville Gulf comprise one of the state's most accessible moose-watching spots (the best chance of seeing these big critters is at dawn or dusk). After 5 miles further north, turn right onto Covered Bridge Rd and cross the bridge into Warren village.

7 Warren & Mad River Valley

This sweet village is the southern gateway into Vermont's picturesque Mad River Valley. The river is popular with swimmers and kayakers, while the surrounding mountains are a mecca for skiers, who flock to the slopes at nearby **Sugarbush** (802-583-6300, 800-537-8427; www.sugarbush.com; 102 Forrest Dr, Warren; lift tickets adult/child $97/77) and **Mad River Glen** (802-496-3551; www.madriverglen.com; VT 17, Waitsfield; lift tickets adult/child weekend $79/63, midweek $65/60).

JIAWANGKUN / SHUTTERSTOCK ©

Stop in at the **Warren Store** (802-496-3864; www.warrenstore.com; 284 Main St, Warren; sandwiches & light meals $5-9; 7:45am-7pm Mon-Sat, to 6pm Sun) in the village center, an animated community hangout with wavy 19th-century wood floors, a deli serving gourmet sandwiches and pastries, and a front porch ideal for sipping coffee while poring over the *New York Times*. The store upstairs sells an eclectic mix of jewelry, toys, Vermont

DETOUR: VERMONT ICELANDIC HORSE FARM

Start: 7 Warren

Icelandic horses are one of the oldest, and some say most versatile, breeds in the world. They're also friendly and affectionate creatures, and are fairly easy to ride even for novices – they tend to stop and think (rather than panic) if something frightens them. The **Vermont Icelandic Horse Farm** (802-496-7141; www.icelandichorses.com; 3061 N Fayston Rd, Waitsfield; 1-3hr rides $60-120, full day incl lunch $220, multiday treks $675-1695; by appointment;), 3 miles west of VT 100 (where the tarmac ends and becomes a dirt road), takes folks on one- to three-hour or full-day jaunts year-round; it also offers two- to five-day inn-to-inn treks (some riding experience required). The farm also runs **Mad River Inn** (802-496-7900, 800-832-8278; www.madriverinn.com; Tremblay Rd, Waitsfield; r incl breakfast & afternoon tea $115-185;), a short trot away.

Head 9 miles north of Warren on VT 100 and follow the signs to the horse farm.

Waterbury Ben & Jerry's Factory

casual clothing and knick-knacks, while the sundeck below overlooks a pretty swimming hole framed by sculpted granite rocks.

p187

The Drive » Continue north 20 miles on VT 100 through pretty farm country to Waterbury, then follow signs for Stowe, crossing the overpass over I-89 to reach Ben & Jerry's.

TRIP HIGHLIGHT

8 Ben & Jerry's

No trip to Vermont would be complete without a visit to the **Ben & Jerry's Factory** (802-882-2047; www.benjerrys.com; 1281 VT 100, Waterbury; adult/child under 13yr $4/free; 9am-9pm Jul–mid-Aug, to 7pm mid-Aug–mid-Oct, 10am-6pm mid-Oct–Jun;), the biggest production center for America's most famous ice cream. Sure, the manufacturing process is interesting, but a visit to the factory also explains how school pals Ben and Jerry went from a $5 ice-cream-making correspondence course to a global enterprise, and offers a glimpse of the fun, in-your-face culture that made these frozen-dessert pioneers so successful. You're treated to a (very) small free taste at the end – if you need a larger dose make a beeline for the on-site scoop shop.

Quaintly perched on a knoll overlooking the parking lot, the Ben & Jerry's Flavor Graveyard's neat rows of headstones pay silent tribute to flavors that flopped, like Makin' Whoopie Pie and Dastardly Mash. Each memorial is lovingly inscribed with the flavor's brief

COVERED BRIDGES OF MONTGOMERY

A 38-mile drive north from Stowe via VT 100 and VT 118 takes you to the covered-bridge capital of Vermont. In an idyllic valley at the confluence of multiple watersheds, the twin villages of Montgomery and Montgomery Center share seven spans crisscrossing the local rivers. Especially beautiful – though challenging to find – is remote Creamery Bridge just off Hill West Rd, which straddles a waterfall with a swimming hole at its base.

life span on the grocery store of this earth and a poem in tribute. Rest in Peace, Holy Cannoli (1997–98)! Adieu, Miss Jelena's Sweet Potato Pie (1992–93)!

The Drive » Wipe that ice-cream smile off your face and replace it with an ear-to-ear grin as you ascend 9 miles up VT 100 to the legendary ski village of Stowe.

❾ Stowe

In a cozy valley where the West Branch River flows into the Little River and mountains rise to the sky in all directions, the quintessential Vermont village of Stowe (founded in 1794) bustles quietly. Nestled in the Green Mountain National Forest, the highest point in Vermont, **Mt Mansfield** (4393ft) towers in the background, juxtaposed against the pencil-thin steeple of Stowe's Community Church, creating *the* classic Vermont picture-postcard scene.

With more than 200 miles of cross-country ski trails, some of the finest mountain biking and downhill skiing in the east and world-class hiking, this is a natural mecca for adrenaline junkies and active families. If shopping and cafe-hopping are more your style, the village center also makes a delightful spot for a leisurely stroll. In addition to winter snow sports, **Stowe Mountain Resort** (☎888-253-4849, 802-253-3000; www.stowe.com; 5781 Mountain Rd; lift tickets adult/child $124/104) opens from spring through to fall with **gondola sky rides**, an **alpine slide** and a scenic auto **toll road** that zigzags to the top of Mt Mansfield.

If *The Sound of Music* is one of your favorite things, the hilltop Trapp Family Lodge (p187) boasts sprawling views and oodles of activities, such as hiking, horse-drawn sleigh and carriage rides, lodge tours detailing the family history (often led by a member of the Trapp family), summer concerts on their meadow and some frothy goodness at the on-site Trapp Family Brewery.

✕ 🛏 p187

Eating & Sleeping

Wilmington ❶

Wahoo's Eatery American **$**

(☎802-464-0110; www.wahooseatery.com; VT 9; sandwiches & salads $6-9; ⊙11am-8pm mid-May–mid-Sep) 'We welcome your business and relish your buns': so reads the sign at this friendly, family-run roadside snack shack less than a mile east of Wilmington on VT 9. A long-standing local institution, it whips up quality burgers ($2 extra for grass-fed Vermont beef), along with hand-cut fries, handmade conch fritters, wraps, sandwiches, hot dogs, salads and ice cream.

Rochester ❻

Liberty Hill Farm B&B **$$**

(☎802-767-3926; www.libertyhillfarm.com; 511 Liberty Hill Rd, Rochester; r incl dinner & breakfast per adult/teen/child $139/82/65) With its magnificent red barn and White River Valley panoramas, this working farm just south of Rochester is a Vermont classic. Overnight stays include dinner and breakfast, served family-style and making ample use of produce from the on-site garden. Other highlights include lounging on the front porch, getting to know the farm animals and sampling the farm's ultra-fresh dairy products.

Warren & Mad River Valley ❼

Peasant Modern American **$$**

(☎802-496-6856; www.peasantvt.com; 40 Bridge St, Waitsfield; mains $23-28; ⊙5:30-9pm Thu-Mon) Living up to its tagline 'a simple feast,' Peasant delivers seasonal farm-to-table treats that can vary from hearty cassoulet in the dead of winter to maple-glazed salmon with locally grown veggies in summer, all complemented by an ample choice of beer, wine and cocktails. Look for it in a cozy slate-blue house in the village center.

Inn at Round Barn Farm Inn **$$$**

(☎802-496-2276; www.roundbarninn.com; 1661 E Warren Rd, Waitsfield; r incl breakfast $179-359;) This place gets its name from the adjacent 1910 round barn – among the few authentic examples remaining in Vermont. The decidedly upscale inn has antique-furnished rooms with mountain views, gas fireplaces, canopy beds and antiques. All overlook the meadows and mountains. In winter guests leave their shoes at the door to preserve the hardwood floors. The country-style breakfast is huge.

Stowe ❾

Hen of the Wood Modern American **$$$**

(☎802-244-7300; www.henofthewood.com; 92 Stowe St, Waterbury; mains $25-33; ⊙5-9pm Tue-Sat) Arguably the finest dining in northern Vermont, this chef-driven restaurant, set in a historic grist mill in Waterbury, gets rave reviews for its innovative farm-to-table cuisine. The ambience is as fine as the food, which features densely flavored dishes like smoked duck breast and sheep's-milk gnocchi.

Trapp Family Lodge Lodge **$$$**

(☎800-826-7000, 802-253-8511; www.trappfamily.com; 700 Trapp Hill Rd; r $225-430, ste $375-630; @) With wide-open fields and mountain vistas, this hilltop lodge 3km southwest of town boasts Stowe's best setting. The Austrian-style chalet, built by Maria von Trapp of *Sound of Music* fame, houses traditional lodge rooms. Alternatively, you can rent one of the modern villas or cozy guesthouses scattered across the property. The 2700-acre spread offers stupendous hiking, snowshoeing and cross-country skiing.

Ivy League Tour

This trip celebrates history and education as it rolls between New England's Ivies, where campus tours sneak behind the gates for an up-close look at the USA's greatest universities.

TRIP HIGHLIGHTS

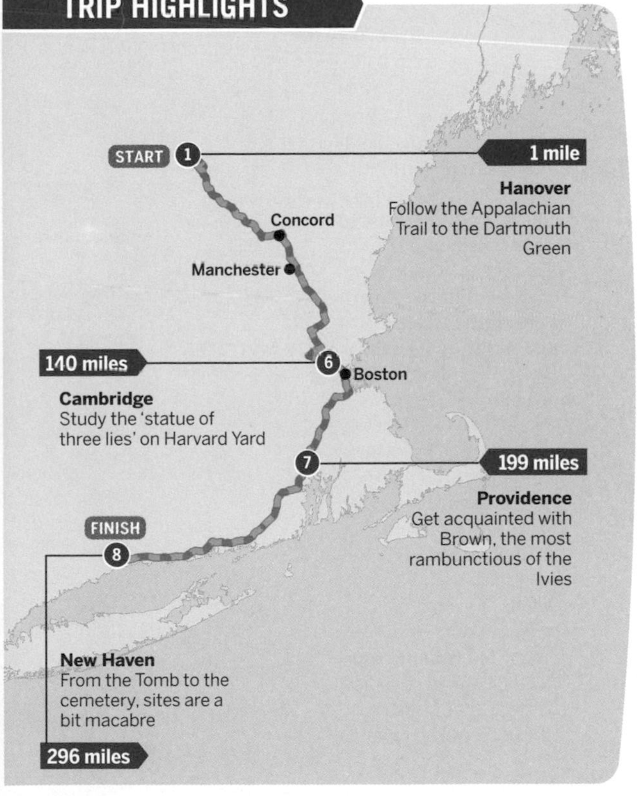

START 1 — 1 mile

Hanover
Follow the Appalachian Trail to the Dartmouth Green

Concord

Manchester

140 miles — 6

Boston

Cambridge
Study the 'statue of three lies' on Harvard Yard

7 — 199 miles

Providence
Get acquainted with Brown, the most rambunctious of the Ivies

FINISH 8

New Haven
From the Tomb to the cemetery, sites are a bit macabre

296 miles

5 DAYS
296 MILES / 476KM

GREAT FOR...

BEST TIME TO GO

Catch student-filled campuses from September to November.

ESSENTIAL PHOTO

Stand beside the statue of John Harvard, the man who didn't found Harvard.

BEST HISTORY

Learn about the USA's oldest university during a Harvard tour.

Cambridge, MA Memorial Hall at Harvard University

14 Ivy League Tour

What's most surprising about a tour of the Ivy League? The distinct personalities of the different campuses, which are symbiotically fused with their surrounding landscapes. Compare fresh-faced Dartmouth, with its breezy embrace of New Hampshire's outdoors, to enclaved Yale, its Gothic buildings fortressed against the urban wilds of New Haven. But the schools all share one trait – vibrant, diverse and engaged students who dispel any notions that they're out-of-touch elites.

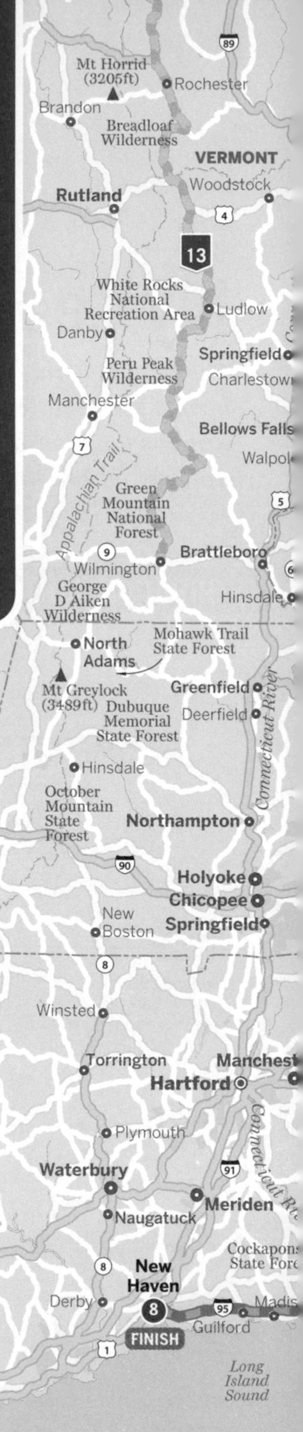

TRIP HIGHLIGHT

1 Hanover, New Hampshire

When the first big snowfall hits **Dartmouth College** (☎603-646-1110; www.dartmouth.edu), an email blasts across campus, calling everyone to the central **Green** for a midnight snowball fight. The Green is also the site of elaborate ice sculptures during Dartmouth's **Winter Carnival** (www.dartmouth.edu; ⏲Feb), a weeklong celebration that's been held annually for more than 100 years.

North of the Green is **Baker Berry Library** (☎603-646-2560; http://dartmouth.edu; 25 N Main St; ⏲8am-2am Mon-Fri, 10am-2am Sat & Sun), which holds an impressive mural called *The Epic of American Civilization*. Painted by Jose Clemente Orozco, it traces the course of civilization in the Americas from the Aztec era to modern times. At 4pm, stop by the adjacent **Sanborn Library** (Dartmouth College; ⏲8am-midnight daily, teatime 4pm Mon-Fri), where tea is served during the academic year for 10¢. This tradition honors a 19th-century English professor who invited students for chats and afternoon tea. For a free student-led **walking tour** (☎603-646-2875; http://dartmouth.edu; 6016 McNutt Hall, 10 N Main St) of the campus, stop by the admissions office on the 2nd floor of McNutt Hall on the west side of the Green. Call or check online to confirm departure times.

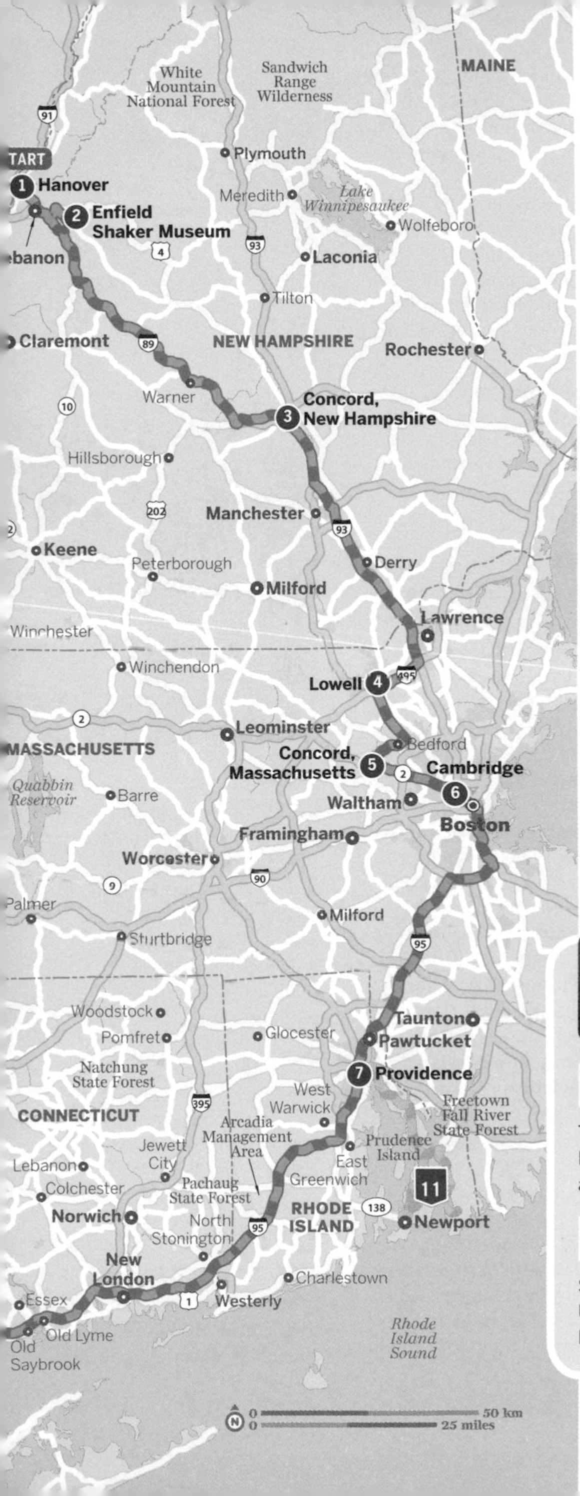

Dartmouth's **Hood Museum of Art** (☎603-646-2808; http://hoodmuseum.dartmouth.edu; 6 E Wheelock St; ⏲10am-5pm Tue & Thu-Sat, to 9pm Wed, noon-5pm Sun) which includes nearly 70,000 items, is closed for restoration through early 2019. The collection is particularly strong in American pieces, including Native American art. A highlight is a set of Assyrian reliefs dating to the 9th century BC.

From the museum, turn left onto E Wheelock St and walk toward the Hanover Inn. You'll soon cross the **Appalachian Trail**, which runs through downtown. From here, it's 431 miles to Mt Katahdin in Maine.

✕ p197

LINK YOUR TRIP

11 Rhode Island: East Bay

Take a detour from Providence for a drive around the East Bay.

13 Vermont's Spine: Route 100

South of Hanover, take US 4 west to hook up with Rte 100 near Killington.

The Drive » From Hanover, follow NH 120 E to I-89 S. Take exit 117 to NH 4 E, following it to NH 4A. Turn right and follow NH 4A 3.5 miles to the museum.

2 Enfield Shaker Museum

The Enfield Shaker site sits in stark contrast to today's college campuses. In fact, the two couldn't be more different – except for the required communal housing with a bunch of nonrelatives. But a trip here is illuminating. Set in a valley overlooking Mascoma Lake, the Enfield Shaker site dates to the late 18th century. At its peak, some 300 members lived in Enfield. Farmers and craftspeople, they built impressive wood and brick buildings and took in converts, orphans and children of the poor – essential for the Shaker future since sex was not allowed in the pacifist, rule-abiding community. By the early 1900s the community had gone into decline and the last family left in 1917.

The **museum** (603-632-4346; www.shakermuseum.org; 447 NH 4A, Enfield; adult/child/youth $12/3/8; 10am-4pm Mon-Sat, noon-4pm Sun Apr–late Dec) centers on the Great Stone Dwelling, the largest Shaker dwelling house ever built. You can also explore the gardens and grounds. The guide might even let you ring the rooftop bell. Spend the night on the 3rd and 4th floor of the building; **accommodations** (603-632-4346; www.shakermuseum.org/staywithus.htm; 447 NH 4A, Enfield; s/d/tr $110/135/160;) feature traditional Shaker furniture, but not phones or TVs, although there is wi-fi.

The Drive » Return to I-89 S. After 54 miles, take I-93 N 3 miles to exit 15E for I-393 E. From there, take exit 1 and follow the signs.

3 Concord, New Hampshire

ZACK FRANK / SHUTTERSTOCK ©

New Hampshire's capital is a trim and tidy city with a wide Main St dominated by the striking **State House** (603-271-2154; www.gencourt.state.nh.us; 107 N Main St; 8am-4pm Mon-Fri), a granite-hewed 19th-century edifice topped with a glittering dome.

Nearby, the New Hampshire schoolteacher Christa McAuliffe, chosen to be America's first teacher-astronaut, is honored at the **McAuliffe-Shepard Discovery Center** (603-271-7827; www.starhop.com; 2 Institute Dr; adult/child $10/7; 10:30am-4pm daily mid-Jun–early Sep, Fri-Sun rest of year). She died in the *Challenger* explosion on January 28, 1986. The museum also honors New Hampshire native Alan B Shepard, a member of NASA's elite *Mercury* corps who became America's first astronaut in 1961. Intriguing exhibits chronicle their lives and spotlight aviation, and earth and space sciences. There's also a planetarium.

p197

The Drive » Return to I-93 S, passing through Manchester before entering Massachusetts. Follow I-495 S toward Lowell.

4 Lowell, Massachusetts

In the early 19th century, textile mills in Lowell churned out cloth by the

Concord, NH State House

mile, driven by the abundant waterpower of Pawtucket Falls. Today, the historic buildings in the city center – connected by the trolley and canal boats – comprise the Lowell National Historic Park, which gives a fascinating peek at the workings of a 19th-century industrial town. Stop first at the **Market Mills Visitors Center** (☎978-970-5000; www.nps.gov/lowe; 246 Market St; ⌚9am-5pm late May–early Oct) to pick up a map and check out the general exhibits. Five blocks northeast along the river, the **Boott Cotton Mills Museum** (☎978-970-5000; www.nps.gov/lowe; 115 John St; adult/child $6/3; ⌚9:30am-5pm late May–early Oct; 👪) has exhibits that chronicle the rise and fall of the industrial revolution in Lowell, including technological changes, labor movements and immigration. The highlight is a working weave room, with 88 power looms. A special exhibit on **Mill Girls & Immigrants** (40 French St; ⌚1:30-5pm late May–early Oct, from 11am mid-Jun–early Sep) examines the lives of working people, while seasonal exhibits are sometimes on display in other historic buildings around town.

The Drive » Take the Lowell Connector to US 3 heading south. In Billerica, exit to Concord Rd. Continue south on Concord Rd (MA 62) through Bedford. This road becomes Monument St and terminates at Monument Sq in Concord center. Walden Pond is about 3 miles south of Monument Sq, along Walden St (MA 126) south of MA 2.

⑤ Concord, Massachusetts

Tall, white church steeples rise above ancient oaks in Colonial Concord, giving the town a stateliness that belies the American Revolution drama that occurred centuries ago. It is easy to see how so many writers found their inspiration here in the 1800s.

Ralph Waldo Emerson was the paterfamilias of literary Concord and the founder of the transcendentalist movement (and, incidentally, a graduate of Harvard College). His home of nearly 50 years, the **Ralph Waldo Emerson Memorial House** (☎978-369-2236; www.facebook.com/EmersonHouseConcord; 28 Cambridge Turnpike; adult/child $9/7; ⏰10am-4:30pm Thu-Sat, 1-4:30pm Sun mid-Apr–Oct), often hosted his renowned circle of friends.

One of them was Henry David Thoreau (another Harvard grad), who put transcendentalist beliefs into practice when he spent two years in a rustic cabin on the shores of **Walden Pond** (☎978-369-3254; www.mass.gov/dcr; 915 Walden St; parking $15; ⏰dawn-dusk). The glacial pond is now a state park, surrounded by acres of forest. A footpath circles the pond, leading to the site of Thoreau's cabin on the northeast side.

The Drive » Take MA 2 east to its terminus in Cambridge. Go left on the Alewife Brook Pkwy (MA 16), then right on Massachusetts Ave and into Harvard Sq. Parking spaces are in short supply, but you can usually find one on the streets around the Cambridge Common.

TRIP HIGHLIGHT

6 Cambridge, Massachusetts

Founded in 1636 to educate men for the ministry, Harvard is America's oldest **college** (www.harvard.edu; Massachusetts Ave; tours free). The geographic heart of the university – where red-brick buildings and leaf-covered paths exude academia – is **Harvard Yard**. For maximum visual impact, enter the yard through the wrought-iron Johnston Gate, which is flanked by the two oldest buildings on campus, **Harvard Hall** and **Massachusetts Hall**.

The focal point of the yard is the **John Harvard statue**, by Daniel Chester French. Inscribed 'John Harvard, Founder of Harvard College, 1638,' it is commonly known as the 'statue of three lies': John Harvard was *not* the college's founder but its first benefactor; Harvard was actually founded in 1636; and the man depicted isn't even Mr Harvard himself! This symbol hardly lives up to the university's motto, *Veritas* (truth).

Most Harvard hopefuls rub the statue's shiny foot for good luck; little do they know that campus pranksters regularly use the foot like dogs use a fire hydrant.

So, what's the best thing about Harvard University? The architecture?

WALTER BIBIKOW / GETTY IMAGES ©

ALL ABOUT HAAAHHHVAAAHHHD

Want to know more? Get the inside scoop from savvy students on the unofficial **Hahvahd Tour** (Trademark Tours; ☎855-455-8747; www.harvardtour.com; tickets purchased on-site adult or child $12, online adult/child $9.95/8.50).

Providence Brown University

The history? Arguably, it's the location. Overflowing with coffeehouses and pubs, bookstores and record stores, street musicians and sidewalk artists, panhandlers and professors, **Harvard Square** exudes energy, creativity and nonconformity – and it's all packed into a handful of streets between the university and the river. Spend an afternoon browsing bookstores, riffling through records and trying on vintage clothing; then camp out in a local cafe.

p197

The Drive » Hop on Memorial Dr and drive east along the Charles River. At Western Ave, cross the river and follow the signs to I-90 E (toll road). Cruise through the tunnel (product of the notorious Big Dig) and merge with I-93 S. Follow I-93 S to I-95 S. Take I-95 S to Providence.

TRIP HIGHLIGHT

7 Providence, Rhode Island

College Hill rises east of the Providence River, and atop it sits **Brown University** (401-863-1000; www.brown.edu), the rambunctious younger child of an uptight New England household. Big brothers Harvard and Yale carefully manicure their public image, while the little black sheep of the family prides itself on staunch liberalism. Founded in 1764, Brown was the first American college to accept students regardless of religious affiliation, and the first to appoint an African American woman, Ruth Simmons, as president in 2001. Of its small 700-strong faculty, five Brown professors, and two alumni, have been honored as Nobel laureates.

The campus, consisting of 235 buildings, is divided into the Main Green and Lincoln Field. Enter through the wrought-iron **Van Wickle Gates** on College St. The oldest building on the campus is **University Hall**, a 1770 brick edifice, which was used as a barracks during the Revolutionary War. Free tours of the campus begin from the **Brown University Admissions Office** (☎401-863-2378; www.brown.edu/admission; Corliss Brackett House, 45 Prospect St).

✕ 🛏 p169, p197

The Drive » Take Memorial Blvd out of Providence and merge with I-95 S. The generally pleasant tree-lined interstate will take you around the periphery of Groton, Old Lyme, Guilford and Madison, where you may want to stop for a coffee or snack. Exit at junction 47 for downtown New Haven.

TRIP HIGHLIGHT

8 New Haven, Connecticut

Gorgeous, Gothic Yale University is America's third-oldest university. Head to the **Yale University Visitor Center** (☎203-432-2300; http://visitorcenter.yale.edu; 149 Elm St; ⌚9am-4:30pm Mon-Fri, 11am-4pm Sat & Sun) to pick up a free map or take a free one-hour tour.

The tour does a good job of fusing historical and academic facts and passes by several standout monuments, including Yale's tallest building, **Harkness Tower**. Guides refrain, however, from mentioning the tombs scattered around the campus. No, these aren't filled with corpses; they're secret hangouts for senior students. The most notorious tomb is the HQ for the **Skull & Bones Club** (64 High St), founded in 1832. Its list of members reads like a who's who of high-powered politicos and financiers over the last two centuries.

New Haven's spacious **green** has been the spiritual center of the city since its Puritan fathers designed it in 1638 as the prospective site for Christ's second coming. Since then it has held the municipal burial grounds – graves were later moved to Grove St Cemetery – several statehouses and an array of churches, three of which still stand.

✕ 🛏 p151, p197

Eating & Sleeping

Hanover, NH ❶

Lou's Diner $

(603-643-3321; www.lousrestaurant.net; 30 S Main St; mains $9-15; 6am-3pm Mon-Fri, 7am-3pm Sat & Sun) A Dartmouth institution since 1947, this is Hanover's oldest establishment, always packed with students meeting for a coffee or perusing their books. From the retro tables or the Formica-topped counter, order typical diner food like eggs, sandwiches and burgers. Breakfast is served all day, and the bakery items are highly recommended (the bakery is open till 5pm, Monday to Saturday).

Concord, NH ❸

Granite Modern American $$

(603-227-9005; www.graniterestaurant.com; 96 Pleasant St; lunch mains $11-19, dinner mains $15-34; 7-10am, 11:30am-2:30pm & 5-9pm Mon-Thu, to 10pm Fri & Sat, 7am-2:30pm & 5-8pm Sun) In a grand turreted Victorian building, Granite serves fine New American cuisine all day long, from breakfasts of smoked turkey and sweet potato hash, to crab cake BLTs with lemon-basil aioli at lunchtime, to braised rabbit stroganoff for dinner.

Cambridge, MA ❻

Café Pamplona Cafe $

(www.cafepamplona.weebly.com; 12 Bow St; 11am-11pm;) Located in a cozy cellar on a backstreet, this no-frills European cafe is the choice among old-time Cantabrigians. In addition to tea and coffee drinks, Pamplona has light snacks, such as gazpacho, sandwiches and biscotti. The tiny outdoor terrace is a delight in summer.

Irving House at Harvard Guesthouse $$

(617-547-4600; www.irvinghouse.com; 24 Irving St; r with/without bath from $255/155; P) Call it a big inn or a homey hotel, this property welcomes the world-weariest of travelers. The 44 rooms range in size, but every bed is covered with a quilt, and big windows let in plenty of light. There is a bistro-style atmosphere in the brick-lined basement, where you can browse books, plan your travels or munch on a free continental breakfast.

Providence, RI ❼

Louis Family Restaurant Diner $

(401-861-5225; www.louisrestaurant.org; 286 Brook St; mains $4-9; 5am-3pm;) Wake up early to watch bleary-eyed students and carpenters eat strawberry-banana pancakes and drink drip coffee at their favorite greasy spoon long before the rest of College Hill shows signs of life.

New Haven, CT ❽

Frank Pepe Pizza $

(203-865-5762; www.pepespizzeria.com; 157 Wooster St; pizzas $7-29; 10:30am-10pm Sun-Thu, to 11pm Fri & Sat;) Pepe's lays claim to baking the 'best pizza in America,' a title it's won three times running. We'll let you be the judge, but can confirm this joint cranks out tasty pies fired in a coal oven, just as it has since 1925; only now it has a bunch of other locations across Connecticut, making consistency harder to master. The white-clam pizza is the pie the people praise. Cash only.

New Haven Hotel Hotel $$

(800-644-6835; www.newhavenhotel.com; 229 George St; d from $169) This robust downtown hotel is both simply stylish and affordable. It's nice to see a private operator raising the bar. The hotel occupies a handsome mid-last-century brick building with bright, modern common areas, while guest rooms are airy with large windows, clean lines, dark woods and sink-into-me bedding. Reasonable rates mean it's understandably popular. Book in advance.

Acadia Byway

For adventurers, Mt Desert Island is hard to beat. Mountain hiking. Coastal kayaking. Woodland biking. Bird-watching. When you're done exploring, unwind by stargazing on the beach.

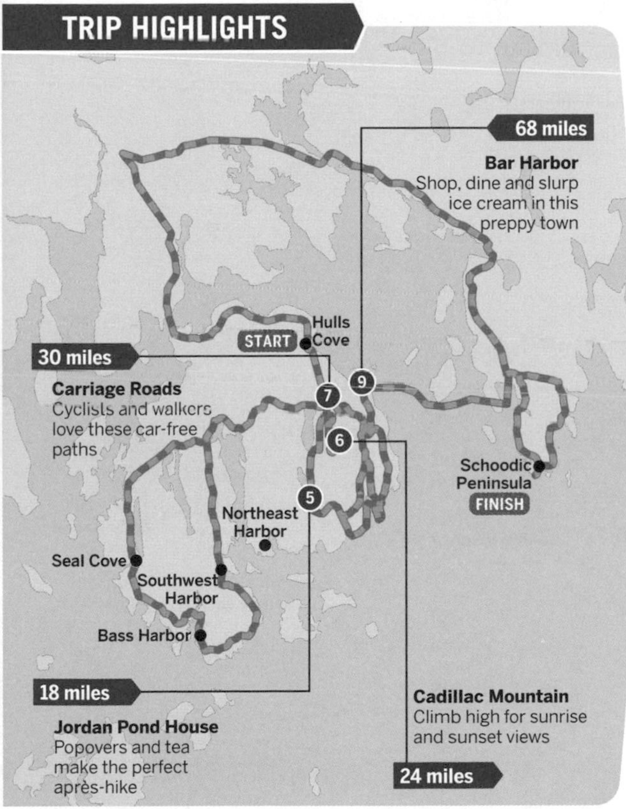

TRIP HIGHLIGHTS

68 miles
Bar Harbor
Shop, dine and slurp ice cream in this preppy town

Hulls Cove
START

30 miles
Carriage Roads
Cyclists and walkers love these car-free paths

9
7
6
5

Schoodic Peninsula
FINISH

Northeast Harbor

Seal Cove

Southwest Harbor

Bass Harbor

18 miles
Jordan Pond House
Popovers and tea make the perfect après-hike

Cadillac Mountain
Climb high for sunrise and sunset views
24 miles

3 DAYS
112 MILES / 180KM

GREAT FOR...

BEST TIME TO GO

May through October for good weather and open facilities.

ESSENTIAL PHOTO

Capture that sea-and-sunrise panorama from atop Cadillac Mountain.

BEST FOR OUTDOORS

Hike a 'ladder trail' up a challenging cliff.

Acadia National Park Sublime lake views

15 Acadia Byway

Drivers and hikers alike can thank John D Rockefeller Jr and other wealthy landowners for the aesthetically pleasing bridges, overlooks and stone steps that give Acadia National Park its artistic oomph. Rockefeller worked diligently with architects and masons to ensure that the infrastructure complemented the surrounding landscape. Today, you tour the wonderful Park Loop Rd by car, but be sure to explore on foot and by bike wherever you can.

❶ Hulls Cove Visitor Center

Whoa, whoa, whoa. Before zooming into Bar Harbor on ME 3, stop at the **park visitor center** (☎207-288-8832; www.nps.gov/acad; ME 3; ⌚8:30am-4:30pm mid-Apr–Jun, Sep & Oct, 8am-6pm Jul & Aug) to get the lay of the land and pay the admission fee. Inside, head directly to the large diorama, which provides a helpful overview of Mt Desert Island (MDI). As you'll see, Acadia National Park shares the island with

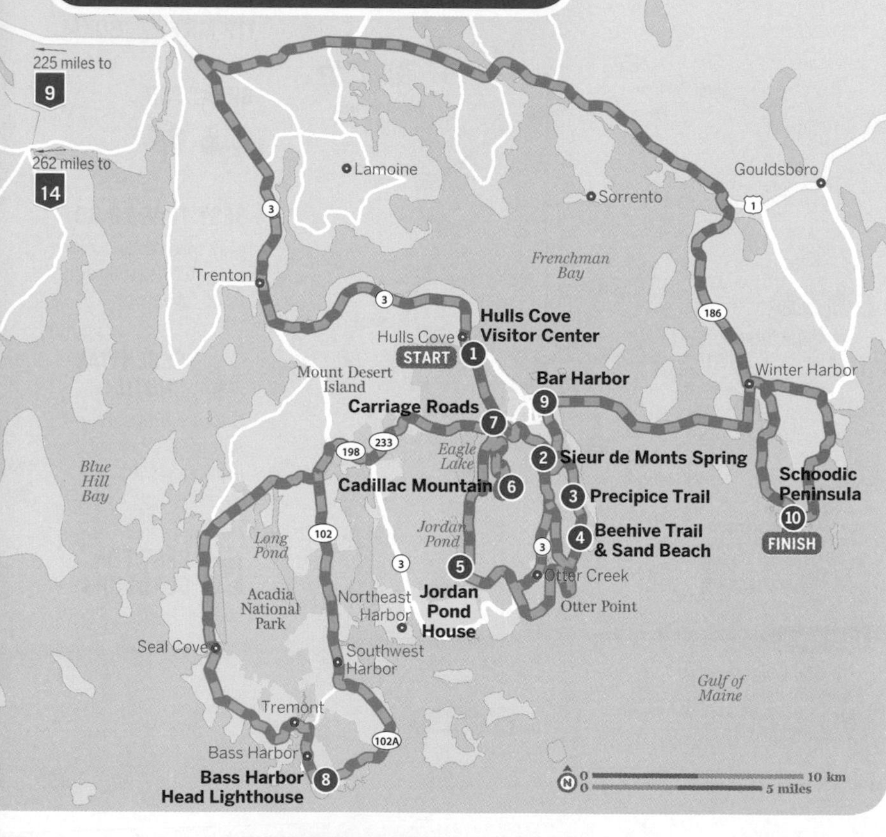

several nonpark communities, which are tucked here and there beside Acadia's borders.

From the visitor center, the best initiation to the park is to drive the 27-mile **Park Loop Road**, which links the park's highlights in the eastern section of MDI. It's one way (traveling clockwise) for most of its length.

The Drive » From the visitor center, turn right onto the Park Loop Rd, not ME 3 (which leads into Bar Harbor). Take in a nice view of Frenchman Bay on your left before passing the spur to ME 233. A short distance ahead, turn left to begin the one-way loop on Park Loop Rd

2 Sieur de Monts Spring

Nature-lovers and history buffs will enjoy a stop at the Sieur de Monts Spring area at the intersection of ME 3 and the Park Loop Rd. Here you'll find a nature center and the summer-only branch of the **Abbe Museum** (207-288-3519; www.abbemuseum.org; ME 3 & Park Loop Rd; adult/child $3/1; 10am-5pm late May–Oct), which sits in a lush, naturelike setting. Twelve of Acadia's biospheres are displayed in miniature at the **Wild Gardens of Acadia** (Park Loop Rd & ME 3), from bog to coniferous woods to meadow. Botany enthusiasts will appreciate the plant labels. There are also some amazing stone-step trails here, appearing out of the talus as if by magic.

The Drive » If you wish to avoid driving the full park loop, you can follow ME 3 from here into Bar Harbor. Push on for the full experience – you won't regret it.

LINK YOUR TRIP

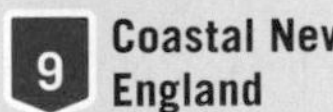

9 Coastal New England

For more scenes from Coastal New England, head south on I-95 to Gloucester.

14 Ivy League Tour

Take I-95 south to Augusta, then head west into New Hampshire. Take I-93 north and I-91 south to Hanover.

3 Precipice Trail

What's the most exciting way to get a bird's-eye view of the park? By climbing up to where the birds are. Two 'ladder trails' cling to the sides of exposed cliffs on the northeastern section of Park Loop Rd, dubbed Ocean Dr. If you're fit and the season's right, tackle the first of the ladder trails, the steep, challenging 1.6-mile Precipice Trail, which climbs the east face of Champlain Mountain on iron rungs and ladders. (Note that the trail is typically closed late spring to mid-August because it's a nesting area for peregrine falcons. If it is closed, you might catch volunteers and staff monitoring the birds through scopes from the trailhead parking lot.) Skip the trail on rainy days.

The Drive » Continue south on Park Loop Rd. The Beehive Trail starts 100ft north of the Sand Beach parking area.

4 Beehive Trail & Sand Beach

Another good ladder trail is the Beehive Trail. The 0.8-mile climb includes ladders, rungs, narrow wooden bridges and scrambling – with steep drop-offs. As with the Precipice Trail, it's recommended that you descend via a nearby walking route, rather than climbing down.

Don't let the crowds keep you away from Sand Beach. It's home to one of the few sandy shorelines in the park, and it's a don't-miss spot. But you don't have to visit in the middle of the day to appreciate its charms. Beat the crowds early in the morning, or visit at night, especially for the **Stars over Sand Beach** program. During these free one-hour talks, lie on the beach, look up at the sky and listen to rangers sharing stories and science about the stars. Even if you miss the talk, the eastern coastline along Ocean Dr is worth checking out at night, when you can watch the Milky Way slip right into the ocean.

The Drive » Swoop south past the crashing waves of Thunder Hole. If you want to exit the loop road, turn right onto Otter Cliff Rd, which hooks up to ME 3 north into Bar Harbor. Otherwise, pass Otter Point then follow the road inland past Wildwood Stables.

TRIP HIGHLIGHT

5 Jordan Pond House

Share hiking stories with other nature-lovers at the lodgelike **Jordan Pond House** (☎207-276-3316; http://acadiajordanpondhouse.com; Park Loop Rd; tea & popovers $11, mains $11-33; ⏲11am-9pm mid-May–mid-Oct), where afternoon tea has been a tradition since the late 1800s. Steaming pots of Earl Grey come with hot popovers (hollow rolls made with egg batter) and strawberry jam. Eat on the broad lawn overlooking the lake. On clear days the glassy waters of 176-acre Jordan Pond reflect the image of Mt Penobscot like a mirror. Take the 3.2-mile nature trail around the pond after finishing your tea.

The Drive » Look up for the rock precariously perched atop South Bubble from the pull-off almost 2 miles north. Continue north to access Cadillac Mountain Rd.

TRIP HIGHLIGHT

6 Cadillac Mountain

Don't leave the park without driving – or hiking – to the 1530ft summit of Cadillac Mountain. For panoramic views of Frenchman Bay, walk the paved 0.5-mile **Cadillac Mountain Summit loop**. The summit is a popular

COLLINS93 / SHUTTERSTOCK ©

place in the early morning because it's long been touted as the first spot in the US to see the sunrise. The truth? It is, but only between October 7 and March 6. The crown is passed to northern coastal towns the rest of the year because of the tilt of the earth. But, hey, the sunset is always a good bet.

The Drive » Drunk on the views, you can complete the loop road and exit the park, heading for your accommodations or next destination. But consider finding a parking lot and tackling walking trails, or heading to Bar Harbor to hire bikes.

TOP TIP: PARK SHUTTLES

With millions of visitors coming to the park each summer, traffic and parking can be a hassle. On arrival, drive the Park Loop Rd straight through for the views and the driving experience. Then leave the driving to others by using the Island Explorer (www.exploreacadia.com), free with park admission. Shuttles run along nine routes that connect visitors to trails, carriage roads, beaches, campgrounds and in-town destinations. They can even carry mountain bikes.

Bass Harbor Head Lighthouse A photographer's favorite

TRIP HIGHLIGHT

7 Carriage Roads

John D Rockefeller Jr, a lover of old-fashioned horse carriages, gifted Acadia with some 45 miles of crisscrossing carriage roads. Made from crushed stone, the roads are free from cars and are popular with cyclists, hikers and equestrians. Several of them fan out from Jordan Pond House; but if the lot is too crowded, continue north to the parking area at **Eagle Lake** on US 233 to link to the carriage road network. If you're planning to explore by bike, the Bicycle Express Shuttle runs to Eagle Lake from the Bar Harbor Village Green from late June through September. Pick up a *Carriage Road User's Map* at the visitor center.

The Drive » Still in the mood for cruising? Before you head for the bright lights of Bar Harbor, take a detour: drive ME 233 toward the western part of MDI, connecting to ME 198 west, then drop south on ME 102 toward Southwest Harbor. Pass Echo Lake Beach and Southwest Harbor, then bear left onto ME 102A for a dramatic rise up and back into the park near the seawall.

8 Bass Harbor Head Lighthouse

There is only one lighthouse on Mt Desert Island, and it sits in the somnolent village of Bass Harbor in the far southwest corner of the park. Built in 1858, the 36ft lighthouse still has a Fresnel lens from 1902. It's in a beautiful location that's a photographers' favorite. The lighthouse is a coastguard residence, so you can't go inside, but you can take photos. You can also stroll to the coast on two easy trails near the property: the **Ship Harbor**

Trail, a 1.2-mile loop, and the **Wonderland Trail**, a 1.4-mile round-trip. These trails are spectacular ways to get through the forest and to the coast, which looks different to the coast on Ocean Dr.

The Drive » For a lollipop loop, return on ME 102A to ME 102 through the village of Bass Harbor. Follow ME 102 then ME 233 all the way to Bar Harbor.

TRIP HIGHLIGHT

9 Bar Harbor

Tucked on the rugged coast in the shadows of Acadia's mountains, Bar Harbor is a busy gateway town with a J Crew joie de vivre. Restaurants, taverns and boutiques are scattered along Main St, Mt Desert St and Cottage St. Shops sell everything from books to camping gear to handicrafts and art. For a fascinating collection of natural artifacts related to Maine's Native American heritage, visit the **Abbe Museum** (207-288-3519; www.abbemuseum.org; 26 Mount Desert St; adult/child $8/4; 10am-5pm May-Oct, 10am-4pm Thu-Sat Nov-Apr). The collection holds more than 50,000 objects, such as pottery, tools, combs and fishing instruments spanning the last 2000 years, including contemporary pieces. (There's a smaller summer-only branch in Sieur de Monts Spring.)

Done browsing? Spend the rest of the afternoon, or early evening, exploring the area by water. Sign up in Bar Harbor for a half-day or sunset sea-kayaking trip. Both **National Park Sea Kayak Tours** (800-347-0940; www.acadiakayak.com; 39 Cottage St; half-day tour $52; late May–mid-Oct) and

ISLAND VISIT PLANNER

Acadia National Park

Orientation & Fees

Park admission is $25 per vehicle (including passengers), $20 per motorcycle and $12 for walk-ins and cyclists. Admission is valid for seven days.

Camping

There are two great rustic campgrounds on Mt Desert Island, with nearly 500 sites between them. Both are densely wooded and near the coast; reservations are essential (except in winter at Blackwoods). **Seawall** (877-444-6777; www.recreation.gov; 668 Seawall Rd, Southwest Harbor; tent sites $22-30, RV sites $30; late May–Sep) is 4 miles south of Southwest Harbor on the 'Quietside' of Mt Desert Island, while **Blackwoods** (877-444-6777; www.recreation.gov; ME 3; tent & RV sites $30; year-round) is closer to Bar Harbor (5 miles south, on ME 3).

Bar Harbor & Mt Desert Island

Before your trip, check lodging availability via the **Acadia Welcome Center** (207-288-5103, 800-345-4617; www.acadiainfo.com; 1201 Bar Harbor Rd/ME 3, Trenton; 9am-5pm Mon-Sat, 10am-4pm Sun late May–mid-Oct, 9am-5pm Mon-Fri mid-Apr–May & mid-Oct–Nov) website, run by the Bar Harbor Chamber of Commerce. Staff can mail you a copy of the visitor guide. Otherwise, stop by the welcome center itself for lodging brochures, maps and local information. It's located north of the bridge onto Mt Desert Island. There is a second **visitors center** (Acadia Welcome Center; 207-801-2558, 800-345-4617; www.barharborinfo.com; cnr Main & Cottage Sts; 8am-8pm mid-Jun–Sep, 9am-5pm Sep–mid-Jun) in Bar Harbor itself.

DAN LOGAN / SHUTTERSTOCK ©

Bar Harbor A waterfront restaurant decorated with floats

Coastal Kayaking Tours (207-288-9605; www.acadiafun.com; 48 Cottage St; 2½hr/4hr/full-day tours $43/53/84; May-Oct) offers guided trips along the jagged coast.

 p207

The Drive » There's another part of the park you haven't yet explored. Reaching it involves a 44-mile drive (north on Rte 3 to US 1, following it about 17 miles to ME 186 S). ME 186 passes through Winter Harbor and then links to Schoodic Point Loop Rd. It's about an hour's drive one way. Alternatively, hop on a Downeast Windjammer ferry from the pier beside the Bar Harbor Inn.

⑩ Schoodic Peninsula

The Schoodic Peninsula is the only section of Acadia National Park that's part of the mainland. It's also home to the Park Loop Rd, a rugged, woodsy drive with splendid views of Mt Desert Island and Cadillac Mountain. You're more likely to see a moose here than on MDI – what moose wants to cross a bridge?

Much of the drive is one-way. There's an excellent **campground** (877-444-6777; www.recreation.gov; campsites $22-40; late May–mid-Oct) near the entrance, then a picnic area at **Frazer Point**. Further along the loop, turn right for a short ride to **Schoodic Point**, a 440ft-high promontory with ocean views.

The full loop from Winter Harbor is 11.5 miles and covers park, town and state roads. If you're planning to come by ferry, you could rent a bike beforehand at **Bar Harbor Bicycle Shop** (207-288-3886; www.barharborbike.com; 141 Cottage St; rental per day $25-50; 8am-6pm) – the Park Loop Rd's smooth surface and easy hills make it ideal for cycling.

In July and August, the Island Explorer Schoodic shuttle bus runs from Winter Harbor to the peninsula ferry terminal and around the Park Loop Rd. It does not link to Bar Harbor.

Eating & Sleeping

Bar Harbor 9

Mount Desert Island Ice Cream — Ice Cream $

(207-801-4006; www.mdiic.com; 325 Main St; ice cream $4-6; 11am-11pm Jun-Aug, to 10pm Sep, shorter hours Apr, May & Oct) A cult hit for innovative flavors like stout beer with fudge, chocolate with wasabi, and blueberry-basil sorbet, this ice-cream counter is a post-dinner must. The small, original outlet is at 7 Firefly Lane, by the Village Green.

2 Cats — Breakfast $

(207-288-2808; http://twocatsbarharbor.com; 130 Cottage St; mains $9-15; 7am-1pm;) It's the most important meal of the day, so 2 Cats channels all its attention to breakfast. On weekends, crowds line up for banana pecan pancakes, smoked-trout omelets, tofu scrambles and homemade muffins at this sunny, arty little cafe. Pick up a kitty-themed souvenir in the gift shop.

Mache Bistro — French $$

(207-288-0447; http://machebistro.com; 321 Main St; mains $20-32; from 5:30pm Tue-Sat May-Oct) A strong contender for Bar Harbor's best midrange restaurant, Mache serves contemporary, French-inflected fare in a stylishly renovated cottage. The changing menu highlights the local riches – think sustainably harvested scallops on fennel salad, rosemary-grilled quail, and wild blueberry trifle. Specialty cocktails add to the appeal. Reservations are suggested, but the bar is open to walk-ins.

Havana — Latin American $$$

(207-288-2822; www.havanamaine.com; 318 Main St; mains $27-39; 5-9pm May-Oct) First things first: order a rockin' Cuba libre or mojito. Once that's done, you can take your time with the menu and the epic global wine list. Havana puts a Latin spin on dishes that highlight local produce, and the kitchen output is accomplished. Signature dishes include crab cakes, paella and a deliciously light lobster *moqueca* (stew). Reservations recommended.

Acadia Inn — Hotel $$

(207-288-3500; https://acadiainn.com; 98 Eden St; r $95-209; mid-Apr–early Nov;) This traditional 95-room hotel with helpful staff sits beside a trail leading into the park. The good-sized rooms are smart and comfortable, there's a laundry and a heated pool, and the park shuttle stops here in summer. It's a good choice if you don't mind being out of the town center.

Moseley Cottage Inn & Town Motel — B&B, Motel $$

(207-288-5548; http://moseleycottage.net; 12 Atlantic Ave; r $175-305;) This two-faced option is down a quiet street just steps from Main St, and covers its bases very well. There are nine large, charming, antique-filled B&B rooms in a traditional 1884 inn (options with fireplace and private porch), plus a small collection of cheaper motel-style units next door. All are of a consistently high standard.

Aysgarth Station Inn — B&B $$

(207-288-9655; www.aysgarth.com; 20 Roberts Ave; r $95-185;) On a quiet side street, this 1895 B&B has six cozy rooms with homey touches. Request the Tan Hill room, which is on the 3rd floor, for a view of Cadillac Mountain, or the Chatsworth room for its private deck.

Bass Cottage Inn — Inn $$$

(207-288-1234; www.basscottage.com; 14 The Field; r $230-440; mid-May–Oct;) If most Bar Harbor B&Bs rate about a '5' in terms of stylishness, this Gilded Age mansion deserves an '11.' The 10 light-drenched guest rooms have an elegant summer-cottage chic, all crisp white linens and understated botanical prints. Tickle the ivories at the parlor's grand piano or read a novel beneath the Tiffany stained-glass ceiling of the wood-paneled sitting room.

STRETCH YOUR LEGS BOSTON

Start/Finish Boston Common

Distance 2.5 miles

Duration Three hours

Everybody knows about its world-class museums and historical sites, but Boston also offers a network of verdant parks, welcoming waterways and delightful shopping streets, making it a wonderful walking city.

Take this walk on Trip

Boston Common

Welcome to the country's oldest **public park** (btwn Tremont, Charles, Beacon & Park Sts; 6am-midnight;), which has a convenient underground parking facility below – what foresight! A **bronze plaque** is emblazoned with the words of the treaty between Governor Winthrop and William Blaxton, who sold this land for £30 in 1634. The **Massachusetts State House** (www.sec.state.ma.us; cnr Beacon & Bowdoin Sts; 8:45am-5pm Mon-Fri, tours 10am-3:30pm Mon-Fri) commands a prominent position in the park's northeastern corner.

The Walk » Follow the busy Bostonians crisscrossing the common. Exit the park from the western side, cross Charles St and enter the tranquil Public Garden.

Public Garden

The **Public Garden** (www.friendsofthepublicgarden.org; Arlington St; dawn-dusk;) is a 24-acre botanical oasis of Victorian flower beds, verdant grass and weeping willows shading a tranquil lagoon. At any time of year, it is an island of loveliness, awash in seasonal blooms, gold-toned leaves or untrammeled snow. Taking a ride on the **Swan Boats** (www.swanboats.com; Public Garden; adult/child $3.50/2; 10am-4pm mid-Apr–mid-Jun, to 5pm late Jun-Aug, noon-4pm 1st half of Sep) in the lagoon has been a Boston tradition since 1877. And don't miss the famous statue **Make Way for Ducklings**, based on the beloved children's book by Robert McCloskey.

The Walk » Cross the bridge and exit the garden through the southwestern gate to Arlington St. Stroll west on swanky Newbury St, perfect for window-shopping and gallery hopping. Take a left on Clarendon St and continue to Boylston St.

Copley Square

Boston's most exquisite architecture is clustered around this stately Back Bay plaza. The centerpiece is **Trinity Church** (www.trinitychurchboston.org; 206 Clarendon St; tours adult/child $7/free; 10am-5pm

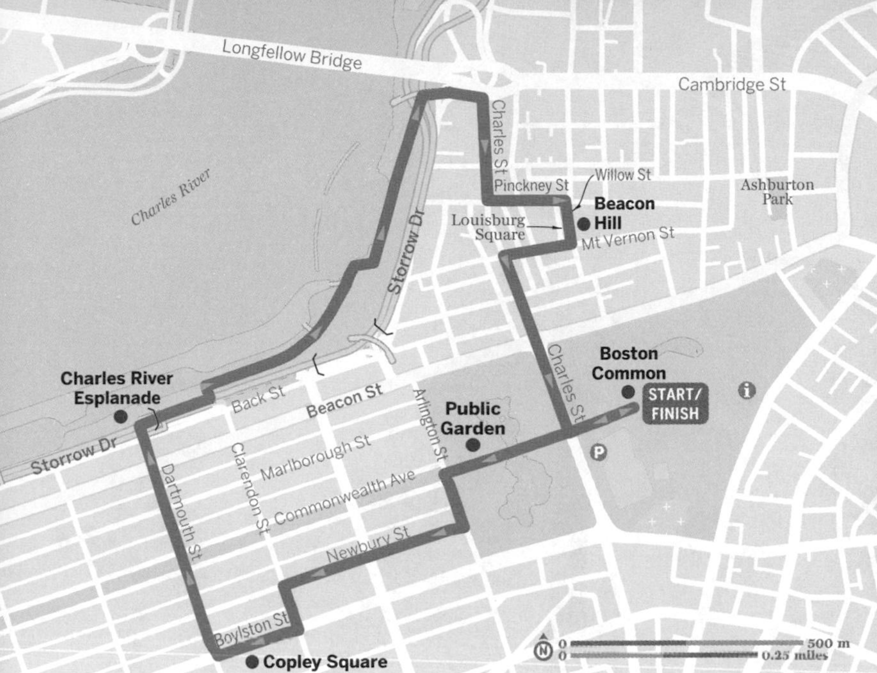

Tue-Sat, 1-5pm Sun Easter-Oct, reduced hours rest of year), famed for its stained-glass windows. It's particularly lovely as reflected in the facade of the modern **John Hancock Tower**. This assemblage faces off against the elegant neo-Renaissance **Boston Public Library** (www.bpl.org; 700 Boylston St; ⏲9am-9pm Mon-Thu, to 5pm Fri & Sat year-round, plus 1-5pm Sun Oct-May).

The Walk » Head north on Dartmouth St, crossing the stately, dual-carriageway Commonwealth Ave, the grandest of Back Bay's grand avenues. Continue three more blocks to Back St, from where a pedestrian walkway crosses Storrow Dr to the esplanade.

Charles River Esplanade

The southern bank of the Charles River Basin is an enticing urban **escape** (www.esplanadeassociation.org; 👪), with grassy knolls and cooling waterways, all designed by Frederick Law Olmsted. The park is dotted with public art, including an oversized bust of **Arthur Fiedler**, the longtime conductor of the Boston Pops. The **Hatch Memorial Shell** (www.hatchshell.com) hosts free outdoor concerts and movies, including the famed July 4 concert by the Boston Pops.

The Walk » Walk northeast along the esplanade, enjoying the breezes and views of the Charles River. It's about a half-mile to the Longfellow Bridge, where you can climb the ramp and find yourself at the top of Charles St.

Beacon Hill

With an intriguing history and iconic architecture, Beacon Hill is Boston's most prestigious address. **Charles Street** is an enchanting spot for browsing boutiques and haggling over antiques. To explore further, wander down the residential streets lit with gas lanterns, admire the brick town houses decked with purple windowpanes and blooming flower boxes, and discover places such as stately **Louisburg Square** that capture the neighborhood's grandeur.

The Walk » Take your time strolling south along charming Charles St. For a glimpse of Louisburg Sq, walk two blocks east on Pinckney St. Then continue south to Boston Common.

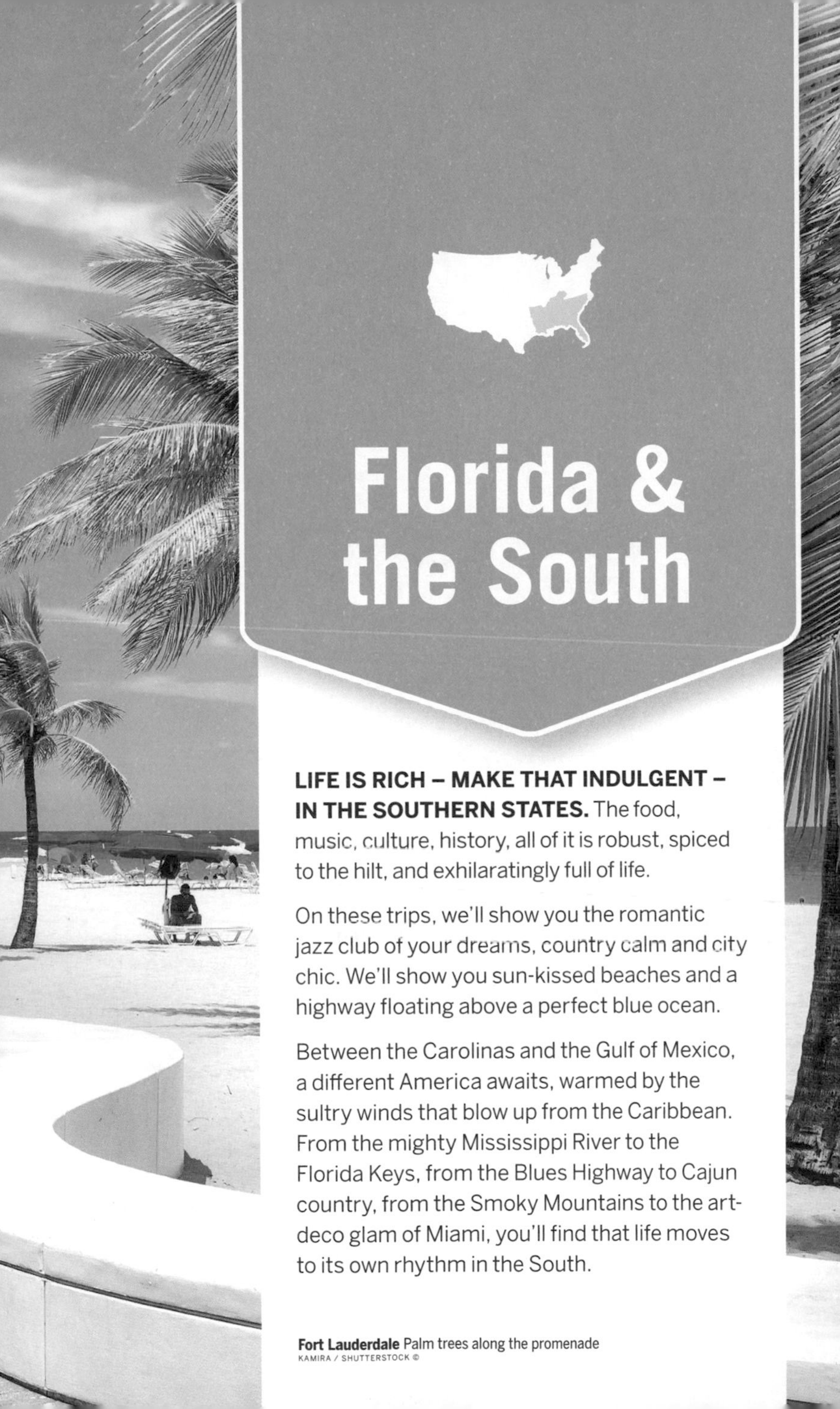

Florida & the South

LIFE IS RICH – MAKE THAT INDULGENT – IN THE SOUTHERN STATES. The food, music, culture, history, all of it is robust, spiced to the hilt, and exhilaratingly full of life.

On these trips, we'll show you the romantic jazz club of your dreams, country calm and city chic. We'll show you sun-kissed beaches and a highway floating above a perfect blue ocean.

Between the Carolinas and the Gulf of Mexico, a different America awaits, warmed by the sultry winds that blow up from the Caribbean. From the mighty Mississippi River to the Florida Keys, from the Blues Highway to Cajun country, from the Smoky Mountains to the art-deco glam of Miami, you'll find that life moves to its own rhythm in the South.

Fort Lauderdale Palm trees along the promenade
KAMIRA / SHUTTERSTOCK ©

Florida & the South

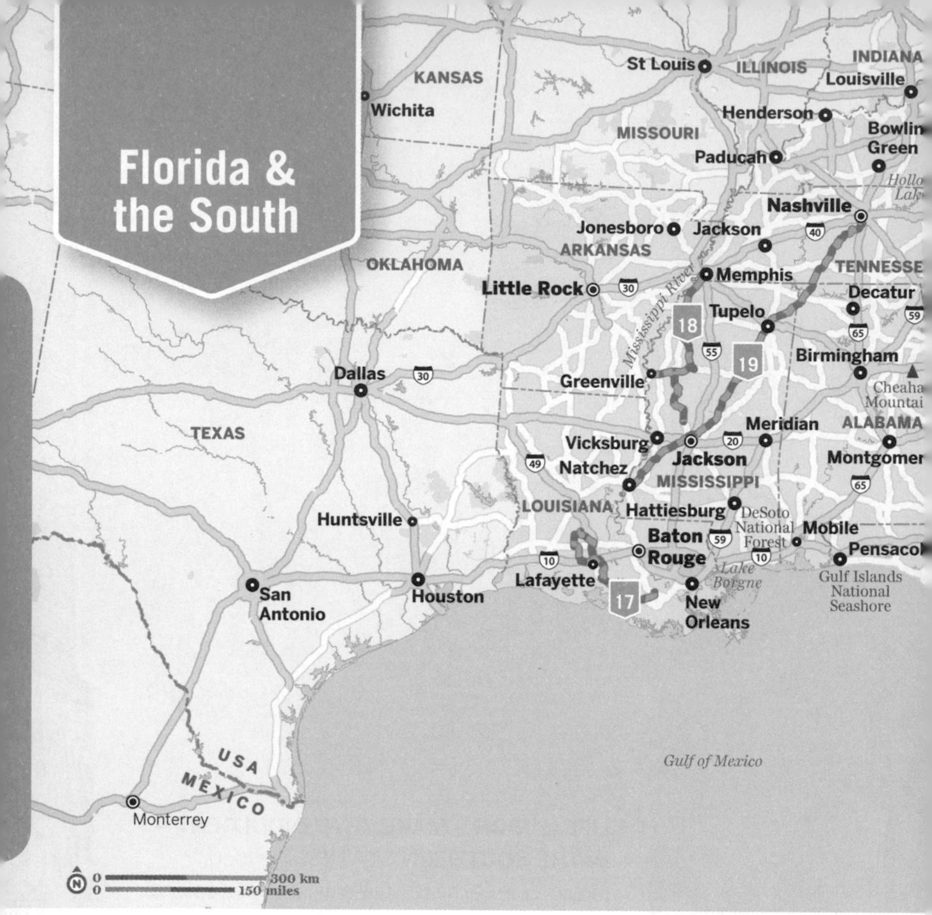

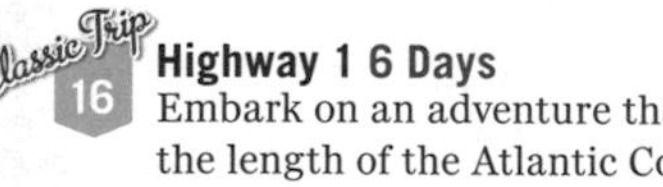

Classic Trip 16 **Highway 1 6 Days**
Embark on an adventure that runs the length of the Atlantic Coast. (p215)

17 **Cajun Country 4 Days**
Explore bayous, dance halls, crawfish boils and folk ways in Louisiana's idiosyncratic Acadiana region. (p227)

18 **The Blues Highway 3 Days**
A soulful ramble to the roots of American popular music. (p235)

19 **Natchez Trace Parkway 3 Days**
The journey south from Nashville stuns with natural beauty and American history. (p245)

Classic Trip 20 **Blue Ridge Parkway 5 Days**
The beloved byway explores the craggy, misty depths of the Appalachians. (p257)

21 **The Great Smokies 4–5 Days**
Raft over rapids, scan for wildlife and drive two fantastic nature loops. (p269)

Miami Beach Detail of fountain on Ocean Drive

DON'T MISS

Fort George Island

Peek into old Florida at this Cultural State Park, one of several historical stop-offs in Trip 16

Biltmore Legacy

For less of the formality and more of the family, visit the new 'Vanderbilts at Home and Abroad' exhibit on Trip 20

Museum of the Cherokee Indian

Learn about three Cherokee chiefs who journeyed to England and met with King George III on Trip 21

Clarksdale

The hub of the Delta has the Crossroads, a spectacular juke joint and comfortable digs from which to explore the blues. Visit it on Trip 18

Natchez

This laid-back river town is an antebellum time capsule, and a charming respite for a few days of strolling and contemplation. See it on Trip 19

AVALON
700

Classic Trip

Highway 1

Glittering Miami provides a spectacular grand finale to this epic coastal road trip featuring miles and miles of beaches interspersed with fascinating historical sights.

TRIP HIGHLIGHTS

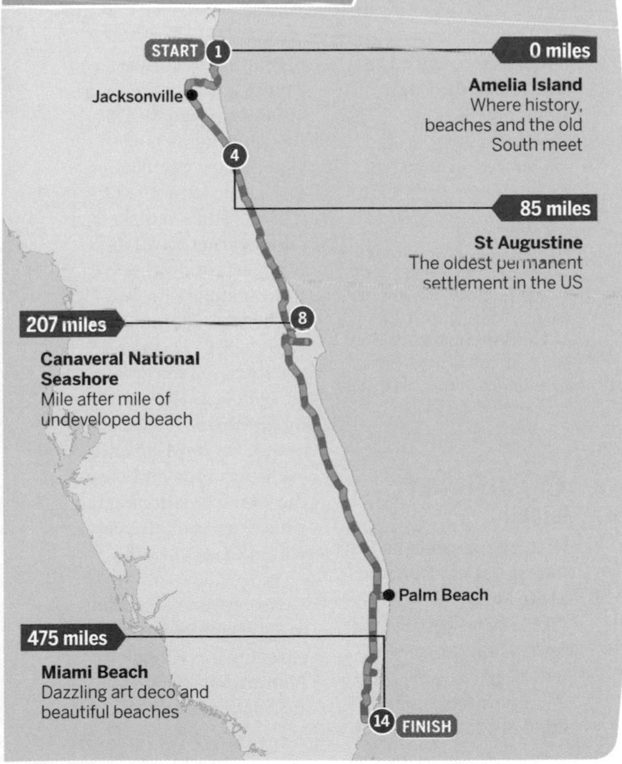

START 1 — 0 miles

Amelia Island
Where history, beaches and the old South meet

Jacksonville

4 — 85 miles

St Augustine
The oldest permanent settlement in the US

8 — 207 miles

Canaveral National Seashore
Mile after mile of undeveloped beach

Palm Beach

14 FINISH — 475 miles

Miami Beach
Dazzling art deco and beautiful beaches

6 DAYS
475 MILES / 764KM

GREAT FOR...

BEST TIME TO GO

November to April, when it's warm but not too hot.

ESSENTIAL PHOTO

Rows of colorful art-deco hotels along Ocean Ave at Miami Beach.

BEST FOR HISTORY

St Augustine is the oldest permanent settlement in the US.

Miami Beach Art-deco architecture

Classic Trip

16 Highway 1

Drive the length of Florida all the way down the coast and you'll get a sampling of everything we love about the Sunshine State. You'll find the oldest permanent settlement in the United States, family-friendly attractions, the Latin flavor of Miami and – oh, yeah – miles and miles of beaches right beside you, inviting you to stop as often as you want.

TRIP HIGHLIGHT

1 Amelia Island

Start your drive just 13 miles south of the Georgia border on Amelia Island, a glorious barrier island with the moss-draped charm of the Deep South. Vacationers have been flocking here since the 1890s, when Henry Flagler's railroad converted the area into a playground for the rich. The legacy of that golden era remains visible today in Amelia's central town of Fernandina Beach, with 50 blocks of historic buildings, Victorian B&Bs and restaurants housed in converted fishing cottages. The best introduction to the town is a half-hour horse-drawn carriage tour with the **Old Towne Carriage Company** (☎904-277-1555; www.ameliacarriagetours.com; 115 Beech St, Fernandina Beach; half-hour adult/child $15/7).

✕ 🛏 p224

The Drive » Meander down Hwy 1A for about half an hour, passing both Big and Little Talbot Island State Parks. After you enter Fort George Island, take the right fork in the road to get to the Ribault Club.

2 Fort George Island

History runs deep at **Fort George Island Cultural State Park** (☎904-251-2320; www.floridastateparks.org/fortgeorgeisland; 11241 Fort George Rd; ⏰8am-sunset; 🅿). Enormous shell middens date the island's habitation by Native Americans to more than 5000 years ago. In 1736 British general James Oglethorpe erected a fort in the area, though it's long since vanished and its exact location is uncertain. In the 1920s flappers flocked to the ritzy **Ribault Club** (☎904-251-2802; www.nps.gov/timu; 11241 Fort George Rd; ⏰9am-5pm Wed-Sun) for Gatsby-esque bashes with lawn bowling and yachting. Today it houses the island's visitor center, which can provide you with a CD tour of the area.

Perhaps most fascinating – certainly most sobering – is **Kingsley Plantation** (☎904-251-3537; www.nps.gov/timu;

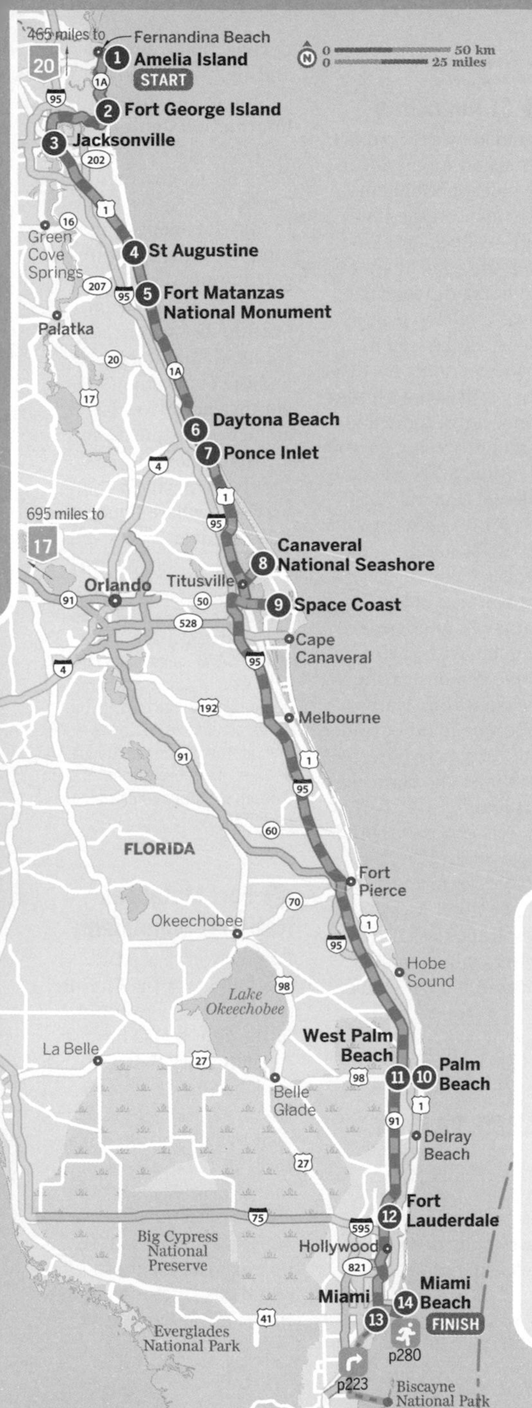

11676 Palmetto Ave; 9am-5pm; P), Florida's oldest plantation house, built in 1798. Because of its remote location, it's not a grand Southern mansion, but it does provide a fairly unflinching look at slavery through exhibits and the remains of 23 slave cabins.

The Drive » Follow Hwy 105 inland 15 miles to I-95, then shoot straight south into downtown Jacksonville, a distance of about 24 miles.

3 Jacksonville

With its high-rises, freeways and chain hotels, Jacksonville is a bit of a departure from our coastal theme, but it offers lots of dining options, and its restored historic districts are worth a wander. Check out the Five Points and San Marco neighborhoods; both are charming, walkable areas lined

LINK YOUR TRIP

17 Cajun Country Follow I-10 west, then head south from Baton Rouge to Thibodaux to start your Cajun Country trip.

20 Blue Ridge Parkway Take the I-95 north along the coast and head inland on I-26 through Columbia. From there take Hwy 321 all the way to Boone.

with bistros, boutiques and bars.

It's also a good chance to work in a little culture at the **Cummer Museum of Art** (www.cummer.org; 829 Riverside Ave; adult/student $10/6; ⏲10am-9pm Tue, to 4pm Wed-Sat, noon-4pm Sun), which has a genuinely excellent collection of American and European paintings, Asian decorative art and antiquities; or the **Museum of Modern Art Jacksonville** (MOCA; ☎904-366-6911; www.mocajacksonville.org; 333 N Laura St; adult/child $8/2.50; ⏲11am-5pm Tue-Sat, to 9pm Thu, noon-5pm Sun), which houses contemporary paintings, sculptures, prints, photography and film.

p224

The Drive » Take Hwy 1 southwest for an hour straight into St Augustine, where it becomes Ponce de Leon Blvd.

TRIP HIGHLIGHT

4 St Augustine

Founded by the Spanish in 1565, St Augustine is the oldest permanent settlement in the US. Tourists flock here to stroll the ancient streets, and horse-drawn carriages clip-clop past townsfolk dressed in period costume. It's definitely touristy, with tons of museums, tours and attractions vying for your attention. Start with the **Colonial Quarter** (☎904-342-2857; www.colonialquarter.com; 33 St George St; adult/child $13/7; ⏲10am-5pm), a re-creation of 18th-century St Augustine complete with craftspeople demonstrating blacksmithing, leather working and other trades.

While you're here, don't miss the **Lightner Museum** (☎904-824-2874; www.lightnermuseum.org; 75 King St; adult/child $10/5; ⏲9am-5pm) located in the former Hotel Alcazar. We love the endless displays of everything from Gilded Age furnishings to collections of marbles and cigar-box labels.

Stop by the **Visitor Information Center** (☎904-825-1000; www.floridashistoriccoast.com; 10 W Castillo Dr; ⏲8:30am-5:30pm) to find out about your other options, including ghost tours, the Pirate and Treasure Museum, Castillo de San Marcos National Monument, and the Fountain of Youth, a goofy tourist attraction disguised as an archaeological park that is purportedly the very spot where Ponce de Leon landed.

p224

The Drive » Take the Bridge of Lions toward the beach then follow Hwy 1A south for 13 miles to Fort Matanzas. To catch the 35-person ferry, go through the visitor center and out to the pier. The ride lasts about five minutes and launches hourly from 9:30am to 4:30pm, weather permitting.

5 Fort Matanzas National Monument

By now you've seen firsthand that the Florida coast isn't all about fun in the sun; it also has a rich history that goes back hundreds of years. History buffs will enjoy a visit to this tiny Spanish **fort** (☎904-471-0116; www.nps.gov/foma; 8635 Hwy A1A, Rattlesnake Island; ⏲9am-5:30pm; P) built in 1742. Its purpose? To guard Matanzas Inlet – a waterway leading straight up

TOP TIP: THE ROAD LESS TAKEN

Despite its National Scenic Byway designation, oceanfront Hwy A1A often lacks ocean views, with wind-blocking vegetation growing on both sides of the road. Unless you're just moseying up or down the coast, Hwy 1 or I-95 are often better choices for driving long-distance.

to St Augustine – from British invasion.

On the lovely (and free) boat ride over, park rangers narrate the fort's history and explain the gruesome origins of the name. ('Matanzas' means 'slaughters' in Spanish; let's just say things went badly for a couple hundred French Huguenot soldiers back in 1565.)

The Drive » Hopping over to I-95 will only shave a little bit off the hour-long trip; you might as well enjoy putting along Hwy 1A to Daytona Beach, 40 miles south.

6 Daytona Beach

With typical Floridian hype, Daytona Beach bills itself as 'The World's Most Famous Beach.' But its fame is less about quality – the beach is actually mediocre – than the size of the parties this expansive beach has witnessed during spring break, Speedweeks and motorcycle events when half a million bikers roar into town. One Daytona title no one disputes is 'Birthplace of NASCAR,' which started here in 1947. Its origins go back as far as 1902 to drag races held on the beach's hard-packed sands.

NASCAR is the main event here. Catch a race at the **Daytona International Speedway** (800-748-7467; www.daytonainternationalspeedway.com; 1801 W International Speedway Blvd; tours from $18; tours 9:30am-3:30pm). When there's no race, you can wander the massive stands for free or take a tram tour of the track and pit area. Race-car fanatics can indulge in the **Richard Petty Driving Experience** (800-237-3889; www.drivepetty.com; from $109; dates vary) and feel the thrill of riding shotgun or even taking the wheel themselves.

p224

The Drive » Take South Atlantic Ave 10 miles south along the coast to get to Ponce Inlet.

7 Ponce Inlet

What's a beach road trip without a good lighthouse? About 6 miles south of Daytona Beach is the **Ponce de Leon Inlet Lighthouse & Museum** (386-761-1821; www.ponceinlet.org; 4931 S Peninsula Dr; adult/child $7/2; 10am-6pm Sep-May, to 9pm Jun-Aug; P). Stop by for a photo op with the handsome red-brick tower built in 1887, then climb the 203 steps to the top for great views of the surrounding beaches. A handful of historic buildings comprise the museum portion of your tour, including the lightkeeper's house and the Lens House, where they show off a collection of Fresnel Lenses.

The Drive » Backtrack up Atlantic, then cut over to Hwy 1/FL 5 and head south for 20 minutes. Pre-planning pays here, because your route depends on where you're heading. One road goes 6 miles south from New Smyrna Beach, and another 6 miles north from the wildlife refuge. Both dead-end, leaving 16 miles of beach between them.

TRIP HIGHLIGHT

8 Canaveral National Seashore

These 24 miles of pristine, windswept beaches comprise the longest stretch of undeveloped beach on Florida's east coast. On the north end is family-friendly Apollo Beach, which shines in a class of its own with gentle surf and miles of solitude. On the south end, Playalinda Beach is surfer central.

Just west of (and including) the beach, the 140,000-acre **Merritt Island National Wildlife Refuge** (321-861-5601; www.fws.gov/merrittisland; Black Point Wildlife Dr, off FL 406; vehicle $10; dawn-dusk) is an unspoiled oasis for birds and wildlife. It's one of the country's best birding spots, especially from October to May (early morning and after 4pm), and more endangered and threatened species of wildlife inhabit the swamps, marshes and hardwood hammocks here than at any other site in the continental US.

Stop by the visitor center for more information; an easy quarter-mile boardwalk will

Classic Trip

MICHAELWARRENPIX / GETTY IMAGES ©

DENNIS K. JOHNSON / GETTY IMAGES ©

WHY THIS IS A CLASSIC TRIP

MARIELLA KRAUSE, WRITER

Who doesn't love cruising down the coast? This trip is a natural for shoreline, seafood and sunshine – but it doesn't rely solely on beach culture. It's a remarkably well-rounded drive that culminates in the world-class city of Miami, with diversions along the way that include worthwhile art exhibits, peaceful nature preserves and some of the United State's oldest historical sites.

Top: Canaveral National Seashore
Left: Rocket Garden at Kennedy Space Center
Right: The historic Spanish settlement of St Augustine

SAMOT / SHUTTERSTOCK ©

whet your appetite for everything the refuge has to offer. Other highlights include the Manatee Observation Deck, the 7-mile Black Point Wildlife Drive, and a variety of hiking trails.

The Drive » Although Kennedy Space Center is just south of the Merritt Island Refuge, you have to go back into Titusville, travel south 5 miles on Hwy 1/FL 5, then take the Nasa Causeway back over to get there.

9 Space Coast

The Space Coast's main claim to fame (other than being the setting for the iconic 1960s TV series *I Dream of Jeannie*) is being the real-life home to the **Kennedy Space Center** (866-737-5235; www.kennedyspacecenter.com; NASA Pkwy, Merritt Island; adult/child 3-11yr $50/40; 9am-6pm) and its massive visitor complex. Once a working spaceflight facility, Kennedy Space Center is shifting from a living museum to a historical one since the end of NASA's space shuttle program in 2011.

✕ p225

The Drive » Hop back onto the freeway (I-95) for the 2½-hour drive south to Palm Beach.

10 Palm Beach

History and nature give way to money and culture as you reach the southern part of the coast, and

Palm Beach looks every inch the playground for the rich and famous that it is. But fear not: the 99% can stroll along the beach – kept pleasantly seaweed-free by the town – ogle the massive gated compounds on A1A or window-shop in uber-ritzy Worth Ave, all for free.

The best reason to stop here is **Flagler Museum** (561-655-2833; www.flaglermuseum.us; 1 Whitehall Way; adult/child $18/10; 10am-5pm Tue-Sat, noon-5pm Sun), housed in the spectacular, beaux-art-styled Whitehall Mansion built by Henry Flagler in 1902. You won't get many details about the railroad mogul himself, but you will get a peek into his opulent lifestyle, including his own personal train car.

The Drive » When you're ready to be back among the commoners, head back inland. West Palm Beach is just a causeway away.

⓫ West Palm Beach

While Palm Beach has the money, West Palm Beach has the largest art museum in Florida, the **Norton Museum of Art** (561-832-5196; www.norton.org; 1451 S Olive Ave; adult/child $12/5; noon-5pm Tue-Sun). The Nessel Wing features a colorful crowd-pleaser: a ceiling made from nearly 700 pieces of handblown glass by Dale Chihuly. Across the street, the **Ann Norton Sculpture Garden** (561-832-5328; www.ansg.org; 253 Barcelona Rd; adult/child $15/7; 10am-4pm Wed-Sun) is a real West Palm gem.

Come evening, if you're not sure what you're in the mood for, head to **CityPlace** (561-366-1000; www.cityplace.com; 700 S Rosemary Ave; 10am-10pm Mon-Sat, noon-6pm Sun), a massive outdoor shopping and entertainment center. There you'll find a slew of stores, about a dozen restaurants, a 20-screen movie theater and the Harriet Himmel Theater – not to mention free concerts in the outdoor plaza.

p225

The Drive » Fort Lauderdale is a straight shot down I-95, 45 miles south of Palm Beach. Taking Hwy 1A will add more than half an hour to your trip.

⓬ Fort Lauderdale

Fort Lauderdale Beach isn't the spring-break destination it once was, although you can still find outposts of beach-bummin' bars and motels in between the swanky boutique hotels and multimillion-dollar yachts. Few visitors venture far inland except maybe to dine and shop along Las Olas Blvd; most spend the bulk of their time on the coast, frolicking at water's edge. The promenade – a wide, brick, palm-tree-dotted pathway swooping along the beach – is a magnet for runners, in-line skaters, walkers and cyclists. The white-sand beach, meanwhile, is one of the nation's cleanest and best.

The best way to see Fort Lauderdale is from the water. Hop on board the **Carrie B** (954-642-1601; www.carriebcruises.com; 440 N New River Dr E; tours adult/child $24/13; tours 11am, 1pm & 3pm, closed Tue & Wed May-Sep) for a 1½-hour riverboat tour that lets you get a glimpse of the ginormous mansions along the Intracoastal and New River. Or, for the best unofficial tour of the city, hop on the **Water Taxi** (954-467-6677; www.watertaxi.com; day pass adult/child $26/12), whose drivers

3, 2, 1...BLASTOFF!

Along the Space Coast, even phone calls get a countdown, thanks to the local area code: 321. It's no coincidence; in 1999 residents led by Robert Osband petitioned to get the digits in honor of the rocket launches that took place at Cape Canaveral.

offer lively narration of the passing scenery.

 p225

The Drive » Things are heating up. Miami is just half an hour south of Fort Lauderdale down I-95.

13 Miami

Miami moves to a different rhythm from anywhere else in the USA, with pastel-hued, subtropical beauty and Latin sexiness at every turn. Just west of downtown on Calle Ocho (8th St), you'll find Little Havana, the most prominent community of Cuban Americans in the US. One of the best times to come is the last Friday of the month during **Viernes Culturales** (Cultural Fridays; www.viernesculturales.org; ⏲7-11pm last Fri of month), a street fair showcasing Latino artists and musicians. Or catch the vibe at **Máximo Gómez Park** (cnr SW 8th St & SW 15th Ave; ⏲9am-6pm), where old-timers gather to play dominoes to the strains of Latin music.

Wynwood and the Design District are Miami's official arts neighborhoods; don't miss the amazing collection of murals at **Wynwood Walls** (www.thewynwoodwalls.com; NW 2nd Ave, btwn 25th & 26th Sts), surrounded by blocks and blocks of even more murals that form sort of a drive-though art gallery.

p225

The Drive » We've saved the best for last. Cross over the Julia Tuttle Causeway or the MacArthur Causeway to find yourself in art-deco-laden Miami Beach.

DETOUR: BISCAYNE NATIONAL PARK

Start: 14 Miami Beach

About an hour's drive south of Miami Beach, **Biscayne National Park** (☎305-230-1144, boat tours 786-335-3644; www.nps.gov/bisc; 9700 SW 328th St; boat tours adult/child $35/25; ⏲7am-5:30pm) is a protected marine sanctuary harboring amazing tropical coral reef systems, most within sight of Miami's skyline. It's only accessible by water: you can take a glass-bottomed-boat tour, snorkel or scuba dive, or rent a canoe or kayak to lose yourself in this 300-sq-mile system of islands, underwater shipwrecks and mangrove forests.

TRIP HIGHLIGHT

14 Miami Beach

Miami Beach dazzles at every turn. It has some of the best beaches in the country, with white sand and warm, blue-green water, and it's world-famous for its people-watching. Then there's the deco. Miami Beach has the largest concentration of deco anywhere in the world, with approximately 1200 buildings lining the streets around Ocean Dr and Collins Ave. Arrange a tour at the **Art Deco Welcome Center** (☎305-672-2014; www.mdpl.org; 1001 Ocean Dr, South Beach; ⏲9:30am-5pm Fri-Wed, to 7pm Thu) or pick up a walking-tour map in the gift shop.

Running alongside the beach, Ocean Ave is lined with cafes that spill out onto the sidewalk; stroll along until you find one that suits your cravings. Another highly strollable area is Lincoln Road Mall, a pedestrian promenade that's lined with stores, restaurants and bars.

Get a taste of all Miami Beach has to offer on our walking tour, p280.

p225

Classic Trip

Eating & Sleeping

Amelia Island 1

Café Karibo & Karibrew Fusion $$
(904-277-5269; www.cafekaribo.com; 27 N 3rd St, Fernandina Beach; mains $8-26; 11am-3pm Mon, to 9pm Tue-Sat, 10:30am-3pm Sun;) This funky side-street favorite serves a large and eclectic menu of sandwiches, soups, salads and healthy treats in a sprawling two-story space with a shady patio hung with twinkling Christmas lights. Down a Sloppy Skip's Stout at the adjacent Karibrew brewpub.

Elizabeth Pointe Lodge B&B $$$
(904-277-4851; www.elizabethpointelodge.com; 98 S Fletcher Ave, Fernandina Beach; r/ste from $299/380; P) Atmosphere oozes from this eccentric yet stylish 1890s Nantucket-shingle-style maritime inn, perched on the ocean 2 miles from downtown. Porches offer the best seats on the island for sunrise. Elegant rooms have plush beds and oversized tubs.

Jacksonville 3

Black Sheep Restaurant Modern American $$
(904-380-3091; www.blacksheep5points.com; 1534 Oak St; lunch/dinner mains from $9/14; 10:30am-10pm Mon-Thu, to 11pm Fri & Sat, 9:30am-3pm Sun;) Good, local ingredients, delicious food, a rooftop bar and a craft cocktail menu. Try miso-glazed duck confit, citrus-marinated tofu, pastrami sandwiches or crispy skinned fish cooked in brown butter, or cardamom pancakes and salmon bagels for Sunday brunch.

Bistro Aix French, Mediterranean $$$
(904-398-1949; www.bistrox.com; 1440 San Marco Blvd; mains $14-37; 11am-10pm Mon-Thu, to 11pm Fri, 5-11pm Sat, 5-9pm Sun) Dine with fashionable foodies on fusion Mediterranean dishes bursting with global flavors, from wine-braised chicken to duck cassoulet. More than 250 wines by the bottle, and 50 by the glass. Reservations recommended.

St Augustine 4

Spanish Bakery & Cafe Bakery $
(904-342-7859; www.spanishbakerycafe.com; 42½ St George St; mains $4-6.50; 10am-5pm Sun-Thu, to 8pm Fri & Sat) This diminutive stucco bakeshop serves empanadas, sausage rolls and other conquistador-era favorites. Sells out quick.

Floridian Modern American $$
(904-829-0655; www.thefloridianstaug.com; 39 Cordova St; mains $14-25; 11am-3pm Wed-Mon, 5-9pm Mon-Thu, to 10pm Fri & Sat) Oozing hipster-locavore earnestness, this farm-to-table restaurant serves whimsical neo-Southern creations. Service and vibe may be too cool for school, but it's hard to fault the food: fried green tomato bruschetta and seafood zucchini linguine pair perfectly. No reservations means long waits.

Casa Monica Historic Hotel $$$
(904-827-1888; www.casamonica.com; 95 Cordova St; r $200-280, ste from $440; P) Built in 1888, this is *the* luxe hotel in town, with turrets and fountains adding to the Spanish-Moorish castle atmosphere. Rooms are richly appointed, with wrought-iron triple-sheeted beds and Bose sound systems. Some suites have Jacuzzis, and the location can't be beaten.

Daytona Beach 6

Dancing Avocado Kitchen Cafe $
(386-947-2022; www.dancingavocadokitchen.com; 110 S Beach St; mains $8-14; 8am-4pm Tue-Sat;) Delicious gluten-free and mostly vegetarian-friendly items feature at this colorful kitchen, but you'll still find a spicy jerk chicken wrap and obligatory mahi sandwich basket.

Tropical Manor Resort $
(386-252-4920; www.tropicalmanor.com; 2237 S Atlantic Ave, Daytona Beach Shores; r $88-135; P) This immaculate, family-friendly beachfront property is like a playful pastel vision of Candy Land. A variety of configurations from motel rooms to suites and cottages are available.

Space Coast 9

Fat Snook Seafood $$$

(☎321-784-1190; www.thefatsnook.com; 2464 S Atlantic Ave; mains $22-33; ⏰5:30-10pm) Hidden inside an uninspired building, tiny Fat Snook stands out as an oasis of fine cooking. Gourmet seafood is expertly prepared with unexpected herbs and spices influenced by Caribbean flavors. Reservations strongly recommended.

West Palm Beach 11

Rhythm Cafe Fusion $$$

(☎561-833-3406; www.rhythmcafe.cc; 3800 S Dixie Hwy; mains $21-30; ⏰5:30-10pm Tue-Sat, to 9pm Sun & Mon) There's no lack of flair at this colorful, upbeat bistro set in a converted drugstore in West Palm's antiques district. The equally vibrant menu ranges from goat's cheese pie to 'the best tuna tartare ever' to a pomegranate-infused catch of the day.

Hotel Biba Motel $

(☎561-832-0094; www.hotelbiba.com; 320 Belvedere Rd; r $149-179;) This place lacks a bit of color but is one of the better budget options around. It's clean and well located a block from the Intracoastal, perched on the edge of the El Cid district.

Fort Lauderdale 12

BREW Urban Cafe Next Door Cafe $

(☎954-357-3934; www.facebook.com/brewnextdoor; 537 NW 1st Ave; ⏰7am-7pm;) Despite its unwieldy name, Brew is the coolest thing going in Fort Lauderdale: a kick-ass cafe located in a weird, semi-abandoned studio space filled with bookshelves. Worth it for the coffee.

Le Tub American $$

(☎954-921-9425; www.theletub.com; 1100 N Ocean Dr; mains $9-20; ⏰11am-1am Mon-Fri, noon-2am Sat & Sun) Decorated exclusively with flotsam collected along Hollywood Beach, this quirky burger joint is routinely named 'Best in America.' Everything is prepared from scratch and in a small kitchen so expect a wait. It's worth it.

Riverside Hotel Hotel $$

(☎954-467-0671; www.riversidehotel.com; 620 E Las Olas Blvd; r/ste from $219/479; P) This well-located Fort Lauderdale landmark (c 1936) with plush floral carpet and an air of grandeur has two room types: larger, executive rooms in the newer 12-story tower, and those in the historic 1936 building. Classic rooms overlooking Las Olas are the pick. Valet parking is a hefty $27 per night.

Miami 13

Biltmore Hotel Historic Hotel $$$

(☎855-311-6903; www.biltmorehotel.com; 1200 Anastasia Ave; r/ste from $409/560; P) Though the Biltmore's standard rooms can be small, a stay here is a chance to sleep in the lap of US luxury. Explore palatial grounds, read a book in the opulent lobby, sun underneath enormous columns and take a dip in the largest hotel pool in continental USA.

Miami Beach 14

11th St Diner Diner $

(☎305-534-6373; www.eleventhstreetdiner.com; 1065 Washington Ave; mains $10-20; ⏰7am-midnight Sun-Wed, 24hr Thu-Sat) You've seen the art-deco landmarks, now eat in one: a Pullman-car diner trucked down from Wilkes-Barre, PA. Classics include oven-roasted turkey, baby back ribs and mac 'n' cheese – plus breakfast all hours.

Pubbelly Fusion $$

(☎305-532-7555; www.pubbellyboys.com/miami/pubbelly; 1418 20th St; sharing plates $11-24, mains $19-30; ⏰6pm-midnight Tue-Thu & Sun, to 1am Fri & Sat;) Delicious Pubbelly skews between Asian, North American and Latin American, gleaning the best from all cuisines. Hand-crafted cocktails go down a treat.

Clay Hotel Hotel $$

(☎305-250-0759; www.clayhotel.com; 1438 Washington Ave; r $140-250;) Packaged in a 100-year-old Spanish-style villa, the Clay has clean and comfortable rooms in a medina-like maze of adjacent buildings. If you're on a budget but don't want a dorm/hostel atmosphere, head here.

Pelican Hotel Boutique Hotel $$$

(☎305-673-3373; www.pelicanhotel.com; 826 Ocean Dr; r $260-420;) A mad experiment of 29 themed rooms that come off like a fantasy-suite hotel dipped in hip. From the cowboy-hipster chic to jungly electric tiger stripes, all the rooms are completely different, and include quality sound systems and high-end fixtures.

Cajun Country

Enter a maze of bayous, lakes, swamps and prairies where the crawfish boils, and all-night jam sessions and dance parties don't end.

TRIP HIGHLIGHTS

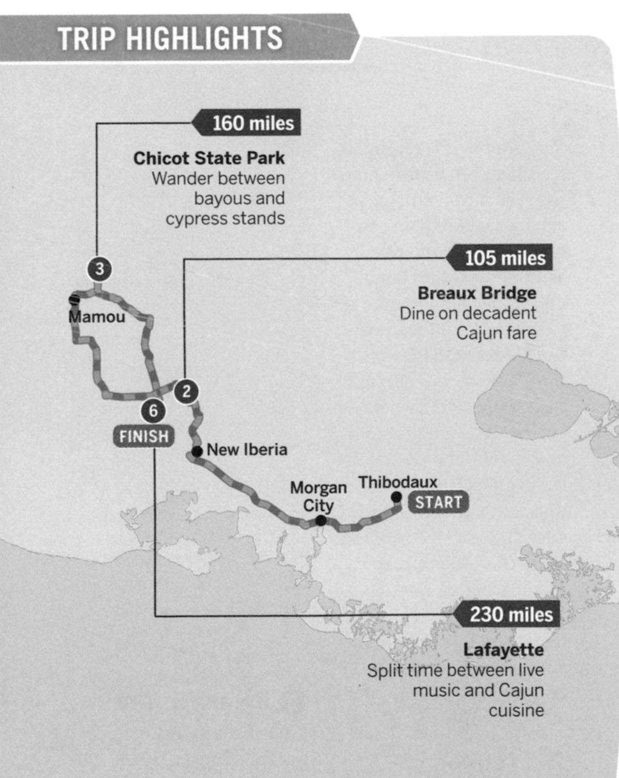

4 DAYS
230 MILES / 370KM

GREAT FOR...

BEST TIME TO GO

March to June is festival season in Acadiana; warm weather and lots of parties.

ESSENTIAL PHOTO

Cajun concerts rock Fred's Lounge every Saturday morning.

BEST FOR CULTURE

The unique folkways of Acadiana permeate south Louisiana.

Lake Martin Home to the great egret

17 Cajun Country

Cross into south Louisiana, and you venture into a land that's intensely, immediately unique. You will drive past dinosaur-laced wetlands where standing water is uphill from the floodplain, through villages where French is still the language of celebration, and sometimes, the home, and towns that love to fiddle, dance, two-step and, most of all, eat well. Bienvenue en Louisiane: this is Cajun Country, a waterlogged, toe-tapping nation unto itself.

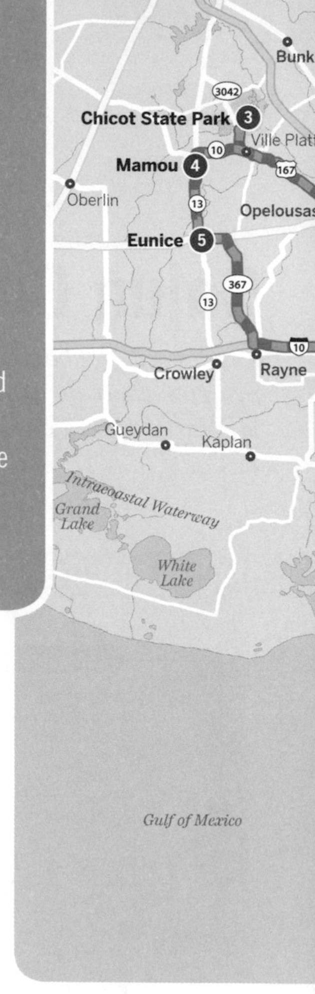

❶ Thibodaux

Thibodaux (tib-ah-*doe*), huddled against the banks of **Bayou Lafourche**, is the traditional gateway to Cajun country for those traveling from New Orleans. Thanks to a city center lined with historic homes, it's a fair bit more attractive than nearby Houma, which is often also cited as a major Cajun Country destination but is in reality more of a charmless oil town. The main attraction in Thibodaux is the **Wetlands Acadian Cultural Center** (985-448-1375; www.nps.gov/jela; 314 St Mary St; 9am-7pm Mon & Tue, to 5pm Wed-Fri;), part of the Jean Lafitte National Park system. NPS rangers lead boat tours from here into the bayou during spring and fall; you can either chug to the **ED White Plantation** home on Wednesday (10am to noon; $5) or head to the **Madewood Plantation** on Saturday (10am to 2:30pm; $32), where you're given a house tour and lunch. The center also hosts an excellent on-site museum and helpful staff who provide free walking tours of Thibodaux town (2pm, Monday, Tuesday and Thursday). If you're lucky, you'll land here on a Monday evening, when Cajun musicians jam out (5:30pm to 7pm).

p233

The Drive » Get on Hwy 90 and drive to Breaux Bridge. It's about two hours nonstop, but don't be afraid to occasionally peel off and check out some side roads.

TRIP HIGHLIGHT

❷ Breaux Bridge

Little Breaux Bridge boasts a pretty 'downtown' of smallish side

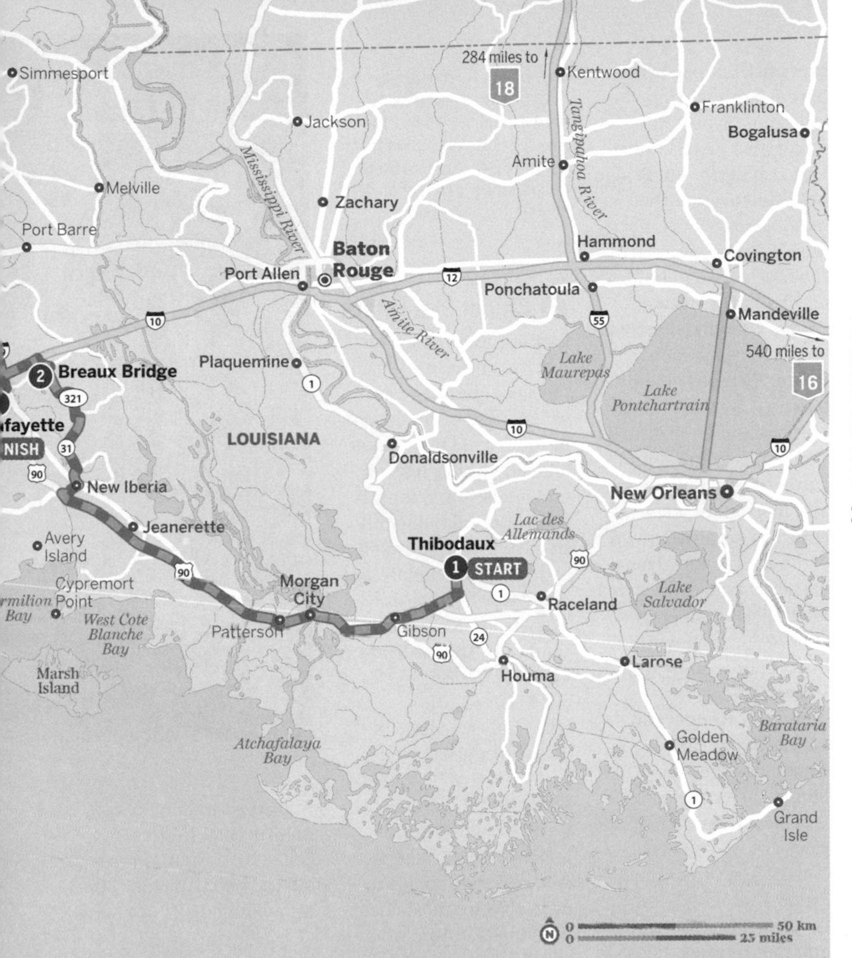

streets, Cajun hospitality and a silly amount of good food. Your main objective is to eat at the ridiculously delicious Café des Amis (p233), where sinfully good Cajun fare is often served alongside local live music. The shows are scheduled for Wednesday nights and Sunday mornings (zydeco

LINK YOUR TRIP

16 Highway 1

From Thibodaux make your way to Baton Rouge then head east on the I-12 and I-10 all the way to the start of your Florida coast cruise.

18 The Blues Highway

From Thibodaux head north to Baton Rouge then east on I-12. At Hammond, head north on the I-55 to Memphis.

brunch!), but performers have a habit of dropping in unexpectedly. Otherwise there's not a lot to do in Breaux Bridge but stroll around the handsome town center and, if you're here during the first weekend in May, check out the **Breaux Bridge Crawfish Festival**.

Three miles south of Breaux Bridge is **Lake Martin** (Lake Martin Rd), a bird sanctuary that hosts thousands of great and cattle egrets, blue heron and more than a few gators. A small walkway extends over the algae-carpeted black water and loops through a pretty cypress swamp, while birds huddle in nearby trees.

Stop by **Henderson**, 8 miles northeast of Breaux Bridge. On Sunday afternoons, **Whiskey River** (☎337-228-8567; www.whiskeyriverla.com; 1365 Henderson Levee Rd; cover varies; ⌚3-9pm Sun) rocks to zydeco and Cajun tunes. It's a small house, and it gets packed. Locals dance on tables, on the bar and in the water. Nearby **Pat's** (☎337-228-7512; www.patsfishermanswharf.com; 1008 Henderson Levee Rd; mains $12-26; ⌚11am-9:30pm Sun-Thu, to 10:30pm Fri & Sat; P) serves decent seafood of the fried variety, and dancing of the two-step and Cajun genre.

✕ 🛏 p233

The Drive » From Breaux Bridge you can take Hwy 49 north for about 24 miles, then Hwy 167 north to Ville Platte, then LA 3042 to Chicot State Park, a total trip time of about 80 minutes.

TRIP HIGHLIGHT

❸ Chicot State Park

Cajun Country isn't just a cultural space – it's a physical landscape as well, a land of shadowy, moss-draped pine forest and slow-water bayous and lakes. Sometimes it can be tough seeing all this from the roadways, as roads have understandably been built away from floodable bottomlands. **Chicot State Park** (☎337-363-2403, 888-677-2442; www.crt.louisiana.gov/louisiana-state-parks/parks/chicot-state-park; 3469 Chicot Park Rd, Ville Platte; per person $3; ⌚6am-9pm Sun-Thu, to 10pm Fri & Sat; P 👪 🐾) is a wonderful place to access the natural beauty of Cajun Country. An excellent interpretive center is fun for kids and informative for adults, and deserves enormous accolades for its open, airy design. Miles of **trails** extend into the nearby forests, cypress swamps and wetlands. If you can, stay for early evening; the sunsets over the Spanish-moss-draped trees that fringe **Lake Chicot** are superb. There are **campsites** ($16 per night October to March, $20 April to September), **cabins** (six-/15-person $85/120) and **boat rentals** (per hour/day $5/20) all available.

JAYL / SHUTTERSTOCK ©

The Drive » Head back towards Ville Platte, then turn onto LA 10 west. After 7 miles turn south onto LA 13; it's about 4 miles more to Mamou.

❹ Mamou

Deep in the heart of Cajun Country, Mamou is a typical south Louisiana small town six days of the week, worth a peek and a short stop before rolling to Eunice. But on Saturday mornings, Mamou's hometown

Chicot State Park Bald cypress swamp

hangout, little **Fred's Lounge** (420 6th St; ⌚8:30am-2pm Sat), becomes the apotheosis of a Cajun dancehall.

OK, to be fair: Fred's is more of a dance shack than hall. It's a little bar and it gets more than a little crowded from 8:30am to 2pm-ish, when owner 'Tante' (auntie) Sue and her staff host a Francophone-friendly music morning, with bands, beer, cigarettes and dancing (seriously, it gets smoky in here. Fair warning). Sue herself will often take to the stage to dispense wisdom and song in Cajun French, all while taking pulls off a bottle of brown liquor she keeps in a pistol holster.

The Drive » Eunice is only 11 miles south of Mamou; just keep heading straight on LA 13.

5 Eunice

Eunice lies in the heart of the Cajun prairie, its associated folkways, and music. Musician Mark Savoy builds accordions at his **Savoy Music Center** (☎337-457-9563; www.savoymusiccenter.com; 4413 Hwy 190; ⌚9am-5pm Tue-Fri, to noon Sat), where you can also pluck some CDs and catch a Saturday-morning jam session. Saturday night means the **Rendez-Vous Cajuns** are playing the **Liberty Theater** (☎337-457-6577; www.eunice-la.com/index.php/things-to-do/liberty-schedule; 200 Park Ave; $5; ⌚6-7:30pm), which is just two blocks from the **Cajun Music Hall of Fame & Museum** (☎337-457-6534; www.cajunfrenchmusic.org; 230 S CC Duson Dr; ⌚9am-5pm) – a small affair, to be sure, but charming in its way. The NPS-run **Prairie Acadian Cultural Center** (☎337-457-8499; www.nps.gov/jela; 250 West Park Ave; ⌚9:30am-4:30pm Wed-Fri, to 6pm Sat) is another worthy stop, and

CAJUNS & CREOLES

A lot of tourists in Louisiana use the terms 'Cajun' and 'Creole' interchangeably, but the two cultures are different and distinct. 'Creole' refers to descendants of the original European settlers of Louisiana, a blended mix of mainly French and Spanish ancestry. The Creoles tend to have urban connections to New Orleans and considered their own culture refined and civilized. Many (but not all) were descended from aristocrats, merchants and skilled tradespeople.

The Cajuns can trace their lineage to the Acadians, colonists from rural France who settled Nova Scotia. After the British conquered Canada, the proud Acadians refused to kneel to the new crown, and were exiled in the mid-18th century – an act known as the Grand Dérangement. Many exiles settled in south Louisiana; they knew the area was French, but the Acadians ('Cajun' is an English bastardization of the word) were often treated as country bumpkins by the Creoles. The Acadians-cum-Cajuns settled in the bayous and prairies, and to this day self-conceptualize as a more rural, frontier-stye culture.

Adding confusion to all of the above is the practice, standard in many post-colonial French societies, of referring to mixed-race individuals as 'creoles.' This happens in Louisiana, but there is a cultural difference between Franco-Spanish Creoles and mixed-race creoles, even as these two communities very likely share actual blood ancestry.

often hosts music nights and educational lectures.

The Drive » Head east on Hwy 190 (Laurel Ave) and turn right onto LA 367. Follow LA 367 for around 19 miles (it becomes LA 98 for a bit), then merge onto I-10 eastbound. Follow I-10 for around 14 miles, then take exit 101 onto LA 182/N University Ave; follow it into downtown Lafayette.

TRIP HIGHLIGHT

6 Lafayette

Lafayette, capital of Cajun Country and fourth-largest city in Louisiana, has a wonderful concentration of good eats and culture for a city of its size (around 120,000). On most nights you can catch fantastic zydeco, country, blues, funk, swamp rock and even punk blasting out of the excellent **Blue Moon Saloon** (☎337-234-2422; www.bluemoonpresents.com; 215 E Convent St; cover $5-8; ⌚5pm-2am Tue-Sun); the crowd here is young, hip and often tattooed, but they'll get down to a fiddle as easily as drum-and-bass. During the last weekend in April Lafayette hosts **Festival International de Louisiane** (www.festivalinternational.org; ⌚Apr), the largest Francophone musical event in the Western Hemisphere.

Vermilionville (☎337-233-4077; www.bayouvermiliondistrict.org/vermilionville; 300 Fisher Rd; adult/student $10/6, boat tour $12/8; ⌚10am-4pm Tue-Sun; P 👪), a restored/re-created 19th-century Cajun village, wends its way along the bayou near the airport. Costumed docents explain Cajun, Creole and Native American history, local bands perform on Sundays and boat tours of the bayou are offered. The not-as-polished **Acadian Village** (☎337-981-2364; www.acadianvillage.org; 200 Greenleaf Dr; adult/student $8/6; ⌚10am-4pm Mon-Sat; P 👪) offers a similar experience, minus the boat tours. Next to Vermilionvile, the NPS runs the **Acadian Cultural Center** (☎337-232-0789; www.nps.gov/jela; 501 Fisher Rd; ⌚9am-4:30pm Tue-Fri, 8:30am-noon Sat; P 👪), containing exhibits on Cajun life; it's a little dry compared to the above, but still worth a visit.

✕ 🛏 p233

Eating & Sleeping

Thibodaux ❶

✕ Fremin's — Cajun $$

(☎985-449-0333; www.fremins.net; 402 W Third St; mains $12-37; ⏰11am-2pm Tue-Fri, 5-9pm Tue-Thu, to 10pm Fri & Sat) Fremin's is one of the great-granddaddies of high-end, classic Cajun cuisine. The menu doesn't change much, and while there are some items that could use an update, overall this is a solid menu. Case in point: soft-shell crab served over pasta with a very good mushroom brandy sauce.

Breaux Bridge ❷

✕ Café des Amis — Cajun $$

(☎337-332-5273; www.cafedesamis.com; 140 E Bridge St; mains $17-26; ⏰11am-2pm Tue, 11am-9pm Wed & Thu, 7:30am-9pm Fri & Sat, 8am-2pm Sun; 👪) In the compact, crawfish lovin' town of Breaux Bridge, you'll find this utterly unexpected cafe, where you can relax amid funky local art as waiters trot out sumptuous weekend breakfasts, all set to live zydeco music on Saturday morning. Dig in to Cajun classics with a contemporary twist like pecan-crusted catfish or eggs with crawfish étoufée.

🛏 Bayou Cabins — Cabin $

(☎337-332-6158; www.bayoucabins.com; 100 W Mills Ave; cabin $80-150; P 📶) The wonderful Bayou Cabins, situated on Bayou Teche, feature 14 completely individualized cabins, some with 1950s retro furnishings, others decked out in regional folk art. The included breakfast is delicious, but the smoked meats may shave a few years off your life.

Lafayette ❻

✕ Dwyer's — Diner $

(☎337-235-9364; 323 Jefferson St; mains $6-14; ⏰6am-2pm; 👪) This family-owned joint serves Cajun diner fare, finally bringing gumbo for lunch and pancakes for breakfast into one glorious culinary marriage. It's especially fun on Wednesday mornings when a French-speaking table is set up and local Cajuns shoot the breeze in their old-school dialect. Rotating lunch mains include smothered pork chops, fried chicken and shrimp stew.

✕ French Press — Breakfast $

(☎337-233-9449; www.thefrenchpresslafayette.com; 214 E Vermillion; mains $9-15; ⏰7am-2pm Mon-Fri, 9am-2pm Sat & Sun; 📶) This French-Cajun hybrid is one of the best culinary things going in Lafayette. Breakfast is mind-blowing, with a sinful Cajun Benedict (boudin instead of ham), cheddar grits (that will kill you dead) and organic granola (to offset the grits). Lunch ain't half bad either; the fried shrimp melt, doused in Sriracha mayo, is gorgeously decadent.

🛏 Blue Moon Guest House — Guesthouse $

(☎337-234-2422; www.bluemoonpresents.com; 215 E Convent St; dm $18, r $70-90; P ❄ @ 📶) This tidy home is one of Louisiana's travel gems: an upscale hostel-like hangout just walking distance from downtown. Snag a bed and you're on the guest list for Lafayette's most popular down-home music venue (p232), located in the backyard. The friendly owners, full kitchen and camaraderie among guests create a unique music-meets-migration environment catering to backpackers, flashpackers and those in transition (flashbackpackers?). Prices skyrocket during festival time. Decidedly not quiet.

Gibson
Lucille

The Blues Highway

Listen to living blues legends howl their sad enlightenment and pay homage to the music that saturated northern Mississippi for a century and bloomed into rock and roll.

TRIP HIGHLIGHTS

START
Memphis
Helena

100 miles
Clarksdale
The inviting hub of Delta blues country

115 miles
Tutwiler
Pay homage to the tiny town that sprouted the blues

Greenwood

185 miles
Indianola
Home to our favorite museum in the Delta

Bentonia
FINISH

3 DAYS
350 MILES / 563KM

GREAT FOR...

BEST TIME TO GO

Blues festivals bloom in the Delta in May and June, and October is an obscenely pleasant month.

Snap Red's smoky glow while a bluesman wails on stage.

The Mississippi Delta is cultural immersion – with an epic soundtrack.

Indianola Replica of Lucille, BB King's guitar, at the BB King Museum & Delta Interpretive Center

18 The Blues Highway

In the plains, along Hwy 61, American music took root. It arrived from Africa in the souls of slaves, morphed into field songs, and wormed into the brain of a sharecropping troubadour waiting for a train. In Clarksdale, at the crossroads, Robert Johnson made a deal with the devil and became America's first guitar hero. But to fully grasp its influence, start in Memphis.

❶ Memphis

The Mississippi Delta and Memphis have always been inextricably linked. Memphis was a beacon for the Delta bluesmen, both because it's the region's biggest city, but also because Memphis meant a certain amount of freedom, African American–owned businesses, and the bright lights and foot-stomping crowds of Beale St, which is still rocking. **Rum Boogie** (www.rumboogie.com; 182 Beale St; ⏰11am-1am) is a Cajun-themed blues bar with a terrific house band.

The original **BB King's** (☎901-524-5464; www.bbkingclubs.com; 143 Beale St; ⏰11am-11:30pm Mon-Thu, noon-2am Fri, 11am-midnight Sat, 11am-11pm Sun) is a living monument to the Mississippi genius who made good here. And it was in Memphis where WC Handy was first credited with putting the blues to paper when he wrote 'Beale Street Blues' in 1916. You can visit the **house** (www.wchandymemphis.org; 352 Beale St; adult/child $6/4; ⏰11am-4pm Tue-Sat winter, 10am-5pm summer) where Handy lived. The Mississippi Delta legacy bubbles up at **Sun Studio** (☎800-441-6249; www.sunstudio.com; 706 Union Ave; adult/child $12/free; ⏰10am-6:15pm), where you can tour the label that launched Elvis – whose interpretation of the blues birthed rock and roll. And it's running through the veins of the wonderful **Stax Museum of American Soul Music** (☎901-942-7685; www.staxmuseum.com; 926 E McLemore Ave; adult/child $13/10; ⏰10am-5pm Tue-Sat, 1-5pm Sun). Those connections are explained perfectly at the **Memphis Rock 'n' Soul Museum** (www.memphisrocknsoul.org; 191 Beale St; adult/child $12/9; ⏰10am-7pm).

✕ 🛏 p243

The Drive » Hwy 61 begins in Memphis, where it is a wide avenue snaking through the city's rough seam. Eventually urbanity gives way to flat farmland, and the highway goes rural as you enter Mississippi. It's about 30 miles to Tunica.

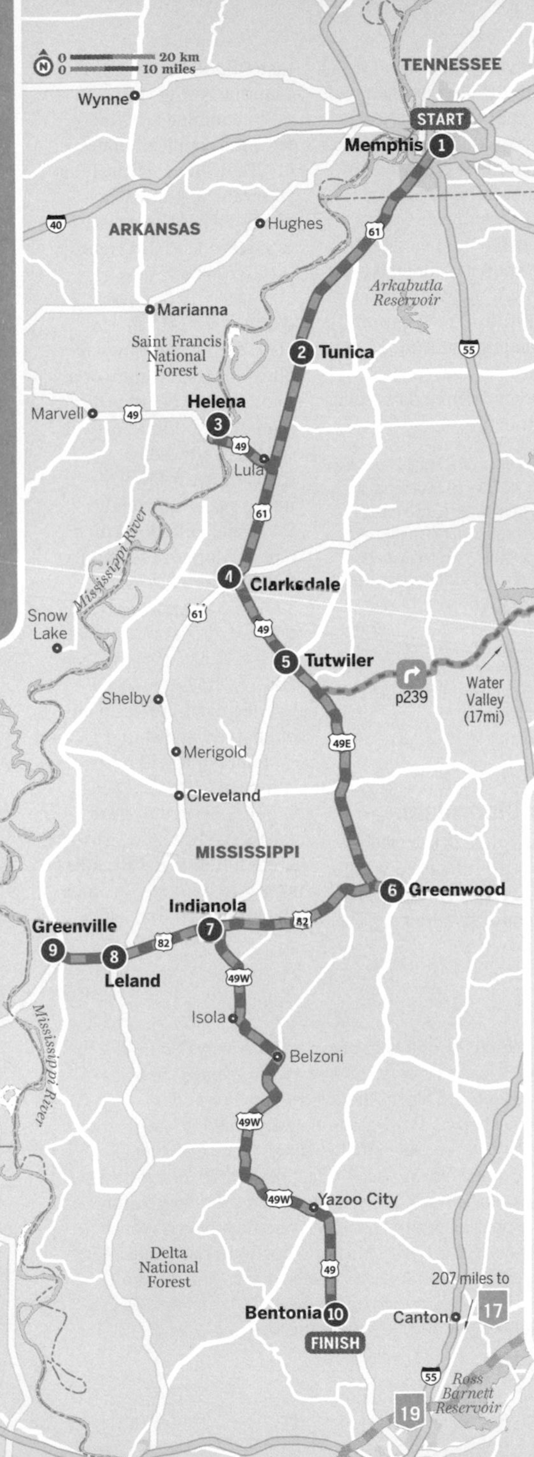

2 Tunica

A collection of casinos rests near the riverbanks in Tunica, Hwy 61's most-prosperous and least-authentic town. Nevertheless, it is the gateway to the blues and home to their juke-joint mock-up of a **Visitor Center** (☎888-488-6422; www.tunicatravel.com; 13625 US 61, Robinsonville; ⊙8am-5:30pm Mon-Fri, from 10am Sat, 1-5pm Sun), where a cool interactive digital guide comes packed with information on famed blues artists and the **Mississippi Blues Trail** itself. It's a good place to get inspired about what you are about to experience, and perhaps do some plotting and

LINK YOUR TRIP

17 Cajun Country

From Bentonia take Hwy 49 to Jackson and then south on I-55 until Hammond. From there head west to Baton Rouge and then south to Thibodaux and Cajun Country.

19 Natchez Trace Parkway

From Memphis head east on I-40 to Nashville where the Natchez Trace trail begins.

planning. Unless you play cards, however, Tunica is not otherwise noteworthy.

The Drive » Continue on the arrow-straight road for 19 miles, then veer west on Hwy 49 and drive 10 miles over the Mississippi River into Helena, AR.

3 Helena

Helena, AR, a depressed mill town 32 miles north and across the Mississippi River from Clarksdale, was once the home of blues legend Sonny Boy Williamson. He was a regular on *King Biscuit Time,* America's original blues radio show. It still broadcasts out of the **Delta Cultural Center** (☎870-338-4350; www.deltaculturalcenter.com; 141 Cherry St; ⏰9am-5pm Tue-Sat; P), a worthwhile blues museum.

Down the street you'll find the Delta's best record store, **Bubba's Blues Corner** (☎870-338-3501; 105 Cherry St; ⏰9am-5pm Tue-Sat). Delightfully disorganized, it's supposedly a regular stop on Robert Plant's personal blues pilgrimages. Bubba himself is warm and friendly and offers a wealth of knowledge. If the shop isn't open when you fall by, give Bubba a ring, and he'll happily open up. The King Biscuit Blues Festival (p242) is held over three days each October.

The Drive » Hwy 49 converges with the Hwy 61 in Mississippi, and from there it's 30 miles south until you reach the Crossroads. Peeking out above the trees on the northeast corner of Hwy 61 and Hwy 49, where the roads diverge once again, is the landmark weathervane of three interlocking blue guitars. You have arrived in the Delta's beating heart.

TRIP HIGHLIGHT

4 Clarksdale

Clarksdale is the Delta's most useful base – with more comfortable hotel rooms and modern, tasteful kitchens here than the rest of the Delta combined. It's also within a couple of hours of all the blues sights. If you want to know who's playing where, come see Roger Stolle at **Cat Head** (☎662-624-5992; www.cathead.biz; 252 Delta Ave; ⏰10am-5pm Mon-Sat). He also sells a good range of blues souvenirs, and is the main engine behind the annual Juke Joint Festival (p242). Wednesday through Saturday, live music sweeps through Clarksdale like a summer storm. Morgan Freeman's **Ground Zero** (☎662-621-9009; www.groundzeroblues club.com; 252 Delta Ave; ⏰11am-2pm Mon & Tue, to 11pm Wed & Thu, to 2am Fri & Sat) has the most professional bandstand and sound system, but it will never compare to **Red's** (☎662-627-3166; 395 Sunfl ower Ave; cover $10; ⏰live music 9pm Fri & Sat), a funky, red-lit, juke joint run with in-your-face charm by Red himself.

BB KING'S BLUES

BB King grew up in the cotton fields on the outskirts of Indianola, a leafy middle-class town, and it didn't take long before he learned what it meant to have the blues. His parents divorced when he was four, and his mother died when he was nine. His grandmother passed away when he was 14. All alone, he was forced to leave Indianola – the only town he ever knew – and live with his father in Lexington, MS. He quickly became homesick, and made his way back, riding his bicycle for two days to return to Indianola. As a young man he was convinced he would become a cotton farmer. There weren't many other possibilities to consider. Or so he thought. When he went to Memphis for the first time in the 1940s, his world opened. From there he drifted into West Memphis, AR, where he met Sonny Boy Williamson, who put the young upstart on the radio for the first time, launching his career. When King died in 2015, it felt as if the entire Delta took a few days to mourn the loss of a legend.

He'll fire up his enormous grill outside on special occasions. The **Delta Blues Museum** (☎662-627-6820; www.deltabluesmuseum.org; 1 Blues Alley; adult/child $10/8; ⏰9am-5pm Mon-Sat), set in the city's old train depot, has a fine collection of blues memorabilia, including Muddy Waters' reconstructed Mississippi cabin. The creative, multimedia exhibits also honor BB King, John Lee Hooker, Big Mama Thornton and WC Handy.

p243

The Drive » From Clarksdale, take Hwy 49 south from the Crossroads for 15 miles to the tiny town of Tutwiler.

TRIP HIGHLIGHT

5 Tutwiler

Sleepy Tutwiler is where WC Handy heard that ragged guitar man in 1903. Handy, known as the 'father of the blues,' was inspired to (literally) write the original blues song, in 12 bars with a three chord progression and AAB verse pattern, in 1912, though he wasn't widely recognized as an originator until 'Beale Street Blues' became a hit in 1916. That way-back divine encounter, which birthed blues and jazz, is honored along the **Tutwiler Tracks** (Front & Hancock Sts; 🚻), where the train station used to be. The mural also reveals the directions to **Sonny Boy Williamson's Grave** (off Prairie Rd, 34.018481, -90.457624). He's buried amid a broken-down jumble of gravestones and Williamson's headstone is set back in the trees. Rusted harmonicas, candles and half-empty whiskey bottles have been left here out of respect.

The Drive » Continue on the other blues highway, Hwy 49 south, through more farmland for 42 miles, across the Yazoo River and into the tiny town of Greenwood.

6 Greenwood

Greenwood is the Delta's most prosperous town that doesn't involve slot machines. The financial backbone here is the Viking Range Corporation which builds its magnificent cooking ranges in town and whose wares you can buy in upmarket showrooms. There is also a fantastic cafe and a fine hotel – the best in the Delta – within these city

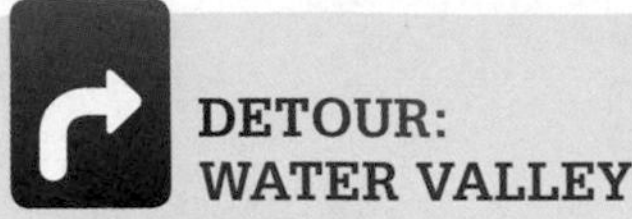

DETOUR: WATER VALLEY

Start: 5 Tutwiler

From Tutwiler, take MS 32 east for about 55 miles to reach Water Valley, a town that's about as pretty as its name implies. This was once a depressed railroad hub, but young professionals and artists from Oxford – just 20 miles north – came here attracted by a glut of gorgeous, if crumbling, historical homes. Veritable mansions were bought and restored for the cost of less than a year's rent in New York, yielding a small-town civic revival that's a joy to soak up. Wander along Main St and pop into galleries and restaurants, or marvel at the architecture of restored homes on Leland and Panola streets.

KING BISCUIT TIME

Sonny Boy Williamson was the host of *King Biscuit Time* when BB King was a young buck. King recalls listening to the lunch-hour program, and dreaming of possibilities. When he moved to Memphis as a teenager and began playing Beale St gigs, Williamson invited King to play on his radio show, and a star was born. Williamson remained an important mentor for King as his career took off. The radio show, which begins weekdays at 12:15pm, is still running, and has been hosted by Sunshine Sonny Payne since 1951.

Above: Beale Street, Memphis
Below: Delta Blues Museum
Right: Juke Joint Festival performance

F11PHOTO / SHUTTERSTOCK ©

DELTA BLUES MUSEUM ©

SCOTT OLSON / GETTY IMAGES ©

limits. As far as history goes, Greenwood happens to be the hometown of Byron De La Beckwith, the murderer of Medgar Evers and, at the time of his crime, a member of the local White Citizens Council.

p243

The Drive » From Greenwood, take Hwy 82 east for 30 miles, over the Yazoo River, through leafy horse country, and through an ugly commercial bloom of big chain stores and kitchens, into Indianola.

TRIP HIGHLIGHT

7 Indianola

You have reached the home town of arguably the Delta's biggest star. When BB King was still a child, Indianola was home to **Club Ebony** (404 Hannah St; from 8pm Thu), a fixture on the so-called 'chitlin circuit.' Ebony gave BB his first steady work, and hosted legends like Howlin' Wolf, Muddy Waters, Count Basie and James Brown. The corner of Church and 2nd is where BB used to strum his beloved guitar, Lucille, for passersby. Nearby, the **BB King Museum & Delta Interpretive Center** (662-887-9539; www.bbkingmuseum.org; 400 Second St; adult/child 5-7yr/under 5yr $15/$10/ free; 10am-5pm Tue-Sat, noon-5pm Sun & Mon) is set in a complex around the old Indianola cotton gin. The experience starts with a 12-minute film covering

King's work. Afterward you are free to roam halls packed with interactive exhibits, tracing King's history and his musical influences – African, gospel and country. Other interactive exhibits demonstrate his influence on the next generation of artists, including Jimi Hendrix and the Allman Brothers. Oh, and BB's 12 Grammy awards are here, too.

The Drive » From Indianola, go west through 15 miles of fast-food jumble along Hwy 82 into Leland.

8 Leland

Leland is a small, down-on-its-luck town, but one with a terrific museum. The **Hwy 61 Blues Museum** (☎662-686-7646; www.highway61blues.com; 307 N Broad St; $7; ⏲10am-5pm Mon-Sat) offers details on local folks like Ruby Edwards and David 'Honeyboy' Edwards.

Luminary Jim Henson, the creator of the Muppets, is also from Leland, and his life and work are celebrated at the Jim Henson Exhibit on the bank of Deer Creek.

The Drive » Head west on Hwy 82 for 25 miles until it ends near the river.

9 Greenville

The Mississippi River town of Greenville was a fixture on the riverboat route and has long been a gambling resort area. For years it supported blues and jazz musicians who played the resorts. Although it's scruffy around the edges, Greenville can be pleasant along the river. But the real reason to visit is to try the steaks, tamales and chili at **Doe's Eat Place** (☎662-334-3315; www.doeseatplace.com; 502 Nelson St; mains $22-40; ⏲5-9pm Mon-Sat) – a classic hole-in-the-wall joint you may never forget.

The Drive » Return to Indianola then drive south on Hwy 49W to humble Bentonia; it's about a 90-mile drive.

10 Bentonia

Bentonia, once a thriving farming community, now has fewer than 100 people and the downtown is gutted, but it's still home to one of Mississippi's most historic jukes. The Holmes family opened the **Blue Front** (☎662-528-1900; www.facebook.com/bluefrontcafeblues; 107 E Railroad Ave; ⏲9am-8pm Mon-Thu, to 10pm Fri & Sat, 1-8pm Sun) during the Jim Crow period, when African Americans weren't even allowed to sip Coca-Cola. The Holmes sold house-stilled corn liquor (to blacks and whites) during Prohibition and welcomed all the Delta blues artists of the day: Sonny Boy, Percy Smith and Jack Owens among them. The joint still opens in the evenings, but live blues only blooms during Bentonia's annual festival when the town comes back to life, if ever so briefly.

FAVORITE BLUES FESTS

To make the most of your music-loving dollar, hit the Delta during one of its many blues festivals. Rooms can be scarce. Book well in advance.

Juke Joint Festival (www.jukejointfestival.com; tickets $15; ⏲Apr) Clarksdale

Bentonia Blues Festival (☎662-763-5306; www.facebook.com/BentoniaBluesFestival; tickets $10; ⏲mid-Jun) Bentonia

Sunflower River Blues & Gospel Festival (www.sunflowerfest.org; ⏲Aug) Clarksdale

Mighty Mississippi Music Festival (Warfield Point Park; weekend pass adult/student/child $70/35/20; ⏲late Sep) Greenville

King Biscuit Blues Festival (☎870-572-5223; www.kingbiscuitfestival.com; tickets $45; ⏲Oct) Helena

Eating & Sleeping

Memphis 1

Arcade — Diner $

(www.arcaderestaurant.com; 540 S Main St; mains $7-10; 7am-3pm Sun-Wed, to 11pm Thu-Sat) Step inside this ultra-retro diner, Memphis' oldest, and wander to the Elvis booth, strategically located near the rear exit. The King used to sit here and eat griddle-fried peanut butter and banana sandwiches and would bolt out the door if fan-instigated pandemonium ensued. Crowds still pack in for sublime sweet-potato pancakes – as fluffy, buttery and addictive as advertised.

Gus's World Famous Fried Chicken — Fast Food $

(www.gusfriedchicken.com; 310 S Front St; plates $6-12; 11am-9pm Sun-Thu, to 10pm Fri & Sat) Fried-chicken connoisseurs across the globe twitch in their sleep at night, dreaming about the gossamer-light fried chicken at this downtown concrete bunker, with a fun, neon-lit interior and vintage jukebox. On busy nights, waits can top an hour.

Charlie Vergos' Rendezvous — Barbecue $$

(901-523-2746; www.hogsfly.com; 52 S 2nd St; mains $8-20; 4:30-10:30pm Tue-Thu, 11am-11pm Fri, from 11:30am Sat) Tucked in its own namesake alleyway off Monroe Ave, this subterranean institution sells an astonishing 5 tons of its exquisite dry-rubbed ribs weekly. The ribs don't come with any sauce, but the pork shoulder does, so try a combo and you'll have plenty of sauce to enjoy. The beef brisket is also tremendous. Expect a wait.

Madison Hotel — Boutique Hotel $$$

(901-333-1200; www.madisonhotelmemphis.com; 79 Madison Ave; r from $279; P @) If you're looking for a sleek treat, check into these swanky, music-themed boutique sleeps. The rooftop Sky Terrace ($10 for non-guests) is one of the best places in town to watch a sunset, and stylish rooms have nice touches like hardwood entryways, high ceilings and Italian linens. Parking is $29.

Clarksdale 4

Abe's Bar-B-Q — Barbecue $

(662-624-9947; www.abesbbq.com; 616 State St; sandwiches $4-6, plates $6-14; 10am-8:30pm Mon-Sat, to 8pm Sun; P) Abe's has served zesty pork sandwiches, vinegary slaw and slow-burning tamales at the Crossroads since 1924.

Lofts at the Five & Dime — Apartment $$

(888-510-9604; www.fiveanddimelofts.com; 211 Yazoo St; lofts from $150;) Set in a 1954 building are plush, loft-style apartments with molded-concrete counters in the full kitchen, massive flat-screens in the living room and bedroom, terrazzo showers, and free sodas and water throughout your stay. They sleep up to four people comfortably.

Greenwood 6

Delta Bistropub — Southern US $$

(662-459-9345; www.deltabistro.com; 222 Howard St; mains $13-26; 11am-2pm & 5-9pm Tue-Fri, 11am-9pm Sat) A tasty upmarket cafe serving Southern treats like fried catfish and barbecue shrimp po'boys and crab bisque, as well as fine departures like local shrimp with lemon zest and fried basil, and a seared duck breast served with pork belly and grilled baby asparagus. This is the best kitchen in the Delta.

Alluvian — Boutique Hotel $$$

(662-453-2114; www.thealluvian.com; 318 Howard St; r $200-235, ste $300; P @) This stunning four-star boutique hotel includes a gallery of Delta art, a gushing fountain in the courtyard, and spacious rooms and suites with all the trimmings: soaker tubs, high ceilings, granite washbasins and checkerboard parlor floors in the bathrooms. Some rooms have courtyard views. Others overlook downtown Greenwood. Book ahead.

Natchez Trace Parkway

With emerald mounds, opulent mansions and layers of American history, the Natchez Trace Parkway winds 444 gorgeously wooded miles from Nashville all the way to southern Mississippi.

TRIP HIGHLIGHTS

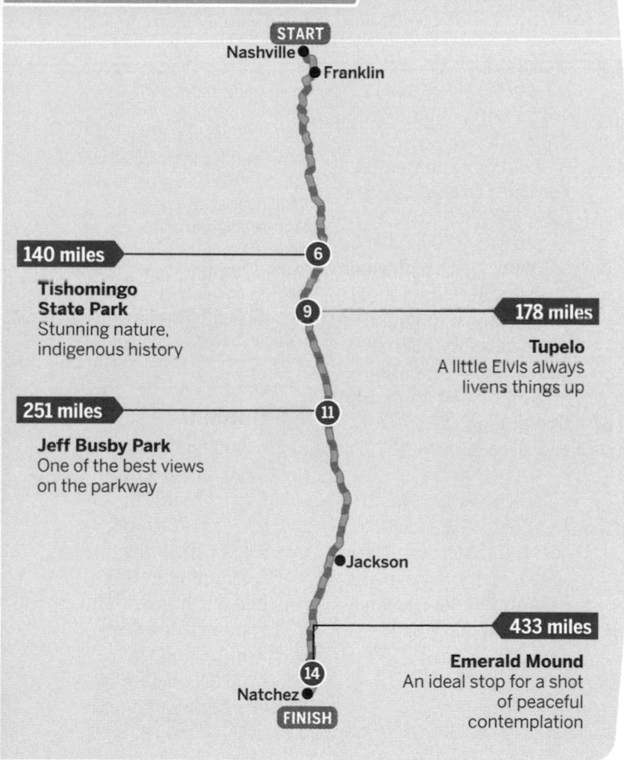

START
Nashville
Franklin

140 miles
6
Tishomingo State Park
Stunning nature, indigenous history

178 miles
9
Tupelo
A little Elvis always livens things up

251 miles
11
Jeff Busby Park
One of the best views on the parkway

Jackson

433 miles
Emerald Mound
An ideal stop for a shot of peaceful contemplation

14
Natchez
FINISH

3 DAYS
444 MILES / 714KM

GREAT FOR...

BEST TIME TO GO

The climate is lovely in spring (April to June) and fall (September to November).

ESSENTIAL PHOTO

Emerald Mound, second-largest Native American mound in the world, is magical just before sunset.

BEST FOR HISTORY

Glimpse indigenous ways and echoes of a pioneering past.

Natchez Trace Parkway The iconic Double-Arch Bridge

19 Natchez Trace Parkway

America grew from infancy to childhood then adolescence in the late 18th and 19th centuries. Early American settlers explored, expanded and traded, clashed with Native Americans, and confronted their own shadow during the Civil War. Evidence of this drama can be found along the Natchez Trace, but before you begin, hit the honky-tonks and enjoy a little night music.

1 Nashville

Although this leafy, sprawling Southern city – with its thriving economy and hospitable locals – has no scarcity of charms, it really is all about the music. Boot-stomping honky-tonks lure aspiring stars from across the country in the hopes of ascending into royalty, of the type on display at the **Country Music Hall of Fame** (www.countrymusichalloffame.com; 222 5th Ave S; ⏲9am-5pm; adult/child $25/15). Don't miss **Bluebird Cafe** (☎615-383-1461; www.bluebirdcafe.com; 4104 Hillsboro Rd; cover free-$30): tucked into a suburban strip mall, this singer-songwriter haven was made famous in the recent television series *Nashville*. No chitchat or you will get bounced. Enjoy a less-controlled musical environment at **Tootsie's Orchid Lounge** (☎615-726-7937; www.tootsies.net; 422 Broadway; ⏲10am-2:30am), a glorious dive smothered with old photographs and handbills from the Nashville Sound glory days. Bluegrass fans will adore **Station Inn** (☎615-255-3307; www.stationinn.com; 402 12th Ave S; ⏲open mike 7pm, live bands 9pm), where you'll sit at one of the small cocktail tables, swill beer (only), and marvel at the lightning fingers of fine bluegrass players.

✕ 🛏 p254

The Drive » The next day head south, and you will traverse the Double-Arch Bridge, 155ft above the valley, before settling in for a pleasant country drive on the parkway. You'll notice dense woods encroaching and arching elegantly over the baby-bottom-smooth highway for the next 444 miles. It's about 10 miles from Nashville to Franklin.

2 Franklin

Before you embark on the Trace, make a little side trip to Franklin. Although it's just 10 miles outside of Nashville, it's worth stopping in this tiny historic hamlet. The Victorian-era downtown is charming and the nearby artsy enclave of **Leiper's Fork** is fun and eclectic. But you're in the area to check out one of the Civil War's bloodiest battlefields. On November 30, 1864, 37,000 men (20,000 Confederates and 17,000 Union soldiers) fought over a 2-mile stretch of Franklin's outskirts. Nashville's sprawl has turned much of that battlefield into suburbs, but the **Carter House** (615-791-1861; www.boft.org; 1140 Columbia Ave; adult/child 6-15yr/child under 6yr $18/8/free; 9am-5pm Mon-Sat, 11am-5pm Sun;) property is a preserved 8-acre chunk of the **Battle of Franklin**. The house is still riddled with 1000-plus bullet holes.

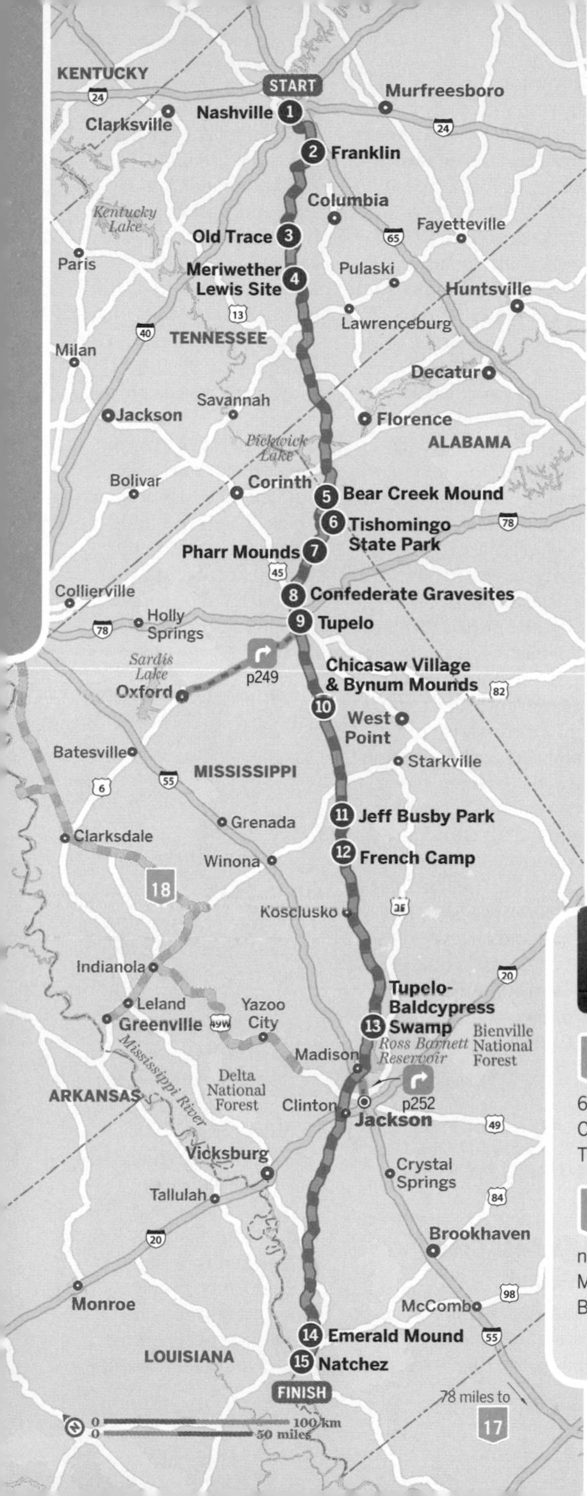

The Drive » The parkway carves a path through dense woodland as you swerve past another historic district at Leiper's Fork, before coming to the first of several Old Trace turnouts after approximately 40 miles.

LINK YOUR TRIP

17 Cajun Country

Head south on Hwy 61 from Natchez to Cajun Country's launching point in Thibodaux.

18 The Blues Highway

At Tupelo head northwest on I-78 to Memphis to link up with the Blues Highway.

3 Old Trace

At Mile 403.7 (yes that's right – don't worry about the 'backward' mile markers; we think a north–south route works best) you'll find the first of several sections of the Old Trace.

In the early 19th century, Kaintucks (boatspeople from Ohio and Pennsylvania) floated coal, livestock and agricultural goods down the Ohio and Mississippi Rivers aboard flat-bottom boats. Often their boats were emptied in Natchez, where they disembarked and began the long walk home up the Old Trace to Nashville, where they could access established roads further north. This walking path intersected Choctaw and Chicasaw country, which meant it was hazardous. In fact, indigenous travelers were the first to beat this earth. You can walk a 2000ft section of that original trail at this turnout.

The Drive » There's beaucoup beauty on a 20-mile stretch of road, as the parkway flows past Jackson Falls and the Baker Bluff overlook, which offers views over the Duck River.

4 Meriwether Lewis Site

At Mile 385.9 you'll come to the Meriwether Lewis Site, where the famed explorer and first governor of the Louisiana territory died mysteriously at nearby **Grinders Inn**. His fateful journey began in September 1809, and his plan was to travel to Washington, DC, to defend his spending of government funds (think of it as an early-days subpoena before a Congressional committee). At Fort Pickering, a remote wilderness outpost near modern-day Memphis, he met up with a Chicasaw agent named James Neely, who was to escort the Lewis party safely through Chicasaw land. They traveled north, through the bush, and along the Old Trace to **Grinder's Stand**, and checked into the inn run by the pioneering Grinder family. Mrs Grinder made up a room for Lewis and fed him, and after he retired, two shots rang out. The legendary explorer was shot in the head and chest and died at 35. Lewis' good friend, Thomas Jefferson, was convinced it was suicide. His family disagreed.

The Drive » It's about 77 miles to your next stop. Continue on and you will cross into Alabama at Mile 341.8, and Mississippi at Mile 308.

5 Bear Creek Mound

Just across the Alabama state line and in Mississippi, at Mile 308.8, you'll find Bear Creek Mound, an ancient indigenous ceremonial site. There are seven groups of Indian mounds found along the parkway, all of them in Mississippi. They varied in shapes from Mayan-like pyramids to domes to small rises, and were used for worship and burying the dead; some were seen as power spots for local chiefs who sometimes lived on top of them. That was arguably the case at Bear Creek, which was built between 1100 and 1300 AD. Archaeologists are convinced that there was a temple and/or a chief's dwelling on the top of the rise.

The Drive » The highway bisects Tishomingo State Park at Mile 304.5.

TRIP HIGHLIGHT

6 Tishomingo State Park

This state park is named for the Chicasaw Indian Chief Tishomingo. If you're taking it slow, you may want to **camp** (☎662-438-6914; www.mississippistateparks.reserveamerica.com; Mile 304.5 Natchez Trace Pkwy; campsite $18; 24hr;) here, among the evocative, moss-covered sandstone cliffs and rock formations, fern gullies and waterfalls of Bear Creek canyon. Hiking trails abound, canoes are available for rent if you wish to paddle

Bear Creek, and spring wildflowers bloom once the weather warms. It's a special oasis, and one that was utilized by the Chicasaw and their Paleo Indian antecedents. There is evidence of their civilization in the park dating back to 7000 BC.

The Drive » Just under 20 miles of more wooded beauty leads from Tishimongo State Park to the next in a series of Native American mounds at Mile 286.7.

7 Pharr Mounds

The Pharr Mounds is a 2000-year-old, 90-acre complex of eight indigenous burial sites. Four of them were excavated in 1966 and found to have fireplaces and low platforms where the dead were cremated. Ceremonial artifacts were also found, along with copper vessels, which raised some eyebrows. Copper is not indigenous to Mississippi, and its presence here indicated an extensive trade network with other nations and peoples.

The Drive » About 17 miles on, at Mile 269.4, you'll come across a turnout that links up to another section of the Old Trace and offers a bit more recent history.

8 Confederate Gravesites

Just north of Tupelo, on a small rise overlooking the Old Trace, lies a row of 13 graves of unknown Confederate soldiers. What led to their fate has been lost in time, but theories range from their having died during the Confederate retreat from Corinth, MS, following the legendary Battle of Shiloh. Others believe they were wounded in the nearby Battle of Brice's Crossroads, and buried by their brothers, here.

The Drive » Less than 10 miles later you will loop into the comparatively large hamlet of Tupelo, at Mile 266, where you can gather road supplies for the southward push.

TRIP HIGHLIGHT

9 Tupelo

Here, the **Natchez Trace Parkway Visitors Center** (☎800-305-7417, 662-680-4025; www.nps.gov/natr; Mile 266 Natchez Trace Pkwy; ⌚8am-5pm, closed Christmas;) is a fantastic resource with well-done natural- and American-history displays, and detailed parkway maps. Music buffs will know that Tupelo is world famous for its favorite son. **Elvis Presley's Birthplace** (☎662-841-1245; www.elvispresleybirthplace.com; 306 Elvis Presley Dr; adult/senior/child $17/14/8, house only adult/child $8/5; ⌚9am-5pm Mon-Sat, 1-5pm Sun; P) is a pilgrimage site for those who kneel before the King. The original structure has a new roof and furniture, but no matter the decor, it was within these humble walls that Elvis was born on January 8, 1935, where he learned to play the guitar and began to dream big. His family's church, where Elvis was first bit by the music bug, has been transported and restored here, as well.

The Drive » Just barely out of Tupelo, at Mile 261.8, is Chicasaw Village. The Bynum Mounds are another nearly 30 miles south. You'll see the turnoff just after leaving the Tombigbee National Forest.

DETOUR: OXFORD

Start: 9 Tupelo

If you plan on driving the entire Natchez Trace from Nashville to Natchez, you should make the 50-mile detour along Hwy 6 to Oxford, MS, a town rich in culture and history. This is Faulkner country, and Oxford is a thriving university town with terrific restaurants and bars. Don't miss the catfish dinner at Taylor Grocery (p255), 15 minutes south of Oxford, via County Rd 303.

Above: French Camp Museum
Left: Nine-banded armadillo
Right: Emerald Mound

LEAH SMALLEY / SHUTTERSTOCK ©

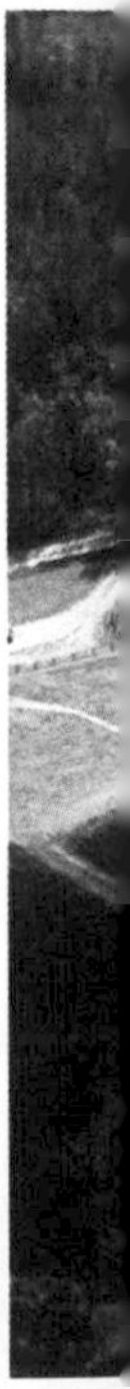

DANITA DELIMONT / GETTY IMAGES ©

FRANKE KEATING / GETTY IMAGES ©

⑩ Chicasaw Village & Bynum Mounds

South from Tupelo, the Trace winds past the Chickasaw Village Site, where you'll find displays documenting how the Chickasaw lived and traveled during the fur-trade heydays of the early 19th century. It was 1541 when Hernando de Soto entered Mississippi under the Spanish flag. They fought a bitter battle, and though De Soto survived, the Chickasaw held strong. By the 1600s the English had engaged the Chickasaw in what became a lucrative fur trade. Meanwhile, the French held sway just west in the massive Louisiana territory. As an ally to England, the Chickasaw found themselves up against not only the French, but their Choctaw allies.

Further down the road are the site of six 2100-year-old Bynum Mounds. Five were excavated just after WWII, and copper tools and cremated remains were found. Two of the mounds have been restored for public viewing.

The Drive » It's about 39 miles from the Bynum Mounds to Jeff Busby Park, which can be found at Mile 193.1.

TRIP HIGHLIGHT

⓫ Jeff Busby Park

Don't miss this hilltop park with picnic tables and a fabulous overlook taking in low-lying, forested hills that extend for miles, all the way to the horizon. Exhibits at the top include facts and figures about local flora and fauna, as well as a primer on indigenous tools. **Little Mountain Trail**, a half-mile loop that takes 30 minutes to complete, descends from the parking lot into a shady hollow. Another half-mile spur trail branches from that loop to the campground below.

The Drive » Thirteen miles down the road, at Mile 180, the forest clears and an agrarian plateau emerges, jade and perfect, as if this land has been cultivated for centuries.

⓬ French Camp

The site of a former French pioneer settlement, here you can tour an antebellum two-story home, built by Revolutionary War veteran Colonel James Drane. An end table is set for tea, aged leather journals are arranged on the desk and Drane's original US flag is in an upstairs bedroom along with an antique loom. Even more noteworthy is the ornate stagecoach of Greenwood LeFlore, which carried the last chief of the Choctaw nation east of the Mississippi on his two trips to Washington to negotiate with President Andrew Jackson. For more recent French camp history you can peruse the **French Camp Museum**. Set in a vintage log cabin, there are a number of historic photos on the porch, as well as framed newspaper articles and maps in the museum itself.

p255

The Drive » As you head south, the forest clears for snapshots of horses in the prairie, before the trees encroach again and again. The next stop is about 55 miles down the Trace.

⓭ Tupelo-Baldcypress Swamp

At Mile 122, you can examine some of these trees up close as you tour the stunning Tupelo-Baldcypress Swamp. The 20-minute **trail** snakes through an abandoned channel and continues on a boardwalk over the milky green swamp shaded by water tupelo and bald cypresses. Look for turtles on the rocks and gators in the murk.

The Drive » The swamp empties into the Ross R Barnett Reservoir, which you'll see to the east as you speed toward and through the state capital of Jackson. The next intriguing sight is just 10.3 miles from Natchez, accessible by graded road that leads west from the parkway.

DETOUR: JACKSON

Start: ⓭ Tupelo-Baldcypress Swamp

Twenty-two miles south of the swamp, and just a bit further along the interstate, is Mississippi's capital. With its fine downtown museums and artsy-funky **Fondren District** – home to Mississippi's best kitchen – Jackson offers a blast of Now if you need a pick-me-up. The city's two best sites are the **Mississippi Museum of Art** (www.msmuseumart.org; 380 South Lamar St; ⏲10am-5pm Tue-Sat, noon-5pm Sun; special exhibitions $5-12), which promotes homegrown artists and offers rotating exhibitions, and the **Eudora Welty House** (www.eudorawelty.org; 1119 Pinehurst St; ⏲tours 9am, 11am, 1pm & 3pm Tue-Fri; adult/student/child $5/3/free). This is where the literary giant, and Pulitzer Prize winner, crafted every last one of her books. And do not leave town without enjoying lunch or dinner at Walker's Drive-In (p255).

TRIP HIGHLIGHT

14 Emerald Mound

Emerald Mound is by far the best of the indigenous mound sites. Using stone tools, pre-Columbian ancestors to the Natchez people graded this 8-acre mountain into a flat-topped pyramid. It is now the second-largest mound in America. There are shady, creekside picnic spots here, and you can and should climb to the top where you'll find a vast lawn along with a diagram of what the temple may have looked like. It would have been perched on the secondary and highest of the mounds. A perfect diversion on an easy spring afternoon just before the sun smolders, when birdsong rings from the trees and comingles with the call of a distant train.

The Drive » Drive on for about 22 more miles. As you approach Natchez, the mossy arms of southern oaks spread over the roadway, and the air gets just a touch warmer and more moist. You can almost smell the river from here.

15 Natchez

When the woods part, revealing historic antebellum mansions, you have reached Natchez, MS. In the 1840s, Natchez had more millionaires per capita than any city in the world (because the plantation owners didn't pay their staff). Yes, old cotton money built these homes with slave labor, but they are graced all the same with an opulent, *Gone With the Wind* charm. 'Pilgrimage season' is in the spring and fall, when the mansions open for tours, though some are open year-round. The brick-red **Auburn Mansion** (☎601-446-6631; www.auburnmuseum.org; 400 Duncan Ave; adult/child $15/10; ⏲11am-3pm Tue-Sat, last tour departs 2:30pm; 👪) is famous for its freestanding spiral staircase. Built in 1812, the architecture here influenced countless mansions throughout the South.

Natchez has dirt under its fingernails, too. When Mark Twain came through town (and he did on numerous occasions), he crashed in a room above the local watering hole. **Under the Hill Saloon** (☎601-446-8023; 25 Silver St; ⏲10am-late), across the street from the mighty Mississippi River, remains the best bar in town, with terrific (and free) live music on weekends.

✕ 🛏 p255

Eating & Sleeping

Nashville ❶

✕ Prince's Hot Chicken Fast Food $

(123 Ewing Dr; quarter/half/whole chicken $5/11/22; ⏲11:30am-10pm Tue-Thu, 11:30am-4am Fri, 2pm-4am Sat; P) Tiny, faded, family-owned Prince's serves Nashville's most legendary 'hot chicken.' It's set in a gritty, northside strip mall and attracts everyone from hipsters to frat boys to entire immigrant families to local heads to hillbillies. Fried up mild (total lie), medium (what a joke), hot (verging on insanity), Xhot (extreme masochism) and XXXHot (suicide), its chicken will burn a hole in your stomach, and take root in your soul. Cash only.

✕ City House Southern US $$

(☎615-736-5838; www.cityhousenashville.com; 1222 4th Ave N; mains $15-29; ⏲5-10pm Mon & Wed-Sat, to 9pm Sun) This signless brick building in Nashville's smart Germantown district hides one of the city's best restaurants. The food, cooked in an open kitchen in the warehouse-like space, is a crackling bang-up of Italy meets New South. On offer are tangy kale salads, a tasty smoked lamb with chard, lemon and pecorino, pastas featuring twists like octopus ragu, or baked grits in cauliflower ragu. The folk at City House cure their own sausage and salamis, and take pride in their cocktail and wine list. Save room for dessert. Sunday supper features a stripped-down menu. The bar, pizza counter and screened-in porch are saved for walk-ins.

✕ Monell's Southern US $$

(☎615-248-4747; www.monellstn.com; 1235 6th Ave N; all you can eat $14-21; ⏲8am-3pm Mon, 8am-3pm & 5-8:30pm Tue-Sat, 8am-4pm Sun) In an old brick house just north of downtown, Monell's is beloved for down-home Southern food served family style. This is not just a meal, it's an experience, as platter after platter of skillet-fried chicken, pulled pork, corn pudding, baked apples, mac 'n' cheese and mashed potatoes keep coming...and coming. Clear your afternoon schedule!

🛏 Hutton Hotel Boutique Hotel $$

(☎615-340-9333; www.huttonhotel.com; 1808 West End Ave; r from $279; P ❄ @ 📶) One of our favorite Nashville boutique hotels riffs on mid-century modern design with bamboo-paneled walls and reclaimed WWI barn wood flooring. Sizable rust- and chocolate-colored rooms are well appointed with electrically-controlled marble rain showers, glass washbasins, king beds, ample desk space, wide flat-screens and high-end carpet and linens. Don't miss daily complimentary happy hours with local wineries, distilleries and breweries. Sustainable luxury abounds. Take a free spin in the hotel's electric Tesla!

🛏 Hotel Indigo Boutique Hotel $$

(☎615-891-6000; www.hotelindigo.com; 301 Union St; r from $189; P ❄ @ 📶) Part of a boutique international chain, the Indigo has a fun, pop-art look, with 161 rooms (30 of which are brand new). Avoid the original (but tacky) Terrazo floor rooms in favor of those spacious King Rooms, with brand new hardwood floors, high ceilings, flat-screens, leather headboards and office chairs.

🛏 Union Station Hotel Hotel $$$

(☎615-726-1001; www.unionstationhotelnashville.com; 1001 Broadway; r from $300; P ❄ 📶) This soaring Romanesque gray stone castle was Nashville's train station back in the days when rail travel was a grand affair; today it's downtown's most iconic hotel. The vaulted lobby is dressed in peach and gold with inlaid marble floors and a stained-glass ceiling. All rooms have just been tastefully modernized with new smart TVs, cowhide headboards and chicken wire chandeliers (upper floors).

Oxford

Taylor Grocery — Seafood $$

(☎662-236-1716; www.taylorgrocery.com; 4 1st St; dishes $9-15; ⏰5-10pm Thu-Sat, to 9pm Sun; P) Be prepared to wait at this splendidly rusticated catfish haunt. Order fried or grilled (either way, it's amazing) and bring a marker to sign your name on the wall. It's about 7 miles from downtown Oxford, south on Old Taylor Rd.

French Camp 12

French Camp B&B — B&B $$

(☎662-547-6835; www.frenchcamp.org; Mile 180.7 Natchez Trace Pkwy; r $95-145; P ❄ 👪) Stay the night in a log cabin built on a former French pioneer site that was further developed by a Revolutionary War hero. Rustic rooms and cabins will have you feeling close to nature – which is plentiful, gorgeous and all around you.

Jackson

Walker's Drive-In — Southern US $$$

(☎601-982-2633; www.walkersdrivein.com; 3016 N State St; lunch mains $8-17, dinner $29-37; ⏰11am-2pm Mon-Fri & from 5:30-10pm Tue-Sat) This retro masterpiece has been restored with love and infused with new Southern foodie ethos. Lunch is diner 2.0 fare with grilled redfish sandwiches, tender burgers and grilled oyster po'boys, as well as an exceptional seared, chili-crusted tuna salad, which comes with spiced calamari and seaweed.

Natchez 15

Magnolia Grill — Southern US $$

(☎601-446-7670; www.magnoliagrill.com; 49 Silver St; mains $13-22; ⏰11am-9pm, to 10pm Fri & Sat; 👪) Down by the riverside, this attractive wooden storefront grill with exposed rafters and outdoor patio is a good place for a pork tenderloin po'boy, or a fried crawfish spinach salad.

Cotton Alley — Cafe $$

(☎601-442-7452; www.cottonalleycafe.com; 208 Main St; mains $10-20; ⏰11am-2pm & 5:30-9pm Mon-Sat) This cute whitewashed dining room is chockablock with knickknacks and artistic touches and the menu borrows from local tastes. Think: grilled chicken sandwich on Texas toast and jambalaya pasta, but it does a nice chicken Caesar and a tasty grilled salmon salad too.

Mark Twain Guesthouse — Guesthouse $

(☎601-446-8023; www.underthehillsaloon.com; 33 Silver St; r without bath $65-85; ❄ 📶) Mark Twain used to crash in room 1, above the bar at the current Under the Hill Saloon (p253), when he was a riverboat pilot passing through town. There are three rooms in all, sharing one bath and laundry facilities.

Historic Oak Hill Inn — Inn $$

(☎601-446-2500; www.historicoakhill.com; 409 S Rankin St; r $135-160, ste $235; P ❄ 📶) Ever wish you could sleep in one of those historic homes? At the Historic Oak Hill Inn, you can sleep in an original 1835 bed and dine on pre–Civil War porcelain under 1850 Waterford crystal gasoliers – it's all about purist antebellum aristocratic living at this classic Natchez B&B.

Classic Trip

Blue Ridge Parkway

This drive on the USA's favorite byway curves through the leafy Appalachians, where it swoops up the East Coast's highest peak and stops by the nation's largest mansion.

TRIP HIGHLIGHTS

START Valle Crucis

5 6 10 11

FINISH Waterrock Knob Visitor Center

21 miles

Grandfather Mountain
Cross a mile-high suspension bridge for a parkway panorama

35 miles

Linville Falls
A family friendly hike leads to views of a 90ft waterfall

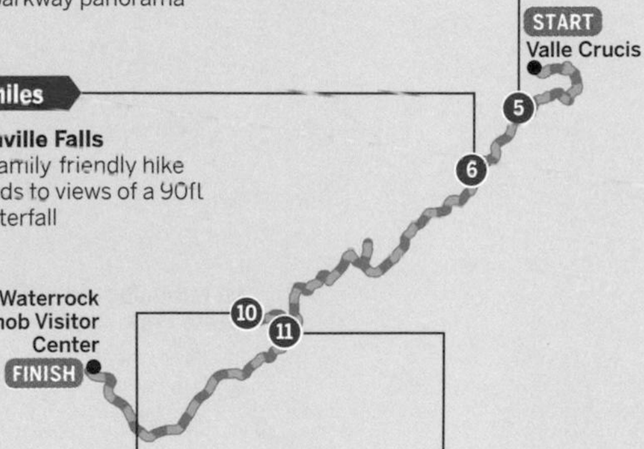

Downtown Asheville
Enjoy indie shops and microbreweries

101 miles

Biltmore Estate
Peer at gargoyles, dumbwaiters and a bowling alley

109 miles

5 DAYS
210 MILES / 338KM

GREAT FOR...

BEST TIME TO GO

May to October for leafy trees and open attractions.

ESSENTIAL PHOTO

The mile-high suspension bridge at Grandfather Mountain.

BEST FOR FAMILIES

Enjoy a steam-train ride, gem mining, easy hiking and old-fashioned candy.

Grandfather Mountain The famed 228ft-long suspension bridge

Classic Trip

20 Blue Ridge Parkway

The Blue Ridge Parkway stretches 469 miles, from Shenandoah National Park in Virginia to Great Smoky Mountains National Park in North Carolina. In the Tar Heel State, the road carves a sinuous path through a rugged landscape of craggy peaks, crashing waterfalls, thick forests and charming mountain towns. Three things you'll see? Whitetail deer, local microbrews and signs for Grandfather Mountain. And one piece of advice: at breakfast, never say no to a biscuit.

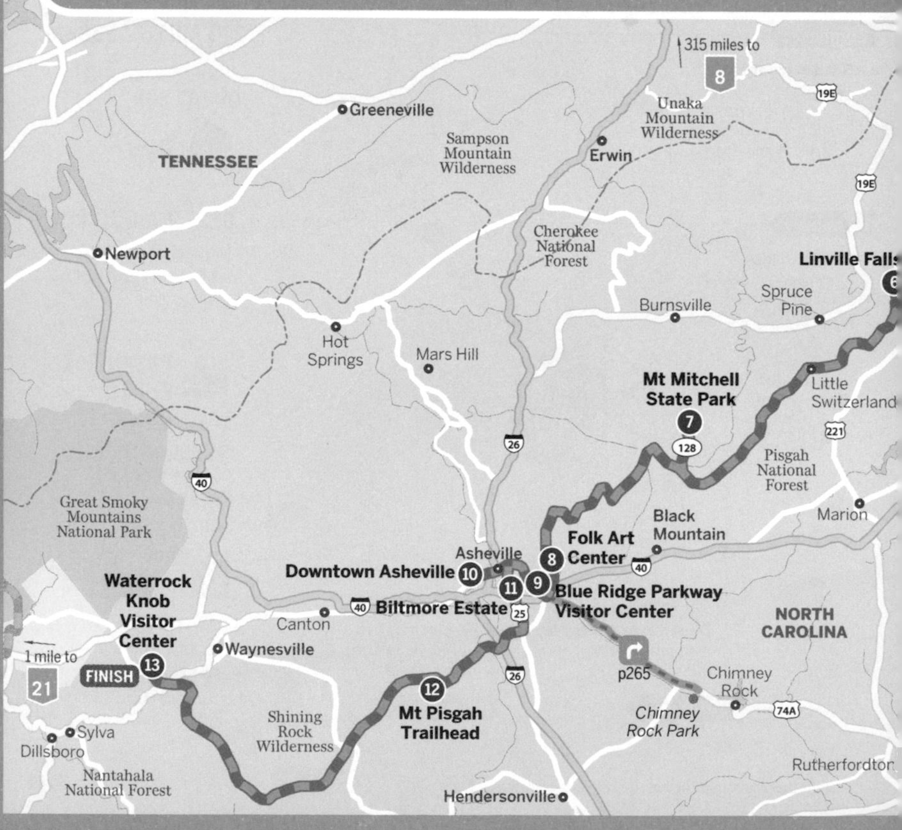

❶ Valle Crucis

How do you start a road trip through the mountains? With a good night's sleep and all the right gear. You'll find both in Valle Crucis, a bucolic village west of Boone. After slumbering beneath sumptuous linens at the Mast Farm Inn (p266), a 200-year-old farmhouse, ease into the day sipping coffee from a rocking chair on the inn's front porch.

Down the road is the **Original Mast General Store** (☎828-963-6511; www.mastgeneralstore.com; Hwy 194; ⏲10am-6pm Mon-Sat, noon-6pm Sun; 👪) and its **Annex** (⏲7am-6:30pm Mon-Sat, noon-6pm Sun). The first of several Mast general stores across the region, the original sells many of the same products that it did when it opened in 1883. Today you'll find bacon and hard candy as well as hiking shoes and French country hand towels. The Annex building, just south on Hwy 194, sells outdoor apparel and hiking gear.

p266

The Drive » Drive south on Hwy 194, also known as Broadstone Rd, through 3 miles of rural splendor. At Hwy 105 turn left.

❷ Boone

If you're traveling with kids or wannabe prospectors, stop at **Foggy Mountain Gem Mine** (☎828-963-4367; www.foggymountaingems.com; 4416 Hwy 105 S; buckets $30-325; ⏲10am-5pm; 👪) to pan for semiprecious stones, which are sold by the bucketload. There are several gem-mining spots near the parkway, but Foggy Mountain, a smaller company, is operated by graduate gemologists who may take their craft a bit more seriously. After sifting your rocks in a miner's flume line, the gemologists will cut and mount your favorite finds in any number of settings.

In downtown Boone, home of Appalachian State, you'll find shopping and dining on **King St**. Keep an eye out for the bronze statue of local bluegrass legend Doc Watson. He's strumming a Gallagher guitar like nobody's business at the corner of King and Depot Sts.

p266

The Drive » From King St, turn on to Hwy 321 just past the Dan'l Boone Inn restaurant. Drive 4 miles then turn right at the theme park.

LINK YOUR TRIP

8 Skyline Drive

Head north from Asheville on I-26 till you reach I-81. Follow that northeast for 300 miles to Strasburg where you'll take I-66 east to Front Royal.

21 The Great Smokies

From Waterrock Knob Visitor Center, head north until you reach Hwy 19. Follow this west through Cherokee to the start of the Great Smokies at Nantahala Outdoor Center.

3 Blowing Rock

The parkway runs just above the village of Blowing Rock, which sits at an elevation of 4000ft. On a cloudy morning, drive south on Hwy 321 to the top of the mountain to check out the cloud-capped views of surrounding peaks. The eastern continental divide runs through the bar at the Green Park Inn (p266), a white-clapboard grand hotel that opened in 1891. They say author Margaret Mitchell worked on *Gone with the Wind* while staying here.

A rite of passage for every North Carolina child is the **Tweetsie Railroad** (☎800-526-5740; www.tweetsie.com; 300 Tweetsie Railroad Lane; adult $45, child 3-12yr $30; ⏲9am-6pm daily Jun–mid-Aug, Fri-Sun mid-Apr–May, mid-Aug–Oct; 👪), a theme park where Appalachian culture meets the Wild West. The highlight? A 1917 coal-fired steam locomotive that chugs past marauding Indians and heroic cowboys. Midway rides, fudge shops and family-friendly shows round out the fun.

✕ 🛏 p266

The Drive » The entrance to the Blue Ridge Parkway is in Blowing Rock, 2.3 miles south of the Tweetsie Railroad. Once on the parkway, drive south 2 miles.

4 Moses H Cone Memorial Park

Hikers and equestrians share 25 miles of carriage roads on the former **estate** (Mile 294) of Moses H Cone, a wealthy philanthropist and conservationist who made his fortune in denim. His mansion and grounds were given to the national park service in the 1950s. His Colonial Revival mansion, completed in 1901, now houses the **Parkway Craft Center** (☎828-295-7938; www.southernhighlandguild.org; Mile 294; ⏲9am-5pm mid-Mar–Nov). The shop sells high-end crafts made by members of the Southern Highland Craft Guild. Free tours of the 2nd floor of

BLUE RIDGE PARKWAY TRIP PLANNER

Construction of the parkway began in 1935, during the Great Depression, after the government harnessed the strength of thousands of out-of-work young men in the Civilian Conservation Corps. The parkway wasn't fully linked together until 1987, when the Lynn Cove Viaduct opened.

» The maximum speed limit is 45mph.

» Long stretches of the road close in winter and may not reopen until March. Many visitor centers and campgrounds are closed until May. Check the park service website (www.nps.gov/blri) for the latest information about road closures and the opening dates for facilities.

» The North Carolina section of the parkway begins at Mile 216.9, between the Blue Ridge Mountain Center in Virginia and Cumberland Knob in North Carolina.

» There are 26 tunnels on the parkway in North Carolina (and just one in Virginia). Watch for signs to turn on your headlights.

» For more trip-planning tools, check the websites for the Blue Ridge Parkway Association (www.blueridgeparkway.org) and the Blue Ridge National Heritage Area (www.blueridgeheritage.com).

the mansion, Flat Top Manor, are offered on Saturdays and Sundays June through mid-October at 10am, 11am, 2pm and 3pm. Tours fill up. To reserve a spot call ☎828-295-3782 on the Friday before your visit.

The Drive » Head south on the parkway, passing split rail fences, stone walls, streams and meadows. Just south of Mile 304 the parkway curves across the Linn Cove Viaduct, the last section of the parkway to be completed, in 1987, because of the terrain's fragility. Exit on to Hwy 221 at Mile 305 and drive 1 mile south.

TRIP HIGHLIGHT

5 Grandfather Mountain

Don't let a fear of heights keep you from driving up to the famed swinging bridge near the peaks of **Grandfather Mountain** (☎828-733-4337; www.grandfather.com; Blue Ridge Pkwy Mile 305, Linville; adult $20, child 4-12yr $9; ⏲8am-7pm Jun-Aug, closes earlier fall, winter & spring). Yes, the 228ft-long bridge is 1 mile above sea level and yes, you can hear its steel girders 'sing' on gusty days, but the ground is just 80ft below the span. Nothing to sneeze at, for sure, but it's not the Grand Canyon, and the views of nearby mountains are superb. The small nature museum spotlights local flora and fauna as well as regional explorer Daniel Boone. Behind the museum, black bears, deer and otters roam a small animal habitat. Grandfather Mountain is a Unesco Biosphere Reserve.

Park attractions have been privately managed by the Morton family since the 1950s. The North Carolina State Park System purchased the mountain's backcountry lands in 2008, and Grandfather Mountain State Park (www.ncparks.gov) was established the following year. State park trails can be accessed from the parkway for free, or from parking lots inside the attraction with paid admission. The strenuous but varied Grandfather Trail runs 2.4 miles from the suspension bridge parking lot along the mountain's crest, ending atop Calloway Peak; the trail includes cables and ladders.

The Drive » Follow the parkway south and turn left just south of Mile 316 to reach Linville Falls.

TRIP HIGHLIGHT

6 Linville Falls

Have time for just one hike? Then hop out of your car for the moderate 1.6-mile Erwin's View Trail (round-trip) at popular Linville Falls. Here, the Linville River sweeps over two separate falls before crashing 2000ft through a rocky gorge. The trail crosses the river then follows it downstream. At half a mile, a spur trail leads to a view of the Upper Falls. The 90ft Lower Falls are visible from the Chimney View and Gorge View overlooks just ahead. At the latter you'll also see the imposing Linville Gorge. Ponder the scope of it all at the trail's last stop, the Erwin's View Overlook.

The Drive » Drive south on the parkway and turn right, south of Mile 355, on to NC 128. Follow NC 128 into the park.

7 Mt Mitchell State Park

Be warned. A trip to **Mt Mitchell** (☎828-675-4611; www.ncparks.gov; 2388 State Hwy 128; ⏲7am-10pm May-Aug, closes earlier rest of year) might lead to a fight. Will you drive to the top of the highest mountain east of the Mississippi, or will you hike there? Make your decision at the park office (open 8am to 5pm daily April to October; closed weekends November to March), which sits beside a 2-mile trail to the 6684ft summit.

At the top you'll see the grave of the mountain's namesake, Dr Elisha Mitchell. A dedicated professor from the University of North Carolina, he died after a fall while trying to verify the height of the mountain in 1857. A circular ramp beside the grave

Classic Trip

ALEX GRICHENKO / GETTY IMAGES ©

MARY TERRIBERRY / SHUTTERSTOCK ©

WHY THIS IS A CLASSIC TRIP

KEVIN RAUB, WRITER

As a card-carrying member of the road-trip fan club, I rank the iconic Blue Ridge Parkway right up there with the best of the great American four-wheeled journeys. In the fall, the parkway comes alive in a kaleidoscopic barrage of intense color, turning one of the country's most fabled roads into a fantastical passageway of deep ruby red and burnt-orange foliage.

Top: View across Lake Lure
Left: Linville Lower Falls
Right: Bluegrass musicians, Asheville

MATT MUNRO / LONELY PLANET ©

leads to panoramic views of the surrounding Black Mountains and beyond.

The Drive » Return to the parkway and drive south to Mile 382. During the last two weeks of June look for blooming rhododendrons.

8 Folk Art Center

As you enter the lobby at the **Folk Art Center** (828-298-7928; www.southernhighlandguild.org; Mile 382; 9am-6pm Apr-Dec, to 5pm Jan-Mar), look up. A row of handcrafted Appalachian chairs hangs from the walls above. They're an impressive calling card for the gallery here, which is dedicated to Southern artisanship. The chairs are part of the Southern Highland Craft Guild's permanent collection, which holds more than 2400 traditional and modern crafts. Items from the collection – pottery, baskets, quilts, woodcarvings – are displayed on the 2nd floor. The Allanstand Craft Shop on the 1st floor sells a range of fine traditional crafts.

The Drive » Turn right on to the parkway and drive south. After crossing the Swannanoa River and I-40, continue to Mile 384.

9 Blue Ridge Parkway Visitor Center

Sit back and let the scenery come to you at this helpful **visitor center**

(☎828-298-5330; www.nps.gov/blri; Mile 384; ⏰9am-5pm), where a big-screen film, *Blue Ridge Parkway – America's Favorite Journey*, captures the beauty and wonder of the drive. A park service representative can provide details about trails along the parkway at the front desk. For a list of regional sites and activities, slide the digital monitor across the interactive I-Wall map at the back of the main hall. The adjacent regional information desk has brochures and coupons for Asheville area attractions.

The Drive » Drive north, backtracking over the interstate and river, and exit at Tunnel Rd, which is Hwy 70. Drive west to Hwy 240 west and follow it to the exits for downtown Asheville.

TRIP HIGHLIGHT

⑩ Downtown Asheville

Hippies. Hipsters. Hikers. And a few high-falutin' preppies. This 4H Club gives Asheville its funky charm. Just look around. Intellectual lefties gather at **Malaprop's Bookstore & Cafe** (☎828-254-6734; www.malaprops.com; 55 Haywood St; ⏰9am-9pm Mon-Sat, to 7pm Sun; 📶), where the shelves stretch from banned books to Southern cooking. And the hipsters? They're nibbling silky truffles at **Chocolate Fetish** (www.chocolatefetish.com; 36 Haywood St; truffles $2.25; ⏰11am-7pm Mon-Thu, to 9pm Fri & Sat, noon-6pm Sun) or sipping homegrown ale at microbreweries like the convivial – and hoppy – **Wicked Weed** (www.wickedweedbrewing.com; 91 Biltmore Ave; pints $4.50-6.40; ⏰11:30am-11pm Mon & Tue, to midnight Wed & Thu, to 1am Fri & Sat, noon-11pm Sun; 📶). At the engaging **Thomas Wolfe Memorial** (www.wolfememorial.com; 52 N Market St; museum free, house tour adult $5, child 7-17yr $2; ⏰9am-5pm Tue-Sat), the city celebrates its most famous angsty son, Thomas Wolfe, who penned the Asheville-inspired novel *Look Homeward, Angel.*

Hikers can shop for new boots at the impressive **Tops for Shoes** (www.topsforshoes.com; 27 N Lexington Ave; ⏰10am-6pm Mon-Sat, 1-5pm Sun) and outdoor gear at **Mast General Store** (www.mastgeneralstore.com; 15 Biltmore Ave; ⏰10am-6pm Mon-Thu, to 9pm Fri & Sat, noon-6pm Sun). And the preppies? They're working inside the downtown banks and law firms – and checking out the same places as everybody else.

The finishing touch? The sidewalk busker fiddling a high-lonesome mountain tune. It'll put a spring in your step while maybe just breaking your heart.

✕ 🛏 p266

BLUEGRASS & MOUNTAIN MUSIC

For locally grown fiddle-and-banjo music, grab your dance partner and head deep into the hills of the High Country. Regional shows and music jams are listed on the Blue Ridge Music Trails (www.blueridgemusic.org) and the Blue Ridge National Heritage Area (www.blueridgeheritage.com) websites.

Here are three to get you started:

Mountain Home Music Concert Series (www.mountainhomemusic.com) Spring through fall, enjoy shows by Appalachian musicians in Boone on scheduled Saturday nights.

Isis Music Hall (www.isisasheville.com) Local bluegrass greats are known to pop into the Tuesday-night sessions, an Asheville tradition.

Historic Orchard at Altapass (www.altapassorchard.org) On weekends May through October, settle in for an afternoon of music at Little Switzerland, at Mile 328.

The Drive » Follow Asheland Ave, which becomes McDowell St, south. After crossing the Swannanoa River, the entrance to the Biltmore Estate is on the right.

TRIP HIGHLIGHT

11 Biltmore Estate

The destination that put Asheville on the map is the 175,000-sq-ft **Biltmore Estate** (☎800-411-3812; www.biltmore.com; 1 Approach Rd; adult $65, child 10-16yr $32.50; ⊙house 9am-4:30pm, with seasonal variations). The French château-style megamansion, built by shipping and railroad heir George Vanderbilt II, was completed in 1895 after six years of work by hundreds of artists, craftspeople and educated professionals. The Vanderbilt-Cecil family still owns the estate. The entrance fee is steep, so arrive early to get your money's worth, and note that tours of the house are self-guided. The $11.75 audio tour is worth purchasing for the extra details. For an additional $20 you can take a general guided tour or join a specialized behind-the-scenes guided tour focusing on architecture, the family or the servants. Children aged 10 to 16 are free June through August with an adult paid admission.

In addition to the mansion there are gardens, trails, lakes, restaurants, two top-end hotels and a winery, with complimentary wine tasting. At the estate's Antler Hill Village, romantics shouldn't miss the new **Fashionable Romance: 60 Years of Vanderbilt Family Wedding Fashion** exhibit in the Biltmore Legacy building.

DETOUR: CHIMNEY ROCK PARK

Start: 10 Downtown Asheville

The American flag flaps in the breeze atop this popular park's namesake 315ft granite monolith. The top can be reached by elevator or by stairs – lots and lots of stairs. Once on top, look east for amazing views of Lake Lure. Another draw is the hike around the cliffs to 404ft Hickory Nut Falls. Scenes from the *Last of the Mohicans* were filmed at the **park** (www.chimneyrockpark.com; Hwy 64/74A; adult $15, child 5-15yr $7; ⊙8:30am-6pm mid-Mar–Nov, 10am-4:30pm Fri-Tue Dec–mid-Mar). There's a small exhibit about the movie inside the Sky Lounge. From Asheville, follow Hwy 74A east for 20 scenic, but very curvy, miles.

The Drive » After exiting the grounds, turn right on to Hwy 25 and continue to the parkway, not quite 3.5 miles, and drive south.

12 Mt Pisgah Trailhead

For a short hike to a panoramic view, pull into the parking lot beside the Mt Pisgah Trailhead just beyond Mile 407. From here, a 1.6-mile trail (one-way) leads to the mountain's 5721ft summit, which is topped by a lofty TV tower. The trail is steep and rocky in its final stretch, but you'll be rewarded with views of the French Broad River Valley and Cold Mountain, the latter made famous by Charles Frazier's novel of the same name. One mile south is a campground, a general store, a restaurant and an inn.

The Drive » The drive south passes the Graveyard Fields Overlook, which has short trails to scenic waterfalls. The 6047ft Richland-Balsam Overlook at Mile 431.4 is the highest point on the parkway. From here, continue south another 20 miles.

13 Waterrock Knob Visitor Center

This trip ends at the Waterrock Knob Visitor Center (Mile 451.2), which sits at an elevation of nearly 6000ft. With a four-state view, this scenic spot is a great place to see where you've been and to assess what's ahead. Helpful signage attaches a name to the mountains on the distant horizons.

Eating & Sleeping

Valle Crucis 1

Mast Farm Inn — B&B $$

(828-963-5857; www.themastfarminn.com; 2543 Broadstone Rd; r/cottage from $109/205;) In the beautiful hamlet of Valle Crucis, this restored farmhouse defines rustic chic with worn hardwood floors, claw-foot tubs and handmade toffees on your bedside table. Nine cabins and cottages also available. Settle into the 1806 Loom House log cabin, fire up the wood-burning fireplace and never leave. Rates include an evening happy hour with local cheeses and sweets.

Boone 2

Dan'l Boone Inn — Southern US $$

(828-264-8657; www.danlbooneinn.com; 130 Hardin St; breakfast adult $11, child $6-8, dinner adult $18, child $7-11; 11:30am-8:30pm Mon-Thu, to 9pm Fri & Sat, to 8:30pm Sun Jun-Oct, hours vary rest of year;) Quantity is the name of the game at this restaurant, and the family-style meals are a Boone (sorry) for hungry hikers. Open since 1959. Cash or check only.

Melanie's Food Fantasy — Cafe $$

(www.melaniesfoodfantasy.com; 664 W King St; breakfast $6-10, lunch & dinner $9-14; 8am-2pm Mon-Wed, 8am-2pm & 5-9pm Thu-Fri, 8am-2:30pm & 5-9pm Sat, 8:30am-2:30pm Sun;) On cutesy King St hippie types gobble up serious breakfast dishes (scrambles, eggs Benedict, omelets, waffles, pancakes) with a side of home fries at this farm-to-fork favorite, always with a vegetarian option (tempeh, soysage etc). Later in the day, excellent creative Southern fare (chipotle-honey salmon and grits, blackened pimento-cheese burger) is on the menu.

Blowing Rock 3

Bistro Roca — Modern American $$

(828-295-4008; www.bistroroca.com; 143 Wonderland Trail; lunch $9-16, dinner $9-34; 11am-3pm & 5-10pm Wed-Mon;) This cozy, lodge-like bistro, tucked just off Main St, occupies a Prohibition-era building and does upscale New American fare (lobster or pork-belly mac 'n' cheese, kicked-up habanero burgers, wood-fired pizzas, mountain-trout banh-mi sandwiches) with an emphasis on local everything. Order anything with the duck bacon and you're all set.

Cliff Dwellers Inn — Motel $$

(828-414-9596; www.cliffdwellers.com; 116 Lakeview Tce; r/apt from $99/149;) From its perch above town, this well-named motel lures guests with good service, reasonable prices, stylish rooms and balconies with sweeping views.

Green Park Inn — Historic Hotel $$

(828-414-9230; www.greenparkinn.com; 9239 Valley Blvd; r $89-299;) The eastern continental divide runs through the bar at this white-clapboard grand hotel that opened in 1891. They say author Margaret Mitchell worked on *Gone with the Wind* while staying here.

Asheville 10

12 Bones — Barbecue $

(www.12bones.com; 5 Foundy St; dishes $5.50-22; 11am-4pm Mon-Fri) How good is this BBQ? Well, former president Obama and wife Michelle stopped by a few years ago for a meal. The slow-cooked meats are smoky tender, and the sides, from the jalapeño-cheese grits to the smoked-potato salad, will bring you to the brink of the wild heart of life.

Sunny Point Cafe — Cafe $

(www.sunnypointcafe.com; 626 Haywood Rd; breakfast $3.50-11, mains $6.50-14.50; 8am-2:30pm Sun-Mon, to 9:30pm Tue-Sat) In the morning, solos, couples and ladies-who-breakfast fill this bright West Asheville spot that's loved for its hearty, homemade fare. The insanely good and towering huevos rancheros, with feta cheese and chorizo sausage, should come with an instruction manual! The cafe and its alt-hippie waitstaff embraces the organic and fresh, and even has its own garden. The biscuits are divine.

Admiral — Modern American $$

(828-252-2541; www.theadmirainc.com; 400 Haywood Rd; small plates $12-17, large plates $17-34; 5-10pm;) This concrete bunker beside a car junkyard looks divey on the outside. But inside? That's where the magic happens. This low-key West Asheville spot is one of the state's finest New American restaurants, serving wildly creative dishes – saffron tagliatelle with lima beans, zucchini and basil pesto – that taste divine.

Tupelo Honey — Southern US $$

(828-255-4863; www.tupelohoneycafe.com; 12 College St; brunch $6-17, lunch & dinner $9.50-30; 11am-9pm Mon-Fri, 9am-9pm Sat & Sun) This Asheville-based chain is a long-time favorite known for New Southern fare such as shrimp and grits with goat's cheese. Tupelo-born Elvis would have surely loved the fried-chicken BLT with apple-cider bacon! Brunches are superb, but no matter the meal, say yes to the biscuit. And add a drop of honey.

Sweet Peas Hostel — Hostel $

(828-285-8488; www.sweetpeashostel.com; 23 Rankin Ave; dm/pod $32/40, r with/without bath $105/75;) This spick-and-span hostel gleams with IKEA-like style, with shipshape steel bunk beds and blond-wood sleeping 'pods.' The loft-like space is very open and can be noisy (the downstairs Lexington Ave Brewery adds to the ruckus but hey, there's a discount) – what you lose in privacy and quiet, you gain in style, cleanliness, sociability and an unbeatable downtown location.

Campfire Lodgings — Campground $$

(828-658-8012; www.campfirelodgings.com; 116 Appalachian Village Rd; tent sites $35-40, RV sites $50-70, yurts $115-135, cabins $160; P) All yurts should have flat-screen TVs, don't you think? Sleep like the world's most stylish Mongolian nomad in one of these furnished multiroom tents, on the side of a wooded hill. Cabins and tent sites are also available. RV sites have stunning valley views and wi-fi access.

Aloft Asheville — Hotel $$$

(828-232-2838; www.aloftasheville.com; 51 Biltmore Ave; r from $250-450; P @) With a giant chalkboard in the lobby, groovy young staff, and an outdoor clothing store on the 1st floor, this place looks like the seventh circle of hipster. The only thing missing is a wool-cap-wearing bearded guy drinking a hoppy microbrew – oh, wait, over there. We jest. Once settled, you'll find the staff knowledgeable and the rooms colorful and spacious.

Omni Grove Park Inn — Historic Hotel $$$

(828-252-2711; www.omnihotels.com; 290 Macon Ave; r $149-419; P @) This titanic arts-and-crafts-style historic stone lodge beckons a bygone era of Americana mountain glamor and, with its hale-and-hearty look, sets a tone for adventure. Did you notice the lobby fireplaces? Of course you did: the 36ft-wide behemoths can accommodate a standing grown man inside their hearths and there is an elevator ascending to the chimney within each!

The Great Smokies

Alas, Hobbiton and Narnia don't exist. But if you crave a land of wonders, take this drive through the Smokies, home to technicolor greenery, strutting wildlife, whispering waterfalls and the irrepressible Dollywood.

TRIP HIGHLIGHTS

FINISH
Sevierville
Dollywood
Pigeon Forge
Gatlinburg
Bryson City
START

85 miles
Cades Cove
Wild animals, old cabins and, well, Sunday drivers

115 miles
Roaring Fork Motor Nature Trail
Follow an old wagon road past hardwoods and waterfalls

50 miles
Clingmans Dome
The last half-mile is a doozy on the hike to the summit

25 miles
Museum of The Cherokee Indian
Stories of triumph and tragedy are movingly told

4–5 DAYS
160 MILES / 257KM

GREAT FOR...

BEST TIME TO GO

April to June for greenery and waterfalls, and September and October for colorful leaves.

ESSENTIAL PHOTO

Leave your car to photograph tree-covered mountains from the Newfound Gap Overlook.

BEST FOR OUTDOORS

Bike the Cades Cove loop on an official 'no-car' morning.

Great Smoky Mountains National Park An elk roams in the mist

21 The Great Smokies

While the beauty of the Great Smokies can be seen from your car, the exhilarating, crash-bang, breathe-it-in wonder of the place can't be fully appreciated until you leave your vehicle. Hold tight as you bounce over Nantahala rapids. Give a nod to foraging black bears as you bicycle Cades Cove. And press your nose against windows in downtown Gatlinburg, where ogling short stacks is the best way to choose the right pancake place.

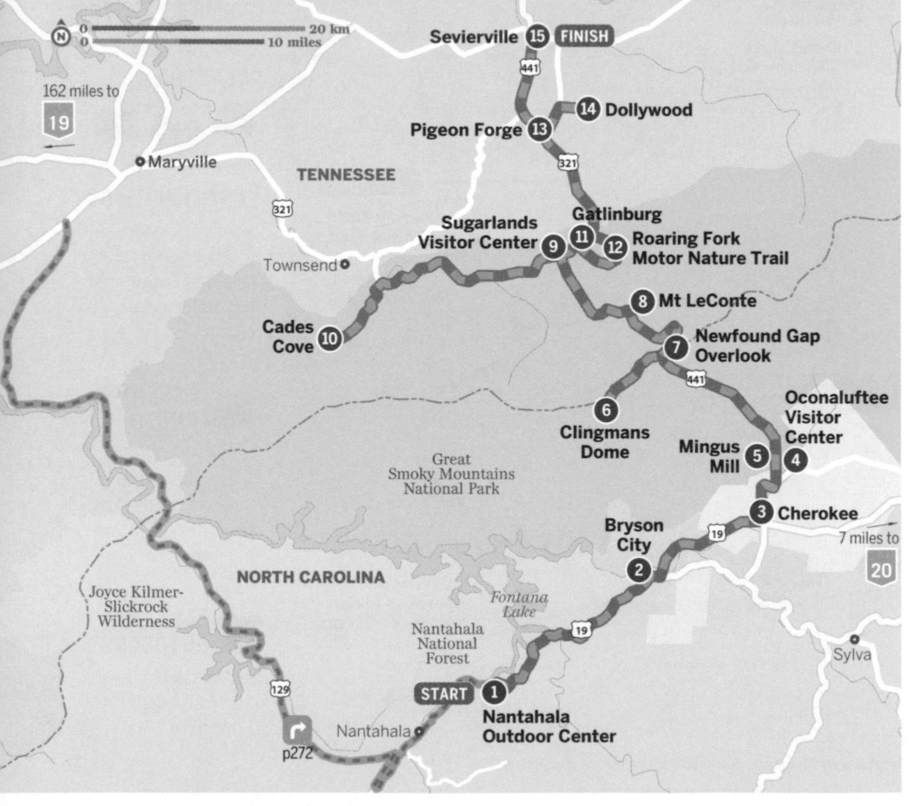

❶ Nantahala Outdoor Center

Splash, bang, wheeeeee... there's no easing into this trip, which starts in the mountain-fed rivers and rugged valleys of western North Carolina, a region famed for its fantastic kayaking and white-water rafting.

The **Nantahala Outdoor Center** (NOC; ☎828-785-5082, 828-785-4850; www.noc.com; 13077 Hwy 19 W; ducky rental per day $35, guided trips $50-200; ⏲8am-8pm Jun-Jul, earlier Aug-May) launches trips on the class II and III rapids of the Nantahala River from its sprawling outpost near Bryson City. Ride a group raft or a two-person ducky through the wide, brown river gorge. The company also offers white-water trips on six other Appalachian rivers. Experienced paddlers can brave the 9-mile trip down the roiling class IV-V Cheoah ($169 to $189), launching from nearby Robbinsville.

At the Adventure Center, which is part of the NOC campus, sign up to zip line or to climb an alpine tower. Also on-site is an outdoor store, a year-round restaurant and lodging, which includes campsites, cabins, a hostel and an inn. The Appalachian Trail crosses the property, and the Great Smoky Mountain Railroad stops here.

The Drive » Follow Hwy 19 north about 12.5 miles on a twisty, wooded path that winds past rafting companies and oh-so-many signs for boiled peanuts. Take exit 67 into downtown Bryson City.

❷ Bryson City

This friendly mountain town is a great base camp for exploring the North Carolina side of the Smokies. The marquee attraction is the historic **Great Smoky Mountains Railroad** (☎800-872-4681; www.gsmr.com; 226 Everett St; Nantahala Gorge trip adult from $55, child 2-12yr from $31), which departs from downtown and plows through the dramatic Nantahala Gorge and across the Fontana Trestle. The former Murphy Branch Line, built in the late 1800s, brought unheard-of luxuries such as books, factory-spun cloth and oil lamps. Themed trips on the red-and-yellow trains include a Great Pumpkin–themed trip in the fall and the Christmastime Polar Express, which stops at the North Pole to pick up Santa.

✕ 🛏 p278

The Drive » Continue 10 miles north on Hwy 19.

TRIP HIGHLIGHT

❸ Cherokee

The Cherokee people have lived in this area since the last ice age, though many died on the Trail of Tears. The descendants of those who escaped or returned are known as the Eastern Band of the Cherokee. Make time for the **Museum of the Cherokee Indian** (☎828-497-3481; www.cherokeemuseum.org; 589 Tsali Blvd/Hwy 441, at Drama Rd; adult $11, child 6-12yr $7; ⏲9am-5pm daily, to 7pm Mon-Sat Jun-Aug). The earth-colored halls trace the history of the tribe, with artifacts such as pots, deerskins, woven skirts and an animated exhibit on Cherokee myths. The tribe's modern story is particularly compelling, with a detailed look at the tragedy and injustice of the Trail of Tears. This mass exodus occurred in the 1830s, when President Andrew Jackson ordered more than

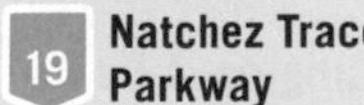

Head northwest on Hwy 321/Rte 73 from Maryville until you reach I-40. Take this west until you hit on musical Nashville.

Continue east on Hwy 19 from Cherokee to link up with Blue Ridge Parkway.

16,000 Native Americans removed from their southeastern homelands and resettled in what's now Oklahoma. The museum also spotlights a fascinating moment in Colonial-era history: the 1760s journey of three Cherokees to England, where they met with King George III.

The Drive » Drive 3 miles north on Hwy 441, passing the Blue Ridge Parkway.

4 Oconaluftee Visitor Center

If they're offering samples of regional preserves at the **Oconaluftee Visitor Center** (828-497-1904; www.nps.gov/grsm; 1194 Newfound Gap Rd, North Cherokee; 8am-7:30pm Jun-Aug, hours vary Sep-May), say yes. But pull out your money because you'll want to take a jar home. Here you'll also find interactive exhibits about the park's history and ecosystems. Helpful guides ($1) about specific attractions are also available. For this trip, the *Day Hikes* pamphlet and the guides to Cades Cove and the Roaring Fork Motor Nature Trail are helpful supplements.

Behind the visitor center, the pet-friendly Oconaluftee River Trail follows the river for 1.5 miles to the boundary of the Cherokee reservation. Pick up a free backcountry camping permit if you plan to go off-trail. The adjacent **Mountain Farm Museum** (www.nps.gov/grsm; 9am-5pm daily mid-Mar–mid-Nov, plus Thanksgiving weekend) is a 19th-century farmstead assembled from buildings from various locations around the park. The worn, wooden structures, including a barn, a blacksmith shop and a smokehouse, give a glimpse into the hardscrabble existence of Appalachian settlers.

The Drive » Drive half a mile north on Hwy 441. The parking lot is on the left.

5 Mingus Mill

Interested in old buildings and 1800s commerce? Then take the short walk to **Mingus Mill** (Mingus Creek Trail, Cherokee; 9am-5pm daily mid-Mar–mid-Nov, plus Thanksgiving weekend). This 1886 gristmill was the largest in the Smokies. If the miller is there, he can explain how the mill grinds corn into cornmeal. Outside, the 200ft-long wooden millrace directs water to the building. There's no waterwheel here because the mill used a cast-iron turbine.

The Drive » Return to Hwy 441 and turn left, continuing toward Gatlinburg. Turn left and drive 7 miles on Clingmans Dome Rd.

TRIP HIGHLIGHT

6 Clingmans Dome

At 6643ft, Clingmans Dome is the third-highest mountain east of the Mississippi. You can drive almost all the way to the top, but the final climb to the summit's Jetsons-like observation tower requires a half-mile walk on a paved trail. It's a very steep ascent, but there are resting spots

DETOUR: TAIL OF THE DRAGON

Start: 1 Nantahala Outdoor Center

A dragon lurks in the rugged foothills of the southwestern Smokies. This particular monster is an infamous drive that twists through Deals Gap beside the national park. According to legend, the 11-mile route, known as the Tail of the Dragon, has 318 curves. From the Nantahala Outdoor Center, drive south on Hwy 19/74 to Hwy 129. Follow Hwy 129 north. The dragon starts at the North Carolina and Tennessee state line. Godspeed and drive slowly. And may you tame the dragon like a Targaryen.

GREAT SMOKY MOUNTAINS NATIONAL PARK TRIP PLANNER

Established in 1934, **Great Smoky Mountains National Park** (www.nps.gov/grsm) attracts more than nine million travelers per year, making it the most-visited national park in America.

Newfoundland Gap Rd/Hwy 441 is the only thoroughfare crossing the entire 521,000-acre park, traversing 33 miles of deep oak and pine forest, and wildflower meadows. The park sits in two states: North Carolina and Tennessee. The Oconaluftee Visitor Center welcomes visitors arriving on Hwy 441 in North Carolina; Sugarlands Visitor Center is the Tennessee counterpart.

Orientation & Fees

Great Smoky charges no admission fee, nor will it ever; this proviso was written into the park's original charter as a stipulation for a $5 million Rockefeller family grant. Stop by a visitor center to pick up a park map and the free *Smokies Guide* newspaper. The park is open all year although some facilities are only open seasonally, and roads may close due to bad weather. Leashed pets are allowed in campgrounds and on roadsides, but not on trails, with the exception of the Gatlinburg and Oconaluftee River trails.

Camping

The park currently operates seven developed campgrounds. None have showers or hookups. **Reservations** (☎877-444-6777; www.recreation.gov) are required at Cataloochee Campground, and they may be made at Elkmont, Smokemont, Cosby and Cades Cove. Big Creek and Deep Creek are first-come, first-served.

Traffic

If you're visiting on a summer weekend, particularly on the Tennessee side, accept that there is going to be a lot of traffic. Take a break by following trails into the wilderness.

along the way. The trail crosses the 2174-mile Appalachian Trail, which reaches its highest point on the dome.

From the tower, on a clear day, enjoy a 360-degree view that sweeps in five states. Spruce- and pine-covered mountaintops sprawl for miles. The **visitor station** (☎865-436-1200; Clingmans Dome Rd; ⏰10am-6pm Apr-Oct, 9:30am-5pm Nov) beside the parking lot has a bookstore and a shop.

The weather here is cooler than at lower elevations, and rain can arrive quickly. Consider wearing layers and bringing a rain poncho. And in case you're wondering, a dome is a rounded mountain.

The Drive » Follow Clingmans Dome Rd back to Hwy 441. Cross Hwy 441 and pull into the overlook parking area.

---

7 Newfound Gap Overlook

There's a lot going at the intersection of US 441 and Clingmans Dome Rd. Here, the **Rockefeller Monument** pays tribute to a $5 million donation from the Rockefeller Foundation that helped to complete land purchases needed to create the park. President Franklin D Roosevelt formally dedicated Great Smoky Mountains National Park in this spot in 1940. The overlook sits at the border of North Carolina and Tennessee, within the 5046ft Newfound Gap. Enjoy expansive mountain views from the parking area or hop on the **Appalachian Trail** for a stroll.

The Drive » From here, follow Hwy 441 north into Tennessee for about 5 miles to the parking lot.

SEAN PAVONE / GETTY IMAGES ©

8 Mt LeConte

Climbing 6593ft Mt LeConte is probably the park's most popular challenge, sure to give serious hamstring burn. The **Alum Cave Trail**, one of five routes to the peak, starts from the Alum Cave parking area on the main road. Follow a creek, pass under a stone arch and wind your way steadily upward past thickets of rhododendron, myrtle and mountain laurel. It's a 5.5-mile hike to LeConte Lodge, where you can join the Rainbow Falls Trail to the summit.

p278

The Drive » Continue on Newfound Gap Rd. Turn left into the parking lot at Little River Rd.

9 Sugarlands Visitor Center

At the juncture of Little River and Newfound Gap Rds is the **Sugarlands Visitor Center** (865-436-1291; www.nps.gov/grsm; 107 Park Headquarters Rd; 8am-7:30pm Jun-Aug, hours vary Sep-May), the park headquarters and main Tennessee entrance. Step

Left: Sunset at Newfound Gap Overlook
Right: Clingmans Dome

DIGIDREAMGRAFIX / GETTY IMAGES ©

inside for exhibits about plant and animal life (there's a stuffed wild boar only a mama boar could love), and a bookstore. Several ranger-led talks and tours meet at Sugarlands.

p278

The Drive » Turn on to Little River Rd for a gorgeous 25-mile drive beside lively flowing waterways. The road passes Elkmont Campground then becomes Laurel Creek Rd. Watch for cars stopping suddenly as drivers pull over to look at wildlife.

TRIP HIGHLIGHT

10 Cades Cove

This secluded valley contains the remnants of a 19th-century settlement. It's accessed by an 11-mile, one-way loop road that has numerous pull-offs. From these, you can poke around old churches and farmhouses or hike trails through postcard-perfect meadows filled with deer, wild turkeys and the occasional bear. For good wildlife viewing, come in the late afternoon when the animals romp with abandon.

The narrow loop road has a speed limit of 10mph and can get crowded (and maddeningly slow) in high season. For a more tranquil experience, ride your bike, or walk, on a Wednesday or Saturday morning from early May through late September – cars are banned from the road between 7am and 10am. Rent a bike at the Cades Cove Campground Store ($4 to $6 per hour). Also recommended is the 5-mile round-trip hike to **Abrams Falls**. Trailhead parking is after the Elijah Oliver Place.

Stop by the **Cades Cove Visitor Center** (☎865-436-7318; Cades Cove Loop Rd; ⏰9am-7:30pm May-Jul, closes earlier rest of year) for ranger talks.

🛏 p278

The Drive » Return to the Sugarlands Vistor Center then turn left on to Hwy 441, which is called parkway between Gatlinburg and Sevierville. Drive 2 miles to Gatlinburg.

⓫ Gatlinburg

Driving out of the park on the Tennessee side is disconcerting. All at once you pop out of the tranquil green tunnel of trees and into a blinking, shrieking welter of cars, motels, pancake houses, minigolf courses and Ripley's Believe It or Not Museums. Welcome to Gatlinburg. It's Heidi meets Hillbilly in this vaguely Bavarian-themed tourist wonderland, catering to Smokies visitors since the 1930s. Most of the tourist attractions are within the compact, hilly little downtown.

Once it's repaired after fire damage, the **Gatlinburg Sky Lift** (☎865-436-4307; www.gatlinburgskylift.com; 765 Parkway; adult/child $16.50/13; ⏰9am-11pm Jun-Aug, varies rest of year), a repurposed ski-resort chairlift, will whisk you high over the Smokies. You'll fill up your camera's memory card with panoramic snapshots.

🍴 🛏 p278

The Drive » From the parkway in downtown Gatlinburg, turn right on to Historic Nature Trail/Airport Rd at the Gatlinburg Convention Center. Follow it into the national park, continuing to the marked entrance for the one-way Roaring Fork Motor Nature Trail.

TRIP HIGHLIGHT

⓬ Roaring Fork Motor Nature Trail

Built on the foundations of a 150-year-old wagon road, the 6-mile Roaring Fork loop twists through strikingly lush forest. Sights include burbling cascades, abundant hardwoods, mossy boulders and old cabins once inhabited by farming families. The isolated community of Roaring Fork was settled in the mid-1800s, along a powerful mountain stream. The families that lived here were forced to move when the park was established about 100 years later.

For a waterfall hike, try the 2.6-mile round-trip walk to **Grotto Falls** from the Trillium Gap Trailhead. Further down the road, check out the Ephraim Bales cabin, once home to 11 people.

The *Roaring Fork Auto Tour Guide*, for sale for $1 in the Oconaluftee and Sugarlands visitor centers, provides details about plant life and buildings along the drive. No buses, trailer or RVs are permitted on the motor road.

The Drive » At the end of Roaring Fork Rd turn left on to E Parkway. Less than 1 mile ahead, turn right at Hwy 321S/Hwy 441. Drive 7 miles to Pigeon Forge.

⓭ Pigeon Forge

The town of Pigeon Forge is an ode to that big-haired, big-busted angel of East Tennessee, Dolly Parton – who's known to be a pretty cool chick.

Born in a one-room shack in the nearby hamlet of Locust Ridge, Parton started performing on Knoxville radio at age 11 and moved to Nashville at 18 with all her worldly belongings in a cardboard suitcase. She's made millions singing about her Smoky Mountain roots and continues to be a huge presence in her hometown, donating money to local causes and riding a glittery float in the annual Dolly Parade.

Wacky museums and over-the-top dinner shows line the parkway, the main drag.

The Drive » Turn right on to the parkway and drive 2 miles southeast. Then turn left on to Dollywood Lane/Veterans Blvd and follow signs to Dollywood, about 2.5 miles away.

WATERFALLS OF THE SMOKIES

The Smokies are full of waterfalls, from icy trickles to roaring cascades. Here are a few of the best:

Grotto Falls You can walk behind these 25ft-high falls, off Trillium Gap Trail.

Laurel Falls This popular 80ft fall is located down an easy 2.6-mile paved trail.

Mingo Falls At 120ft, this is one of the highest waterfalls in the Appalachians.

Rainbow Falls On sunny days, the mist here produces a rainbow.

14 Dollywood

Dolly Parton's theme park **Dollywood** (☎865-428-9488; www.dollywood.com; 2700 Dollywood Parks Blvd, Pigeon Forge; adult/child $67/54; ⏰Apr-Dec) is an enormous love letter to mountain culture. Families pour in to ride the country-themed thrill rides and see demonstrations of traditional Appalachian crafts. You can also tour the bald-eagle sanctuary or worship at the altar of Dolly in the Chasing Rainbows life-story museum. The adjacent Dollywood's Splash Country takes these themes and adds water.

The Drive » Return to the parkway and follow it north 4.5 miles into downtown Sevierville. Turn left on to Bruce St and drive one block to Court Ave.

15 Sevierville

On the front lawn of the downtown courthouse (125 Court Ave) you might see a few happy folks getting their pictures taken in front of the statue of a young Dolly Parton. Wearing a ponytail, her guitar held loose, it captures something kind of nice. You know where's she's from, where her music is going to take her, and how it all ties in to this tough, but always beautiful, mountain country.

Eating & Sleeping

Bryson City 2

Cork & Bean — Cafe $$

(828-488-1934; www.brysoncitycorkandbean.com; 16 Everett St; brunch $6.50-12.50, lunch $8-11.50, dinner $18-35.50; 4:30-9pm Mon-Thu, 11am-9pm Fri, 9am-9pm Sat & Sun, hours vary outside summer;) Big windows frame the Cork & Bean, a chic restaurant-bar in downtown Bryson City. With its emphasis on locally grown and organic fare, you'll feel less guilty digging into the eatery's crepes and sandwiches after your local hike. Look for eggs Benedict and huevos rancheros on the weekend brunch menu, Andouille sausage, duck and wild-boar étoufée at dinner and local craft beers on tap.

Fryemont Inn — Inn $$

(828-488-2159; www.fryemontinn.com; 245 Fryemont St; lodge/ste/cabin incl breakfast & dinner from $165/$205/260; nonguest breakfast $10-12, dinner $20-31; restaurant 8am-10am & 6-8pm Sun-Tue, 6-9pm Fri & Sat mid-Apr–late Nov; P) The view of Bryson City and the Smokies from the porch of the lofty Fryemont Inn is hard to beat. This historic family-owned mountain lodge feels like summer camp with its bark-covered main building and a common area flanked by a stone fireplace. No TVs or air-con in the lodge rooms. Wi-fi is available in the lobby, cottage and balcony suites. The room rate includes breakfast and dinner at the on-site restaurant, which is open to the public.

Mt LeConte 8

LeConte Lodge — Cabin $

(865-429-5704; www.lecontelodge.com; cabins per person incl breakfast & dinner adult/4-12yr $145/85; mid-Mar–mid-Nov) The park's only non-camping accommodation is LeConte Lodge, and the only way to get to the lodge's rustic, electricity-free cabins is via five uphill hiking trails varying in length from 5.5 (Alum Cave Trail) to 8 miles (Boulevard), it's so popular you need to reserve up to a year in advance.

Sugarlands Visitor Center 9

Elkmont Campground — Campground $

(865-436-1271; www.recreation.gov; Little River Rd; tent/RV sites $17-23; early Mar-Nov;) The park's largest campground is on Little River Rd, 5 miles west of Sugarlands Visitor Center. Little River and Jakes Creek run through this wooded campground and the sound of rippling water adds tranquility. There are 200 tent and RV campsites and 20 walk-in sites. All are reservable beginning May 15. Like other campgrounds in the park, there are no showers, or electrical or water hookups. There are restrooms.

Cades Cove 10

Cades Cove Campground — Campground $

(865-448-2472; www.recreation.gov; tent/RV sites $17/20) This woodsy campground with 159 sites is a great place to sleep if you want to get a jump on visiting Cades Cove. There's a camp store, drinking water and bathrooms, but no showers. There are 29 tent-only sites.

Gatlinburg 11

Pancake Pantry — Breakfast $

(www.pancakepantry.com; 628 Parkway; breakfast $8-12, lunch $8-11; 7am-3pm;) Gatlinburg has a thing for pancakes, and this is the place that started it all. The Pantry's secret is simple: real butter, honest-to-goodness fresh whipped cream and everything made from scratch. We recommend the Swedish pancakes, with lashings of lingonberry jam. At lunch there's gourmet sandwiches with funny names like The Polish Aristocrat, which can be ordered ahead for picnics by the waterfalls of Great Smoky.

Smoky Mountain Brewery American $$

(www.smoky-mtn-brewery.com; 1004 Parkway; mains $8.50-24; 11:30am-11pm Sun-Thu, to midnight Fri & Sat;) American pub grub like quesadillas, chicken fingers, pizzas, burgers and pasta dishes are A-OK, but it's the microbrewed beer (nine on tap), multiple TV sets and raucous ski-lodge atmosphere that really packs in the crowds.

Wild Boar Saloon & Howard's Steakhouse Steak $$

(865-436-3600; www.facebook.com/TheWildBoarSaloon; 976 Parkway; mains $10-37; 11am-11pm Apr-Jan, to 9pm winter;) Since 1946 this dark creekside saloon has been serving burgers, ribs and a tasty pulled-pork shoulder drenched in homemade sauce. But it's known for its steaks and Bloody Marys and for being the oldest joint in town. On an nice day, the creekside patio is a winner.

Bearskin Lodge Lodge $$

(877-795-7546; www.thebearskinlodge.com; 840 River Rd; d $79-220; P) This shingled riverside lodge is blessed with timber accents and a bit more panache than other Gatlinburg comers. All of the 96 spacious rooms have flat-screen TVs and some come with gas fireplaces and private balconies jutting over the river.

Hampton Inn Hotel $$

(865-436-4878; www.hamptoninn3.hilton.com; 967 Parkway; d $89-269; P @) Yep, it's part of a chain, but the hotel sits in the thick-of-the-action on Parkway. Decor is modern, and furnishings include an easy chair and ottoman. Rooms with king beds have a fireplace. Ahhh.

STRETCH YOUR LEGS MIAMI BEACH

Start/Finish Ocean Dr

Distance 3 miles

Duration Three hours

Greater Miami sprawls, but compact Miami Beach packs in the sights, making it perfect for an afternoon of exploring on foot. Get a taste of its famous art-deco district, as well as its luscious, white-sand beaches.

Take this walk on Trip

16

Ocean Drive

Ocean Dr is the classic Miami strip, where neon-accented art-deco buildings line the way for an endless parade of cars, in-line skaters and pedestrians. Stop at the **Art Deco Museum** (www.mdpl.org/welcome-center/art-deco-museum; 1001 Ocean Dr; $5; ⌚10am-5pm Tue-Sun, to 7pm Thu) for an overview of South Beach architectural style, from its tropical and nautical motifs to those eye-catching cantilevered eyebrows.

The Walk » Head north. To fully appreciate the architecture, stick to the park side of the street. At 13th St, note the Carlyle Hotel, where *The Birdcage* was filmed. Cross Lummus Park to get to the beach.

Lummus Park & South Beach

Take off your shoes and dig your toes into some of the most luscious sand you've ever felt, and stare out at (or run straight toward) the teal-green water that's shallow and warm enough to splash around in for hours. Run up and down if you must – cartwheels in the sand would not be inappropriate – but be sure to notice the six floridly colored lifeguard stands that stretch along this strip.

The Walk » Walk (or wade) up the beach and find the path that takes you to Lincoln Rd just past the Loews Hotel. (If you get to the Sagamore you've gone too far.) Walk two blocks west along Lincoln until you reach Washington Ave.

Lincoln Road Mall

Calling Lincoln Rd a mall is technically accurate, but misses the point. Yes, you can shop, and there are sidewalk cafes galore. But this outdoor pedestrian promenade between Alton Rd and Washington Ave is really about seeing and being seen; there are times when it feels less like a road and more like a runway.

The Walk » Head south down busy Collins Ave, another thoroughfare that's lined with deco treasures. At 13th St, hop over one block to Washington Ave.

Miami Beach Post Office

Ahhh, Miami Beach. Even its municipal buildings are treasured works of art. A fine example of Streamline Moderne, the **Miami Beach Post Office** (1300 Washington Ave; ⌚8am-5pm Mon-Fri, 8:30am-2pm Sat) was built in 1937 as part of the Works Progress Administration (WPA). Duck inside to mail some postcards and check out the striking ceiling mural of a stylized night sky.

The Walk » Just two blocks down – and they're not very interesting blocks, so we're tempted to send you back over to Collins – is a vintage dining experience.

11th St Diner

Many art-deco buildings evoke modes of transportation, such as planes, trains or ships. Well, the shiny little 11th St Diner (p225) does more than evoke: it's actually housed in a classic Pullman train car. Pull over for refreshments; the inside is as cute as the outside.

The Walk » Now that you're refreshed, head just a few doors down; your next stop is in the same block.

Wolfsonian-FIU

A fascinating museum that's part of Florida International University, the **Wolfsonian-FIU** (☎305-531-1001; www.wolfsonian.org; 1001 Washington Ave; adult/child $10/5, 6-9pm Fri free; ⌚10am-6pm Mon, Tue, Thu & Sat, to 9pm Fri, noon-6pm Sun, closed Wed) showcases artifacts from the height of the Industrial Revolution from the late 19th to mid-20th century. The exhibits span transportation, urbanism, industrial design, advertising and political propaganda, and give some intriguing insight as to what was going on in the world while all that deco was being built.

The Walk » It's just two short blocks along 10th St to get back to Ocean Dr. Between 7th and 8th is a fetching strip of buildings including the Colony Hotel, which you'll recognize instantly if you've ever watched anything set in Miami Beach.

STRETCH YOUR LEGS SAVANNAH

Start/Finish Sentient Bean, Forsyth Park

Distance 3.3 miles

Duration Three hours

Savannah is a living museum of Southern architecture and antebellum charm. Gorgeous and full of Old South charisma, its historical heart is freckled with pleasant squares shaded by spreading oaks dripping with Spanish moss. This town was made for walking.

Sentient Bean

Savannah is a coffee-loving town, and there's no better place to start your morning than **Sentient Bean** (www.sentientbean.com; 13 E Park Ave; ⌚7am-9pm; 📶), a fabulous, bohemian cafe with terrific coffee, gourmet scones, hipster clientele and baristas with attitude (the good kind). Plus, it's just across the street from Forsyth Park.

The Walk » Step across the street and stroll through Savannah's most central, and most beautiful, park.

Forsyth Park

Gushing with fountains, draped with mossy oaks, unfurled with vast lawns and basketball and tennis courts, this is one dynamite city park. The **visitor center** has a number of brochures and maps that delve into local architecture and history and is worth stopping by.

The Walk » From the north end of the park continue straight to elegant Monterey Sq, your first of such rectangular oases of European charm.

Mercer-Williams House

The location of an infamous homicide, the **Mercer-Williams House** (☎912-236-6352; www.mercerhouse.com; 429 Bull St; adult/student $12.50/8; ⌚10:30am-4:10pm Mon-Sat, noon-4pm Sun) was purchased and restored by eccentric art dealer Jim Williams in 1969. Inside you'll find the room in which Danny Hansford was murdered in 1981. That story is at the heart of *Midnight in the Garden of Good and Evil,* the book and subsequent film that put Savannah (and Kevin Spacey) on the map.

The Walk » From Monterey Sq, take Bull St north for four blocks, past a row of historic homes to E Charlton St on Madison Sq.

Shop SCAD

Creative impulse charges through Savannah's veins, thanks in large part to the **Savannah College of Art and Design** (SCAD). SCAD students are legion, its graduates often settling in town to paint or open flower shops,

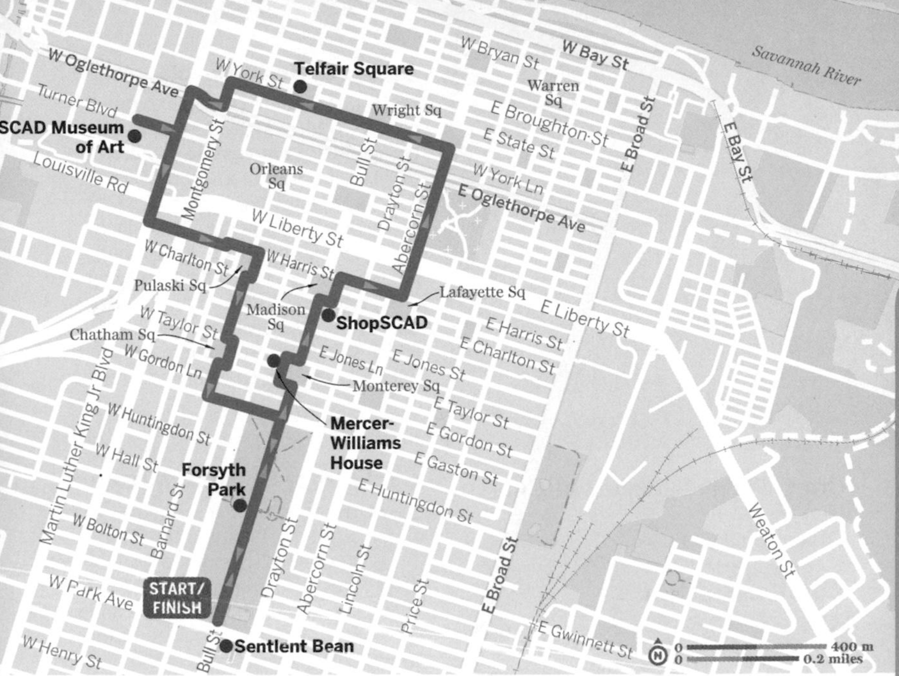

textile depots or design businesses. All the wares on sale at **ShopSCAD** (912-525-5180; www.shopscadonline.com; 340 Bull St; 9am-5:30pm Mon-Fri, 10am-6pm Sat, noon-5pm Sun) – the throw pillows, the canvases and art books, the jewelry and T-shirts – were imagined by SCAD students, alumni or faculty.

The Walk » Make a right on Harris St and wander past Lafayette Sq (one of our favorites) then make a left on Abercorn St.

Telfair Square

Two of Savannah's most popular museums are set around this leafy residential plaza. The **Telfair Academy of Arts & Sciences** (912-790-8800; www.telfair.org; 121 Barnard St; adult/child $20/15; noon-5pm Sun & Mon, 10am-5pm Tue-Sat) is filled with 19th-century American art and silver, and a smattering of European pieces. Nearby, **Jepson Center for the Arts** (912-790-8800; www.telfair.org/visit/jepson; 207 W York St; noon-5pm Sun & Mon, 10am-5pm Tue-Sat; adult/child $20/15) has 20th- and 21st-century art.

The Walk » Take York St west to Montgomery, head south one block to Oglethorpe and head west again. Cross Martin Luther King Jr Blvd, one of town's major thoroughfares, and walk two long blocks south to Turner Blvd.

SCAD Museum of Art

More than the sum of its parts, the **SCAD Museum of Art** (www.scadmoa.org; 601 Turner Blvd; 10am-5pm Tue-Wed, to 8pm Thu, to 5pm Fri & Sat, noon-5pm Sun; adult/child under 14yr $10/free) is a brick, steel, concrete and glass longhouse carved with groovy, creative sitting areas inside and out, and filled with fun rotating exhibitions. We saw an installation of video screens strobing various karaoke interpretations of Madonna's *Lucky Star*. It has intriguing mixed-media pieces, and an inviting cafe.

The Walk » Your 1.25 mile walk back to the start follows MLK Blvd to Harris St. Make a left to Barnard, and head south, through Pulaski and Chatham Sqs. Make a left on Gaston to re-enter Forsyth Park.

STRETCH YOUR LEGS NEW ORLEANS

Start/Finish St Augustine Church

Distance 2.2 miles

Duration Three hours

Few destinations have as many sensational ways to kill time as the Crescent City. Its history runs deep, the colonial architecture is exquisite, and there's mouthwatering Cajun and Creole food, historic dive bars, gorgeous countryside and lashings of great free live music.

St Augustine Church

We'll start in the Tremé, one of the country's oldest African American neighborhoods, at **St Augustine's Church** (☎504-525-5934; www.staugchurch.org; 1210 Governor Nicholls St; ⏰mass 10am Sun & 5pm Wed), home to one of the oldest black congregations in the US. Even if only appreciated from the outside, the church is a fascinating window into the African American experience in Louisiana, which stands out from the rest of the US due to the French-colonial connection.

The Walk » Proceed southeast along Governor Nicholls St then turn right onto Henriette Delille St.

Backstreet Cultural Museum

New Orleans is often described as both the least American city in the US and the northernmost city in the Caribbean. This is due to a unique colonial history that preserved the bonds between black New Orleanians and Africa and the greater black diaspora. Learn about this deep culture at the **Backstreet Cultural Museum** (☎504-522-4806; www.backstreetmuseum.org; 1116 Henriette Delille St; $10; ⏰10am-4pm Tue-Sat), a small but fascinating peek into the street-level music, ritual and communities that underlay the singular New Orleans experience.

The Walk » Get on Governor Nicholls St and continue walking southeast. Once you cross busy Rampart St, you've entered the French Quarter. Turn right onto Royal St, a pretty lane with cute art galleries, antique shops and onderful architecture.

Historic New Orleans Collection

The **Historic New Orleans Collection** (THNOC; ☎504-523-4662; www.hnoc.org; 533 Royal St; admission free, tours $5; ⏰9:30am-4:30pm Tue-Sat, 10:30am-4:30pm Sun, tours 10am, 11am, 2pm & 3pm Tue-Sat) is an interesting museum, spread over several exquisitely restored buildings and packed with thoughtfully curated exhibits. Rotating exhibitions are inevitably fascinating.

The Walk » Continue in the same, southerly direction on Royal St; at the 400 block, you'll pass the marbled magnificence of the Louisiana

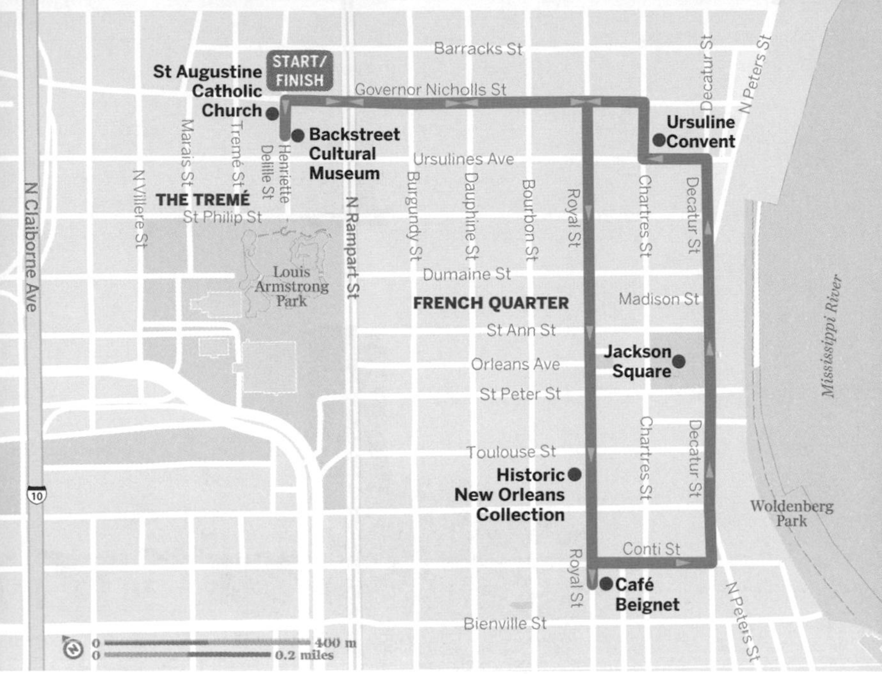

State Supreme Court. It's only about 500ft to the next stop.

Café Beignet

You've likely heard about the beignets (fried, sugar-covered donuts) at Café du Monde. They're good, but the place is horribly crowded. For the romantic experience of sipping coffee at a wrought-iron table while surrounded by lazy cats, head to **Café Beignet** (504-524-5530; www.cafebeignet.com; 334 Royal St; meals $6-8; 7am-10pm). Watch pedestrians stroll by, and try a beignet; they're delicious.

The Walk » Turn around and turn right (east) on Conti St, follow it for two blocks, then turn left (north) on Decatur St. To your right, over the levee, is the Mississippi River. Walk north four blocks to get to Jackson Sq.

Jackson Square

Stroll over to **Jackson Square** (Decatur & St Peter Sts), the city green. Lovers lanes and trimmed hedges surround a monument to Andrew Jackson, the hero of the Battle of New Orleans and the seventh president of the USA. But the real stars are the magnificent, French-style St Louis Cathedral, flanked by the Cabildo and Presbytère. The former houses a Louisiana state-history museum; the latter a permanent exhibition on the Mardi Gras holiday.

The Walk » Continue north on Decatur St for three blocks, then turn left onto Ursulines Ave. After one block, turn right onto Chartres St (pronounced 'Charters') for the convent.

Ursuline Convent

In 1727, 12 Ursuline nuns arrived in New Orleans to care for the French garrison's 'miserable little hospital' and to educate the young girls of the colony. Between 1745 and 1752 the French colonial army built the **Ursuline Convent** (504-503-0361; www.stlouiscathedral.org; 1112 Chartres St; adult/student $8/6; 10am-4pm Mon-Fri, 9am-3pm Sat), which is now the oldest structure in the Mississippi River Valley and the only remaining French building in the Quarter. Take in rotating exhibits and beautiful St Mary's chapel.

The Walk » Walk up Chartres St and turn left on Governor Nicholls St. From here it's a half-mile back to the Tremé and your starting point.

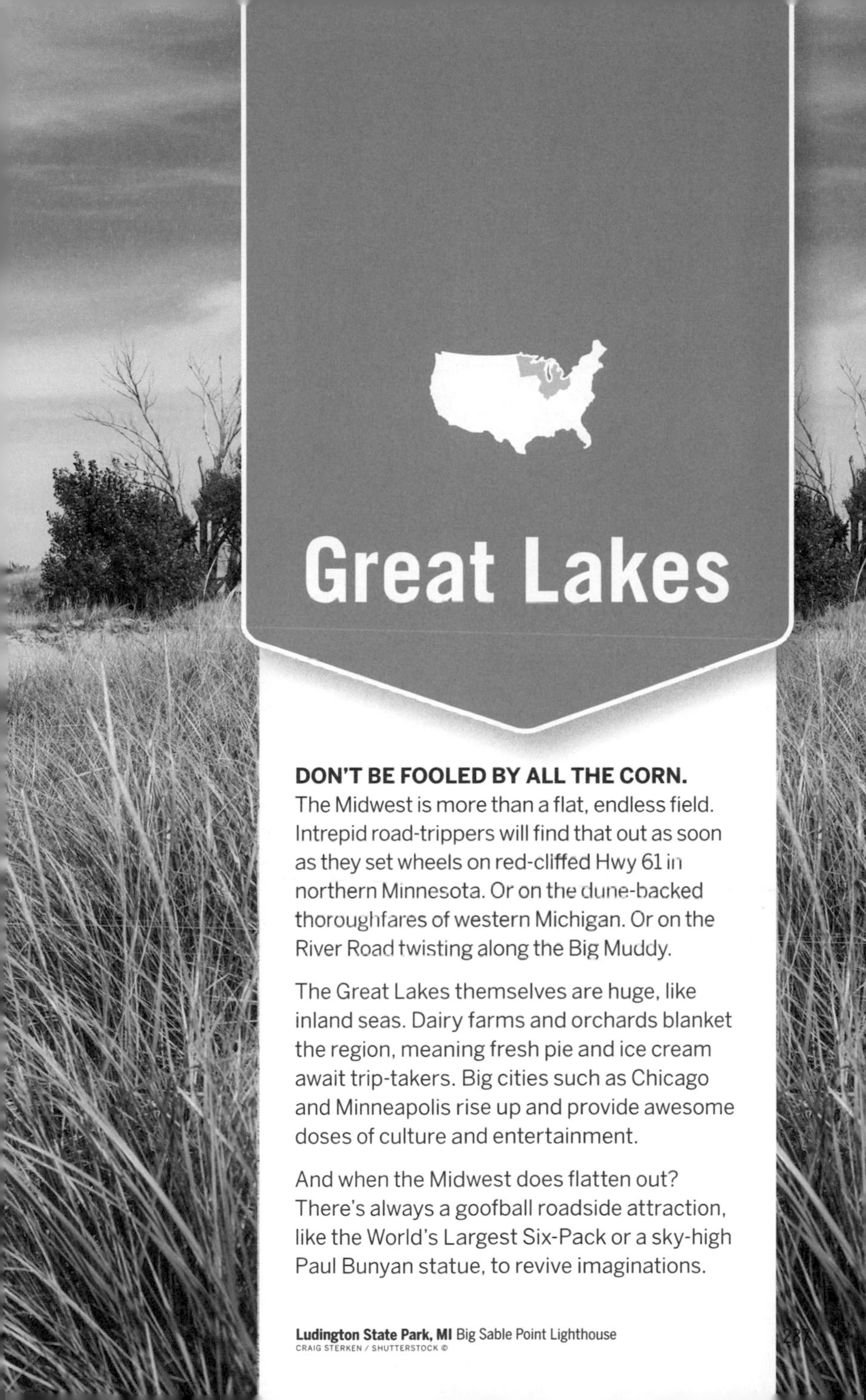

Great Lakes

DON'T BE FOOLED BY ALL THE CORN. The Midwest is more than a flat, endless field. Intrepid road-trippers will find that out as soon as they set wheels on red-cliffed Hwy 61 in northern Minnesota. Or on the dune-backed thoroughfares of western Michigan. Or on the River Road twisting along the Big Muddy.

The Great Lakes themselves are huge, like inland seas. Dairy farms and orchards blanket the region, meaning fresh pie and ice cream await trip-takers. Big cities such as Chicago and Minneapolis rise up and provide awesome doses of culture and entertainment.

And when the Midwest does flatten out? There's always a goofball roadside attraction, like the World's Largest Six-Pack or a sky-high Paul Bunyan statue, to revive imaginations.

Ludington State Park, MI Big Sable Point Lighthouse
CRAIG STERKEN / SHUTTERSTOCK ©

Great Lakes

0 200 km
0 100 miles
Thunder Bay
Lake Superior
CANADA
USA
Boundary Waters Canoe Area Wilderness
Grand Portage
Tofte
Superior National Forest
Bemidji
Chippewa National Forest
Grand Rapids
Leech Lake Indian Reservation
MINNESOTA
24
Apostle Islands
Isle Royale Wilderness
Houghton
Duluth
Superior
Fond du Lac Indian Reservation
Ashland
Ironwood
MICHIGAN
Marquette
Ottawa National Forest
Mille Lacs Lakes
23
35
Chequamegon National Forest
Lake Chippewa
Lac du Flambeau Indian Reservation
Hiawatha National Forest
Mackinaw City
94
St Cloud
Saint Croix National Scenic Riverway
Escanaba
Nicolet National Forest
Petoskey
WISCONSIN
Menominee
Boyne City
Minneapolis
St Paul
Wausau
Menominee Indian Reservation
Sleeping Bear Dunes National Lakeshore
Eau Claire
Mississippi River
Green Bay
Traverse City
Mankato
Rochester
Appleton
Manistee
Cadillac
Winona
Oshkosh
Manitowoc
90
Albert Lea
La Crosse
Lake Winnebago
43
Manistee National Forest
Isabella Indian Reservation
Fond Du Lac
Sheboygan
22
Mason City
Lake Michigan
Port Washington
Praire Du Chien
Muskegon
Grand Rapids
Fort Dodge
IOWA
Madison
Milwaukee
Janesville
Holland
Lansing
Jewell
Dubuque
Kenosha
Waterloo
Benton Harbor
Kalamazoo
Rockford
Freeport
Marshall
Cedar Rapids
Cedar River
New Buffalo
Chicago
80
Des Moines
Iowa City/Coralville
Rock River
Gary
South Bend
Davenport
Three Oaks
Des Moines River
Wilmington
Kankakee
Fort Wayne
Galesburg
Fort Madison
Burlington
Peoria
INDIANA
Illinois River
Bloomington
MISSOURI
Lafayette
Muncie
55
Danville
Quincy
Champaign
Urbana
Chillicothe
Hannibal
Springfield
Decatur
Indianapolis
Richmond
Moberly
ILLINOIS
Terre Haute
Litchfield
Columbia
Columbus
St Louis

Dubuque, IA

DON'T MISS

Pie

The region's prolific orchards result in flaky, scrumptious desserts at hot spots such as Crane's Pie Pantry and Betty's Pies. Try them out on Trips 22 24

Hemingway Haunts

Literary buffs can find the places Papa wrote about and the bars where he tossed back drinks during his days in northern Michigan. Retrace the writer's steps on Trip 22

Harbor View Cafe

It's in the middle of nowhere, but foodies have been trekking to check out the riverside cafe's chalkboard menu for 30-plus years. Make a visit on Trip 23

Judge CR Magney State Park

You've never seen a waterfall like Devil's Kettle, where half the flow disappears down a hole. Scientists can't determine where it comes out. See it for yourself on Trip 24

Paula Red
Mollies

Michigan's Gold Coast

They don't call it the Gold Coast for nothing. Michigan's western shoreline features endless stretches of beach, dunes, wineries, orchards and B&B-filled towns that boom in summer.

TRIP HIGHLIGHTS

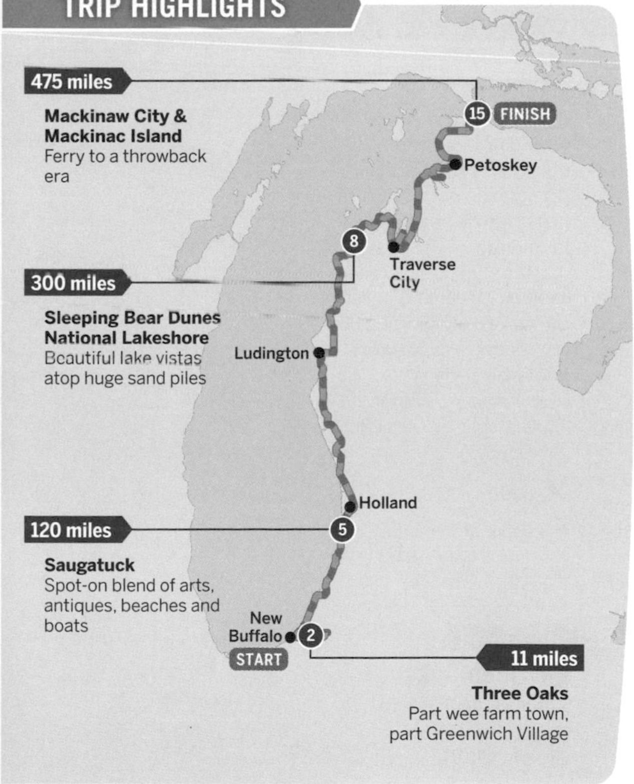

475 miles

Mackinaw City & Mackinac Island
Ferry to a throwback era

15 FINISH

Petoskey

8

Traverse City

300 miles

Sleeping Bear Dunes National Lakeshore
Beautiful lake vistas atop huge sand piles

Ludington

Holland

5

120 miles

Saugatuck
Spot-on blend of arts, antiques, beaches and boats

New Buffalo 2

START

11 miles

Three Oaks
Part wee farm town, part Greenwich Village

4 DAYS
475 MILES / 765 KM

GREAT FOR...

BEST TIME TO GO

July through October for pleasant weather and orchard harvests.

ESSENTIAL PHOTO

Atop the Dune Climb at Sleeping Bear Dunes.

BEST FOR FOODIES

Traverse City has artisan food shops selling local wines, ciders and produce.

Local produce A fruit stand on the Old Mission Peninsula

22 Michigan's Gold Coast

While Michigan's shore has been a holiday hot spot for over a century, it still surprises: the Caribbean-azure water, the West Coast surfing vibe, the French-style cider house that pops up by the road. Ernest Hemingway used to spend summers in the northern reaches, and he never forgot it. Even after traveling the world, he once wrote that the best sky is in 'Northern Michigan in the fall.'

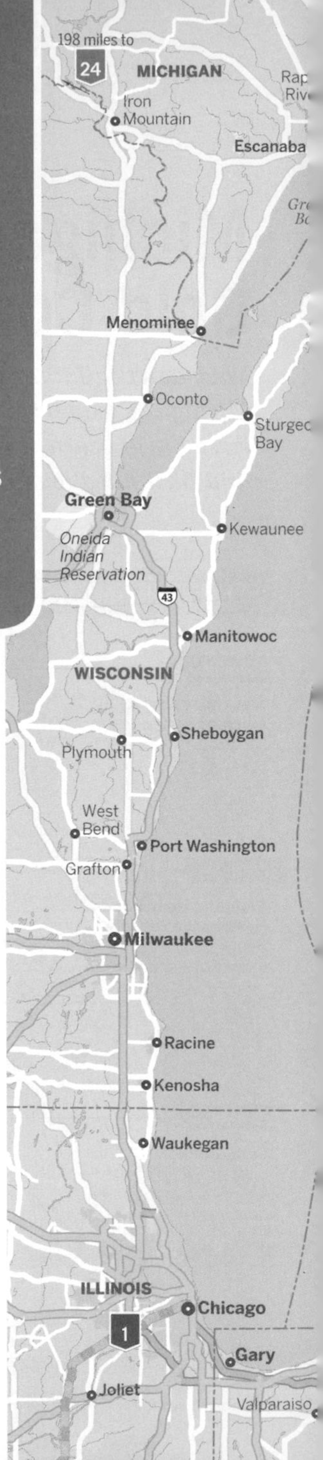

❶ New Buffalo

Hit the waves first in New Buffalo. While it looks like a typical resort town, it's also the Midwest's surfing hub. You heard right. You can surf Lake Michigan, and the groovy folks at **Third Coast Surf Shop** (☎269-932-4575; www.thirdcoastsurfshop.com; 110 N Whittaker St; ⌚10am-7pm Sun-Thu, to 8pm Fri & Sat Jun-Aug, reduced hours Apr-May & Sep-Dec, closed Jan-Mar) will show you how. They rent wetsuits and boards (per half day \$20 to \$25). For novices they offer two-hour private lessons (\$75 including equipment) from the public beach a few blocks from the front door. Reserve in advance.

Not a surfer? Not a problem. Lounge on the wide, sandy beach (lifeguards patrol in summer); watch boats glide in and out of the busy marina; lick an ice-cream cone or three; and peruse the festive shops and the town's popular **farmers market** (www.facebook.com/newbuffalofarmersmarket; 107 N Whittaker St; ⌚4-8pm Thu Jun-early Sep).

✕ p299

The Drive » Follow Hwy 12 as it curves inland for 6 miles to the wee town of Three Oaks.

TRIP HIGHLIGHT

❷ Three Oaks

Three Oaks is where Green Acres meets Greenwich Village in

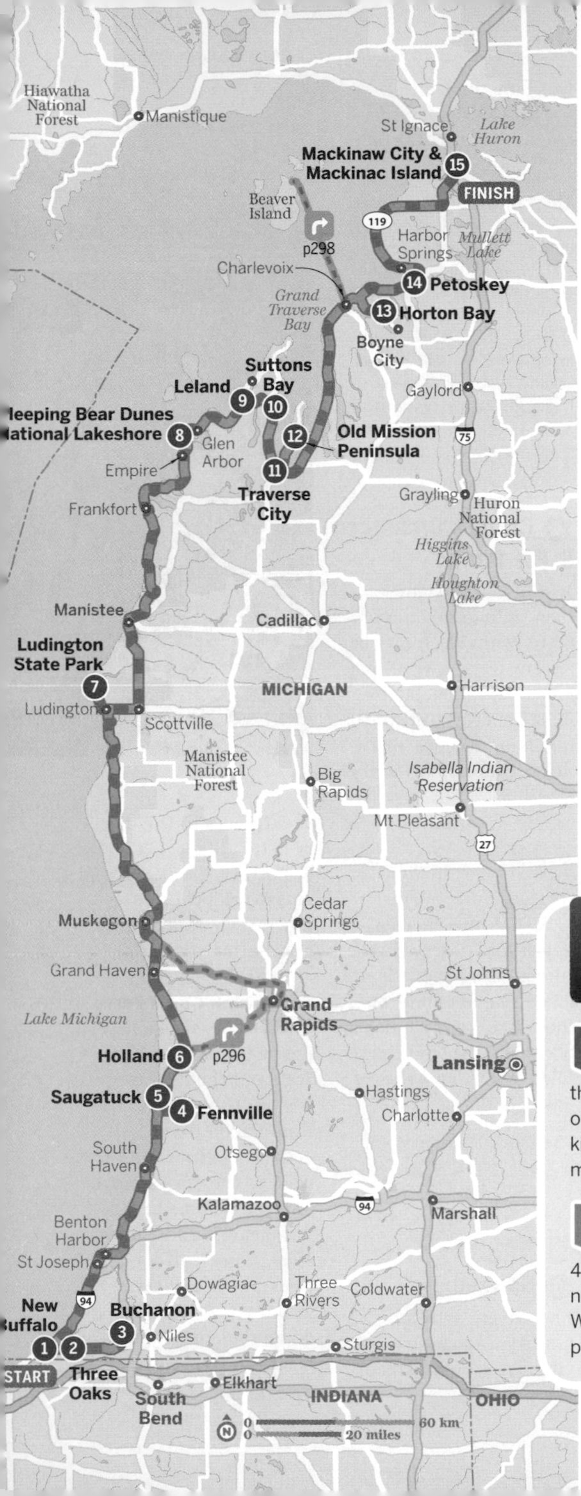

a funky farm-and-arts blend. Rent bikes at **Dewey Cannon Trading Company** (☎269-756-3361; www.facebook.com/deweycannontradingcompany; 3 Dewey Cannon Ave; ⏲9am-5pm Tue-Fri, to 7pm Sat, to 3pm Sun, reduced hours Oct-Apr) and cycle lightly used rural roads past orchards and vineyards. In the evening, catch a provocative play or art-house flick at Three Oaks' theaters.

Or just swing by for an hour or two to putter around the antique stores and concrete lawn ornament shops. The whole town spans about five blocks. Be sure to stop in at **Drier's Meat Market** (☎269-756-3101; www.driers.com; 14 S Elm St; ⏲9am-5pm Mon-Sat, 11am-5pm Sun), a butcher shop that has been around since Civil War days. It's filled with antique grinders and

LINK YOUR TRIP

1 Route 66

The time-warped thoroughfare is America's original road trip, and it kicks off in Chicago, 70 miles west of New Buffalo.

24 Highway 61

Ready to drive? It's 420 miles across the wild northwoods of Michigan and Wisconsin to your starting point in Duluth.

cleavers, as well as the famous smoked meats.

The Drive » Head north on Elm St, which becomes Three Oaks Rd. After about 5 miles you'll zig left onto Sawyer Rd, then right onto the Red Arrow Hwy. About 1 mile later, turn right on Browntown Rd. When it ends at Hills Rd turn left, and then right on Mt Tabor Rd.

3 Buchanon

By now you've noticed all the wineries around. A dozen or so cluster between New Buffalo and Saugatuck. Connoisseurs often regard **Tabor Hill Winery** (☎800-283-3363; www.taborhill.com; 185 Mt Tabor Rd; tours free, tastings $9; ⏲tours noon-4:30pm, tasting room 10am-5pm Mon-Fri, 10am-9pm Fri & Sat, noon-6pm Sun) as the region's best. The vintner provides tours and lets you belly up in the tasting room for swigs of its blood-red Cabernet Franc and crisp sparkling wines. There's also a restaurant overlooking the vineyard.

A mile north (take Hills Rd), **Round Barn Winery** (☎269-422-1617; www.roundbarnwinery.com; 10983 Hills Rd, Baroda; tastings $12-15; ⏲11am-6pm Mon-Sat, from noon Sun May-Oct, reduced hours Nov-Apr; 🐾) goes beyond vino with its grapes. It also uses the fruit to make DiVine Vodka, a smoother elixir than the kind made with grains or potatoes. Try it in the tasting room. During the week, you're welcome to picnic on the grounds; a food truck serves snacks on weekends.

The Drive » Return to the Red Arrow Hwy. Head north until it intersects with I-94 and Business I-94. Follow the latter through downtown St Joseph. Soon it converges with shore-hugging Hwy 63, which meets the Blue Star Hwy (aka County Rd A-2). This scenic thoroughfare moseys north to South Haven, a fine ice-cream stop, and onward to Saugatuck.

4 Crane's Orchards & Pie Pantry

Just before Saugatuck, turn right (east) on Hwy 89 to Fennville. It may be a teeny farm town with a lone traffic light, but pie fanatics have been swarming in for decades. The draw: **Crane's Pie Pantry** (☎269-561-2297; www.cranespiepantry.com; 6054 124th Ave; pie slices $4.50; ⏲9am-8pm Mon-Thu, to 9pm Fri & Sat, 11am-8pm Sun). Sure, you can pick your own cherries, apples and peaches in the surrounding orchards (open 10am to 6pm), but those in need of a quick fix beeline to the tchotchke-filled bakery for a slice of flaky goodness.

The Drive » Return to the Blue Star Hwy. Drive north for 4 miles to Saugatuck.

TRIP HIGHLIGHT

5 Saugatuck

The strong arts community and gay-friendly vibe draw boatloads of vacationers to this pretty little village. Galleries of pottery, paintings and glasswork proliferate downtown along Water and Butler Sts. Climb aboard the clackety **Saugatuck Chain Ferry** (end of Mary St; one-way $1; ⏲9am-9pm late May-early Sep), and the operator will pull you across the Kalamazoo River.

On the other side, walk to the dock's right and you'll come to Mt Baldhead, a 200ft-high sand dune. Huff up the stairs to see the grand view, then race down the north side to beautiful **Oval Beach**

THOMAS BARRAT / SHUTTERSTOCK ©

Holland Veldheer Tulip Gardens

(Oval Beach Dr; ⌚8am-10pm). Can't get enough sand? **Saugatuck Dune Rides** (☎269-857-2253; www.saugatuckduneride.com; 6495 Blue Star Hwy; adult/child $20/11; ⌚10am-7:30pm Jul & Aug, reduced hours May, Jun, Sep & Oct, closed Nov-Apr) provides a half-hour of good, cheesy fun zipping over nearby mounds.

p299

The Drive » The Blue Star Hwy makes its slowpoke, two-lane way northeast through farmland. It becomes Washington Ave, then Michigan Ave, then River Ave before reaching downtown Holland 12 miles later.

6 Holland

You don't have to cross the ocean for tulips, windmills and clogs. Holland, MI, has the whole kitschy package. **Veldheer Tulip Gardens** (☎616-399-1900; www.veldheer.com; 12755 Quincy St; ⌚9am-5pm Mon-Sat, 10am-4pm Sun, reduced hours in winter) is a popular place to immerse in all things Dutch. A wooden-shoe factory and traditional blue-and-white pottery workshop are also on-site. While it veers from the Dutch theme, be sure to stop by the **New Holland Brewing Company Pub** (☎616-355-6422; www.newhollandbrew.com; 66 E 8th St; ⌚11am-midnight Mon-Thu, to 1am Fri & Sat, to 10pm Sun). The microbrewery is known for its robust beers, such as Dragon's Milk stout (10% alcohol), and its housemade rums. The pub is the place to sample them.

The Drive » From Holland to Grand Haven, Lake Shore Ave is the back-road alternative to Hwy 31. Pick it up from Ottawa Beach Rd just before entering Holland State Park, and you're golden for 22 miles. After Grand Haven, filter back onto Hwy 31 for 75 miles to Ludington. Take exit 166 for the park.

7 Ludington State Park

It's time to stretch the legs at **Ludington State Park** (☎231-843-2423; per car $9), beyond the city limits on Hwy 116. If you don't have one already, buy a vehicle permit (per day/year $9/32) at the entrance booth, valid at all Michigan parks. Once inside, people simply pull over on the roadside and make a break for the beautiful stretches of beach. There's also a top-notch trail system and the renovated **Big Sable Point Lighthouse** to hike to (or live in, as the volunteer lighthouse keeper). Tours of the 112ft fog-buster cost $5.

The Drive » Get back on Hwy 31 and head to Manistee. Three miles beyond, hop on Hwy 22 which clasps the coast for the next 115 miles. Inland lakes, clapboard towns and historic lighthouses flash by en route to the Sleeping Bear Dunes.

TRIP HIGHLIGHT

8 Sleeping Bear Dunes National Lakeshore

Stop at the park's **visitor center** (☎231-326-4700; www.nps.gov/slbe; 9922 W Front St; 8am-6pm Jun-Aug, 8:30am-4pm Sep-May) in Empire for information, trail maps and vehicle entry permits (week/annual $15/30). Then steer north for 2 miles to Hwy 109 and the **Pierce Stocking Scenic Drive**. The 7-mile, one-lane, picnic-grove-studded loop is one way to absorb the stunning lake vistas. Another is the **Dune Climb**, which entails trudging up a 200ft-high sand pile. It's likewise on Hwy 109. There's also the **Sleeping Bear Heritage Trail**, which paves 17 miles from Empire north past the Dune Climb and onward by the water; it's a view-a-licious jaunt, which is why walkers and cyclists are all over it.

The Drive » Hwy 109 ends in bustling Glen Arbor, a good choice for lodging. Rejoin Hwy 22 for 18 miles as it continues through the national lakeshore and hugs the coast to Leland.

9 Leland

Little Leland is cute as a button. Grab a bite at a waterfront restaurant downtown, and poke around atmospheric Fishtown with its weather-beaten fishing-shanties-cum-shops. Ferries depart from here for the forest-cloaked Manitou Islands; day trips are doable in July and August. Check with **Manitou**

DETOUR: GRAND RAPIDS

Start: 6 Holland

The second-largest city in Michigan, Grand Rapids – once known for office-furniture manufacturing – has become a mecca for beer tourism. Twenty craft breweries operate in the area. Grand Rapids Convention and Visitors Bureau (www.experiencegr.com) has maps and self-guided tour information online.

If you've only got time for one brewery, make it rock-and-roll **Founders Brewing Co** (☎616-776-1195; www.foundersbrewing.com; 235 Grandville Ave SW; 11am-2am Mon-Sat, noon-midnight Sun; wi-fi). The ruby-tinged Dirty Bastard Ale is good swillin'. Want to try one more? Head to **Brewery Vivant** (☎616-719-1604; www.breweryvivant.com; 925 Cherry St SE; 3-11pm Mon-Thu, to midnight Fri, 11am-midnight Sat, noon-10pm Sun), which specializes in Belgian-style beers. It's set in an old chapel with stained glass, a vaulted ceiling and farmhouse-style communal tables.

The city lies 29 miles inland from Holland via I-196.

Island Transit (☎231-256-9061; www.manitoutransit.com), which also runs a sunset cruise (per adult/child $25/15) along the lighthouse-dotted shoreline four days per week.

✕ p299

The Drive » Take Hwy 22 north for 4 miles. Zig right on N Eagle Hwy, then left on E Kolarik Rd. A mile onward, take the first right you come to, which is Setterbo Rd. You'll spy the cider house 3.5 miles later.

⑩ Suttons Bay

On the outskirts of Suttons Bay, **Tandem Ciders** (☎231-271-0050; www.tandemciders.com; 2055 Setterbo Rd; ⏲noon-6pm Mon-Sat, to 5pm Sun) pours delicious hard ciders in its cozy tasting room on the family farm. Pull up a stool at the bar and sip elixirs such as Cidre Royale (tart and high-powered) and Honey Pie (sweetened by a local beekeeper's wares). Tastings cost $2 for three 2oz pours.

In town, **Grand Traverse Bike Tours** (☎231-421-6815; www.grandtraverse-biketours.com; 318 N St Joseph St; ⏲9am-5:30pm Mon-Fri, to 5pm Sat, 10am-4pm Sun) offers guided rides (four-hour tour is $79) to local wineries, as well as self-guided tours (per person $65) for which staff provide route planning and van pick-up of your wine purchases.

The Drive » Hwy 22 rides down the Leelanau Peninsula and eventually rolls into Traverse City.

⑪ Traverse City

Traverse City is the region's 'big' city, with an unabashed love for cherries. It's a happening place with kiteboarding and sailing, music and movie festivals, and brewpubs and chic restaurants.

Front St is the main drag to wander and for window shopping. Be sure to pop in to **Cherry Republic** (☎231-932-9205; www.cherryrepublic.com; 154 E Front St; ⏲9am-9pm). It's touristy but a hoot to see all the products: cherry ketchup, cherry-dusted tortillas, cherry butter, cherry wine – you get the point. Most of it tastes better than you think. And the shop is *very* generous with samples (hence the crowds).

✕ p299

The Drive » Take Front St (aka Hwy 31) heading east out of town. When you get to Garfield Ave, turn left. It soon becomes Hwy 37, sallying through the grape- and cherry-planted Old Mission Peninsula.

⑫ Old Mission Peninsula

Taste tripping through the peninsula's wineries is a popular pastime. With nine vineyards in 19 miles, you won't go thirsty. **Chateau Grand Traverse** (☎231-938-6120; www.cgtwines.com; 12239 Center Rd; ⏲10am-7pm Mon-Sat, to 6pm Sun) and **Chateau Chantal** (☎800-969-4009; www.chateauchantal.com; 15900 Rue de Vin; ⏲11am-7pm Mon-Sat, to 6pm Sun) pour crowd-pleasing Chardonnay and Pinot Noir.

Peninsula Cellars (☎231-933-9787; www.peninsulacellars.com; 11480 Center Rd; ⏲10am-6pm), in an old schoolhouse, makes fine whites and is often less crowded. Whatever bottle you buy, take it out to Lighthouse Park beach at the peninsula's tip and enjoy it with the waves chilling your toes.

🛏 p299

The Drive » Retrace your path back to Hwy 31 and head north. In roughly 50 miles, north of yacht-riddled Charlevoix, look for Boyne City Rd. It skirts Lake Charlevoix and eventually arrives at the Horton Bay General Store.

⑬ Horton Bay General Store

Ernest Hemingway fans will recognize the **Horton Bay General Store** (☎231-582-7827; www.hortonbaygeneralstore.com; 5115 Boyne City Rd; ⏲8am-2pm Sun-Thu, 8am-2pm & 5-9pm Fri & Sat, closed mid-Oct–mid-May), with its 'high false front,' from his short story 'Up in Michigan.' Hemingway idled away some youthful summers telling fish stories on the big porch. His family

DETOUR: BEAVER ISLAND

Start: ⑬ Horton Bay

For an alternative to Mackinac Island, sail to quieter **Beaver Island** (www.beaverisland.org), an Irish-influenced enclave, home to 600 people, that offers hiking, fishing, kayaking and snorkeling to shipwrecked schooners. The **ferry** (☎231-547-2311; www.bibco.com; 103 Bridge Park Dr; ⌚mid-Apr–late Dec) departs from downtown Charlevoix. The two-hour journey costs $32.50/105 one-way per person/car.

had a cottage on nearby Walloon Lake.

The Drive » Head east on Boyne City Rd. Take the second left onto Sumner Rd, and then left again on Camp Daggett Rd. The latter meets Hwy 31 in 6 miles, which carries you to Petoskey.

---

⑭ Petoskey

Petoskey is yet another resort town with a yacht-filled marina and compact downtown dotted with gourmet restaurants and gift boutiques. It also has a couple of Hemingway sights. The **Little Traverse History Museum** (☎231-347-2620; www.petoskeymuseum.org; 100 Depot Ct; $3; ⌚10am-4pm Mon-Sat, closed mid-Oct–late May) has a collection dedicated to the author, including rare first-edition books that Hemingway autographed for a friend when he visited in 1947. Afterward, toss back a drink at **City Park Grill** (☎231-347-0101; www.cityparkgrill.com; 432 E Lake St; ⌚11:30am-9pm Sun-Thu, to 1:30am Fri & Sat), where Hemingway was a regular. Just north of town you can hunt for famed Petoskey stones (honeycomb-patterned fragments of ancient coral) at **Petoskey State Park** (☎231-347-2311; 2475 Hwy 119; per car $9).

The Drive » Time for a choice on this final stretch: take the 'fast' way to Mackinaw City via Hwy 31, or dawdle on narrow Hwy 119. The latter dips and curves through thick forests and along bluffs as part of the Tunnel of Trees scenic route.

TRIP HIGHLIGHT

⑮ Mackinaw City & Mackinac Island

Touristy Mackinaw City serves mainly as the jump-off point to Mackinac Island, but it does have an intriguing sight: **Colonial Michilimackinac** (☎231-436-5564; www.mackinacparks.com; 102 W Straits Ave; adult/child $12/7; ⌚9am-7pm Jun-Aug, to 5pm May & Sep–mid-Oct; 👪), a National Historic Landmark that features a reconstructed stockade first built in 1715 by the French; the visitor center is beneath the enormous Mackinac Bridge.

Mackinac Island floats a few miles offshore and is the big draw up here. Cars are banned, and all travel on the 3.8-sq-mile isle is by horse-drawn carriage or bicycle. It's a charming, old-time place, speckled with fudge shops, Victorian cottages and 18th-century forts. The ferry ride over takes 20 minutes, so it's easy to do as a day trip. Better yet, spend the night.

Two ferry companies – **Shepler's** (☎800-828-6157; www.sheplersferry.com) and **Star Line** (☎800-638-9892; www.mackinacferry.com) – make frequent trips and charge the same rates: round-trip adult/child $26/14. They have parking lots where you can leave your car.

✕ 🛏 p299

Eating & Sleeping

New Buffalo 1

Redamak's — Burgers $

(269-469-4522; www.redamaks.com; 616 E Buffalo St, New Buffalo; burgers $6-12; noon-10:30pm Mon-Sat, to 10pm Sun Mar–mid-Oct) It's a rightfully lauded, longstanding spot to get a wax-paper-wrapped cheeseburger, spicy curly fries and cold beer in New Buffalo. Cash only.

South Haven

Sherman's Dairy Bar — Ice Cream $

(269-637-8251; www.shermanicecream.com; 1601 Phoenix Rd; cones from $3.50; noon-9pm Sun-Thu, to 10pm Fri & Sat, closed Nov-Feb;) Beloved Sherman's scoops massive cones in 50 flavors (try the Mackinac Island fudge). It can't get any fresher, since it's made in the on-site factory. Lines can be lengthy.

Saugatuck 5

Wicks Park Bar & Grill — American $$

(269-857-2888; www.wickspark.com; 449 Water St; mains $11-25; noon-10pm Sun-Thu, to 1am Fri & Sat) Located by the chain ferry, Wicks gets props for its lake perch and live music.

Pines Motorlodge — Motel $$

(269-857-5211; www.thepinesmotorlodge.com; 56 Blue Star Hwy; r $139-249;) Retro-cool tiki lamps, pinewood furniture and communal lawn chairs add up to a fun, social ambience amid the firs in Douglas.

Leland 9

Cove — Seafood $$$

(231-256-9834; www.thecoveleland.com; 111 River St; mains $22-32; 11am-10pm, closed Nov-Apr) The Cove's specialty is whitefish that it prepares four ways (baked with almonds, stuffed with crab, encrusted with garlic, and foil-baked with peppers), all served at a good-time, waterside location.

Traverse City 11

Folgarelli's — Deli $

(231-941-7651; www.folgarellis.net; 424 W Front St; sandwiches $8-11; 9:30am-6:30pm Mon-Fri, to 5:30pm Sat, 11am-4pm Sun) After a day of fun in the sun, refresh with sandwiches at gastronome favorite Folgarelli's.

North Peak Brewing Company — Pub Food $$

(231-941-7325; www.northpeak.net; 400 W Front St; mains $10-20; 11am-11pm Mon-Thu, to midnight Fri & Sat, noon-10pm Sun) Munch pizzas, mussels and pretzel-crusted walleye with the housemade suds. A five-beer sampler costs $7. Not a brew drinker? North Peak also makes root beer.

Old Mission Peninsula 12

Grey Hare Inn — B&B $$$

(231-947-2214; www.greyhareinn.com; 1994 Carroll St; r $200-300;) The Grey Hare is an intimate, three-room B&B on a working vineyard, with French-style decor and bay views. Rooms are large with wrought iron or canopy beds and heavy antique furnishings.

Mackinac Island 15

Horn's Bar — Mexican $$

(906-847-6154; www.hornsbar.com; 7300 Main St; mains $12-20; 10:30am-2am) Horn's saloon serves American burgers and south-of-the-border fare. There's live entertainment nightly.

Cloghaun B&B — B&B $$

(906-847-3885; www.cloghaun.com; Market St; r $134-204, without bath $89-119; mid-May–late Oct) Cloghaun sees lots of return customers. The immaculate Victorian home offers 11 rooms done up with antiques and a bit of frill. Two rooms share a bathroom, while all others have a private bath. Peaceful gardens, a bountiful cooked breakfast and afternoon tea are all part of the package. It's well located downtown.

POSTED
KEEP OUT
POSTED
NO TRESPASSING
KEEP OUT

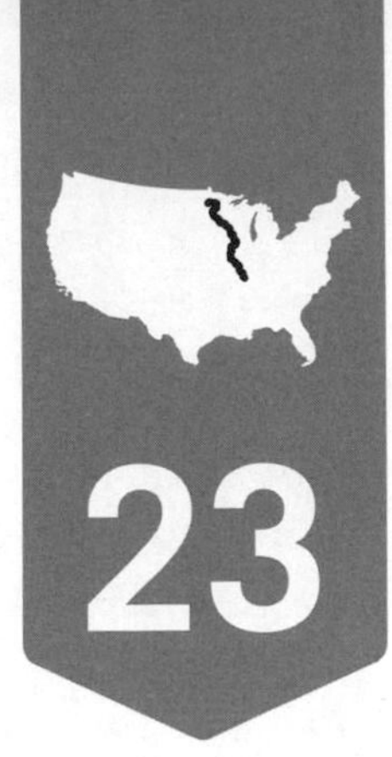

Along the Great River Road

The epic roadway edges the Mississippi River. In its northern half, it passes pine forests and eagles' nests, 18th-century forts and the World's Largest Six-Pack.

TRIP HIGHLIGHTS

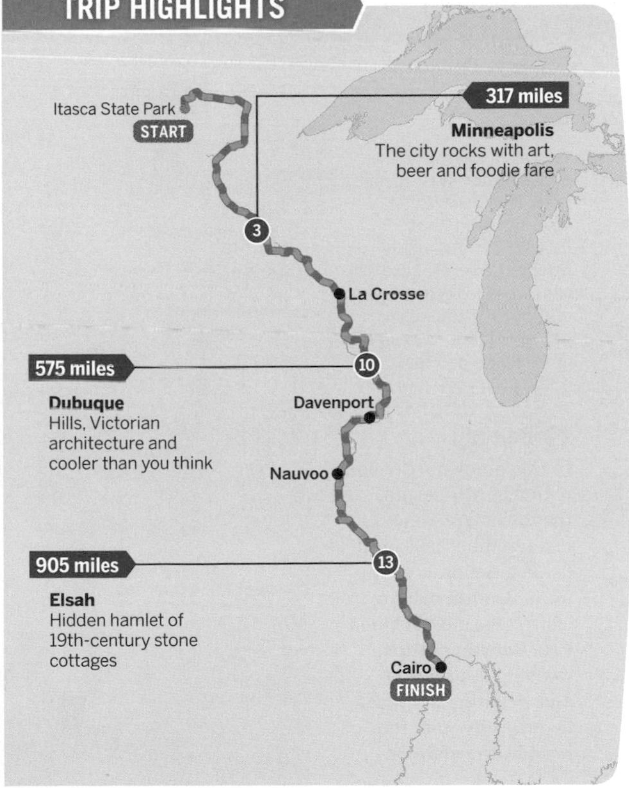

Itasca State Park
START

317 miles
Minneapolis
The city rocks with art, beer and foodie fare

3

La Crosse

575 miles
Dubuque
Hills, Victorian architecture and cooler than you think

10

Davenport

Nauvoo

905 miles
Elsah
Hidden hamlet of 19th-century stone cottages

13

Cairo
FINISH

6–7 DAYS
1075 MILES / 1730KM

GREAT FOR...

BEST TIME TO GO

June through September for snow-free weather.

ESSENTIAL PHOTO

Paul Bunyan and his blue ox Babe in Bemidji.

BEST TWO DAYS

The road between stops four and 10 offers bluff-strewn scenery, historic towns and foodie pit stops.

Dubuque, IA The 4th Street Elevator

23 Along the Great River Road

It happens time and again. The road curves around a bluff and Old Man River appears, wider than you remember, a swift-moving expanse dotted with woodsy islands and behemoth barges. An eagle swoops overhead, diving to the water and rising with a floppy fish. Every once in a while you reach a city, say Minneapolis or Dubuque, but mostly the road unfurls through forgotten towns where it becomes Main Street.

1 Itasca State Park, MN

Begin where the river begins, in Minnesota's **Itasca State Park** (☎218-699-7251; www.dnr.state.mn.us/itasca; off Hwy 71 N; per car $5). A carved pole denotes the headwaters of 'the Mighty Mississippi' – a good thing, because it's puny enough to mistake for a creek. Wade in the knee-deep flow and hop over a couple of stepping stones, then boast you walked across the Father of Waters. The park also offers canoeing, hiking, biking and camping, plus a lodge and hostel, all operated according to the principles of 'Minnesota nice' (the state's proverbial hospitality).

🛏 p309

The Drive » Drive northeast, zigzagging on various county roads. Take County Rd 2 to 40 to 9, through Becida. Turn left onto 169th Ave, which becomes County Rd 7 and rolls into Bemidji (an overall trip of 30 miles). For free maps that help navigation, see www.mnmississippiriver.com.

2 Bemidji

In this piney northwoods region of Minnesota, the towns are known for lakes, lumberjacks and fishing. A classic example is Bemidji, where an enormous, mustachioed **Paul Bunyan statue** awaits. Standing 18ft and weighing 2.5 tons, he raises his concrete head by the **visitors**

center (☎218-759-0164; www.visitbemidji.com; 300 Bemidji Ave N; ⏰8am-5pm, 10am-5pm Sat, 11am-3pm Sun Jun-Aug, closed Sat & Sun Sep-May), flanked by Babe, his faithful blue ox. Together they make a mighty photo op. Did we mention they created the Mississippi? As legend has it, Babe was hauling the tank wagon that paved the winter logging roads with ice. One day it sprang a leak, which trickled down to New Orleans and formed the Big Muddy.

The Drive » The road drifts east then south for 350 miles, taking strides on remote Forest Service lanes, gravel roads and county highways that skirt wee communities like Palisade, a sweet cafe stop, and Cuyuna, home to wood-tick races each June. The road eventually drops into glassy, high-rise Minneapolis.

LINK YOUR TRIP

1 Route 66
Join the Mother Road in St Louis and mosey 2100 miles southwest to LA or 300 miles northeast to Chicago.

28 The Mighty Mo
Here's another one to pick up in St Louis, a history-studded trip along the Missouri River heading northwest to the Dakotas.

TRIP HIGHLIGHT

3 Minneapolis

The Riverfront District at downtown's northern edge makes a fine pause with its parks, museums, bars and polka clubs. At the foot of Portland Ave is the car-free **Stone Arch Bridge** over the Mississippi, from which you can view the cascading St Anthony Falls. A few blocks east is the cobalt-blue **Guthrie Theater** (☎612-377-2224; www.guthrietheater.org; 818 2nd St S). Make your way up to its 'Endless Bridge,' a cantilevered walkway overlooking the river. You don't need a theater ticket – it's intended as a public space.

A stone's throw downstream, 50,000 students hit the books (and live-music venues) at the University of Minnesota. The university's **Weisman Art Museum** (☎612-625-9494; www.wam.umn.edu; 333 E River Rd; ⏰10am-5pm Tue, Thu & Fri, to 8pm Wed, 11am-5pm Sat & Sun) occupies a swooping, silver waterfront structure by architect Frank Gehry. It's worth a peek for its airy galleries of American art.

✕ p309

The Drive » Take I-94 E to exit 241B for downtown St Paul. It's about a 10-mile drive.

4 St Paul

Smaller and quieter than its twin city Minneapolis, St Paul has more of a historic character. The **Mississippi River Visitors Center** (☎651-293-0200; www.nps.gov/miss; 120 W Kellogg Blvd; ⏰9:30am-5pm Sun & Tue-Thu, to 9pm Fri & Sat) occupies an alcove in the science museum's lobby. Stop by to pick up trail maps and see what sort of ranger-guided activities are going on.

GMSTOCKSTUDIO / SHUTTERSTOCK ©

Up on Cathedral Hill, named for – that's right – the hulking church that marks the spot, a string of Gilded Age mansions lines **Summit Avenue**. This is the old stomping ground of author F Scott Fitzgerald, who lived in the brownstone at 599 Summit Ave when he published *This Side of Paradise*. A block south, Grand Ave holds a slew of foodie cafes and shops.

✕ 🛏 p309

The Drive » Twenty-five miles beyond St Paul, near Hastings, the River Road splits

ROAD RESOURCES

Turn-by-turn directions for the Great River Road are complex, spanning an incredible number of highways and byways. We've provided some road information here, but for nitty-gritty instructions you'll need additional resources. Minnesota (www.mnmississippiriver.com), Wisconsin (www.wigrr.com), Illinois (www.greatriverroad-illinois.org) and Iowa (www.iowagreatriverroad.com) each maintain their own River Road website. Or check the America's Byways (www.fhwa.dot.gov/byways/byways/2279) for designated sections. The one constant, wherever you are: the green paddle-wheel sign that marks the way.

Minneapolis Stone Arch Bridge

into eastern and western sections as the Mississippi becomes the border between states. It's the Minnesota–Wisconsin line at this juncture, and our trip starts flip-flopping between the two to cover the best sights.

5 Pepin, WI

Stay on the Minnesota side (Hwy 61) of the river to shoe and pottery purveyor Red Wing, then cross to Wisconsin (Hwy 35) where some of the Mississippi Valley's prettiest landscapes begin. A great stretch of road edges the bluffs around Pepin. *Little House on the Prairie* fans can make a pit stop at the **Laura Ingalls Wilder Museum** (715-513-6383; www.lauraingallspepin.com; 306 3rd St; adult/child $5/2; 10am-5pm mid-May–mid-Oct). This is where she was born and the abode that starred in *Little House in the Big Woods*. There's not a lot in the museum (and the building itself is a replica), but die-hards will appreciate being on the authentic patch of land once homesteaded by Ma and Pa Ingalls.

p309

The Drive » Continue 8 miles southeast on Hwy 35 to Nelson.

6 Nelson, WI & Wabasha, MN

These two towns are across the river from each other. Nelson is on the Wisconsin side and home to the **Nelson Cheese Factory** (715-673-4725; www.nelsoncheese.com; S237 Hwy 35; ice-cream scoops from $2; 9am-6pm;). The name is a bit misleading: the refurbished building no longer produces cheese, but the shop carries a big stash of Wisconsin hunks, and the cozy wine bar serves 'em on tasting plates. The queues, though, are for the ice cream (emphasis on cream, which is used in abundance in the mega-rich treat).

Across the water in Wabasha, MN, is the **National Eagle Center** (☎651-565-4989; www.nationaleaglecenter.org; 50 Pembroke Ave, Wabasha; adult/child $8/6; ⏰10am-5pm; 👪). Large populations of bald eagles flock to the area each winter, where they nest in waterside trees and catch themselves fat silvery fish. The center has the lowdown. It also introduces you to Donald, Angel and the other rehabilitated birds who live on-site.

✕ p309

The Drive » From Wabasha, stay on Hwy 61 as it opens into a gorgeous drive for nearly 60 miles past sandbars, marshes and untamed green hills en route to La Crescent, MN.

7 La Crescent, MN

It's no wonder it's nicknamed 'the Apple Capital.' Orchards sprout from the land and roadside stands sell the tart wares, particularly bountiful from August through October. Strawberries, sweet corn and pumpkins fill baskets during other seasons. Hardy **Bauer's Market** (☎507-895-4583; www.bauersmarketplace.com; 221 N 2nd St; ⏰8am-8pm Mon-Fri, to 6pm Sat & Sun) is open all year round selling local produce as well as garden supplies and giftware – say, a fish-toting gnome or giant mushroom – many painted by a local artist.

The Drive » Cross the Mississippi again via Hwy 61 to La Crescent's twin city La Crosse, WI.

8 La Crosse, WI

The road (which becomes 3rd St S on the Wisconsin side) swings by the **World's Largest Six-Pack** (cnr 3rd St S & Mississippi St). The 'cans' are actually storage tanks for City Brewery, formerly G Heileman Brewing, maker of Old Style lager. As the sign in front says: they hold enough to fill 7.3 million cans, or enough to provide one lucky person with a six-pack a day for 3351 years. Yowza.

The historic center of La Crosse nestles several restaurants and pubs downtown around Main St. **Grandad Bluff** (3020 Grandad Bluff Rd) offers grand views of the river. It's east of town along Main St (which becomes Bliss Rd); follow Bliss Rd up the hill and then turn right on Grandad Bluff Rd.

The Drive » Return to Hwy 35, which clasps the river for 24 miles to the Iowa border, then 35 miles more to the old fur-trading post of Prairie du Chien. Continue to Bloomington, then turn right on Hwy 133 for 40 rural, rolling miles to Potosi.

9 Potosi

The River Road becomes Main St as it moseys into town. The **Potosi Brewing Company** (☎608-763-4002; www.potosibrewery.com; 209 S Main St; ⏰10:30am-9pm Mon-Sat, 9am-3pm Sun, closed Mon & Tue Jan-Mar) is your one-stop shop for food, drink, memorabilia and historical information. The thick-stone building began brewing beer in 1852. Imbibe indoors amid neon-lit beer signs or outdoors in the pretty beer garden. Supplement with a burger and the famous beer cheese soup.

The building also holds the **National Brewery Museum** (admission $5), stuffed with old beer bottles, cans, coasters and advertising signs, and a **transportation museum** (admission free) that shows early beer-hauling equipment. And there's one more item of interest inside: the **Great River Road interpretation center**, offering maps, history and internet kiosks.

The Drive » Go east on Hwy 133 to Hwy 35/61; turn right. Follow it for 8 miles to the junction with Hwy 151. The three roads merge into one for 10 miles. Veer off for Dubuque at the 9th St–11th St exit.

TRIP HIGHLIGHT

10 Dubuque, IA

Dubuque has some surprises up its sleeve. Nineteenth-century

Victorian homes line its narrow and lively streets between the Mississippi River and seven steep limestone hills. The **4th Street Elevator** (www.fenelonplaceelevator.com; cnr 4th St & Bluff; round-trip adult/child $3/1.50; ⌚8am-10pm Apr-Nov), built in 1882, climbs a steep hill for huge views. Ring the bell to begin the ride.

At the **National Mississippi River Museum & Aquarium** (☎563-557-9545; www.rivermuseum.com; 350 E 3rd St; adult/child $15/10; ⌚9am-6pm Jun-Aug, 10am-5pm Sep-May), learn about life of all sorts on the Big Muddy. Exhibits span steamboating, aquatic creatures and indigenous Mississippi River dwellers. An American alligator lurks in the Bayou aquarium, one of six creature-filled habitats.

🛏 p309

The Drive » Take Hwy 52 south for 45 miles toward Sabula, then follow Hwy 67 to Davenport for 55 miles.

⓫ Davenport

Davenport is arguably the coolest of the 'Quad Cities' (www.visitquadcities.com), a foursome that also includes Bettendorf in Iowa and Moline and Rock Island in Illinois. Downtown, the glass-walled **Figge Art Museum** (☎563-326-7804; www.figgeartmuseum.org; 225 W 2nd St; adult/child $7/4; ⌚10am-5pm Tue, Wed, Fri & Sat, to 9pm Thu, noon-5pm Sun) sparkles above the River Road. The museum's Midwest Regionalist Collection includes many works by Iowa native (and *American Gothic* painter) Grant Wood; you can also stroll through the world-class Haitian and Mexican Colonial collections.

The Drive » A leisurely network of roads continue south in Iowa, with Hwy 61 rolling into Fort Madison. Cross the Mississippi on the Fort Madison Toll Bridge ($2), a double-decker swing-span accommodating trains and cars on separate levels. On the Illinois side, take Hwy 96 into striking Nauvoo.

⓬ Nauvoo, IL

Little Nauvoo (www.beautifulnauvoo.com) has long been a pilgrimage site for Mormons. Joseph Smith, the religion's founder, brought his flock here in 1839 after they were kicked out of Missouri. Nauvoo (Hebrew for 'beautiful place') grew quickly. Almost 12,000 Mormons took up residence, rivaling Chicago's population. By 1846 they were gone. Tension rose, Smith was killed, and Brigham Young led the group west to Utah. Today the tiny town is a historic district loaded with impressive structures, such as the homes of Smith and Young. The centerpiece is the gleaming white temple, built in 2002 on the site of the Mormons' burned-down original sanctuary.

The Drive » Follow Hwy 96 south to I-72, taking it west across the Mississippi to Hannibal, MO, hometown of writer Mark Twain. Back in Illinois, take Hwy 96 to Hwy 100. The road becomes incredibly scenic around Grafton. As you slip under wind-hewn bluffs, watch for the turnoff to Elsah.

TRIP HIGHLIGHT

⓭ Elsah

You can't help but slow down in itty-bitty Elsah (www.escapetoelsah.com), a hidden hamlet of 19th-century stone cottages, wood-buggy shops and farmhouses. Most of the town sits on two parallel streets. Around the bend lies Principia College, a small liberal arts school and one of the few for Christian Scientists. Outdoors enthusiasts can zipline and cycle bluff-side trails.

🛏 p309

The Drive » Take Hwy 100 to Alton. After that, the River Road gets lost around St Louis (take a walking tour if you plan to make it a stop). A good place to pick up the trail again is Ellis Grove, IL, 75 miles south via I-255, Hwy 159 and Hwy 3.

⓮ Fort Kaskaskia

A few miles south of Ellis Grove, **Fort Kaskaskia** (☎618-859-3741; 4372 Park Rd; ⌚8am-4pm) sits on a bluff beside the river. The French built it around

DETOUR: CYPRESS CREEK NATIONAL WILDLIFE REFUGE

Start: ⓯ Cairo

You certainly don't expect to find Southern-style swampland, complete with moss-draped cypress trees and croaking bullfrogs in Illinois. But it's here, at **Cypress Creek National Wildlife Refuge** (618-634-2231; www.fws.gov/refuge/cypress_creek). For River Road-trippers who aren't going onward to Louisiana, this is an opportunity to see the eerie swamp ecosystem in action. From Cairo drive north 25 miles on Hwy 37 to Cypress, and stop in at the **Cache River Wetlands Center** (618-657-2064; www.friendsofthecache.org; 8885 Hwy 37; 9am-4pm Wed-Sun). Staff can sort you out with hiking, biking and canoeing information.

1759 to defend against British attacks. All that remains today are lonely earthworks around the perimeter, a cemetery from the late 1800s and a view-tastic overlook. It's a great spot for a picnic, with tables and grills. If you're into French colonial architecture, take the footpath down to ogle the Pierre Menard Home, built in 1802 for the gent who eventually became Illinois' first lieutenant governor. Trivia tip: the town of Kaskaskia was Illinois' first capital, though its tenure barely lasted a year.

The Drive » About 6 miles down Hwy 3 you'll roll through Chester. It's the hometown of EC Segar, creator of the cartoon character Popeye – hence the statues of the spinach-eating sailor and pals Wimpy, Olive Oyl and Swee'Pea throughout town. Continue south on Hwy 3 for 85 miles until it ends at Cairo.

⓯ Cairo

It's the end of the line for the Great River Road's northern half. The town – pronounced kay-ro – has seen better days, but the surrounding area's swampy parklands are nifty. For those continuing on the thoroughfare, this is roughly the halfway point. The next 1000 miles meander past blues joints and barbecue shacks, steamboats and plantations, en route to New Orleans.

Eating & Sleeping

Itasca State Park 1

Douglas Lodge Lodge $$

(866-857-2757; www.dnr.state.mn.us/itasca; r $105-150;) If you want a little rustic luxury, try the venerable Douglas Lodge, operated by Itasca State Park. The facility also has cabins and two good dining rooms.

Palisade

Palisade Cafe American $

(218-845-2214; 210 Main St, Palisade; mains $5-11; 6am-7pm Mon-Sat, to 2pm Sun) This woodsy little joint in the middle of nowhere is a welcome respite, whipping up stuffed hash browns (as in stuffed with gooey cheese) and killer pies. It's in teeny Palisade, on the Great River Road midway between Grand Rapids and Brainerd.

Minneapolis 3

Butcher & the Boar American $$$

(612-238-8888; www.butcherandtheboar.com; 1121 Hennepin Ave; mains $32-48; 5-10:30pm Mon-Thu, to 11pm Fri & Sat, to 10pm Sun;) Get your carving knife ready for wild-boar ham with country butter, chicken-fried veal sausage and many more house-crafted meats. The 30 taps flow with regional brews, backed up by a lengthy bourbon list (flights available). Make reservations, or opt for small plates in the beer garden.

St Paul 4

Mickey's Diner Diner $

(651-222-5633; www.mickeysdiningcar.com; 36 W 7th St; mains $4-9; 24hr) Mickey's is a downtown classic, the kind of place where the friendly waitress calls you 'honey' and satisfied regulars line the bar with their coffee cups and newspapers. The food has timeless appeal, too: burgers, malts and apple pie.

Hotel 340 Boutique Hotel $$

(651-280-4120; www.hotel340.com; 340 Cedar St; r $109-189; P @) Hotel 340 delivers old-world ambiance aplenty, and it's usually a great deal to boot. The 56 rooms in the stately old building have hardwood floors and plush linens. The two-story lobby stokes a grand fireplace and nifty little bar (the desk staff double as bartenders). Continental breakfast is included. Parking costs $17 per night.

Pepin 5

Harbor View Cafe American $$$

(715-442-3893; www.harborviewpepin.com; 314 First St; mains $19-33; 11am-2:30pm Thu-Mon, closed mid-Nov–mid-Mar) The book-stuffed Harbor View is a Slow Food stalwart. Staff write the changing menu on a chalkboard twice daily – once for lunch, once for dinner. Cross your fingers the list shows the four-cheese stuffed mushrooms, caper-sauced halibut and lemon cake with ginger. No reservations.

Nelson 6

Stone Barn Pizza $$

(715-673-4478; www.thenelsonstonebarn.com; S685 County Rd KK; pizzas $18-25; 5-8pm Fri, 4-8pm Sat & Sun mid-May–late Sep) Browse the antique store or amble through the herb garden while waiting for your pizza to emerge from the wood-fired oven. All tables are set outdoors, surrounded by hilly farmland.

Dubuque 10

Hotel Julien Historic Hotel $$

(563-556-4200; www.hoteljuliendubuque.com; 200 Main St; r $120-250;) The eight-story hotel was built in 1914 and was once a refuge for Al Capone. A lavish renovation has turned it upscale and it's a real antidote to chains.

Elsah 13

Maple Leaf Cottage Inn B&B $$

(618-374-1684; www.mapleleafcottageinn.com; 12 Selma St, Elsah; r $119-149;) Iron-rail beds, claw-foot tubs, headboards made from Victorian gables and other antique accoutrements throw the Maple Leaf back in time. A cooked breakfast and free bicycles for roaming are included in the price.

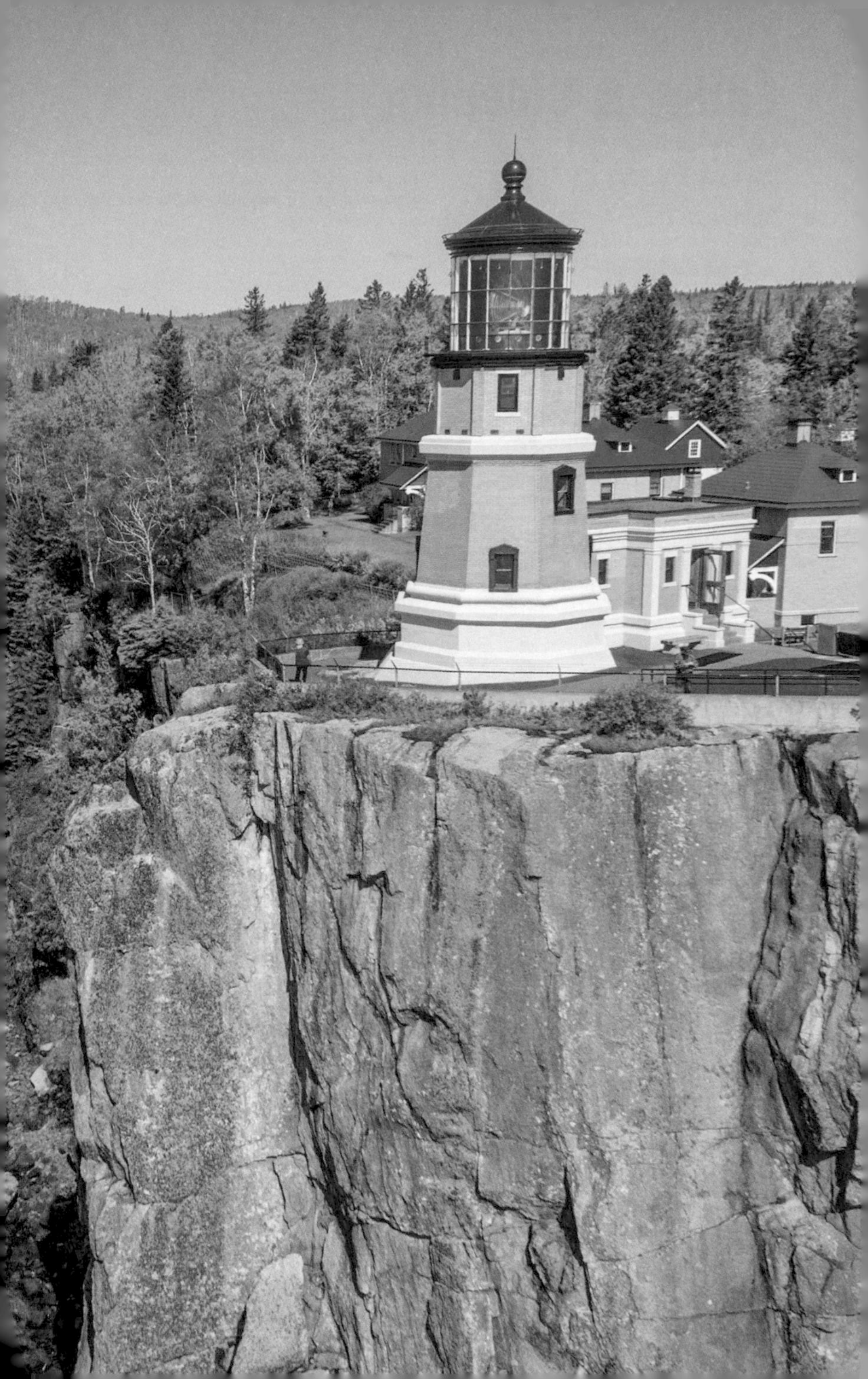

Highway 61

Waterfalls, moose and Bob Dylan vestiges roll by on Minnesota's Hwy 61. The road grips Lake Superior's shore, tucked between red-tinged cliffs and towering firs from Duluth to Canada's edge.

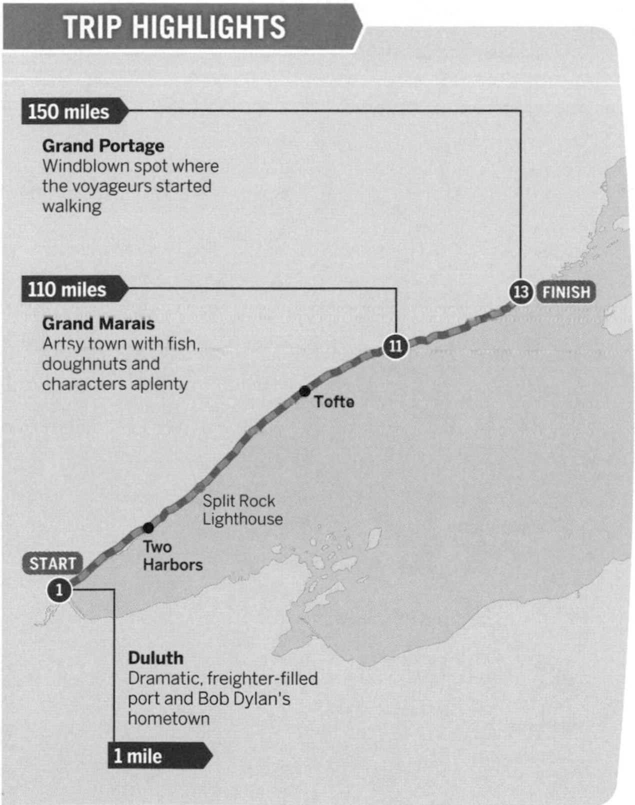

TRIP HIGHLIGHTS

150 miles

Grand Portage
Windblown spot where the voyageurs started walking

110 miles

Grand Marais
Artsy town with fish, doughnuts and characters aplenty

13 FINISH

11

Tofte

Split Rock Lighthouse

Two Harbors

START

1

Duluth
Dramatic, freighter-filled port and Bob Dylan's hometown

1 mile

2–3 DAYS
150 MILES / 241KM

GREAT FOR...

BEST TIME TO GO

July to mid-October for pleasant weather and fall colors.

ESSENTIAL PHOTO

Split Rock Lighthouse on its perfect cliff top.

BEST FOR WILDLIFE

Drive the Gunflint Trail and watch for moose.

Split Rock Lighthouse The most visited spot on the North Shore

24 Highway 61

Mention Hwy 61 and many folks hum Bob Dylan. But this North Shore road is not about murder, poverty or any other mean-street mumblings from his 1965 album *Highway 61 Revisited*. Instead it's a journey dominated by water, where ore-toting freighters ply the ports, little fishing fleets haul in the day's catch, and wave-bashed cliffs offer Superior views if you're willing to trek.

TRIP HIGHLIGHT

1 Duluth

Dramatically spliced into a cliff that tumbles down to Lake Superior, Duluth is one of the busiest ports in the nation. Canal Park downtown is a good spot to see the action. Start at the **Aerial Lift Bridge**, Duluth's landmark that raises its mighty arm to let horn-bellowing ships into port. About 1000 freighters a year glide through. The screens outside the **Maritime Visitor Center** (☎218-

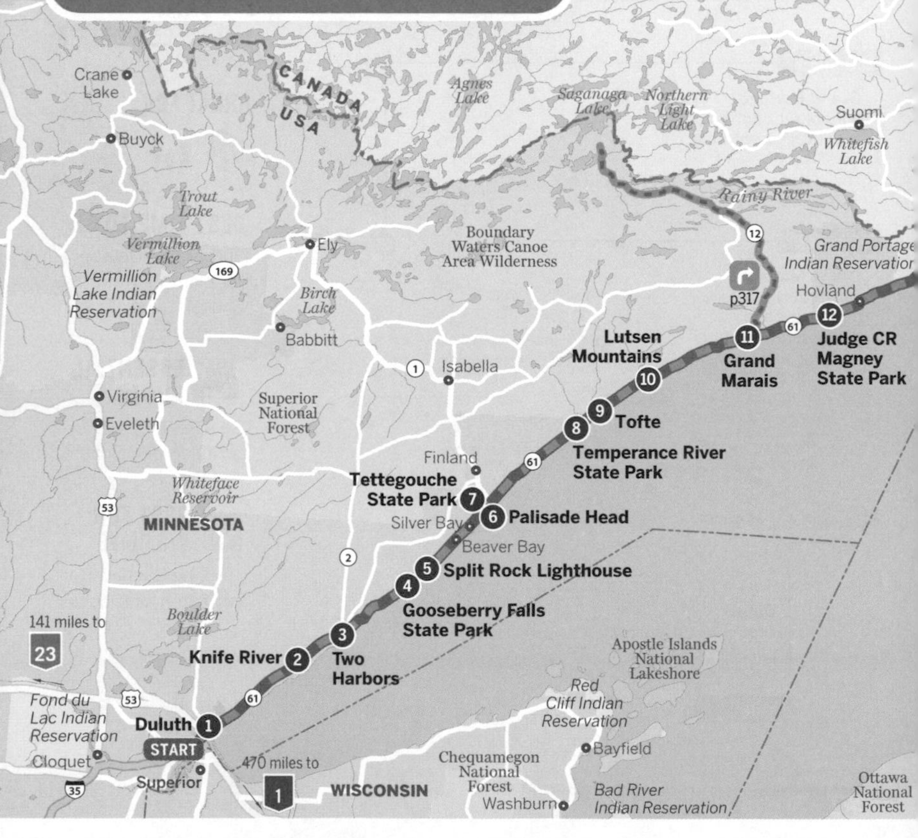

720-5260; www.lsmma.com; 600 S Lake Ave; ⏲10am-9pm Jun-Aug, reduced hours Sep-May) announce when the big boats come and go; inside holds first-rate exhibitions on Great Lakes shipping and shipwrecks.

Duluth is also the birthplace of Bob Dylan, though the town is pretty laid-back about its famous son. You're on your own to find **Dylan's childhood home** (519 N 3rd Ave E), up a hill a few blocks northeast of downtown. Dylan lived on the top floor until age six, when his family moved inland to Hibbing. It's a private residence (and unmarked), so all you can do is check it out from the street.

✕ 🛏 p319

The Drive » Take London Rd, aka Hwy 61, heading northeast out of town. Follow the signs for the North Shore Scenic Dr (also called Scenic 61 or Old Hwy 61). There's a Hwy 61 expressway that also covers the next 20 miles, but steer clear and dawdle on the original, curvy, two-lane route instead.

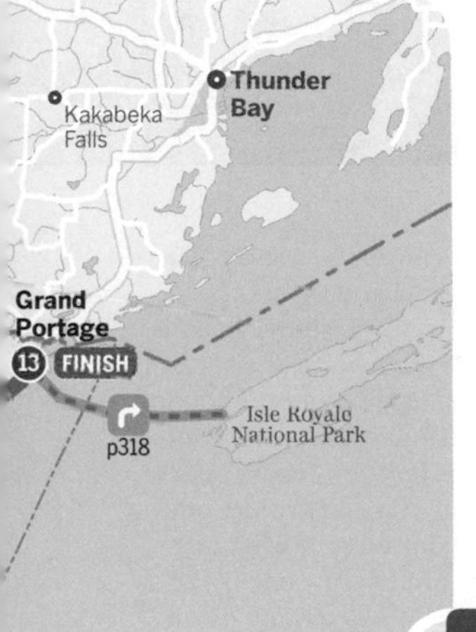

❷ Knife River

Unspoiled shoreline and fisherfolk casting at river mouths are your companions along the way until you reach **Russ Kendall's Smoke House** (☎218-834-5995; 149 Scenic Dr; ⏲9:30am-5:30pm) in Knife River. A groovy neon sign beckons you in. Four generations of Kendall folk have cooked up the locally plucked trout and line-caught Alaskan salmon. Buy a brown-sugar-cured slab; staff will wrap it in newspaper, and you'll be set for picnics for miles to come.

The Drive » Continue northeast on Hwy 61. OK, so the Knife River fish is demolished by the time you reach Two Harbors, a couple of miles up the road.

❸ Two Harbors

Minnesota's only operating **lighthouse** (www.lakecountyhistoricalsociety.org; $5; ⏲10am-6pm Mon-Sat, to 4pm Sun) rises up over Agate Bay. The 1892 fog-buster sticks to a rhythm – 0.4-second flash, 4.6 seconds of darkness, 0.4-second flash, 14.6 seconds of darkness. That's how it goes all day, every day; check it out. You can also watch iron-ore freighters maneuvering around the docks that jut into Agate Bay, and there's an old tugboat you can tour (per person $3). Oh, the other harbor that gives the town its name? Burlington Bay, around the point to the north.

Hiking buffs should stop in the **Superior Hiking Trail Headquarters**

LINK YOUR TRIP

Route 66

It's a haul to Chicago – 470 miles – but the payoff is a slowpoke ride on America's Main Street.

Along the Great River Road

Pick up the Mississippi River–edged route in Grand Rapids, about 83 miles east via Hwy 2.

(☎218-834-2700; www.shta.org; 731 7th Ave; ⏰9am-4:30pm Mon-Fri, 10am-4pm Sat, noon-4pm Sun, closed Sat & Sun mid-Oct–mid-May). The awesome 290-mile footpath follows the lake-hugging ridgeline between Duluth and the Canadian border. Trailheads with parking lots pop up every 5 to 10 miles, making it ideal for day hikes. Overnight hikers will find 81 backcountry campsites and several lodges along the way. The headquarters has maps and information.

🍴🛏 p319

The Drive » Motor onward on Hwy 61, past the hamlet of Castle Danger (named for a boat that ran aground nearby) to Gooseberry Falls State Park, a 13-mile drive.

4 Gooseberry Falls State Park

The five cascades, scenic gorge and easy trails draw carloads of visitors to **Gooseberry Falls State Park** (☎218-834-3855; www.dnr.state.mn.us; 3206 Hwy 61; per car $5; ⏰8am-10pm; 👪). Several cool stone and log buildings, built by Civilian Conservation Corps in the 1930s, dot the premises and hold exhibits and concessions.

The **Lower and Middle Falls** offer the quickest access via a 0.6-mile paved walkway. Hardier types can trek the 2-mile **Gooseberry River Loop**, which is part of the Superior Hiking Trail. To embark, leave your car at the visitor center lot (at Mile 38.9). Follow the trail to the Upper Falls, then continue upstream on the Fifth Falls Trail. Cross the bridge at Fifth Falls, then return on the river's other side to where you started. Voila! It's one of the simplest Superior trail jaunts you'll find.

The Drive » Yep, it's back to Hwy 61 heading northeast, this time for 6 miles.

5 Split Rock Lighthouse

The most visited spot on the entire North Shore is **Split Rock Lighthouse State Park** (☎218-595-7625; www.dnr.state.mn.us; 3755 Split Rock Lighthouse Rd; per car $5, lighthouse per adult/child $10/6; ⏰10am-6pm mid-May–mid-Oct, 11am-4pm Thu-Mon mid-Oct–mid-May). The shiner itself is a state historic site with a separate admission fee. Guided tours are available (they depart hourly), or you can explore on your own. If you don't mind stairs, say 170 or so each way, tramp down the cliff to the beach for incredible views of the lighthouse and surrounding shore.

The lighthouse was built after a whopping storm in November 1905 battered 29 ships in the area. Modern navigation equipment rendered it obsolete by 1969. No

C. CHASE TAYLOR / GETTY IMAGES ©

HWY 61'S OTHER INCARNATION

Hwy 61 is also used to reference the fabled Blues Hwy (p235) that tracks the Mississippi River en route to New Orleans. That road is actually US 61, and it starts near St Paul, MN. Our Hwy 61 is the state scenic road that starts in Duluth.

Gooseberry Falls Middle Falls

matter. It remains one of the most picture-perfect structures you'll come across.

The Drive » Onward on Hwy 61 for 10 miles. Not long after cruising by taconite-crazed Silver Bay, watch for the sign to Palisade Head.

6 Palisade Head

Palisade Head is an old lava flow that morphed into some awesomely sheer, rust-red cliffs. A narrow road winds around to the top, where there's a small parking lot. The view that unfurls is tremendous. On a clear day you can see Wisconsin's Apostle Islands. Rock climbers love the Head, and you'll probably see a lot of them hanging around.

The Drive » Return to Hwy 61. Palisade Head is actually part of Tettegouche State Park, though it's not contiguous. The park's main span begins 2 miles up the road.

7 Tettegouche State Park

Like most of the parks dotting the North Shore, **Tettegouche State Park** (☎218-353-8800; www.dnr.state.mn.us; 5702 Hwy 61; per car $5; ⏲9am-8pm) offers fishing, camping, paddling, and hiking trails to waterfalls and little lakes, plus skiing and snowshoe trails in winter.

There are two unique to-do's, both accessed near the park entrance (Mile 58.5). Leave your car in the parking lot by the visitor center, then hit the trail to **Shovel Point**. It's a 1.5-mile round-trip jaunt over lots of steps and boardwalks. It pays off with sublime views of the rugged landscape from the point's tip. Watch the lake's awesome power as waves smash below. And keep an eye out for peregrine falcons that nest in the area. Tettegouche's other cool feature is the idyllic **swimming hole** at the Baptism River's mouth. Walk along the picnic area by the visitor center and you'll run into it.

The Drive » Hwy 61 rolls by more birch trees, parks and cloud-flecked skies for the next 22 miles. Not far past Taconite Harbor (now used to load and unload coal for the adjacent power plant), you'll come to Temperance River.

8 Temperance River State Park

Get ready for another gorgeous, falls-filled landscape. The eponymous waterway at **Temperance River State Park** (☎218-663-3100; www.dnr.state.mn.us; 7620 Hwy 61; per car $5; ⏰9am-8pm) belies its moderate name and roars through a narrow, twisting gorge. The scene is easy to get to, with highway-side parking. Then hike over footbridges and around rock pools to see the action.

The Drive » It's a quick 2 miles up Hwy 61 to Tofte.

9 Tofte

The teeny town of Tofte is worth a stop to browse the **North Shore Commercial Fishing Museum** (☎218-663-7050; www.commercialfishingmuseum.org; 7136 Hwy 61, Tofte; adult/child $3/1; ⏰9am-3pm Sun-Thu, 9am-5pm Fri & Sat mid-May–mid-Oct, noon-5pm Fri, 9am-5pm Sat mid-Oct–mid-May). The twin-gabled red building holds fishing nets, a fishing boat and other tools of the trade, as well as intriguing photos, most of them from the original Norwegian families who settled and fished here in the late 1800s.

Nearby **Sawtooth Outfitters** (☎218-663-7643; www.sawtoothoutfitters.com; 7216 Hwy 61; ⏰8am-6pm early May–late Oct & mid-late Dec, 8am-6pm Thu-Mon Jan–early Apr) offers guided kayaking tours (half-/full-day tours $55/110) for all levels of paddling. It has trips on the Temperance River and out on Lake Superior, as well as easier jaunts on wildlife-rich inland lakes. Sawtooth also rents mountain bikes (per day from $22) to pedal over the many trails in the area, including the popular Gitchi Gami State Bike Trail (www.ggta.org).

The Drive » Get back on Hwy 61 and head 7 piney miles northeast.

10 Lutsen Mountains

Lutsen (☎218-406-1320; www.lutsen.com; ⏰10am-5pm) is a ski resort – the biggest alpine ski area in the Midwest, in fact. So it bustles in winter when skiers and snowboarders pile in for the 95 runs on four mountains.

In summer, visitors come for the **aerial gondola** (round-trip adult/child $20/12) to the top of Moose Mountain. The red cars glide at treetop level into the valley and over the Poplar River before reaching the mountain top 1000ft later. Gape at the view from the chalet and hike the paths. The Superior Hiking Trail cuts through and you can take it plus a spur for the 4.5-mile trek back down the mountain.

Kids go crazy for the **alpine slide** (per person $12) on Eagle Mountain; it's accessed by chairlift. The resort also arranges family-friendly canoe trips in voyageur-style vessels (per person $15; times vary) on the Poplar River.

The Drive » Back to Hwy 61, past maple- and birch-rich Cascade River State Park (particularly pretty in fall), for 20 miles to Grand Marais.

TRIP HIGHLIGHT

11 Grand Marais

Artsy little Grand Marais makes an excellent base to explore the region. Stroll the waterfront, watch the small fishing fleet head out, and take advantage of the characterful local eateries. DIY enthusiasts can learn to build boats, tie flies or harvest wild rice at the **North House Folk School** (☎218-387-9762; www.northhouse.org; 500 Hwy 61). The course list, which strives to preserve local traditions, is phenomenal – as is the school's two-hour sailing trip aboard the Viking-esque schooner *Hjordis* (per person $45).

✕ 🛏 p319

The Drive » Beyond Grand Marais Hwy 61 widens, you see fewer people, and the lake reveals itself more. After 14 miles, you'll arrive at Judge CR Magney State Park.

⓬ Judge CR Magney State Park

The namesake of the **park** (☎218-387-6300; www.dnr.state.mn.us; 4051 Hwy 61; per car $5; ⏰9am-8pm) was a former mayor of Duluth and Minnesota Supreme Court justice who helped preserve the area. His own patch of land is a beauty. Hiking to **Devil's Kettle**, the famous falls where the Brule River splits around a huge rock, is a must. Half of the flow drops 50ft in a typically gorgeous North Shore gush, but the other half disappears down a huge hole and flows underground. Where it goes is a mystery – scientists have never been able to determine the water's outlet. It's a moderately breath-sapping 1.1-mile walk each way.

Across the road from the park is **Naniboujou Lodge**. Built in the 1920s, the property was once a private club for Babe Ruth and his contemporaries, who smoked cigars in the Great Hall, warmed by the 20ft-high stone fireplace. The pièce de résistance is the hall's massive domed ceiling painted with mind-blowing, psychedelic-colored Cree Indian designs. The hall is now the lodge's dining room, and you're welcome to walk in for a peek (or meal).

🛏 p319

The Drive » The final 26-mile stretch of highway passes through the Grand Portage Indian Reservation and, finally, Grand Portage National Monument.

TRIP HIGHLIGHT

⓭ Grand Portage

Named for the early voyageurs who had to carry their canoes around the Pigeon River rapids, **Grand Portage National Monument** (☎218-475-0123; www.nps.gov/grpo; 170 Mile Creek Rd; ⏰9am-5pm Jun–mid-Oct)

DETOUR: GUNFLINT TRAIL

Start: ⓫ Grand Marais

The Gunflint Trail (www.gunflint-trail.com), aka Hwy 12, slices inland from Grand Marais and ends near Saganaga Lake. The paved, 57-mile-long byway dips into the Boundary Waters Canoe Area Wilderness (www.fs.usda.gov/attmain/superior/specialplaces), the legendarily remote paddlers' paradise. For Boundary permits and information, visit the **Gunflint Ranger Station** (☎218-387-1750; 2020 Hwy 61; ⏰8am-4:30pm, closed Sat & Sun Oct-Apr), a stone's throw southwest of Grand Marais on Hwy 61.

Even if you're not canoeing, the road has excellent hiking, picnicking and moose-viewing. Look for the big antlered guys and gals around dawn or dusk in wet, swampy areas.

It takes 1½ hours to drive the Gunflint Trail one way, but you'll want longer for hiking, ziplining and moose stops. There aren't any towns along the route, but several lodges tuck in woods where you can grab a meal or snack.

DETOUR: ISLE ROYALE NATIONAL PARK

Start: 13 Grand Portage

Isle Royale National Park (www.nps.gov/isro) is technically part of Michigan, but it's easily accessed from Grand Portage by daily **ferries** (218-475-0024; www.isleroyaleboats.com; Upper Rd, Grand Portage; day trip adult/child $67/61) between May and October. The unspoiled, 210-sq-mile island is totally free of vehicles and roads, and gets fewer visitors in a year than Yellowstone National Park gets in a day – which means the 1600 moose creeping through the forest are all yours.

The ferry ride takes 90 minutes. Day trips leave Grand Portage in the morning, spend four hours on the island, then return by 3:30pm.

Wilderness buffs will want to linger. Around 165 miles of hiking trails lace the island and connect dozens of campgrounds along Lake Superior and inland waterways. It's a full-on wilderness adventure for which you'll need a tent, camping stove, sleeping bag, food and water filter. Or you can bunk at the island's lone accommodations, the **Rock Harbor Lodge** (906-337-4993; www.rockharborlodge.com; r & cottages $224-256; late May-early Sep).

was the center of a far-flung fur-trading empire, and the reconstructed 1788 trading post and Ojibwe village show how the little community lived in the harsh environment. Learn how the original inhabitants prepared wild rice and pressed beaver pelts as you wander through the Great Hall, kitchen, canoe warehouse and other buildings with costumed interpreters. A big powwow takes place the second weekend in August.

The half-mile paved path that goes to Mt Rose rewards with killer views. Or make like a voyageur and walk the 17-mile round-trip Grand Portage Trail that traces the early fur-men's route.

Grand Portage is impressively lonely and windblown – fitting for the end of the road. Because with that, Hwy 61 stops cold at the Canadian border.

Eating & Sleeping

Duluth 1

Duluth Grill — American $

(218-726-1150; www.duluthgrill.com; 118 S 27th Ave W; mains $10-17; 7am-9pm;) The garden in the parking lot is the tip-off that the Duluth Grill is a sustainable, hippie-vibed place. The diner-esque menu ranges from eggy breakfast skillets to curried polenta stew to bison burgers, with plenty of vegan and gluten-free options. It's a couple miles southwest of Canal Park, near the bridge to Superior, Wisconsin.

New Scenic Cafe — American $$

(218-525-6274; www.newsceniccafe.com; 5461 North Shore Dr; sandwiches $13-16, mains $24-29; 11am-9pm Sun-Thu, to 10pm Fri & Sat) Foodies travel from far and near to New Scenic Cafe, 8 miles beyond Duluth on Old Hwy 61. There, in a humble wood paneled room, they fork into rustic salmon with creamed leeks or a slice of triple-berry pie, all served with a generous helping of lake views. Make reservations.

Fitger's Inn — Hotel $$

(218-722-8826; www.fitgers.com; 600 E Superior St; r $185-290;) Fitger's created its 62 large rooms, each with slightly varied decor, from an old brewery. Located on the Lakewalk, the pricier rooms have great water views. Continental breakfast is included. The free shuttle to local sights is handy.

Two Harbors 3

Betty's Pies — American $

(218-834-3367; www.bettyspies.com; 1633 Hwy 61; pie slices $4.50-5; 7:30am-9pm) Racks of pie are Betty's claim to fame, though there's a lengthy menu of sandwiches, burgers and omelets, too. Try a fruit-filled, crunch-topping slice.

Lighthouse B&B — B&B $$

(888-832-5606; www.lighthousebb.org; r $145-160) You can't beat this real-deal lighthouse for nautical ambience and lake views. Three rooms share a bathroom; there's a fourth en suite room in a separate building. A cooked breakfast is included.

Grand Marais 11

Dockside Fish Market — Deli $

(218-387-2906; www.docksidefishmarket.com; 418 Hwy 61; mains $8-11; 9am-6pm Mon-Sat, to 5pm Sun) The boat heads out in the morning, and by noon the freshly caught herring has been fried into fish and chips at the deli counter. Seven tables are scattered on the outdoor deck, and another seven indoors. Before leaving, check the freezer case for briny-tanged Superior Gold Caviar (aka herring roe), a local delicacy.

Sven and Ole's — American $

(218-387-1713; www.svenandoles.com; 9 Wisconsin St; pizzas $10-20; 11am-8pm, to 9pm Thu-Sat) It's a classic for sandwiches and pizza, plus beer at the attached Pickled Herring Pub. Go ahead: ask about the lutefisk pizza.

Harbor Inn — Hotel $$

(218-387-1191; www.harborinnhotel.com; 207 Wisconsin St; r $110-145;) The rooms look plain-Jane, but they're comfy and well located in town.

Judge CR Magney State Park 12

Naniboujou Lodge — Lodge $$

(218-387-2688; www.naniboujou.com; 20 Naniboujou Trail; r $115-160; late May–late Oct) Built in the 1920s, the property was once a private club for Babe Ruth and his contemporaries, who smoked cigars in the Great Hall, warmed by the 20ft-high stone fireplace. The pièce de résistance is the hall's massive domed ceiling painted with mind-blowing, psychedelic-colored Cree Indian designs. Rooms vary in decor, but each offers an away-from-it-all experience. It's 14 miles northeast of Grand Marais.

STRETCH YOUR LEGS CHICAGO

Start/Finish: Millennium Park

Distance: 2 miles

Duration: Three hours

The Windy City will blow you away with its blend of high culture and earthy pleasures. This walk swoops through the action-packed downtown Loop, highlighting Chicago's revered art and architecture.

Take this walk on Trip

Millennium Park

Where to start amid the mod designs of **Millennium Park** (312-742-1168; www.millenniumpark.org; 201 E Randolph St; 6am-11pm;)? Pritzker Pavilion, Frank Gehry's rippling silver band shell? Crown Fountain, Jaume Plensa's splashy waterwork, where images of locals spout gargoyle-style? Or 'the Bean' (officially *Cloud Gate*), Anish Kapoor's 110-ton, silver-drop sculpture? That's the one. Join the visitors swarming it to see the skyline reflections.

The Walk » Walk across Monroe St to the Art Institute's Modern Wing entrance. You can also take the silvery pedestrian bridge that rises from Millennium Park and arches over the street. It deposits you at the institute's free, 3rd-floor sculpture garden.

Art Institute of Chicago

The **Art Institute of Chicago** (312-443-3600; www.artic.edu; 111 S Michigan Ave; adult/child $25/free; 10:30am-5pm Fri-Wed, to 8pm Thu;) is the second-largest art museum in the country. The collection of impressionist and post-impressionist paintings is second only to those in France, and the number of surrealist works is tremendous. Download the free app for DIY tours. It offers several quick-hit jaunts, from highlights to architecture to pop art tours.

The Walk » Walk south on Michigan Ave to Jackson Blvd; turn right. Pass under the rumbling L train. Four business-y blocks later you'll pass the 1930 art-deco Board of Trade (look for Ceres, the goddess of agriculture, on top). Turn right on LaSalle St.

Rookery

The 1888 **Rookery** (312-994-4000; www.flwright.org; 209 S LaSalle St; 9am-5pm Mon-Fri) looks fortresslike from the outside, but the inside is light and airy thanks to Frank Lloyd Wright, who overhauled the atrium. You can walk in and look around for free. The Frank Lloyd Wright Preservation Trust has a groovy shop in the lobby and offers tours ($10 to $15) at 11am, noon and 1pm weekdays.

The Walk » Continue on LaSalle St, the heart of Chicago's financial district, to Washington St. Turn right and behold what rises up when you get to Daley Plaza.

The Picasso

Pablo Picasso's abstract sculpture is the granddaddy of Chicago's public art. Baboon, dog, woman? Picasso couldn't decide either, which is why it's officially titled **Untitled** (50 W Washington St).

The Walk » Stay on Washington St, passing the Alise Chicago hotel (at 1 W Washington). The building is an 1890s landmark that set the bar for modern skyscraper design. A block and a half later you'll reach Toni's place.

Toni Patisserie & Cafe

Parisian-style **Toni Patisserie & Cafe** (☎312-726-2020; www.tonipatisserie.com; 65 E Washington St; ⏰7am-7pm Mon-Fri, 8am-7pm Sat, 9am-5pm Sun) provides a refuge from the Loop hullabaloo. Order a coffee to sip at the close-set tables while you try to resist the eclairs, macarons and tiered cakes tempting from the glass case.

The Walk » Walk a half block down Washington St and cross the street.

Chicago Cultural Center

There's always something cool and free going on at the **Chicago Cultural Center** (☎312-744-6630; www.chicagoculturalcenter.org; 78 E Washington St; ⏰9am-7pm Mon-Thu, to 6pm Fri & Sat, 10am-6pm Sun): art exhibitions, foreign films, lunchtime jazz and classical concerts. The grand building also contains the world's largest Tiffany stained-glass dome and StoryCorps' recording studio (where folks tell their tale and have it preserved in the Library of Congress).

The Walk » Depart from the Cultural Center's Randolph St exit, and you're back where you started.

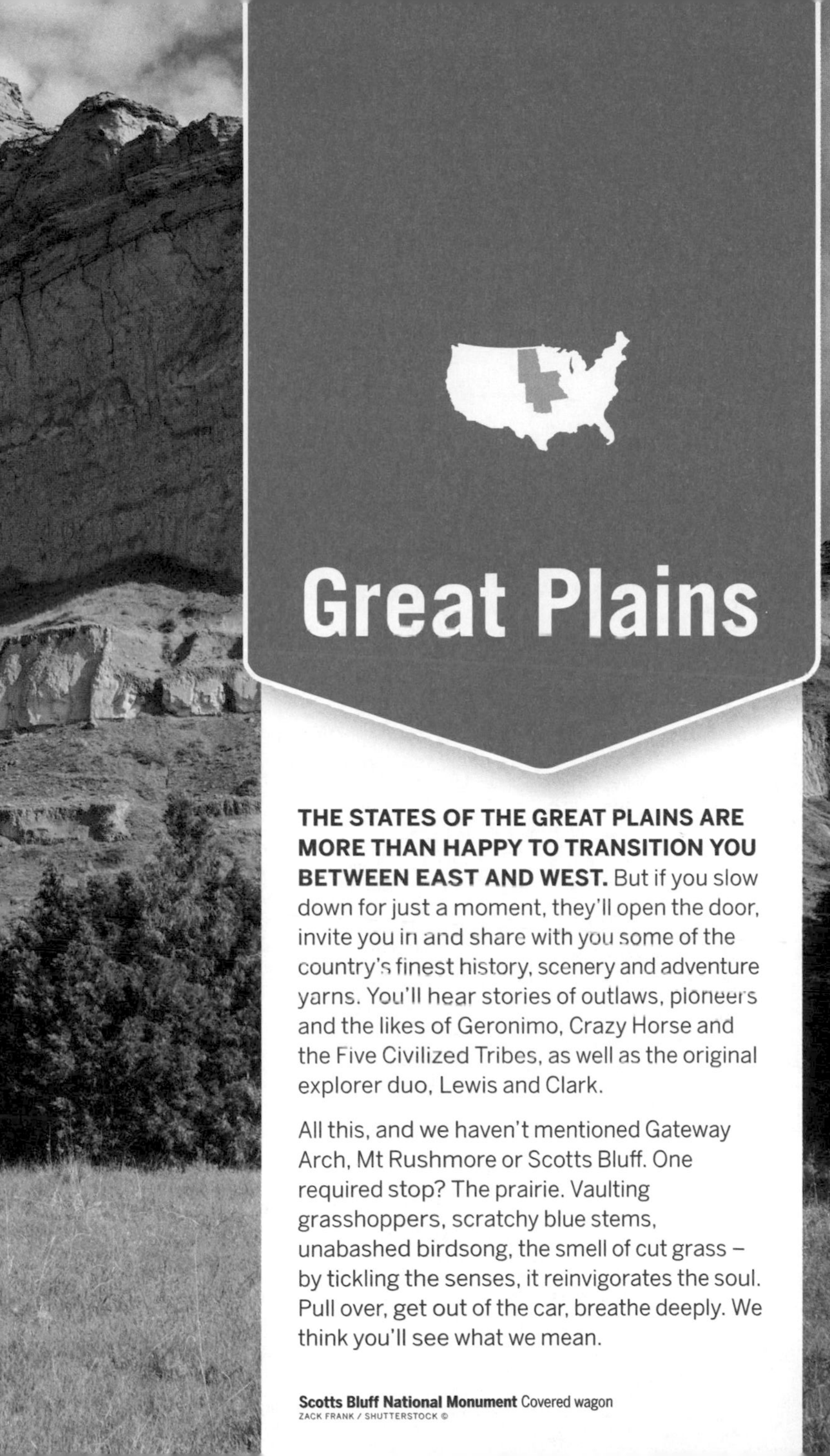

Great Plains

THE STATES OF THE GREAT PLAINS ARE MORE THAN HAPPY TO TRANSITION YOU BETWEEN EAST AND WEST. But if you slow down for just a moment, they'll open the door, invite you in and share with you some of the country's finest history, scenery and adventure yarns. You'll hear stories of outlaws, pioneers and the likes of Geronimo, Crazy Horse and the Five Civilized Tribes, as well as the original explorer duo, Lewis and Clark.

All this, and we haven't mentioned Gateway Arch, Mt Rushmore or Scotts Bluff. One required stop? The prairie. Vaulting grasshoppers, scratchy blue stems, unabashed birdsong, the smell of cut grass – by tickling the senses, it reinvigorates the soul. Pull over, get out of the car, breathe deeply. We think you'll see what we mean.

Scotts Bluff National Monument Covered wagon
ZACK FRANK / SHUTTERSTOCK ©

Great Plains
MANITOBA
Lake Manitoba
ONTARIO
Lake Nipigon
Winnipeg
CANADA
USA
Thunder Bay
Williston
Minot
Devils Lake
Grand Forks
Theodore Roosevelt National Park
Lake Sakakawea
Washburn
White Earth Indian Reservation
Superior Nationa Park
Lake Superior
Jamestown
Superior
Little Missouri National Grassland
Bismarck
NORTH DAKOTA
Fargo
MINNESOTA
Brainerd
Standing Rock Indian Reservation
Ellendale
Lake Traverse Indian Reservation
Alexandria
MONTANA
Grand River National Grassland
Aberdeen
WISCONSIN
Cheyenne River Indian Reservation
Willmar
Eau Claire
Redfield
Watertown
Minneapolis
Green Bay
Spearfish
Rapid City
Pierre
SOUTH DAKOTA
Brookings
Mitchell
Sioux Falls
Madison
WYOMING
Badlands National Park
Rosebud Indian Reservation
Missouri River
Hot Springs
Chadron
Yankton
IOWA
Dubuque
Valentine
Sioux City
Waterloo
Rockford
Crawford
O'Neill
Cedar Rapids
Alliance
Norfolk
Marshalltown
NEBRASKA
Des Moines
Iowa City/Coralville
Scottsbluff
North Platte
Columbus
Des Moines River
Sidney
Ogallala
Grand Island
Lincoln
Omaha
Burlington
Platte River
Hastings
Auburn
ILLINOIS
Fort Morgan
McCook
Beatrice
MISSOURI
Mississippi River
St Joseph
Springfield
Norton
Topeka
Columbia
Burlington
Wa Keeney
Kansas City
St Louis
Salina
KANSAS
Jefferson City
Great Bend
Emporia
Lamar
Dodge City
Newton
Iola
Cape Girardeau
COLORADO
Arkansas River
Wichita
Pratt
Springfield
Joplin
Mark Twain National Forest
Osage Indian Reservation
Boise City
Guymon
Alva
Bartlesville
Enid
Tulsa
Dalhart
Canadian River
OKLAHOMA
ARKANSAS
Muskogee
Pampa
Clinton
Memphis
Amarillo
Oklahoma City
Little Rock
NEW MEXICO
Wichita Mountains
Lawton
Frederick
Ardmore
Durant
Wichita Falls
Lubbock
Texarkana
Brazos River
MISSISSIPPI
TEXAS
Dallas
Shreveport
LOUISIANA
Meridian
0 400 km
0 200 miles

Pigtailing loop Needles Hwy, SD

DON'T MISS

Washita Battlefield National Historic Site

General George Custer surprised this peaceful Native American camp during a dawn raid in 1868. A great new National Park Service facility tells the tragic story; visit this evocative and unchanged site on Trip 25

Homestead National Monument of America

The Homestead Act of 1862 opened up much of the American West to settlers. Among the earliest were the Freeman's, whose story is evocatively recalled here on Trip 26

Iron Mountain Road

A real-life roller coaster, this road passes through beautiful Custer State Park on Trip 27

Lewis & Clark Historical Trail Visitors Center

Part of the vibrant new riverfront on the Missouri River in Omaha, this center lets you plan your own journey of discovery as part of Trip 28

Oklahoma's Tribal Trails

Oklahoma's flag is the only state flag that honors Native Americans. What's the history behind the tribal heritage? This trip uncovers the answers from Tahlequah to Washita.

TRIP HIGHLIGHTS

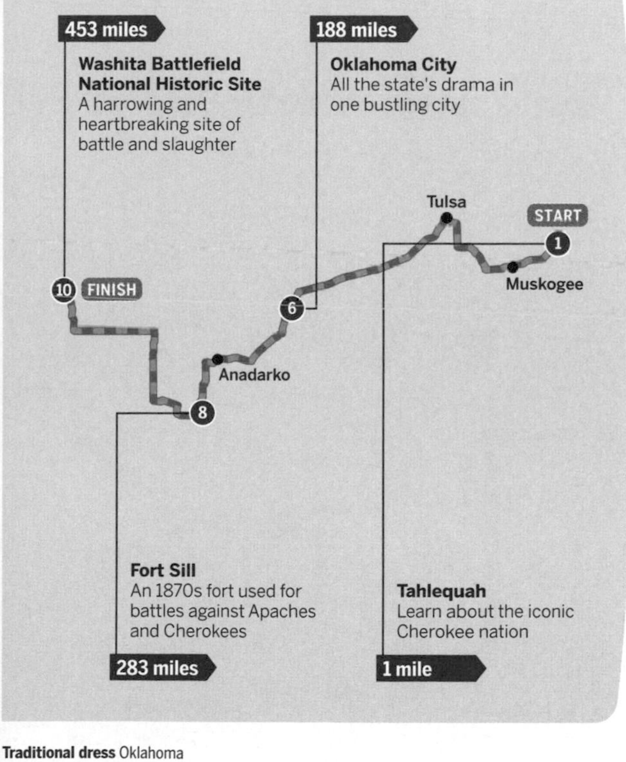

453 miles
Washita Battlefield National Historic Site
A harrowing and heartbreaking site of battle and slaughter

188 miles
Oklahoma City
All the state's drama in one bustling city

Tulsa
START
1
Muskogee
10 FINISH
6
Anadarko
8

Fort Sill
An 1870s fort used for battles against Apaches and Cherokees
283 miles

Tahlequah
Learn about the iconic Cherokee nation
1 mile

4–5 DAYS
453 MILES / 729KM

GREAT FOR...

ESSENTIAL PHOTO

Dawn at Washita Battlefield National Historic Site.

BEST TIME TO GO

Enjoy this trip April to October, when the weather can be lovely.

BEST FOR HISTORY

The unmissable Cherokee Heritage Center with its moving displays in Tahlequah.

Traditional dress Oklahoma

25 Oklahoma's Tribal Trails

There's no soft-pedaling the Trail of Tears, the forced removal and march of five Indian tribes from the southeastern US to what was then called the Indian Territory in present-day eastern Oklahoma. The tales of death, deception and duplicity are sobering. You can visit sites connected to these tragedies (and others) across Oklahoma. In addition you can learn about the vital role of Native Americans in the state today.

TRIP HIGHLIGHT

1 Tahlequah

Subtle, forested hills interspersed with lakes and iconic red dirt cover Oklahoma's northeast corner, aka Green Country (www.greencountryok.com), which includes Tahlequah, the Cherokee capital since 1839.

Of the tragedies visited on Indian tribes, perhaps none is more tragic than the relocation of the Cherokees. The history and horror behind the forced march is movingly

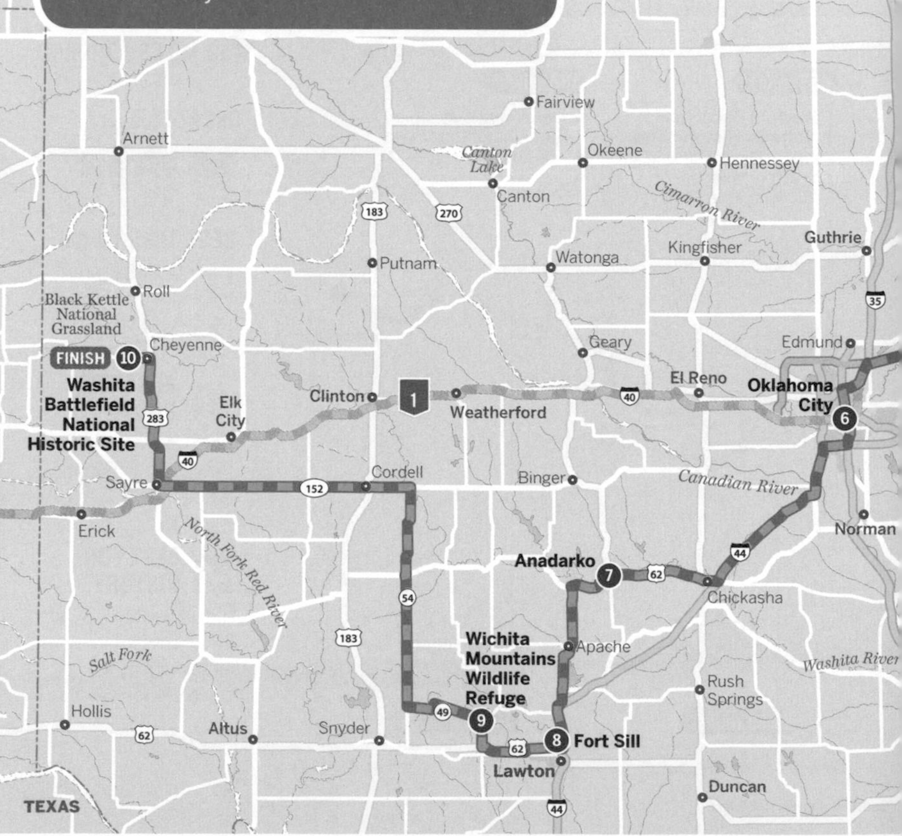

traced at the six-gallery **Cherokee Heritage Center** (918-456-6007; www.cherokeeheritage.org; 21192 S Keeler Dr; adult/child $8.50/5; 9am-5pm Mon-Sat Jun-Aug, Tue-Sat Sep-May) outside of town. Interactive displays describe key events, including court battles and stockade imprisonment, that preceded the forced removal, then focus on the army-commanded marches between 1838 and 1839. Disease, starvation and the cold killed scores on the 800-mile journey.

Outside, at the **Ancient Village**, visitors can learn what life was like in a Cherokee community before the arrival of Europeans. The one-hour guided tour includes pottery-making and blowgun demonstrations.

The Drive » The Cherokee Heritage Center is on the south side of Tahlequah. From here it is a short drive (1 mile) south on South Keeler Dr to your next stop.

LINK YOUR TRIP

1 Route 66

Already one of the richest states for Route 66 sites, the Native American heritage of Oklahoma makes an excellent add-on.

On the Pioneer Trails

See yet more ways people spread out across the US, for better and worse. Take I-49 and I-29 430 miles north to Omaha, NE.

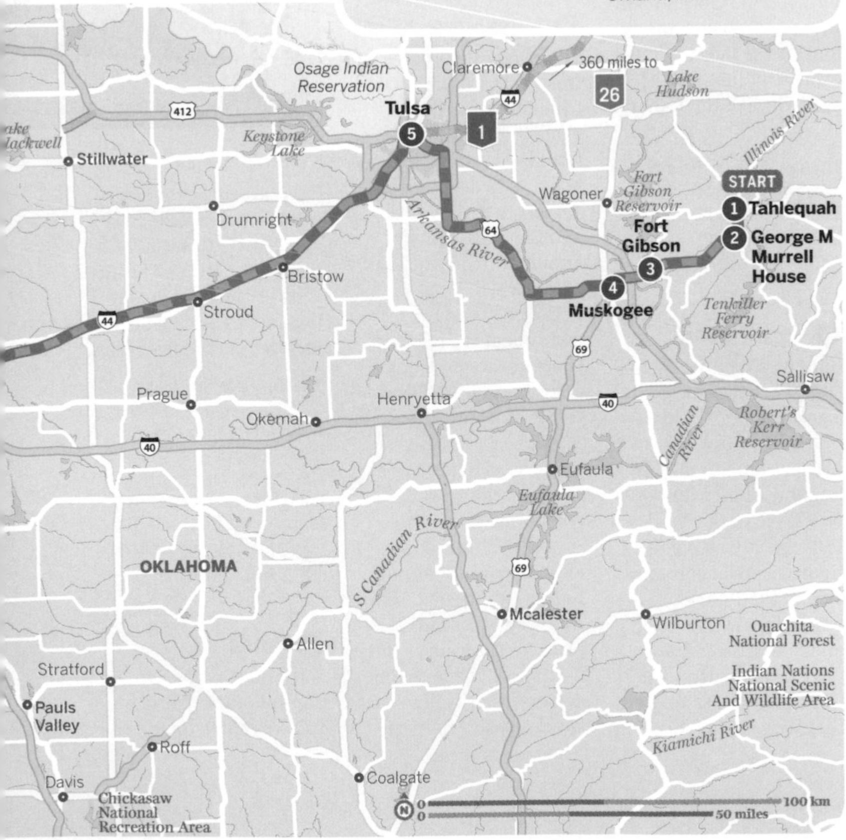

2 George M Murrell House

A large estate from the mid-19th century, this historic **house** (19479 E Murrel Home Rd, Park Hill; donation requested; ⏲10am-5pm Wed-Sat, 1-5pm Sun Mar-Oct, Sat & Sun only Nov-Feb) belies some of the images of the Cherokees as downtrodden. Murrell, who was of European descent, was married to Minerva Ross, a member of a prominent Cherokee family (her father was principal chief of the tribe from 1828 to 1866). He moved with his family at the time of the forced removals and built this estate, which offers a look at the more genteel aspects of life in the early days of the Indian Territory.

The Drive » The third stop on the tour is an easy 18 miles southwest along US 62. Enjoy the gently rolling countryside and iconic red Oklahoma earth.

3 Fort Gibson

Built as a frontier fort in 1824, **Fort Gibson** (907 N Garrison Rd, Fort Sill; adult/child $7/4; ⏲10am-5pm Tue-Sat) came to play an integral – and notorious – role in the Trail of Tears. It was home to the removal commission in the 1830s and is where surviving Creek and Seminole Indians were brought after the forced march. From here they were dispatched around the Indian Territory. You can get a good sense of military life 180 years ago at the restored grounds and buildings. Fort Gibson is a National Historic Landmark managed by the Oklahoma Historical Society.

Washington Irving wrote his landmark *A Tour of the Prairies* in 1835 based on trips he took with Fort Gibson troops in 1832 and 1833 looking for local bands of Native Americans.

The Drive » Continue southwest on US 62 to Muskogee, 9 miles away.

4 Muskogee

The namesake of Merle Haggard's 1969 hit 'Okie from Muskogee,' this place is a bit different from the rest of Oklahoma. It is deep in the Arkansas River valley and there are hints of humid air from the Gulf of Mexico.

Here you can learn more about the relocated tribes at the small but engaging **Five Civilized Tribes Museum** (☎918-683-1701; www.fivetribes.org; 1101 Honor Heights Dr, Agency Hill; adult/student $3/1.50; ⏲10am-5pm Mon-Fri, to 2pm Sat). The museum is located in a 1875 former Indian Agency office that was used as a meeting place for the leaders of the five tribes. The museum dedicates one wall to each tribe; displays cover an

MARILYN ANGEL WYNN / GETTY IMAGES ©

eclectic array of topics from Choctaw code talkers in WWI to variations in lacrosse sticks. The gift shop sells pottery, painting and jewelry made by members of the five tribes.

The Drive » Skip the tolls and monotony of the Muskogee Turnpike and opt instead for US 64, which wanders through classic small towns such as Haskell that give a timeless sense of rural Oklahoma. The 60-mile drive to Tulsa will take about 90 minutes.

5 Tulsa

Self-billed as the 'Oil Capital of the World,' Tulsa is home to scores

Muskogee Five Civilized Tribes Museum

of energy companies that make their living drilling for oil, selling it or supplying those who do. The wealth this provides once helped create Tulsa's richly detailed art-deco downtown and has funded some excellent museums that give the state's Native American heritage its due.

The superb **Gilcrease Museum** (☎918-596-2700; www.gilcrease.org; 1400 Gilcrease Museum Rd; adult/child $8/free; ⏰10am-5pm Tue-Sun) has a great story: it sits on the manicured estate of Thomas Gilcrease, a part–Native American who grew up on Creek tribal lands. He was later eligible for a tribal allotment that contained a little surprise – oil! Over his life, Gilcrease built up one of the world's great collections of art and artifacts relating to the American West cultures. The museum is northwest of downtown, off Hwy 64.

South of town is another oil magnate's property, a converted Italianate villa also ringed by fabulous foliage. It houses some fine Native American works at the **Philbrook Museum of Art** (☎918-749-7941; www.philbrook.org; 2727 S Rockford Rd; adult/child $9/free; ⏰10am-5pm Tue, Wed & Fri-Sun, to 8pm Thu, guided tours 2pm).

✖ 🛏 p335

The Drive » Link Oklahoma's two largest cities via the quick route of I-44, otherwise known as the Turner Turnpike. In return for the tolls you'll minimize your time between the big-name attractions as you zip along slightly more than 100 miles.

TRIP HIGHLIGHT

6 Oklahoma City

At the impressive **Oklahoma History Center** (www.okhistory.org/historycenter; 800 Nazih Zuhdi Dr; adult/child $7/4; ⏰10am-5pm Mon-Sat) you can explore the heritage of the 39 tribes headquartered in the state. Artifacts include an 1890 cradle-board, a Kiowa pictorial calendar and an original letter from Thomas Jefferson that Lewis and Clark gave to the Otoe tribe. In it, Jefferson invites the tribe to the nation's capital. Be sure to look up before you leave – there's a Pawnee star chart on the ceiling.

You can experience the frontier in a manner more familiar to anyone who has seen an old Western movie at the **National Cowboy & Western Heritage Museum** (405-478-2250; www.nationalcowboymuseum.org; 1700 NE 63rd St; adult/child $12.50/6; 10am-5pm Mon-Sat, noon-5pm Sun).

p335

The Drive » A 40-mile drive southwest on I-44 (the Bailey Turnpike toll road) leads to Chickasha at exit 83. Head 20 miles west on US 62 through Native American lands to Anadarko.

7 Anadarko

Eight tribal lands are located in this area, and students from many more tribes are enrolled in Anadarko schools. The town regularly hosts powwows and Native American events.

To mix a little shopping with your learning, visit **Oklahoma Indian Arts & Crafts Co-Op** (405-247-3486; 214 NW 2nd St; 10am-4pm Mon-Fri), which sells museum-quality crafts, including jewelry, dolls and beadwork items (barrettes, purses and moccasins). About 85% of the store's customers are Native American. Nearby is the **Southern Plains Indian Museum** (405-247-6221; www.doi.gov/iacb/southern-plains-indian-museum; 715 E Central Blvd; 9am-4:30pm Mon-Fri;), which houses a small but diverse collection of Plains Indian clothing, weaponry and musical instruments.

Just east is the **National Hall of Fame for Famous American Indians** (405-247-5555; 901 E Central Blvd, Hwy 62; site 24hr, visitor center 9am-5pm Mon-Sat, from 1pm Sun). A short outdoor walk leads past the bronze busts of well-known Native Americans including Pocahontas, Geronimo and Sitting Bull. The visitor center has a good

TRAIL OF TEARS ACROSS THE US

From Alabama to Oklahoma, across nine states, the National Park Service administers the **Trail of Tears National Historic Trail** (www.nps.gov/trte), which features important sites from the tragedy. Among the highlights:

Alabama – Fort Payne Cabin Site. Dates to 1838 when federal troops arrived to force the Cherokee to Oklahoma.

Georgia – Rockdale Plantation. An 18th-century plantation building once owned by a slave-owning Cherokee man.

Tennessee – Brainerd Mission Cemetery. The remains of a mission for the Cherokees near Chattanooga. Most of the missionaries accompanied the tribe's removal to Oklahoma.

Kentucky – Trail of Tears Commemorative Park. Used as a cemetery for chiefs who died during the removals.

Illinois – Trail of Tears State Forest. A bleak forest where hundreds of Native Americans died during the winter of 1838–39.

Missouri – Trail of Tears State Park. Another natural area that commemorates the horrible events of the removals.

selection of books on Oklahoma Indians.

The Drive » US 62 continues to figure prominently in this tour as you drive 35 miles south to Fort Sill. The historic portion is just west of US 62 on the edge of this very active military base.

TRIP HIGHLIGHT

8 Fort Sill

Oklahoma isn't just home to eastern tribes. Numerous western and Plains tribes, including the Apache, Comanche, Kiowa and Wichita, were also forced here as the US expanded west. The US Army built Fort Sill in 1869 in Kiowa and Comanche territory to prevent raids into settlements in Texas and Kansas. By the 1880s and 1890s its role had changed, and the fort was serving as a protective sanctuary for many tribes.

The **Fort Sill National Historic Landmark & Museum** (☎580-442-5123; 6701 Sheridan Rd, Visitor Control Center, Fort Sill; ⏰9am-5pm Tue-Sat), which fills several original stone buildings, explores the history of the fort. Another highlight is the 1872 **Post Guardhouse**, the center of law enforcement for the Indian Territory. Step inside to see where Apache leader Geronimo was detained on three separate occasions. Geronimo's grave is on fort grounds a few miles from the guardhouse.

THE CHOCTAWS & OKLAHOMA'S IDENTITY

The Choctaws were skilled farmers living in brick and stone homes in Mississippi and Alabama in the early 1800s. They were relocated to Oklahoma in the 1830s – after 16 broken treaties with the US. Oklahoma's name derives from the Choctaw words for 'red man,' and the state flag is derived in part from a flag carried by Choctaw soldiers fighting for the Confederacy during the Civil War.

Fort Sill remains an active army base. You'll need to register at the Visitor Control Center before passing through the gates to view the historic sites.

The Drive » Leave booming artillery in your wake as you roll west on Hwy 62 to state Hwy 115 north. Black-eyed Susans, scrubby trees and barbed-wire fences line the two-lane byway as it unfurls from tiny Cache toward the hill-dappled Wichita Mountains Wildlife Refuge.

9 Wichita Mountains Wildlife Refuge

Southwest Oklahoma opens into expansive prairie fields all the way to Texas. Beautiful mountains provide texture.

The 59,020-acre **Wichita Mountains Wildlife Refuge** (☎580-429-3222; http://wichitamountains.fws.gov; 20539 State Hwy 115, Cache; ⏰visitor center 9am-5pm; 👪🐾) protects bison, elk, longhorn cattle and a super-active prairie dog town. Wildlife is abundant; observant drivers might even see a spindly, palm-sized tarantula tiptoeing across the road. At the visitor center, informative displays highlight the refuge's flora and fauna. A massive glass window yields inspiring views of prairie grasslands. For a short but scenic hike, try the creek-hugging **Kite Trail** to the waterfalls and rocks at the **Forty Foot Hole**. It starts at the Lost Lake Picnic Area.

✕ p335

The Drive » After 15 miles on Hwy 49, turn north on Hwy 54, which runs through tribal lands. Look for schools, tiny towns and small farms on the 38.5 miles. At Hwy 152, just north of Cloud Chief village, turn west for 44 miles to US 283. Go north for 24 miles to Cheyenne and follow the signs to the Washita site.

TRIP HIGHLIGHT

10 Washita Battlefield National Historic Site

Marking the place where George Custer's troops launched a dawn attack on November 27, 1868 on

FIVE CIVILIZED TRIBES

Two of eastern Oklahoma's earliest known tribes, the Osage and the Quapaw, ceded millions of acres to the US government in the 1820s. The US then gave the land to five east-coast tribes: the Cherokee, Chickasaw, Choctaw, Creek and Seminole. Because these five tribes had implemented formal governmental and agricultural practices in their communities, they were collectively called the Five Civilized Tribes.

The Five Civilized Tribes were forced to move to the Oklahoma area, known then as the Indian Territory, after settlers in the southern states decided they wanted the tribes' fertile farmlands for themselves. Between 1830 and 1850, the five tribes were forcibly relocated; their routes are collectively known as the Trail of Tears.

How many people died in this forced march is unknown; however, records suggest deaths were in the tens of thousands. Often overlooked are the thousands of African Americans who were held as slaves by the Native Americans. Scores died during the removals.

As for their new homes in the Indian Territory, the US government said it would belong to the five tribes as long as the stars shine and rivers flow. The reality? More like 70 years. In the mid-1800s the country was quickly expanding west, and white settlers wanted the land. Through legislative maneuvering, certain Indian-owned lands were deemed 'unassigned,' opening them up for settlement. The Oklahoma Land Rush began on April 22, 1889, when 50,000 would-be settlers made a mad dash for their own 160-acre allotment.

the peaceful village of Chief Black Kettle, **Washita Battlefield National Historic Site** (☎580-497-2742; www.nps.gov/waba; Hwy 47A, Cheyenne; ⏰site dawn-dusk, visitor center 8am-5pm) was a slaughter of men, women, children and domestic animals, an act some would say led to karmic revenge on Custer eight years later. Among those who died was the peace-promoting chief, Black Kettle. Even today, you may encounter current members of the US military studying what exactly transpired here that cold, pre-winter morning.

Self-guiding **trails** traverse the site of the killings, which is remarkably unchanged. A new visitor center 0.7 miles away contains a good **museum**. Seasonal tours and talks are very worthwhile. A small garden shows how traditional plants were grown for medicine, spiritual rituals and food.

Eating & Sleeping

Tulsa 5

Ike's Chili House — Diner $

(918-838-9410; www.ikeschilius.com; 1503 E 11th St; mains $5-9; 10am-7pm Mon-Fri, to 3pm Sat) Ike's has been serving chili for more than 100 years and its classic version is much-loved. You can get it straight or over Fritos, a hot dog, fries or spaghetti. Top with red peppers, onions, jalapeños, saltines and cheddar cheese for pure joy.

Tavern — American $$

(918-949-9801; www.taverntulsa.com; 201 N Main St; mains $15-38; 11am-11pm Sun-Thu, to 1am Fri & Sat) This beautiful pub is a top choice in the Brady Arts District and serves excellent fare. The hamburgers are legendary or you can opt for steaks, salads or seasonal specials. The bartenders are true mixologists and there's a good wine list.

Hotel Campbell — Hotel $$

(918-744-5500; www.thecampbellhotel.com; 2636 E 11th St; r $140-210; P) Restored to its 1927-era Route 66 splendor, this historic hotel east of downtown has 26 luxurious rooms with hardwood floors and plush period furniture. Ask for a tour.

Oklahoma City 6

Tucker's Onion Burgers — Burgers $

(405-609-2333; www.tuckersonionburgers.com; 324 NW 23rd St; mains $5.50-10; 11am-9pm) A new kind of burger joint with an old-time Route 66 vibe, Tucker's has high-quality food (locally sourced) that includes iconic Oklahoma onion burgers, fresh-cut fries and shakes. It even has a green ethos and a fine patio.

Cattlemen's Steakhouse — Steak $$

(405-236-0416; www.cattlemensrestaurant.com; 1309 S Agnew Ave; mains $7-30; 6am-10pm Sun-Thu, to midnight Fri & Sat) OKC's most storied restaurant, this Stockyards City institution has been feeding cowpokes and city slickers slabs of beef since 1910. Deals are still cut at the counter (where you can jump the wait for tables) and back in the luxe booths.

Picasso's Cafe — Modern American $$

(405-602-2002; www.picassosonpaseo.com; 3009 Paseo; mains $10-20; 11am-late;) Picasso's is renowned for its Bloody Mary's at noon and masterfully plated farm-fresh meals. The place has an artistic sensibility, with works by local artists on display. Grab a table outside.

Colcord Hotel — Boutique Hotel $$

(405-601-4300; www.colcordhotel.com; 15 N Robinson Ave; r $170-240; P) OKC's first skyscraper, built in 1911, is now a luxurious 12-story hotel. Many original flourishes, such as the marble-clad lobby, survive, while the 108 rooms have a stylish, contemporary touch. It's near Bricktown.

Wichita Mountains Wildlife Refuge 9

Meers Store & Restaurant — Burgers $

(580-429-8051; Hwy 115; mains $4-11; 10:30am-8:30pm Thu-Mon;) Meers Store & Restaurant is a ramshackle burger-and-beer joint hunkered at the end of a twisty, country-road junction on the far side of Lake Lawtonka from Medicine Park. Its smashed-flat, 7in Meers burger – made from the beef of the restaurant's own longhorns – is a must-eat in the region.

On the Pioneer Trails

Follow in the wagon tracks of thousands of pioneers who crossed Nebraska on iconic treks like the Oregon Trail. Visit windswept settlements of those who stayed behind.

TRIP HIGHLIGHTS

575 miles

Scotts Bluff National Monument
An iconic stop for caravans of covered wagons

260 miles

Grand Island
It's 1890 all over again at this re-created pioneer town

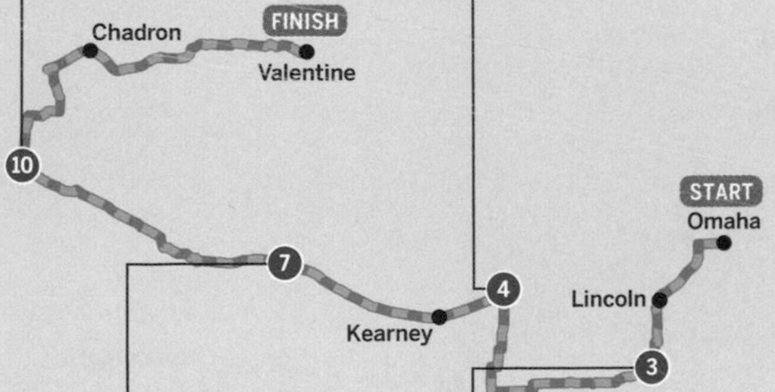

Chadron
FINISH
Valentine
10
START
Omaha
7
4
Lincoln
Kearney
3

Homestead National Monument of America
See how America's homesteaders settled a continent

92 miles

North Platte
Trains jam the hub of America's oldest railroad

398 miles

5–7 DAYS
802 MILES / 1290KM

GREAT FOR...

BEST TIME TO GO

May to September when everything is open and the wildflowers are in bloom.

ESSENTIAL PHOTO

The postcard-worthy buttes of Scotts Bluff.

BEST FOR EXPLORING

Off-the-beaten-path explorations of a land many blithely whiz through.

Covered wagon Oregon Trail

26 On the Pioneer Trails

Balmy days driving through lush green valleys and barren buttes; nights hanging outside a small-town ice-cream stand recalling the day's adventures to the background sound of crickets. These are just some of the charms of exploring the back roads of Nebraska, which, like the ubiquitous state plant, corn, when left on the fire, pops with attractions. Eschew I-80 and be a modern-day pioneer.

1 Omaha

Omaha's location on the Missouri River and proximity to the Platte made it an important stop on the Oregon, California and Mormon trails. Many heading west paused here before plunging into Nebraska and you should do the same. Learn tales from these pioneer trails at the beautiful **Durham Museum** (☎402-444-5071; www.durhammuseum.org; 801 S 10th St; adult/child $11/7; ⏰10am-8pm Tue, to 5pm Wed-Sat, 1-5pm Sun),

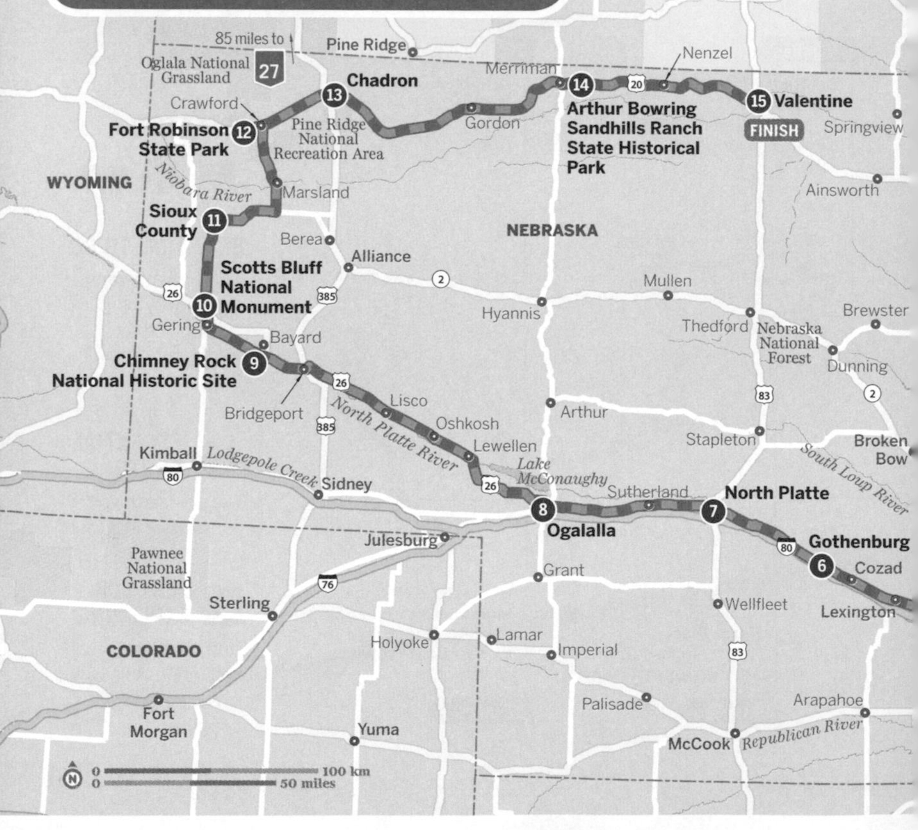

housed in the once-bustling Union Station.

p345, p367

The Drive » Scoot along US 6 with its old drive-ins still peddling soft-serve cones and other pleasures for the 57 miles to Lincoln.

2 Lincoln

Home to the historic **Haymarket District** and the huge downtown campus of the University of Nebraska, the capital city is a good place to get the big picture of the state's story. You can almost hear the wagon wheels creaking and the sound of sod busting at the **Museum of Nebraska History** (☎402-471-4782; www.nebraskahistory.org; 131 Centennial Mall N; ⏰9am-4:30pm Mon-Fri, 1-4:30pm Sat & Sun).

p345

The Drive » Drive 35 miles south of Lincoln on Hwy 77 to Beatrice.

LINK YOUR TRIP

27 Black Hills Loop
A trip of icons, colorful history and natural beauty. Take US 20, then US 18 west, then go north on scenic US 385.

28 The Mighty Mo
Follow in the tracks of famous explorers Lewis and Clark along America's longest river. Join the trip right in Omaha.

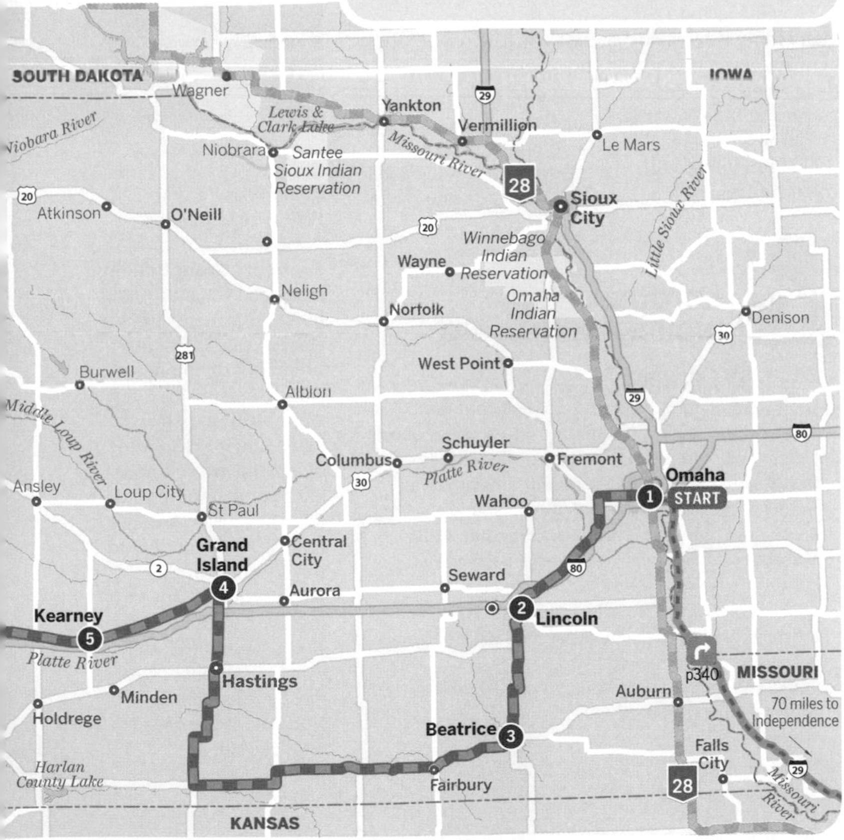

TRIP HIGHLIGHT

3 Homestead National Monument of America

The **Homestead National Monument** (☎402-223-3514; www.nps.gov/home; off Hwy 4, Beatrice; ⌚heritage center 9am-5pm, trails dawn-dusk) just west of Beatrice is on the site of the very first homestead granted under the landmark Homestead Act of 1862, which opened much of the US to settlers who received land for free if they made it productive.

The pioneering Freeman family is buried here and you can see their reconstructed log house and hike the site. The heritage center is a striking building with good displays.

The Drive » An even 100 miles west on US 136 takes you through near ghost towns, where the solitary gas stations serve as town centers and quaint brick downtowns slowly crumble. Head north at Red Cloud and drive for 68 miles on US 281.

TRIP HIGHLIGHT

4 Grand Island

For a wide-ranging introduction to pioneer life, spend a few hours at the 200-acre **Stuhr Museum of the Prairie Pioneer** (☎308-385-5316; www.stuhrmuseum.org; 3133 W Hwy 34, I-80 exit 312; adult/child $8/6; ⌚9am-5pm Mon-Sat, noon-5pm Sun, closed Mon Jan-Mar; 👪) in Grand Island. In summer, period reenactors go about their business in an 1890s railroad town, answering questions about their jobs and home life. Also on view: an 1860s log-cabin settlement, a one-room schoolhouse and a Pawnee earth lodge.

On the 2nd floor of the museum's **Stuhr Building**, a covered wagon overflows with furniture and clothes – an inspiring symbol of the pioneers' can-do optimism. A few steps away, a display of black-and-white photos of a primitive sod house and a prairie funeral depict the darker, harsher realities lurking behind the romance of the pioneer dream. Interesting fact? In 1880, 20% of Nebraska's population was foreign born, with most settlers emigrating from Germany, Sweden and Ireland.

RICHARD CUMMINS / GETTY IMAGES ©

DETOUR: INDEPENDENCE, MO

Start: 1 Omaha

Long associated with colorful US president Harry S Truman, Independence, Missouri, was also a popular jumping-off point for pioneers preparing to follow the Oregon and California trails. For an enjoyable history of these two trails and others, spend an hour or two at the city's **National Frontier Trails Museum** (☎816-325-7575; www.frontiertrailsmuseum.org; 318 W Pacific Ave; adult/child $6/3; ⌚9am-4:30pm Mon-Sat, 12:30-4:30pm Sun). Exhibits include a wall-sized map of the major trail routes, a mock general store and diary entries from the pioneers.

Independence is near Kansas City, 200 miles south of Omaha off I-29.

Grand Island Stuh Museum of the Prairie Pioneer

The Drive ›› The leaves of cottonwoods shimmer in the sunlight on this lonely yet lush 42 miles of US 30.

❺ Kearney

A shimmering brown arch sweeps across four lanes of I-80 like an imposing medieval drawbridge. This horizon-breaking distraction – it depicts a setting Nebraska sun – is the **Great Platte River Road Archway Monument** (☎308-237-1000; www.archway.org; 3060 E 1st St, near exit 275; adult/child $12/6; ⏲9am-6pm Mon-Sat, noon-6pm Sun May-Sep, reduced hours Oct-Apr; 👪). A little bit hokey, a little bit history, it's a relentlessly cheery ode to the West that puts a high-tech, glossy spin on the pioneer journey and western travel, sweeping in everything from stampeding buffalo to the gold-seeking forty-niners. The mini-adventure begins with a dramatic escalator ride up to the enclosed, two-story bridge.

Kearney's compact, cute and walkable downtown, near US 30 and the busy UP main line, has good cafes and bars.

🍴 🛏 p345

The Drive ›› Count the corn silos and see if they outnumber the passing trains along the next 60 miles of US 30.

❻ Gothenburg

The Pony Express (1860–61) was the FedEx of its day, using a fleet of young riders and swift horses to carry letters between Missouri and California in an astounding 10 days. Each horseman rode full-bore for almost six hours – changing horses every 10 miles – before passing the mail to the next rider. Their route through Nebraska generally followed the Oregon Trail.

TOP TIP: AVOID I-80

I-80 zips across Nebraska for 455 miles. But while it speeds travelers on their way, it does the state no favors. Here are some fine alternatives: take US 6 out of Omaha to Lincoln, US 34 on to Grand Island and then historic US 30 all the way to Wyoming.

In Gothenburg, step inside what some researchers think is an original **Pony Express Station** (☎308-537-9876; www.ponyexpressstation.org; 1500 Lake Ave, Gothenburg; ⏰9am-3pm Apr & Oct, 9am-7pm May-Sep, by appointment Nov-Mar), one of just a few still in existence. The engaging array of artifacts includes a mochila, the rider's mail-holding saddlebag. Afterward, wander a few of the streets downtown lined with beautiful old Victorian houses.

The Drive » A never-ending procession of UP trains zips along the world's busiest freight line for the next 36 miles of US 30.

TRIP HIGHLIGHT

7 North Platte

North Platte, a railfan mecca, is home to the **Buffalo Bill Ranch State Historical Park** (☎308-535-8035; www.outdoornebraska.gov/buffalobillranch; 2921 Scouts Rest Ranch Rd; house adult/child $2/1, vehicle permit $5; ⏰9am-5pm Jun-Aug, 10am-4pm Sat & Sun late Apr–May & Sep–early Oct), 2 miles north of US 30. Once the home of Bill Cody – an iconic figure of the American West and the father of rodeo and the famed Wild West Show – it has a fun museum that reflects his colorful life.

Enjoy sweeping views of Union Pacific's **Bailey Yard**, the world's largest railroad classification yard, from the **Golden Spike Tower** (☎308-532-9920; www.goldenspiketower.com; 1249 N Homestead Rd; adult/child $7/5; ⏰9am-7pm May-Sep, to 5pm Oct-Apr), an eight-story observation tower with indoor and outdoor decks.

The Drive » Set the cruise control on 'chill' as you cruise a straight line 52 miles due west on US 30.

8 Ogalalla

Set your clocks to mountain time just west of Sutherland. Ogalalla was once known as the 'Gomorrah of the Cattle Trail.' It now has all the salacious charm of a motel's nightstand Bible.

The Oregon and California trails turn north near here, following the Platte River toward Wyoming and the wild blue yonder.

The Drive » Cornfields give way to untamed prairie grasses and desolate bluffs on two-lane US 26, known as Nebraska's Western Trails Historic & Scenic Byway. Look right soon after leaving Ogalalla to glimpse sparkling Lake McConaughy through the low hills. Otherwise, cattle herds, passing trains with coal from Wyoming and tumbleweed towns are the biggest distractions for the next 101 miles.

9 Chimney Rock National Historic Site

Heading west, you see centuries-old bluff formations rise up from the horizon, their striking presence a visual link connecting modern-day travelers (and Oregon Trail gamers) with their pioneer forebears. One of these links is Chimney Rock, located inside the **Chimney Rock National Historic Site** (☎308-586-2581; Chimney Rock Rd, Bayard; adult/child $3/free; ⏰9am-5pm). It's visible 12 miles after Bridgeport off Hwy 92. Chimney Rock's fragile 120ft spire was an inspiring landmark for pioneers, and it was mentioned in hundreds of journals. It also marked the end of the first leg of the journey and the beginning of the tough – but final – push to the coast.

The Drive » Stay on Hwy 92 for 21 miles west after Chimney Rock. As you enter Gering, just south of the city of Scottsbluff, continue straight onto M St, which leads to Old Oregon Trail Rd. It follows the actual route of the trail and leads straight to Scotts Bluff National Monument after just 3 miles.

TRIP HIGHLIGHT

⑩ Scotts Bluff National Monument

Spend a few minutes in the visitor center of this picturesque **monument** (☎308-436-9700; www.nps.gov/scbl; 190276 Old Oregon Tr, Gering; per car $5; ⏲visitor center 8am-6pm Jun-Aug, to 5pm Sep-May) run by the National Park Service – there's a nice collection of Western art in the William Henry Jackson Gallery – then hit the trail. You can hike the 1.6-mile (one way) **Saddle Rock Trail** or drive the same distance up to the South Overlook for bird's-eye views of Mitchell Pass.

Before you leave, spend a few moments hiking the trail through Mitchell Pass itself. The covered wagons on display here look unnervingly frail as you peer through the bluff-flanked gateway, a narrow channel that spills onto the Rocky Mountain–bumping plains. For pioneers, reaching this pass was a significant milestone; it marked the completion of 600 miles of Great Plains trekking.

✕ p345

The Drive » From Scottsbluff, leave the Great Platte River Rd and head north to a historic military fort and a lonely trading post, important bastions that paved the way for long-term settlers. Along the way, revel in Nebraska's prairie, which is aptly described as a 'sea of grass.' This analogy proves true on the 52-mile drive north on Hwy 71.

⑪ Sioux County

Prairie grasses bend and bob as strong winds sweep over low-rolling hills, punctuated by the occasional wooden windmill or lonely cell-phone tower as you drive through Sioux County, named for the Plains tribe that hunted and traveled throughout Nebraska.

Enjoy the drive: this is roll-down-your-window-and-breathe-in-America country.

The Drive » Like bristles on the visage of a trail-weary pioneer, trees begin appearing amid the rolling grasslands as you head north for 27 miles on Hwy 2.

⑫ Fort Robinson State Park

Sioux warrior Crazy Horse was fatally stabbed on the grounds of Fort Robinson, now **Fort Robinson State Park** (☎308-665-2900; www.outdoornebraska.gov; Hwy 20, Crawford; vehicle permit $8; ⏲park dawn-dusk, visitor center 8am-5pm daily Apr-Nov, Mon-Fri Dec-Mar), on

GO WEST!

An estimated 400,000 people trekked west across America between 1840 and 1860, lured by tales of gold, promises of religious freedom and visions of fertile farmland. They were also inspired by the expansionist credo of President James Polk and the rallying cry of New York editor John O'Sullivan, who urged Americans in 1845 to 'overspread the continent allotted by Providence for the free development of our yearly multiplying millions.'

These starry-eyed pioneers became the foot soldiers of manifest destiny, eager to pursue their own dreams while furthering America's expansionist goals. The movement's success depended on the safe, reliable passage of these foot soldiers through the Great Plains and beyond. The California, Oregon and Mormon pioneer trails served this purpose well, successfully channeling the travelers and their prairie schooners on defined routes across the country.

September 5, 1877, at the age of 35. The fort – in operation between 1874 and 1948 – was the area's most important military post during the Indian Wars.

In summer, visitors descend on the 22,000-acre park for stagecoach rides, steak cookouts, trout fishing and hiking. There are two museums on the grounds – the **Fort Robinson Museum** and the **Trailside Museum** – as well as the reconstructed **Guardhouse** where Crazy Horse spent his final hours.

The Drive » If you prefer your historic digs in an urban setting, drive 20 miles east to Chadron.

⓭ Chadron

Chadron's **Museum of the Fur Trade** (☎308-432-3843; www.furtrade.org; 6321 US 20; adult/child $5/free; ⏰8am-5pm May-Oct; 👪) is a well-curated tribute to the mountain men and trappers who paved the way for the pioneers. For a small museum, it holds a fascinating array of artifacts: from 1820s mountain-man leggings and hand-forged animal traps to blankets, pelts and liquor bottles. Kit Carson's shotgun is displayed beside the world's largest collection of Native American trade guns.

Out the back, there's a reproduction of the Bordeaux Trading Post; it was in operation here from 1837 to 1876. The harsh reality of life on the plains is evident the moment you step inside the squat, unnervingly cramped building. Though it's not the original structure, the reproduction is so precisely done it's listed on the National Register of Historic Places.

The Drive » Continue east to the Sandhills for 77 miles on US 20, known as the Bridges to Buttes Byway. The little towns along here are just hanging on amid the buttes, canyons and rolling hills of the often-dramatic landscape.

⓮ Arthur Bowring Sandhills Ranch State Historical Park

The hardscrabble lives of Nebraskan ranchers is faithfully recalled at this preserved 1920s ranch near the South Dakota border. Owned by the Bowring clan, it includes an early sod house that makes it clear that *any* farmhouse was a major step up. Still, you'll find comforts here as Eva Bowring, who lived here for much of her long life, collected drool-worthy crystal, china and antique furniture. Her story is an interesting one: in 1954 she took a break from chasing cows to represent Nebraska in the US Senate, where she served for a brief period after another senator died.

The Drive » Keep the camera ready for moody shots of lonely windmills amid the sandy bluffs on the 60 miles east on US 20 to Valentine.

⓯ Valentine

What better way to literally immerse yourself in a timeless Nebraska from before the pioneer days than floating down a scenic river – especially on a steamy summer day.

Valentine sits on the edge of the Sandhills and is a great base for canoeing, kayaking and inner-tubing the winding canyons of the federally protected **Niobrara National Scenic River** (www.nps.gov/niob). The river crosses the **Fort Niobrara National Wildlife Refuge** (☎402-376-3789; www.fws.gov/fortniobrara; Hwy 12; ⏰visitor center 8am-4:30pm daily Jun-Aug, Mon-Fri Sep-May). Driving tours take you past bison, elk and more.

Floating down the river draws scores of people through the summer. Sheer limestone bluffs, lush forests and spring-fed waterfalls along the banks shatter any 'flat Nebraska' stereotypes. Most float tours are based in Valentine (www.visitvalentine.com).

🛏 p345

Eating & Sleeping

Omaha 1

Ted & Wally's Ice Cream Ice Cream $

(402-341-5827; www.tedandwallys.com; 1120 Jackson St; ice cream from $3; 11am-11pm Jun-Aug, to 10pm Sep-May) Ultra-creamy ice cream in myriad flavors made fresh daily right before your very eyes. Vegans should try the coconut-based creations.

Upstream Brewing Company American $$

(402-344-0200; www.upstreambrewing.com; 514 S 11th St; mains $10-30; 11am-1am Mon-Thu, to 2am Fri & Sat, 10am-midnight Sun) In a big old firehouse, the beer here is also big on flavor. The Caesar salads have enough garlic to propel you over the Missouri to Iowa. Steaks are thick and up to local standards. There are sidewalk tables, a rooftop deck and a huge bar.

Grey Plume Modern American $$$

(402-763-4447; www.thegreyplume.com; 220 S 31st Ave; mains bar $9-18, restaurant $25-42; 5-10pm Mon-Sat) West of downtown in Midtown Crossing, chef Clayton Chapman has upturned perceptions of Great Plains cuisine with his fiercely local and seasonal dishes. Winners: the bar burger, the duck-fat fries, the steaks and anything with trout.

Magnolia Hotel Historic Hotel $$

(402-341-2500; www.magnoliahotelomaha.com; 1615 Howard St; r $140-220;) Not far from Old Market, the Magnolia is a boutique hotel housed in a restored 1923 Italianate high-rise. The 145 rooms have a vibrant, modern style. Get ready for bedtime milk and cookies.

Lincoln 2

Indigo Bridge Cafe $

(402-477-7770; www.indigobridgebooks.com; 701 P St; mains $4-8; 8am-10pm Mon-Sat, noon-6pm Sun;) This fine Haymarket cafe in a fantastic bookstore serves excellent coffee, snacks and sandwiches throughout the day. Best of all, 100% of all proceeds from coffee purchases go directly to a local cause.

Rogers House B&B $$

(402-476-6961; www.rogershouseinn.com; 2145 B St; r $90-170;) Close to downtown, the seven spacious rooms here occupy a 100-year-old brick home. Refreshingly, the decor eschews the froufrou silliness of many B&Bs. Expect a hearty two-course breakfast.

Kearney 5

Thunderhead Brewing Co American $

(www.thunderheadbrewing.com; 18 E 21st St; mains $7-15; 11am-1am) The place to go for good IPAs and pizza; located in a brick storefront downtown.

Midtown Western Inn Motel $

(308-237-3153; www.midtownwesterninn.com; 1401 2nd Ave; r $50-80;) A good indie choice near downtown, this vintage motel has huge, clean rooms.

Scottsbluff 10

Emporium Coffeehouse & Café American $$

(308-632-6222; www.emporiumdining.com; 1818 1st Ave, Scottsbluff; mains $12-27; 6:30am-10pm Mon-Sat) This umbrella-fronted vintage house in downtown Scottsbluff is a regional gem. There are great meals, from the pastries at breakfast to late-night steak and seafood plates. The wine and spirits list has more than 100 selections.

Valentine 15

Trade Winds Motel Motel $

(402-376-1600; www.tradewindslodge.com; 1009 E US 20/83; r $65-100;) The classic red-brick Trade Winds Motel has 32 comfy and clean rooms with refrigerators and microwaves. It's a great indie choice with a hot country breakfast.

Classic Trip

Black Hills Loop

27

Shaggy bison lumber across the plains. Giant monuments praise great men. Windswept prairies unfurl below towering mountains. This Black Hills tour embraces the region's heritage in all its messy glory.

TRIP HIGHLIGHTS

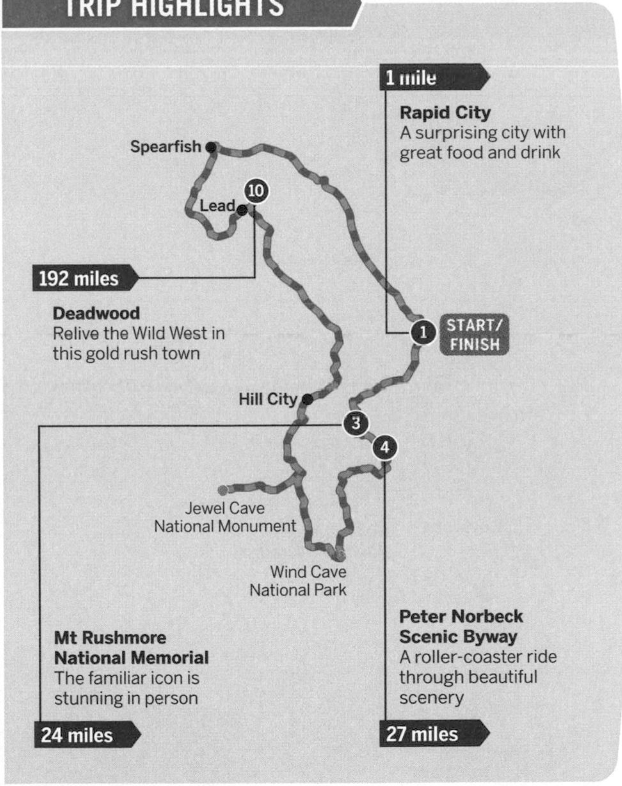

1 mile
Rapid City
A surprising city with great food and drink

Spearfish

10 Lead

192 miles
Deadwood
Relive the Wild West in this gold rush town

1 START/FINISH

Hill City

3

4

Jewel Cave National Monument

Wind Cave National Park

Peter Norbeck Scenic Byway
A roller-coaster ride through beautiful scenery

27 miles

Mt Rushmore National Memorial
The familiar icon is stunning in person

24 miles

2–3 DAYS
265 MILES / 426KM

GREAT FOR...

BEST TIME TO GO

May to September, when all sights are open.

ESSENTIAL PHOTO

Find a new angle on the four mugs at Mt Rushmore.

BEST FOR OUTDOORS

Where buffalo roam is just the start of critter-filled days amid beautiful scenery.

Classic Trip

27 Black Hills Loop

In the early 1800s, 60 million buffalo roamed the plains. Rampant overhunting decimated their ranks and by 1889 fewer than 1000 remained. Today, their numbers have climbed to 500,000; several Black Hills parks manage healthy herds. On this tour you'll see the iconic buffalo and other legendary sights, including the Badlands, Mt Rushmore, the Crazy Horse Memorial, sprawling parks and the town made famous for having no law: Deadwood.

TRIP HIGHLIGHT

1 Rapid City

A worthy capital to the region, 'Rapid' has an intriguing, lively and walkable downtown. Well-preserved brick buildings, filled with quality shops and places to dine, make it a good urban base and hub for your looping tour. Get a walking-tour brochure of Rapid's historic buildings and public art from the visitor center. Check out the watery fun on **Main St Square**.

While strolling, don't miss the **Statues of Presidents** (www.presidentsrc.com; 631 Main St; ⌚info center noon-9pm Mon-Sat Jun-Sep) on downtown street corners. From a shifty-eyed Nixon in repose to a triumphant Harry Truman, lifelike statues dot corners throughout the center. Collect all 42.

Learn about how dramatic natural underground events over the eons have produced some spectacular rocks. See these plus dinosaur bones and some stellar fossils at the **Museum of Geology** (☎605-394-2467; http://museum.sdsmt.edu; 501 E St Joseph St, O'Harra Bldg; ⌚9am-7pm Mon-Sat Jun-Aug, 9am-4pm Mon-Fri, 10am-4pm Sat Sep-May), located at the South Dakota School of Mines & Technology.

✕ 🛏 p356

The Drive » Choose from the commercial charms on Hwys 16 and 16A on the 21-mile drive to Keystone.

2 Keystone

One indisputable fact about the Black Hills? It will always, always, always take longer than you think to reach a key attraction. Trust us. Slow-moving Winnebagos, serpentine byways and kitschy roadside distractions will deaden your pace. And the distractions start early on Hwy 16 where family- friendly and delightfully hokey tourist attractions vie for dollars on the way to Mt Rushmore, including the animal-happy **Bear Country USA** (☎605-343-2290; www.bearcountryusa.com; 13820 Hwy 16; adult/child $17/11; ⌚8am-6pm May-Aug, reduced hours Sep-Nov; 👪) and **Reptile Gardens** (www.reptilegardens.com; 8955 Hwy 16; adult/child $17.50/11.50; ⌚8am-6pm late May-early Sep, reduced hours Mar-late May & early Sep-Nov, closed Dec Feb; 👪).

Kitsch reigns supreme in Keystone, a gaudy town bursting with rah-rah patriotism, Old West spirit and too many

LINK YOUR TRIP

28 The Mighty Mo
Join the route in Pierre, SD, a 170-mile trip east of Rapid City via I-90 plus a scenic leg on US 14.

29 Grand Teton to Yellowstone
More great American parks are west through Montana.

fudgeries. The fuss is directly attributable to its proximity to Mt Rushmore, 3 miles west.

p356

The Drive » It's a mere 3-mile jaunt uphill to Mt Rushmore. Keep yours eyes peeled for the first glimpse of a prez.

TRIP HIGHLIGHT

3 Mt Rushmore National Memorial

Glimpses of Washington's nose from the roads leading to this hugely popular monument never cease to surprise and are but harbingers of the full impact of this mountainside sculpture once you're up close (and past the less impressive parking area and entrance walk). George Washington, Thomas Jefferson, Abraham Lincoln and Theodore Roosevelt each iconically stare into the distance in 60ft-tall granite glory.

It's hugely popular, but you can easily escape the crowds and fully appreciate **Mt Rushmore** (605-574-2523; www.nps.gov/moru; off Hwy 244; parking $10; 8am-10pm Jun-Aug, to 9pm Sep, to 5pm Oct-May) while marveling at the artistry of sculptor Gutzon Borglum and the

DETOUR: BADLANDS NATIONAL PARK & MORE

Start: 1 Rapid City

More than 600 buffalo, also known as North American bison, roam **Badlands National Park** (605-433-5361; www.nps.gov/badl; Hwy 240; 7-day park pass bicycle/car $10/20). The name originated with French trappers and the Lakota Sioux, who described the park's jagged spires and crumbling buttes as 'bad lands.' Today, this crumbling former floodplain is visually compelling, its corrugated hillsides enlivened by an ever-changing palette of reds and pinks.

You can see the eroding rocks up close on the **Notch Trail**, a 1.5-mile (round-trip) leg stretcher that twists through a canyon, scampers up a wooden ladder then curves along a crumbly ridgeline to an expansive view of grasslands and more serrated walls. At the **Ben Reifel Visitor Center** (605-433-5361; www.nps.gov/badl; Hwy 240; 7-day park pass bicycle/car $10/20; 8am-7pm Jun-Aug, to 5pm Apr, May, Sep & Oct, to 4pm Nov-Mar) just down the road, a visually stunning film captures the park's natural diversity with jaw-dropping close-ups of the plants and animals that thrive in the mixed-grass prairie.

From Rapid City, head about 50 miles east on I-90, where **Badlands Loop Rd** (Hwy 240) links with I-90 at exits 131 and 110. The loop stretches west from the visitor center into the park's north unit, curving along a narrow ridge of buttes known as the **Badlands Wall**. It can be driven in an hour, but stopping at the numerous overlooks can easily fill a morning. Exit 110 off I-90 also serves Wall, home to the eponymous **Wall Drug** (605-279-2175; www.walldrug.com; 510 Main St; 7am-6pm;), one of the world's great – and unmissable – tourist traps.

To avoid I-90 back to Rapid City, pick up Hwy 44, which can be accessed at several points from the Badlands. Jagged bluffs give way to rolling prairie on this made-for-convertibles byway that swings through the **Buffalo Gap National Grassland** on its way west.

immense labor of the workers who created the memorial between 1927 and 1941.

The **Presidential Trail** loop passes right below the monument for some fine nostril views and gives you access to the worthwhile Sculptor's Studio. Start clockwise and you're right under Washington's nose in under five minutes. The **nature trail** to the right as you face the entrance connects the viewing and parking areas, passing through a pine forest and avoiding the crowds and commercialism.

The official Park Service **information centers** have excellent bookstores with proceeds going to the park. Avoid the schlocky Xanterra gift shop and the disappointing Carvers Cafe, which looked much better in the scene where Cary Grant gets plugged in *North by Northwest.* The main **museum** is far from comprehensive but the fascinating **Sculptor's Studio** conveys the drama of how the monument came to be.

The Drive » Backtrack slightly from Mt Rushmore and head southwest for the 16 miles of thrills on the Iron Mountain Rd.

TRIP HIGHLIGHT

❹ Peter Norbeck Scenic Byway

Driving the 66-mile Peter Norbeck Scenic Byway is like flirting with a brand-new crush: always exhilarating, occasionally challenging and sometimes you get a few butterflies. Named for the South Dakota senator who pushed for its creation in 1919, the oval-shaped byway is broken into four roads linking the most memorable destinations in the Black Hills (drivers of large RVs should call Custer State Park for tunnel measurements).

Iron Mountain Rd (Hwy 16A) is the real star, beloved for its pigtailing loops, Mt Rushmore–framing tunnels and one gorgeous glide through sun-dappled pines. It's a 16-mile roller coaster of wooden bridges, virtual loop-the-loops, narrow tunnels and stunning vistas. Expect lots of drivers going even slower than you are.

The 14-mile **Needles Hwy** (Hwy 87) swoops below granite spires, careens past rocky overlooks and slings though a super-narrow tunnel.

The Drive » Once past the Iron Mountain Rd, other Peter Norbeck Scenic Byway options aside, it is only 3 miles along Hwy 16 west to the Custer State Park visitor center.

❺ Custer State Park

The only reason 111-sq-mile **Custer State Park** (☎605-255-4515; www.custerstatepark.com; 7-day pass per car $20; ⏲24hr) isn't a national park is that the state grabbed it first. It boasts one of the largest free-roaming bison herds in the world (about 1500), the famous 'begging burros' (donkeys seeking handouts) and more than 200 bird species. Other wildlife include elk, pronghorns, mountain goats, bighorn sheep, coyotes, prairie dogs, mountain lions and bobcats. Meandering over awesome stone bridges and across sublime alpine meadows, the 18-mile **Wildlife Loop Road** allows plenty of spotting.

The **Custer State Park Visitor Center** (☎605-255-4020; www.custerstatepark.com; US 16A; ⏲9am-5pm Jun-Aug, to 4pm Sep-May), situated on the eastern side of the park, contains good exhibits and offers guided nature walks. The nearby **Black Hills Playhouse** (☎605-255-4141; www.blackhillsplayhouse.com; tickets adult/child $34/16; ⏲schedule varies Jun–mid-Aug) hosts summer theater.

Hiking through the pine-covered hills and prairie grassland is a great way to see wildlife and rock formations. Trails through **Sylvan Lake Shore**, **Sunday Gulch**, **Cathedral Spires** and **French Creek Natural Area** are all highly recommended.

The park is named for the notorious George A Custer, who led a scientific expedition into the

Classic Trip

GABI LUKA / SHUTTERSTOCK ©

JESS KRAFT / SHUTTERSTOCK ©

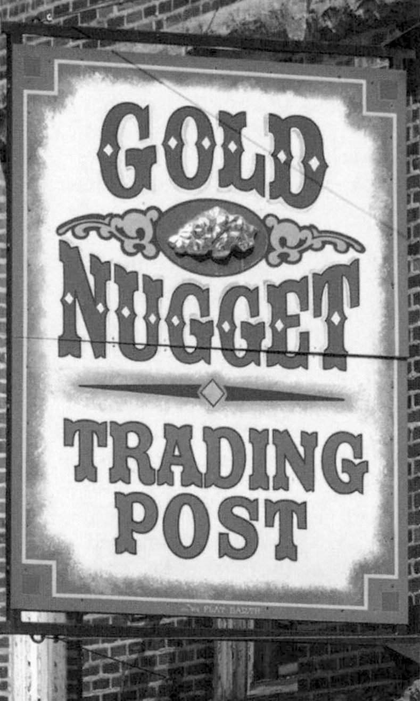

WHY THIS IS A CLASSIC TRIP

MARK JOHANSON, WRITER

Ride the roller-coaster roads into the pine-covered Black Hills, and the golden plains of the American heartland seem a world away. Iconic Mt Rushmore lures most visitors to this remote region, but it's the prismatic caves, herds of bison and Wild West tales of Deadwood's larger-than-life characters that leave lasting memories. Hike or bike near attractive resort towns, then laze away an afternoon in a bubbling thermal spring.

Above: Bison herd, Custer State Park
Left: Shop sign, Deadwood
Right: Rock formations, Black Hills

JASON PATRICK ROSS / SHUTTERSTOCK ©

Black Hills in 1874. The expedition's discovery of gold drew so many new settlers that an 1868 treaty granting the Sioux a 60-million-acre reservation in the area was eventually broken. Crazy Horse and the Lakotas retaliated, killing Custer and 265 of his men at Montana's Battle of the Little Big Horn in 1876.

The Drive » Near the western edge of Custer State Park, head due south on Hwy 87 for 19 miles from US 16. It's a beautiful ride through a long swath of wilderness and park.

6 Wind Cave National Park

This **park** (☎605-745-4600; www.nps.gov/wica; off US 385; tours adult $10-30, child $5-6; ⏰visitor center 8am-7pm Jun-Aug, reduced hours Sep-May), protecting 44 sq miles of grassland and forest, sits just south of Custer State Park. The central feature is, of course, the cave, which contains 147 miles of mapped passages. The cave's foremost feature is its 'boxwork' calcite formations (95% of all that are known exist here), which look like honeycomb and date back 60 to 100 million years. The strong gusts of wind that are felt at the entrance, but not inside, give the cave its name. For an introduction to the cave's history and geology, wander the exhibits at the visitor center prior to one of the ranger-led cave tours (most are one to 1½ hours; the four-hour Wild Cave Tour offers an orgy of spelunking).

Not all of the park's treasures are underground. Wind Cave's above-ground acres abound with bison and prairie dogs.

The Drive » Scenic drives continue as you go from one big hole in the ground to another. Jewel Cave is 38 miles northwest on US 385 and US 16.

7 Jewel Cave National Monument

Another of the Black Hills' many fascinating caves is **Jewel Cave** (☎605-673-8300; www.nps.gov/jeca; off US 16; tours adult $4-31, child free-$8; ⏰visitor center 8am-5:30pm Jun-Sep, 8:30am-4:30pm Oct-May), 13 miles west of Custer on US 16, so named because calcite crystals line many of its walls. Currently 187 miles have been surveyed (3% of the estimated total), making it the third-longest known cave in the world.

Tours range in length and difficulty and are offered on a first-come, first-served basis. Make arrangements at the visitor center.

The Drive » Retrace your route for 13 miles until US 385 joins US 16 and then go north for 5 miles.

8 Crazy Horse Memorial

The world's largest monument, the **Crazy Horse Memorial** (www.crazyhorsememorial.org; 12151 Ave of the Chiefs, off US 385; per person/car $11/28; ⏰7am-10pm Jun-Sep, reduced hours Oct-May) is a 563ft-tall work-in-progress. When finished it will depict the Sioux leader astride his horse, pointing to the horizon saying, 'My lands are where my dead lie buried.'

Never photographed or persuaded to sign a meaningless treaty, Crazy Horse was chosen for a monument that Lakota Sioux elders hoped would balance the presidential focus of Mt Rushmore. In 1948 a Boston-born sculptor, the indefatigable Korczak Ziolkowski, started blasting granite. His family has continued the work since his death in 1982. (It should be noted that many Native Americans oppose the monument as desecration of sacred land.)

No one is predicting when the sculpture will be complete (the face was dedicated in 1998). A rather thrilling laser-light show tells the tales of the monument on summer evenings.

The visitor center complex includes a Native American museum, a cultural center, cafes and Ziolkowski's studio.

The Drive » It's a short 10-mile drive north on US 16/385 to the refreshments of Hill City.

9 Hill City

One of the most appealing towns up in the hills, Hill City (www.hillcitysd.com) is less frenzied than places such as Keystone. Its main drag has cafes and galleries.

1880 Train (☎605-574-2222; www.1880train.com; 222 Railroad Ave; adult/child round-trip $29/14; ⏰mid-May–Dec) is a classic steam train running through rugged country to and from Keystone. An interesting little train museum is next door.

🍴🛏 p356

The Drive » Lakes, rivers, meadows and a few low-key tourist traps enliven the 42 miles on US 385 to Deadwood through the heart of the Black Hills.

TRIP HIGHLIGHT

10 Deadwood

Fans of the iconic HBO TV series may recall that Deadwood was the epitome of lawlessness in the 1870s. Today things have changed, although the 80 gambling halls, big and small, would no doubt put a sly grin on the faces of the hard characters who founded the town.

Deadwood's atmospheric streets are lined with gold-rush-era buildings lavishly restored with gambling dollars. Its storied past is easy to find at its museums and cemeteries. There's eternal devotion to Wild Bill Hickok, who was shot in the back of the head here in 1876 while gambling.

Actors reenact famous **shootouts** (Main St; 2pm, 4pm & 6pm Jun-Aug) on Main St during summer, including the 1877 saloon fight between Tom Smith and David Lunt (who lived for 67 days relatively unbothered by the bullet in his head before finally dropping dead).

p357

The Drive » Lead is just 4 miles uphill from Deadwood, through land scarred by generations hunting for gold.

11 Lead

Lead (pronounced 'leed') has an unrestored charm and still bears plenty of scars from the mining era. Gape at the 1250ft-deep **Homestake Gold Mine** (605-584-3110; www.sanfordlabhomestake.com; 160 W Main St; viewing area free, tours adult/child $8/7; 9am-6pm May-Oct, to 5pm Nov-Apr, tours 10am-4pm May-Oct) to see what open-pit mining can do to a mountain. Nearby are the same mine's shafts, which plunge more than 1.5 miles below the surface and are now being used for physics research.

p357

The Drive » Climb out of steep canyons for 11 miles on US 14A until you plunge back down into Spearfish Canyon.

12 Spearfish

Spearfish Canyon Scenic Byway (www.byways.org) is a waterfall-lined, curvaceous 20-mile road that cleaves from the heart of the hills into Spearfish. There's a sight worth stopping for around every bend; pause for longer than a minute and you'll hear beavers hard at work.

p357

The Drive » It's a quick 22 miles east on I-90 to Sturgis. That solitary headlight in the rearview mirror is a hog hoping to blow past. From Sturgis back to Rapid City is only 36 miles.

13 Sturgis

Neon-lit tattoo parlors, Christian iconography and billboards for ribald biker bars featuring dolled-up models are just some of the cacophony of images of this loud and proud biker town. Shop for leather on Main St, don your American flag bandana and sidle up to the saloon bar to give a toast to the stars and stripes!

Things get even louder for the annual **Sturgis Motorcycle Rally** (605-720-0800; www.sturgismotorcyclerally.com; early Aug), when around 700,000 riders, fans and onlookers take over the town.

Eating & Sleeping

Rapid City 1

Independent Ale House Pub $
(☎605-718-9492; www.independentalehouse.com; 625 St Joseph St; ⏰3pm-late Sun-Thu, 11am-late Fri & Sat) Enjoy a fabulous (and changing) lineup of the best microbrews from the region in this vintage-style bar. The wine list is equally good. Pizzas are excellent (mains $8 to $15).

Murphy's Pub & Grill American $$
(www.murphyspubandgrill.com; 510 9th St; mains $10-25; ⏰food 11am-10pm, bar to 1am) Pub fare with creative flair makes this bustling downtown bar an excellent dining choice. Specials feature seasonal and local ingredients. The vast terrace is matched by the big interior.

Tally's Silver Spoon American $$
(☎605-342-7621; www.tallyssilverspoon.com; 530 6th St; mains $6-30; ⏰7am-9pm) Carter or Reagan? Both statues are visible out front and you can ponder your preference while you savor the upscale diner fare at this slick downtown cafe and bar. Breakfasts are as good as ever; more creative regional fare is on offer at night.

Delmonico Grill Modern American $$$
(☎605-791-1664; www.delmonicogrill.com; 609 Main St; mains lunch $6-15, dinner $24-38; ⏰11am-2pm & 5-9pm Mon-Sat) Fine burgers, sandwiches and salads star at lunch at this casually elegant downtown dining spot. At dinner, choose from superb steaks and other meaty mains from the Plains. Lots of specials by season.

Town House Motel Motel $
(☎605-791-3989; www.townhousemotelssd.com; 210 St Joseph St; r $70-140; ⏰mid-May–mid-Sep; ❄ 📶 🏊) A classic yet clean 40-room motel within walking distance of all the downtown joys. The exterior corridors in the two-story blocks of rooms overlook the parking area and pool.

Hotel Alex Johnson Hotel $$
(☎605-342-1210; www.alexjohnson.com; 523 6th St; r $70-200; ❄ @ 📶) The design of this 1927 classic magically blends Germanic Tudor architecture with traditional Lakota Sioux symbols – note the lobby's painted ceiling and the chandelier made of war lances. The rooftop bar is a delight, while the 143 rooms are modernized retro (some have fabulous views!). Ask at reception about the hotel's role in Hitchcock's *North by Northwest*.

Rushmore Hotel Hotel $$
(☎605-348-8300; www.therushmorehotel.com; 445 Mt Rushmore Rd; r $100-200; P ❄ @ 📶 🐾) This high-rise hotel has been transformed into a high-concept downtown gem with green accents. A lot of the furniture is made from recycled materials yet there's no skimping on comfort. The marble floor in the lobby is a stunner.

Keystone 2

Teddy's Deli Deli $
(☎605-389-3354; www.teddysdeli.com; 236 Winter St; mains $8-12; ⏰11am-7pm May-Sep) Best sandwiches in the region, far better than what you'll get at nearby Mt Rushmore.

Hill City 9

Desperados American $$
(☎605-574-2959; 301 Main St; mains $9-20; ⏰11am-9pm, closed Oct-Apr) Dine amid frontier charm in the oldest hand-hewn log commercial building in South Dakota. Have the burger. Service is quick and casual.

Alpine Inn — Historic Hotel $$

(605-574-2749; www.alpineinnhillcity.com; 133 Main St; r $80-180;) Right in the center, the Alpine Inn dates to 1884 and has comfy rooms in regal red. The **restaurant** (mains $8 to $11; 11am-2:30pm & 5-9pm) serves filling German fare.

Lantern Inn — Motel $$

(605-574-2582; www.lanterninn.com; 580 E Main St; r $70-130; closed Nov-Mar;) Lantern Inn is an 18-room motel-style place spread over two stories fronting attractive grounds.

Deadwood 10

Midnight Star — American $

(605-578-3550; 677 Main St; mains $8-15; food 10am-10pm, closed Mon Nov-Apr) Owned by actor Kevin Costner, this attractive boozer (with 'top shelf Jell-O shots') has costumes and photos from his movies. The restaurant serves sandwiches, pastas and seafood.

Saloon No 10 — Bar $

(800-952-9398; www.saloon10.com; 657 Main St; kitchen 11am-9pm, bar 8am-2am) Dark paneled walls and sawdust on the floor are features of this storied bar. The original, where Hickok literally lost big time, stood across the street, but the building burned to the ground and the owners relocated here. There's a rooftop bar, and decent pub grub and Italian-accented dinners (mains $8 to $25). Hickok's murder is acted out here at 1pm, 3pm, 5pm and 7pm from June to mid-September.

Bullock Hotel — Historic Hotel $$

(605-578-1745; www.historicbullock.com; 633 Main St; r $70-200;) Fans of the TV show will recall the conflicted but upstanding sheriff Seth Bullock. This hotel was opened by the real Bullock in 1895. The 28 rooms are modern and comfortable while retaining the building's period charm.

Deadwood Dick's — Hotel $$

(605-578-3224; www.deadwooddicks.com; 51 Sherman St; r $36-200;) These home-style and idiosyncratic rooms feature furniture from the owner's antique shop, and range in size from small doubles to large suites with kitchens. The unique bar lives up to the town's past.

Lead 11

Town Hall Inn — Historic Hotel $

(605-584-1112; www.townhallinn.com; 215 W Main St; r $50-100;) This 12-room inn occupies Town Hall (built in 1912) and has spacious suites named and themed in honor of their former purpose, from the municipal judge's chamber to the jury room and mayor's office.

Spearfish 12

Spearfish Canyon Lodge — Lodge $$

(605-584-3435; www.spfcanyon.com; US 14A; r $90-220;) For a rural retreat, the Spearfish Canyon Lodge is 13 miles south of Spearfish near trails and streams. The massive lobby fireplace adds charm and the 54 modern piney rooms are cozy.

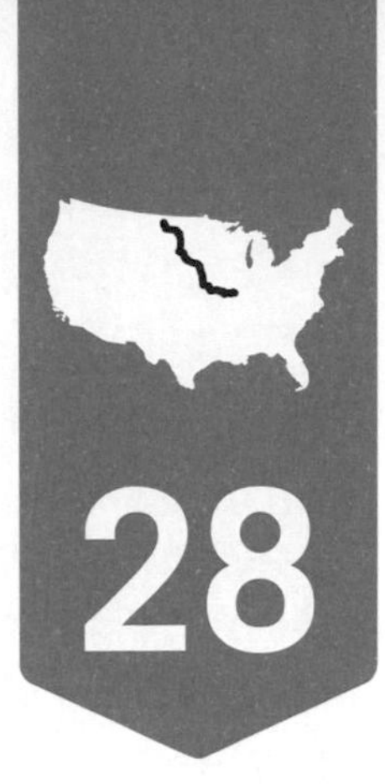

The Mighty Mo

Follow the course of North America's longest river as it runs past great cities, evocative wilderness and sites embedded in US history.

TRIP HIGHLIGHTS

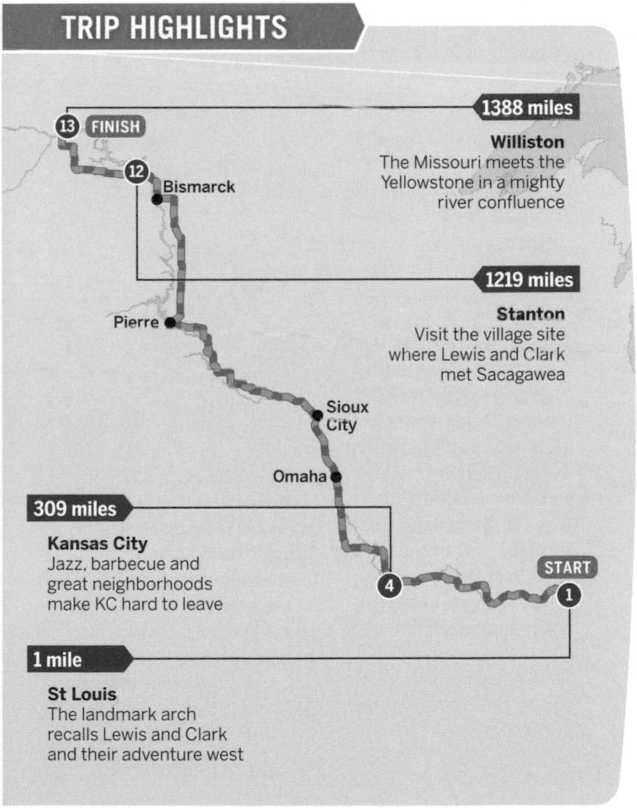

13 FINISH

12 Bismarck

Pierre

Sioux City

Omaha

4

START 1

1388 miles

Williston
The Missouri meets the Yellowstone in a mighty river confluence

1219 miles

Stanton
Visit the village site where Lewis and Clark met Sacagawea

309 miles

Kansas City
Jazz, barbecue and great neighborhoods make KC hard to leave

1 mile

St Louis
The landmark arch recalls Lewis and Clark and their adventure west

7 DAYS
1388 MILES / 2234KM

GREAT FOR...

BEST TIME TO GO

May to September, when all the sights are open.

ESSENTIAL PHOTO

Any shot that shows the Missouri River's impressive girth.

BEST FOR HISTORY

Much of America's 19th-century sense of self was formed by events along the river.

St Louis Gateway Arch

28 The Mighty Mo

In 1804–05, Lewis and Clark followed the Missouri River during the first stages of their legendary journey west. With their Corps of Discovery, they canoed up the river, meeting Native Americans – some friendly, others hostile – and discovering vast expanses of land, untouched for eons and teeming with wildlife. Exploring the river today, you can make your very own discoveries.

TRIP HIGHLIGHT

1 St Louis

Slide into St Louis and revel in the unique vibe of the largest city in the Great Plains. Beer, bowling and baseball are some of the top attractions, but history and culture, much of it linked to the city's unique position as the 'Gateway to the West,' give it texture.

Fur-trapper Pierre Laclede knew prime real estate when he saw it, putting down stakes at the junction of the Mississippi and Missouri Rivers in 1764. The hustle picked up considerably when prospectors discovered gold in California in 1848 and St Louis became the jumping-off point first for get-rich-quick dreamers and later for waves of settlers.

As a symbol for the city, the **Gateway Arch** (☎314-655-1700; www.gatewayarch.com; tram ride adult/child $13/10; ⌚8am-10pm Jun-Aug, 9am-6pm Sep-May, last tram 1hr before closing; 👪) has soared above any expectations its backers could have had in 1965 when it opened. The centerpiece of this National Park Service property, the silvery, shimmering 630ft-high arch is the Great Plains' own Eiffel Tower. A tram ride takes you to the tight confines at the top.

The arch is part of the **Jefferson National Expansion Memorial**, which honors the vision of the namesake president who sponsored the Lewis and Clark expedition. It began here on May 14, 1804 and followed the Missouri River, much as you'll do on this tour.

✕ 🛏 p46, p367

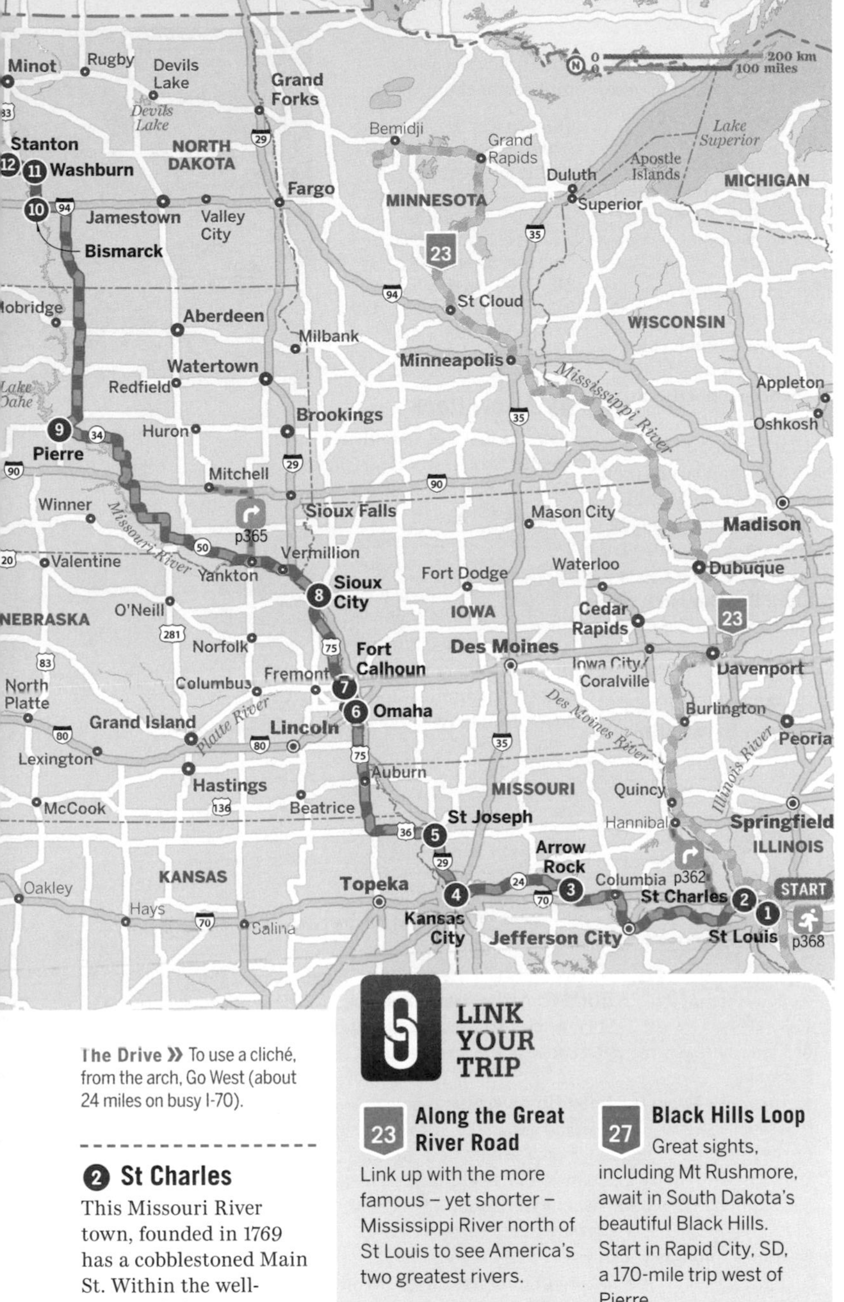

The Drive » To use a cliché, from the arch, Go West (about 24 miles on busy I-70).

❷ St Charles

This Missouri River town, founded in 1769 has a cobblestoned Main St. Within the well-preserved downtown you can visit the **First State**

LINK YOUR TRIP

23 Along the Great River Road

Link up with the more famous – yet shorter – Mississippi River north of St Louis to see America's two greatest rivers.

27 Black Hills Loop

Great sights, including Mt Rushmore, await in South Dakota's beautiful Black Hills. Start in Rapid City, SD, a 170-mile trip west of Pierre.

Capitol (636-940-3322; 200 S Main St; tours adult/child $4.50/3; 10am-4pm Mon-Sat, noon-4pm Sun, closed Mon Nov-Mar, closed Sun Jan & Feb). Ask at the **visitor center** (800-366-2427; www.historicstcharles.com; 230 S Main St; 8am-5pm Mon-Fri, 10am-5pm Sat, noon-5pm Sun) about tours, which pass some rare French colonial architecture in the **Frenchtown neighborhood** just north.

Clark joined Lewis here and they began their epic journey on May 21, 1804. Their encampment is reenacted annually on that date. The **Lewis & Clark Boathouse & Nature Center** (www.lewisandclarkcenter.org; 1050 Riverside Dr; adult/child $5/2; 10am-5pm Mon-Sat, noon-5pm Sun) has displays about the duo and replicas of their boats.

The Drive » Skip the elusive charms of I-70 and instead stay close to the river, first taking Hwy 94 and then cutting north via Columbia (which has good cafes downtown) on US 63. From here take Hwy 740, Hwy 240, US 40 and Hwy 41, in that order, for a total journey of 190 miles.

3 Arrow Rock

Perched just above and west of the Missouri River, **Arrow Rock State Historic Site** (www.mostateparks.com; visitor center 10am-4pm daily Mar-Nov, Fri-Sun Dec-Feb) is a small preserved town that feels little changed since the 1830s when it was on the main stagecoach route west.

MICHAEL RUSSELL / GETTY IMAGES ©

DETOUR: HANNIBAL

Start: 2 St Charles

When the air is sultry in this old river town, you almost expect to hear the whistle of a paddle steamer on that *other* river, the Mississippi. Mark Twain's boyhood home, 100 miles northwest of St Louis, has some authentically vintage areas and plenty of sites where you can get a sense of the muse and his creations, Tom Sawyer and Huck Finn.

The **Mark Twain Boyhood Home & Museum** (573-221-9010; www.marktwainmuseum.org; 120 N Main St; adult/child $11/6; 9am-5pm, reduced hours Jan-Mar) presents eight buildings, including two homes Twain lived in and that of Laura Hawkins, the real-life inspiration for Becky Thatcher. Afterward, float down the Mississippi on the **Mark Twain Riverboat** (573-221-3222; www.marktwainriverboat.com; Center St Landing; 1hr sightseeing cruise adult/child $18/11; Apr-Nov, schedule varies). **National Tom Sawyer Days** (www.hannibaljaycees.org; around weekend of Jul 4) feature frog-jumping and fence-painting contests and much more.

From St Charles, Hannibal is 95 miles northwest through low, rolling hills via US 61.

Kansas City The 'City of Fountains'

The Drive » Hwy 41 followed by US 65 and US 24 take you through rolling Missouri countryside and, after 95 miles, right into the heart of Kansas City.

TRIP HIGHLIGHT

❹ Kansas City

Kansas City (KC) began life in 1821 as a trading post but really came into its own once westward expansion began. The Oregon, California and Santa Fe trails all met steamboats loaded with pioneers here.

KC is famed for its barbecues (100-plus joints smoke it up), fountains (more than 200; on par with Rome) and jazz.

Neighborhoods not to miss include the **Country Club Plaza** (☎816-753-0100; www.countryclubplaza.com), often shortened to 'the Plaza,' a 1920s shopping district and an attraction in itself; **River Market**, home to a large farmers market, immediately north of downtown; and **Westport**, located on Westport Rd, just west of Main St, and filled with alluring locally owned restaurants and bars.

The unpredictable Missouri River claimed hundreds of riverboats. At the **Arabia Steamboat Museum** (☎816-471-1856; www.1856.com; 400 Grand Blvd; adult/child $14.50/5.50; ⏲10am-5pm Mon-Sat, noon-5pm Sun, last tour 90min before closing) you can see 200 tons of salvaged 'treasure' from an 1856 victim.

✕ 🛏 p367

The Drive » Quickly escape KC's endless suburbs by darting north 55 miles on I-29.

❺ St Joseph

The first Pony Express set out in 1860, carrying mail from 'St Jo' 2000 miles west to California, taking just eight days. The service lasted 18 months before telegraph lines made it redundant. The **Pony Express National Museum** (☎816-279-5059; http://ponyexpress.org; 914 Penn St; adult/child $6/3; ⏰9am-5pm Mon-Sat, 11am-4pm Sun) tells the story of the dangerous Express and its riders.

St Jo, just east of the Missouri River, was home to outlaw Jesse James. He was killed at what is now the **Jesse James Home Museum** (☎816-232-8206; www.ponyexpressjessejames.com; 1202 Penn St; adult/child $6/4; ⏰9am-4pm Mon-Sat, noon-4pm Sun). The fateful bullet hole is still in the wall.

Housed in the former 'State Lunatic Asylum No 2,' the **Glore Psychiatric Museum** (☎816-232-8471; www.stjosephmuseum.org; 3406 Frederick Ave; adult/child $6/4; ⏰10am-5pm Mon-Sat, 1-5pm Sun) gives a frightening and fascinating look at lobotomies, the 'bath of surprise' and other discredited treatments.

The Drive » Cross west to Nebraska on US 36 and then head north on US 75. While on this 157-mile-long leg, look for views of the Missouri from old river towns like Nebraska City.

6 Omaha

Home to the brick-and-cobblestoned **Old Market** neighborhood downtown, a lively music scene and several quality museums, Omaha can turn a few hours into a few days.

Omaha's location on the Missouri River and proximity to the Platte River made it an important stop on the Oregon, California and Mormon Trails. Later, the first transcontinental railroad to California stretched west from here. Its history is recounted at the **Union Pacific Railroad Museum** (www.uprrmuseum.org; 200 Pearl St; ⏰10am-4pm Thu-Sat) in nearby Council Bluffs.

The downtown **riverfront** (8th St & Riverfront Dr) has been massively spiffed up. Among the highlights: the architecturally stunning **Bob Kerry Pedestrian Bridge**, which soars over to Iowa; the **Heartland of America Park**, with fountains and lush gardens; and **Lewis & Clark Landing**, where the explorers did just that in 1804. It's home to the **Lewis & Clark National Historical Trail Visitor Center** (☎402-661-1804; www.nps.gov/lecl; 601 Riverfront Dr; ⏰8am-5pm Mon-Fri, from 9:30am Sat & Sun May-Oct, 8am-4:30pm Mon-Fri Nov-Apr), where you can get information and advice for following in their footsteps.

✕ 🛏 p345, p367

The Drive » Just beyond the outer reaches of ever-growing Omaha, Fort Calhoun is 16 miles north on US 75.

7 Fort Calhoun

The small town of Fort Calhoun has two sights that take you back to days long gone on the Missouri. **Fort Atkinson State Historical Park** (www.outdoornebraska.ne.gov; Madison St; adult/child $2/1; ⏰park 8am-5pm, visitor center 10am-5pm Jun-Aug, Sat & Sun May & Sep) preserves the first US military fort built west of the Missouri River. It was built in 1820 on a recommendation of Lewis and Clark, who, besides being explorers, were keen military officers.

Just east of town, **Boyer Chute National Wildlife Refuge** (www.fws.gov/refuge/Boyer_Chute; CR 34; ⏰dawn-dusk) has marshes and other open areas on the river that have changed little in centuries. A looping driving route shows you what the land crossed by the Missouri once looked like before farms and development forever changed things.

The Drive » Farm towns hoping to be remembered by time dot the 84 miles of US 75 north from Fort Calhoun. The road's general route gently bends with the overall course of the Missouri River to the east.

8 Sioux City

On a high bluff, the modest city of Sioux City, IA, has grand views looking west over the Missouri River. There's a good **overlook** at the corner of W Fourth and Burton Sts.

On August 20, 1804, Sergeant Charles Floyd became the only person to die on the Lewis and Clark expedition team, probably from appendicitis. You can learn much more about this and other aspects of the journey at the beautiful **Lewis & Clark Interpretive Center** (www.siouxcitylcic.com; 900 Larsen Park Rd, Sioux City; 9am-5pm Tue-Fri, noon-5pm Sat & Sun), which is right on the river.

The Drive » Enjoy the smallest of rural two-laners to reach the first capitol of the Dakota states. Angle out of Sioux City on Hwy 12, then cross over to South Dakota at Westfield and pick up the alternately sinuous and angular Hwy 50, which closely follows the river. The final 64 miles of this 306-mile-long leg are on Hwy 34.

DETOUR: MITCHELL

Start: 8 Sioux City

Why not honor the starch you'll see growing in profusion in vibrant green fields all along the Missouri? Every year, half a million people pull off I-90 (exit 332) to see the Taj Mahal of agriculture, the all-time-ultimate roadside attraction, the **Corn Palace** (605-995-8430; www.cornpalace.com; 604 N Main St; 8am-9pm Jun-Aug, reduced hours Sep-May). Close to 300,000 ears of corn are used each year to create a tableau of murals on the outside of the building. Ponder the scenes and you may find a kernel of truth or just say 'aw shucks.' Head inside to see photos of how the facade has evolved over the years.

Mitchell is 150 miles northwest of Sioux City via I-29 and I-90. Rejoin the drive at Pierre, 150 miles northwest via I-90 and US 83.

9 Pierre

Pierre (pronounced 'peer'), SD, is just too small (population 14,100) and ordinary to feel like a seat of power. Small-town Victorian homes overlook the imposing 1910 **State Capitol** (605-773-3011; 500 E Capitol Ave; 8am-7pm Mon-Fri, to 5pm Sat & Sun) with its black copper dome.

Hard by the Missouri River, it lies along the Native American Scenic Byway and lonely, stark US 14. Imagine this area when it was rich with bison, beavers, elk and much more.

Exhibits at the **South Dakota Cultural Heritage Center** (605-773-3458; www.history.sd.gov; 900 Governors Dr; adult/child $4/free; 9am-6:30pm Mon-Sat, 1-4:30pm Sun Jun-Aug, to 4:30pm rest of year) include a bloody Ghost Dance shirt from the Battle of Wounded Knee.

At a bend on the river, **Framboise Island** has several hiking trails and plentiful wildlife. It's across from where the Lewis and Clark expedition spent four days in late September, 1804. The expedition was nearly derailed when they inadvertently offended members of the local Brule tribe.

The Drive » Dams cause the Missouri to look like a lake for much of the 208 miles you'll drive north along US 83 to the other Dakota capitol.

10 Bismarck

Compared with the sylvan charms of Pierre, the stark 1930s **State Capitol** (701-328-2480; 600 E Boulevard Ave, Capitol Hill; 8am-4pm Mon-Fri, 9am-4pm Sat, 1-4pm Sun Jun-Aug, 9am-4pm Mon-Fri Sep-May, tours hourly except noon) in Bismarck, ND, is often referred to as the 'skyscraper of the prairie' and looks like a Stalinist school of dentistry.

Behind the Sacagawea (a Native American woman whose friendship proved invaluable to Lewis and Clark) statue, the huge **North Dakota Heritage Center** (701-328-2666; www.history.nd.gov; 612 East Boulevard Ave, Capitol Hill; 8am-5pm Mon-Fri, 10am-5pm Sat & Sun) has details on everything from Norwegian bachelor farmers to the scores of nuclear bombs perched on missiles in silos across the state.

Fort Abraham Lincoln State Park (www.parkrec.nd.gov; off Hwy 1806; per vehicle $5, tours adult/child $6/4; ⌚park 9am-5pm, tours May-Sep), 7 miles south of nearby Mandan on SR 1806, is well worth the detour. Its **On-a-Slant Indian Village** has five re-created Mandan earth lodges, while the fort, with several replica buildings, was Custer's last stop before the Battle of Little Bighorn.

The Drive ›› Maybe pancakes are popular in North Dakota because that's how flat much of the land is. See for yourself on this 40-mile drive north on US 83.

⓫ Washburn

There are several worthwhile attractions near the spot where Lewis and Clark wintered with the Mandan in 1804–05. They offer an evocative look at the lives of the Native Americans and the explorers amid lands that even today seem little changed.

Learn about the duo's expedition and the Native Americans who helped them at the **Lewis & Clark Interpretive Center** (☎701-462-8535; www.fortmandan.com; junction US 83 & ND Hwy 200A, Washburn; adult/child $7.50/3; ⌚9am-5pm Apr-Oct, 9am-5pm Mon-Sat, noon-5pm Sun Nov-Mar).

Fort Mandan, a replica of the fort built by Lewis and Clark, is 2.5 miles west (10 miles downstream from the flooded original site). It sits on a lonely stretch of the Missouri River marked by a monument to Seaman, the expedition's dog.

The Drive ›› Head 22 miles west of Washburn through verdant rolling prairie on Hwy 200 to just north of the small town of Stanton, ND.

TRIP HIGHLIGHT

⓬ Stanton, ND

At **Knife River Indian Villages National Historical Site** (☎701-745-3300; www.nps.gov/knri; off Hwy 200, Stanton; ⌚buildings 8am-5pm Jun-Aug, to 4:30pm Sep-May, trails dawn-dusk) you can still see the mounds left by three earthen villages of the Hidastas, who lived on the Knife River, a narrow tributary of the Missouri, for more than 900 years. The National Park Service has re-created one of the earthen lodges. A stroll through the mostly wide-open and wild site leads to the village where Lewis and Clark met Sacagawea.

The Drive ›› More dams cause the Missouri to balloon out into a tangle of waters that look like a couple of lizards doing a mating dance. Hwy 200 takes you for most of the 169 miles of your final leg.

TRIP HIGHLIGHT

⓭ Williston

Twenty-two miles southwest of Williston along SR 1804, **Fort Buford** (☎701-572-9034; www.history.nd.gov; SR 1804; tours adult/child $5/2.50; ⌚fort buildings 10am-5:30pm Jun-Aug) is the bleak army outpost where Sitting Bull surrendered. The adjacent **Missouri-Yellowstone Confluence Interpretive Center** includes the fort's visitor center and has good views of where the Yellowstone River joins the Missouri, greatly increasing the latter's flow.

About 2 miles west, on the Montana–North Dakota border, the more evocative **Fort Union Trading Post** (☎701-572-9083; www.nps.gov/fous; SR 1804; ⌚8am-6:30pm Central Time Jun-Aug, 9am-5pm Sep-May) is a reconstruction of the American Fur Company post built in 1828.

Over the border in Montana, the Missouri frays out into myriad tributaries. Lewis and Clark had numerous portages as they continued their epic journey west.

Eating & Sleeping

St Louis 1

Crown Candy Kitchen — Cafe $

(314-621-9650; www.crowncandykitchen.net; 1401 St Louis Ave; mains $5-10; 10:30am-8pm Mon-Thu, to 9pm Fri & Sat;) An authentic family-run soda fountain that's been making families smile since 1913. Malts (hot fudge, yum!) come with spoons, the floats, well, float, and you can try the famous BLT. Homemade candies top it off.

Bridge Tap House & Wine Bar — Bar $

(314-241-8141; www.thebridgestl.com; 1004 Locust St; 11am-1am Mon-Sat, to midnight Sun) Slip onto a sofa or rest your elbows on a table at this romantic bar where you can savor fine wine or the best local beer (55 on tap) and nibble a variety of exquisite little bites from a seasonal menu.

Eleven Eleven Mississippi — Modern American $$

(314-241-9999; www.1111-m.com; 1111 Mississippi Ave; mains $9-25; 11am-10pm Mon-Thu, to midnight Fri, 5pm-midnight Sat;) This popular bistro and wine bar fills an old shoe factory. Dinner mains draw on regional specialties with a farm-to-table vibe. Other options on the seasonal menu include sandwiches, pizzas, steaks and veggie dishes.

Moonrise Hotel — Boutique Hotel $$

(314-721-1111; www.moonrisehotel.com; 6177 Delmar Blvd; r $170-450; P) The stylish eight-story Moonrise has a high profile amid the high energy of the Loop neighborhood. Its 125 rooms sport a lunar motif, but are grounded enough to slow things down to comfy.

Kansas City 4

Arthur Bryant's — Barbecue $

(816-231-1123; www.arthurbryantsbbq.com; 1727 Brooklyn Ave; mains $8-15; 10am-9:30pm Mon-Thu, to 10pm Fri & Sat, 11am-8pm Sun; P) Not far from the Jazz District, this famous institution serves up piles of superb BBQ. The sauce is silky and fiery, the staff charming and witty. Get the burnt ends.

Joe's Kansas City Bar-B-Que — Barbecue $

(913-722-3366; www.joeskc.com; 3002 W 47th Ave; mains $6-20; 11am-9pm Mon-Thu, to 10pm Fri & Sat; P) This legendary joint is housed in a brightly lit old gas station and is the best reason to cross the state border – it's actually not far from the Plaza. The pulled pork is pleasure on a plate and vegetarians will appreciate the smoked portobello; expect lines.

Rieger Hotel Grill & Exchange — American $$

(816-471-2177; www.theriegerkc.com; 1924 Main St; mains $11-30; 3-10pm Mon-Thu, to 11pm Fri & Sat) One of KC's most innovative restaurants is housed in what was once a humdrum 1915 vintage hotel in the Crossroads Arts District. Today it's been spiffed up to match the creative fare on Howard Hanna's seasonal menu. (Note the bathroom plaque pointing out where Al Capone once sought release.)

Southmoreland on the Plaza — B&B $$

(816-531-7979; www.southmoreland.com; 116 E 46th St, Country Club Plaza; r $120-235; P) The 12 rooms at this posh B&B are furnished like the home of your rich country-club friends. It's a big old mansion between the art museums and the Plaza.

Omaha 6

Boiler Room — Modern American $$$

(402-916-9274; www.boilerroomomaha.com; 1110 Jones St; mains $28-35; 5.30-9pm Mon Thu, to 10pm Fri & Sat) Global influences and French techniques shape the locally sourced foods that comprise the seasonal dishes at this trendsetting Old Market bistro. It's got an open kitchen and a cocktail bar.

Spencer's — Steak $$$

(402-280-8888; www.spencersomahaforsteaksandchops.com; 102 S 10th St; mains $25-65; 5-10pm) Omaha is famous for steaks and this lavish low-lit restaurant won't disappoint with its seared meat. You can enjoy excellent casual fare in the bar for a fraction of the price.

STRETCH YOUR LEGS ST LOUIS

Start/Finish: Forest Park Visitor & Education Center

Distance: 4 miles

Duration: Three hours

The Gateway Arch downtown is an obvious drawcard but, for real walking pleasure, join the masses in leafy, museum- and attraction-filled Forest Park. The Central West End neighborhood to the east adds to the fun.

Take this walk on Trips

Forest Park

New York City may have Central Park, but St Louis has the bigger (by 528 acres) **Forest Park** (☎314-367-7275; www.forestparkforever.org; bounded by Lindell Blvd, Kingshighway Blvd & I-64; ⏰6am-10pm). The superb, 1371-acre spread was the setting of the 1904 World's Fair. The **Visitor & Education Center** (5595 Grand Dr; ⏰6am-8pm Mon-Fri, to 7pm Sat & Sun) is in an old streetcar pavilion and has a cafe. Park your car here and start your walk, which runs roughly counterclockwise.

The Walk » Walk northwest through the well-tended grounds some 300m.

Missouri History Museum

This **museum** (☎314-746-4599; www.mohistory.org; 5700 Lindell Blvd; ⏰10am-5pm Wed-Mon, to 8pm Tue; P) presents the story of St Louis, starring such worthies as the World's Fair, a replica of Charles Lindbergh's plane and a host of bluesmen. Oral histories from those who fought segregation are very moving.

The Walk » Walk south past the tennis courts to the lake's small marina.

Post-Dispatch Lake

Still showing signs of its central position during the World's Fair, this large lake isn't just for ogling: rent a boat from the **Boathouse** (☎314-367-2224; www.boathouseforestpark.com; 6101 Government Dr; boat rental per hour $17; ⏰11am-approx 1hr before sunset, weather permitting) and explore the placid waters.

The Walk » Walk directly southwest to the art museum, or alternatively take the longer and prettier sinuous path along the north side of the lakes, then drop down south past the Grand Basin and across the grassy expanse of Art Hill.

St Louis Art Museum

A grand beaux-arts palace originally built for the World's Fair, it now houses the storied **St Louis Art Museum** (www.slam.org; 1 Fine Arts Dr; ⏰10am-5pm Tue-Thu, Sat & Sun, to 9pm Fri), which has a collection that spans time and styles, and includes a variety of household names from Picasso to Van Gogh and Warhol.

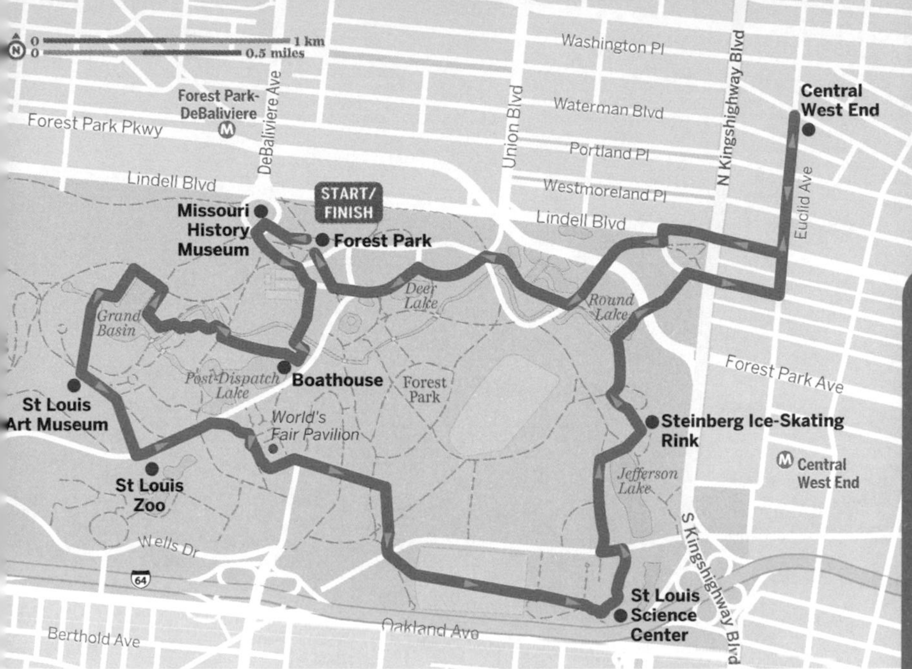

The Walk » A short verdant stroll southeast and you are at the north entrance to the zoo.

St Louis Zoo

A world-class facility, the vast **St Louis Zoo** (314-781-0900; www.stlzoo.org; 1 Government Dr; fee for some exhibits; 9am-5pm daily, to 7pm Fri-Sun May-Sep; P) includes a fascinating River's Edge area with African critters.

The Walk » Walk straight east through the tree-shaded grounds, watching for the planetarium in the distance. You might pause at the beautiful 1909 World's Fair Pavilion, a grand open-air shelter built with proceeds from the 1904 fair.

St Louis Science Center

Live demonstrations, dinosaurs, a planetarium and an IMAX theater are just some of the highlights of the **St Louis Science Center** (314-289-4400; www.slsc.org; 5050 Oakland Ave; 9:30am-4:30pm Mon-Sat, 11am-4:30pm Sun; P), much of which is reached via a dramatic glass walkway over I-64. The park entrance is anchored by the planetarium here.

The Walk » Follow the wide main pedestrian path north past Jefferson Lake.

Steinberg Ice-Skating Rink

If it's too cold to rent a boat, it's probably just right to go ice-skating with lots of other happy skaters at the **Steinberg Ice-Skating Rink** (314-367-7465; www.steinbergskatingrink.com; 400 Jefferson Dr; $7, skate rental $6; 10am-9pm Sun-Thu, to midnight Fri & Sat mid-Nov–Feb).

The Walk » Leave the park, crossing S Kingshighway Blvd, and walk one block to Euclid Ave, the heart of the Central West End neighborhood.

Central West End

This posh center for cafes and shopping is anchored by Euclid Ave. Get a picnic lunch at **Pickles Deli** (314-361-3354; www.picklesdelistl.com; 22 N Euclid Ave; mains $5-10; 9am-7pm Mon-Fri, 10am-3pm Sat;); top ingredients separate this slick spot from humdrum sandwich chains. Nearby is **Left Bank Books** (314-367-6731; www.left-bank.com; 399 N Euclid Ave; 10am-10pm Mon-Sat, 11am-6pm Sun), a great indie bookstore.

The Walk » Return to the car park via some of the nicest gardens in Forest Park. Follow the paths along the waterways linking Round and Deer Lakes.

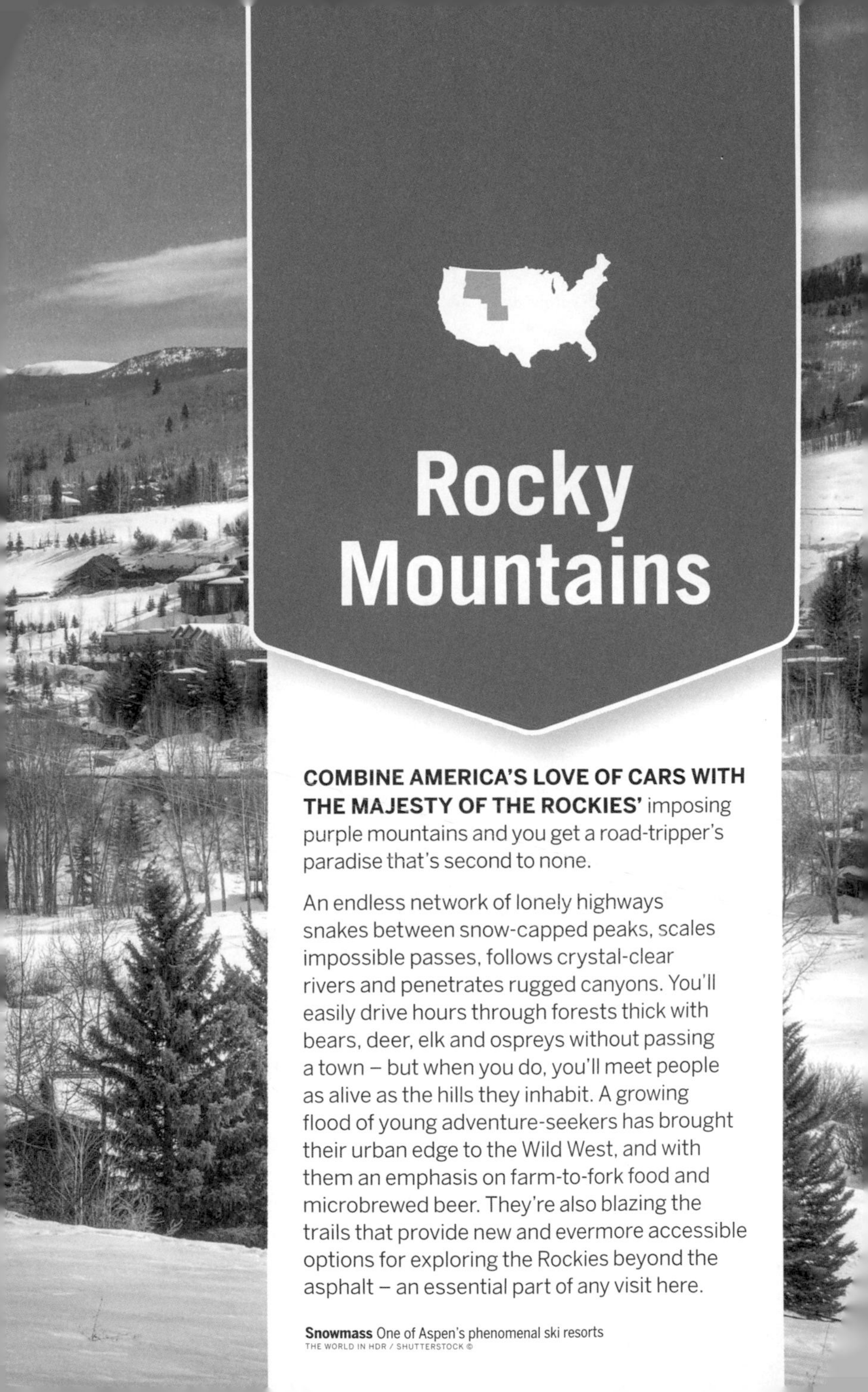

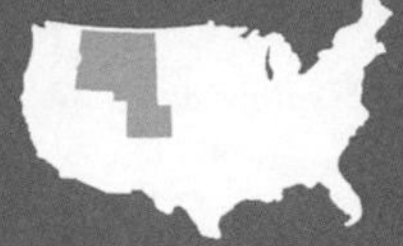

Rocky Mountains

COMBINE AMERICA'S LOVE OF CARS WITH THE MAJESTY OF THE ROCKIES' imposing purple mountains and you get a road-tripper's paradise that's second to none.

An endless network of lonely highways snakes between snow-capped peaks, scales impossible passes, follows crystal-clear rivers and penetrates rugged canyons. You'll easily drive hours through forests thick with bears, deer, elk and ospreys without passing a town – but when you do, you'll meet people as alive as the hills they inhabit. A growing flood of young adventure-seekers has brought their urban edge to the Wild West, and with them an emphasis on farm-to-fork food and microbrewed beer. They're also blazing the trails that provide new and evermore accessible options for exploring the Rockies beyond the asphalt – an essential part of any visit here.

Snowmass One of Aspen's phenomenal ski resorts
THE WORLD IN HDR / SHUTTERSTOCK ©

Rocky Mountains
400 km
200 miles
Saskatoon
Regina
SASKATCHEWAN
Medicine Hat
Cranbrook
Lethbridge
ALBERTA
Estevan
CANADA
USA
Glacier National Park
IDAHO
Sandpoint
Whitefish
Kalispell
30
Rocky Mountains
Shelby
Havre
Fort Peck Indian Reservation
Williston
Lake Sakakawea
NORTH DAKOTA
Coeur d'Alene
Bob Marshall Wilderness
Missouri River
Fort Peck Lake
Great Falls
Glendive
Dickinson
Missoula
Lewistown
Lewiston
Helena
MONTANA
Yellowstone River
Miles City
Standing Rock Indian Reservation
Anaconda
Butte
Billings
Cheyenne River Indian Reservation
Bozeman
Livingston
Crow (Apsaalooke) Indian Reservation
Continental Divide
Dillon
IDAHO
Sheridan
Devil's Tower National Monument
Sawtooth National Recreation Area
29
Yellowstone National Park
Cody
Big Horn Mountains
Buffalo
Gillette
Rapid City
SOUTH DAKOTA
Stanley
Grand Teton National Park
WYOMING
Boise
Idaho Falls
Jackson
Thermopolis
Mountain Home
Craters of the Moon National Monument
Pocatello
Wind River Range
Riverton
Casper
Lander
Douglas
Twin Falls
NEBRASKA
Kemmerer
Rawlins
Brigham City
Evanston
Green River
Rock Springs
Laramie
Cheyenne
Ogden
Elko
Great Salt Lake
Fort Collins
Salt Lake City
Craig
Rocky Mountain National Park
Greeley
Provo
Boulder
UTAH
Glenwood Springs
Vail
Denver
Burlington
Grand Junction
Conifer
Ely
Aspen
Fairplay
31
Crested Butte
Colorado Springs
Montrose
Florence
Pueblo
Lamar
NEVADA
Colorado River
Cedar City
Telluride
Monte Vista
COLORADO
Glen Canyon National Recreation Area
32
Alamosa
Trinidad
Mesa Verde National Park
Durango
Las Vegas
Navajo Indian Reservation
Farmington
Taos
Grand Canyon National Park
Continental Divide
NEW MEXICO
Hualapai Reservation
ARIZONA
Hopi Reservation
Santa Fe
TEXAS
Kingman
Gallup

Yellowstone National Park, WY

DON'T MISS

Balcony House
Often sold out, the most adventurous Mesa Verde cliff dwelling features steep ladder climbs and narrow passageways to crawl through. Take the climb on Trip 32

Wolf-Watching
Get up early to see wolf packs roaming Lamar Valley. Join a biologist-led Yellowstone Institute course to see what you can spot on Trip 29

Maroon Bells
See for yourself these chiseled peaks and you'll forget all about Aspen's glamorous airs on Trip 31

Lake McDonald
Immerse yourself in these immense blue waters ringed by Glacier National Park by renting a rowboat from Glacier Park Boat Co on Trip 30

James Ranch
Dig in to farm-fresh burgers and salads at this roadside farmstand near Durango. Satisfy your hunger on Trip 32

Classic Trip

Grand Teton to Yellowstone

America's most beloved national park, Yellowstone, is conveniently paired with America's most impressive mountain range, the Tetons, in this epic two-for-one journey.

TRIP HIGHLIGHTS

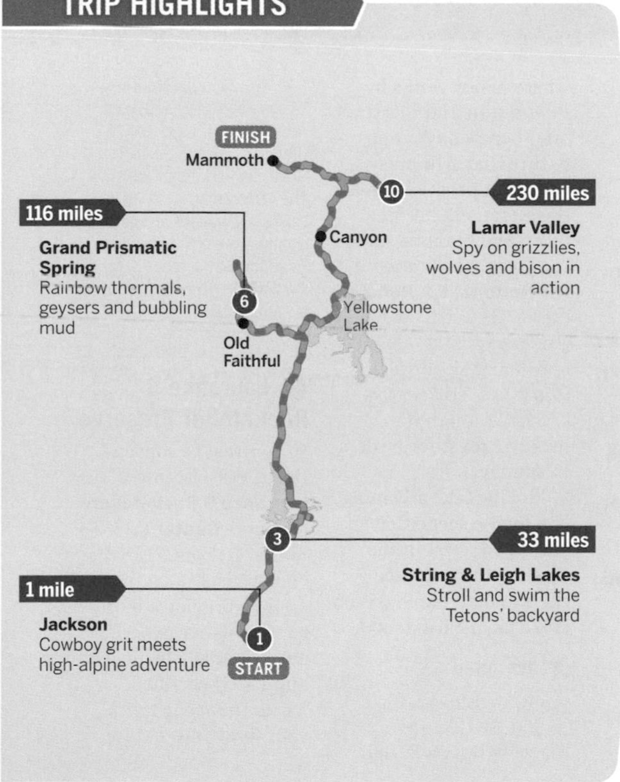

FINISH
Mammoth

230 miles
Lamar Valley
Spy on grizzlies, wolves and bison in action

116 miles
Grand Prismatic Spring
Rainbow thermals, geysers and bubbling mud

Canyon
Yellowstone Lake
Old Faithful

33 miles
String & Leigh Lakes
Stroll and swim the Tetons' backyard

1 mile
Jackson
Cowboy grit meets high-alpine adventure

START

7 DAYS
263 MILES / 423KM

GREAT FOR...

BEST TIME TO GO

June through September are usually snow-free and full of wildlife.

ESSENTIAL PHOTO

Mt Moran reflecting off the placid water of Oxbow Bend.

BEST FOR WILDLIFE

A North American wildlife safari at dawn in the valleys of Yellowstone.

Grand Teton National Park Male (bull) moose antlers can each weigh up to 50lb

Classic Trip

29 Grand Teton to Yellowstone

As if having the world's highest concentration of geysers wasn't enough, Yellowstone also excels in the landscape and wildlife department. You stand a good chance of spotting herds of bison, lumbering grizzlies and packs of wolves as you drive past the country's largest alpine lake and countless gushing waterfalls. Approach from the south and you'll be overwhelmed by the craggy peaks of the Tetons towering above the pristine Snake River valley.

TRIP HIGHLIGHT

1 Jackson

Just south of Grand Teton National Park, the rustic-haute saloon town of Jackson is much more than a park gateway. A destination on its own, this world-class skier magnet is also a summer stunner, with plentiful outdoor activities, galleries and a shopping scene that reaches beyond trinketry with cool boutiques and tailored outdoor gear.

Don't skip the **National Museum of Wildlife Art** (307-733-5771; www.wildlifeart.org; 2820 Rungius Rd; adult/child $14/6; 9am-5pm May-Oct, from 11am Sun & closed Mon Nov-Apr;), where major works by Remington and Bierstadt offer perspectives on nature that will make your skin prickle. Across the street, elk herds, bison and bighorn sheep congregate in winter at the **National Elk Refuge** (307-733-9212; www.fws.gov/refuge/national_elk_refuge; Hwy 89; sleigh ride adult/child $21/15; 10am-4pm Dec-Apr), though it's mostly a feast for birders in summer.

Finally, take advantage of a foodie scene that's among the best in the West, with renowned chefs and an emphasis on local, farm-raised food.

p384

The Drive » Rather than shoot straight north from Jackson on Hwy 26/89/191, take Hwy 22 to the Moose–Wilson Road (Hwy 390) past Teton Village through the Granite Canyon entrance to Grand Teton National Park. The narrow road is closed to trucks and trailers, and grizzly sightings are not uncommon. Turn into the Laurance S Rockefeller Preserve, 18 miles from Jackson.

2 Laurance S Rockefeller Preserve

In contrast to conventional visitor centers, the **Laurance S Rockefeller Preserve Center** (307-739-3654; Moose-Wilson Rd; 9am-5pm Jun-Sep;) aims to provide a more contemplative experience. Sparsely furnished and LEED certified, it sets the scene for your foray into nature

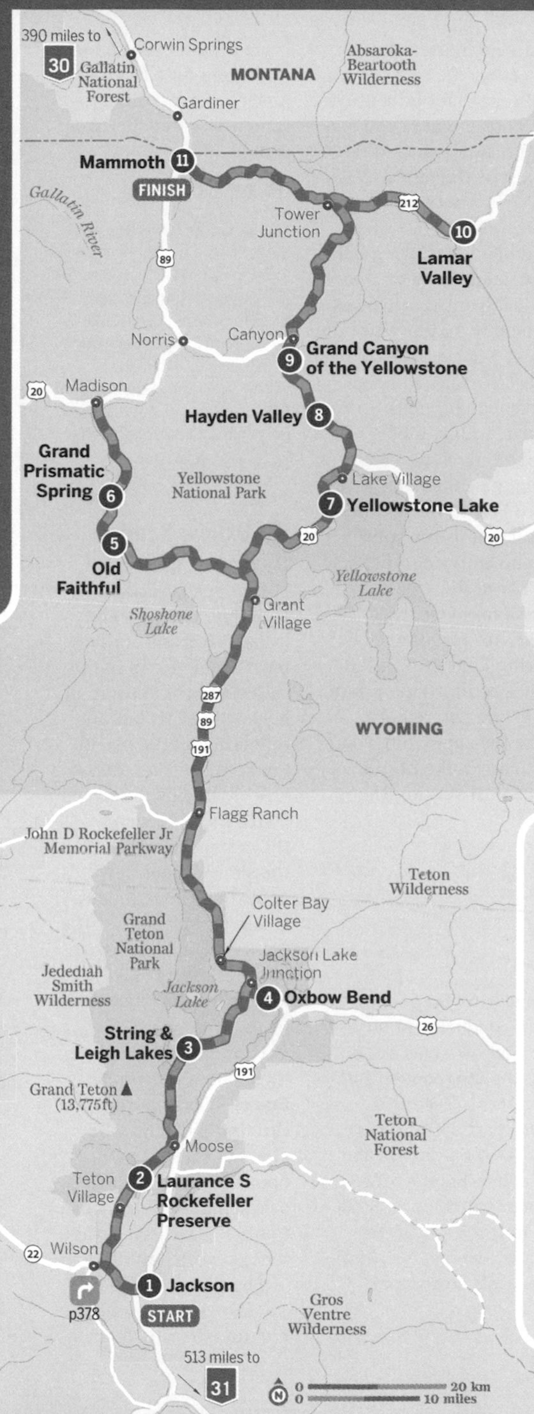

with great quotes from naturalists etched into the walls and a gorgeous conservation library with titles best enjoyed in the leather armchairs.

Oil tycoon John D Rockefeller secretly purchased this land – and much of the Snake River Valley – when fears of a 'massive government land grab' made Grand Teton National Park an unpopular idea among avaricious developers and self-interested locals. He donated it all to the park in the 1930s, save for this ranch which his son handed over in 1990.

From here, you might take an easy stroll to **Phelps Lake**. Any part of the 7-mile loop is spectacular, but a 30ft plunge off Jumping Rock at the far end of the lake is thrilling.

LINK YOUR TRIP

30 Going-to-the-Sun Road

From Mammoth, take Hwy 89 north to I-90, then Hwy 93 north at Missoula – a seven-hour trip to even more spectacular mountain grandeur.

31 Top of the Rockies

From Jackson take US 191 south to I-80 east, then I-25 south to Denver – an eight-hour trip to Colorado high country.

The Drive ›› The road ends in 4 miles at Teton Park Rd. Ultimately you want to go left, but first turn right for the Craig Thomas Discovery & Visitors Center before backtracking. In 16 miles, turn left for Leigh and String Lake trailheads as well as the scenic one-way loop along Jenny Lake that will return you back south a short distance.

TRIP HIGHLIGHT

❸ String & Leigh Lakes

In **Grand Teton** (☎307-739-3300; www.nps.gov/grte; Teton Park Rd, Grand Teton National Park; per vehicle $30) the drive-by views are so dramatic it's hard to keep your eyes on the road. Each turnout affords a better photo op than the last – no matter which direction you're going in.

Prepare for adventure in Moose, where you can rent a canoe or paddleboard at **Dornan's** (☎307-733-2415; www.dornans.com; Moose Village; ⏰9am-6pm) and head for **String Lake and Leigh Lake** trailhead. This adventure involves a mellow paddle through rocky String Lake to a short portage to Leigh Lake which opens up considerably. Float, swim and enjoy views of the craggy peaks from your own beach. Better yet, reserve a waterfront backcountry campsite.

These shores also make for a great, gentle hike, apt for all ages. String Lake trail is 3.3 miles round-trip on foot.

While you're here, take the short loop road to Jenny Lake Lodge (p385). If staying the night is out of your budget, stop in for a casual lunch or formal dinner – a romantic, candlelit, five-course affair.

 p384

The Drive ›› Take a left out of the Jenny or String Lake areas to Teton Park Rd. As you head 13 miles north the landscape turns from sagebrush to pine forest, climbing near densely forested Signal Mt Road (a worthy side trip). At the Jackson Lake Junction go right to Oxbow Bend, almost immediately after the turn on your right.

❹ Oxbow Bend

Located 1.2 miles east of the Jackson Lake Junction, **Oxbow Bend** (N Park Rd) is one of the most scenic views in the valley, with the stunning backdrop of Mt Moran reflecting off the placid Snake River. The oxbow was created as the river's faster water eroded the outer bank while the slower inner flow deposited the sediment. During many sunsets the banks will be lined with photographers looking for the next masterpiece by nature.

Families enjoy rafting the mellow section of **Snake River** that runs through the park, with views of sharp snowbound peaks and the occasional wading moose. Contact a Jackson outfitter to book a half-day trip.

These wet lowlands are also prime wildlife habitat, so bring binocu-

DETOUR: WILSON, WY

Start: ❶ Jackson

Big barns and the open range make this outpost 13 miles from Jackson feel more like Marlboro country – even though the median home price averages a cool three million dollars. Don't miss the **Stagecoach Bar** (☎307-733-4407; www.stagecoachbar.net; 5755 W Hwy 22, Wilson; ⏰11am-2am; 📶), where fun bands have ranch hands mingling with rhinestone cowgirls, hippies and hikers. Thursday is disco night and on Sundays the popular house country band croons until 10pm. Local institution, **Nora's Fish Creek Inn** (☎307-733-8288; 5600 W Hwy 22, Wilson; mains $7-35; ⏰6am-2pm, 5-9:30pm) dishes up heaping country breakfasts, fresh trout and homemade cobbler.

lars. Early morning and dusk are ideal for spotting moose, elk, sandhill cranes, ospreys, bald eagles, trumpeter swans and other birds.

The Drive » From Oxbow Bend, backtrack toward Jackson Lake Lodge before continuing north 65 beautiful but slow miles on Hwy 89/191/287 past Jackson Lake to the Yellowstone. After entering Yellowstone National Park, the straight road climbs to the Continental Divide (7988ft). At West Thumb junction, continue straight. This will take you over Craig Pass (8262ft) toward Old Faithful.

5 Old Faithful

Yellowstone National Park (☎307-344-7381; www.nps.gov/yell; Grand Loop Rd, Mammoth, Yellowstone National Park; $30; north entrance year-round, south entrance May-Oct), America's first – and arguably its most diverse – national park, covers an astounding 3472 sq miles. You could spend a lifetime here and not see it all.

Make a quick stop at **Grant Village Visitor Center** (☎307-242-2650; Grant Village; 8am-7pm late May-late Sep;) to put the 1988 fires that burned one-third of the park into perspective, before heading west on the loop road to the **Old Faithful Visitor Center** (☎307-545-2751; Old Faithful; 8am-8pm Jun-Sep, hours vary spring & fall, 9am-5pm Dec-Mar;), which demystifies geyser plumbing and has predicted times for famous eruptors.

Spouting some 8000 gallons of water over 180ft high, **Old Faithful** (Upper Geyser Basin) pleases the crowds roughly every 90 minutes. If you just missed a show, fill the wait with a 1.1 mile walk to **Observation Hill** for an overview of the entire basin. Loop back via **Solitary Geyser** (who's sudden bursts come every four to eight minutes) before rejoining the boardwalk.

Another prime viewing spot is the porch of historic **Old Faithful Inn** (p385). Even if you're not staying over, treat yourself to a cocktail in the cavernous log lobby.

p385

The Drive » From Old Faithful overpass it's only 16 miles to Madison Junction, but these are action-packed. If driving out and back (to loop back to Yellowstone Lake), you might consider taking all the easterly right-hand turnouts first, and following with the west-side turnouts while heading south the following day after camping at Madison.

TOP TIP: BEAT THE CROWDS

To avoid Yellowstone crowds, visit in May or October. Services may be limited, but the scenery is no less spectacular. Plan your movements around dawn and dusk, which increases your chances of seeing wildlife and decreases the crowds. Pitch your tent in the the wild (permit required) – less than 1% of visitors overnight in Yellowstone's backcountry.

TRIP HIGHLIGHT

6 Grand Prismatic Spring

Exploring **Geyser Country** can take the better part of a day. Unlike the wildlife, these spurting geysers, multi-hued springs and bubbling mud pots are nearly guaranteed to show up for the picture.

Leaving Madison Campground, backtrack south 2 miles and take Firehole Canyon drive on your right past rhyolite cliffs to **Firehole Falls** and swimming area.

Five miles south, a pullout offers fine views of the smoking geysers and pools of **Midway Geyser Basin** to the right, and Firehole Lake Basin to the left, with bison making it a classic Yellowstone vista.

One mile on, take a right for **Fountain Paint Pot** (Lower Geyser Basin), a huge pool of plopping goop and assorted geysers. Try to stop at Midway Geyser Basin with breathtaking

YUN GAO / 500PX ©

PHILLIP RUBINO / SHUTTERSTOCK ©

LOREN BELL
WRITER

Watching the bubbling mud pits is one my first childhood memories. That early Yellowstone road trip infected me with a passion for travel and the outdoors. Every time I drive or bike these roads, I never fail to see something that surprises or amazes me.

Above: Grand Prismatic Spring, Yellowstone National Park
Left: Canoeing on Jackson Lake, Grand Teton
Right: A cinnamon bear

MARK READ / LONELY PLANET ©

rainbow-hued **Grand Prismatic Spring** (Midway Geyser Basin) – Yellowstone's most photogenic pool. If parking is full, consider driving south 1.5 miles to the Fairy Falls trailhead and hiking 1 mile in to a new overlook that gives an elevated view of Grand Prismatic Spring.

The Drive » From Grand Prismatic Spring, drive south toward Old Faithful. The road curves west to climb back over Craig Pass (8262ft) before descending to West Thumb. Go left on the shoreline road to Lake Village, approximately 45 miles away.

7 Yellowstone Lake

At 7733ft above sea level, shimmering **Yellowstone Lake** is the largest high-elevation lake in the United States. Despite there being a number of thermal features under it, however, the temperature remains bitterly cold at 41°F (5°C), and not great for swimming.

Grand Loop Rd hugs much of the western shore. Stop to picnic at Sand Point, where it's worth taking a short walk to the lagoon and black-sand beach, looking beyond to the rugged Absaroka Range.

Continue north and have a rest at the 1891 **Lake Yellowstone Hotel** (p385), the park's oldest building. Enjoy classical concerts and cocktail hour in the sprawling sunroom of

this buttercup-yellow colonial mansion – you may want to return at the day's end.

At the intersection, Hwy 14/16/20 heads east past **Fishing Bridge** (closed to fishing) toward Cody over what Theodore Roosevelt once called the '50 most beautiful miles in America,' but, for the time being, continue north to Hayden Valley.

 p385

The Drive » Drive along Yellowstone Lake to Lake Village, and 10 miles north to Hayden Valley. Bear jams are frequent here; drive slowly and stop only at turnouts.

8 Hayden Valley

Flowing from Yellowstone Lake, the **Yellowstone River** is broad and shallow as it meanders gently through the grasslands of **Hayden Valley**. This is the heart of the Yellowstone Plateau, the largest valley in the park and one of the premier wildlife-watching spots.

A former lake bed, the valley's fine silt and clay keeps shrubs and grasses thriving, attracting elk by the herd. Watch for coyotes, springtime grizzlies, and bison that turn out in the fall for the largest rut in the country. Early morning or near dusk are the best times to spot critters.

Also check out the mud pots and sulphur pits at **Mud Volcano** (near Fishing Bridge), a thermal area 6 miles north of Fishing Bridge Junction. Earthquakes in 1979 generated enough heat and gases in the mud pots to cook nearby lodgepole pines. Follow the 2.3-mile loop boardwalk to see the sights.

The Drive » The road runs for 5 miles north along the Yellowstone River to the Grand Canyon of the Yellowstone. This is another spot famous for bear jams (though the offender is usually bison). After the open valley changes to densely forested terrain, keep watch for the right-hand South Rim Drive with sublime views of the upper and lower falls.

9 Grand Canyon of the Yellowstone

Here the Yellowstone River takes a dive over the Upper Falls (109ft) and Lower Falls (308ft) before raging through

YELLOWSTONE SAFARI

The **Lamar Valley** is dubbed the 'Serengeti of North America' for its large herds of bison, elk and the occasional grizzly or coyote. It's the best place to spot wolves, particularly in spring. Wolf-watchers should ask visitor center staff for the wolf-observation sheet, which differentiates the various packs and individual members.

The central **Hayden Valley** is the other solid wildlife-watching area, where spotters crowd the pullouts around dusk. It's a good place to view large predators like wolves and grizzlies, especially in spring when thawing winter carcasses offer almost guaranteed sightings. Coyotes, elk and bison are all common. The tree line is a good place to scan for wildlife. The more you know about animals' habitats and habits, the more likely you are to catch a glimpse of them.

In general, spring and fall are the best times to view wildlife, but each season has its own highlight. Elk calves and baby bison are adorable in late spring, while bugling bull elk come out in the fall rut. Most animals withdraw to the forests to avoid midday heat, so plan your observations around dawn or dusk.

It's worth having good binoculars or even renting a spotting scope. A high-end telephoto lens will also help you capture that prize-winning grizzly shot at a grizzly-safe distance.

the 1000ft **Grand Canyon of the Yellowstone** (near Canyon Village).

Heading north on Grand Loop Road, take the right-hand turn to South Rim Drive. A steep 500ft descent, **Uncle Tom's Trail** (near Canyon Village), offers the best view of both falls. Hop in the car again to continue to **Artist Point** (South Rim Dr, Canyon). Canyon walls shaded salmon pink, chalk white, ochre and pale green make this a masterpiece. A short 1-mile trail continues here to Point Sublime, worth following just to bask in the landscape.

Returning to the Grand Loop, go north and turn right on North Rim Drive, a 2.5-mile one-way with overlooks. **Lookout Point** (near Canyon Village) offers the best views of the Lower Falls. Hike the steep 500ft trail for closer action. This is where landscape artist Thomas Moran sketched for his famous canyon painting, supposedly weeping over his comparatively poor palette.

The Drive » Heading north on the Grand Loop, the second right is the one-way North Rim Drive, which winds to Canyon Village. Take a right turn to head north here for Dunraven Pass. This section is narrow and curvy with huge drops. It descends to Tower-Roosevelt Junction, where you can head right (east) for Lamar Valley, a total of 35 miles away.

TRIP HIGHLIGHT

⑩ Lamar Valley

Take the winding road to Tower-Roosevelt (open late May to mid-October), stopping at **Washburn Hot Springs Overlook** for views of the Yellowstone Caldera. On clear days you can even see the Teton range. The road climbs Dunraven Pass (8859ft), surrounded by fir and whitebark pines.

There's a short hike to **Tower Fall** (Tower-Roosevelt) just before you get to Tower-Roosevelt Junction. The images of this dramatic drop between volcanic pinnacles helped to inspire congress to create America's first National Park.

At the Tower-Roosevelt junction, head east through **Lamar Valley** (Tower-Roosevelt) a hot spot for wolves, bears, foxes and coyotes. Watching a wolf pack stalk, surround and take down an elk in a matter of seconds is truly one of the most powerful sights in the world, though without the aid of a spotting scope you may have a hard time following the action. Along this road, Buffalo Ranch hosts **Yellowstone Forever Institute** (☎406-848-2400; www.yellowstone.org; Lamar Valley) courses, with biologist-led wildlife-watching. The wolf-watching course is particularly fascinating.

The Drive » To continue to Mammoth, turn around at Pebble Creek campground and return to Tower-Roosevelt. From here it's 18 miles to Mammoth Hot Springs, with a visitor center and full services. Turn left for parking for the upper and lower terraces of Mammoth Hot Springs.

⑪ Mammoth Hot Springs

At over 115,000 years old, **Mammoth Hot Springs** (Mammoth) is North America's oldest and most volatile, continuously active thermal area. Here the mountain is actually turning itself inside-out, depositing dissolved subterranean limestone that builds up in white sculpted ledges. There are no geysers here as the limestone substrate dissolves too readily to build up the necessary pressure.

Take the one-way loop around the **Upper Terraces** for views, but it's best to park at the **Lower Terraces** to walk the hour's-worth of boardwalks, so you can descend back to your car.

End your trip with a dip in the **Boiling River**, a hot-spring swimming hole, reached via an easy half-mile footpath from the eastern side of the road, 2.3 miles north of Mammoth. The hot springs here tumble over travertine rocks into the cool Gardner River. Though it's usually crowded, soaking here is still a treat. Leave the park via the **north entrance** and Gardiner at the Montana state line.

🛏 p385

Classic Trip

Eating & Sleeping

Jackson 1

The Bunnery Bakery & Restaurant — Cafe $

(307-733-5474; www.bunnery.com; 130 N Cache St; mains $9-14; 7am-3pm;) This Jackson mainstay serves breakfast and lunch staples as well as some creative creations – all of which should be chased down with a strawberry–cream-cheese croissant or a slice of caramel–apple-crumble pie. Order anything you can OSM-style (the Bunnery's flour made from oats, sunflower seeds and millet) for a hearty rib-sticking start to the day.

Gun Barrel — Steak $$

(307-733-3287; http://jackson.gunbarrel.com; 852 W Broadway; mains $19-36; 5:30pm-late) The line stretches out the door for Jackson's best steakhouse where the buffalo prime rib and elk chop rival the grilled bone-in rib eye for the title of 'king cut.' For a fun game, try to match the meat with the animal watching you eat it: this place was once the wildlife and taxidermy museum, and many original tenants remain.

Lotus — Fusion $$

(307-734-0882; www.theorganiclotus.com; 140 N Cache St; mains $15-26; 8am-10pm;) In a region where steak and potatoes reign supreme, Lotus pushes back with things like plantain torte, vegan burgers and giant grain-and-veg bowls. There's plenty of meat, too – this is Wyoming – but it's all organic.

Antler Inn — Hotel $$

(307-733-2535; www.townsquareinns.com/antler-inn; 43 W Pearl Ave; r $100-260, ste $220-325;) Right in the midst of the Jackson action, this sprawling complex provides clean and comfortable rooms, some with fireplaces and bathtubs. Stepping in to the cheaper 'cedar log' rooms feels like you're coming home to a cozy Wyoming cabin – mostly because you are: they were hauled here and attached to the back of the hotel.

Wort Hotel — Historic Hotel $$$

(307-733-2190; www.worthotel.com; 50 N Glenwood St; r from $450; @) A distinctly Wyoming vibe permeates this luxury historic hotel that has only gotten better with age. Knotty pine furniture and hand-crafted bedspreads compliment full-size baths and Jacuzzis while the best concierge service in Jackson helps you fill out your itinerary with outdoor adventures. Even if staying here is out of your reach, swing by the antique **Silver Dollar Bar** downstairs.

String & Leigh Lakes 2

Dornan's Pizza & Pasta Company — Pizza $

(ext 204 307-733-2415; www.dornans.com; Moose; mains $10-13, pizza $9-17; 11:30am-9pm;) If there is a more ideal place to have pizza and a beer than sitting on Dornan's rooftop deck looking across the Snake River and Menor's Ferry at the towering Tetons, we've yet to find it. The food is almost as good as the view here at one of the only independently owned restaurants in the park.

Climbers' Ranch — Cabin $

(307-733-7271; www.americanalpineclub.org/grand-teton-climbers-ranch; End Highlands Rd; dm $25; Jun-Sep) Started as a refuge for serious climbers, these rustic log cabins run by the American Alpine Club are now available to hikers who can take advantage of the spectacular in-park location. There is a bathhouse with showers and sheltered cook station with locking bins for coolers. Bring your own sleeping bag and pad (bunks are bare, but still a steal).

Gros Ventre Campground — Campground $

(Gros Ventre Rd; tent/RV sites $24/52; late Apr–mid-Oct) Sprawling but secluded, this campground complex sits near the Gros Ventre River, 11.5 miles southwest of Moose. With the tall cottonwoods for shade and a nearby river, it's fairly attractive. It tends to fill up later in the day, but is usually your best last-minute bet for camping in the park.

Jenny Lake Lodge — Lodge $$$

(307-543-3100; www.gtlc.com; Jenny Lake Rd; cabins from $500; Jun-Sep) Worn timbers, down comforters and colorful quilts imbue these elegant cabins with a cozy atmosphere. It doesn't come cheap, but the Signature Stay package includes breakfast, five-course dinner, bicycle use and guided horseback riding. Rainy days are for hunkering down at the fireplace in the main lodge with a game or book from the stacks.

Old Faithful 5

Old Faithful Lodge Cafeteria — Cafeteria $

(www.yellowstonenationalparklodges.com; Old Faithful Lodge; mains $9-15; 11am-9pm mid-May–early Oct) Providing factory-style functionality rather than fine cuisine, this good-value place churns out solid choices like bison meatloaf and trout *amandine*. It's fast, but get here early before the buffet-style food gets too stewed. The best part is the view of Old Faithful from the side windows and porch rockers.

Old Faithful Inn — Hotel $$

(307-344-7311; www.yellowstonenationalparklodges.com; Old Faithful; old house d with/without bath from $191/119, r $236-277; early May-early Oct) This historic log masterpiece of design and engineering rivals Yellowstone's natural beauty. The lobby alone is worth a visit, just to sit in front of the impossibly large rhyolite fireplace and listen to the pianist upstairs. The cheapest 'Old House' rooms provide the most atmosphere with log walls and original wash basins, but bathrooms are down the hall.

Yellowstone Lake 7

Lake Yellowstone Hotel Dining Room — American $$$

(307-344-7311; www.yellowstonenationalparklodges.com; Lake Village; mains $14-40; 6:30-10am, 11:30am-2:30pm & 5-10pm mid-May–Sep;) Save your one unwrinkled outfit (and an unwrinkled $100 bill) to feast in style at the dining room of the Lake Yellowstone Hotel. Lunch options include trout, a poached-pear salad and sandwiches. Dinner ups the ante with starters of lobster ravioli and mains of bison tenderloin, quail and rack of Montana lamb. Dinner reservations are required.

Lake Yellowstone Hotel — Hotel $$$

(866-439-7375; www.yellowstonenationalparklodges.com; cabins $157, r $245-455; mid-May–early Oct; @) Commanding the northern lake shore, this buttercup-yellow colonial behemoth harks back to a bygone era – though the rooms that cost $4 in 1895 have appreciated somewhat. The spacious main-building rooms were upgraded in 2014, with new carpet and the park's only wired internet connections (per hour $4.75). Lakeside rooms cost extra, sell out first and don't guarantee lake views.

Mammoth Hot Springs 11

Norris Campground — Campground $

(Norris; tent & RV sites $20; mid-May–Sep) Nestled in a scenic, open, lodgepole-pine forest on a sunny hill overlooking the Gibbon River and meadows, this is one of the park's nicest campgrounds. Sites are given on a first-come basis and the few loop-A riverside spots get snapped up quickly. Campfire talks are at 7:30pm and firewood is sold between 7pm and 8:30pm. Generators allowed 8am to 8pm.

Going-to-the-Sun Road

Glacier National Park is the poster child of the Rockies, and there's no easier way to penetrate deep into its heart than this cliff-climbing road – a marvel of engineering.

TRIP HIGHLIGHTS

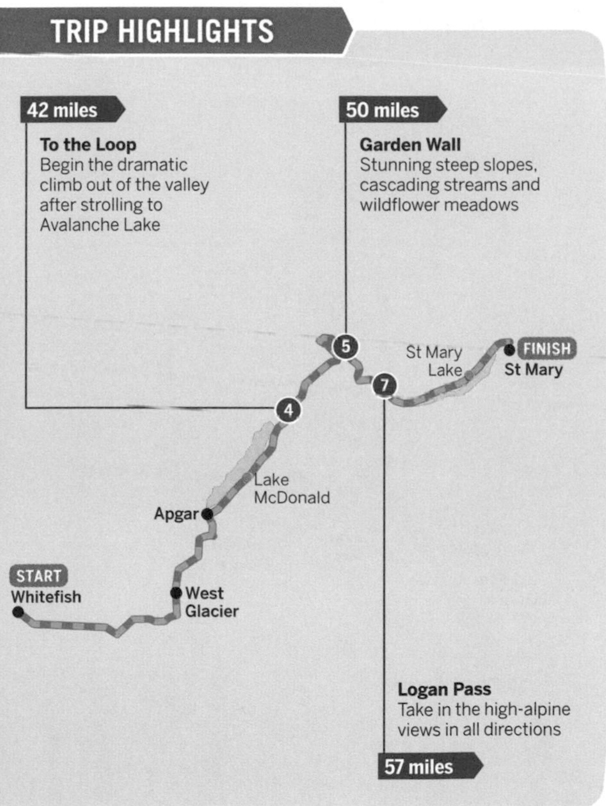

2–3 DAYS
76 MILES / 122KM

GREAT FOR...

BEST TIME TO GO

July through September once the road has been plowed.

ESSENTIAL PHOTO

The view of Bird Woman Falls from the flanks of Haystack Butte.

Spy on elk herds and roaming coyotes at Two Dog Flats.

Glacier National Park Hiker on the Highline Trail

30 Going-to-the-Sun Road

Few national parks are as magnificent and pristine as Glacier, where grizzly bears roam free in a wilderness that's both easily accessible to humans yet authentically wild. It's renowned for its historic 'parkitecture' lodges, intact pre-Columbian ecosystem and the spectacular Going-to-the-Sun Road. This 53-mile mountain route is a National Historic Landmark, purpose-built for you to drive into this wild country.

1 Whitefish

This charismatic and caffeinated New West ski town would merit a long-distance trip itself. It's 1 sq mile of rustic Western chic with welcoming shops and restaurants surrounded by the great outdoors.

Summer at **Whitefish Mountain Resort** (☎406-862-2900; www.skiwhitefish.com; Big Mountain Rd; ski/bike lift $76/38) has intrepid explorers touring the treetops via suspended canopy, mountain-biking white-knuckle trails and

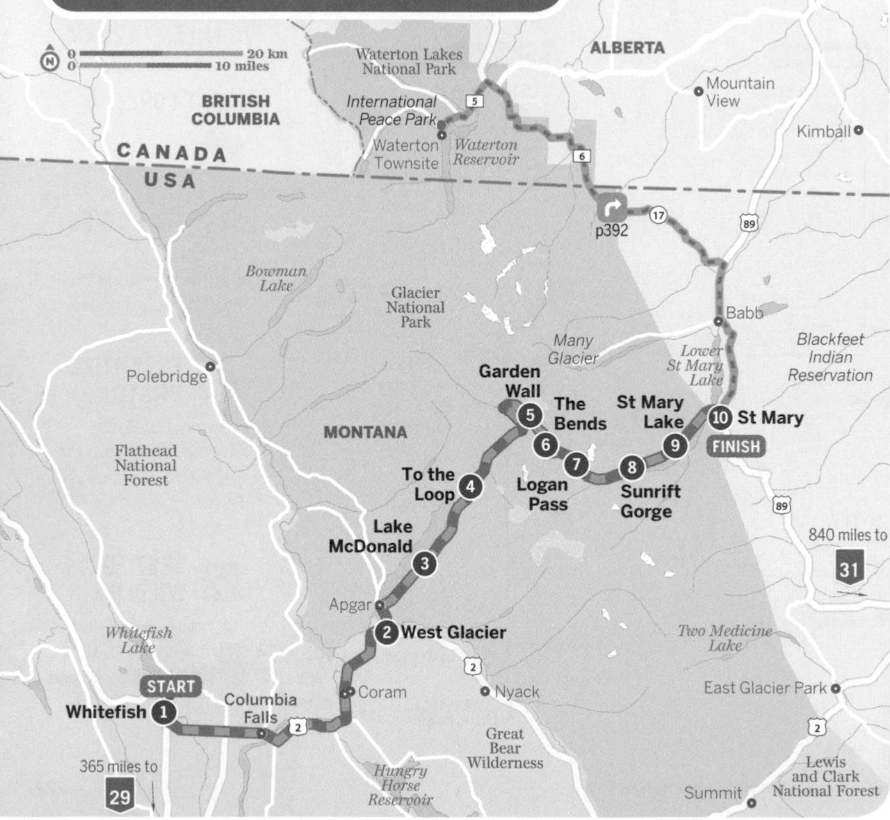

finishing with beers at the Summit House.

 p393

The Drive » From Whitefish head south on Hwy 93 and go left on MT 40 East, which runs into Hwy 2. While early travelers had to lower their wagons down the steep walls of Badrock Canyon just west of Columbia Falls, where the Flathead River slices like a knife through the Swan Range, it's now an easy 26-mile trip to West Yellowstone.

2 West Glacier

West Glacier is little more than a rail depot and an entryway to Glacier National Park. Services, including a **visitor center** (406-888-7939; west end of Going-to-the-Sun Road; 8am-6pm Jun-Aug, hours vary fall, winter, spring) and backcountry permit office, are found in the nearby hub of Apgar. If you have time, check out Apgar's original schoolhouse which dates from 1915. Nearby, the tiny 1929 **Discovery Cabin** acts as a kids' activity center.

In Apgar, you can also ditch your car and travel the rest of this route on the free **hop-on–hop-off shuttle** (www.nps.gov/glac/planyourvisit/shuttles.htm; Apgar Visitor Center to St. Mary Visitor Center; 9am-7pm July-Aug) that stops at all major trailheads and sights.

Mind-boggling amounts of snow must be plowed off **Going-to-the-Sun Road** (www.nps.gov/glac/planyourvisit/goingtothesunroad.htm; mid-Jun–late Sep), and opening times vary. If the road is closed, don't fret, it means you have an excellent opportunity to bicycle one of America's most scenic routes car-free.

p393

The Drive » Apgar is 2.5 miles north of West Glacier on the paved Going-to-the-Sun Road. Services and lodging are left at the intersection, the visitor center is straight and Going-to-the-Sun Road is right. There is a large campground just beyond.

3 Lake McDonald

The lush, verdant glacier-carved valley of Lake McDonald boasts some of the park's oldest temperate rainforest. Paddling your rowboat over the glassy surface of the largest lake in the park may be the best way to experience serenity on a superscale. Rent a boat from **Glacier Park Boat Co** (406-257-2426; www.glacierparkboats.com) at the lodge dock. On the opposite shore, burned areas are evidence of the 2003 Robert Fire.

Shrug off the crowds and sleep under the fragrant pines at **Sprague Creek**, our favorite lakeside campground. There's only tent camping allowed and with just 25 sites you'll feel like the lake belongs to you.

Reaching the eastern end of the shore, rustic **Lake McDonald Lodge** (www.glaciernationalparklodges.com; Lake McDonald) was first built in 1895, though it was replaced with Swiss-style architecture in 1913. Enter via the back door, which faces the lake to welcome the guests who historically arrived by boat.

p393

The Drive » Rimmed by pines, this 11-mile section skirts Lake McDonald's eastern shore, with views of Stanton Mountain beyond the northern shore. Both Sprague Creek and Lake McDonald Lodge are to the left. Note: vehicles over 21ft (6.4m) long, 8ft (2.4m) wide, 10ft (3m) tall are not permitted on Going-to-the-Sun Road beyond Avalanche Creek at the north end of Lake McDonald.

TRIP HIGHLIGHT

4 To the Loop

The road runs parallel to blue-green McDonald Creek and **McDonald Falls**, a seemingly endless

LINK YOUR TRIP

29 Grand Teton to Yellowstone

From Whitefish, it's 400 miles to Yellowstone via Hwy 93 to I-90 before cutting south through Paradise Valley on Hwy 89 to Mammoth.

31 Top of the Rockies

For a Rocky Mountain epic, head south through Yellowstone cutting over to Lander, WY, and on to Denver, CO.

cascade gushing through rock chasms along the longest river in the park.

Though it's often crowded, make the stop to appreciate the old-growth cedars and hemlocks – the easternmost outpost of this decidedly Pacific Northwest forest type – of **Avalanche Creek** (north of Lake McDonald) and consider hiking the pleasant and popular trail to snow-fed Avalanche Lake for superior views for little effort.

The 192ft **West Tunnel** took two years to drill in 1926. An interior sidewalk accesses the view of Heaven's Peak through observation windows.

The sharp hairpin turn known as **the Loop** is an elegant engineering solution to one *very* vertical climb. Instead of making a proposed 15 switchbacks to Logan Pass, this routing allowed a more subtle line that would be easier to plow. The road has a maximum slope of 6%, the grade at which 1920s automobiles could climb without downshifting to second gear.

The Drive » At the Loop, the road breaks from McDonald Creek to angle sharply toward the Garden Wall, a 9000ft spine of the Continental Divide, 14 miles beyond McDonald Falls. In early summer, there may be standing water on the road from the Weeping Wall.

TRIP HIGHLIGHT

5 Garden Wall

Powerful glaciers carved this dramatic arête running parallel to Going-to-the-Sun Road millions of years ago. The steep western slopes of Garden Wall feature lush wildflower meadows traversed by the Highline Trail.

Located 610ft below the Garden Wall, the **Weeping Wall** (Going-to-the-Sun Road) creates seasonal waterfalls, formed when drilling during road construction unleashed a series of mountain springs. Water falls over the lip of a 30ft artificial cliff and frequently gives westbound car passengers a good soaking in early summer. By early August the torrent reverts to its more gentle namesake: weeping.

For a more natural waterfall, look across the valley to the distant **Bird Woman Falls** (Going-to-the-Sun Road), a spectacular 560ft spray emerging from a hanging valley between Mt Oberlin and Mt Cannon. This phenomenon was created when a small glacier from above the falls fed into a larger glacier along Logan Creek. The Logan glacier had significantly more mass, gouging deeper into the rocks as it flowed down Lake McDonald valley.

The Drive » Continue the ascent to Logan Pass. In alpine sections the speed limit is 25mph. Throughout this 2-mile section there is ample evidence of why Going-to-the-Sun Road is renowned as a marvel of civil engineering and use of natural materials. Highlights include Haystack Creek Culvert and Triple Arches which blend almost seamlessly with the landscape.

6 The Bends

Just beyond the Weeping Wall, **Big Bend** features magnificent views of Mt Oberlin, Heaven's Peak and Cannon Mountain amid blooming beargrass and fireweed. It's midway between The Loop and Logan Pass, and is a good spot for a break. Bighorn sheep blend well iwnto the cliffs – grab your binoculars to find them.

Just west of Logan Pass, **Oberlin Bend** sits below the cascading waterfalls of Mt Oberlin. Take the short boardwalk for breathtaking views of hanging valleys and Going-to-the-Sun Road itself. On a clear day, views extend all the way to Canada. It may also be the best spot to see the park's signature mountain goats hanging out on steep rock ledges.

The Drive » The section between The Loop and Logan Pass has views onto the Garden Wall. Stop at designated pullouts along this 3-mile stretch for both Big Bend and Oberlin Bend.

TRIP HIGHLIGHT

7 Logan Pass

The highest point of Going-to-the-Sun Road, panoramic Logan Pass (6646ft) also marks the Continental Divide. Stop at **Logan Pass Visitor Center** (☎406-888-7800; Going-to-the-Sun Rd; ⏲9am-7pm Jun-Aug, 9:30am-4pm Sep) with interesting natural-history displays

COLE STECYK / SHUTTERSTOCK ©

Logan Pass Bear grass in front of Mt Reynolds

and a browse-worthy bookstore. Take the 1.5-mile boardwalk trail behind it to the wildflower meadows of **Hidden Lake Overlook**.

Across the way, the **Highline Trail** (Logan Pass) is lauded as one of America's best hikes and is a highlight for trekkers. Cutting daringly across the famous Garden Wall, this rugged path traces mountain-goat terrain along the Continental Divide with huge vistas of glaciated valleys and jagged peaks. Though it isn't difficult (there's minimal elevation change), the trail is quite exposed. For a classic romp, turn back at Granite Park Chalet, 7.6 miles one-way.

Five early hikers' express shuttles run from Apgar to Logan Pass, leaving between 7am and 7:36am. Many people start here, hike the Highline Trail to The Loop and catch the return shuttle from there.

The Drive » Descend Going-to-the-Sun Road heading east. From here the road makes a relatively straightforward descent, passing through 408ft East Side Tunnel and Siyeh Bend switchbacks on its way to St Mary Lake. The Jackson Glacier overlook comes up on the right 4.7 miles from the pass.

8 Sunrift Gorge

Pull out near Gunsight Pass Trailhead for telescopic views of **Jackson Glacier**. It's a short walk to the overlook of the park's fifth-largest glacier. As it has melted over the years, it has actually split into two glaciers called Jackson and Blackfoot. In 1850 the park had 150 glaciers. Today there are a scant 26, and scientists predict they will completely disappear by 2030.

Just off the road and adjacent to a shuttle stop to your left, **Sunrift Gorge** (Going-to-the-Sun Road) is a narrow canyon

DETOUR: INTERNATIONAL PEACE PARK

Start: ⑩ St Mary Visitor Center

Hello, Canada! This overnight detour takes Hwy 89 north from St Mary Visitor Center to Hwy 17, which becomes Canada's Hwy 6 at Chief Mountain border crossing (open mid-may–Sep, passport for humans and papers for dogs required). Hook a left at Hwy 5 to **Waterton Lakes National Park**, Glacier's sister park in Alberta, Canada. Together these two stunners compose the Waterton Glacier International Peace Park, declared a World Heritage Site in 1995.

From the northern end, the mountains of the Waterton Glacier are arguably even more dramatic than along Going-to-the-Sun Road, and can be enjoyed from daily boat cruises, or the venerable **Prince of Wales Hotel** (☎403-859-2231; www.princeofwaleswaterton.com; Prince of Wales Rd; r from $249; ⏰May-Sep; P 📶), on a hill above the lake. Take in the majestic cross-border landscape on a free International Peace Park Hike (reserve a spot at the St Mary or Waterton Visitor Center up to 3 days in advance).

that's 80ft deep and 800ft long. The picturesque **Baring Bridge** is considered the most beautiful artificial feature on the road. Follow the short quarter-mile wooded trail here to Baring Falls.

The Drive » The road skirts north of St Mary Lake for the remainder of the drive and has a few pulloffs to let other drivers pass. Sun Point is approximately 3.5 miles beyond Jackson Glacier overlook.

⑨ St Mary Lake

Located on the park's dryer eastern side, St Mary Lake fills a deep, glacier-carved valley famous for its astounding views and ferocious winds. Its long shoreline features numerous trailheads and viewpoints.

Windy and spectacular, **Sun Point** (Going-to-the-Sun Road) is a rocky promontory overlooking the lake. Take in views of the magnificent Going-to-the-Sun Mountain (9642ft) to the north. You will also see **Wild Goose Island** (St Mary Lake), a tiny stub in the middle of St Mary Lake. Sun Point was formerly the site of some of the park's earliest and most luxurious Swiss chalets which fell into disarray during WWII when they closed. Lace up your boots if you want to take the trails linking to Baring Falls and St Mary Falls.

The Drive » Services at Rising Sun are 4 miles beyond Sun Point and St Mary Visitor Center is 6 miles further. Note: if you're traveling this route east to west, vehicles over 21ft (6.4m) long, 8ft (2.4m) wide, 10ft (3m) tall are not permitted on Going-to-the-Sun Road beyond Sun Point. Park at Sun Point and take the free park shuttle.

⑩ St Mary Visitor Center

Handy shuttle stop **Rising Sun** has a lovely backdrop, hotel, campground and services. A 1½-hour lake cruise can be combined with a 3-mile hike to St Mary Falls with Glacier Park Boat Co (p389). The amazing biological diversity found at **Two Dog Flats** is a result of the eastern prairies butting against mountains so massive they create their own weather.

The restored 1950s **St Mary Visitor Center** (⏰8am-6pm mid-Jun–mid-Aug, 8am-5pm early Jun & Sep) has classic lines that imitate mountain silhouettes. In addition to offering information, rangers present evening programs here throughout the summer. You can obtain backcountry permits here, too.

✕ 🛏 p393

Eating & Sleeping

Whitefish 1

Loula's — Cafe $

(406-862-5614; www.whitefishrestaurant.com; 300 Second St E, downstairs; mains $9-11; 7am-2pm Mon-Sun & 5-9:30pm Thu-Sun;) Downstairs in the century-old Masonic temple building, this bustling cafe has local art on the wall and culinary artists in the kitchen. The highly recommended lemon-crème-filled French toast dripping with raspberry sauce is a sinfully delicious breakfast, especially paired with the truffle eggs Benedict.

Montana Coffee Traders — Cafe $

(406-862-7667; www.coffeetraders.com; 110 Central Ave; 7am-6pm Mon-Sat, 8am-4pm Sun;) Whitefish's home-grown microroaster runs this always-busy cafe and gift shop in the center of town. The organic, fair-trade beans are roasted in an old farmhouse on Hwy 93 that you can tour (10am Fridays, with reservation).

Garden Wall — B&B $$

(406-862-3440; www.gardenwallinn.com; 504 Spokane Ave; r $155-215, ste $275;) Shoehorned into a shady spot, this elegant home is an efficiently run B&B. Guests enjoy art-deco rooms, log fires blazing in the living room on cold days, and gourmet breakfasts prepared by a chef. The suite sleeps up to four.

Downtowner Inn — Motel $$

(406-862-2535; www.downtownermotel.cc; 224 Spokane Ave; r from $130;) Cozier than the chain motels that line US 93 south of Whitefish, the cheerful Downtowner has spacious rooms, friendly staff and a morning bagel bar. (There's no longer a Jacuzzi and fitness center, though, despite the signs.)

West Glacier 2

West Glacier Restaurant — American $

(406-888-5359; 200 Going-to-the-Sun Rd; mains $6-18; 7am-10pm mid-May–Oct;) Basic diner fare in a classic if drab diner setting, but it's conveniently located close to the park's western entrance. Kids, with their parents' cash in hand, stop in for excellent ice cream.

Lake McDonald 3

Apgar Campground — Campground $

(406-888-7800; www.recreation.gov; tent & RV sites $15-20; May-Oct & Nov-late Mar) This large wooded campground is a good choice for its proximity to the conveniences of Apgar Village and West Glacier, as well as for being only a short stroll to Lake McDonald. It feels, however, far from the wilderness.

Lake McDonald Lodge — Hotel $$

(855-733-4522; www.glaciernationalparklodges.com; r $85-190, cabins $140-205, ste $329; mid-May–Sep;) A huge fireplace, Native American–themed paintings and taxidermied animal heads ensure you know you're out West. Small, old-fashioned rooms are complemented by cottages and a 1950s motel.

Sperry Chalet — Chalet $$

(888-345-2649; www.sperrychalet.com; Lake McDonald Valley; s/d incl full board $135/332; Jul–early Sep) This 17-room historic Swiss-style chalet is a good three-hour hike from the nearest road. Guests must either walk or horseback ride here via an ascending 6.5-mile trail that begins at Lake McDonald Lodge. With no lights, heat or water, staying at Sperry rates alongside a night in the African bush.

St Mary Visitor Center 10

Park Café — American $$

(406-732-9979; www.parkcafe.us; US 89; mains $12-25; 7:30am-9pm Jun-Sep) With its longtime celebrated pie maker gone, along with its previous owner, the Park no longer enjoys the vaunted reputation among locals it once did. Hearty breakfasts, burgers and fairly high-priced mains such as bratwurst and ahi tuna, not to mention homemade pies, remain.

St Mary Campground — Campground $

(406-732-7708; www.recreation.gov; St Mary Campground Rd; tent & RV sites $23; year-round) Cottonwood and aspen dot this mostly flat and exposed campground with reservable sites just west of St Mary entrance station. Showers for registered campers. There's a half-mile walking path to the St Mary Visitor Center.

Top of the Rockies

Ride the Great Divide as you climb past snow-dusted peaks, glitzy resorts, abandoned ghost towns and big-sky wilderness.

TRIP HIGHLIGHTS

242 miles
Aspen
Hollywood glitz and sublime scenery

128 miles
Vail
Colorado's iconic winter playground

Denver
START
7
5
FINISH
12
Leadville
11
Fairplay
Twin Lakes

Independence Pass
Follow hairpin turns to the top of the Rockies
195 miles

Breckenridge
Gold-nugget history and outdoor adventure
96 miles

4–5 DAYS
242 MILES / 389KM

GREAT FOR...

BEST TIME TO GO

June to October, for the sky-high drive over Independence Pass.

ESSENTIAL PHOTO

Maroon Bells, Colorado's most iconic peaks.

BEST TWO DAYS

Head from Breckenridge to Aspen to hit the highlights; Vail is optional.

Aspen Snowboarding is just one popular activity in this ski town

31 Top of the Rockies

This high-altitude adventure follows Colorado's back roads from one spectacular mountain pass to the next. Along the way you'll get a glimpse of countless jagged peaks (including the two tallest in the state, Mt Elbert and Mt Massive), rich veins of Wild West history and alpine gems like Breckenridge, Vail and Aspen. Come here to hike, bike, ski or spot wildlife – for lovers of the great outdoors, this here's paradise.

1 Denver

While Denver has its moments – see the walking tour (p414) for tips on exploring the city – it won't be long before you feel the urge to head up into those alluring snow-capped peaks west of town. But while everyone else will be leaving via the interstate, this trip will introduce you to the Rockies' prettiest back-door secret: Hwy 285.

The Drive » Kenosha Pass is 65 miles southwest of downtown Denver, on Hwy 285.

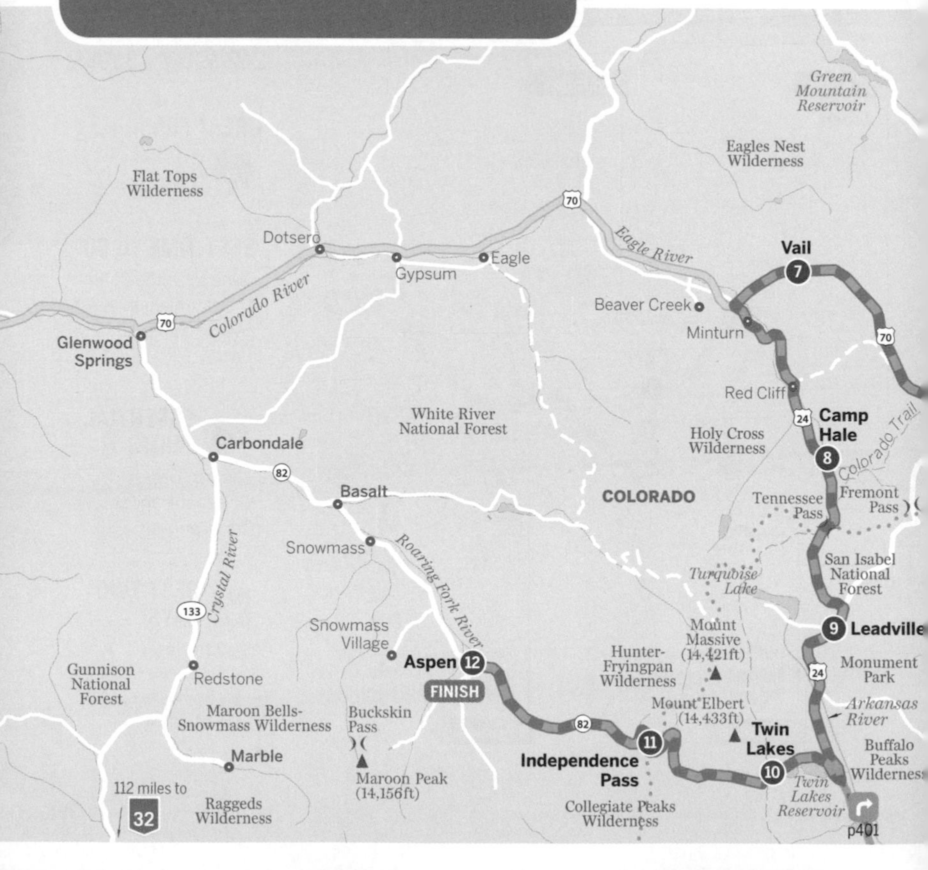

❷ Kenosha Pass

The climb out of Denver is pretty enough, but it's not until you reach Kenosha Pass (10,000ft) that you really start to feel that Rocky Mountain magic. Although there's a scenic overlook at the pass, the best views, ironically, are not at the overlook at all, but after you round the bend on the way down. Suddenly, you'll find yourself looking out over the distant peaks of the Mosquito range, rising mightily above the high-altitude prairie of the South Park basin. Inspired? You're not the first. Walt Whitman wrote about this same view on a trip West in 1879.

The Drive » Fairplay is 21 miles southwest of Kenosha Pass on Hwy 285. When you reach town, turn north onto Hwy 9 to access Main St. Much of the highway between here and Denver follows an old stagecoach road – originally

LINK YOUR TRIP

32 San Juan Skyway & the Million Dollar Highway

Follow a string of gorgeous back roads 250 miles south to the peaks and cliff houses of Telluride and Mesa Verde.

High & Low Roads to Taos

Take Hwy 285 south to enchanted New Mexico and Santa Fe (300 miles), passing Salida and the Great Sand Dunes.

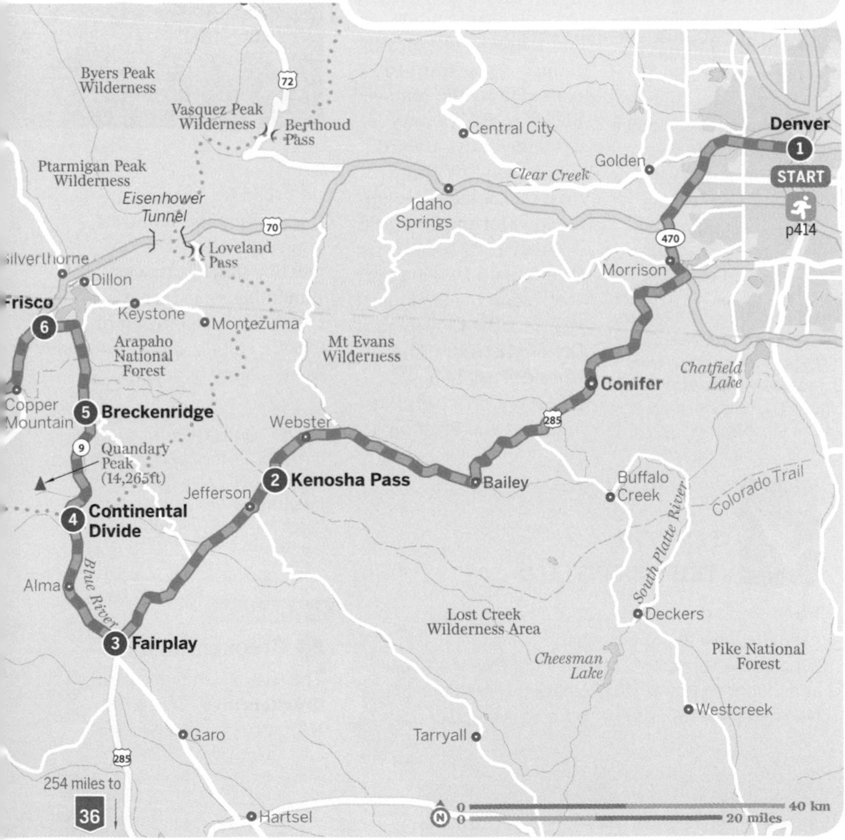

an 18-hour-long journey, broken up over two days.

3 Fairplay

Tiny Fairplay was originally a mining settlement and supply town for Leadville (pack burros used to clop back and forth over 13,000ft Mosquito Pass to the west), and you can stop here to visit **South Park City** (www.southparkcity.org; 100 4th St; adult/child 6-12yr $10/4; ⌚9am-7pm mid-May–mid-Oct, shorter hours early May & late Oct), a re-created 19th-century Colorado boomtown. Get a taste of life back in the good old, bad old days of the gold rush through the 40 restored buildings on display, which range from the general store and saloon to a dentist's office and morgue. And yes, *South Park* fans, Fairplay does bear more than a passing resemblance to the hometown of Kyle, Cartman and the boys.

The Drive » Hoosier Pass and the Continental Divide are 11 miles north of Fairplay on Hwy 9. The pass is hemmed in by Mt Lincoln (14,286ft) to the west and Mt Silverheels (13,822ft) to the east. The latter is named after a dancer who stayed behind to care for the ill during a smallpox epidemic in Alma, eventually succumbing to the disease herself.

4 Continental Divide

The stunning climb up to the Continental Divide begins just north of Fairplay. A mere 5.5-mile drive will bring you to Alma, the highest incorporated town in the United States, at an elevation of 10,578ft. It's surrounded by four '14ers' (mountains over 14,000ft), thousand-year-old bristlecone pines and scores of old mining claims. If you want to explore, follow the unpaved Buckskin Rd (County Rd 8) 6 miles west toward Kite Lake – 4WD and high clearance is recommended for the last mile.

Otherwise, keep climbing up Hwy 9 and you'll soon reach Hoosier Pass and the Continental Divide (11,539ft). The Hoosier Pass Loop (3 miles) is a relatively easy hike that starts off on a dirt road leading out of the parking lot. It allows you to get above the treeline quickly, though remember you started the day at an elevation of 5280ft, so take it easy and drink plenty of water.

ZUMA PRESS, INC. / ALAMY STOCK PHOTO ©

The Drive » Breckenridge is 11 miles north of Hoosier Pass on Hwy 9. On the way down from the pass, you'll pass the turnoff for Quandary Peak (County Rd 850), which is 7.5 miles from Breckenridge.

TOP TIP: TRIP ESSENTIALS

Much of this drive is above 9000ft: don't underestimate the altitude. Essential gear includes sunglasses, sunscreen, a hat, a windbreaker, a fleece and Ibuprofen (known to decrease the likelihood of altitude sickness). Staying hydrated is crucial.

TRIP HIGHLIGHT

5 Breckenridge

The historic downtown of **Breckenridge** (☎800-789-7669; www.breckenridge.com;

Fairplay J.A. Merriam Drug Store at South Park City

lift ticket adult/child $171/111; ⏰8:30am-4pm Nov–mid-Apr; 👪), with its down-to-earth vibe, is a refreshing change from Colorado's glitzier resorts. Its gold-nugget history survives in the numerous heritage buildings scattered around town, but make no mistake, it's the endless outdoor activities that draw the crowds. Regardless of whether it's snow or shine, the BreckConnect Gondola (free) up to the base of Peak 8 is where the fun begins. In winter, skiers can catch the T-bar up to the Imperial Express Superchair, which, at 12,840ft, is the highest chairlift in the US. In summer, kids will rock the **Epic Discovery** (☎800-985-9842; www.epicdiscovery.com; Peak 8; day pass 3-7yr/8yr & over from $47/68; ⏰Jun & Jul; 👪) adventure park, while older teens and adults can hit the hiking and **mountain-bike trails** (☎970-453-5000; www.breckenridge.com; 1 haul/day pass $18/30; ⏰9:30am-5:30pm Jul–mid-Sep). **Quandary Peak** (14,265ft) is a popular 14er to climb, but be prepared for alpine conditions; it's a 6-mile (about eight hours) round-trip hike.

✖ 🛏 p403

The Drive » Follow Hwy 9 north for 10 miles until you reach the turnoff (on your left) for Frisco's Main St.

6 Frisco

Located on the western edge of the Dillon Reservoir and ringed by mountains, tiny Frisco is a worthy stopover on the way to Vail. The main attraction is the **Historic Park and Museum** (www.townoffrisco.com; 120 Main St, cnr 2nd Ave; ⏰10am-4pm Tue-Sat, to 2pm Sun) which has a collection of restored log cabins and the town jail and chapel. Frisco is also a great place to get on two wheels and exercise your lungs – Summit County's paved **bike lanes** (www.summitbiking.org) extend around the reservoir all the way from Vail to Keystone to Breck. Get the scoop on local trails and rent a bike at **Pioneer Sports** (☎970-668-3668; www.pioneersportscolorado.com; 842 N Summit Blvd; ski rental adult/child from $18/13, bikes half-/full-day from $25/48; ⏰8am-6pm; 👪).

The Drive » From Frisco, take I-70 west 27 miles to exit 176 and follow signs to either Vail Village (the main town) or Lionshead further west. Either way, look for the public parking garages ($25 per day in winter, free in summer) – they're the only places to park, unless you're spending the night.

TRIP HIGHLIGHT

7 Vail

Vail Mountain Resort (☎970-754-8245; www.vail.com; lift ticket adult/child $189/130; ⏰9am-4pm Nov–mid-Apr; 👪) is Eagle County's legendary winter playground. This is where the movie stars and tycoons ski, and it's not unusual to see Texans in 10-gallon hats and women in mink coats zipping down the slopes.

Whether you're here for the powdery back bowls or it's your first time on a snowboard, the largest ski resort in the US rarely disappoints – so long as you're prepared for the price tag. There's plenty of action in summer too. For mountain-bike rental see **Bike Valet** (☎970-476-7770; www.bikevalet.net; 616 W Lionshead Cir; bike rental per day from $50; ⏰9am-6pm; 👪), and **Bearcat Stables** (☎970-926-1578; www.bearcatstables.com; 2701 Squaw Creek Rd, Edwards; 1/2/4hr ride $60/90/160; ⏰by reservation) for horseback riding.

Book ahead if you plan on teeing off at the **Vail Golf Club** (☎970-479-2260; www.vailrec.com; 1778 Vail Valley Dr; 9/18 holes May-Oct $60/100), and check out the **Holy Cross Ranger Office** (☎970-827-5715; www.fs.usda.gov/whiteriver; 24747 Hwy 24; ⏰9am-4pm Mon-Fri) for hiking and camping info. Families stay occupied at **Epic Discovery** (☎970-496-4910; www.epicdiscovery.com; day pass Ultimate/Little Explorer $94/54; ⏰10am-6pm Jun-Aug, Fri-Sun only Sep; 👪), which features a plethora of activities 10,000ft up at the top of Eagle Bahn Gondola (access is from Lionshead).

✕ 🛏 p403

The Drive » From Vail, take I-70 west for 4.5 miles to exit 171, and then turn onto Hwy 24 east. After you pass through the town of Minturn, the road begins to wind up along a cliff face, with impressive views of Notch Mt (13,237ft) and the Holy Cross Wilderness on your right. After 17 miles you'll reach the turnoff for Camp Hale – now no more than a grassy meadow.

8 Camp Hale

Established in 1942, **Camp Hale** (Hwy 24) was created specifically for the purpose of training the 10th Mountain Division, the US Army's only battalion on skis. At its height during WWII, there were over 1000 buildings and some 14,000 soldiers housed in the meadow here.

After the war Camp Hale was decommissioned, only to be brought back to life again in 1958, this time by the CIA. Over the next six years, CIA agents trained Tibetan freedom fighters in guerrilla warfare, with the goal of driving the communist Chinese out of Tibet.

In 1965 Camp Hale was officially dismantled, and the land returned to the US Forest Service. Many vets from the 10th Mountain Division returned to Colorado to become involved in the burgeoning ski industry, including Pete Seibert, who co-founded Vail Resort in 1962.

✕ p403

The Drive » Hwy 24 is known as the 'Top of the Rockies Scenic Byway.' On the way down from Tennessee Pass you'll be treated to a panorama of Colorado's two highest peaks – Mt Massive and Mt Elbert – stretching away to the south. All told, it's 16 miles from Camp Hale to Leadville.

9 Leadville

Originally known as Cloud City, Leadville was once Colorado's second-largest municipality. It was silver, not gold, that made the fortunes of many here; the best place to learn about the town's mineral-rich history is at the surprisingly interesting **National Mining Hall of Fame** (www.mininghalloffame.org; 120 W 9th St; adult/student $12/10; 9am-5pm, closed Mon Nov-Apr;), which can be combined with a visit to the exterior of **Matchless Mine** (719-486-1229; www.mininghalloffame.org; E 7th Rd; adult/student with tour $12/10, without tour $6/5; noon-4:45pm mid-May–Sep) in summer.

The historic downtown area makes for a pleasant stroll; check out landmarks like the **Healy House Museum** (719-486-0487; www.leadvilletwinlakes.com; 912 Harrison Ave; adult/child $6/free; 10am-4:30pm late May–Sep) and the **Tabor Opera House** (719-486-8409; www.taboroperahouse.net; 308 Harrison Ave; adult/child $8/2; 10am-5pm Mon-Sat Jun-Aug), where the likes of Houdini and Oscar Wilde once appeared.

p403

The Drive » From Leadville, take Hwy 24 south for 14 miles, following the not-yet-mighty Arkansas River until you reach the turnoff for Hwy 82. Follow Hwy 82 west for 6.5 miles until you reach Twin Lakes.

The turnoff for the Mt Elbert trailhead is actually just south of Leadville on Rte 300. The turnoff for the Interlaken trailhead is 0.6 miles after you turn onto Hwy 82, after Lost Canyon Rd.

10 Twin Lakes

A short drive from Leadville, Twin Lakes has the two largest glacial lakes in the state and is an excellent spot to spend a night. A few cabins are all that's left of Dayton, the original town, but the scenery is fabulous and there are plenty of opportunities to get out and hike or fish. On the south shore of the main lake is Interlaken, the vestiges of what was once Colorado's largest resort, built in 1889. You can get here along the Colorado and Continental Divide trails; it's about 5 miles round-trip with little elevation gain.

If you're up for something more challenging, Colorado's tallest peak, Mt Elbert (14,433ft), is also a possibility. This is a 9-mile round-trip hike with nearly 5000ft of elevation gain, so figure on spending the entire day.

p403

The Drive » It's 17 miles from Twin Lakes to the top of Independence Pass along Hwy 82. The ghost town of Independence is roughly 3 miles west of the summit.

TRIP HIGHLIGHT

11 Independence Pass

Looming at 12,095ft, Independence Pass (open June to October) is one

DETOUR: SALIDA

Start: 10 Twin Lakes

If you're on the road from November to May, chances are Independence Pass will be closed. If this is the case, don't fret – simply follow Hwy 24 and the Arkansas River south for 50 miles until you reach the town of Salida. Home to one of the largest historic downtown areas in the state, funky Salida is Colorado's white-water rafting hub and a great base from which to explore the Collegiate Peaks, whether you're on foot, bike or skis. A favorite with Coloradans, Salida is nevertheless less well-known than the big ski towns and has a much more local, small-town feel.

Alternatively, if you simply can't miss Aspen, retrace your steps from Twin Lakes back to I-70, head west to Glenwood Springs, then follow Hwy 82 east up the Roaring Fork Valley until you reach town. It's roughly 150 miles or three hours of driving.

of the more high-profile passes along the Continental Divide. The views along the narrow ribbon of road range from pretty to stunning to downright cinematic, and by the time you glimpse swatches of glacier just below the knife edge of peaks, you'll be living in your own IMAX film. A paved nature trail leaves the parking area at the top of the pass – you're above the treeline here, so dress warmly. On your way down into Aspen, don't miss the ghost town of **Independence** (www.aspenhistory.org; Hwy 82; $5; guided tours mid-Jun–Aug). Operated and preserved by the Aspen Historical Society, you can see the remains of the old livery, general store and a few cabins.

The Drive » Aspen is 20 miles west of Independence Pass on Hwy 82. Although in theory you can find metered street parking, it's simplest to park in the public garage ($15 per day) next to the Aspen Visitor Center on Rio Grande Pl.

TRIP HIGHLIGHT

⓬ Aspen

A cocktail of cowboy grit, Hollywood glam, Ivy League brains and fresh powder, Aspen is a town unlike any place else in the American West. And whatever the season, you'll find plenty here to keep you occupied.

The **Aspen Skiing Company** (800-525-6200; www.aspensnowmass.com; 4-mountain lift ticket adult/child $164/105; 9am-4pm Dec–mid-Apr;) runs the area's four resorts – Aspen, Snowmass, Buttermilk and the Highlands – while the historic red-brick downtown has some of Colorado's best restaurants, a great **art museum** (970-925-8050; www.aspenartmuseum.org; 637 E Hyman Ave; 10am-6pm Tue-Sun), plenty of galleries and boutiques, and the noteworthy **Aspen Center for Environmental Studies** (ACES; 970-925-5756; www.aspennature.org; 100 Puppy Smith St, Hallam Lake; 9am-5pm Mon-Fri;). Whether you go on a tour with ACES or venture out on your own, the backcountry here is simply spectacular: hikers and bikers have a range of trails to choose from, including several in the iconic Maroon Bells Wilderness Area.

p403

Eating & Sleeping

Breckenridge 5

Hearthstone Modern American $$$
(☎970-453-1148; www.hearthstonebreck.com; 130 S Ridge St; mains $26-45; ⏰4pm-late;) This restored 1886 Victorian churns out creative mountain fare such as blackberry elk and braised buffalo ribs with tomatillos, roasted chilies and polenta. Fresh and delicious; it's worth a splurge.

Abbett Placer Inn B&B $$
(☎970-453-6489; www.abbettplacer.com; 205 S French St; r winter/summer from $179/129; P ❄ @) This violet house has five large rooms decked out with wood furnishings, iPod docks and fluffy robes. It's very low-key. Welcoming hosts cook big breakfasts, and guests can enjoy an outdoor Jacuzzi deck and use of a common kitchenette. Check-in is from 4pm to 7pm.

Vail 7

bōl American $$
(☎970-476-5300; www.bolvail.com; 141 E Meadow Dr; mains $18-27; ⏰2pm-1am;) Half hip eatery, half space-age bowling alley, bōl is the most unusual hangout in Vail. You can go bowling in the back, but it's the eclectic menu that's the real draw: creations range from lamb lollipops and blue corn–crusted chile relleno to duck-confit gnocchi.

Sebastian Hotel Hotel $$$
(☎800-354-6908; www.thesebastianvail.com; 16 Vail Rd; r winter/summer from $800/300; P ❄) Deluxe and modern, this sophisticated hotel showcases tasteful contemporary art and an impressive list of amenities, including a ski valet and luxury spa.

Camp Hale 8

Tennessee Pass Cookhouse Modern American $$$
(☎719-486-8114; www.tennesseepass.com; Tennessee Pass; lunch $12-18, 4-course dinner $89; ⏰lunch Sat & Sun, dinner Dec–mid-Apr, dinner only Thu-Sun late Jun–Sep;) If you've never had a gourmet dinner in a yurt before, this is your chance. Diners get to hike, snowshoe or cross-country ski 1 mile to the yurt, where an elegant four-course meal featuring elk tenderloin, local rack of lamb and rainbow trout awaits. Departures are from the **Tennessee Pass Nordic Center** (☎719-486-1750; Hwy 24; ⏰8:30am-5pm Dec–mid-Apr;), at the base of Ski Cooper. Reservations only.

Leadville 9

Tennessee Pass Cafe Cafe $
(☎719-486-8101; www.tennesseepasscafe.com; 222 Harrison Ave; mains $10-16; ⏰11am-9pm;) This artsy cafe has the most inventive menu in town, with organic specials ranging from buffalo shepherd's pie and baked trout to sweet-potato gnocchi and pizza. (It's unrelated to the Tennessee Pass Cookhouse.)

Twin Lakes 10

Twin Lakes Inn Hotel $$
(☎719-486-7965; www.thetwinlakesinn.com; 6435 Hwy 82; r $109-149; ⏰late May–Sep;) This green-shuttered inn was reopened in 2013 after three years of restoration. Some rooms are on the small side and not all have private bathrooms, but you can't argue with the lakeside location. The downstairs **restaurant** (lunch mains $7 to $12, dinner mains $16 to $26) and saloon is the main hangout in Twin Lakes.

Aspen 12

Justice Snow's American $$
(☎970-429-8192; www.justicesnows.com; 328 E Hyman Ave; mains lunch $12-18, dinner $17-26; ⏰11am-2am Mon-Fri, 9am-2am Sat & Sun;) Located in the historic Wheeler Opera House, Justice Snow's is a retro-fitted old saloon that marries antique wooden furnishings with a deft modern touch. Although nominally a bar, the affordable and locally sourced menu is what keeps the locals coming back.

Hotel Aspen Hotel $$$
(☎970-925-3441; www.hotelaspen.com; 110 W Main St; r winter/summer from $400/300; P ❄) Modern decor features rust-hued walls, a wet bar and stylish furnishings. The heated pool and frothing hot tubs are a plus.

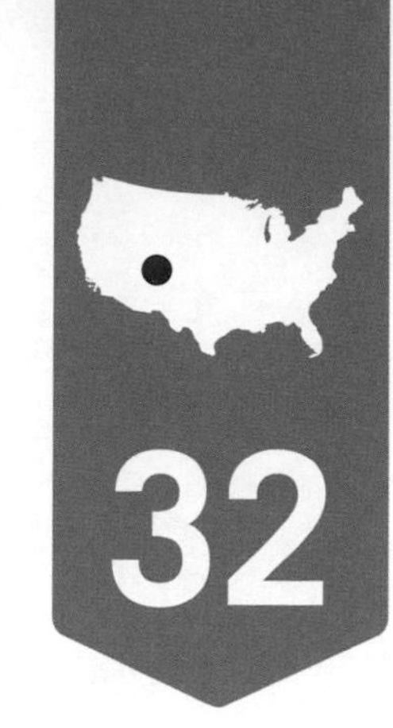

San Juan Skyway & Million Dollar Highway

Encompassing the vertiginous Million Dollar Hwy, the San Juan Skyway loops southern Colorado, traveling magnificent passes to alluring Old West towns.

TRIP HIGHLIGHTS

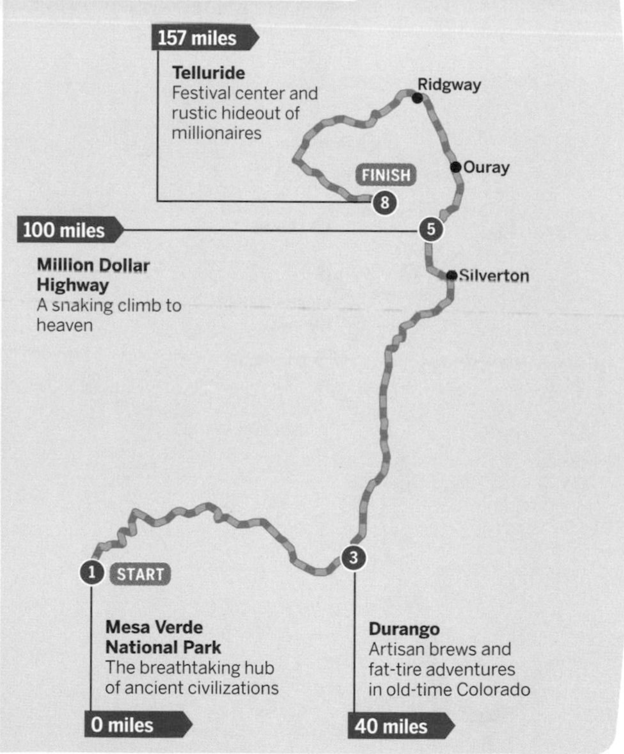

157 miles

Telluride
Festival center and rustic hideout of millionaires

Ridgway

Ouray

FINISH 8

100 miles 5

Million Dollar Highway
A snaking climb to heaven

Silverton

1 START

3

Mesa Verde National Park
The breathtaking hub of ancient civilizations

0 miles

Durango
Artisan brews and fat-tire adventures in old-time Colorado

40 miles

6–8 DAYS
157 MILES/253KM

GREAT FOR...

BEST TIME TO GO

Visit from June to October for clear roads and summer fun.

ESSENTIAL PHOTO

Snap Mesa Verde's dramatic cliff dwellings.

BEST FOR FOODIES

The farm-to-table options in Mancos and Durango.

Mesa Verde National Park Ancestral Puebloan cliff dwellings

32 San Juan Skyway & Million Dollar Highway

This is the West at its most rugged: a landscape of twisting mountain passes and ancient ruins, with burly peaks and gusty high desert plateaus, a land of unbroken spirit. Beyond the thrills of outdoor adventure and the rough charm of old plank saloons, there remains the lingering mystery of the region's earliest inhabitants whose awe-inspiring cliff dwellings make up Mesa Verde National Park.

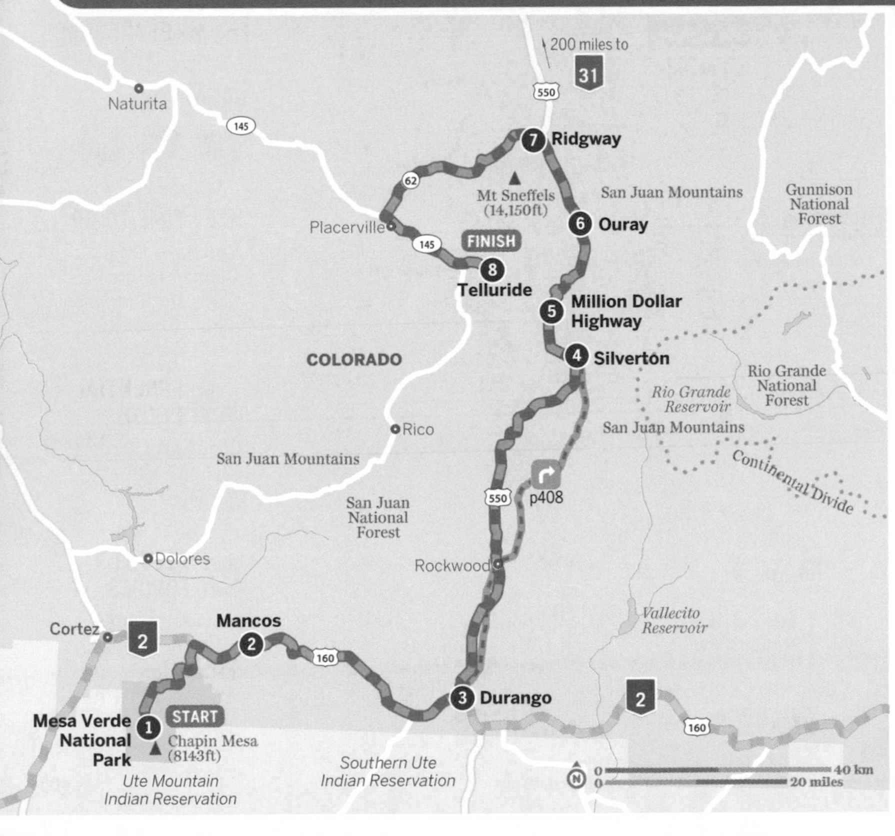

TRIP HIGHLIGHT

❶ Mesa Verde National Park

More than 700 years after Ancestral Puebloans left, the mystery behind their last known home remains. Amateur anthropologists love it; the incredible cultural heritage makes it unique among American national parks. Ancestral Puebloan sites are scattered throughout the canyons and mesas, perched on a high plateau south of Mancos, though many remain off-limits to visitors.

If you only have a few hours, stop at **Mesa Verde Visitor & Research Center** (970-529-5034; www.nps.gov/meve; 8am-7pm Jun–early Sep, to 5pm early Sep–mid-Oct, closed mid-Oct–May;) and drive around **Chapin Mesa** where you can take a ranger-led tour to **Balcony House** (www.recreation.gov; Cliff Palace Loop; 1hr guided tours $5; P), climbing to a well-preserved, hidden cliff dwelling via an exposed ladder. Purchase your ticket a day in advance at the visitor center.

If you have a day or more, buy tickets in advance for popular ranger-led tours of Cliff Palace and Balcony House. These active visits involve climbing rung ladders and scooting through ancient passages. The heat in summer is brutal – go early if you want to hike or cool off at the informative **Chapin Mesa Museum** (970-529-4475; www.nps.gov/meve; Chapin Mesa Rd; admission included with park entry; 8am-6:30pm Apr–mid-Oct, 8am-5pm mid-Oct–Apr; P) near Spruce Tree House.

The Drive » Entering Mesa Verde, go immediately left for the visitor center. Return to the main access road. It takes 45 minutes to reach the main attractions on Wetherill Mesa and the road is steep and narrow in places. Leaving the park, head east on Hwy 160 for Mancos, exit right for Main St and follow to the intersection with Grand Ave.

LINK YOUR TRIP

2 Four Corners Cruise

Join the super-sized Four Corners drive on the U-160 at Durango.

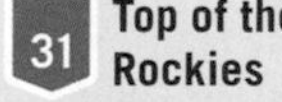

31 Top of the Rockies

Head north from Ridgway on 550 to Grand Junction. Turn right to join I-70 toward Glenwood Springs, then take 82 to Aspen.

❷ Mancos

Blink and you'll miss this hamlet embracing the offbeat, earthy and slightly strange (witness the puppets dangling through the roof of the local coffee shop). With a vibrant arts community and love for locavore food, Mancos is the perfect rest stop. You will find most points of interest in a three-block radius. These include a custom hat shop, galleries and good cooking. During the last Friday of each month, the Arts Walk fires up what locals deem 'downtown.'

The area's oddest accommodations is **Jersey Jim Lookout Tower** (970-533-7060; r $40; mid-May–mid-Oct), a watch tower standing 55ft high with panoramic views. This sought-after lodging is 14 miles north of Mancos at 9800ft. It comes with an Osborne Fire Finder and topographic map.

The Drive » Drive east on Hwy 160. Reaching Durango turn left onto Camino del Rio and right onto W 11th St in half a mile. Main Ave is your second right.

TRIP HIGHLIGHT

❸ Durango

A regional darling, Durango's style straddles its ragtime past and a cool, cutting-edge future where townie bikes, caffeine and farmers markets rule.

Outdoor enthusiasts get ready to be smitten. The **Animas River** floats right through town; float it or fly-fish it, while hundreds of mountain-bike rides range from scenic dirt roads to steep singletrack. When you've gotten your kicks, you can join the summer crowds strolling **Main Ave**, stopping at book stores, boutiques and breweries.

Leave town heading north on the **San Juan Skyway** (Hwy 550), which passes farms and stables as it starts the scenic climb toward Silverton. Bring your hunger to the family-run **James Ranch** (Animas River Valley; mains $6-13; ⌚11am-7pm Mon-Sat) just 10 miles out of Durango. The outstanding farmstand grill features the farm's own organic grass-fed beef, cheese and fresh produce market. Steak sandwiches and focaccia cheese melts with caramelized onions simply rock. Kids dig the goats. Thursday features Burgers & Bands from July to October (adult/child $20/10). A two-hour farm tour ($18) is held on Mondays and Fridays at 9:30am and Tuesdays at 4pm.

p413

The Drive » Take Main Ave heading north. Leaving Durango it becomes Hwy 550, also part of the San Juan Skyway. James Ranch is 10 miles in on the right side. A band of 14,000ft peaks becomes visible to the right and frequent pullouts offer scenic views. Before Silverton the road climbs both Coal Banks Pass (10,640ft) and Molas Pass (10,910ft).

DETOUR: NARROW GAUGE RAILROAD

Start: 3 Durango

Climb aboard the steam-driven **Durango & Silverton Narrow Gauge Railroad** (☎970-247-2733; www.durangotrain.com; 479 Main Ave; return adult/child 4-11yr from $89/55; ⌚May-Oct; 👪) for the train ride of the summer. The train, running between Durango and Silverton, has been in continuous operation for 123 years, and the scenic 45-mile journey north to Silverton, a National Historic Landmark, takes 3½ hours one-way. Most locals recommend taking it one way and returning from Silverton via bus; it's faster. It's most glorious in late September and early October when the Aspens go golden.

4 Silverton

Ringed by snowy peaks and proudly steeped in tawdry mining-town lore, Silverton would seem more at home in Alaska than the lower 48. At 9318ft the air is thin, but that discourages no one from hitting the bar stool.

Explore it all and don't shy away from the mere 500 locals – they're happy to see a fresh face. It's a two-street town, but only respectable **Greene St**, now home to restaurants and trinket shops, is paved. One block over, notorious **Blair St** was a silver-rush hub of brothels and boozing establishments, banished to the back-street where real ladies didn't stroll.

Stop at the **Silverton Museum** (☎970-387-5838; www.silvertonhistoricsociety.org; 1557 Greene St; adult/child $8/3; ⌚10am-4pm Jun-Oct; P 👪), housed in the old San Juan County Jail, to see the original cells. It tells the Silverton story from terrible mining accidents to prostitution, drinking, gambling and robbery, showing the many ways to meet a grisly end in the West.

Most visitors use Silverton as a hub for Jeep tours – sketchy mining roads climbing in all directions offer unreal views. In winter,

Silverton Mountain (970-387-5706; www.silvertonmountain.com; State Hwy 110; daily lift tickets $59, all-day guide & lift tickets $159) offers experts the best in untamed, ungroomed terrain.

 p413

The Drive » Leaving Silverton head north on Hwy 550, the Million Dollar Hwy. It starts with a gentle climb but becomes steeper. Hairpin turns slow traffic at Molas Pass to 25mph. The most hair-raising sections follow, with 15mph speed limits in places. The road lacks guardrails and drops are huge, so stay attentive. Pullouts provide relief between Mile 91 and Mile 93.

LOCAL KNOWLEDGE: COLORADO'S HAUTE ROUTE

An exceptional way to enjoy hundreds of miles of singletrack in summer or virgin powder slopes in winter, **San Juan Hut System** (970-626-3033; www.sanjuanhuts.com; per person $30) continues the European tradition of hut-to-hut adventures with five backcountry mountain huts. Bring just your food, flashlight and sleeping bag – amenities include padded bunks, propane stoves, wood stoves for heating and firewood.

Mountain-biking routes go from Durango or Telluride to Moab, winding through high alpine and desert regions. Or pick one hut as your base. There's terrain for all levels, though skiers should have knowledge of snow and avalanche conditions or go with a guide. The website has helpful tips and information on rental skis, bikes and (optional) guides based in Ridgway or Ouray.

TRIP HIGHLIGHT

5 Million Dollar Highway

The origin of the name of this 24-mile stretch between Silverton and Ouray is disputed – some say it took a million dollars a mile to build it in the 1920s; others claim the roadbed contains valuable ore.

Among America's most memorable drives, this breathtaking stretch passes old mine-head frames and larger-than-life alpine scenery. Though paved, its blind corners, tunnels and narrow turns would put the Roadrunner on edge. It's often closed in winter, when it's said to have more avalanches than the entire state of Colorado. Snowfall usually starts in October.

Leaving Silverton, the road ascends Mineral Creek Valley, passing the Longfellow mine ruins 1 mile before **Red Mountain Pass** (11,018ft), with sheer drops and hairpin turns slowing traffic to 25mph.

Descending toward Ouray, visit **Bear Creek Falls**, a large turnout with a daring viewing platform over the crashing several-hundred-foot falls. A difficult 8-mile trail here switchbacks to even greater views – not for vertigo sufferers.

Stop at the **lookout** over Ouray at Mile 92. Turn right for the lovely **Amphitheater Campground** (877-444-6777; www.recreation.gov; Hwy 550; tent sites $20; Jun-Aug).

The Drive » The Million Dollar Hwy makes a steep descent into Ouray and becomes Main St.

6 Ouray

A well-preserved mining village snug beneath imposing peaks, Ouray breeds enchantment. It's named after the legendary Ute chief who kept the peace between the white settlers and the crush of miners invading the San Juan Mountains in the early 1870s, by relinquishing the Ute tribal lands. The area is rife with hot springs. One cool cave spring, now located underneath the **Wiesbaden Hotel** (970-325-4347; www.wiesbadenhotsprings.com; 625 5th St; r $132-347;),

Above: Mesa Verde National Park
Left: Telluride
Right: Hiking in the mountains near Telluride

CHRISTIAN ASLUND / GETTY IMAGES ©

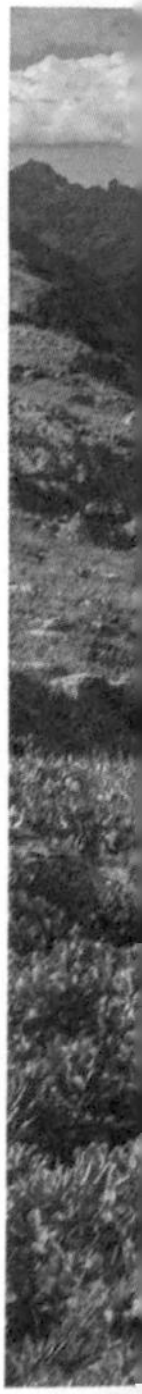

SHAWN MITCHELL PHOTO / SHUTTERSTOCK ©

WHIT RICHARDSON / GETTY IMAGES ©

was favored by Chief Ouray. Now you can soak there by the hour.

The annual **Ouray Ice Festival** (☎970-325-4288; www.ourayicefestival.com; donation for evening events; ⏲Jan; 👪) draws elite climbers for a four-day competition. But the town also lends thrills to hikers and 4WD fans. If you're skittish about driving yourself, **San Juan Scenic Jeep Tours** (☎970-325-0089; www.sanjuanjeeptours.com; 206 7th Ave; half-day adult/child $59/30; 👪) takes open-air Jeeps into the high country, offering special wildflower or ghost-town trips. It's worth hiking up to **Box Canyon Falls** (off Box Canyon Rd; adult/child $4/2; ⏲8am-8pm Jun-Aug; P 👪) from the west end of 3rd Avenue. A suspension bridge leads you into the belly of this 285ft waterfall. The surrounding area is rich in birdlife – look for the protected black swift, which nests in the rock face.

✕ 🛏 p413

The Drive » Leave Ouray heading north via Main St, which becomes Hwy 550 N. It's a flat 10-mile drive to Ridgway's only traffic light. Turn left onto Sherman St. The center of town is spread over the next half-mile.

7 Ridgway

Wide open meadows backed by snowcovered San Juans and the stellar

TELLURIDE FESTIVALS

Telluride is mountain magic in the summer when bluebird skies converge with stellar festival opportunities. For more information, see www.visittelluride.com/festivals-events.

Mountainfilm (late May) A four-day screening of high-caliber outdoor adventure and environmental films.

Telluride Bluegrass Festival (late Jun) Thousands enjoy a weekend of top-notch rollicking alfresco bluegrass going well into the night.

Telluride Film Festival (early Sep) National and international films are premiered throughout town, and the event attracts big-name stars.

Mt Sneffels, Ridgway is an inviting blip of a burg. The backdrop of John Wayne's 1969 cowboy classic *True Grit*, today it sports a sort of neo-Western charm.

Sunny rock pools at **Orvis Hot Springs** (☎970-626-5324; www.orvishotsprings.com; 1585 County Rd 3; per hour/day $18/22) make this clothing-optional hot spring hard to resist. Though it gets its fair share of exhibitionists, a variety of soaking areas (100°F to 114°F/37°C to 45°c) mean you can probably scout out the perfect quiet spot. Less appealing are the private indoor pools lacking fresh air. It's 9 miles north of Ouray, outside Ridgway.

The Drive » Leaving town heading west, Sherman St becomes CO 62. Take this easy drive 23 miles. At the crossroads go left onto CO 145 S for Telluride. Approaching town there's a traffic circle; take the second exit onto W Colorado Ave. The center of Telluride is in half a mile.

TRIP HIGHLIGHT

8 Telluride

Surrounded on three sides by mastodon peaks, exclusive Telluride was once a rough mining town. Today it's dirtbag-meets-diva – where glitterati mix with ski bums, and renowned music and film festivals create a frolicking summer atmosphere.

The very renovated center still has palpable old-time charm. Stop into the plush **New Sheridan Bar** (☎970-728-3911; www.newsheridan.com; 231 W Colorado Ave, New Sheridan Hotel; ⏰5pm-2am) to find out the story of those old bullet holes in the wall and the plucky survival of the bar itself, even as the adjoining hotel sold off chandeliers to pay the heating bills during waning mining fortunes.

Touring downtown, check out the **free box** where you can swap unwanted items; the tradition is a point of civic pride. Then take a free 15-minute **gondola** (S Oak St; ⏰7am-midnight; 🐾) ride up to the Telluride Mountain Village, where you can rent a mountain bike, dine or just bask in the panoramas.

If you are planning on attending a festival, book your tickets and lodging months in advance.

✕ 🛏 p413

Eating & Sleeping

Durango 3

Antlers on the Creek — B&B $$$

(970-259-1565; www.antlersonthecreek.com; 999 Lightner Creek Rd; r from $249; P) Tuck yourself into this peaceful creekside setting surrounded by sprawling lawns and cottonwoods and you may never want to leave. Between the spacious main house and the carriage house there are seven tasteful rooms with jetted tubs, plush bed linens and gas fireplaces. There's also a decadent three-course breakfast and hot tub in the outdoor gazebo. It's open year-round.

Silverton 4

Rum Bar — Bar $

(970-769-8551; www.silvertonrumbar.com; 1309 Greene St; mains $6-14; 11am-2am) This regional favorite delivers rum bliss in a spacious minimalist bar on Greene St. On a summer day, score a seat on the rooftop deck. Bartenders here can talk you into anything, crafting exotic cocktails with homemade syrups and award-winning rum. Note: low season hours change.

Inn of the Rockies at the Historic Alma House — B&B $$

(970-387-5336, toll-free 800-267-5336; www.innoftherockies.com; 220 E 10th St; r $129-173; P) Opened by a local named Alma in 1898, this inn has nine unique rooms furnished with Victorian antiques. The hospitality is first rate and the New Orleans–inspired breakfasts, served in a chandelier-lit dining room, merit special mention. Cheaper rates are available without breakfast. There's also a garden hot tub for soaking after a long day.

Ouray 6

Bon Ton Restaurant — French, Italian $$$

(970-325-4419; www.bontonrestaurant.com; 426 Main St; mains $16-40; 5:30-11pm Thu-Mon, brunch 9:30am-12:30pm Sat & Sun;) Bon Ton has been serving supper for a century in a beautiful room under the historic St Elmo Hotel. The French-Italian menu includes specialties like roast duck in cherry peppercorn sauce and tortellini with bacon and shallots. The champagne brunch comes recommended.

Box Canyon Lodge & Hot Springs — Lodge $$

(800-327-5080, 970-325-4981; www.boxcanyonouray.com; 45 3rd Ave; r $189;) It's not every hotel that offers geothermal heating, not to mention pineboard rooms that are spacious and fresh, and spring-fed barrel hot tubs – perfect for a romantic stargazing soak. With good hospitality that includes free apples and bottled water, it's popular, so book ahead.

Telluride 8

Chop House — Modern American $$$

(970-728-4531; www.newsheridan.com; 231 W Colorado Ave, New Sheridan Hotel; mains $26-62; 5pm-2am) With superb service and a chic decor of embroidered velvet benches, this is an easy pick for an intimate dinner. Start with a cheese plate, but from there the menu gets Western with exquisite elk shortloin and ravioli with tomato relish and local sheep-milk ricotta.

Telluride Town Park Campground — Campground $

(970-728-2173; 500 E Colorado Ave; campsite with/without vehicle space $28/17; mid-May–mid-Oct;) Right in the center of town, this convenient creekside campground has 43 campsites, along with showers, swimming and tennis. Sites are all on a first-come, first-served basis, unless it is festival time (consult ahead with festival organizers). Fancy some nightlife with your camping? Why not.

STRETCH YOUR LEGS DENVER

Start/Finish LoHi neighborhood

Distance 4 miles

Duration Three hours

The Mile High City has winsome walking paths, world-class art museums, brewpubs aplenty, urban white-water parks, Rocky Mountain–chic boutiques and eateries, and a new urban scene that is transforming this classic Western city.

Take this walk on Trip

31

LoHi

One of Denver's hottest neighborhoods, Lower Highlands – LoHi to locals – sits conveniently next to I-70, offering a bird's-eye view of the city and free parking (two-hour on the main drag, unlimited on side streets). Here, check out some hipster boutiques, laid-back brewpubs and great lunchtime restaurants, like **Tamales by La Casita** (303-477-2899; www.tamalesbylacasita.net; 3561 Tejon St; dishes $3-10; 7am-7pm Mon-Fri, from 9am Sat;), before heading into the city.

The Walk » Trundle over to the 16th St pedestrian bridge, which passes over I-70, and past John McEnroe's pile of public art known as *National Velvet*. Cross another pedestrian bridge to Commons Park.

Commons Park

Affording views of the city and a bit of fresh air, spacious and hilly **Commons Park** (www.denvergov.org/parksandrecreation; cnr 15th & Little Raven Sts;) has bike paths, benches, river access and plenty of people-watching. A lyrical curving stairway to nowhere known as **Common Ground** by artist Barbara Grygutis is an undeniable centerpiece.

The Walk » Meander through the park, then cross over the pedestrian-only Millennium Bridge, with its 200ft sloped 'mast' and laser-like cables. Take in the views of Coors Field and Union Station, before plunging into Lower Downtown (LoDo).

Union Station

Beautifully restored, the 19th-century **Union Station** (303-592-6712; www.unionstationindenver.com; 1701 Wynkoop St; P) is LoDo's crown jewel. A transportation hub, the waiting area doubles as an urban chic lounge. Swanky restaurants and bars line the building along with classy boutiques and cool coffee shops.

The Walk » Poke around Union Station – sip a cappuccino or window-shop. From here, head southeast to 16th St Mall. The town's favorite bookstore, the Tattered Cover, marks its start.

16th Street Mall

The 16th St pedestrian mall is a bustling stretch of downtown Denver with restaurants, retail shops and old-school tourist traps. There are a few gems though – **I Heart Denver** (www.iheartdenverstore.com; ⌚10am-9pm Mon-Sat, 11am-6pm Sun) for one – and the occasional street performer too.

The Walk » Cruise southeast on 16th St to the end of the pedestrian mall. From there, hop across Colfax Ave to Civic Center Park. To save time, take the free bus that runs the length of the mall.

Civic Center Park

In the shadow of the State Capitol's golden dome, **Civic Center Park** (cnr Broadway & Colfax Ave; 👪) hosts food trucks, public events and some of the most iconic sculptures in the city, including the 1920 **Bronco Buster**, whose model was arrested for cattle rustling before the statue was finished (the artist bailed him out). If you have time, head to the **State Capitol** for a free tour plus a selfie with the 13th step, which sits exactly a mile above sea level.

The Walk » Head south past the whimsical *Yearling* statue (how did that horse get onto that chair?) and the postmodern Denver Public Library before you hit the iconic Denver Art Museum.

Denver Art Museum

Truly a don't-miss museum, **DAM** (☎720-865-5000; www.denverartmuseum.org; 100 W 14th Ave; adult/child $13/free, 1st Sat of month free; ⌚10am-5pm Tue-Thu, Sat & Sun, to 8pm Fri; P 👪) is home to one of the largest American Indian art collections in the country plus it hosts a variety of special multimedia exhibits. There's a large family area, and it always has several interactive exhibits, which kids love. When you're done, grab a **B-Cycle** (www.denverbcycle.com; 1-day membership $9; ⌚5am-midnight; 👪) here and pedal back to LoHi.

The Walk » Go past the Convention Center's Big Blue Bear, continuing west down Champa St past the Denver Performing Arts Complex and its signature *Dancers* statue. From there, take the Cherry Creek Bike Path to Confluence Park and back to LoHi.

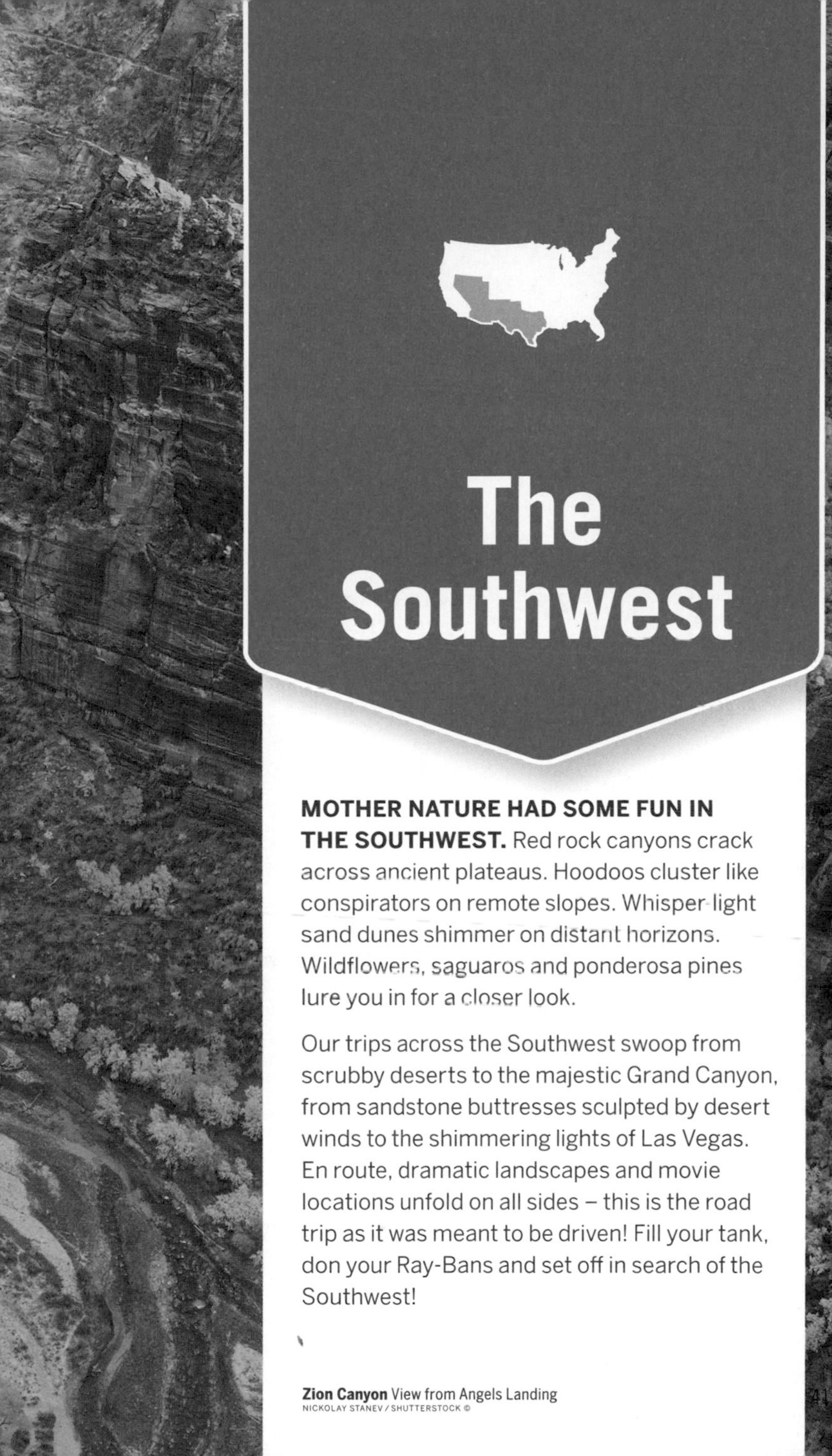

The Southwest

MOTHER NATURE HAD SOME FUN IN THE SOUTHWEST. Red rock canyons crack across ancient plateaus. Hoodoos cluster like conspirators on remote slopes. Whisper-light sand dunes shimmer on distant horizons. Wildflowers, saguaros and ponderosa pines lure you in for a closer look.

Our trips across the Southwest swoop from scrubby deserts to the majestic Grand Canyon, from sandstone buttresses sculpted by desert winds to the shimmering lights of Las Vegas. En route, dramatic landscapes and movie locations unfold on all sides – this is the road trip as it was meant to be driven! Fill your tank, don your Ray-Bans and set off in search of the Southwest!

Zion Canyon View from Angels Landing
NICKOLAY STANEV / SHUTTERSTOCK ©

The Southwest

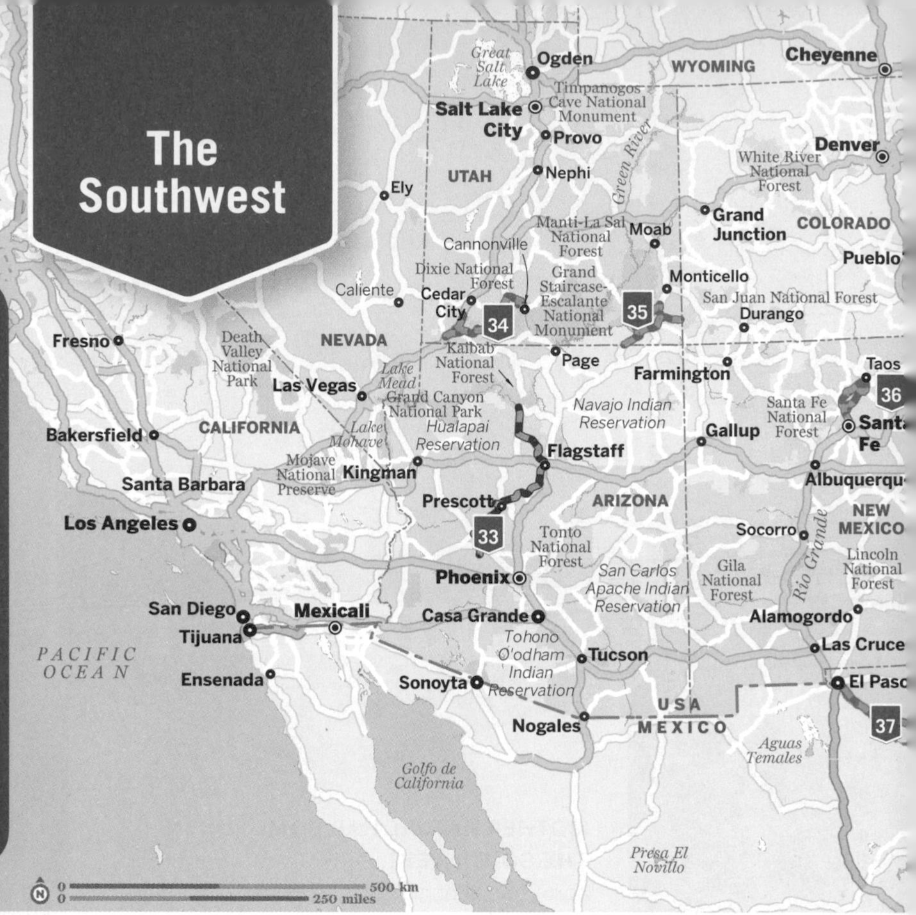

Classic Trip

33 Fantastic Canyon Voyage 4–5 Days
Cowboy up in Wickenburg, enjoy views in Jerome, then applaud the Grand Canyon. (p421)

34 Zion & Bryce National Parks 6 Days
Red rock grandeur and untouched wilderness in two stunning national parks. (p433)

35 Monument Valley & Trail of the Ancients 5 Days
Ancient and modern-day indigenous tribal cultures on display. (p443)

36 High & Low Roads to Taos 1–4 Days
Take the mountains up and the canyons down, looping between iconic destinations. (p451)

37 Big Bend Scenic Loop 5–7 Days
Minimalist art, mystery lights and star parties lead the way to Big Bend. (p461)

38 Hill Country 2–5 Days
This country drive strings together some of Texas' most welcoming towns. (p469)

San Antonio, TX The Alamo

DON'T MISS

Santuario de Chimayó

This 1816 adobe church is home to miracle healings and is the site of the largest Catholic pilgrimage in the US. Find it on Trip 36

Beer Drinking

Grab an ice-cold Shiner Bock and join the locals at Gruene Hall or on the Terlingua Porch, on Trips 37 38

Canyoneering

Rock-climb up then rappel down through narrow slot canyons on Trip 34

Airport Mesa

It's an easy scramble to a sweeping 360-degree view of Sedona's monolithic red rocks on Trip 33

Classic Trip

Fantastic Canyon Voyage

The Old West meets the New on this scenic sojourn to the Grand Canyon. Visit cowboy country and mining towns, wineries and red rocks, before the grand finale at the Big Ditch.

33

TRIP HIGHLIGHTS

FINISH
Grand Canyon Village

15

235 miles
Bright Angel Trail
The descent? It's easy. The climb out? Very wheezy

132 miles
Arizona Stronghold
Get cozy at this welcoming wine-tasting room

Flagstaff

6 9 3

113 miles
Jerome
This cliff-hugging former mine town now peddles good wine, food and art

Congress
Yarnell
Wickenburg
START

Prescott
Drink like Wyatt Earp on Whiskey Row
90 miles

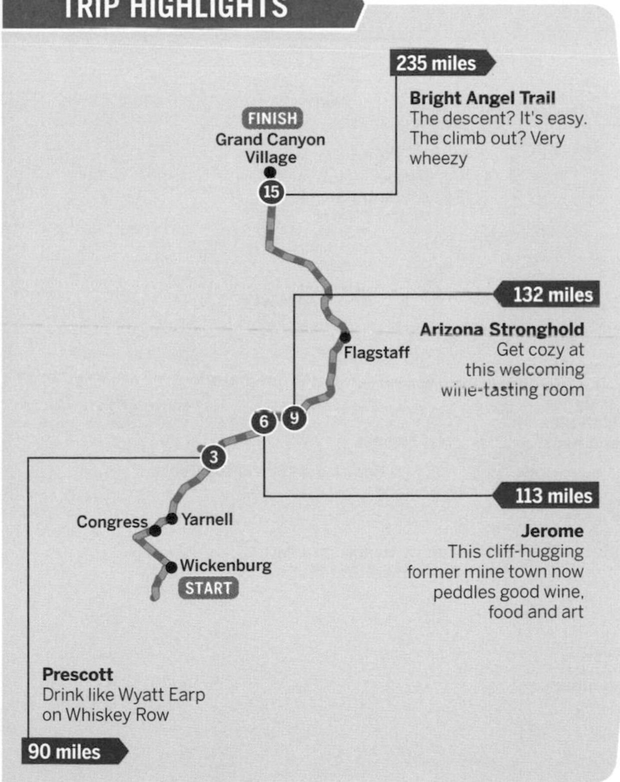

4–5 DAYS
235 MILES/378KM

GREAT FOR…

BEST TIME TO GO

Visit in fall and spring, to beat the heat and summer crowds.

ESSENTIAL PHOTO

The Grand Canyon from Mather Point.

BEST FOR HISTORY & CULTURE

Push through the swinging doors of history in Wickenburg, Prescott and Jerome.

Classic Trip

33 Fantastic Canyon Voyage

This road trip steers you through the greatest hits of Central Arizona, en route to the incomparable Grand Canyon. It's pretty, it's wild and it carries a decent whack of Arizona's rough-and-tumble history. Scenic trails wind past sandstone buttes, ponderosa pines and canyon views. Wild West adventures include horseback rides, saloon crawls and fathomless mine shafts. But this route isn't all about the past: a burgeoning wine scene and great contemporary dining add 21st-century allure.

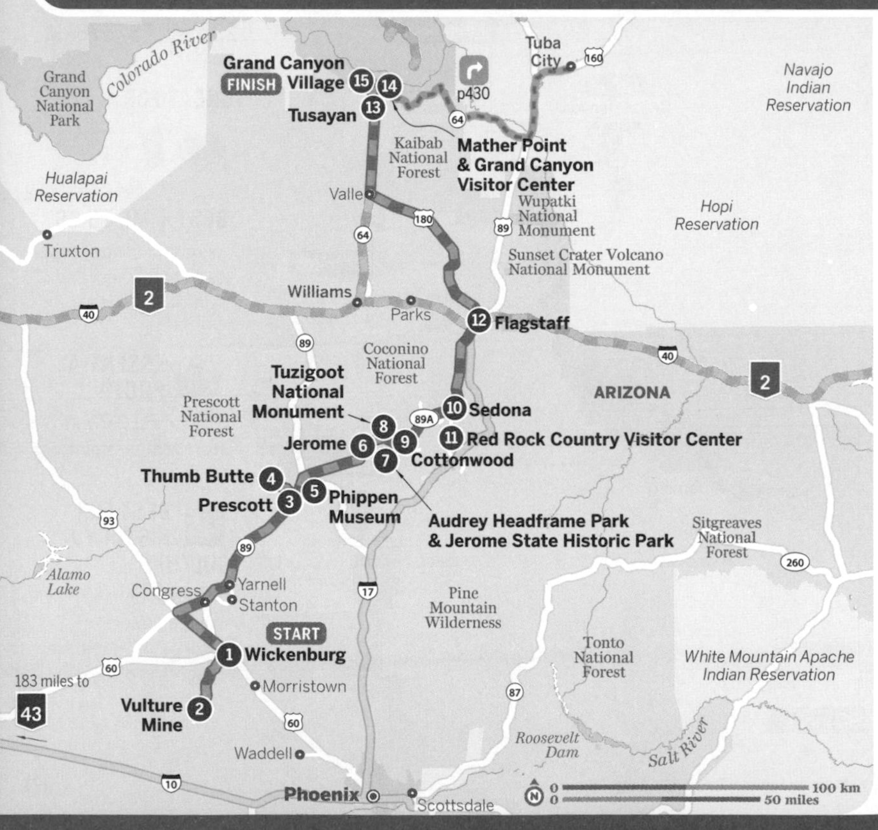

❶ Wickenburg

With its saddle shops and Old West storefronts, Wickenburg looks like it fell out of the sky – directly from the 1890s. At the ever-popular **Desert Caballeros Western Museum** (☎928-684-2272; www.westernmuseum.org; 21 N Frontier St; adult/senior/child 17yr & under $12/10/free; ⌚10am-5pm Mon-Sat, noon-4pm Sun, closed Mon Jun-Aug), the artwork celebrates the West and the lives of those that won it. The Hays *Spirit of the Cowboy* collection examines the raw materials behind the cowboy myth, showcasing rifles, ropes and saddles. The *Cowgirl Up!* exhibit and sale in March and April is a fun and impressive tribute to an eclectic array of Western women artists.

Scattered across downtown are statues of the town's founders and colorful characters. One of the latter was George Sayers, a 'bibulous reprobate' who was chained to the **Jail Tree** on Tegner St in the late 1800s. Press the button to hear his tale, then head over the road to the locally loved Nana's Sandwich Shoppe (p431) for a feed.

Wickenburg is pleasant anytime but summer, when temperatures regularly top 110°F (43°C).

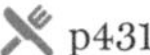

p431

The Drive » Head west on Hwy 60, turn left onto Vulture Mine Rd. Saguaros and cattle guards mark the lonely 14-mile drive to the mine.

❷ Vulture Mine Road

At the remote and dusty **Vulture Mine** (www.vultureminetours.com; 36610 N 355 Ave, off Vulture Mine Rd; donation $10; ⌚tours 8:30am Sat early May–mid-Oct, 10am Sat mid-Oct–early May), Austrian immigrant Henry Wickenburg staked his claim and made his fortune. The site holds the main shaft, where $30 million worth of gold was mined, the blacksmith shop and other decrepit old buildings, and the Hanging Tree. You can visit by guided tour on Saturday mornings between late October and May.

On the way back into town, consider spending the night at the Flying E dude ranch (p431), where guests can sign up for two-hour trail rides.

🛏 p431

The Drive » From downtown Wickenburg, pick up Hwy 93 north and drive 5 miles to 89N. Continuing north, the route leaves the Sonoran Desert and tackles the Weaver Mountains, climbing 2500ft in 4 miles. It's 59 miles to Prescott.

TRIP HIGHLIGHT

❸ Prescott

Fire raged through Whiskey Row in downtown Prescott ('press-kit') on July 14, 1900. Quick-thinking locals saved the town's most prized possession: the 24ft-long Brunswick Bar that anchored the **Palace Saloon** (☎928-541-1996; www.historicpalace.com; 120 S Montezuma St; ⌚11am-10pm Sun-Thu, to 11pm Fri & Sat). After lugging the solid oak bar onto **Courthouse Plaza**, they grabbed their drinks and continued the party. Prescott's cooperative spirit lives on, infusing the city with a welcoming vibe.

The Palace is at the centre of Prescott's **Historic Downtown** and **Whiskey Row**, where 40 drinking establishments once supplied suds and sour mash to rough-hewn cowboys, miners and wastrels.

LINK YOUR TRIP

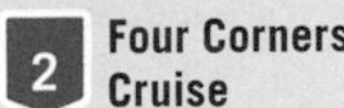

2 Four Corners Cruise

Trade natural wonders for Sin City wows by driving west on I-40 to Hwy 93 north.

43 Palm Springs & Joshua Tree Oases

From Wickenburg, take Hwy 60 west to I-10 for lush desert getaways and outdoor fun.

To learn more about Prescott, which was Arizona's first territorial capital, visit the engaging **Sharlot Hall Museum** (928-445-3122; www.sharlot.org; 415 W Gurley St; adult/child 13-17yr $9/5; 10am-5pm Mon-Sat, noon-4pm Sun May-Sep, shorter hours Oct-Apr), named for its 1928 founder, pioneer woman Sharlot Hall. The city is also home to the **World's Oldest Rodeo** (928-445-3103; www.worldsoldestrodeo.com; 840 Rodeo Dr; tickets $12-25; Jul), which dates to 1888 and is held the week before July 4.

p431

The Drive » From the County Courthouse downtown, drive west on Gurley St, which turns into Thumb Butte Rd, an overall drive of just 4 miles.

4 Thumb Butte

Prescott sits in the middle of the Prescott National Forest, a 1.2-million-acre playground bursting with scenic slopes, lakes and ponderosa pines. The **Prescott National Forest Office** (928-443-8000; www.fs.usda.gov/prescott; 344 S Cortez St; 8am-4:30pm Mon-Fri) has information about local hikes, drives, picnic areas and campgrounds. A day-use fee is required – and payable – at many area trailheads. Intra-agency passes, including the America the Beautiful pass, cover this fee.

For a short hike, head to the hard-to-miss Thumb Butte. The 1.75-mile **Thumb Butte Trail #33** is a moderate workout and offers nice views of the town and mountains. Leashed dogs are OK.

The Drive » Follow Hwy 89N out of Prescott, passing the Granite Dells rock formations on the 11-mile drive. Granite Dells Rd leads to a trail through the granite boulders on the Mile High Trail System (cityofprescott.net/services/parks/trails).

5 Phippen Museum

Strutting its stuff like a rodeo champ, the thoroughly engaging **Phippen Museum** (928-778-1385; www.phippenartmuseum.org; 4701 Hwy 89 N; adult/student/child 12yr & under $7/5/free; 10am-4pm Tue-Sat, 1-4pm Sun) ropes in visitors with an entertaining mix of special exhibits spotlighting cowboy and Western art. Named for the late George Phippen, a local self-taught artist who helped put Western art on the map, it's worth a stop to see what's brewing. As you'll discover, Western art is broader than oil paintings of weather-beaten faces under broad hat brims – although you might see some of those, as well.

The Drive » Just north, leave Hwy 89 for Hwy 89A. This 27-mile serpentine road brooks no distraction as it approaches hillside Jerome, tucked in the Mingus Mountains. If you dare, glance east for stunning glimpses of the Verde Valley.

6 Jerome

As the road snakes down steep **Cleopatra Hill**, it can be hard to tell whether the buildings are winning or losing their battle with gravity. Just take the **Sliding Jail** – it's waaaay down there at the bottom of town.

Now shabbily chic, this resurrected ghost town was known as the 'Wickedest Town in the West' during its late-1800s copper-mining heyday. In those days it teemed with brothels, saloons and opium dens. When the mines petered out in 1953, Jerome's population plummeted. Then came the '60s, when scores of hippies snapped up crumbling, atmospheric buildings for pennies, more or less restored them and injected the town with a groovy joie de vivre.

Join the party with a stroll past the galleries, indie shops, old buildings and wine-tasting rooms that are scattered up and down the hillside. Local artists sell their work at the **Jerome Artists Cooperative Gallery** (928-639-4276; www.

jeromecoop.com; 502 N Main St; ⏲10am-6pm) while burly but friendly-enough bikers gather at the **Spirit Room Bar** (☎928-634-8809; www.spiritroom.com; 166 Main St; ⏲11am-1am).

🛏 p431

The Drive » Follow Main St/ Hwy 89A out of downtown then turn left onto Douglas Rd.

7 Audrey Headframe Park & Jerome State Historic Park

Jerome's darkly humorous embrace of its industrial past is clear at this former minehead, which boasts the largest surviving timber framehead in the state. The glass platform covering the mining shaft at **Audrey Headframe Park** (www.jeromehistoricalsociety.com; 55 Douglas Rd; ⏲8am-5pm) isn't your everyday roadside attraction: it's death staring you in the face. If the cover shattered, the drop is 1910ft – a mere 650ft longer than from atop the Empire State Building.

Sufficiently disturbed? Chill out next door at the excellent **Jerome State Historic Park** (☎928-634-5381; www.azstateparks.com; 100 Douglas Rd; adult/child 7-13yr $7/4; ⏲8:30am-5pm), which explores the town's mining past. The museum is inside the 1916 mansion of eccentric mining mogul Jimmy 'Rawhide' Douglas. The folksy video is worth watching before you explore the museum.

The Drive » Hwy 89A drops to tranquil Clarkdale. At the traffic circle, take the second exit onto the Clarkdale Pkwy and into town. Follow Main St east to S Broadway then turn left onto Tuzigoot Rd, a total drive of just 7 miles.

8 Tuzigoot National Monument

Squatting atop a ridge east of Clarkdale, **Tuzigoot National Monument** (☎928-634-5564; www.nps.gov/tuzi; adult/child 15yr & under $10/free; ⏲8am-5pm; P 👪), a pueblo built by the prehistoric Sinaguan people (Spanish for 'without water'), is believed to have been inhabited from AD 1000 to 1400. At its peak as many as 225 people lived in its 110 rooms. Stop by the informative visitor center to examine tools, pottery and arrowheads, then climb a short, steep trail (not suitable for wheelchairs) for memorable views of the Verde River Valley.

The Drive » Return to S Broadway and follow it south into Old Town Cottonwood, just 3 miles south of Tuzigoot.

TRIP HIGHLIGHT

9 Cottonwood

Cottonwood has kicked up its cool quotient, particularly around the pedestrian-friendly **Old Town District**. On this low-key strip there are loads of good restaurants and wine-tasting rooms, and several interesting indie stores. The inviting tasting room **Arizona Stronghold** (☎928-639-2789; www.azstronghold.com; 1023 N Main St; wine tasting $9; ⏲noon-7pm Sun-Thu, to 9pm Fri & Sat) has welcoming staff, comfy couches, and live music on Friday nights. Enjoy a few more wine samples across the street at the chocolate-and-wine-pairing **Pillsbury Wine Company** (☎928 639-0646; www.pillsburywine.com; 1012 N Main St; wine tasting $10-12; ⏲11am-6pm Sun-Thu, to 9pm Fri & Sat). For wet-and-wild wine tasting in Cottonwood, join a Water to Wine kayak tour ($97) with **Sedona Adventure Tours** (☎877-673-3661; www.sedonaadventuretours.com; 👪) on the Verde River to **Alcantara Vineyards** (☎928-649-8463; www.alcantaravineyard.com; 3445 S Grapevine Way; wine tasting $10-15; ⏲11am-5pm).

The Drive » Follow Main St south to reconnect with Hwy 89A, then drive a further 20 miles to Sedona. At the roundabout at the junction of Hwy 89A and Hwy 179, called the Y, continue into uptown Sedona. The main visitor center sits at the junction of Hwy 89A and Forest Rd.

Classic Trip

JEFFREY MURRAY / GETTY IMAGES ©

WELTREISENDERTJ / SHUTTERSTOCK ©

WHY THIS IS A CLASSIC TRIP

HUGH MCNAUGHTAN, WRITER

Yes, the landscape's spectacular, but much of this state's charm lies in how it's translated a rough-and-ready past into a characterful and appealing present. Central Arizona is packed with former mining, railroad and lumber towns that have taken the demise of traditional industries in their stride, developing wine, food and cultural scenes that keep the lifeblood pumping. Enjoy Prescott, Jerome, Cottonwood, Flagstaff and Sedona on your way to the canyon.

Above: Sunset over Sedona
Left: The atmospheric Jerome
Right: Desert View Watchtower, Grand Canyon

DIANA GRAMLICH / SHUTTERSTOCK ©

⑩ Sedona

The stunning red rocks here have an intensely spiritual pull for many visitors. Some New Age believers even think that the sandstone formations hold 'vortices' that vibrate to the frequencies of the 'deepest earth energies.' Judge for yourself atop **Airport Mesa** (Airport Rd), the vortex most convenient to downtown. Here, a short scramble leads to a lofty view of the surrounding sandstone monoliths, which blaze a psychedelic red and orange at sunset. To get to the viewpoint, drive up Airport Rd for half a mile and look for a small parking area ($3) on the left.

Another arresting site is the **Chapel of the Holy Cross** (☎928-282-4069; www.chapeloftheholycross.com; 780 Chapel Rd; ⏰9am-5pm Dec-Feb, to 6pm Mar-Nov), a church tucked between spectacular red-rock columns 3 miles south of town. This modern Catholic chapel was built by Marguerite Brunwig Staude in the tradition of Frank Lloyd Wright.

The Drive » Follow Hwy 179 9 miles south, past Bell Rock, through the village of Oak Creek to the Red Rock Country Visitor Center.

11 Red Rock Country Visitor Center

Outdoor adventurers love the super-scenic hiking and biking trails in and around Sedona. The US Forest Service provides the helpful and free *Recreation Guide to Your National Forest*, which has brief descriptions of popular trails and a map pinpointing their routes and trailheads. Pick one up at the **Red Rock Country Visitor Center** (☎928-203-2900; www.redrockcountry.org; 8375 Hwy 179; ⏰9am-4:30pm), just south of the village of Oak Creek. Staff can guide you to less populated trails, or those best suited to your interests.

The Drive » Hwy 89A rolls north through the riparian greenery of scenic Oak Creek Canyon, where red cliffs and pine forest rear spectacularly from either side of the road. Once out of the canyon pick up I-17 north. The total drive to Flagstaff is 39 miles.

12 Flagstaff

Flagstaff's charms are myriad, from its pedestrian-friendly historic downtown to high-altitude pursuits like skiing and hiking. **Humphrey's Peak** (www.fs.usda.gov), the highest point in the state, provides an inspiring backdrop. Start at the downtown visitor center (☎928-7293-2951; www.flagstaffarizona.org; 1 E Rte 66; ⏰8am-5pm Mon-Sat, 9am-4pm Sun), which has free brochures for walking tours, including a guide to Flagstaff's haunted places.

The fascinating **Lowell Observatory** (☎main phone 928-774-3358, recorded information 928-233-3211; www.lowell.edu; 1400 W Mars Hill Rd; adult/senior/child 5-17yr $15/14/8; ⏰10am-10pm Mon-Sat, to 5pm Sun; 👪), built in 1894 and site of the first official sighting of Pluto (in 1930), sits on a hill just outside downtown. During the day you can take a guided tour, while at night, weather permitting, there's stargazing. Flagstaff's microbreweries are the stars on the one-mile **Flagstaff Ale Trail** (www.flagstaffaletrail.com). But if walking seems too pedestrian, climb aboard the **Alpine Pedaler** (☎928-213-9233; www.alpinepedaler.com; seats from $17; ⏰11am-11pm), a 14-passenger 'party on wheels' that brakes for bars and breweries.

🛏 p431

The Drive » The next morning – and mornings are best for the 90-mile trip – take Hwy 180 west and enjoy the views of the San Francisco Peaks through the treetops. When you reach Hwy 64 at the town of Valle, turn right and drive the remainder of the journey north on the broad uplands of the Coconino Plateau.

13 Tusayan

This little town, sitting 1 mile south of the Grand Canyon's South Entrance on Hwy 64, is basically a half-mile strip of canyon-focused hotels and restaurants. Stop at the **National Geographic Visitor Center & IMAX Theater** (☎928-638-2203; www.explorethecanyon.com; 450 Hwy 64; adult/child $14/11; ⏰visitor center 8am-10pm Mar-Oct, 10am-8pm Nov-Feb, theater 8:30am-8:30pm Mar-Oct, 9:30am-6:30pm Nov-Feb; 🚌Tusayan) to pre-pay the $30 per-vehicle park fee and save yourself what could be a long wait at the entrance. Always screening in the IMAX theater is the terrific 34-minute film *Grand Canyon – The Hidden Secrets*. With exhilarating river-running scenes and virtual-reality drops off canyon rims, the film plunges you into the history and geology of the canyon through the eyes of ancient American Indians, first explorer John Wesley Powell and a soaring eagle.

In summer, you can leave your car here and catch the Tusayan shuttle into the park.

The Drive » Follow Hwy 64 1 mile north to the park entrance. Admission to the national park is $30 per vehicle, $25 for motorcycles or $15 for pedestrians or bikes, and is good for seven days. All up, it's a serene 7 miles to Mather Point.

ED FREEMAN / GETTY IMAGES ©

Grand Canyon National Park Mather Point

⓮ Mather Point & Grand Canyon Visitor Center

Park at the **visitor center** (☎928-638-7888; www.nps.gov/grca; Visitor Center Plaza, Grand Canyon Village; ⏰9am-5pm; 🚌Village, 🚌Kaibab/Rim) but don't go inside. Not yet. Walk (or run) directly to **Mather Point**, the first overlook after the South Entrance. It's usually packed elbow-to-elbow with a global array of tourists, but even with the crowds there's a sense of communal wonder that keeps things civil. You'll see – the sheer immensity of the canyon just grabs you, then holds you as you scan the endless details – rugged mesas, sculpted spires, and an almost overwhelming sense of scale.

Once your sense of wonder is surfeited, head back to the main visitor center, with its theater and bookstore. On the plaza, bulletin boards and kiosks display information about ranger programs, the weather, tours and hikes. Inside is a ranger-staffed information desk and a lecture hall, where rangers offer daily talks on a variety of subjects. The theater screens a 20-minute movie, *Grand Canyon: A Journey of Wonder*, on the hour and half-hour.

From here, explore the park via park shuttle, a **bike** (928-638-3055, 928-814-8704; www.bikegrandcanyon.com; 10 S Entrance Rd, Visitor Center Plaza; 24hr rental adult/child 16yr & under $40/30, 5hr rental $30/20, wheelchair $10, s/d stroller up to 8hr $18/27; 7am-5pm Mar-Oct; Village, Kaibab/Rim), or your own four wheels. In summer, parking can be a challenge in Grand Canyon Village.

The Drive » The Village Loop Rd leads into Grand Canyon Village. Pass El Tovar, Kachina and Thunderbird Lodges on the 2-mile drive to Bright Angel Lodge. The Bright Angel Trailhead is just west of the lodge.

DETOUR: DESERT VIEW DRIVE

Start: 14 Mather Point & Grand Canyon Visitor Center

This scenic road meanders 25 miles to the East Entrance on Hwy 64, passing some of the park's finest viewpoints, picnic areas and historic sites. **Grand View Point** marks the trailhead where miner Peter Berry opened the aptly named Grand View Hotel in 1897 – it really is one of the Grand Canyon's most stunning viewpoints. Another captivating view awaits at **Moran Point** (www.nps.gov/grca; Desert View Dr;), named for the landscape painter whose work helped secure the Grand Canyon national monument status in 1908. Further along is **Tusayan Museum & Ruin** (www.nps.gov/grca; Desert View Dr; 9am-5pm), where you can walk around the remains of an excavated Puebloan village dating to 1185. At the end of the road is the **Desert View Watchtower** (www.nps.gov/grca; Desert View, East Enrance; 8am-sunset mid-May–Aug, 9am-6pm Sep–mid-Oct, 9am-5pm mid-Oct–Feb, 8am-6pm Mar–mid-May), designed by Mary Jane Colter and inspired by ancient Puebloan structures – the terrace provides panoramic views of the canyon and river. The circular staircase inside leads past Hopi murals to 360-degree views on the top floor.

TRIP HIGHLIGHT

15 Grand Canyon Village

The **Bright Angel Trail** is the most popular of the South Rim corridor trails, and its steep and scenic 8-mile descent to the Colorado River has four logical turn-around points: Mile-and-a-Half Resthouse, Three Mile Resthouse, Indian Garden and Plateau Point. Summer heat can be crippling and the climb is steep. Day hikers should turn around at one of the two resthouses (a 3- to 6-mile round-trip).

If you're more interested in history and geography than strenuous hiking, follow the easy **Rim Trail** east from here. Heading west, the Rim Trail passes every overlook on the way to **Hermits Rest** (www.nps.gov/grca; Hermit Rd; Hermits Rest), offering spectacular views. The Hermits Rest shuttle runs parallel to the trail, so hike until you're tired, then hop aboard to continue or return. But be sure to hop off for the sunset, which is best at **Hopi Point** (which draws crowds) or **Pima Point**.

p431

Eating & Sleeping

Wickenburg ❶

✕ Nana's Sandwich Shoppe — Sandwiches $

(☎928-684-5539; nanassandwichsaloon.com; 48 N Tegner St; sandwiches $7-9; ⏲7:30am-3pm Mon-Sat; 📶) Order at the counter of this busy sandwich shop in the heart of Wickenburg. The god-fearing folks here load 'em up right, from the Mustang (hot pastrami, Swiss cheese, house dressing, lettuce, tomato and red onion) to the Cowboy (roast beef, Swiss cheese and horseradish).

Vulture Mine ❷

🛏 Flying E Ranch — Ranch $$$

(☎928-684-2690; www.flyingeranch.com; 2801 W Wickenburg Way; s/d/house from $205/280/330; ⏲Nov-Apr; 📶🏊) The coolest place at this down-home working cattle ranch is the boot room, which is lined with scuffed-up cowboy boots and hats that guests can borrow on their rides. Sitting on 20,000 acres in the Hassayampa Valley, the ranch is a big hit with families and also works well for groups. Two-hour horseback rides cost $50 (or $80 for two).

Prescott ❸

✕ Iron Springs Cafe — American, Cajun $$

(☎928-443-8848; www.ironspringscafe.com; 1501 Iron Springs Rd; brunch & lunch $11-13, dinner $16-20; ⏲11am-8pm Wed-Sat, 9am-2pm Sun) Cajun and Southwestern specialties mingle delightfully inside this former train station – from the N'awlins muffuletta with sliced ham, salami and mortadella to the crab cakes and thick, spicy sausage and okra gumbo, it's all delicious, and served with real warmth. Train decor, colorful blankets and easy-bantering waitstaff enliven three tiny rooms.

🛏 Motor Lodge — Bungalow $$

(☎928-717-0157; www.themotorlodge.com; 503 S Montezuma St; r/ste/apt from $109/129/139; ❄📶) Set three blocks south of Courthouse Plaza, the 12 snazzy bungalows here form a bright and welcoming horseshoe around a central driveway. Inside, the rooms, whimsical prints and comfy bedding add to the overall appeal, making the Motor Lodge a top choice. Rooms and bathrooms, built in 1936, can be snug, but many have kitchens and porches.

Jerome ❻

🛏 Jerome Grand Hotel — Hotel $$

(☎928-634-8200; www.jeromegrandhotel.com; 200 Hill St; r/ste $225/325; ❄📶) This former hospital looks like the perfect setting for a sequel to *The Shining*. Built in 1926 for the mining community, the sturdy fortress plays up its unusual history. The halls are filled with relics of the past, from incinerator chutes to patient call lights. There's even a key-operated Otis elevator. Victorian-style rooms are more traditionally furnished.

Flagstaff ⓬

🛏 Hotel Monte Vista — Historic Hotel $$

(☎928-779-6971; www.hotelmontevista.com; 100 N San Francisco St; r/ste from $115/145; ❄📶) A huge, old-fashioned neon sign towers over this 1926 landmark hotel, hinting at what's inside: feather lampshades, vintage furniture, bold colors and eclectic decor. Rooms are named for the movie stars who stayed here, including the 'Humphrey Bogart,' with dramatic black walls, yellow ceiling and gold-satin bedding. Several resident ghosts supposedly make regular appearances.

Grand Canyon Village ⓯

🛏 El Tovar — Lodge $$$

(☎888-297-2757, ext 6380, front desk & reservations within 48hrs 928-638-2631; www.grandcanyonlodges.com; Village Loop Dr; r/ste from $187/381; ⏲year-round; P❄📶; 🚌Village) Stuffed mounts. Thick pine walls. Sturdy fireplaces. Is this the fanciest hotel on the South Rim or a backcountry hunting lodge? Despite renovations, this rambling 1905 wooden lodge hasn't lost a lick of its genteel historic patina, or its charm.

Zion & Bryce National Parks

From canyon floor to cliff-top perches, the red rock country in southwestern Utah will delight your eyes and challenge your muscles.

TRIP HIGHLIGHTS

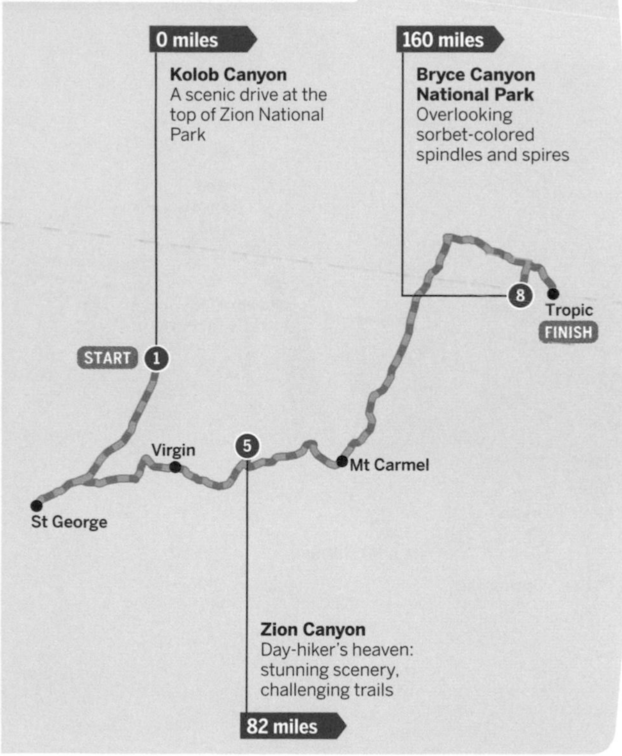

0 miles

Kolob Canyon
A scenic drive at the top of Zion National Park

160 miles

Bryce Canyon National Park
Overlooking sorbet-colored spindles and spires

START 1

Virgin

5

Mt Carmel

8

Tropic

FINISH

St George

Zion Canyon
Day-hiker's heaven: stunning scenery, challenging trails

82 miles

6 DAYS
178 MILES/286KM

GREAT FOR...

BEST TIME TO GO

In April and September you'll likely have warm weather both at low and high elevations.

ESSENTIAL PHOTO

The amphitheater's color at sunrise on Fairyland Point.

BEST FOR HIKING

Zion Canyon has easy river walks to strenuous, canyon-climbing hikes.

34 Zion & Bryce National Parks

Meet red rock country in all its heart-soaring, sculpted splendor. From the sheer wall of Zion to the pastel sentinels of hoodoos that form Bryce Canyon, these are the landscapes that no one traveling in the Southwest should miss. This trip takes in the parks' classic highlights as well as tiny Western towns and off-the-beaten-path nature sanctuaries where the screech of a hawk breaks the silence of the trail.

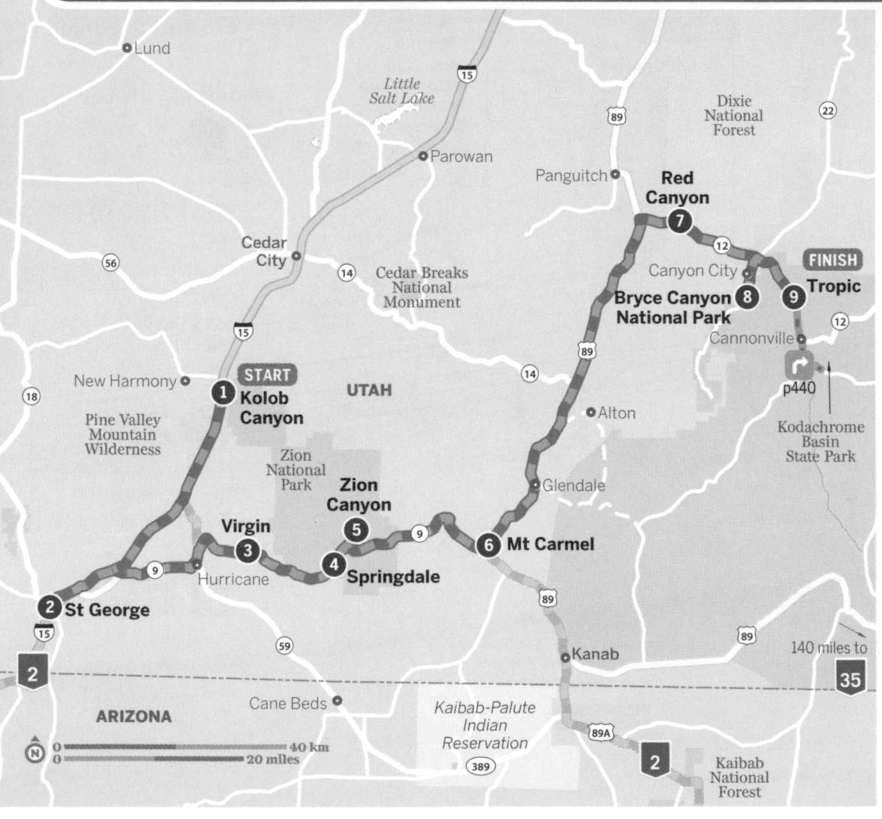

TRIP HIGHLIGHT

1 Kolob Canyon

Start your visit at the **Kolob Canyons Visitor Center** (435-586-0895; www.nps.gov/zion; Kolob Canyons Rd; 8am-7.30pm late May-Sep, to 5pm rest of year), gateway to the less-visited, higher elevation section of Zion National Park off I-15. Even in peak season you'll see relatively few cars on the scenic 5-mile **Kolob Canyons Rd**, a high-plateau route where striking canyon and rangeland views alternate. The road terminates at **Kolob Canyons Viewpoint** (6200ft); from there the **Timber Creek Overlook Trail** (1-mile round-trip) follows a 100ft ascent to a small peak with great views of the Pine Valley Mountains beyond. In early summer the trail area is covered with wildflowers. Note that the upper section of the road may be closed due to snow from November through May.

The best longer hike in this section of the park is the **Taylor Creek Trail** (5-mile round-trip), which passes pioneer ruins and crisscrosses a creek, with little elevation change.

The Drive » Distant rock formations zoom by as you cruise along at 70-plus mph on I-15. St George is 41 miles south.

LINK YOUR TRIP

2 Four Corners Cruise

Twist east from Zion on Hwy 9 then follow Hwys 89 and 89A south to the Grand Canyon North Rim.

35 Monument Valley & Trail of the Ancients

For majestic monoliths, take Hwy 9 then Hwy 89 southeast to Page then follow Hwys 98 and 160 east to Hwy 163 north.

2 St George

A spacious Mormon town with an eye-catching temple and a few pioneer buildings, St George sits about equidistant between the two halves of Zion. The **Chamber of Commerce** (435-628-1658; www.stgeorgechamber.com; 97 E St George Blvd; 9am-5pm Mon-Fri) can provide information on the historic downtown. Otherwise, use this time to stock up on food and fuel in this trip's only real city (population 77,000). Eleven miles north of town, **Snow Canyon State Park** (435-628-2255; stateparks.utah.gov; 1002 Snow Canyon Dr, Ivins; per vehicle $6; day use 6am-10pm;) is a 7400-acre sampler of southwest Utah's famous land features. Easy trails that are perfect for kids lead to tiny slot canyons, cinder cones, lava tubes and fields of undulating slickrock.

The Drive » Off the interstate, Hwy 9 leads you into canyon country. You'll pass the town of Hurricane before sweeping curves give way to tighter turns (and slower traffic). Virgin is 27 miles east of St George.

3 Virgin

The tiny-tot town of Virgin, named after the river (what else?), has an odd claim to fame – in 2000 the city council passed a largely symbolic law requiring every resident (about 600 of them) to own a gun. You can't miss **Fort Zion** (435-635-3455; 1000 W Hwy 9; village $2; 9am-7pm), which sells homemade fudge, ice cream and every Western knickknack known to the free world. Stop and have your picture taken in the 'Virgin Jail' or 'Wild Ass Saloon' in the replica Old West village here. It's pure, kitschy fun.

The Drive » Springdale is 14 miles further along Hwy 9 (55 minutes from St George).

4 Springdale

Stunning orangish-red mountains, including the **Watchman** (6555ft), form the backdrop for a perfect little park town. Here eclectic cafes and eateries are big on locally sourced ingredients. Galleries and artisan shops line the long main drag, interspersed with indie motels, lodges and a few B&Bs. Make this your base for three nights exploring Zion Canyon and surrounds. Outfitters **Zion Guru** (☎435-632-0432; www.utahcanyonoutdoors.com; 792 Zion Park Blvd; half-day canyoneering from $150; ⏰9am-7pm) and **Zion Adventure Company** (☎435-772-1001; www.zionadventures.com; 36 Lion Blvd; canyoneering day from $177; ⏰8am-8pm Mar-Oct, 9am-noon & 4-7pm Nov-Feb) lead canyoneering, climbing and 4WD trips outside the park; the latter has inner-tube rentals for summer float trips. They both outfit for backcountry hikes through Zion National Park's popular **Narrows**.

At **Zion Canyon Giant Screen Theatre** (☎435-772-2400; www.zioncanyontheatre.com; 145 Zion Park Blvd; admission varies) the 40-minute *Zion Canyon: Treasure of the Gods* screens three times daily. The film is short on substance but long on beauty.

p441

The Drive » The entrance to the Zion Canyon section of Zion National Park is only 2 miles east of Springdale. Note that here you're at about 3900ft, the lowest (and hottest) part of your trip.

TRIP HIGHLIGHT

5 Zion Canyon

More than 100 miles of trails cut through the surprisingly well-watered, deciduous-tree-covered Virgin River canyon section of Zion National Park. Map out your routes at the **Zion Canyon Visitor Center** (☎435-772-3256; www.nps.gov/zion; Hwy 9, Zion National Park; ⏰8am-7:30pm late May-early Sep, 8am-5pm rest of year). Your first activity should be the 6-mile **Scenic Drive**, which pierces the heart of the park. From April through October, using the free shuttle is mandatory, but you can hop off and on at any of the scenic stops and trailheads along the way.

The paved, 2.2 mile return **Riverside Walk** (👪), at the end of the road, is an easy stroll. When the trail ends, you can continue hiking along in the Virgin River for 5 miles. Alternatively, a half-mile one-way trail leads up to the lower of the **Emerald Pools** where water

LOCAL KNOWLEDGE: EAST MESA TRAIL

It feels deliciously like cheating to wander through open stands of tall ponderosa pines and then descend to Observation Point instead of hiking more than 2100ft uphill from the Zion Canyon floor. On East Mesa Trail (6.4 miles round-trip, moderate difficulty) you can do just that, because your vehicle does all the climbing. North Fork Rd is about 2.5 miles beyond the park's east entrance; follow it 5 miles north up Hwy 9 from there. Getting to the trailhead in some seasons requires 4WD; inquire about conditions and maps at the Zion Canyon Visitor Center. Nearby **Zion Ponderosa Ranch Resort** (☎800-293-5444; www.zionponderosa.com; Twin Knolls Rd; luxury tent $119, RV site $55, cabin $139-199; 📶🏊), which also has accommodations and activities, can provide hiker shuttles. Note that at 6500ft, these roads and the trail may be closed due to snow November through May.

tumbles from above a steep overhang stained by desert varnish.

The strenuous, 5-mile round-trip **Angels Landing Trail** (four to five hours, 1488ft elevation gain) is a vertigo-inducer with narrow ridges and 2000ft sheer drop-offs. Succeed and the exhilaration is unsurpassed. Canyon views are even more phenomenal from the top of the even higher **Observation Point** (8 miles round-trip; 2148ft elevation change).

For the longer trips down through the **Narrows** – spectacular slot canyons of the Virgin River – you need to plan ahead. An outfitter shuttle and gear plus a backcountry permit from the park are required; make advance reservations via the park website.

p441

The Drive » Driving east, Hwy 9 undulates over bridges and up 3.5 miles of tight switchbacks before reaching the impressive gallery-dotted Zion–Mt Carmel Tunnel. From there until the east park entrance, the canyon walls are made of etched, light-colored slickrock, including Checkerboard Mesa. Mt Carmel lies 26 miles (45 minutes) northwest of Zion Canyon.

6 Mt Carmel

Several little towns line Hwy 89 north of the Hwy 9 junction. As you drive, look for little rock shops, art galleries and home-style cafes. Stop into the **Maynard Dixon Living History Museum** (www.thunderbirdfoundation.com; 2200 S State St; self-guided/docent tour $10/20; 10am-5pm Mar-Nov) in Mt Carmel to explore the rustic retreat of this seminal Western artist. The Great Depression–era painter created breathtaking, light-infused landscapes and scenes of social struggle. Guides lead visitors through the log home and studio where solitude fueled the artist's imaginative drive.

The Drive » Hwy 89 is a fairly straight shot through pastoral lands; turn off from there onto Scenic Byway 12 where the red rock meets the road. Red Canyon is 45 miles northeast of Mt Carmel.

7 Red Canyon

Impossibly red monoliths rise up roadside as you reach **Red Canyon** (435-676-2676; www.fs.usda.gov/recarea/dixie; Scenic Byway 12, Dixie National Forest; park 24hr, visitor center 9am-6pm Jun-Aug, 10am-4pm May & Sep). These parklands provide super-easy access to eerie, intensely colored formations. Check out the excellent geologic displays and pick up maps at the visitor center, where several moderate hiking trails begin. The 0.7-mile one-way **Arches Trail** passes 15 arches as it winds through a canyon. Legend has it that outlaw Butch Cassidy once rode in the area; a tough 8.9-mile hiking route, **Cassidy Trail**, bears his name.

The Drive » Stop to take the requisite photo before you drive through two blasted-rock arches to continue on. Bryce Canyon National Park is only 9 miles down the road.

TRIP HIGHLIGHT

8 Bryce Canyon National Park

The pastel-colored, sandcastle-like spires and hoodoos of **Bryce Canyon National Park** (435-834-5322; www.nps.gov/brca; Hwy 63; 7-day pass per vehicle $30; 24hr, visitor center 8am-8pm May-Sep, to 4:30pm Oct-Apr) look like something straight out of Dr Seuss' imagination. The 'canyon' is actually an amphitheater of formations eroded from the cliffs. **Rim Road Scenic Drive** (18 miles one-way) roughly follows the canyon rim past the visitor center (8000ft), the lodge, incredible overlooks and trailheads, ending at **Rainbow Point** (9115ft). From early May through early October, an optional free shuttle bus (8am until at least 5:30pm) departs from a staging area just north of the park.

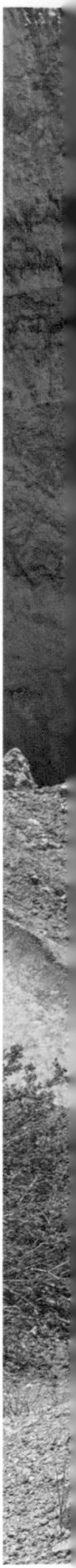

LEFT: FOTOS593 / SHUTTERSTOCK ©; RIGHT: PEERASITH PATRICK TRIRATPADOONGPHOL / SHUTTERSTOCK ©

Above: Zion National Park
Left: Bighorn sheep, Zion National Park
Right: Bryce Canyon National Park

ALASKAPHOTO / SHUTTERSTOCK ©

DETOUR: KODACHROME BASIN STATE PARK

Start: 9 Tropic

Dozens of red, pink and white sandstone chimneys punctuate **Kodachrome Basin State Park** (435-679-8562; www.stateparks.utah.gov; off Cottonwood Canyon Rd; day use per vehicle $8; day use 6am-10pm), named for its photogenic landscape by the National Geographic Society in 1948. The moderately easy, 3-mile round-trip **Panorama Trail** provides an overview of the otherworldly formations. Be sure to take the side trails to **Indian Cave**, where you can check out the handprints on the wall (cowboys' or Indians'?), and **Secret Passage**, a short spur through a narrow slot canyon. **Red Canyon Trail Rides** (800-892-7923, 435-834-5441; www.redcanyontrailrides.com; Hwy 12, Bryce Canyon Pines; 2hr ride $60; Mar-Nov) offers horseback riding in Kodachrome.

The park lies 26 miles southeast of Bryce Canyon National Park, off Cottonwood Canyon Rd, south of Cannonville.

The easiest walk would be to follow the **Rim Trail** that outlines Bryce Amphitheater from Fairyland Point to Bryce Point (up to 5.5 miles one-way). Several sections are paved and wheelchair accessible, the most level being the half-mile between Sunrise and Sunset Points.

A number of moderate trails descend below the rim to the maze of fragrant juniper and undulating high-mountain desert. The **Navajo Loop** drops 521ft from Sunset Point. To avoid a super-steep ascent, follow the **Queen's Garden Trail** on the desert floor and hike up 320ft to Sunrise Point. From there take the shuttle, or follow the Rim Trail back to your car (2.9-mile round-trip).

Note that the high altitude means cooler temperatures here – 80°F (27°C) average in July – than at scorching Zion National Park.

p441

The Drive » Only 11 miles east of Bryce Canyon, the town of Tropic is 2000ft lower in elevation – so expect it to be 10 degrees warmer.

---

9 Tropic

A farming community at heart, Tropic does offer a few services for park goers. There's a grocery store, a couple of restaurants and several motels. Basing yourself here for two nights is definitely less expensive than staying in the park. Note that the town is entirely seasonal: many businesses shut their doors tight from October through March.

p441

Eating & Sleeping

St George 2

Painted Pony Modern American $$$
(☎435-634-1700; www.painted-pony.com; 2 W St George Blvd, Ancestor Sq; lunch $10-12, dinner mains $25-36; ⏰11:30am-10pm Mon-Sat, 4-10pm Sun) Expect gourmet comfort food such as meatloaf with a port wine reduction and rosemary mashed potatoes.

Seven Wives Inn B&B $$
(☎435-628-3737, 800-600-3737; www.sevenwivesinn.com; 217 N 100 W; r $120-199;) Two 1800s homes and a cottage feature lovely bedrooms and suites surrounded by well-tended gardens and a small pool. The name comes from settler's times, when one of the owners harbored fugitive polygamists (including one with seven wives) in the 1880s.

Red Mountain Resort & Spa Resort $$$
(☎435-673-4905, 877-246-4453; www.redmountainresort.com; 1275 E Red Mountain Circle; retreats per person from $220;) A Zen-chic sensibility pervades this low-profile yogacentric adobe resort, right down to the silk pillows that echo the copper color of surrounding cliffs. It's located 7 miles northwest of town off Snow Canyon Pkwy.

Springdale 4

King's Landing American $$$
(☎435-772-7422; www.klbzion.com; 1515 Zion Park Blvd, Driftwood Lodge; mains $16-38; ⏰5-9pm) Bison fettuccine with truffle oil, charred octopus and verdant greens entice. Locals love its intimacy. There are also good burgers, vegetarian fare that does not bore and beautiful desserts. Reserve ahead.

Red Rock Inn B&B $$
(☎435-772-3139; www.redrockinn.com; 998 Zion Park Blvd; cottages $199-259;) Five romantic country-contemporary cottages spill down the desert hillside, backed by incredible red rock. Enjoy the full hot breakfast (egg dish and pastries) that appears at the door.

Zion Canyon 5

Zion Lodge Lodge $$
(☎888-297-2757, 435-772-7700; www.zionlodge.com; Zion Canyon Scenic Dr; cabin/r $227/217;) We love the location in the middle of Zion Canyon (along with the red permit that allows you to drive to the lodge in shuttle season). But be warned: today's reconstructed lodge is not as grand as other national-park lodges (the 1920s original burned down in 1966). Nevertheless, you'll need to reserve months ahead.

Bryce Canyon National Park 8

Bryce Canyon Lodge Lodge $$
(☎435-834-8700, 877-386-4383; www.brycecanyonforever.com; Hwy 63; r & cabin $208-270; ⏰Apr-Oct;) Built in the 1920s, the main park lodge exudes rustic mountain charm, with a large stone fireplace and exposed roof timbers. The retro-cool Western cabins have gas fireplaces and creaky porches. No TVs.

Tropic 9

Stone Hearth Grille American $$$
(☎435-679-8923; www.stonehearthgrille.com; 1380 W Stone Canyon Lane; mains $22-38; ⏰5-10pm) In a lovely rural setting staring out at the bluffs, this upscale lodge restaurant serves rib-eye steaks, quinoa-stuffed peppers and satisfying green salads alongside a decent wine list. It's the best dinner option in the area. The deck seating offers a heavy dose of romance.

Buffalo Sage B&B B&B $$
(☎435-679-8443; www.buffalosage.com; 980 N Hwy 12; d $120; ⏰May-Sep;) Up on a bluff west of town, three exterior-access rooms lead out to an expansive, upper-level deck or ground-level patio with great views. The owner's background in art is evident in the decor. Do note that the communal living area is shared by cats and a dog. The full breakfast accommodates vegetarians.

Monument Valley & Trail of the Ancients

Extreme desert isolation has preserved rocky natural wonders and numerous Ancestral Puebloan sites in far southeastern Utah and into Arizona.

TRIP HIGHLIGHTS

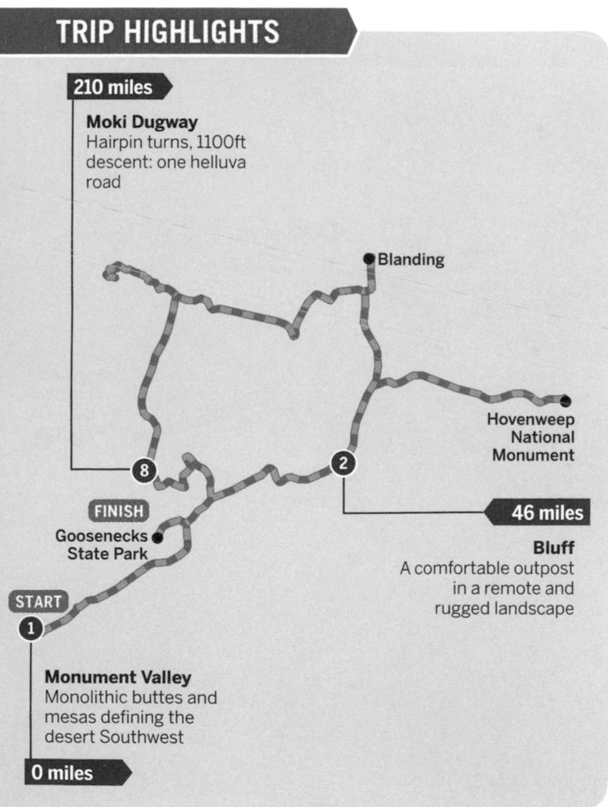

5 DAYS
262 MILES/422KM

GREAT FOR...

BEST TIME TO GO

October through April to avoid scorching desert heat.

ESSENTIAL PHOTO

Monument Valley's monolithic buttes at sunrise or sunset.

BEST FOR ANCIENT SITES

Hire a guide in Bluff or Monument Valley to help you see amazing rock art and ruins.

Valley of the Gods Hot air balloons float over the desert

35 Monument Valley & Trail of the Ancients

The red rock beauty found here is no exception to southern Utah, but those who come this way want something more. Ancestral Puebloan history courses through the veins of these dusty-hued canyons, pocked with ruins of cliff dwellings and granaries and marked with rock art. Photo highlights include the Valley of the Gods and Goosenecks. Much of this area is now protected in the new Bears Ears National Monument.

TRIP HIGHLIGHT

❶ Monument Valley

Don't worry if you feel like you've seen this place before. Monument Valley's monolithic chocolate-red buttes and colossal, colorful mesas have stared in countless films, TV shows and commercials. The most famous formations are conveniently visible from the 17-mile, rough-dirt **scenic drive** looping through **Monument Valley Navajo Tribal**

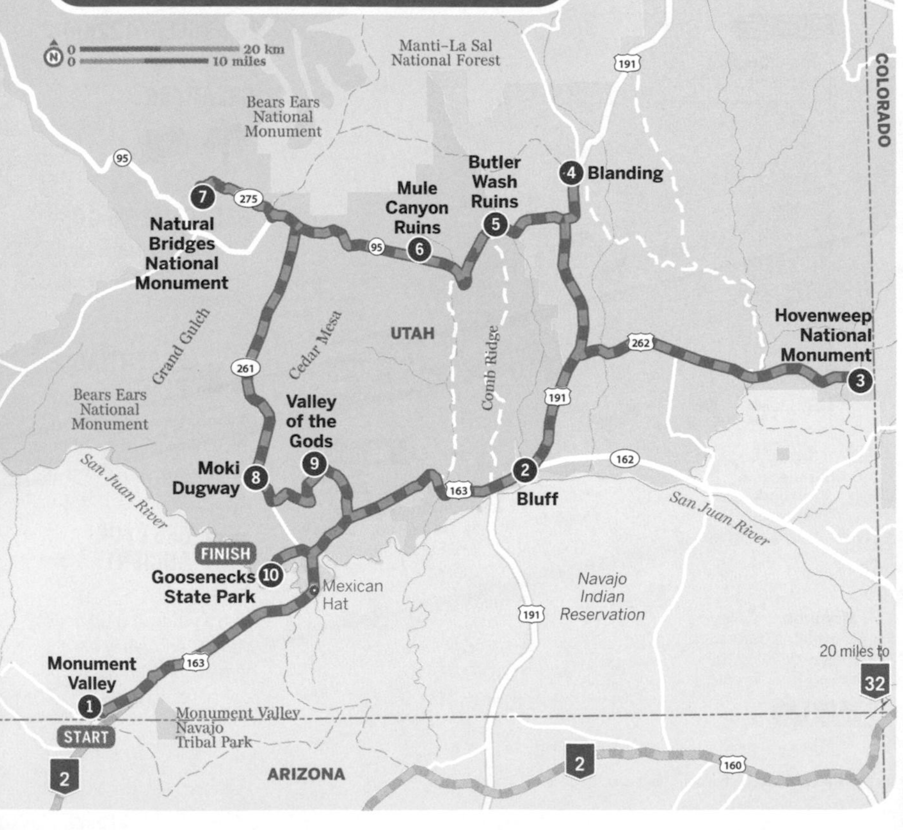

Park (☎435-727-5870; www.navajonationparks.org; per 4-person vehicle $20; ⌚drive 6am-7pm Apr-Sep, 8am-4:30pm Oct-Mar, visitor center 6am-8pm Apr-Sep, 8am-5pm Oct-Mar; P), down a 4-mile spur road south of **Goulding's Lodge** (☎435-727-3231; www.gouldings.com; Hwy 163; r from $130, tent/RV sites $25/36;), which has a small museum and also offers tours. Note that the park and scenery straddle the Utah–Arizona line.

The only way to get into the backcountry to see rock art, natural arches and coves is by taking a Navajo-led tour on foot, on horseback or by vehicle. Easygoing guides have booths set up in the parking lot at the visitor center. Tours are peppered with details about Diné culture, life on the reservation, movie trivia and whatever else comes to mind.

p59, p449

The Drive » The monument's mesas diminish then disappear in your rearview mirror as you head north, crossing the San Juan River and continuing along its valley the 45 total miles to Bluff, UT.

TRIP HIGHLIGHT

2 Bluff

Tiny tot Bluff (population 320) isn't much, but a few good motels and a handful of restaurants – surrounded by stunning red rock – make it a cool little base for exploring. We've set up the trip for two nights in Monument Valley, two here in Bluff and one in Mexican Hat or back in the Valley. But distances are short enough that you could spend every night in Bluff and take daily forays to area sights.

Descendants of the town's pioneers re-created a tourable log cabin settlement called **Bluff Fort** (www.hirf.org/bluff.asp; 5 E Hwy 191; ⌚9am-6pm Mon-Sat). Three miles west of town on public lands, the accessible **Sand Island Petroglyphs** (www.blm.gov; Sand Island Rd, off Hwy 163; ⌚24hr) were created between 800 and 2500 years ago.

A few outfitters in town lead backcountry excursions that access rock art and ruins. **Far Out Expeditions** (☎435-672-2294; www.faroutexpeditions.com; day tours $295) offers single and multiday hikes. **Wild Rivers Expeditions** (☎800-422-7654; www.riversandruins.com; half-day trip adult/child $89/69), a history- and geology-minded outfit, rafts along the San Juan. And **Buckhorn Llama** (☎435-672-2466; www.llamapack.com; guided trip per day $250) leads five- and six-day, llama-supported treks – really, llamas.

p449

The Drive » The best route to Hovenweep is the paved Hwy 262 (past Hatch Trading Post, turn off onto Hwy 191 and follow the signs). From Bluff to the main entrance is a slow, 42-mile drive total (1¼ hours).

3 Hovenweep National Monument

Meaning 'deserted valley' in the Ute language, the archaeological sites of **Hovenweep National Monument** (www.nps.gov/hove; Hwy 262; tent & RV sites $10; ⌚park dusk-dawn, visitor center 8am-6pm Jun-Sep, 9am-5pm Oct-May) exist in splendid isolation. Most of the eight towers and unit houses you'll see in the **Square Towers Group**, accessed near the visitor center, were built from 1230 to 1275 CE. Imagine stacking each clay-formed block to create such tall structures on tiny ledges. You could easily spend a half day or

LINK YOUR TRIP

32 **San Juan Skyway & Million Dollar Highway**

Swap Utah's ancient wonders for Colorado cliff dwellings via Hwy 162 southeast and Hwy 160E.

2 **Four Corners Cruise**

With the Mittens Buttes in the rearview mirror, pick up US 163 south to Hwy 160 East.

more hiking around the gorge's ruins. Other sites, which lie across the border in Colorado, require long hikes.

The Drive » Bluff is the only base in the area, so you'll have to drive both to Hovenweep and back in one day. Moving on to Blanding, 28 miles north of Bluff, Hwy 191 is a rural road unimpeded by too many twists or turns.

JULIEN HAUTCOEUR / SHUTTERSTOCK ©

❹ Blanding

A special museum elevates small, agriculturally oriented Blanding a little above its totally drab name. The **Edge of the Cedars State Park Museum** (☎435-678-2238; www.stateparks.utah.gov; 660 W 400 N; adult/child $5/3; ⏰9am-5pm Mon-Sat, 10am-4pm Sun) is where you can learn more about the area's ancients, with its trove of archaeological treasures that have been gathered from across southeastern Utah. Outside, climb down the rickety ladder into a dark, earthy-smelling ceremonial kiva (an Ancestral Puebloan ceremonial structure) from c 1100 CE. Can you feel a power to the place? (Just ignore the encroaching subdivision noise.)

Blue Mountain Artisans (www.bluemountainartisans.com; 215 E Center St; ⏰11am-6pm Wed-Sat) sells professional photographs of area archaeological and geological sites, plus local jewelry.

🛏 p449

The Drive » Heading west on Hwy 95, the scenery gets up close and personal. Butler Wash is only 14 miles along on free public lands; look for the signs.

❺ Butler Wash Ruins

No need to hike for days into the backcountry here: it's only a half-mile tramp to views of the freely accessible Butler Wash Ruins, a 20-room cliff dwelling on public lands. Scramble over the slickrock boulders (follow the cairns) to see the sacred kivas, habitation and storage rooms associated with the Ancestral Puebloan (or Anasazi) Kayenta group of northern Arizona c 1300 CE.

Monument Valley

The Drive » Continue west on Hwy 95. After the road veers north, look for a sign announcing more ruins – about 25 miles along.

6 Mule Canyon Ruins

Though not particularly well preserved or evocative, the base of the tower, kiva and 12-room Mule Canyon Ruins sit almost roadside. Pottery found here links the population (c 1000 to 1150 CE) to the Mesa Verde group in southern Colorado.

The Drive » Continue along through the cliffs and canyons of Hwy 95 until you branch off onto the even smaller Hwy 275. The monument is located 26 miles west of Mule Canyon.

7 Natural Bridges National Monument

The views at **Natural Bridges** (www.nps.gov/nabr; Hwy 275; 7-day pass per vehicle $10, tent & RV sites $10; ⌚24hr, visitor center 8am-6pm May-Sep, 9am-5pm Oct-Apr) are of a white sandstone canyon (it's not red!). All three impressive and easily accessible bridges are

TAKE ONLY PICTURES

Sadly enough, many invaluable archaeological sites in the area have been vandalized by thieves. Even casual visitors do irreparable damage by climbing on old dwelling walls or picking up 'just one' little pot shard. The old maxim 'take only pictures' bears repeating. Do not touch, move or remove any artifacts; it's against the law. The best way to explore ancient backcountry sites is with a well-informed, responsible guide.

visible from a 9-mile winding **Scenic Drive** loop with overlooks. The oldest is also the closest: take a half-mile hike to the beautifully delicate **Owachomo Bridge**, spanning 180ft at only 9ft thick. Note that trails to Kachina and Siapu bridges are not long, but they require navigating super-steep sections or ladders. Near the end of the drive, don't skip the 0.3-mile trail to the **Horsecollar Ruin** cliff dwelling overlook.

The Drive » Ocher-yellow to reddish-orange sandstone canyons surround you as you wend your way south on Rte 261. To your right is Cedar Mesa–Grand Gulch primitive area, a seriously challenging wilderness environment now part of the new Bears Ears National Monument. To drive the 36 miles to Moki Dugway will take at least an hour.

TRIP HIGHLIGHT

8 Moki Dugway

Along a roughly paved, hairpin-turn-filled section of road, Moki Dugway descends 1100ft in just 3 miles. Miners 'dug out' the extreme switchbacks in the 1950s to transport uranium ore. Note that the road is far from wide by today's standards, but there are places to pull out. You can't always see what's around the next bend, but you can see down the sheer drop-offs. Those afraid of heights (or in trailers over 24ft long), steer clear.

The Drive » At the bottom of the dugway, prepare yourself for another wild ride. The turnoff for Valley of the Gods is less than 5 miles ahead on your left.

9 Valley of the Gods

Think of the gravel road through the freely accessible **Valley of the Gods** (www.blm.gov) as a do-it-yourself roller coaster, with sharp, steep hills and quick turns around some amazing scenery. Locals call it 'mini–Monument Valley.' Download the public lands office pamphlet from www.blm.gov to identify the strangely shaped sandstone monoliths and pinnacles (Seven Sailors, Lady on a Tub, Rooster Butte...). Allow an hour-plus for the 17 miles between Hwys 261 and 163. Do not attempt it without a 4WD if it's rained recently.

The Drive » Once you emerge from the valley, follow Hwy 163 back west and take the little jog up Hwy 261 to the Goosenecks State Park spur, a total of 8 miles away.

10 Goosenecks State Park Overlook

Following the 4-mile spur to **Goosenecks State Park** (stateparks.utah.gov; vehicle $5, campsite $10) brings you to a mesmerizing view. From 1000ft above you can see how the San Juan River's path carved tight turns through sediment, leaving gooseneck-shaped spits of land untouched. The dusty park itself doesn't have much to speak of besides pit toilets and picnic tables.

Eating & Sleeping

Monument Valley 1

Stagecoach Dining Room — American $$

(435-727-3231; www.gouldings.com; Goulding's Trading Post Rd; mains $12-20; 6:30am-9:30pm, shorter hours in winter) Goulding Lodge's restaurant, Stagecoach Dining Room, is a replica of a film set built for John Ford's 1949 Western *She Wore a Yellow Ribbon*. Get a vitamin kick from the salad bar before tucking into the steaks or Navajo tacos piled high with chile and cheese. At lunchtime it often swarms with coach tourists.

Bluff 2

Comb Ridge Bistro — Cafe $

(435-485-5555; www.combridgebistro.com; 680 S Hwy 191; breakfast mains $5-7, dinner mains $10-17; 8am-3pm & 5-9pm Tue-Sun;) An adobe gallery and cafe with standout single-pour coffee, blue-corn pancakes and breakfast sandwiches loaded with peppers and eggs. Dinner includes pasture-raised beef in the form of homemade meatloaf or whiskey burgers, organic salads and good vegetarian options.

Valley of the Gods B&B — B&B $$

(970-749-1164; www.valleyofthegodsbandb.com; off Hwy 261; s/d $145/175, cabin $195) Spend a secluded night at one of the original ranches in the area, 6.5 miles north of Hwy 163. Exposed wood-and-stone rooms have simple rustic beds, and the on-site cabin is just magical. Water is trucked in and solar power is harnessed out of necessity here (leave your hair dryer at home).

Blanding 4

Stone Lizard Lodge — Motel $$

(435-678-3323; www.stonelizardlodging.com; 88 W Center St; r $104-109, ste $155-249;) More than a motel, with spacious rooms sporting Southwestern themes, homemade cinnamon rolls for breakfast and a huge back garden with strawberries for the picking. The suites feel like a welcoming home. Wander into the office to borrow a book from the great regional library.

Mexican Hat

San Juan Inn — Motel $

(435-683-2220; www.sanjuaninn.net; Hwy 163; r from $84, apt $265, yurt from $90;) The cliffside San Juan Inn perches high above the river. These basic motel rooms are the nicest in town, with quilted comforters and flat-screen TVs. There's also a **trading post** (7am-9pm) and restaurant on-site. Yurt accommodations are in round tents decked out with air-conditioning, wi-fi and views.

High & Low Roads to Taos

Santa Fe. Taos. The Rio Grande. The Sangre de Cristos. And all the adobe villages, galleries, Spanish Colonial churches and burrito stands in between make this loop a classic.

TRIP HIGHLIGHTS

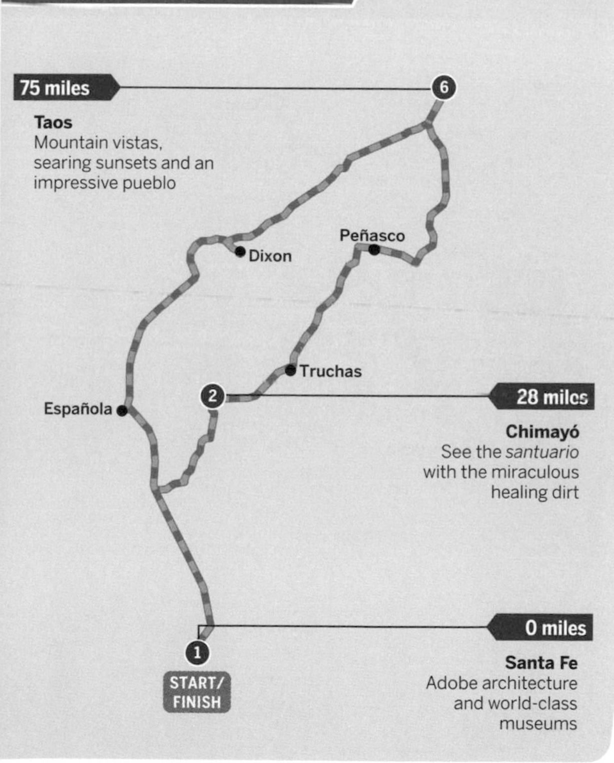

75 miles

Taos
Mountain vistas, searing sunsets and an impressive pueblo

Dixon

Peñasco

Truchas

Española

28 miles

Chimayó
See the *santuario* with the miraculous healing dirt

0 miles

Santa Fe
Adobe architecture and world-class museums

START/
FINISH

1–4 DAYS
150 MILES/241KM

GREAT FOR…

BEST TIME TO GO

June to March, when temps are not too hot.

ESSENTIAL PHOTO

Capture the gorge and mountains at once, from Hwy 68 near Taos.

BEST FOR CULTURE

The 'miracle church' – and the chile – in Chimayó.

Chimayó El Santuario de Chimayó

36

High & Low Roads to Taos

Starting in hip, historic Santa Fe, you'll rise from scrub-and-sandstone desert into ponderosa forests, snaking between the villages at the base of the 13,000ft Sangre de Cristos, until you reach the Taos Plateau. After checking out this little place that's lured artists, writers and hippies for the past century, head back south through the ruggedly sculpted Rio Grande Gorge, with the river coursing alongside you.

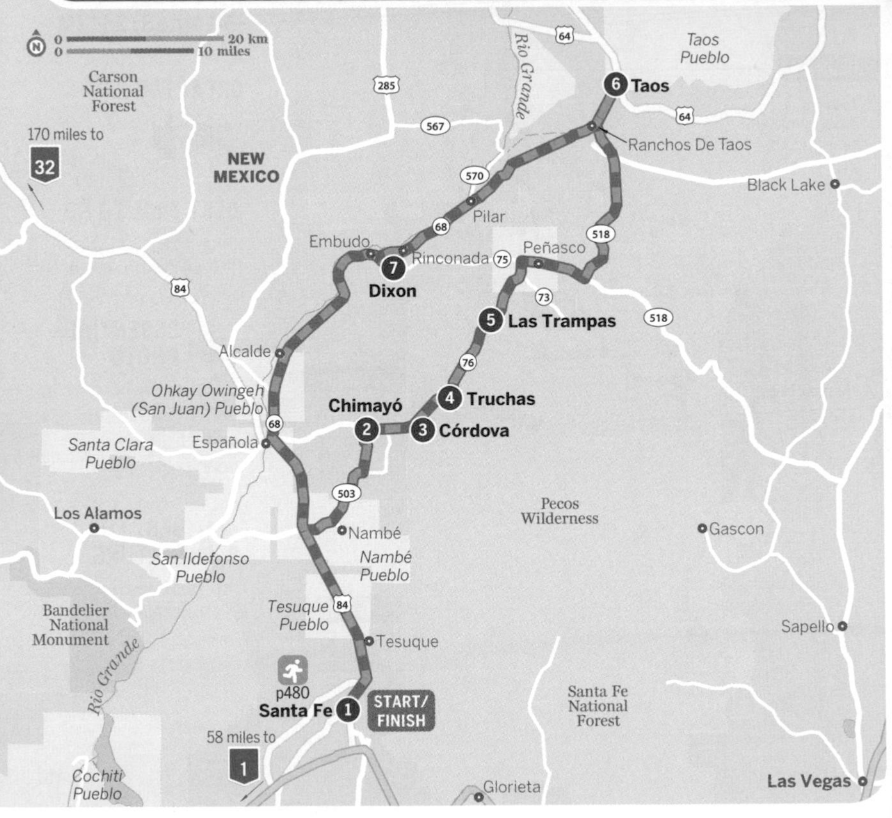

❶ Santa Fe

TRIP HIGHLIGHT

Walking among the historic adobe neighborhoods, and even around the tourist-filled plaza, there's no denying that 400-year-old Santa Fe has a timeless, earthy soul. Known as 'the city different,' it seamlessly blends historical and contemporary styles and casts a spell that's hard to resist: it's the second-oldest city in the US, the oldest state capital, and throws the oldest annual party (Fiesta) while boasting the second-largest art market in the nation, plus gourmet restaurants, world-class museums, opera, spas and more. At 7000ft above sea level, Santa Fe is also the highest state capital in the US, and a fantastic base for hiking, mountain biking, backpacking and skiing. The plaza area (p480) has the highest concentration of sights but it's also worth a trip to Museum Hill, where you'll find the fantastical **Museum of International Folk Art** (☎505-827-6344; www.internationalfolkart.org; 706 Camino Lejo; adult/child $12/free; ⊙10am-5pm, closed Mon Nov-Apr) and the excellent **Museum of Indian Arts & Culture** (☎505-476-1250; www.indianartsandculture.org; 710 Camino Lejo; adult/child $12/free; ⊙10am-5pm, closed Mon Sep-May), among others.

p59, p459

HIGH/LOW ROAD FESTIVALS

Try to catch – or avoid, if you hate crowds – some of the highlights from around the year on the High and Low Roads. Check websites for exact dates each year:

Easter (Chimayó) – March/April

Taos Pueblo Pow-Wow (www.taospueblopowwow.com) – July

International Folk Art Market (www.folkartmarket.org; Santa Fe) – July

Spanish Market (www.spanishcolonial.org; Santa Fe) – July

Indian Market (www.swaia.org; Santa Fe) – August

Santa Fe Fiesta (www.santafefiesta.org) – September

High Road Art Tour (www.highroadnewmexico.com; Hwy 76 to Peñasco) – September

Dixon Studio Tour (www.dixonarts.org) – November

Christmas on Canyon Rd – December

LINK YOUR TRIP

32 San Juan Skyway & Million Dollar Highway

The landscape becomes the art after leaving Española on US 84 north to US 160 east to Mesa Verde.

1 Route 66

From Santa Fe drive south on I-25 to Albuquerque for green chili specialties on Route 66.

The Drive » For this 28-mile leg, take Hwy 84/285 north, then exit right onto Hwy 503 towards Nambé. Turn left onto Juan Medina Rd, toward the Santauario de Chimayó.

TRIP HIGHLIGHT

❷ Chimayó

Tucked into this little village is the so-called 'Lourdes of America,' **El Santuario de Chimayó** (☎505-351-9961; www.elsantuariodechimayo.us; ⊙9am-6pm May-Sep, to 5pm Oct-Apr), one of the most important cultural sites in New Mexico. In 1816, this two-towered adobe chapel was built over a spot of earth said to have miraculous healing properties. Even today, the faithful come to rub the *tierra bendita* (holy dirt) from a small pit inside the church on whatever hurts; some mix it with water and drink it. The walls of the dirt room are covered with crutches, left behind by those healed by the dirt. During Holy Week, about 30,000 pilgrims walk to Chimayó from Santa Fe, Albuquerque and beyond in the largest Catholic pilgrimage in the US. The artwork in the *santuario* is worth a trip on its own.

Chimayó also has a centuries-old tradition of producing some of the finest weavings in the area and has a handful of family-run galleries. Irvin Trujillo, a seventh-generation weaver, whose carpets are in collections at the Smithsonian in Washington, DC, and the Museum of Fine Arts in Santa Fe, works out of his gallery **Centinela Traditional Arts** (☎505-351-2180; www.chimayoweavers.com; Hwy 76; ⊙9am-6pm Mon-Sat, 10am-5pm Sun). Naturally dyed blankets, vests and pillows are sold, and you can watch the artists weaving on handlooms.

✕ 🛏 p459

The Drive » Follow Hwy 76 north for a few miles, and take the right-side turnoff to Córdova.

WINTER THRILLS

One of the biggest winter draws to this part of New Mexico is the skiing and snowboarding, and **Taos Ski Valley** (☎866-968-7386; www.skitaos.org; lift ticket adult/teen/child $98/81/61; ⊙9am-4pm) is the premier place to hit the slopes. There's just something about the abundant powder, wicked steeps and laid-back atmosphere that makes this mountain a wintery heaven-on-earth – that is, if heaven has a 3274ft vertical drop.

Offering some of the most difficult terrain in the US, it's a fantastic place to zip down steep tree glades into untouched powder bowls. Seasoned skiers luck out, with more than half of the 70-plus trails at the Taos Ski Valley ranked expert; but there's also an award-winning ski school, so complete beginners thrive here too. The resort has a peak elevation of 12,481ft and gets an average of more than 300in of snowfall annually. The resort also has a skier-cross obstacle course at its popular terrain park.

That said, **Ski Santa Fe** (☎505-982-4429, snow report 505-983-9155; www.skisantafe.com; lift ticket adult/teen/child $75/60/52; ⊙9am-4pm Dec-Mar) is no slouch. Less than 30 minutes from the Santa Fe plaza, it boasts the same fluffy powder (though usually a little less), with an even higher base elevation (10,350ft). Briefly admire the awesome desert and mountain vistas, then fly down chutes, steep bump runs or long groomers. The resort caters to families and expert skiers alike with its varied terrain. The quality and length of the ski season can vary wildly from year to year depending on how much snow the mountain gets (you can almost always count on a good storm in late March).

❸ Córdova

Down in the Rio Quemado Valley, this little town is best known for its unpainted, austere *santos* (saint) carvings created by local masters such as George Lopez, Jose Delores Lopez and Sabinita Lopez Ortiz – all members of the same artistic family. Stop and see their work at the **Sabinita Lopez Ortiz shop** (☎505-351-4572; County Rd 1317; ⊙hours vary) – one of a few galleries in town.

The Drive » Hop back on Hwy 76 north, and climb higher into the Sangre de Cristo Mountains, for about 4 miles.

❹ Truchas

Rural New Mexico at its most sincere is showcased in Truchas, originally settled by the Spaniards in the 18th century. Robert Redford's *The Milagro Beanfield War* was filmed here (but don't bother with the movie – the book it's based on, by John Nichols, is waaaay better). Narrow roads, many unpaved, wend between century-old adobes. Fields of grass and alfalfa spread toward the sheer walls and plunging ridges that define the western flank of the Truchas Peaks. Between the rundown homes are some wonderful art galleries, which double as workshops for local weavers, painters, sculptors and other artists. The best place to get an overview of who's painting/sculpting/carving/weaving what is the **High Road Marketplace** (505-689-2689; 1642 Hwy 76; 10am-5pm, to 4pm winter), a cooperative art gallery with a huge variety of work by area artists.

The Drive » Continue north on Hwy 76 for around 8 miles, transecting the little valleys of Ojo Sarco and Cañada de los Alamos.

LOCAL KNOWLEDGE: NATURE CALLS

Want to see the scenery without a pane of glass in front of your face? Off the High Road, take a stroll on the **Santa Barbara Trail**, which follows a trout-filled creek through mixed forest into the Pecos Wilderness; it's pretty flat and easygoing. To reach the trailhead, take Hwy 73 from Peñasco and follow the signs.

Off the Low Road, turn onto Hwy 570 at Pilar and check out the **Orilla Verde Recreation Area** (575-758-8851; Hwy 570; day-use $3, tent/RV sites $7/15), where you can hang out or camp along the Rio Grande (or tube or fish in it). Hike up to the rim on Old 570, a dirt road blocked by a landslide, with expansive vistas of the Taos Plateau and the Sangre de Cristos.

Some of the best views in the state are from the top of **Lake Peak** (12,409ft), which can be reached on a day hike starting at the Santa Fe Ski Basin.

From Taos Ski Valley, you can day hike to the top of **Wheeler Peak** (13,161ft), New Mexico's highest summit (the views are pretty good up there, too). For trail maps and more information, go to the **Travel Bug** (505-992-0418; www.mapsofnewmexico.com; 839 Paseo de Peralta; 7:30am-5:30pm Mon-Sat, 11am-4pm Sun;) bookshop in Santa Fe or the **Taos Visitor Center** (575-758-3873; taos.org; 1139 Paseo del Pueblo Sur; 9am-5pm;).

❺ Las Trampas

Completed in 1780 and constantly defended against Apache raids, the **Church of San José de Gracia** (505-351-4360; Hwy 76; by appointment, call ahead) is considered one of the finest surviving 18th-century churches in the USA and is a National Historic Landmark. Original paintings and carvings remain in excellent condition, and self-flagellation bloodstains from Los Hermanos Penitentes (a 19th-century religious order with a strong following in the northern mountains of New Mexico) are still visible. On your way out of town, look right to see the amazing irrigation aqueduct, carved from tree trunks!

The Drive » Continue north on Hwy 76, through lovely Chamisal. At the T, turn right onto Hwy 75 and stay on it through Peñasco and Vadito. At Hwy 518, turn left toward Taos. At the end of the road,

Fajitas El Molero Fajitas
El Molero Fajitas
Cathedral Basilica of St Francis
IAIA Museum
Cathedral Park
Visitor Information
City Hall
Community Convention Center
Palace of the Governors
NM History Museum
NM Museum of Art
Chicken Fajita
Beef Fajita
Chicken & Pork Tamales
Bienvenidos
El Molero

COBH / GETTY IMAGES ©

Above: Taos Pueblo
Left: Food stand in Santa Fe
Right: Textiles for sale, Santa Fe

LEFT: ANDRIY BLOKHIN / SHUTTERSTOCK ©; RIGHT: DOUGLAS KNIGHT / SHUTTERSTOCK ©

turn right on Paseo del Pueblo Sur/Hwy 68 and take it on into Taos – around 32 miles in total.

TRIP HIGHLIGHT

6 Taos

Taos is a place undeniably dominated by the power of its landscape: 12,300ft often-snowcapped peaks rise behind town, a sage-speckled plateau unrolls to the west before plunging 800ft straight down into the Rio Grande Gorge. The sky can be a searing sapphire blue or an ominous parade of rumbling thunderheads. And then there are the sunsets ...

The pueblo here is one of the oldest continuously inhabited communities in the United States and it roots the town in a long history with a rich cultural legacy – including conquistadors, Catholicism and cowboys. Taos remains a relaxed and eccentric place, with classic mud-brick buildings, quirky cafes and excellent restaurants. It's both rural and worldly, and a little bit otherworldly.

The best thing to do is walk around the plaza area soaking in the aura of the place. But you also won't want to miss **Taos Pueblo** (☎575-758-1028; www.taospueblo.com; Taos Pueblo Rd; adult/child $16/free; ⏰8am-4:30pm Mon-Sat, 8:30am-4:30pm Sun, closed mid-Feb–mid-Apr). Built around 1450 and continuously inhabited ever since, it's the largest existing multistoried pueblo structure in the USA and one of the best surviving examples of traditional adobe construction. Also well worth a visit is the **Millicent Rogers Museum** (☎575-758-2462; www.millicentrogers.org; 1504 Millicent Rogers Rd; adult/child $10/2; ⏰10:10am-5pm Apr-Oct, closed Mon Nov-Mar), filled with pottery, jewelry, baskets and textiles from the private collection of a model and oil heiress who moved to Taos in 1947 and acquired one of the best collections of American Indian and Spanish Colonial art in the USA.

✕ 🛏 p459

The Drive » On this 26-mile leg, cruise the Low Road back toward Santa Fe by taking Hwy 68 south. Just before the road drops downhill, there's a large pullout with huge views, so hop out and see what you're leaving behind. Then head down into the Rio Grande Gorge. Go left on Hwy 75 to Dixon.

7 Dixon

This small agricultural and artistic community is spread along the gorgeous Rio Embudo valley. It's famous for its apples but plenty of other crops are grown here too, including some of the grapes used by two award-winning local wineries, **Vivac** (☎505-579-4441; www.vivacwinery.com; 2075 Hwy 68; tasting $8; ⏰10am-6pm Mon-Sat, from noon Sun) and **La Chiripada** (☎505-579-4437; www.lachiripada.com; Hwy 75; tasting $10; ⏰11am-5pm Mon-Sat, from noon Sun), both of which have tasting rooms. In summer and fall, there's a farmers market on Wednesday afternoons, with food fresh from the fields. Our favorite art gallery is actually on Hwy 68, in Rinconada, just north of Hwy 75: **Rift Gallery** (☎505-579-9179; www.saxstonecarving.com; 2249 Hwy 68; ⏰10am-5pm Wed-Sun May-Sep, shorter hours rest of year) features masterful ceramics and stonework. On the first weekend in November, local artists open their homes and studios to the public in New Mexico's oldest studio tour. In summer, ask at the local food co-op and some kind soul might point you to the waterfalls, up a nearby dirt road.

p459

The Drive » Back on Hwy 68, head south along the river, through Embudo (a great lunch stop) and out of the gorge. Continue through Española, where you'll meet Hwy 84/285, which you can take back to Santa Fe. This leg is around 47 miles.

Eating & Sleeping

Santa Fe 1

Harry's Roadhouse — American, New Mexican $$

(505-989-4629; www.harrysroadhousesantafe.com; 96 Old Las Vegas Hwy; lunch $8-14, dinner $9-23; 7am-9:30pm;) This casual longtime favorite on the southern edge of town feels like a rambling cottage with its various rooms and patio garden – and there's also a full bar. And, seriously, *everything* here is good. Especially the desserts.

El Paradero — B&B $$

(505-988-1177; www.elparadero.com; 220 W Manhattan Ave; r from $155;) Each room in this 200-year-old adobe B&B, south of the river, is unique and loaded with character. Two have their own bathrooms across the hall, the rest are en suite; our favorites are rooms 6 and 12. The full breakfasts satisfy, and rates also include afternoon tea. A separate casita holds two kitchenette suites that can be combined into one.

Chimayó 2

Rancho de Chimayó — New Mexican $

(505-984-2100; www.ranchodechimayo.com; County Rd 98; mains $7-11, dinner $10-25; 11:30am-9pm, closed Mon Nov-Apr) Half a mile north of the Santuario, this bright, spacious garden-set restaurant serves classic New Mexican cuisine, courtesy of the Jaramillo family's famed recipes. Best of all is the basket of warm, fluffy *sopaipillas* (puffed-up pastries) that comes with each dish. The same management offers cozy B&B rooms (from $79) across the street.

Casa Escondida — B&B $$

(505-351-4805; www.casaescondida.com; 64 County Rd 100; r from $130;) Set on 6 acres, a mile or so north of Chimayó, this unpretentious and highly recommended B&B features eight beautiful rooms, all en suite and furnished in Southwestern style. Some have outdoor decks, all share use of a communal covered porch and a hot tub.

Taos 6

Lambert's — Modern American $$$

(505-758-1009; www.lambertsoftaos.com; 123 Bent St; lunch $11-14, dinner $23-38; 11:30am-close;) Consistently hailed as the 'Best of Taos,' this charming old adobe just north of the Plaza remains what it's always been – a cozy, romantic local hangout where patrons relax and enjoy sumptuous contemporary cuisine, with mains ranging from lunchtime's barbecue pork sliders to dinner dishes such as chicken mango enchiladas or Colorado rack of lamb.

Historic Taos Inn — Historic Hotel $$

(575-758-2233; www.taosinn.com; 125 Paseo del Pueblo Norte; r from $119;) Lovely and always lively old inn, where the 45 characterful rooms have Southwest trimmings such as heavy-duty wooden furnishings and adobe fireplaces (some functioning, some for show). The famed **Adobe Bar** (11am-11pm, music 6:30-10pm) spills into the cozy central atrium, and features live music every night – for a quieter stay, opt for one of the detached separate wings – and there's also a good **restaurant** (breakfast & lunch $7-15, dinner $15-28; 11am-3pm & 5-9pm Mon-Fri, 7:30am-2:30pm & 5-9pm Sat & Sun).

Dixon 7

Zuly's Cafe — Cafe $

(505-579-4001; 234 Hwy 75; mains $6-14; 7:30am-3pm Tue-Thu, 7:30am-8pm Fri, 9am-8pm Sat) This superfriendly place, run by Dixon native Chalako Chilton, serves some of the best green chile you'll find anywhere, plus espresso coffees.

Tower Guest House — Guesthouse $

(505-579-4288; www.vrbo.com/118083; cottage $95;) Located on a garlic farm, this lovely cottage is close to the Rio Embudo. Sleeps three.

Big Bend Scenic Loop

Although it's known for wide open spaces, west Texas is packed with surprising experiences that makes this a supremely well-rounded drive.

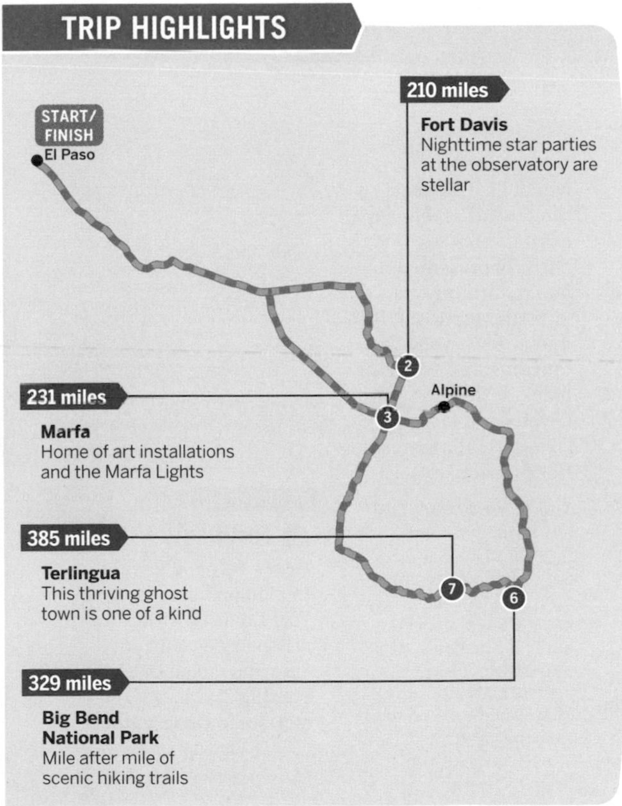

TRIP HIGHLIGHTS

START/ FINISH El Paso

210 miles
Fort Davis
Nighttime star parties at the observatory are stellar

Alpine

231 miles
Marfa
Home of art installations and the Marfa Lights

385 miles
Terlingua
This thriving ghost town is one of a kind

329 miles
Big Bend National Park
Mile after mile of scenic hiking trails

5–7 DAYS
690 MILES/1110KM

GREAT FOR...

BEST TIME TO GO

Best between February and April – before the heat sets in.

ESSENTIAL PHOTO

Prada Marfa, a quirky roadside art installation.

BEST FOR OUTDOORS

McDonald Observatory's nighttime star parties.

Fort Davis McDonald Observatory

37 Big Bend Scenic Loop

Getting to visit Big Bend National Park and experience the endless vistas straight out of an old Western are reason enough to make this trip. But you'll also have plenty of fun along the way, exploring the quirky small towns that are prime road-trip material. Unforgettable experiences in west Texas include minimalist art installations, nighttime astronomy parties and thriving ghost towns.

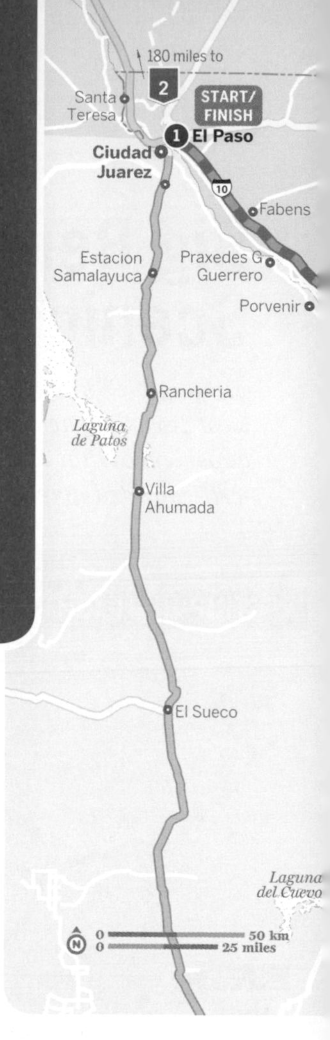

❶ El Paso

Start your trip in El Paso, a border city that's wedged into a remote corner of west Texas. While here, take advantage of the great Mexican food you can find all over the city – it's right across the river from Mexico – and enjoy El Paso's many free museums. Downtown, the **El Paso Museum of Art** (☎915-212-0300; www.elpasoartmuseum.org; 1 Arts Festival Plaza; ⏲9am-5pm Tue-Sat, to 9pm Thu, noon-5pm Sun) has a terrific Southwestern collection.

And don't miss the **El Paso Holocaust Museum** (☎915-351-0048; www.elpasoholocaustmuseum.org; 715 N Oregon St; ⏲9am-5pm Tue-Fri, 1-5pm Sat & Sun), which hosts amazingly thoughtful and moving exhibits that are imaginatively presented for maximum impact.

To the west, you'll find several good restaurants and watering holes in the new and developing Montecillo commercial and residential district.

The Drive » Head east on I-10 for two hours, then turn onto TX 118 toward Fort Davis. The area is part of both the Chihuahuan Desert and the Davis Mountains, giving it a unique setting where the endless horizons are suddenly interrupted by rock formations springing from the earth.

TRIP HIGHLIGHT

❷ Fort Davis

Here's why you'll want to plan on being in Fort Davis on either a Tuesday, Friday or Saturday: to go to an evening star party at **McDonald Observatory** (☎432-426-3640; www.mcdonaldobservatory.org;

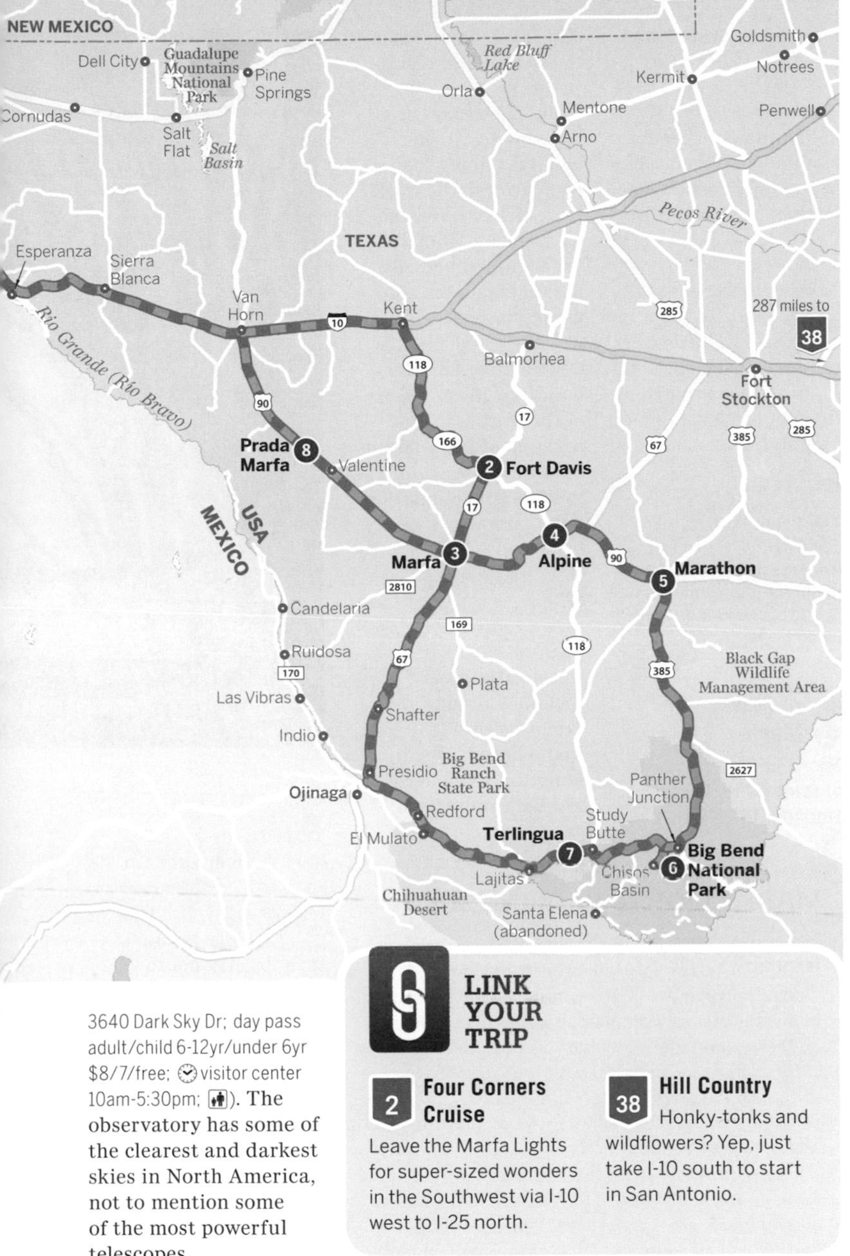

3640 Dark Sky Dr; day pass adult/child 6-12yr/under 6yr $8/7/free; visitor center 10am-5:30pm;). The observatory has some of the clearest and darkest skies in North America, not to mention some of the most powerful telescopes.

Besides that, nature lovers will enjoy **Davis**

LINK YOUR TRIP

2 Four Corners Cruise

Leave the Marfa Lights for super-sized wonders in the Southwest via I-10 west to I-25 north.

38 Hill Country

Honky-tonks and wildflowers? Yep, just take I-10 south to start in San Antonio.

Mountains State Park (☎432-426-3337; www.tpwd.state.tx.us; Hwy 118; adult/child under 13yr $6/free), and history buffs can immerse themselves at the 1854 **Fort Davis National Historic Site** (☎432-426-3224; www.nps.gov/foda; Hwy 17; adult/child under 16yr $7/free; ⏰8am-5pm; 🐾), a well-preserved frontier military post that's impressively situated at the foot of Sleeping Lion Mountain.

🛏 p467

The Drive » Marfa is just 20 minutes south on TX 17, a two-lane country road where tumbleweeds bounce slowly by and congregate around the barbed-wire fences.

TRIP HIGHLIGHT

3 Marfa

Marfa got its first taste of fame when Rock Hudson, Elizabeth Taylor and James Dean came to town to film *Giant* (1956).

But these days, this tiny town with one stoplight draws visitors from around the world for a different reason: its art scene. Donald Judd single-handedly put Marfa on the art-world map in the 1980s when he used a bunch of abandoned military buildings to create one of the world's largest permanent installations of minimalist art at the **Chinati Foundation** (☎432-729-4362; www.chinati.org; 1 Calvary Row; Full Collection Tour adult/student $25/10, Selections Tour adult/student $20/10; ⏰by guided tour 10am & 2pm Wed-Sun).

Art galleries are sprinkled around town, exploring everything from photography to sculpture to modern art. **Ballroom Marfa** (☎432-729-3600; www.ballroommarfa.org; 108 E San Antonio St; suggested donation $5; ⏰10am-6pm Wed-Sat, to 3pm Sun) is a great gallery to catch the vibe. Try not to visit on a Monday or Tuesday, when many businesses are closed.

HEATHER DRAKE / LOOP IMAGES / GETTY IMAGES ©

🍴🛏 p467

The Drive » Alpine is about 30 minutes east of Marfa on Hwy 90/67.

4 Alpine

The biggest little town in the area, Alpine is the county seat, a college

MARFA LIGHTS VIEWING AREA

The Marfa Lights that flicker beneath the Chinati Mountains have captured the imagination of many a traveler over the decades, with accounts of mysterious lights that appear and disappear on the horizon that go all the way back to the 1800s. Numerous studies have been conducted to explain the phenomenon, but the only thing scientists all agree on is that they have no idea what causes the apparition.

Catch the show at the Marfa Lights Viewing Area, on the south side of the road between Marfa and Alpine. From the platform, look south and find the red blinking light (that one's real). Just to the right is where you will (or won't) see the Marfa Lights doing their ghostly thing.

Terlingua Starlight Theater

town (Sul Ross University is here) and the best place to stock up on whatever you need before you head down into the Chihuahuan Desert.

Stop by the **Museum of the Big Bend** (☎432-837-8143; www.museumofthebigbend.com; 400 N Harrison St; donations accepted; ⏰9am-5pm Tue-Sat, 1-5pm Sun) to brush up on the history of the Big Bend region. But don't expect it to be dry and dusty. The multimedia exhibits are big and eye-catching, and display-reading is kept to a minimum. Most impressive? The enormous replica wing bone of the Texas pterosaur found in Big Bend – the largest flying creature ever found, with an estimated wing span of more than 50ft.

✕ 🛏 p467

The Drive » Keep heading east. In 15 miles, look south for the guerilla art installation Target Marathon, a fun nod to Prada Marfa. In another 15 miles you'll reach the seriously tiny town of Marathon (mar-a-thun). The views aren't much during this stretch of the drive, but Big Bend will make up for all that.

5 Marathon

This tiny railroad town has two claims to fame. It's the closest town to Big Bend's north entrance – providing a last chance to fill up your car and your stomach – and it's got the **Gage Hotel** (☎432-386-4205; www.gagehotel.com; 102 NW 1st St/Hwy 90; r $229-279; ❄@📶🏊), a true Texas treasure that's worth a peek, if not an overnight stay.

The Drive » Heading south on Hwy 385, it's 40 miles to the northern edge of Big

Bend, and 40 more to get to the Chisos Basin, the heart of the park. The flat road affords miles and miles of views for most of the drive.

TRIP HIGHLIGHT

6 Big Bend National Park

At 1252 sq miles, this national park is almost the size of Rhode Island. Some people duck in for an afternoon, hike a quick trail and leave, but we recommend staying at least two nights to hit the highlights.

Seventeen miles south of the Persimmon Gap Visitor Center, pull over for the new **Fossil Discovery Exhibit** (www.nps.gov/bibe), which spotlights the dinosaurs and other creatures that inhabited this region beginning 130 million years ago.

With more than 200 miles of trails to explore, it's no wonder hiking is one of the most popular activities, with many of the best hikes leaving from the Chisos Basin. Hit the short, paved **Window View Trail** at sunset, then hike the 4.4-mile **Window Trail** the next morning before it gets too hot. Spend the afternoon hiking the shady 4.8-mile **Lost Mine Trail**, or take a scenic drive to see the eerily abandoned **Sam Nail Ranch** or the scenic **Santa Elena Canyon**.

p467

The Drive » From the west park entrance, turn left after 3 miles then follow the signs for Terlingua Ghost Town, just past Terlingua proper. It's about a 45-minute drive from the middle of the park.

TRIP HIGHLIGHT

7 Terlingua

Quirky Terlingua is a unique combination: it's both a ghost town and a social hub. When the local cinnabar mines closed down in the 1940s, the town dried up and blew away like a tumbleweed, leaving buildings that fell into ruins.

But the area has slowly repopulated, businesses have been built on top of the ruins, and locals gather here for two daily rituals. In the late afternoon, everyone drinks beer on the porch of **Terlingua Trading Company** (☎432-371-2234; terlinguatradingco.homestead.com; 100 Ivey St; ⏲10am-9pm). And after the sun goes down, the party moves next door to Starlight Theatre (p467), where there's live music every night.

p467

The Drive » Continue west on Rte 170, also known as the River Road, for a gorgeous drive along the Rio Grande inside Big Bend Ranch State Park. In 60 miles or so you'll reach Presidio. Head north on Hwy 67 to return to Marfa, then cut west on Hwy 90.

8 Prada Marfa

So you're driving along a two-lane highway out in the middle of nowhere, when suddenly a small building appears in the distance like a mirage. You glance over and see ... a Prada store? Known as the 'Prada Marfa' (although it's really closer to Valentine) this art installation set against the backdrop of dusty west Texas is a tongue-in cheek commentary on consumerism.

The Drive » Take Hwy 90 back to I-10 and head west to El Paso.

Eating & Sleeping

Fort Davis 2

Indian Lodge — Inn $$

(lodge 432-426-3254, reservations 512-389-8982; www.tpwd.texas.gov; Hwy 118; r $95-125, ste 135-$150; P) Located inside Davis Mountains State Park (p464), this historic, 39-room inn was built by the Civilian Conservation Corps in the 1930s. It has 18in-thick adobe walls, hand-carved cedar furniture and ceilings of pine viga and *latilla* that give it the look of a Southwestern pueblo – that is, one with a swimming pool and gift shop. Reserve early.

Marfa 3

Cochineal — American $$$

(432-729-3300; www.cochinealmarfa.com; 107 W San Antonio St; small plates $9-12, mains $22-42; 5:30-10pm) Foodies flock to this stylish but minimalist eatery for a changing menu that showcases high-quality organic ingredients. Portions are generous, so don't be afraid to share a few small plates – maybe along the lines of brisket tacos, oyster mushroom risotto or house-made ramen with duck breast – in lieu of a full dinner.

El Cosmico — Campground $

(432-729-1950; www.elcosmico.com; 802 S Highland Ave; tent site per person $30, safari tents $95, tipis & yurts $165, trailers $165-210; P) One of the funkiest choices in all of Texas, where you can sleep in a stylishly converted travel trailer, tipi, safari tent, or even a yurt. It's not for everyone: the grounds are dry and dusty, you might have to shower outdoors, and there's no air-con (luckily, it's cool at night). But when else can you sleep in a tipi?

Alpine 4

Reata — Steak $$

(432-837-9232; www.reata.net; 203 N 5th St; lunch $10-15, dinner $13-40; 11:30am-2pm & 5-10pm Mon-Sat) Reata turns on the upscale ranch-style charm – at least in the front dining room, where the serious diners go. Step back into the lively bar area or onto the shady patio for a completely different vibe, where you can feel free to nibble your way around the menu and enjoy a margarita.

Holland Hotel — Historic Hotel $$

(432-837-2800; www.thehollandhoteltexas.com; 209 W Holland Ave; r incl breakfast $150-225, ste $170-250;) Built in 1928, this beautifully renovated Spanish Colonial building has elegantly furnished rooms set with carved wood furniture, Western-style artwork and sleek modern bathrooms. The lobby, with its stuffed leather chairs and wood-beamed ceiling, is a classy place to unwind; there's a good high-end restaurant attached.

Big Bend National Park 6

Chisos Basin Campground — Campground $

(877-444-6777; www.nps.gov/bibe; tent & RV sites $14) The most centrally located of the main campgrounds, this 60-site place has stone shelters and picnic tables, with bathroom facilities nearby. It's located right near the **Chisos Lodge Restaurant** (www.chisosmountainlodge.com; lunch $7-12, dinner $10-22; 7-10am, 11am-4pm & 5-8pm) and the **Basin Store** (432 477 2291; 7am 9pm), as well as several popular trails. Twenty-six sites are available for advance reservations from November 15th through May at www.recreation.gov; the rest are first-come, first-served.

Terlingua 7

Starlight Theatre — American $$

(432-371-3400; www.thestarlighttheatre.com; 631 Ivey Rd; mains $10-27; 5pm-midnight Sun-Fri, to 1am Sat) You'd think a ghost town would be dead at night (pardon the pun), but the Starlight Theatre keeps things lively. This former movie theater fell into roofless disrepair (thus the 'starlight') before being converted into a restaurant. There's live music nearly every night in spring and fall.

Hill Country

Gently rolling hills are blanketed with wildflowers and dotted with vineyards. Friendly locals enjoy an easy way of life, with dance halls, lazy rivers and local art adding to the fun.

TRIP HIGHLIGHTS

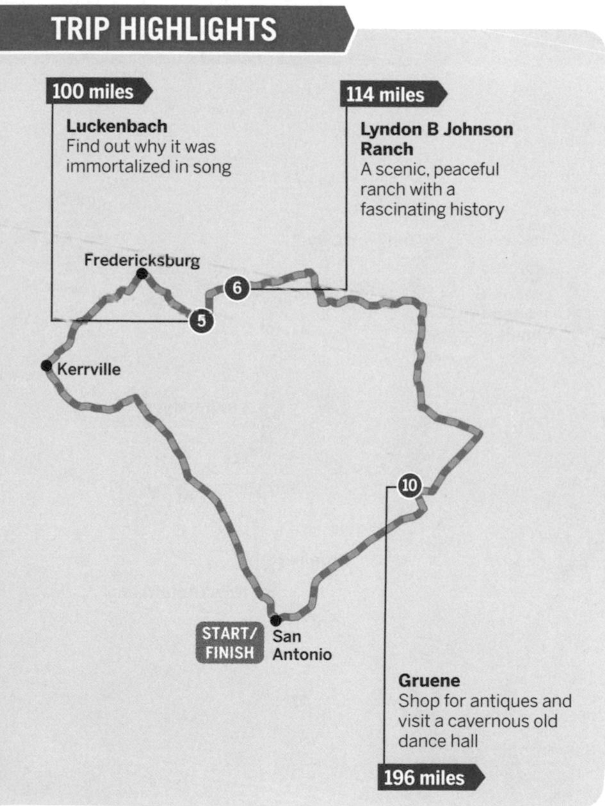

2–5 DAYS
229 MILES/369KM

GREAT FOR...

BEST TIME TO GO

In March and April for wildflower season.

ESSENTIAL PHOTO

Bluebonnets – pose your kids or yourself in a field full of wildflowers.

BEST FOR CULTURE

Two-stepping at Texas' oldest dance hall in Gruene.

Texas bluebonnets

38 Hill Country

In March and early April when wildflowers are blooming, this is one of the prettiest drives in all of Texas – perfect for a day trip or a meandering and low-stress vacation. Along this route, you can rummage through antique stores, listen to live music, dig in to a plate of barbecue, and learn about the US president who called this area home.

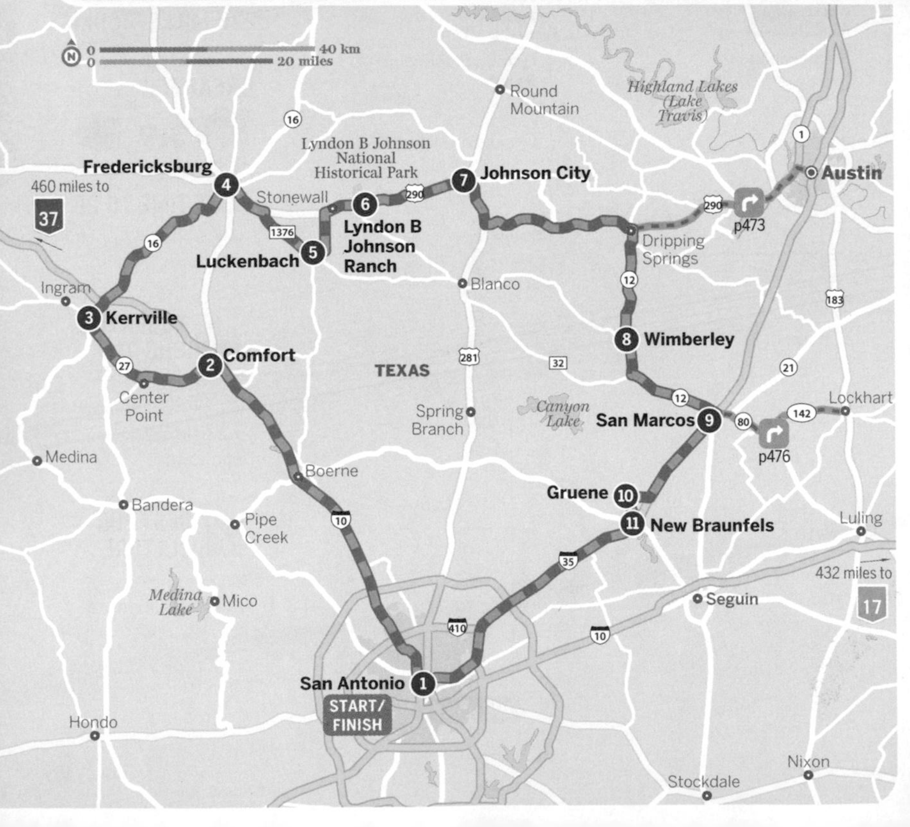

❶ San Antonio

While sprawling San Antonio isn't part of the Hill Country, it's a great launching point for your trip. Don't miss the lovely, European-style River Walk, a paved canal that winds its way through downtown and is lined with colorful cafes, hotel gardens and stone footbridges. It stretches north to the museum district and south to the missions, adding pretty mileage for walking and cycling. For the best overview, hop on a Rio San Antonio cruise.

Whatever you do, pay your respects at the **Alamo** (☎210-225-1391; www.thealamo.org; 300 Alamo Plaza; ⏰9am-5:30pm Sep-Feb, to 9pm Mar-Aug), the beloved historical site where revolutionaries fought for Texas' independence from Mexico.

The Drive » Ready to get out of town? Head northwest on I-10 to get to Comfort, less than an hour from downtown San Antonio. When the wildflowers are blooming, detouring north on Waring-Welfare Rd then back on TX 473 makes a nice scenic drive.

❷ Comfort

Remarkably under the tourist radar, Comfort is a 19th-century German settlement and perhaps the most idyllic of the Hill Country bunch, with rough-hewn limestone homes from the late 1800s and a beautifully restored historic center in the area around High and 8th Sts.

Shopping for antiques is the number-one activity, but you'll also find a few good restaurants, a winery and, as the town's name suggests, an easy way of life. Start at the **Comfort Antique Mall** (☎830-995-4678; www.visitcomfortantiquemall.com; 734 High St; ⏰10am-5pm), where you can pick up a map of antique stores, or go to the Comfort chamber of commerce website (www.comfort-texas.com) to discover your options.

🛏 p477

The Drive » The interstate is a straight shot, but we prefer the back road of TX 27 west to Kerrville that takes you through serene farmland.

❸ Kerrville

The Hill Country can feel a bit fussy at times, but not Kerrville. What it lacks in historic charm, it makes up for in size, offering plenty of services for travelers, as well as easy access to kayaking, canoeing and swimming on the Guadalupe River. Stretch your legs on the new **River Trail** (www.kerrvilletx.gov; ⏰dawn-dusk; 🐾), which runs alongside the Guadalupe River for several miles. The best place to hop in the water is **Kerrville-Schreiner Park** (☎830-257-5300; www.kerrvilletx.gov; 2385 Bandera Hwy; adult/child 3-12yr/senior $4/1/2; ⏰office 8am-5pm, day use to 10pm).

Check out an eye-catching collection of cowboy art at the **Museum of Western Art** (☎830-896-2553; www.museumofwesternart.com; 1550 Bandera Hwy; adult/student/child under 8yr $7/5/free; ⏰10am-4pm Tue-Sat). The building itself is beautiful, with hand-made mesquite parquet floors and unique vaulted domes overhead.

✕ p477

The Drive » Take TX 16 northeast of town for half an hour to get to Fredericksburg.

❹ Fredericksburg

The unofficial capital of the Hill Country, Fredericksburg is a

LINK YOUR TRIP

17 Cajun Country For po'boys and crawfish, take I-10 east to Lafayette then head south on US 90 with a left to Thibodaux.

37 Big Bend Scenic Loop West Texas? Breath-taking, quirky, and big. Head northwest on I-10 to El Paso.

19th-century German settlement that specializes in 'quaint.' The town packs a lot of charm into a relatively small amount of space, with a boggling array of welcoming inns and B&Bs and a main street lined with historic buildings housing German restaurants, biergartens, antique stores and shops. The informative **National Museum of the Pacific War** (830-997-8600; www.pacificwarmuseum.org; 340 E Main St; adult/child $14/7; 9am-5pm) spotlights the Pacific Theater in WWII. Admiral Chester Nimitz, Commander of the US fleet there during the war, grew up in Fredericksburg.

Many of the shops are typical tourist-town offerings, but there are enough interesting stores to make it fun to wander. Plus, the town is a great base for checking out the surrounding peach orchards and vineyards. A few miles east of town, **Wildseed Farms** (830-990-1393; www.wildseedfarms.com; 100 Legacy Dr; 9:30am-5pm) has cultivated fields of wildflowers and sells seed packets along with wildflower-related gifts.

p477

The Drive » Five miles southeast of town on Hwy 290, turn right on Ranch Rd 1376 and follow it 4.5 miles into Luckenbach. There are only a handful of buildings here, so don't worry that the actual town is somewhere else.

TRIP HIGHLIGHT

5 Luckenbach

You won't find a more laid-back place than Luckenbach, where the main activity is sitting at a picnic table under an old oak tree with a cold bottle of Shiner Bock and listening to guitar pickers (who are often accompanied by roosters). Come prepared to relax and get to know some folks while basking in the small-town atmosphere.

Start at the old trading post established back in 1849 – now the **Luckenbach General Store** (830-997-3224; www.luckenbachtexas.com; 412 Luckenbach Town Loop; 9am-11pm Sun-Thu, to midnight Fri, to 1am Sat), which also serves as the local post office, saloon and community center. Out back you'll find the picking circle, and there's often live music on the weekends in the old dance hall; go online to check out the town's music schedule (www.luckenbachtexas.com).

The Drive » Take Luckenbach Rd back north to Hwy 290. The LBJ Ranch is just 7 miles down and the entrance is right off the highway.

TRIP HIGHLIGHT

6 Lyndon B Johnson Ranch

You don't have to be a history buff to appreciate the family home of the 36th president of the United States. Now the **LBJ Ranch** (national park visitor center 830-868-7128, state park visitor center 830-644-2252; www.nps.gov/lyjo; Hwy 290, Stonewall; tour adult/child under 18yr $3/free; ranch grounds 9am-5:30pm, house tours 10am-4:30pm), this beautiful piece of Texas land is where Lyndon B Johnson was born, lived and died.

SCENIC DRIVE: WILDFLOWER TRAILS

You know spring has arrived in Texas when you see cars pulling up roadside and families climbing out to take the requisite picture of their kids surrounded by bluebonnets, Texas' state flower. From March to April in Hill Country, Indian paintbrushes, winecups and bluebonnets are at their peak.

Check the **Wildflower Hotline** (800-452-9292) to find out what's blooming where. Taking Rte 16 and FM 1323, north from Fredericksburg and east to Willow City, is usually a good route.

The park includes the Johnson birthplace, the one-room schoolhouse where he briefly attended school and a neighboring farm that now serves as a living history museum. The centerpiece of the park is the ranch house where LBJ and Lady Bird lived and where he spent so much time during his presidency that it became known as the 'Texas White House.'

You can also see the Johnson family cemetery, where LBJ and Lady Bird are both buried under sprawling oak trees.

Stop by the visitor center to get your free park permit and a map.

The Drive » LBJ's childhood home is just 15 minutes east on Hwy 290.

DETOUR: AUSTIN

Start: 7 Johnson City

Since this trip is all about winding your way through the Hill Country, we didn't list Austin as a stop. After all, it warrants its own whole trip, which we hope your central Texas itinerary already includes.

However, we'd be remiss if we didn't mention that when you get to Dripping Springs, you're only half an hour from the Texas state capital. While you're there, it's well worth doing some exploring and stretching your legs.

7 Johnson City

You might assume Johnson City was named after President Johnson, but the bragging rights go to James Polk Johnson, a town settler back in the late 1800s. The fact that James Johnson's grandson went on to become president of the United States was just pure luck.

Here you'll find **Lyndon B Johnson's Boyhood Home** (☎830-868-7128; www.nps.gov/lyjo; 200 E Elm St; ⊙tours half hourly 9am-noon & 1-4:30pm), which Johnson himself had restored for personal posterity. Park rangers from the **visitor center** (☎830-868-7128; www.nps.gov/lyjo; 100 E Ladybird Lane, cnr E Ladybird Lane & Ave G; ⊙9am-5pm) – where you can also find local information and exhibits on the president and first lady – offer free guided tours every half-hour that meet on the front porch. On the surface, it's just an old Texas house, but it's fascinating when you think about the boy who grew up there.

The Drive » Follow Hwy 290 south toward Blanco then east toward Dripping Springs. At Dripping Springs, turn right on Ranch Rd 12 towards Wimberley.

8 Wimberley

A popular weekend spot for Austinites, this artists community gets absolutely bonkers during summer weekends – especially on the first Saturday of each month from March to December, when local art galleries, shops and craftspeople set up booths for **Wimberley Market Days**, a bustling collection of live music, food and more than 475 vendors at Lion's Field on RR 2325. Keep an eye out for the 50 painted cowboy boots scattered around town (www.bootifulwimberley.com).

For excellent scenic views of the surrounding limestone hills, take a drive on FM 32, otherwise known as the Devil's Backbone. From Wimberley, head south on RR 12 to FM 32, then turn right toward Canyon Lake. The road gets steeper, then winds out onto a craggy ridge – the 'backbone' – with a 360-degree vista.

Afterwards, cool off at Wimberley's famous **Blue Hole** (☎512-660-9111; www.cityofwimberley.com; 100 Blue Hole Lane; adult/child 4-12yr/under 4 $9/5/free; ⊙park 8am-dusk, swimming area

Above: Luckenbach General Store
Left: Old license plates
Right: Country store, Wimberley

STEPHEN SAKS / GETTY IMAGES ©

CRACKERCLIPS STOCK MEDIA / SHUTTERSTOCK ©

FOTOLUMINATE LLC/SHUTTERSTOCK ©

10am-6pm Sat & Sun May, daily Jun-Aug), one of the Hill Country's best swimming holes. It's a privately owned spot in the calm, shady and crystal-clear waters of Cypress Creek.

✕ p477

The Drive » Keep going south on Ranch Rd 12; San Marcos is about 15 minutes southeast through some more (mostly) undeveloped countryside.

9 San Marcos

Around central Texas, 'San Marcos' is practically synonymous with 'outlet malls.' Bargain shoppers can make a full day of it at two side-by-side shopping meccas. It's not exactly in keeping with the spirit of the Hill Country, but it's a popular enough activity that we had to point it out.

The fashion-oriented **San Marcos Premium Outlets** (☎512-396-2200; www.premiumoutlets.com; 3939 S IH-35, exit 200; ⏱10am-9pm Mon-Sat, to 7pm Sun) is enormous and enormously popular – with 140 name-brand outlets. Across the street, **Tanger Outlets** (☎512-396-7446; www.tangeroutlet.com/sanmarcos; 4015 S IH-35, exit 200; ⏱9am-9pm Mon-Sat, 10am-7pm Sun) has more modest offerings, with brands that aren't that expensive to start with, but it's still fun to hunt for deals.

DETOUR: LOCKHART

Start: 9 San Marcos

People travel from all over the state to dig into brisket, sausage and ribs in Lockhart, officially designated in 1999 as the Barbecue Capital of Texas. Lucky for you, you only have to detour 18 miles to experience the smoky goodness. You can eat very well for under $15 at the following places:

Black's Barbecue (512-398-2712; www.blacksbbq.com; 215 N Main St; sandwiches $10-13, brisket per pound $16.50; 10am-8pm Sun-Thu, to 8:30pm Fri & Sat) A longtime Lockhart favorite since 1932, with sausage so good Lyndon Johnson had them cater a party at the nation's capital.

Kreuz Market (512-398-2361; www.kreuzmarket.com; 619 N Colorado St; brisket per pound $16.49; 10:30am-8pm Mon-Sat, to 6pm Sun) Serving Lockhart since 1900, the barn-like Kreuz Market uses a dry rub, which means you shouldn't insult them by asking for barbecue sauce – they don't serve it, and the meat doesn't need it.

Smitty's Market (512-398-9344; www.smittysmarket.com; 208 S Commerce St; brisket per pound $14.90; 7am-6pm Mon-Fri, to 6:30pm Sat, 9am-6:30pm Sun) The blackened pit room and homely dining room are all original (knives used to be chained to the tables). Ask them to trim off the fat on the brisket if you're particular about that.

The Drive » Shoot 12 miles down I-35 to the turnoff for Canyon Lake. Gruene is just a couple of miles off the highway.

TRIP HIGHLIGHT

10 Gruene

Get a true taste of Texas at **Gruene Hall** (830-606-1281; www.gruenehall.com; 1280 Gruene Rd; 11am-midnight Mon-Fri, 10am-1am Sat, 10am-9pm Sun), a dance hall where folks have been congregating since 1878, making it Texas' oldest. It opens early, so you can stop by anytime to toss back a longneck, two-step on the well-worn wooden dance floor or play horseshoes out in the yard. There's only a cover charge on weekend nights and when big acts are playing, so at least stroll through and soak up the vibe.

The town is loaded with antique stores and shops selling housewares, gifts and souvenirs, and **Old Gruene Market Days** are held the third weekend of the month, February through November, and the first weekend of December.

p477

The Drive » You don't even have to get back on the interstate; New Braunfels is just 3 miles south.

11 New Braunfels

The historic town of New Braunfels was the first German settlement in Texas. In summer, visitors flock here to float down the Guadalupe River in an inner tube – a Texas summer tradition. There are lots of outfitters in town, like **Rockin' R River Rides** (830-629-9999; www.rockinr.com; 1405 Gruene Rd; tube rental $20). Their rental prices include shuttle service, and for an additional fee they can also hook you up with an ice chest to keep your drinks cold and a tube to float it on.

p477

The Drive » From New Braunfels it's 32 miles on I-35 back to San Antonio.

Eating & Sleeping

Comfort 2

Hotel Faust B&B $$

(830-995-3030; www.hotelfaust.com; 717 High St; r $139-169, 2-bedroom cottage $250;) For some true historic charm, spend the night at Hotel Faust. The limestone building dates from the late 1800s, but the rooms have all been gutted and beautifully restored. For a special treat, stay in their Ingenhuett Log Cabin ($210 per night), built in the 1820s and moved to its present location from Kentucky.

Kerrville 3

Francisco's American $$$

(830-257-2995; www.franciscos-restaurant.com; 201 Earl Garrett St; lunch mains $7.25-10, dinner mains $13-38; 11am-3pm Mon-Sat & 5:30-9pm Thu-Sat) Colorful, bright and airy, this bistro and sidewalk cafe is housed in an old limestone building in the historic district. It's packed at lunch, and is one of the swankiest places in town for a weekend dinner.

Fredericksburg 4

Cotton Gin Village Cabin $$

(830-990-8381; www.cottonginlodging.com; 2805 S Hwy 16; cabins incl breakfast $229; P) Rustic on the outside, posh on the inside. Oh yes, we like it here. Just south of town, this cluster of stone-and-timber cabins offers guests a supremely private stay away from both the crowds and the other guests. Cabins come with a stone wood-burning fireplace. Romantic getaway? Start packing.

Wimberley 8

Leaning Pear American $

(512-847-7327; www.leaningpear.com; 111 River Rd; lunch mains $7-13, dinner mains $11-24; 11am-9pm Tue-Sat, to 3pm Sun) Get out of the crowded downtown area for a relaxed lunch. This cafe exudes Hill Country charm like a cool glass of iced tea, with salads and sandwiches served in a restored stone house.

Gruene 10

Gristmill Restaurant American $$

(830-606-1287; www.gristmillrestaurant.com; 1287 Gruene Rd; mains $10-24; 11am-9pm Sun-Thu, to 10pm Fri & Sat, closes 1hr later summer) Conscientious service and juicy steaks topped with lemon-butter are highlights here, where a pre-show dinner (it's behind Gruene Hall, p476) transforms into a memorably pleasant experience. Right under the water tower, the restaurant is located within the brick remnants of a long-gone gristmill. Indoor seating affords a rustic ambience, while outdoor tables get a view of the river.

Gruene Mansion Inn Inn $$$

(830-629-2641; www.gruenemansioninn.com; 1275 Gruene Rd; r incl breakfast from $225; P) This cluster of buildings is practically its own village, with rooms in the mansion, a former carriage house and the old barns. Richly decorated in a style the owners call 'rustic Victorian elegance,' the rooms feature lots of wood, floral prints and pressed-tin ceiling tiles. The hot breakfast buffet is fantastic. Gruene Hall is next door. Two-night minimum.

New Braunfels 11

Huisache Grill & Wine Bar American $$

(830-620-9001; www.huisache.com; 303 W San Antonio St; mains $10-25; 11am-10pm) Located in a former home, this cozy, stylish eatery breaks with local tradition by not being even remotely German. An impressively lengthy wine list is one of the draws, as is the variety of choices on the menu – everything from sandwiches to seafood and steaks.

STRETCH YOUR LEGS LAS VEGAS

Start/Finish: Bellagio

Distance: 1.8 miles/2.9km

Duration: Four hours

This loop takes in the most dazzling sites on the Strip: the canals of Venice, the graceful Eiffel Tower, the world's tallest Ferris wheel and a three-story chandelier. And remember, objects on the Strip are further away than they appear.

Take this walk on Trip

2

Bellagio

For floral inspiration, pause in the lobby at the ever-stylish **Bellagio** (☎888-987-6667; www.bellagio.com; 3600 S Las Vegas Blvd; 24hr; P 🐾) to admire the room's showpiece: a Dale Chihuly sculpture composed of 2000 hand-blown glass flowers in vibrant colors. Just beyond the lobby, the **Bellagio Conservatory & Botanical Gardens** (24hr; P 👪) dazzles passersby with gorgeously ostentatious floral designs that change seasonally. If you're hankering for fine art, see what's on display at the **Bellagio Gallery of Fine Art** (☎702-693-7871; adult/child under 12yr $18/free; 10am-8pm, last entry 7:30pm; P 👪), which hosts blockbuster traveling exhibits.

The Walk » Walk north on S Las Vegas Blvd (The Strip) and cross E Flamingo Rd. Caesar's Palace will be just ahead on your left.

Caesars Palace

It's easy to get lost inside this labyrinth-like Greco-Roman **fantasyland** (☎866-227-5938; www.caesarspalace.com; 3570 S Las Vegas Blvd; 24hr; P) where maps are few (and not oriented to the outside). The interior is captivating, however, with marble reproductions of classical statuary, including a 4-ton Brahma shrine near the front entrance. Towering fountains, goddess-costumed cocktail waitresses and the swanky haute couture of the Forum Shops ante up the glitz. For lunch, consider the fantastic buffet at **Bacchanal** (☎702-731-7928; www.caesars.com; buffet per adult $30-58, child 4-10yr $15-27; 8am-10pm; P ❄ 🍸 👪), a gastronomic celebration of global proportions. You'll love every bite of it.

The Walk » Continue north on S Las Vegas Blvd, passing the Mirage. At night, its faux-Polynesian volcano erupts. Just north, take the walkway over The Strip.

Venetian

The spectacular **Venetian** (☎702-414-1000; www.venetian.com; 3355 S Las Vegas Blvd; 24hr; P) is a facsimile of a doge's palace, inspired by the splendor of

Italy's most romantic city. It features roaming mimes and minstrels in period costume, hand-painted ceiling frescoes and full-scale reproductions of the Italian port's famous landmarks. Flowing canals, vibrant piazzas and stone walkways attempt to capture the spirit of La Serenissima Repubblica, reputedly the home of the world's first casino. Take a **gondola ride** or stroll through the atmospheric **Grand Canal Shoppes**.

The Walk » It's a 0.7-mile trek to Paris, but sights along the way should keep it interesting, particularly the $55 million LINQ shopping and entertainment district, home to the 550ft-tall High Roller, billed as the world's tallest Ferris wheel.

Paris Las Vegas

Evoking the gaiety of the City of Light, **Paris Las Vegas** (☎877-603-4386; www.parislasvegas.com; 3655 S Las Vegas Blvd; ⏲24hr; 🅿) strives to capture the essence of the grande dame by recreating her landmarks. Fine likenesses of the Opera, the Arc de Triomphe, the Champs-Élysées, the soaring Eiffel Tower and even the Seine frame the property. The signature attraction is the **Eiffel Tower Experience** (☎888-727-4758; www.caesars.com; adult/child 12yr & under/family $19/14/49, after 7:15pm $22/17/67; ⏲9:30am-12:30am Mon-Fri, to 1am Sat & Sun, weather permitting; 🅿 👪). Ascend in a glass elevator to the observation deck for panoramic views of the Strip, notably the Bellagio's dancing fountains.

The Walk » Walk a short distance south on S Las Vegas Blvd. Cross the boulevard on Paris Dr.

The Cosmopolitan

The twinkling three-story chandelier inside this sleek addition to the Strip isn't purely decorative. Nope, it's a 'step inside, sip a swanky cocktail and survey your domain' kind of place, worthy of your wildest fairy tale. A bit much? Not really. Like the rest of Vegas, the **Cosmopolitan** (☎702-698-7000; www.cosmopolitanlasvegas.com; 3708 S Las Vegas Blvd; ⏲24hr; 🅿 ❄) is just having fun.

The Walk » From here, walk north on S Las Vegas Blvd to catch the dazzling choreographed dancing fountain show at Bellagio's.

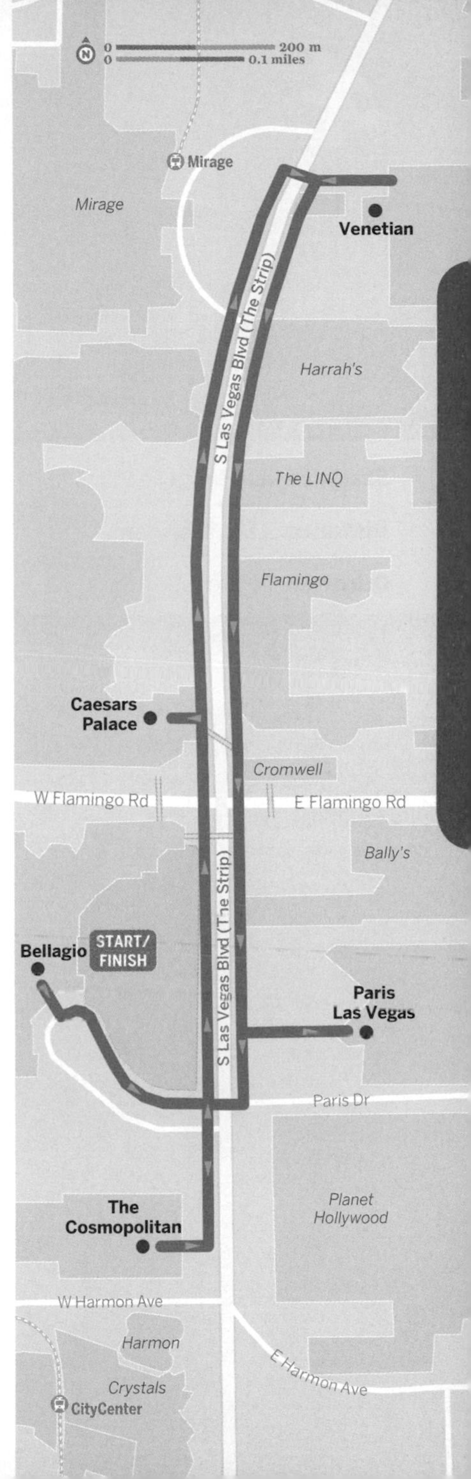

STRETCH YOUR LEGS

SANTA FE

Start/Finish Santa Fe Plaza

Distance 2.5 miles/4km

Duration Two to four hours

The only way to see the best of Santa Fe is on foot, strolling through its old adobe soul and into its renowned museums, churches, art galleries and historic buildings.

Take this walk on Trips

New Mexico Museum of Art

At the plaza's northwest corner, the **New Mexico Museum of Art** (☎505-476-5072; www.nmartmuseum.org; 107 W Palace Ave; adult/child $12/free; ⏰10am-5pm Tue-Sun) features collections of the Taos Society of Artists, Santa Fe Society of Artists and other legendary collectives – it's a who's who of the geniuses who put this dusty town on par with Paris and New York.

The Walk » Cross Lincoln Ave.

Palace of the Governors

Built in 1610, the **Palace of the Governors** (☎505-476-5100; www.palaceofthegovernors.org; 105 W Palace Ave; adult/child $12/free; ⏰10am-5pm, closed Mon Oct-May) is one of the oldest public buildings in the USA. It displays a handful of historic relics, but most of its holdings are now shown in an adjacent exhibition space called the **New Mexico History Museum**, a glossy, 96,000-sq-ft expansion that opened in 2009.

The Walk » Browse the selection of American Indian pottery and jewelry, talking to the artisans about their work. Then cross Palace Ave.

Shiprock

In a 2nd-floor loft at the northeast corner of the Plaza, **Shiprock** (www.shiprocktrading.com; 53 Old Santa Fe Trail; ⏰10am-5pm Mon-Fri, noon-5pm Sat) has an extraordinary collection of Navajo rugs. Run by a fifth-generation Southwest Indian art trader, its vintage pieces are the real deal.

The Walk » Walk one block south, then turn left on E San Francisco St. If you're hungry, first make a pit stop across the plaza at the casual Plaza Cafe.

St Francis Cathedral

Jean Baptiste Lamy was sent to Santa Fe by the pope with orders to tame the Wild Western outpost town through culture and religion. Convinced that the town needed a focal point for religious life, he began construction of **St Francis Cathedral** (www.cbsfa.org; 131 Cathedral

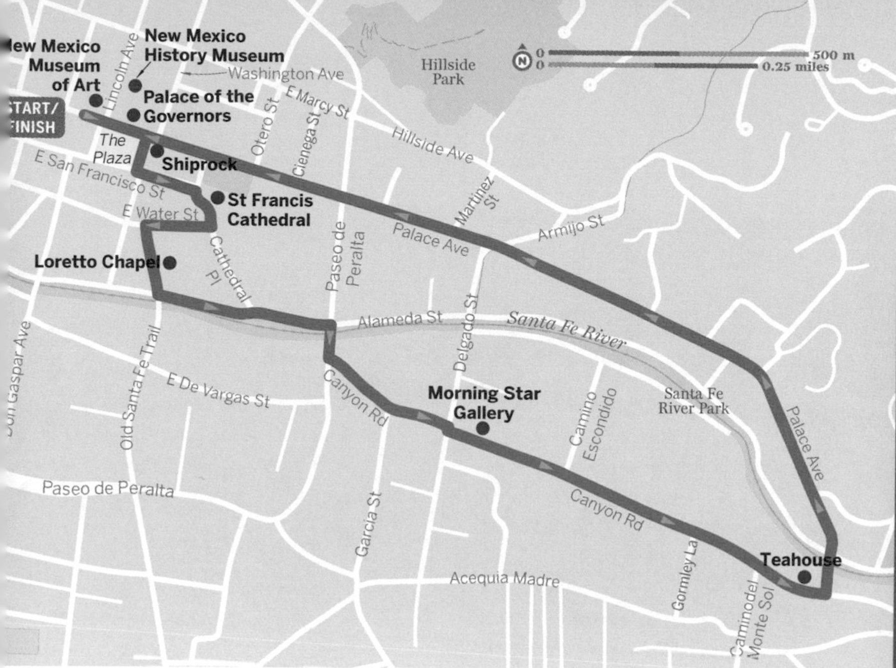

Pl; ⏲8:30am-4:30pm) in 1869. Inside is a small chapel that houses the oldest Madonna statue in North America.

The Walk » Just south of the cathedral, turn right on Water St, to the corner with Old Santa Fe Trail.

Loretto Chapel

Modeled on Sainte-Chapelle in Paris, **Loretto Chapel** (☎505-982-0092; www.lorettochapel.com; 207 Old Santa Fe Trail; $3; ⏲9am-5pm Mon-Sat, 10:30am-5pm Sun) was built between 1873 and 1878 for the Sisters of Loretto, the first nuns to come to New Mexico. Today the chapel is a museum popular for **St Joseph's Miraculous Staircase** – which seems to defy the laws of physics by standing with no visible support.

The Walk » Walk south and turn left on E Alameda St. Turn right on Paseo de Peralta, then left onto Canyon Rd – the legendary heart of Santa Fe's gallery scene.

Morning Star Gallery

Of all the Canyon Rd shops dealing in American Indian antiquities, **Morning Star** (☎505-982-8187; www.morningstargallery.com; 513 Canyon Rd; ⏲9am-5pm Mon-Sat) remains the best: weaving, jewelry, beadwork, kachina (Hopi spirit) dolls and even a few original ledger drawings are just some of the stars at this stunning gallery, which specializes in pre-WWII Plains Indian ephemera. Some artifacts here are finer than those in most museums and sell for hundreds of thousands of dollars.

The Walk » Meander on down Canyon Rd, stopping into whichever galleries catch your eye.

Teahouse

Prepare for a dilemma – at the **Teahouse** (☎505-992-0972; www.teahousesantafe.com; 821 Canyon Rd; ⏲9am-9pm; wi-fi), you'll be confronted with the list of 150 types of tea. There's coffee too, and a great food menu, from baked polenta with poached eggs to wild mushroom porcini panini to grilled salmon salad. And freshly baked desserts. It's a perfect last stop on Canyon Rd.

The Walk » Turn left on Palace Ave and walk it back to the plaza.

California

ONLY CALIFORNIA GIVES GREAT AMERICAN ROAD TRIPS A HOLLYWOOD ENDING. Ever since the early days of Spanish conquistadors and gold rush pioneers, the eternal quest for fortune and fame has inevitably led to California's golden shores. But even gold will seem overrated once you've seen the platinum glint of the Pacific, and no movie star will ever be as big as California's mighty old-growth redwoods or giant sequoia trees.

Hang tight around curves that hug the coastline on legendary Hwy 1, stringing together sandy beaches, surf and seafood shacks. Follow country lanes to famous Napa and Sonoma Valley vineyards. Take a head-spinning trip on Sierra Nevada byways past jagged peaks and glacial lakes. Honestly, there's no such thing as a wrong turn here.

In California, dreaming comes with the territory.

Napa Valley Vineyards in the fall
MICHAEL WARWICK / SHUTTERSTOCK ©

California

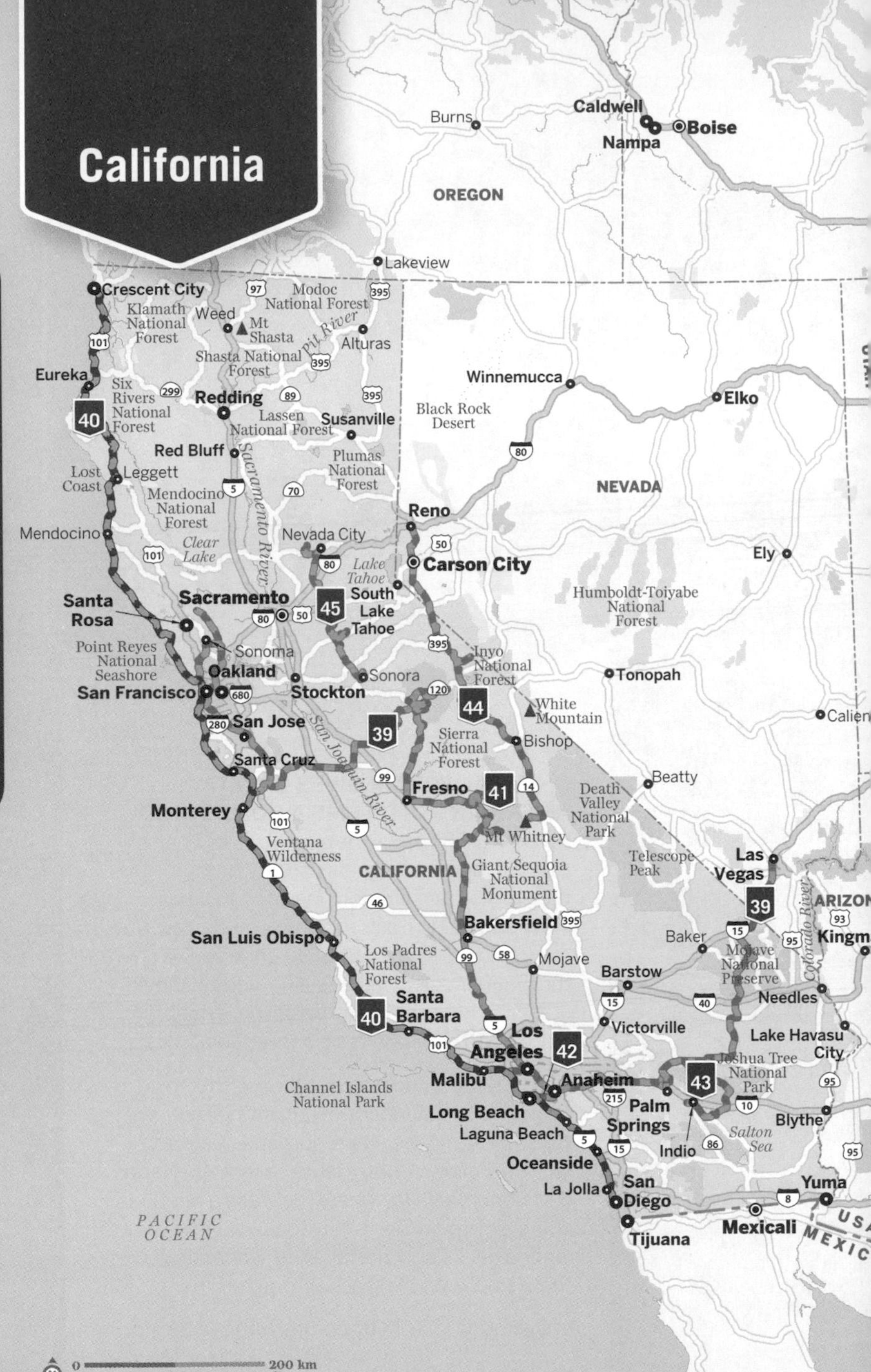

Burns
Caldwell
Nampa
Boise
OREGON
Lakeview
Crescent City
Modoc National Forest
Klamath National Forest
Weed
Mt Shasta
Pit River
Alturas
Shasta National Forest
Eureka
Six Rivers National Forest
Redding
Lassen National Forest
Susanville
Winnemucca
Elko
Black Rock Desert
Red Bluff
Sacramento River
Plumas National Forest
Lost Coast
Leggett
Mendocino National Forest
NEVADA
Reno
Mendocino
Clear Lake
Nevada City
Lake Tahoe
Carson City
Ely
Santa Rosa
Sacramento
South Lake Tahoe
Humboldt-Toiyabe National Forest
Point Reyes National Seashore
Sonoma
Oakland
Inyo National Forest
Sonora
Tonopah
San Francisco
Stockton
White Mountain
San Jose
Sierra National Forest
Bishop
Santa Cruz
San Joaquin River
Beatty
Fresno
Death Valley National Park
Monterey
Mt Whitney
Ventana Wilderness
Telescope Peak
Las Vegas
CALIFORNIA
Giant Sequoia National Monument
Colorado River
ARIZON
Bakersfield
San Luis Obispo
Baker
Kingm
Los Padres National Forest
Mojave
Mojave National Preserve
Barstow
Santa Barbara
Needles
Victorville
Los Angeles
Lake Havasu City
Joshua Tree National Park
Malibu
Anaheim
Channel Islands National Park
Palm Springs
Long Beach
Blythe
Laguna Beach
Salton Sea
Indio
Oceanside
La Jolla
San Diego
Yuma
Tijuana
Mexicali
USA
MEXIC
PACIFIC OCEAN
0 200 km
0 100 miles

39 California's Greatest Hits & Las Vegas 12–15 Days
This epic trip from the Golden State to Nevada's Las Vegas covers all the highlights. (p487)

40 Pacific Coast Highways 7–10 Days
The ultimate coastal road trip takes in beaches, redwood forests and more. (p501)

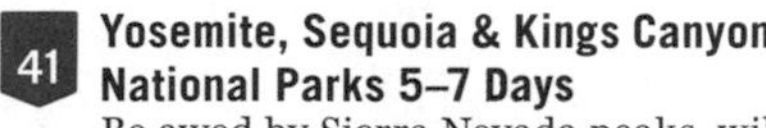

41 Yosemite, Sequoia & Kings Canyon National Parks 5–7 Days
Be awed by Sierra Nevada peaks, wildflower meadows, sequoias and waterfalls. (p515)

42 Disneyland & Orange County Beaches 2–4 Days
Meet Mickey Mouse, then surf the sun-bronzed OC coast. (p527)

43 Palm Springs & Joshua Tree Oases 2–3 Days
Where palm trees shade hot springs and watering holes for wildlife. (p537)

44 Eastern Sierra Scenic Byway 3–5 Days
A rugged wilderness gateway to hot springs, hikes and ghost towns. (p545)

45 Highway 49 Through Gold Country 3–4 Days
Head for the hills and California's historic pioneer mining towns. (p555)

DON'T MISS

Kings Canyon Scenic Byway

Wind down into the USA's deepest river canyon carved by glaciers to Road's End in Cedar Grove on Trip 41

Point Arena

Ascend 145 corkscrew steps inside the tallest lighthouse in California that you can still climb to the top of on Trip 40

Alabama Hills

Where famous Western movies and TV shows were filmed outside of Lone Pine, just below Mt Whitney, on Trip 44

Seal Beach

Slow way down for this old-fashioned beach town, squeezed between LA and the OC, where you can learn to surf by the weather-beaten wooden pier on Trip 42

Classic Trip

California's Greatest Hits & Las Vegas

Like a top-10 playlist, this epic road trip hits the all-time greats of the Golden State (and some fascinating in-between spots), ultimately stopping in glitzy Las Vegas, Nevada.

TRIP HIGHLIGHTS

0 miles

San Francisco
A kaleidoscope of neighborhoods by a breezy bay

540 miles

Yosemite National Park
Nature's temple in the Sierra Nevada Mountains

Sacramento

1 START

4

Kings Canyon National Park

Fresno

FINISH

11

Big Sur

Palm Springs

7

Joshua Tree National Park

1125 miles

Los Angeles
Go from glam Hollywood to bohemian beaches

1600 miles

Las Vegas, Nevada
Neon-lit casino playground on Sin City's Strip

12–15 DAYS
1600 MILES / 2575KM

GREAT FOR...

BEST TIME TO GO

June to September for sunny days and snow-free mountain roads.

ESSENTIAL PHOTO

Waterfalls and iconic peaks from Tunnel View in Yosemite Valley.

BEST FOR FOOD & DRINK

Napa Valley wineries and star chefs' tables.

Yosemite National Park The iconic Tunnel View

Classic Trip

39 California's Greatest Hits & Las Vegas

California is a big place, so seeing its most famous spots all in one trip could mean resigning yourself to driving dead-boring multilane freeways for hours on end. But you don't have to do that. Instead, this epic drive takes scenic state highways and local back roads to connect the dots, with a minimum of mind-numbing empty miles between San Francisco, Yosemite National Park, Los Angeles and Las Vegas.

TRIP HIGHLIGHT

1 San Francisco

In two action-packed days, explore **Golden Gate Park** (www.golden-gate-park.com; btwn Stanyan St & Great Hwy; P 👪 🐾), spy on sea lions lolling around **Pier 39** (www.pier39.com; cnr Beach St & the Embarcadero; ⏰24hr; 👪) at Fisherman's Wharf and saunter through the streets of busy Chinatown (p566) to the Italian sidewalk cafes of **North Beach**.

Feast on an overstuffed burrito in the **Mission District** after wandering its mural-splashed alleys. Queue up at Powell and Market Sts for a ride on a bell-clanging cable car (fare $7) and then cruise to the infamous prison island of **Alcatraz** (☎415-981-7625; www.nps.gov/alcatraz; tours adult/child 5-11yr day $37.25/23, night $44.25/26.50; ⏰call center 8am-7pm, ferries depart Pier 33 half-hourly 8:45am-3:50pm, night tours 5:55pm & 6:30pm; 👪) out in the bay. Book Alcatraz tickets online at least two weeks ahead.

At the foot of Market St, indulge your inner epicure at the food stalls of the **Ferry Building** (☎415-983-8030; www.ferrybuildingmarketplace.com; cnr Market St & the Embarcadero; ⏰10am-7pm Mon-Fri, 8am-6pm Sat, 11am-5pm Sun; 👪), and stop by its

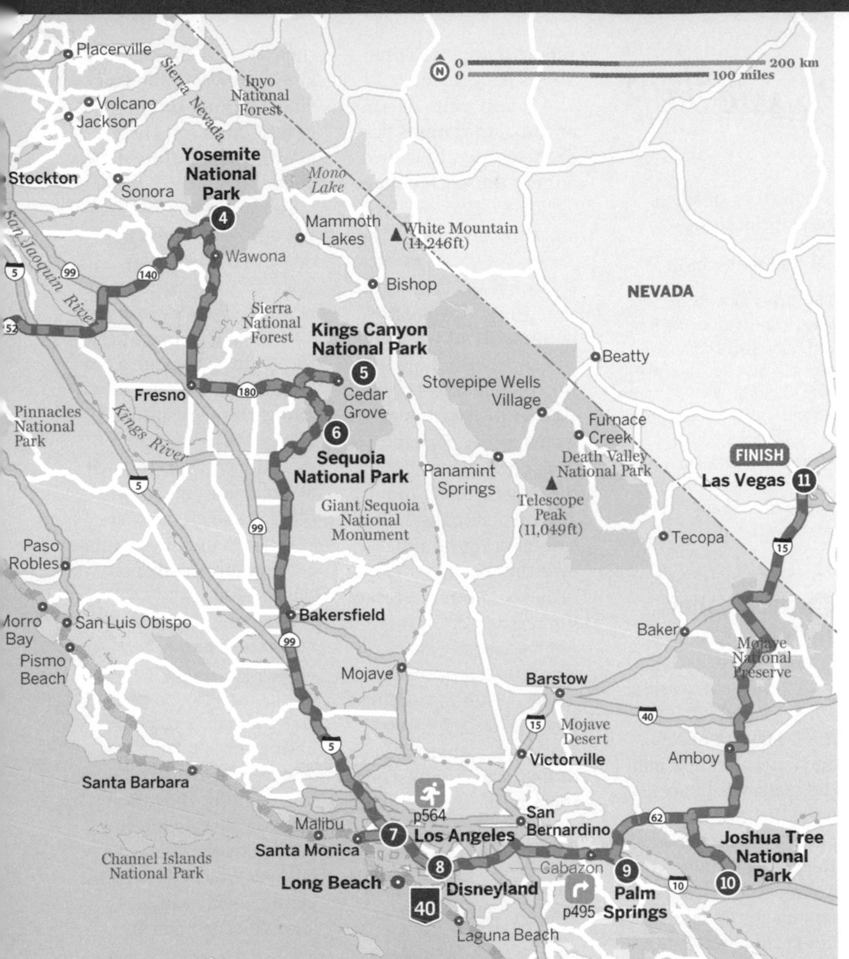

LINK YOUR TRIP

40 Pacific Coast Highways

California's most famous driving route hugs the Pacific Ocean from Mexico to Oregon. Join up in San Francisco, Big Sur or LA.

farmers market (☎415-291-3276; www.cuesa.org; street food $3-12; ⏰10am-2pm Tue & Thu, from 8am Sat; ✎ 👪) year-round to wallow in the bounty of California-grown produce and gourmet prepared foods.

Inside the historic **Castro Theatre** (☎415-621-6120; www.castrotheatre.com; 429 Castro St; ⏰Tue-Sun), the crowd goes wild when the great organ rises from the floor and pumps out show tunes until the movie starts, and the sumptuous chandelier complements

a repertory of silver-screen classics.

p498, p513

The Drive » Without traffic jams, it's an hour's drive from San Francisco to Napa, the nexus of Wine Country. Take Hwy 101 north over the soaring Golden Gate Bridge, stopping at the Vista Point on the far side of the bridge, and into Marin County. Zigzag northeast on Hwys 37, 121, 12 and 29 to reach downtown Napa.

2 Napa Valley

The Napa Valley is famous for regal Cabernet Sauvignon, château-like wineries and fabulous food. The city of Napa anchors the valley, but the real work happens up-valley. Scenic towns along Hwy 29 include St Helena, Yountville and Calistoga – the last more famous for its natural hot-springs water than its wine.

Start by the river in downtown Napa, where the **Oxbow Public Market** (707-226-6529; www.oxbowpublicmarket.com; 610 & 644 1st St; 9am-9pm; P) showcases all things culinary – produce stalls, kitchen shops, and everywhere something to taste – with emphasis on seasonal eating and sustainability. Come hungry, and top it all off with a scoop of organic Three Twins Ice Cream.

A dozen miles north of Napa, tour buses flock to the corporate-owned winery **Robert Mondavi** (707-226-1395; www.robertmondaviwinery.com; 7801 Hwy 29, Oakville; tasting/tour from $5/25; 10am-5pm, store to 6pm; P); if you know nothing about wine and can cope with crowds, the worthwhile tours provide excellent insight into winemaking. Driving back down-valley, follow the bucolic Silverado Trail, which passes several other landmark, over-the-top wineries, including **Robert Sinskey Vineyards** (707-944-9090; www.robertsinskey.com; 6320 Silverado Trail; bar tasting $40, seated food & wine pairings $70-175; 10am-4:30pm; P), where a dramatic hilltop tasting room resembles a small cathedral.

The Drive » From Napa, it's a four-hour drive of nearly 200 miles to the dramatic Big Sur coast. Head south over the Carquinez Bridge to Berkeley, then sail over the Bay Bridge into San Francisco, taking Hwy 101 south toward Silicon Valley. Detour on Hwy 17 over the mountains to Santa Cruz, then join Hwy 1 south past Monterey and Carmel-by-the-Sea.

3 Big Sur

Highway 1 along Big Sur coast may be the most famous stretch of highway in the entire state. The road twists and turns a thousand feet above the vast blue Pacific, hugging the skirts of mile-high sea cliffs, above which California condors fly.

In the 1950s and '60s, Big Sur – so named by Spanish settlers who referred to the wilderness as *el país grande del sur* (the big country to the south) – became a bohemian retreat for artists and writers, including Henry Miller and the Beat Generation. Today it attracts new-age mystics, hippies and city slickers seeking to unplug on this emerald-green edge of the continent.

All along Hwy 1 in Big Sur's **state parks** (www.parks.ca.gov; parking fee $10, valid for same-day admission to all other parks), you'll find hiking trails through forests of redwoods (incidentally, the tallest trees on earth) and to magical waterfalls – don't miss **McWay Falls**, which picturesquely tumbles onto an ocean beach.

p498

The Drive » It's about a five-hour, 220-mile trip from Big Sur to Yosemite Valley. Backtrack north on coastal Hwy 1 past Monterey, then veer inland through California's agricultural valleys, taking Hwy 152 east past San Luis Reservoir and crossing I-5, then continuing east toward Hwy 99. Outside Merced, join Hwy 140 – an all-weather highway normally open year-round – to Yosemite National Park.

TRIP HIGHLIGHT

4 Yosemite National Park

With wild rock formations, astonishing waterfalls, vast swaths of granite and humbling Sierra Nevada peaks, **Yosemite National Park** (visitor center 209-372-0200; 9035 Village Dr, Yosemite Village; 9am-5pm;) is no less than perfect. On your way in, stop at **Tunnel View** to drink in views of the Yosemite Valley, with the iconic Half Dome and plunging Bridalveil Fall in the distance. Go deeper into the valley to see triple-decker **Yosemite Falls** up close, or to hike the **Mist Trail**, which climbs a rocky staircase beside mighty **Vernal and Nevada Falls**. Drive up to **Glacier Point** (p518) to catch a brilliant sunset.

The next day, detour along high-elevation Tioga Rd (closed in winter and spring) to wildflower-strewn **Tuolumne Meadows**, encircled by skyscraping peaks and granite domes. Picnic beside sparkling **Tenaya Lake** and pull over at roadside **Olmsted Point** for panoramic views over the rooftop of the Sierra Nevada. Then backtrack down to the valley and take Hwy 41 south, exiting the park near the **Mariposa Grove** (p520) of giant sequoia trees.

p524

The Drive » It's a straight shot south on Hwy 41 from Yosemite's south entrance to Fresno, then head east on Hwy 180, which eventually winds uphill and gains over 6000ft in elevation to enter Kings Canyon National Park. The 120-mile trip to Grant Grove Village takes about 2½ hours, without traffic.

5 Kings Canyon National Park

From giant sequoia crowns down into one of the USA's deepest canyons, the twisting scenic drive in **Kings Canyon National Park** (559-565-3341; www.nps.gov/seki; 7-day entry per car $30; P) is an eye-popping, jaw-dropping revelation.

At the northern end of the Generals Hwy, take a walk in **General Grant Grove**, encompassing the world's third-largest living tree, then wash off all that sweat with a dip down the road at **Hume Lake** (Hume Lake Rd). Get back on the **Kings Canyon Scenic Byway** (Hwy 180; closed in winter and spring), which makes a precipitous descent, and make sure you pull over to survey the canyon depths and lofty Sierra Nevada peaks from **Junction View**.

At the bottom of the canyon, cruise past Cedar Grove Village. Admire striking canyon views from verdant **Zumwalt Meadow**, a

LOCAL KNOWLEDGE: HIKING HALF DOME

Just hold on, don't forget to breathe and – whatever you do – don't look down. A pinnacle so popular that hikers need a permit to scale it, Half Dome lives on as Yosemite Valley's must reach it obsession for millions. It's a day hike longer than an average work day, an elevation gain equivalent to almost 480 flights of stairs, and a final stretch of near-vertical steps that melts even the strongest legs and arms to masses of quivering jelly.

Reaching the top can only be done when the fixed cables are up, usually from late May until mid-October. To stem lengthy lines (and increasingly dangerous conditions) on the vertiginous cables, the park now requires that all day and overnight hikers obtain an advance permit. Half Dome permits go on sale by a preseason lottery in early spring, with a limited number available via another daily lottery two days in advance during the hiking season. Permit regulations and prices are subject to change; check the park website (www.nps.gov/yose/planyourvisit/hdpermits.htm) for current details.

TUNATURA / SHUTTERSTOCK ©

AE PICTURES INC / GETTY IMAGES ©

WHY THIS IS A CLASSIC TRIP

SARA BENSON, WRITER

If you've only got one shot at seeing everything California is famous for – wine, beaches, mountains, deserts, big trees and even bigger cities – take this trip. It even includes a short hop across the Nevada state line to the casino capital of Las Vegas, a favorite weekend getaway for Californians year-round. The Sierra Nevada Mountains are best visited in summer; spring brings wildflower blooms to the deserts.

Above: Wildflowers, Sierra Nevada
Left: Napa Valley vineyard
Right: Tunnel Log, Sequoia National Park

wildlife-watching hot spot with a boardwalk nature trail. At **Road's End** (usually 7am-3:45pm late May-late Sep), cool off by the sandy Kings River beach or make an 8-mile round-trip hike to **Mist Falls**, which roars in late spring and early summer.

p525

The Drive » It's only a 60-mile drive from Cedar Grove to the Giant Forest in Sequoia National Park, but it can take nearly two hours, thanks to hairpin turns and gawking drivers. Backtrack along the Kings Canyon Scenic Byway (Hwy 180) to Grant Grove, then wind south on the Generals Hwy through the sun-dappled forests of the Giant Sequoia National Monument.

6 Sequoia National Park

Big trees, deep caves and high granite domes are all on the agenda for this day-long tour of **Sequoia National Park** (559-565-3341; www.nps.gov/seki; 7-day entry per car $30; P). Arriving in the Giant Forest, let yourself be dwarfed by the majestic **General Sherman Tree**, the world's largest. Learn more about giant sequoias at the **Giant Forest Museum** (559-565-4480; www.nps.gov/seki; cnr Generals Hwy & Crescent Meadow Rd; 9am-4:30pm; P). Snap a photo of your car driving through the **Tunnel Log**, or better yet, leave your car behind and hop on the park shuttle for a wildflower walk around **Crescent Meadow** and to climb the puff-and-pant stairway up **Moro Rock**, granting bird's-eye canyon and peak views.

Picnic by the river at Lodgepole Village, then get back in the car and make your way to the chilly underground wonderland of **Crystal Cave** (www.explorecrystalcave.com; Crystal Cave Rd; tours adult/child/youth from $16/5/8; ⏰May-Sep; P 👪), where you can marvel at delicate marble formations while easing through eerie passageways. You must book tour tickets online in advance. Before sunset, take the dizzyingly steep drive down the Generals Hwy into the **Foothills** area, stopping at riverside swimming holes.

 p525

The Drive » After a few days in the wilderness, get ready to zoom down to California's biggest city. The fastest route to Los Angeles takes at least 3½ hours to cover 200 miles. Follow Hwy 198 west of Three Rivers to Hwy 65 south through the valley. In Bakersfield, join Hwy 99 south to I-5, which streams south toward LA.

TRIP HIGHLIGHT

7 Los Angeles

Make a pilgrimage to **Hollywood**, with its pink-starred sidewalks, blingy nightclubs and restored movie palaces. Long ago, the TV and movie biz (locals just call it 'the Industry') decamped over the hills to the San Fernando Valley. Peek behind the scenes on a **Warner Bros Studio Tour** (☎877-492-8687, 818-972-8687; www.wbstudiotour.com; 3400 W Riverside Dr, Burbank; tours adult/child 8-12yr from $62/52; ⏰8:30am-3:30pm, extended hours Jun-Aug), or get a thrill along with screaming tweens at **Universal Studios Hollywood** (☎800-864-8377; www.universalstudioshollywood.com; 100 Universal City Plaza, Universal City; admission from $99, child under 3yr free; ⏰daily, hours vary; P 👪).

Downtown LA is a historical, multilayered and fascinating city within a city, known for its landmark architecture. Wander through the old town of **El Pueblo** (☎213-628-1274; www.elpueblo.lacity.org; Olvera St; ⏰tours 10am, 11am & noon Tue-Sat; 👪), then be awed by the museum of art **Broad** (☎213-232-6200; www.thebroad.org; 221 S Grand Ave; free, but reservations required; ⏰11am-5pm Tue & Wed, to 8pm Thu & Fri, 10am-8pm Sat, to 6pm Sun; P 👪) before partying at the entertainment complex **LA Live** (☎866-548-3452, 213-763-5483; www.lalive.com; 800 W Olympic Blvd; P 👪) and worshiping at the star-spangled altar of the **Grammy Museum** (☎213-765-6800; www.grammymuseum.org; 800 W Olympic Blvd; adult/child $13/11; ⏰10:30am-6:30pm Mon-Fri, from 10am Sat & Sun; P 👪).

Don't leave town without hitting LA's sunny beaches. In laid-back **Santa Monica** and hipper **Venice**, you can mix with the surf rats, skate punks, muscled bodybuilders, yogis and street performers along a stretch of sublime coastline cradling the city.

p498

The Drive » It's a tedious 25-mile trip south on I-5 between Downtown LA and Anaheim. The drive can take well over an hour, especially in rush-

TOP TIP: SAFE DRIVING IN ALL WEATHER

If you plan on driving this route in winter, be prepared for snow in the Sierra Nevada; carry tire chains in your car. During summer, the deserts can be dangerously hot; avoid overheating your car by not running the air-conditioning and by traveling in the cooler morning and late-afternoon hours.

hour traffic. As you approach Anaheim, follow the freeway signs and take exit 110b for Disneyland Dr.

8 Disneyland

When Walt Disney opened Disneyland on July 17, 1955, he declared it the 'Happiest Place on Earth.' More than 60 years later, it's hard to argue with the ear-to-ear grins on the faces of kiddos, grandparents, honeymooners and everyone else here in Anaheim.

If you've only got one day to spend at **Disneyland** (☎714-781-4636; www.disneyland.com; 1313 Harbor Blvd; adult/child 3-9yr 1-day pass from $97/91, 2-day park-hopper pass $244/232; ⏲daily, seasonal hours vary), buy tickets online in advance and arrive early. Stroll **Main Street USA** toward Sleeping Beauty Castle. Enter **Tomorrowland** to ride Space Mountain. In **Fantasyland** don't miss the classic 'it's a small world' ride or racing downhill on the Matterhorn Bobsleds. Grab a FASTPASS for the **Indiana Jones Adventure** or the **Pirates of the Caribbean** before lunching in **New Orleans Square**. Plummet down Splash Mountain, then visit the Haunted Mansion before the **Fantasmic!** show and fireworks begin.

The Drive » A few different routes from Anaheim to Palm Springs all eventually funnel onto I-10 eastbound from Los Angeles. It's a trip of almost 100 miles, which should take less than three hours without traffic jams. Watch for the towering wind turbines on the hillsides as you shoot through San Gorgonio Pass. Take Hwy 111 south to downtown Palm Springs.

DETOUR: WORLD'S BIGGEST DINOSAURS

Start: 9 Palm Springs

West of Palm Springs, you may do a double take when you see the **World's Biggest Dinosaurs** (☎951-922-8700; www.cabazondinosaurs.com; 50770 Seminole Dr, Cabazon; adult/child $10/9; ⏲10am-4:30pm Mon-Fri, 9am-6:30pm Sat & Sun; P 👪). Claude K Bell, a sculptor for Knott's Berry Farm, spent over a decade crafting these concrete behemoths, now owned by Christian creationists who contend that God created the original dinosaurs in one day, along with the other animals, as part of his 'intelligent design.' In the gift shop you'll find the sort of dino-swag you might find at science museums.

9 Palm Springs

In the 1950s and '60s, Palm Springs was the swinging getaway of Sinatra, Elvis and dozens of other stars. Now a new generation has fallen in love with the city's mid-century modern charms: steel-and-glass bungalows designed by famous architects, boutique hotels with vintage decor and kidney-shaped pools, and hip bars serving perfect martinis.

North of downtown 'PS,' ride the revolving **Palm Springs Aerial Tramway** (☎760-325-1391, 888-515-8726; www.pstramway.com; 1 Tram Way; adult/child $26/17, parking $5; ⏲1st tram up 10am Mon-Fri, 8am Sat & Sun, last tram down 9:45pm daily, varies seasonally; P 👪), which climbs 6000ft vertically in under 15 minutes. It's 30°F to 40°F (up to 22°C) cooler as you step out into pine forest at the top, so bring warm clothing – the ride up from the desert floor is said to be the equivalent (in temperature) of driving from Mexico to Canada.

Down-valley in Rancho Mirage, **Sunnylands** (☎760-202-2222; www.sunnylands.org; 37977 Bob Hope Dr; tours $20-45, center & gardens free; ⏲9am-4pm Thu-Sun, closed early Jun–mid-Sep; P) was the glamorous modern estate of the Annenberg family. Explore the magnificent desert gardens or book ahead for tours of the stunning house with its art collection.

p499, p543

The Drive » North of Palm Springs, take I-10 west to Hwy 62, which winds northeast to the high desert around Joshua Tree. The 35-mile trip goes by quickly; it should take you less than an hour to reach the park's west entrance. Resupply and fuel up first in the town of Joshua Tree – there's no gas, food or water inside the park.

⑩ Joshua Tree National Park

Taking a page from a Dr Seuss book, whimsical-looking Joshua trees (actually tree-sized yuccas) symbolize this **national park** (760-367-5500; www.nps.gov/jotr; 7-day entry per car $25; 24hr; P) at the convergence of the Colorado and Mojave Deserts. Allegedly, it was Mormon settlers who named the trees because the branches stretching up toward heaven reminded them of the biblical prophet pointing the way to the promised land.

Rock climbers know 'JTree' as the best place to climb in California, but kids and the young at heart also welcome the chance to scramble up, down and around the giant boulders. Hikers seek out hidden, shady, desert-fan-palm oases fed by natural springs and small streams. Book ahead for fascinating guided tours of **Keys Ranch** (760-367-5500; www.nps.gov/jotr; tour adult/child $10/5; tour schedules vary; P), built by a 20th-century desert homesteader.

Scenic drives worth taking inside the park include the side road to panoramic **Keys View** (760-367-5500; www.nps.gov/jotr; Keys View Rd; P) and the **Pinto Basin Rd** (760-367-5500; www.nps.gov/jotr), which winds down to Cottonwood Spring, letting you watch nature transition from the high Mojave Desert to the low Colorado Desert.

p499, p543

The Drive » It's a gloriously scenic back-road adventure to Las Vegas, three hours and nearly 200 miles away. From Twentynine Palms, Amboy Rd barrels east then north, opening up desert panoramas. At Amboy, head east on Route 66 and north on Kelbaker Rd across I-40 into the Mojave National Preserve. North of the preserve, join I-15 northbound to Las Vegas.

TRIP HIGHLIGHT

⑪ Las Vegas, NV

Vegas is the ultimate escape. It's the only place in the world where you can spend the night partying in ancient Rome, wake up in Egypt and brunch under the Eiffel Tower, watch an erupting volcano at sunset and get married in a pink Cadillac at midnight.

Double down with the high rollers, pick up some tacky souvenirs and sip a neon 3ft-high margarita as you stroll along the **Strip**. Traipse through mini versions of New York, Paris and Venice before riding the **High Roller** (702-322-0591; www.caesars.com/linq; LINQ Prom-

FOTOS593 / SHUTTERSTOCK ©

Las Vegas Fremont Street Experience

enade; adult/child from $22/9, after 5pm $32/19; ⏲11:30am-2am; P 👪), the world's tallest Ferris wheel (for now). After dark, go glam at ultra-modern casino resorts like Cosmopolitan and Wynn.

Do you like old-school casinos, vintage neon signs and dive bars more than celebrity chefs and clubbing? No problem. Head downtown to historic 'Glitter Gulch' along the **Fremont Street Experience** (☎702-678-5600; www.vegasexperience.com; Fremont St Mall; ⏲shows hourly dusk-midnight or 1am), a pedestrian-only zone with the **Slotzilla zip-line canopy** (www.vegasexperience.com/slotzilla-zip-line; lower line $25, upper line $45; ⏲1pm-1am Sun-Thu, to 2am Fri & Sat; 👪), near the **Mob Museum** (☎702-229-2734; www.themobmuseum.org; 300 Stewart Ave; adult/child $24/14; ⏲9am-9pm; P). Afterward, mingle with locals at hip hangouts in the **Fremont East** entertainment district.

✕ 🛏 p59, p499

Classic Trip

Eating & Sleeping

San Francisco 1

La Taqueria — Mexican $

(415-285-7117; 2889 Mission St; items $3-11; 11am-9pm Mon-Sat, to 8pm Sun;) SF's definitive burrito has no saffron rice, spinach tortilla or mango salsa – just perfectly grilled meats, slow-cooked beans and tomatillo or mesquite salsa wrapped in a flour tortilla. They're purists at James Beard Award–winning La Taqueria. You'll pay extra to go without beans, because they add more meat – but spicy pickles and *crema* (sour cream) bring burrito bliss. Worth the wait, always.

Hotel Bohème — Boutique Hotel $$

(415-433-9111; www.hotelboheme.com; 444 Columbus Ave; r $235–295;) Eclectic, historic and unabashedly poetic, this quintessential North Beach boutique hotel has jazz-era color schemes, pagoda-print upholstery and photos from the Beat years on the walls. The vintage rooms are smallish, some face noisy Columbus Ave (quieter rooms are in back) and bathrooms are teensy, but novels beg to be written here – especially after bar crawls. No elevator or parking lot.

Big Sur 3

Big Sur Roadhouse — Californian $

(831-667-2370; www.bigsurroadhouse.com; 47080 Hwy 1; snacks & mains $7-15; 8am-2:30pm;) This modern roadhouse glows with color-splashed artwork and an outdoor fire pit. At riverside tables, fork into upscale California-inspired pub grub like spicy wings, pork sliders and gourmet burgers, with craft beer on tap. It's also a top spot for coffee and cake.

Ripplewood Resort — Cabin $$

(831-667-2242; www.ripplewoodresort.com; 47047 Hwy 1; cabins $140-250;) North of Pfeiffer Big Sur State Park, Ripplewood has gotten behind fiscal equality by charging the same rates year-round. Throwback Americana cabins mostly have kitchens and sometimes even wood-burning fireplaces. Quiet riverside cabins are surrounded by redwoods, but roadside cabins can be noisy. Wi-fi in restaurant only.

Los Angeles 7

Connie & Ted's — Seafood $$$

(323-848-2722; www.connieandteds.com; 8171 Santa Monica Blvd, West Hollywood; mains $13-44; 4-10pm Mon & Tue, 11:30am-10pm Wed & Thu, 11:30am-11pm Fri, 10am-11pm Sat, 10am-10pm Sun; P) At this modernized version of a New England seafood shack by acclaimed chef Michael Cimarusti, there are always up to a dozen oyster varieties at the raw bar, classics such as fried clams, grilled fish (wild and sustainably raised), lobsters and steamers, lobster rolls served cold with mayo or hot with drawn butter, and shellfish marinara is a sacred thing.

Palihouse — Boutique Hotel $$$

(310-394-1279; www.palihousesantamonica.com; 1001 3rd St; r/studios from $315/350; P) LA's grooviest hotel brand (not named Ace) occupies the 38 rooms, studios and one-bedroom apartments of the 1927 Spanish Colonial Embassy Hotel, with antique-meets-hipster-chic style. Each comfy room is slightly different, but look for picnic-table-style desks and wallpaper with intricate sketches of animals. Most rooms have full kitchens (and we love the coffee mugs with lifelike drawings of fish).

Palm Springs 9

Cheeky's — Californian $

(760-327-7595; www.cheekysps.com; 622 N Palm Canyon Dr; mains $9-14; 8am-2pm Thu-Mon, last seating 1:30pm;) Waits can be long and service only so-so at this breakfast and lunch spot, but the farm-to-table menu dazzles with witty inventiveness. The kitchen tinkers with the menu on a weekly basis but perennial faves such as custardy scrambled eggs and grass-fed burger with pesto fries keep making appearances.

Ace Hotel & Swim Club — Hotel $$

(☎760-325-9900; www.acehotel.com/palmsprings; 701 E Palm Canyon Dr; r $180-230, ste $300-679, $31 daily resort fee; P) Palm Springs goes Hollywood – with all the sass, sans the attitude – at this former Howard Johnson motel turned hipster hangout. The 176 rooms (many with patio) sport a glorified tent-cabin look and sport such lifestyle essentials as big flat-screen TVs and MP3 plug-in radios. Happening pool scene, low-key spa, an on-site restaurant and bar to boot.

Joshua Tree ⑩

La Copine — American $

(www.lacopinekitchen.com; 848 Old Woman Rd, Flamingo Heights; mains $10-16; 9am-3pm Thu-Sun; P) It's a long road from Philadelphia to the high desert, but that's where Nikki and Claire decided to take their farm-to-table brunch cuisine from pop-up to brick and mortar. Their roadside bistro serves zeitgeist-capturing dishes such as the signature salad with smoked salmon and poached egg, homemade crumpets and gold milk turmeric tea. Expect a wait on weekends.

Harmony Motel — Motel $

(☎760-367-3351, 760-401-1309; www.harmonymotel.com; 71161 29 Palms Hwy/Hwy 62, Twentynine Palms; r $65-85; P) This well-kept 1950s motel, run by the charming Ash, was where U2 stayed while working on the *Joshua Tree* album. It has a small pool and seven large, cheerfully painted rooms (some with kitchenette) set around a tidy desert garden with serenely dramatic views. A light breakfast is served in the communal guest kitchen.

Las Vegas, NV ⑪

Container Park — Fast Food $

(☎702-359-9982; www.downtowncontainerpark.com; 707 Fremont St; items $3-12; restaurants 11am-11pm Mon-Thu, to 1am Fri & Sat, 10am-11pm Sun, shopping center daily 11am-9pm;) With food-truck-style menus, outdoor patio seating and late-night hours, food vendors inside the cutting-edge Container Park sell something to satisfy everyone's appetite. When we last stopped by, the ever-changing lineup included **Pinches Tacos** for Mexican flavors, Southern-style **Big Ern's BBQ**, raw-food and healthy vegan cuisine from **Simply Pure**, and salads and panini at **Bin 702** wine bar.

Wicked Spoon Buffet — Buffet $$$

(☎702-698-7870; www.cosmopolitanlasvegas.com; Cosmopolitan; per person $26-51; 8am-2pm & 5-9pm Mon-Thu, 8am-10pm Fri & Sat, 8am-9pm Sun;) Wicked Spoon makes casino buffets seem cool again, with freshly prepared temptations served on individual plates for you to grab and take back to your table. The spread has all the expected meat, sushi, seafood and desserts, but with global upgrades – think roasted bone marrow and a gelato bar. Weekend brunch adds unlimited champagne mimosas or Bloody Marys (surcharge $10).

Cosmopolitan — Casino Hotel $$$

(☎702-698-7575, 702-698-7000; www.cosmopolitanlasvegas.com; 3708 S Las Vegas Blvd; r/ste from $250/300; P @) With at least eight distinctively different and equally stylish room types to choose from, Cosmo's digs are the hippest on the Strip. Ranging from oversized to decadent, about 2200 of its 2900 or so rooms have balconies (all but the entry-level category), many sport sunken Japanese tubs and all feature plush furnishings and design quirks you'll delight in uncovering.

Classic Trip

Pacific Coast Highways

Our top pick for classic California dreamin' snakes along the Pacific coast for more than 1000 miles. Uncover beaches, seafood shacks and piers for catching sunsets over boundless ocean horizons.

TRIP HIGHLIGHTS

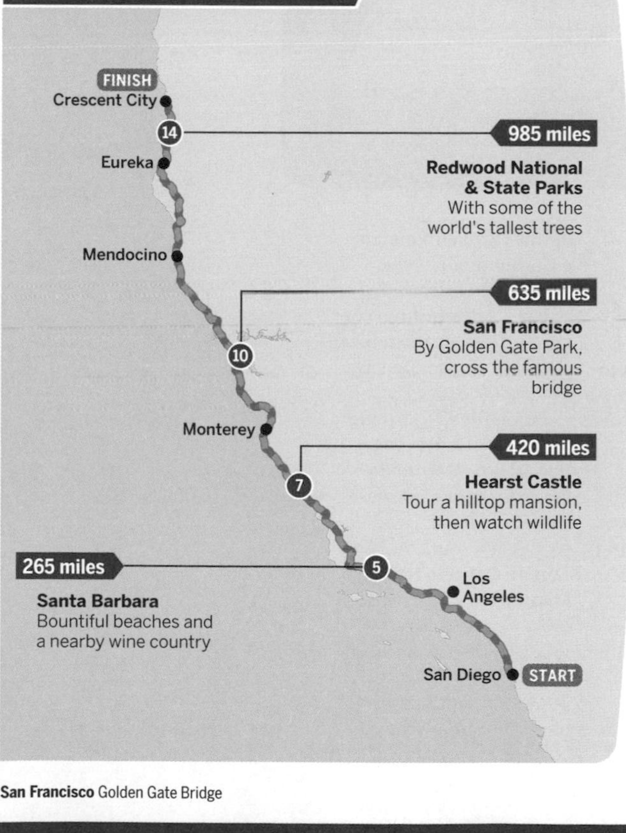

FINISH
Crescent City

14 — 985 miles
Redwood National & State Parks
With some of the world's tallest trees

Eureka

Mendocino

10 — 635 miles
San Francisco
By Golden Gate Park, cross the famous bridge

Monterey

7 — 420 miles
Hearst Castle
Tour a hilltop mansion, then watch wildlife

5 — 265 miles
Santa Barbara
Bountiful beaches and a nearby wine country

Los Angeles

San Diego
START

7–10 DAYS
1030 MILES / 1658KM

GREAT FOR...

BEST TIME TO GO

Year-round, but July to October for the sunniest skies.

ESSENTIAL PHOTO

Golden Gate Bridge over San Francisco Bay.

BEST TWO DAYS

Santa Barbara north to Monterey via Big Sur.

San Francisco Golden Gate Bridge

Classic Trip

40 Pacific Coast Highways

Make your escape from California's tangled, traffic-jammed freeways and cruise in the slow lane. Once you get rolling, it'll be almost painful to leave the ocean behind. Officially, only the short, sun-loving stretch of Hwy 1 through Orange and Los Angeles Counties can legally call itself Pacific Coast Highway (PCH). But never mind those technicalities, because equally bewitching ribbons of Hwy 1 and Hwy 101 await all along this route.

❶ San Diego

Begin at the bottom of the state map, where the pretty peninsular beach town of **Coronado** is connected to the San Diego mainland by the white-sand beaches of the **Silver Strand**. If you've seen Marilyn Monroe cavort in *Some Like It Hot,* you'll recognize the **Hotel del Coronado** (☎619-435-6611; www.hoteldel.com; 1500 Orange Ave; P 👪), which has hosted US presidents, celebrities and royalty, including the former Prince of Wales who gave up his throne to marry a Coronado divorcée. Wander the turreted palace's labyrinthine corridors, then quaff tropical cocktails at ocean-view Babcock & Story Bar.

Be thrilled by driving over the 2.1-mile-long **San Diego–Coronado Bridge**. Detour inland to **Balboa Park**. Head west, then south to Point Loma's **Cabrillo National Monument** (☎619-557-5450; www.nps.gov/cabr; 1800 Cabrillo Memorial Dr; per car $10; ⏰9am-5pm; P 👪) for captivating bay panoramas from the

19th-century lighthouse and monument to the West Coast's first Spanish explorers. Roll north of **Mission Beach** and the old-fashioned amusement park at **Pacific Beach**, and suddenly you're in hoity-toity **La Jolla**, beyond which lie North County's beach towns.

p512

The Drive » It's a 70-mile trip from La Jolla north along coastal roads then I-5 into Orange County (aka the 'OC'), passing Camp Pendleton Marine Corps Base and buxom-shaped San Onofre Nuclear Generating Station. Exit at San Clemente and follow Avenida del Mar downhill to the beach.

2 San Clemente

Life behind the conservative 'Orange Curtain' is far different than in most other laid-back, liberal California beach towns. Apart from glamorous beaches where famous TV shows and movies have been filmed, you can still uncover the

LINK YOUR TRIP

42 Disneyland & Orange County Beaches

Soak up the SoCal sunshine in glam beach towns along PCH, then take the kids to Anaheim's world-famous theme parks.

California beach culture of yesteryear here in off-the-beaten-path spots like San Clemente. Home to living surfing legends, top-notch surfboard companies and *Surfer* magazine, this may be the last place in the OC where you can authentically live the surf lifestyle. Ride your own board or swim at the city's main beach beside San Clemente Pier. A fast detour inland, the community's **Surfing Heritage & Culture Center** (949-388-0313; www.surfingheritage.org; 110 Calle Iglesia; suggested donation $5; 11am-4pm Mon-Sat; P) exhibits surfboards ridden by the greats, from Duke Kahanamoku to Kelly Slater.

The Drive » Slingshot north on I-5, exiting onto Hwy 1 near Dana Point. Speed by the wealthy artists' colony of Laguna Beach, wild Crystal Cove State Park, Newport Beach's yacht harbor and 'Surf City USA' Huntington Beach. Turn west off Hwy 1 near Naples toward Long Beach, about 45 miles from San Clemente.

3 Long Beach

In Long Beach, the biggest stars are the **Queen Mary** (877-342-0738; www.queenmary.com; 1126 Queens Hwy; tours adult/child from $27/17.50; tours 10am-6pm or later; P), a grand (and allegedly haunted) British ocean liner permanently moored here, and the giant **Aquarium of the Pacific** (tickets 562-590-3100; www.aquariumofpacific.org; 100 Aquarium Way; adult/senior/child $30/27/19; 9am-6pm; P), a high-tech romp through an underwater world in which sharks dart and jellyfish float. Often overlooked, the **Long Beach Museum of Art** (562-439-2119; www.lbma.org; 2300 E Ocean Blvd; adult/seniors & students/child $7/6/free, Fri free; 11am-8pm Thu, to 5pm Fri-Sun; P) focuses on California modernism and contemporary mixed-media inside a 20th-century mansion by the ocean, while the urban **Museum of Latin American Art** (562-437-1689; www.molaa.org; 628 Alamitos Ave; adult/senior & student/child $10/7/free, Sun free; 11am-5pm Wed, Thu, Sat & Sun, to 9pm Fri; P) shows off contemporary south-of-the-border art.

The Drive » Wind slowly around the ruggedly scenic Palos Verdes Peninsula. Follow Hwy 1 north past the South Bay's primetime beaches. Curving around LAX airport and Marina del Rey, Hwy 1 continues north to Venice, Santa Monica and all the way to Malibu, almost 60 miles from Long Beach.

4 Malibu

Leaving traffic-jammed LA behind, Hwy 1 breezes northwest of Santa Monica to Malibu. You'll feel like a movie star walking around on the public beaches, fronting gated compounds owned by Hollywood celebs. One mansion you can actually get a look inside is the **Getty Villa** (310-430-7300; www.getty.edu; 17985 Pacific Coast Hwy, Pacific Palisades; 10am-5pm Wed-Mon; P), a hilltop showcase of Greek, Roman and Etruscan antiquities and manicured gardens. Next to **Malibu Lagoon State Beach** (Surfrider Beach; 310-305-9503, 310-457-8143; www.parks.ca.gov; 3999 Cross Creek Rd; per car $12; 8am-sunset; P), west of the surfers by Malibu Pier, **Adamson House** (310-456-8432; www.adamsonhouse.org; 23200 Pacific Coast Hwy; adult/child $7/2; 11am-3pm Thu-Sat; P) is a Spanish-Moorish villa lavishly decorated with locally made hand-painted tiles.

Motoring further west along the coast, where the Santa Monica Mountains plunge into the sea, take time out for a frolic on Malibu's mega-popular beaches like sandy Point Dume, Zuma or Leo Carrillo.

p512

The Drive » Hwy 1 crosses into Ventura County, winding alongside the ocean and windy Point Mugu. In Oxnard join Hwy 101 northbound. Motor past Ventura, a jumping-off point for boat trips to Channel Islands National Park, to Santa Barbara, just over 90 miles from Malibu Pier.

TRIP HIGHLIGHT

5 Santa Barbara

Seaside Santa Barbara has almost perfect weather and a string of idyllic beaches, where surfers, kite flyers, dog walkers and surfers mingle. Get a close-up of the city's iconic Spanish Colonial Revival–style architecture along **State St** downtown or from the **county courthouse** (805-962-6464; http://sbcourthouse.org; 1100 Anacapa St; 8am-5pm Mon-Fri, 10am-5pm Sat & Sun), its tower rising above the red-tiled rooftops. Gaze south toward the busy harborfront and **Stearns Wharf** (www.stearnswharf.org; open daily, hours vary; P) or north to the historic Spanish **Mission Santa Barbara** (805-682-4713; www.santabarbaramission.org; 2201 Laguna St; adult $9, child 5-17yr $4; 9am-5pm, last entry 4:15pm; P). Santa Barbara's balmy climate is also perfect for growing grapes. A 45-minute drive northwest along Hwy 154, visit Santa Barbara's **wine country**, made famous by the 2004 movie *Sideways*. Hit wine-tasting rooms in **Los Olivos**, then take Foxen Canyon Rd north past more wineries to rejoin Hwy 101.

p512

The Drive » Keep following fast Hwy 101 northbound or detour west onto slow Hwy 1, which squiggles along the Pacific coastline past Guadalupe, gateway to North America's largest sand dunes. Both highways meet up again in Pismo Beach, 100 miles northwest of Santa Barbara.

6 Pismo Beach

A classic California beach town, Pismo Beach has a long, lazy stretch of sand for swimming, surfing and strolling out onto the pier at sunset. After digging into bowls of clam chowder and baskets of fried seafood at surf-casual cafes, check out the retro family fun at the bowling alley, billiards halls and bars uphill from the beach, or dash 10 miles up Hwy 101 to San Luis Obispo's vintage **Sunset Drive-In** (805-544-4475; www.facebook.com/sunsetdrivein; 255 Elks Lane; adult/child 5-11yr $9/4;), where you can put your feet up on the dash and munch on bottomless bags of popcorn while watching Hollywood blockbuster double-features.

p512

The Drive » Follow Hwy 101 north past San Luis Obispo, exiting onto Hwy 1 west to landmark Morro Rock in Morro Bay. North of Cayucos, Hwy 1 rolls through bucolic pasture lands, only swinging back to

DETOUR: CHANNEL ISLANDS NATIONAL PARK

Start: 4 Malibu

Imagine hiking, kayaking, scuba diving, camping and whale-watching, and doing it all amid a raw, end-of-the-world landscape. Rich in unique flora and fauna, tide pools and kelp forests, the islands of this **national park** (805-658-5730; www.nps.gov/chis) are home to nearly 150 plant and animal species found nowhere else in the world, earning them the nickname 'California's Galápagos.' Anacapa and Santa Cruz, the most popular islands, are within an hour's boat ride of Ventura Harbor, off Hwy 101 almost 40 miles northwest of Malibu on the way to Santa Barbara. Reservations are essential for weekends, holidays and summer trips. Before you shove off from the mainland, stop by the park's **visitor center** (Robert J Lagomarsino Visitor Center; 805-658-5730; www.nps.gov/chis; 1901 Spinnaker Dr, Ventura; 8:30am-5pm;) for educational natural history exhibits, a free 25-minute nature film and family-friendly activities.

Classic Trip

STILL LIFE PHOTOGRAPHY / SHUTTERSTOCK ©

ED-NI PHOTO / SHUTTERSTOCK ©

WHY THIS IS A CLASSIC TRIP

SARA BENSON, WRITER

From the perfect sun-kissed beaches of Southern California to towering coast redwoods in foggy Northern California, this slice of Pacific Coast is a knockout. I've driven every mile of this route – in some spots, dozens of times – and never tired of the seascapes and surf. My favorite stretches are around Laguna Beach, Big Sur, north of Santa Cruz, and from Jenner to Mendocino and Westport.

Above: Carousel, Santa Cruz Beach Boardwalk
Left: Malibu surfing
Right: Big Sur

the coast at Cambria. Ten miles further north stands Hearst Castle, about 60 miles from Pismo Beach.

TRIP HIGHLIGHT

7 Hearst Castle

William Randolph Hearst, the 19th- and 20th-century newspaper magnate, entertained Hollywood stars and royalty at **Hearst Castle** (info 805-927-2020, reservations 800-444-4445; www.hearstcastle.org; 750 Hearst Castle Rd; tours adult/child 5-12yr from $25/12; from 9am; P), a fantasy estate furnished with European antiques, accented by shimmering pools and surrounded by flowering gardens.

Tour reservations are recommended in advance year-round.

About 4.5 miles further north along Hwy 1, park at the signposted vista point and amble the boardwalk to view the enormous **elephant seal colony** that breeds, molts, sleeps, plays and fights on the beach. Seals haul out year-round, but the winter birthing and mating season peaks on Valentine's Day. Nearby, **Piedras Blancas Light Station** (805-927-7361; www.piedrasblancas.gov; off Hwy 1; tours adult/child 6-17yr $10/5; tours 9:45am Mon-Tue & Thu-Sat mid-Jun–Aug, 9:45am Tue, Thu & Sat Sep–mid-Jun) is an outstandingly scenic spot.

p512

The Drive » Fill your car's gas tank before plunging north into the redwood forests of the remote Big Sur coast, where precipitous cliffs dominate the seascape, and tourist services are few and far between. Hwy 1 keeps curving north to the Monterey Peninsula, approximately a three-hour, 95-mile trip from Hearst Castle.

8 Monterey

As Big Sur loosens its condor's talons on the coastal highway, Hwy 1 rolls gently downhill toward Monterey Bay. The fishing community of Monterey is the heart of Nobel Prize–winning writer John Steinbeck's country, and although **Cannery Row** today is touristy claptrap, it's worth strolling down to step inside the mesmerizing **Monterey Bay Aquarium** (info 831-648-4800, tickets 866-963-9645; www.montereybayaquarium.org; 886 Cannery Row; adult/child 3-12yr/youth 13-17yr $50/30/40; 10am-6pm;), inhabiting a converted sardine cannery on the shores of a national marine sanctuary. All kinds of aquatic denizens swim in giant tanks here, from sea stars to pot-bellied seahorses and comical sea otters.

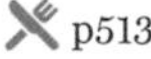
p513

The Drive » It's a relatively quick 45-mile trip north to Santa Cruz. Hwy 1 traces the crescent shoreline of Monterey Bay, passing Elkhorn Slough wildlife refuge near Moss Landing boat harbor, Watsonville's strawberry and artichoke farms, and a string of tiny beach towns in Santa Cruz County.

9 Santa Cruz

Here, the flower power of the 1960s lives on, and bumper stickers on surfboard-laden woodies shout 'Keep Santa Cruz weird.' Next to the ocean, **Santa Cruz Beach Boardwalk** (831-423-5590; www.beachboardwalk.com; 400 Beach St; per ride $4-7, all-day pass $37-82; daily Apr-early Sep, seasonal hours vary; P) has a glorious old-school Americana vibe and a 1911 Looff carousel. Its fun-for-all atmosphere is punctuated by squeals from nervous nellies on the stomach-turning Giant Dipper, a 1920s wooden roller coaster that's a national historic landmark, as seen in the vampire cult-classic movie *The Lost Boys*.

A kitschy, old-fashioned tourist trap, the **Mystery Spot** (831-423-8897; www.mysteryspot.com; 465 Mystery Spot Rd; $8; 10am-4pm Mon-Fri, to 5pm Sat & Sun Sep-May, 10am-6pm Mon-Fri, 9am-7pm Sat & Sun Jun-Aug; P) makes compasses point crazily, while mysterious forces push you around and buildings lean at odd angles; call for directions, current opening hours and tour reservations.

p513

The Drive » It's a blissful 75-mile coastal run from Santa Cruz up to San Francisco past Pescadero, Half Moon Bay and Pacifica, where Hwy 1 passes through the tunnels at Devil's Slide. Merge with heavy freeway traffic in Daly City, staying on Hwy 1 north through the city into Golden Gate Park.

TRIP HIGHLIGHT

10 San Francisco

Gridlock may shock your system after hundreds of lazy miles of wide-open, rolling coast. But don't despair. Hwy 1 runs straight through the city's biggest, most breathable greenspace: **Golden Gate Park** (www.golden-gate-park.com; btwn Stanyan St & Great Hwy; P). You could easily spend all day in the

TROUBLE-FREE ROAD-TRIPPING

In coastal areas, thick fog may impede driving – slow down, and if it's too soupy, get off the road. Along coastal cliffs, watch out for falling rocks and mudslides that could damage or disable your car if struck. For current highway conditions, including road closures (which aren't uncommon during the rainy winter season) and construction updates, call 800-427-7623 or visit www.dot.ca.gov.

conservatory of flowers, arboretum and botanical gardens, or perusing the **California Academy of Sciences** (415-379-8000; www.calacademy.org; 55 Music Concourse Dr; adult/student/child $35/30/25; 9:30am-5pm Mon-Sat, from 11am Sun; P) and the fine arts **de Young Museum** (415-750-3600; http://deyoung.famsf.org; 50 Hagiwara Tea Garden Dr; adult/child $15/free, 1st Tue of month free; 9:30am-5:15pm Tue-Sun, to 8:45pm Fri Apr-Nov;). Then follow Hwy 1 north over the **Golden Gate Bridge**. Guarding the entry to San Francisco Bay, this iconic bridge is named after the strait it spans, not for its 'International Orange' paint job. Park in the lots on the bridge's south or north side, then traipse out onto the pedestrian walkway for a photo.

For a walking tour of the city, see p566.

p498, p513

The Drive » Past Sausalito, leave Hwy 101 in Marin City for slow-moving, wonderfully twisted Hwy 1 along the Marin County coast, passing nearby Point Reyes. Over the next 100 miles from Bodega Bay to Mendocino, revel in a remarkably uninterrupted stretch of coastal highway. More than halfway along, watch for the lighthouse road turnoff north of Point Arena town.

DETOUR: POINT REYES

Start: 10 San Francisco

A rough-hewn beauty, **Point Reyes National Seashore** (415-654-5100; www.nps.gov/pore; P) lures marine mammals and birds, as well as scores of shipwrecks. It was here that Sir Francis Drake repaired his ship the *Golden Hind* in 1579 and, while he was at it, claimed the indigenous land for England.

Follow Sir Francis Drake Blvd west out to the point's edge-of-the-world **lighthouse** (415-669-1534; www.nps.gov/pore; 10am-4:30pm Fri-Mon, lens room 2:30-4pm Fri-Mon; P), whipped by ferocious winds, where you can observe migrating whales in winter. The lighthouse is about 20 miles west of Point Reyes Station off Hwy 1 along Marin County's coast.

11 Around Point Arena

The fishing fleets of Bodega Bay and Jenner's harbor-seal colony are the last things you'll see before PCH dives into California's great rural northlands. Hwy 1 twists and turns past the Sonoma Coast's state parks packed with hiking trails, sand dunes and beaches, as well as underwater marine reserves, rhododendron groves and a 19th-century Russian fur-trading fort.

At **Sea Ranch**, don't let exclusive-looking vacation homes prevent you from following public-access trailhead signs and staircases down to empty beaches and across ocean bluffs. Further north, guarding an unbelievably windy point since 1908, **Point Arena Lighthouse** (707-882-2809; www.pointarenalighthouse.com; 45500 Lighthouse Rd; adult/child $7.50/1; 10am-3:30pm mid-Sep–mid-May, to 4:30pm mid-May–mid-Sep; P) is the only lighthouse in California where you can actually climb to the top. Check in at the museum, then ascend the 115ft tower to inspect the Fresnel lens, and panoramas of the sea and the jagged San Andreas Fault below.

p513

The Drive » It's an hour-long, 35-mile drive north along Hwy 1 from the Point Arena Lighthouse turnoff to Mendocino, crossing the Navarro, Little and Big Rivers. Feel free to stop and stretch at wind-tossed state beaches, parklands crisscrossed by hiking trails and tiny coastal towns along the way.

ALEKSEI POTOV / SHUTTERSTOCK ©

12 Mendocino & Fort Bragg

Looking more like Cape Cod than California, the quaint maritime town of **Mendocino** has white picket fences surrounding New England–style cottages with blooming gardens and redwood-built water towers. Its dramatic headlands jutting into the Pacific, this yesteryear timber town and shipping port was 'discovered' by artists and bohemians in the 1950s and has served as a scenic backdrop in over 50 movies.

Once you've browsed the souvenir shops and art galleries selling everything from driftwood carvings to homemade fruit jams, escape north to workaday **Fort Bragg**, with its simple fishing harbor and brewpub, stopping first for a short hike on the ecological staircase and pygmy forest trail at oceanfront **Jug Handle State Natural Reserve** (707-937-5804; www.parks.ca.gov; Hwy 1, Caspar; sunrise-sunset; P).

The Drive » About 25 miles north of Mendocino, Westport is the last hamlet along this rugged stretch of Hwy 1. Rejoin Hwy 101 northbound at Leggett for another 90 miles to Eureka, detouring along the Avenue of the Giants and, if you have more time to spare, to the Lost Coast.

13 Eureka

Hwy 101 trundles alongside **Humboldt Bay National Wildlife Refuge** (707-733-5406; www.fws.gov/refuge/humboldt_bay; 1020 Ranch Rd, Loleta; 8am-5pm; P), a major stopover for migratory birds on the Pacific Flyway. Next comes the sleepy railroad town of Eureka.

As you wander downtown, check out the ornate **Carson Mansion** (Ingomar Club; www.ingomar.org; 143 M St), built in the 1880s by a timber baron and adorned with dizzying Victorian turrets, towers, gables and gingerbread details. **Blue Ox Millworks & Historic Park** (707-444-3437; www.blueoxmill.com; 1 X St; adult/child 6-12yr $10/5; 9am-5pm Mon-Fri year-round, plus 9am-4pm Sat Apr-Nov;) still creates Victorian detailing by hand using traditional carpentry and 19th-century equipment.

Back by Eureka's harborfront, climb aboard the blue-and-white 1910 **Madaket** (Madaket Cruises; 707-445-1910; www.humboldtbaymaritimemuseum.com; 1st St; narrated cruises adult/child $22/18; 1pm, 2:30pm & 4pm Wed-Sat, 1pm & 2:30pm Sun-Tue mid-May–mid-Oct;), docked at the foot of C St. Sunset cocktail cruises serve from California's smallest licensed bar.

p513

The Drive » Follow Hwy 101 north past the Rastafarian-hippie college town of Arcata and turnoffs for Trinidad State Beach and Patrick's Point State Park. Hwy 101 drops out of the trees beside marshy Humboldt Lagoons State Park, rolling north toward Orick, just over 40 miles from Eureka.

Redwood forest

TRIP HIGHLIGHT

14 Redwood National & State Parks

At last, you'll reach **Redwood National Park** (707-465-7335; www.nps.gov/redw; Hwy 101; P 👪). Get oriented to the tallest trees on earth at the coastal **Thomas H Kuchel Visitor Center** (707-465-7765; www.nps.gov/redw; Hwy 101, Orick; 9am-5pm Apr-Oct, to 4pm Nov-Mar; 👪), just south of the tiny town of Orick. Then commune with the coastal giants on their own mossy turf inside **Lady Bird Johnson Grove** or the majestic **Tall Trees Grove** (free drive-and-hike permit required). For more untouched redwood forests, wind along the 8-mile **Newton B Drury Scenic Parkway** in **Prairie Creek Redwoods State Park** (707-488-2039; www.parks.ca.gov; 9am-5pm May-Sep, to 4pm Wed-Sun Oct-Apr; 👪), passing grassy meadows where Roosevelt elk roam, then follow Hwy 101 all the way north to **Crescent City**, the last pit stop before the Oregon border.

Eating & Sleeping

San Diego 1

Pearl — Motel $$

(☎619-226-6100; www.thepearlsd.com; 1410 Rosecrans St; r $125-199; P ❄ 📶 🏊) The mid-century-modern Pearl feels more Palm Springs than San Diego. The 23 rooms in its 1959 shell have soothing blue hues, trippy surf motifs and fishbowls. There's a lively pool scene (including **'dive-in' movies** on Wednesday nights), or you can play Jenga or Parcheesi in the groovy, shag-carpeted lobby. Light sleepers: request a room away from busy street traffic. On-site parking is limited and costs $12.

Malibu 4

Neptune's Net — Seafood $$

(☎310-457-3095; www.neptunesnet.com; 42505 Pacific Coast Hwy; mains $7-21; ⏰10:30am-8pm Mon-Thu, to 9pm Fri, 10am-8pm Sat & Sun, closes 1hr earlier Oct-Apr; 👪 🐾) Not far past the Malibu line in Ventura County, Neptune's Net catches Range Rovers, road bikes and rad choppers with fried-shrimp-and-beer hospitality on inviting wooden porches.

Santa Barbara 5

Santa Barbara Shellfish Company — Seafood $$

(☎805-966-6676; http://shellfishco.com; 230 Stearns Wharf; dishes $4-19; ⏰11am-9pm; 👪 🐾) 'From sea to skillet to plate' sums up this end-of-the-wharf seafood shack that's more of a buzzing counter joint than a sit-down restaurant. Chase away the seagulls as you chow down on garlic-baked clams, crab cakes and coconut-fried shrimp at wooden picnic tables outside. Awesome lobster bisque, ocean views and the same location for almost 40 years.

Santa Barbara Auto Camp — Campground $$

(☎888-405-7553; http://autocamp.com/sb; 2717 De La Vina St; d $175-215; P ❄ 📶 🐾) Ramp up the retro chic and bed down with vintage style in one of five shiny metal Airstream trailers parked near upper State St, north of downtown. All five architect-designed trailers have unique perks, such as a claw-foot tub or extra twin-size beds for kiddos, as well as full kitchen and complimentary cruiser bikes to borrow.

Pismo Beach 6

Ember — Californian $$$

(☎805-474-7700; www.emberwoodfire.com; 1200 E Grand Ave, Arroyo Grande; shared dishes $12-26, mains $26-36; ⏰4-9pm Wed-Thu & Sun, to 10pm Fri & Sat) Chef Brian Collins, who once cooked at Alice Waters' revered Chez Panisse, has returned to his roots in San Luis Obispo County. Out of this heart-warming restaurant's wood-burning oven come savory flatbreads, artfully charred squid and hearty red-wine-smoked short ribs. No reservations, so show up at 4pm or after 7:30pm, or be prepared for a very long wait for a table.

Hearst Castle 7

Sebastian's — American $

(☎805-927-3307; www.facebook.com/SebastiansSanSimeon; 442 SLO–San Simeon Rd; mains $9-14; ⏰11am-4pm Tue-Sun) Down a side road across Hwy 1 from Hearst Castle, this tiny historic market sells cold drinks, Hearst Ranch beef burgers, giant deli sandwiches and salads for beach picnics at San Simeon Cove. Hearst Ranch Winery tastings are available at the copper-top bar.

Monterey 8

Alvarado Street Brewery Brewery $

(831-655-2337; www.alvaradostreetbrewery.com; 426 Alvarado St; small plates $6-13, large plates $13-16; 11:30am-10pm Sun-Wed, to 11pm Thu-Sat) Vintage beer advertising punctuates Alvarado Street's brick walls, but that's the only concession to earlier days at this excellent craft-beer pub. Innovative brews harness new hop strains, sour and barrel-aged beers regularly fill the taps, and superior bar food includes Thai-curry mussels and truffle-crawfish mac 'n' cheese. In summer, adjourn to the alfresco beer garden out back.

Santa Cruz 9

Adobe on Green B&B B&B $$

(831-469-9866; www.adobeongreen.com; 103 Green St; r $179; P) Peace and quiet are the mantras at this place, a short walk from Pacific Ave. The hosts are practically invisible, but their thoughtful touches are everywhere, from boutique-hotel amenities in spacious, stylish and solar-powered rooms to breakfast spreads from their organic gardens.

San Francisco 10

Greens Vegetarian, Californian $$

(415-771-6222; www.greensrestaurant.com; Fort Mason Center, 2 Marina Blvd, Bldg A; mains lunch $16-19, dinner $20-28; 11:45am-2:30pm & 5:30-9pm) Career carnivores won't realize there's zero meat in the hearty black-bean chili, or in Greens' other flavor-packed vegetarian dishes, made using ingredients from a Zen farm in Marin. And, oh, what views! The Golden Gate rises just outside the window-lined dining room. The on-site cafe serves to-go lunches, but for sit-down meals, including Sunday brunch, reservations are essential.

Argonaut Hotel Boutique Hotel $$$

(415-563-0800; www.argonauthotel.com; 495 Jefferson St; r from $389; P) Fisherman's Wharf's top hotel was built as a cannery in 1908 and has century-old wooden beams and exposed-brick walls. Rooms sport an over-the-top nautical theme, with porthole-shaped mirrors and plush, deep-blue carpets. Though all rooms have the amenities of an upper-end hotel – ultra-comfy beds, iPod docks – some are tiny with limited sunlight. Parking is $59.

Around Point Arena 11

Mar Vista Cottages Cabin $$$

(707-884-3522; www.marvistamendocino.com; 35101 Hwy 1, Anchor Bay; cottages $190-310; P) These elegantly renovated 1930s fishing cabins offer a simple, stylish seaside escape with a vanguard commitment to sustainability. The harmonious environment is the result of pitch-perfect details: linens are line-dried over lavender, guests browse the organic vegetable garden to harvest their own dinner and chickens cluck around the grounds laying the next morning's breakfast. It often requires two-night stays.

Eureka 13

Carter House Inns B&B $$$

(707-444-8062; www.carterhouse.com; 301 L St; r $184-384; P) Constructed in period style, this aesthetically remodeled hotel is a Victorian lookalike. Rooms have all modern amenities and top-quality linens; suites have in-room Jacuzzis and marble fireplaces. The same owners operate four other sumptuously decorated lodgings: a single-level house, two honeymoon hideaway cottages and a replica of an 1880s San Francisco mansion, which the owner built himself, entirely by hand.

Yosemite, Sequoia & Kings Canyon National Parks

Drive up into the lofty Sierra Nevada, where glacial valleys and ancient forests overfill the windshield scenery. Go climb a rock, pitch a tent or photograph wildflowers and wildlife.

TRIP HIGHLIGHTS

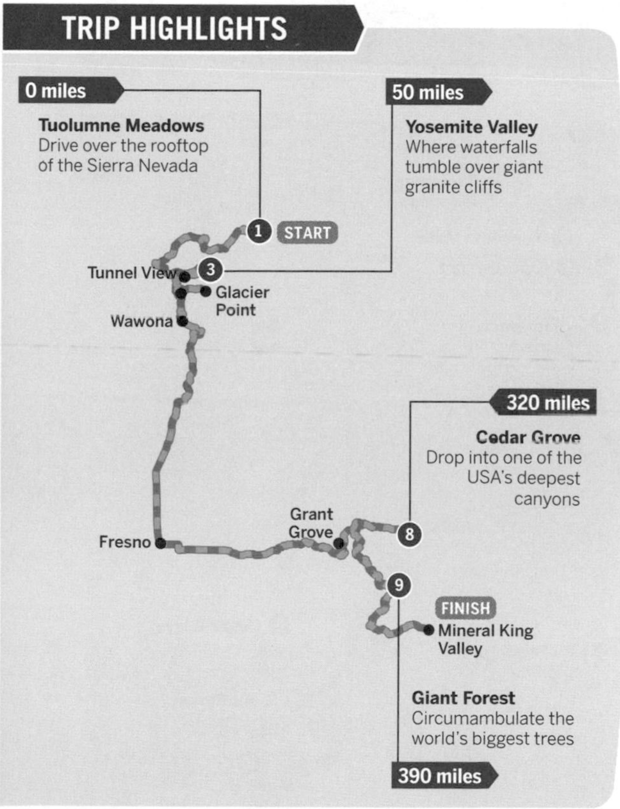

5–7 DAYS
450 MILES / 725KM

GREAT FOR...

BEST TIME TO GO

April and May for waterfalls; June to September for full access.

ESSENTIAL PHOTO

Yosemite Valley from panoramic Tunnel View.

Kings Canyon Scenic Byway to Cedar Grove.

Yosemite National Park Cycling past Yosemite Falls

41 Yosemite, Sequoia & Kings Canyon National Parks

Glacier-carved valleys resting below dramatic peaks make Yosemite an all-ages playground. Here you can witness earth-shaking waterfalls, clamber up granite domes and camp out by meadows where wildflowers bloom in summer. Home to the USA's deepest canyon and the biggest tree on the planet, Sequoia and Kings Canyon National Parks justify detouring south into the Sierra Nevada, which conservationist John Muir called 'The Range of Light.'

TRIP HIGHLIGHT

1 Tuolumne Meadows

Tuolumne Meadows makes for an impressive introduction to the Yosemite area. These are the Sierra Nevada's largest subalpine meadows, with fields of wildflowers, bubbling streams, ragged granite peaks and cooler temperatures at an elevation of 8600ft. Hikers can find a paradise of trails to tackle, or unpack a picnic basket by the stream-fed meadows.

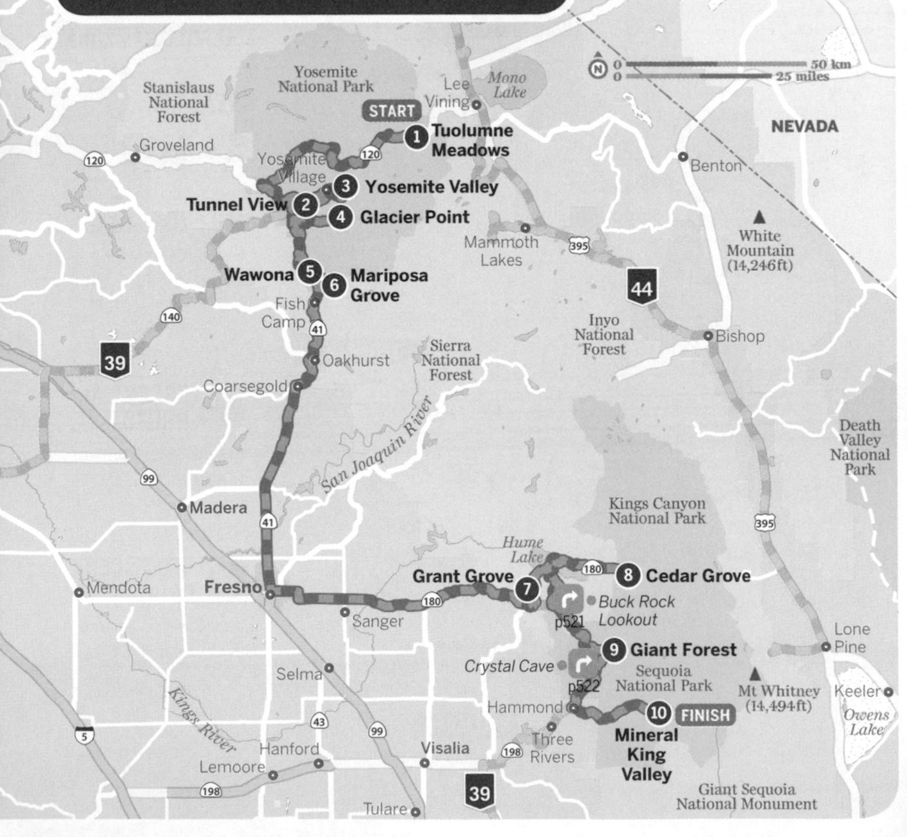

Note that the route crossing the Sierra and passing by the meadows, **Tioga Rd** (a 19th-century wagon road and Native American trading route), is completely closed by snow in winter. It usually reopens in May/June and remains passable until October or November.

Nine miles west of the meadows, a sandy half-moon beach wraps around **Tenaya Lake**, tempting you to brave some of the park's coldest swimming. Sunbathers lie upon rocks that rim the lake's northern shore. A few minutes further west stop at **Olmsted Point**. Overlooking a lunar-type landscape of glaciated granite, you can gaze deeply down Tenaya Canyon to Half Dome's backside.

LINK YOUR TRIP

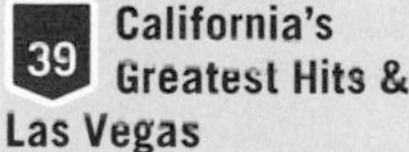

39 California's Greatest Hits & Las Vegas

After a few days in the wilderness, head south to LA and then across the desert to Nevada.

44 Eastern Sierra Scenic Byway

From Yosemite's Tuolumne Meadows, roll over high-elevation Tioga Pass and downhill towards Mono Lake, a 20-mile trip.

p524

The Drive » From Tuolumne Meadows it's 50 miles to Yosemite Valley, following Tioga Rd (Hwy 120), turning south onto Big Oak Flat Rd, then east onto El Portal Rd. There's one must-do stop before entering the valley proper, Tunnel View, so follow Wawona Rd west for a few miles where it forks with Southside Dr. You'll know you've arrived when you see all the other parked cars.

TRIP HIGHLIGHT

2 Tunnel View

For your first, spectacular look into Yosemite Valley, pull over at Tunnel View, a vista that has inspired painters, poets, naturalists and adventurers for centuries. On the right, Bridalveil Fall swells with snowmelt in late spring, but by late summer, it's a mere whisper, often lifted and blown aloft by the wind.

Spread below you are the pine forests and meadows of the valley floor, with the sheer face of El Capitan rising on the left and, in the distance straight ahead, iconic granite Half Dome.

The Drive » Merge carefully back onto eastbound Wawona Rd, which continues downhill into Yosemite Valley, full of confusingly intersecting one-way roads. Drive east along the Merced River on Southside Dr past the Bridalveil Fall turnoff. Almost 6 miles from Tunnel View, turn left and drive across Sentinel Bridge to Yosemite Village's day-use parking lots. Ride free shuttle buses that circle the valley.

TRIP HIGHLIGHT

3 Yosemite Valley

From the bottom looking up, this dramatic valley cut by the meandering Merced River is song-inspiring, and not just for birds: rippling meadow grasses; tall pines; cool, impassive pools reflecting granite monoliths; and cascading, glacier-cold whitewater ribbons.

At busy Yosemite Village, start inside the **Yosemite Valley Visitor Center** (☎209-372-0200; 9035 Village Dr; ⊙9am-5pm; 👪), with its thought-provoking history and nature displays and free *Spirit of Yosemite* film screenings. At the nearby **Yosemite Museum** (www.nps.gov/yose; 9037 Village Dr; ⊙9am-5pm summer, 10am-4pm rest of year, often closed noon-1pm), Western landscape paintings are hung beside Native American baskets and beaded clothing.

The valley's famous waterfalls are thunderous cataracts in May, but mere trickles by late July. Triple-tiered **Yosemite Falls** is North America's tallest, while **Bridalveil Fall** is hardly less impressive. A strenuous, often slippery staircase beside Vernal Fall leads you, gasping, right to the top edge of the waterfall, where rainbows pop in clouds of mist. Keep hiking up the same Mist

Trail to the top of **Nevada Fall** for a heady 5.5-mile round-trip trek.

In midsummer, you can rent a raft at Half Dome Village and float down the Merced River. The serene stretch between Stoneman Bridge and Sentinel Beach is gentle enough for kids. Or take the whole family to see the stuffed wildlife mounts at the hands-on **Nature Center at Happy Isles** (www.nps.gov/yose; ⏲9am-5pm late May-Sep; 👪), east of Half Dome Village.

✕ 🛏 p524

The Drive » Use Northside Dr to loop round and join Wawona Rd again. Follow Wawona Rd/Hwy 41 up out of the valley. After 9 miles, turn left onto Glacier Point Rd at the Chinquapin intersection, driving 15 more miles to Glacier Point.

4 Glacier Point

In just over an hour, you can zip from Yosemite Valley up to head-spinning Glacier Point. Note that the final 10 miles of Glacier Point Rd is closed by snow in winter, usually from November through April or May. During winter, the road remains open as far as the Yosemite Ski & Snowboard Area, but snow tires and tire chains may be required.

Rising over 3000ft above the valley floor, dramatic Glacier Point (7214ft) practically puts you at eye level with Half

PAVEL TVRDY / SHUTTERSTOCK ©

HIKING HALF DOME & AROUND YOSEMITE VALLEY

Over 800 miles of hiking trails in Yosemite National Park fit hikers of all abilities. Take an easy half-mile stroll on the valley floor or underneath giant sequoia trees, or venture out all day on a quest for viewpoints, waterfalls and lakes in the mountainous high country.

Some of the park's most popular hikes start right in Yosemite Valley, including to the top of **Half Dome** (16-mile round-trip), the most famous of all. It follows a section of the John Muir Trail and is strenuous, difficult and best tackled in two days with an overnight in Little Yosemite Valley. Reaching the top can only be done in summer after park rangers have installed fixed cables; depending on snow conditions, this may occur as early as late May and the cables usually come down in mid-October. To limit the cables' notorious human logjams, the park now requires permits for day hikers, but the route is still nerve-wracking because hikers must share the cables. Advance permits go on sale by a preseason lottery in early spring, with a limited number available via another daily lottery two days in advance during the hiking season. Check the park website (www.nps.gov/yose) for current regulations and prices.

The less ambitious or physically fit will still have a ball following the **Mist Trail** as far as Vernal Fall (2.5-mile round-trip), the top of Nevada Fall (5.5-mile round-trip) or idyllic Little Yosemite Valley (8-mile round-trip). The **Four Mile Trail** (9-mile round-trip) up to Glacier Point is a strenuous but satisfying climb to a glorious viewpoint. If you've got the kids in tow, nice and easy valley walks include to **Mirror Lake** (2-mile round-trip) and viewpoints at the base of thundering **Yosemite Falls** (1-mile round-trip) and lacy **Bridalveil Fall** (0.5-mile round-trip).

Glacier Point View of Half Dome

Dome. Glimpse what John Muir and US President Teddy Roosevelt saw when they camped here in 1903: the waterfall-strewn Yosemite Valley below and the distant peaks ringing Tuolumne Meadows. To get away from the crowds, hike a little way down the Panorama Trail, just south of the crowded main viewpoint.

On your way back from Glacier Point, take time out for a 2-mile hike up **Sentinel Dome** or out to **Taft Point** for incredible 360-degree valley views.

The Drive » Drive back downhill past Yosemite Ski & Snowboard Area, turning left at the Chinquapin intersection and winding south through thick forest on Wawona Rd/Hwy 41. After almost 13 curvy miles, you'll reach Wawona, with its lodge, visitor center, general store and gas station, all on your left.

5 Wawona

At Wawona, a 45-minute drive south of the valley, drop by the **Pioneer Yosemite History Center** (☎209-372-0200; www.nps.gov/yose; rides adult/child $5/4; ⊙24hr, rides Wed-Sun Jun-Sep; P 👪), with its covered bridge, pioneer-era buildings and historic Wells Fargo office. In summer you can take a short, bumpy stagecoach ride and really feel like you're living in the past. Peek inside the **Wawona Visitor Center** (☎209-375-9531; ⊙8:30am-5pm May-Oct) at the re-created studio of 19th-century artist Thomas Hill, hung with romantic Sierra Nevada landscape paintings. On summer evenings, imbibe a civilized cocktail in the lobby lounge of the Big Trees Lodge (p525), where pianist Tom Bopp often plays tunes from Yosemite's bygone days.

🛏 p525

The Drive » By car, follow Wawona Rd/Hwy 41 south for 4.5 miles to the park's south

WINTER WONDERLANDS

When the temperature drops and the white stuff falls, there are still tons of fun outdoor activities around the Sierra Nevada's national parks. In Yosemite, strap on some skis or a snowboard and go tubing downhill off Glacier Point Rd; plod around Yosemite Valley on a ranger-led snowshoe tour; or just try to stay upright on ice skates at Half Dome Village. Further south in Sequoia and Kings Canyon National Parks, the whole family can go snowshoeing or cross-country skiing among groves of giant sequoias. Before embarking on a winter trip to the parks, check road conditions on the official park websites or by calling ahead. Don't forget to put snow tires on your car, and always carry tire chains too.

entrance, where you must leave your car at the new parking lot. A free shuttle will take you to Mariposa Grove.

6 Mariposa Grove

Wander giddily around the Mariposa Grove, home of the 1800-year-old Grizzly Giant and 500 other giant sequoias that tower above your head. Nature trails wind through this popular grove, but you can only hear yourself think above the noise of vacationing crowds during the early morning or evening.

Notwithstanding a cruel hack job back in 1895, the walk-through California Tunnel Tree continues to survive, so pose your family in front and snap away. If you've got the energy, make a round-trip pilgrimage on foot to the fallen Wawona Tunnel Tree in the upper grove.

The Drive » From Yosemite's south entrance station, it's a 115-mile, three-hour trip to Kings Canyon National Park. Follow Hwy 41 south 60 miles to Fresno, then slingshot east on Hwy 180 for another 50 miles, climbing out of the Central Valley back into the mountains. Keep left at the Hwy 198 intersection, staying on Hwy 180 toward Grant Grove.

7 Grant Grove

Through **Sequoia and Kings Canyon National Parks** (559-565-3341; www.nps.gov/seki; 7-day entry per car $30; P), roads seem barely to scratch the surface of the twin parks' beauty. To see real treasures, you'll need to get out and stretch your legs. North of Big Stump entrance station in Grant Grove Village, turn left and wind downhill to **General Grant Grove**, where you'll see some of the park's landmark giant sequoia trees along a paved path. You can walk right through the Fallen Monarch, a massive, fire-hollowed trunk that's done duty as a cabin, hotel, saloon and horse stable. For views of Kings Canyon and the peaks of the Great Western Divide, follow a narrow, winding side road (closed in winter; no RVs or trailers) starting behind the John Muir Lodge for over 2 miles up to **Panoramic Point**.

p525

The Drive » Kings Canyon National Park's main visitor areas, Grant Grove and Cedar Grove, are linked by the narrow, twisting Kings Canyon Scenic Byway (Hwy 180), which dramatically descends into the canyon. Expect spectacular views all along this outstandingly scenic 30-mile drive. Note: Hwy 180 from the Hume Lake turnoff to Cedar Grove is closed during winter (usually mid-November through mid-April).

TRIP HIGHLIGHT

8 Cedar Grove

Serpentining past chiseled rock walls laced with waterfalls, Hwy 180 plunges down to the Kings River, where roaring white-water ricochets off the granite cliffs of North America's deepest canyon, technically speaking. Pull over partway down at **Junction View** overlook for an eyeful, then keep rolling down along the river to **Cedar Grove Village**. East of the village, **Zumwalt Meadow** is the place for spotting birds, mule deer and black bears.

If the day is hot and your swimming gear is handy, stroll from Road's End to **Muir Rock**, a large flat-top river boulder where John Muir once gave outdoor talks, now a popular summer swimming hole. Starting from **Road's End**, a very popular day hike climbs 4 miles each way to **Mist Falls**, which thunders in late spring.

The Drive » Backtrack from Road's End nearly 30 miles up Hwy 180. Turn left onto Hume Lake Rd. Curve around the lake past swimming beaches and campgrounds, turning right onto 10 Mile Rd. At Hwy 198, turn left and follow the Generals Hwy (often closed from January to March) south for about 23 miles to the Wolverton Rd turnoff on your left.

TRIP HIGHLIGHT

9 Giant Forest

We dare you to try hugging the trees in Giant Forest, a 3-sq-mile grove protecting the park's most gargantuan specimens. Park off Wolverton Rd and walk downhill to reach the world's biggest living tree, the **General Sherman Tree**, which towers 275ft into the sky. With sore arms and sticky sap fingers, you can lose the crowds on any of many forested trails nearby. The trail network stretches all the way south to Crescent Meadow, a 5-mile one-way ramble.

By car, drive 2.5 miles south along the Generals Hwy to get schooled on sequoia ecology and fire cycles at the **Giant Forest Museum** (☎559-565-4480; www.nps.gov/seki; cnr Generals Hwy & Crescent Meadow Rd; ⏰9am-4:30pm; P 🚻). Starting outside the museum, Crescent Meadow Rd makes a 6-mile loop into the Giant Forest, passing right through **Tunnel Log**. For 360-degree views of the Great Western Divide, climb the steep quarter-mile staircase up **Moro Rock**. Note: Crescent Meadow Rd is closed to traffic by winter snow; during summer, ride the free shuttle buses around the loop road.

The Drive » Narrowing, the Generals Hwy drops for more than 15 miles into the Sierra Nevada foothills, passing Amphitheater Point and exiting the park beyond Foothills Visitor Center. Before reaching the town of Three Rivers, turn left on Mineral King Rd, a dizzyingly scenic 25-mile road (partly unpaved; no trailers or RVs allowed and closed in winter) that switchbacks up to Mineral King Valley.

10 Mineral King Valley

Navigating over 700 hairpin turns, it's a winding 1½-hour drive up to the glacially sculpted Mineral King Valley (7500ft), a 19th-century silver-mining camp and lumber settlement, and later a mountain retreat.

Trailheads into the high country begin at the end of Mineral King Rd,

DETOUR: BUCK ROCK LOOKOUT

Start: 8 Cedar Grove

To climb one of California's most evocative fire lookouts, drive east of the Generals Hwy on Big Meadows Rd into the Sequoia National Forest between Grant Grove and the Giant Forest. Follow the signs to staffed **Buck Rock Fire Lookout** (www.buckrock.org; FR-13S04; ⏰9:30am-6pm May-Oct). Constructed in 1923, this active fire lookout allows panoramic views from a dollhouse-sized cab lording it over the horizon from 8500ft atop a granite rise, reached by 172 spindly stairs. It's not for anyone with vertigo. Opening hours may vary seasonally, and the lookout closes during lightning storms and fire emergencies.

DETOUR: CRYSTAL CAVE

Start: 9 Giant Forest

Off the Generals Hwy, about 2 miles south of the Giant Forest Museum, turn right (west) onto twisting 6.5-mile-long Crystal Cave Rd for a fantastical walk inside 10,000-year-old **Crystal Cave** (www.explorecrystalcave.com; tours adult/child/youth from $16/5/8; May-Sep; P), carved by an underground river. Stalactites hang like daggers from the ceiling, and milky-white marble formations take the shape of ethereal curtains, domes, columns and shields. Bring a light jacket – it's 50°F (10°C) inside the cave. Buy tour tickets a month or more in advance online at www.recreation.gov; during October and November, tickets are only sold in person at the Giant Forest Museum and Foothills Visitor Center. Tour tickets are *not* available at the cave itself.

where historic private cabins dot the valley floor flanked by massive mountains.

Your final destination is just over a mile past the ranger station, where the valley unfolds all of its hidden beauty, and hikes to granite peaks and alpine lakes beckon.

Note that Mineral King Rd is typically open only from late May through late October. In summer, Mineral King's marmots like to chew on parked cars, so wrap the undercarriage of your vehicle with a tarp and rope (which can be bought, though not cheaply, at the hardware store in Three Rivers).

MEINZAHN / GETTY IMAGES ©

Sequoia National Park Crystal Cave

Eating & Sleeping

Tuolumne Meadows 1

Tuolumne Meadows Lodge Cabin $$
(reservations 888-413-8869; www.travelyosemite.com; tent cabins $137; mid-Jun–mid-Sep) Set amid the magnificent high country, about 50 miles from Yosemite Valley off Tioga Rd, this option attracts hikers to its 69 canvas tent cabins with two or four beds each, a wood-burning stove and candles (no electricity). Breakfast and dinner are available (surcharge applies; dinner reservations required). A fork of the Tuolumne River runs through the property.

Yosemite Valley 3

Degnan's Loft Pizza $$
(www.travelyosemite.com; Yosemite Village) Above the new Degnan's Kitchen, off Village Dr, the Loft retains its old name but has also received a top-to-bottom remodeling. Kick back and enjoy artisan pizzas, specialty appetizers and desserts, and beer and wine in this space with high-beamed ceilings and a many-sided fireplace.

Mountain Room Restaurant American $$$
(209-372-1403; www.travelyosemite.com; Yosemite Valley Lodge, 9006 Yosemite Lodge Dr; mains $20-36; 5:30-10pm Mon-Sat, 9am-1pm & 5:30-10pm Sun;) With a killer view of Yosemite Falls, the window tables at this casual yet elegant contemporary restaurant are a hot commodity. Plates of flat-iron steak, cider-brined pork chops and locally caught mountain trout woo diners, who are seated beside gallery-quality nature photographs. Reservations accepted only for groups larger than eight.

Half Dome Village Cabin $$
(reservations 888-413-8869; www.travelyosemite.com; tent cabins from $143, r from $260, cabins with shared/private bath from $170/225; daily mid-Mar–late Nov, Sat & Sun early Jan–mid-Mar; P) Founded in 1899 as summertime Camp Curry, Half Dome Village has hundreds of units squished together beneath towering evergreens. The canvas cabins (heated or unheated) are basically glorified tents, so for more comfort, quiet and privacy get one of the cozy wood cabins, which have vintage posters. There are 18 motel-style rooms in Stoneman House, including a loft suite that sleeps six.

Majestic Yosemite Hotel Historic Hotel $$$
(reservations 888-413-8869; www.travelyosemite.com; 1 Ahwahnee Dr; r/ste from $480/590; P @) The crème de la crème of Yosemite's lodging, this sumptuous historic property (formerly called the Ahwahnee) dazzles with soaring ceilings and atmospheric lounges with mammoth stone fireplaces. Classic rooms have inspiring views of Glacier Point and (partial) Half Dome. Cottages are scattered on the immaculately trimmed lawn next to the hotel. For high season and holidays, book a year in advance.

Yosemite Valley Campground Reservation Office Accommodation Services $
(877-444-6777, information 209-372-8502, reservations 518-885-3639; www.nps.gov/yose; tent & RV sites $26; 8am-5pm) The main campground reservation office for Yosemite Valley can be found off Southside Dr in the Half Dome Village parking lot. If you couldn't reserve a campsite in advance (go to www.recreation.gov), head here first thing in the morning to get on the list for available valley sites from no-shows and cancellations.

Yosemite Valley Lodge Motel $$$
(reservations 888-413-8869; www.travelyosemite.com; 9006 Yosemite Lodge Dr; r from $260; P @) Situated a short walk from Yosemite Falls, this large complex contains a wide range of eateries, a lively bar, a big pool and other handy amenities. The rooms, spread out over 15 buildings, feel somewhat lodge-like, with rustic wooden furniture and striking nature photography. All have cable TV, telephone, fridge and coffeemaker, and great patio or balcony panoramas.

Wawona 5

Big Trees Lodge — Historic Hotel $$

(☎reservations 888-413-8869; www.travelyosemite.com; 8308 Wawona Rd; r with shared/private bath from $150/220; ⊙mid-Mar–late Nov & mid-Dec–early Jan; P ⊖ ☏ ≋) This National Historic Landmark, dating from 1879, is a collection of six graceful, whitewashed New England–style buildings flanked by wide porches. The 104 rooms – with no phone or TV – have Victorian-style furniture and other period items, and about half the rooms share bathrooms, with nice robes provided for the walk there. Wi-fi is available in the annex building only.

Kings Canyon National Park

Sentinel Campground — Campground $

(www.nps.gov/seki; Hwy 180, Cedar Grove Village; tent & RV sites $18; ⊙late Apr–mid-Nov; P 🐾) Sentinel is Cedar Grove's busiest and most centrally located campground, near the visitor center and campfire ranger programs in summer. Premier riverside sites at the beginning of the first loop fill fastest.

John Muir Lodge — Lodge $$

(☎866-807-3598; www.visitsequoia.com; Grant Grove Village; r from $225; P ⊖ ☏) An atmospheric building hung with historical black-and-white photographs, this is a place to lay your head and still feel like you're in the forest. Wide porches have rocking chairs, and homespun rooms, completely renovated a couple of years ago, contain rough-hewn wooden furniture and patchwork bedspreads. On chilly nights, cozy up to the big stone fireplace with a board game.

Sequoia High Sierra Camp — Cabin $$

(☎866-654-2877; www.sequoiahighsierracamp.com; tent cabins without bath incl all meals adult/child $250/150; ⊙mid-Jun–mid-Sep) A mile's hike deep into the Sequoia National Forest, this off-the-grid, all-inclusive resort is nirvana for those who don't think luxury camping is an oxymoron. Canvas bungalows are spiffed up with pillow-top mattresses, feather pillows and cozy wool rugs. Restrooms and a shower house are shared. Reservations are required, and there's usually a two-night minimum stay.

Sequoia National Park

Lodgepole Market Center — Market, Deli $

(☎559-565-3301; www.visitsequoia.com; Lodgepole Village; mains $5-10; ⊙market 8am-9pm early May–mid-Sep, 9am-6pm mid-Apr–early May & mid-Sep–mid-Oct, grill & deli hours vary early May–mid-Sep) Inside is the park's biggest general store, selling groceries, camping supplies and snacks; a fast-food grill slinging pizza, burgers and breakfast burritos; and a deli serving food that's a tad healthier: focaccia sandwiches, wraps and salads.

Peaks Restaurant — American $$

(☎559-565-4070; www.visitsequoia.com; Wuksachi Lodge, 64740 Wuksachi Way; mains lunch $8-15, dinner $12-34; ⊙dining room 7-10am, 11:30am-3pm & 5-9:30pm, lounge 4-10pm, shorter hours low season; ☏ 👪) The lodge's dining room has an excellent breakfast buffet and soup-and-salad lunch fare, but dinners aim somewhat successfully to be more gourmet, with mains like pan-seared trout and seared venison. In the lounge, nosh on appetizers like grilled flatbreads and swill cocktails, beer and wine. Non-guests are welcome, but reservations are available for Wuksachi guests only.

Lodgepole Campground — Campground $

(www.nps.gov/seki; Lodgepole Rd; tent & RV sites $22; ⊙late Apr–Nov; 🐾) Closest to the Giant Forest area, with over 200 closely packed sites, this place fills quickly because of its proximity to Kaweah River swimming holes and Lodgepole Village amenities. The 16 walk-in sites are more private. Reservations are recommended from late May through late September.

Wuksachi Lodge — Lodge $$

(☎information 866-807-3598, reservations 317-324-0753; www.visitsequoia.com; 64740 Wuksachi Way; r $215-290; P ⊖ ☏ 🐾) Built in 1999, Wuksachi Lodge is the park's most upscale option. But don't get too excited: the wood-paneled atrium lobby has an inviting stone fireplace and forest views, but the motel-style rooms are fairly generic, with coffeemakers, minifridges, oak furniture and thin walls. The location near Lodgepole Village, however, can't be beat, and staff members are friendly and accommodating.

Disneyland & Orange County Beaches

On this fun coastal getaway, let the kids loose at the 'Happiest Place on Earth,' then strike out for sunny SoCal beaches – as seen on TV and the silver screen.

TRIP HIGHLIGHTS

0 miles
START 1
Disneyland
Party with Mickey Mouse and the Pixar gang

Seal Beach

Sunset Beach

30 miles
3
Huntington Beach
Laze on the golden sands of Surf City USA

40 miles
4
Newport Beach
Show off your bikini on Balboa Peninsula

Crystal Cove State Park

55 miles
7
Laguna Beach
An artist's dreamy seascape

FINISH
Dana Point

2–4 DAYS
65 MILES / 105KM

GREAT FOR...

BEST TIME TO GO

June to September for summer beach season.

Surfers at Huntington Beach Pier.

Corona del Mar's Lookout Point.

Huntington Beach Surfing by the pier

42 Disneyland & Orange County Beaches

It's true you'll find gorgeous sunsets, prime surfing breaks and just-off-the-boat seafood when road-tripping down the OC's sun-kissed coastal Hwy 1. Yet it's the unexpected and serendipitous discoveries you'll remember long after you've left this blissful 42 miles of surf and sand behind. Start it all off with a day or two at Disneyland's theme parks and let's call it a wrap for the perfect SoCal family vacation.

TRIP HIGHLIGHT

1 Disneyland

No SoCal theme park welcomes more millions of visitors every year than **Disneyland** (714-781-4636; www.disneyland.com; 1313 Harbor Blvd; adult/child 3-9yr 1-day pass from $97/91, 2-day park-hopper pass $244/232; open daily, seasonal hours vary). From the ghostly skeletons of Pirates of the Caribbean to the screeching monkeys of the Indiana Jones Adventure, there's magical detail every-

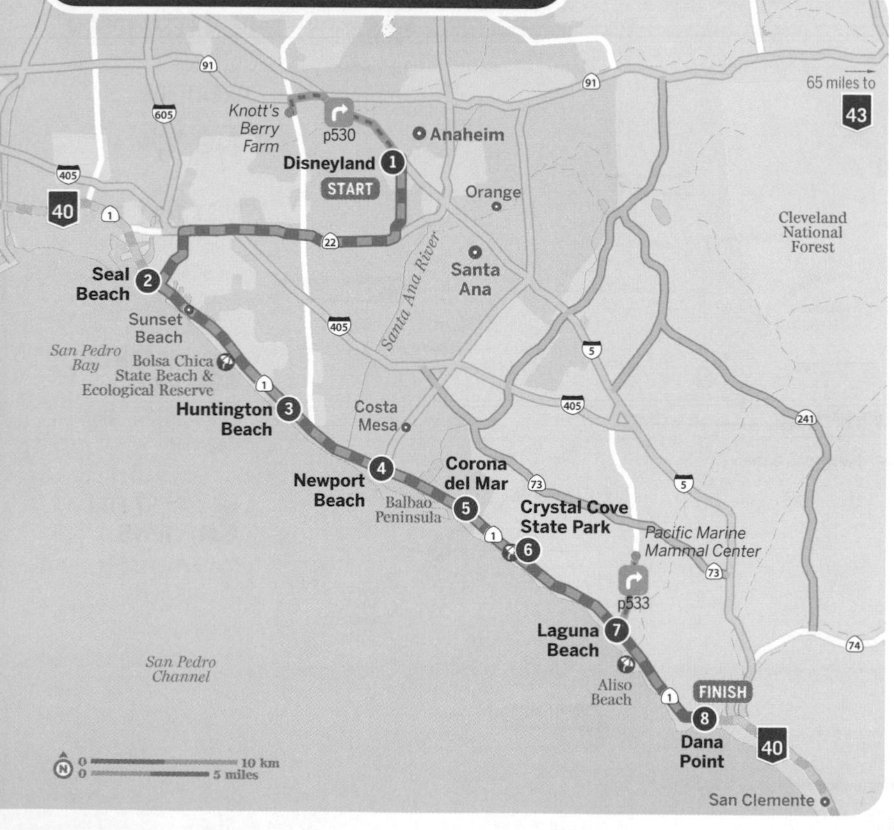

where. Retro-futuristic Tomorrowland is the home of the Finding Nemo Submarine Voyage and the *Star Wars*-themed Star Tours and Jedi Training: Trials of the Temple. Use the FASTPASS system and you'll be hurtling through Space Mountain – still the park's best adrenaline pumper – in no time. After dark, watch fireworks explode over Sleeping Beauty's Castle.

Any fear of heights? Then ditch the Twilight Zone Tower of Terror at **Disney California Adventure** (DCA; ☎714-781-4565; https://disneyland.disney.go.com; 1313 Harbor Blvd, Anaheim; single day ticket prices vary daily, 2-day pass adult/child from $199/187; P 👪), Disneyland's younger neighbor. DCA's lightheartedly themed areas highlight the best of the Golden State, while plenty of adventures like Route 66–themed Cars Land don't involve losing your lunch. An exception is rockin' California Screamin' at Paradise Pier: this whip-fast coaster looks like an old-school carnival ride, but from the moment it blasts forward with a cannon-shot whoosh, this monster never lets go. Catch the enthusiasm of the Pixar Play Parade by day and World of Color special-effects show at night.

Just outside the parks, **Downtown Disney** pedestrian mall is packed with souvenir shops, family restaurants, after-dark bars and entertainment venues.

🛏 p534

The Drive » Follow I-5 south, then take Hwy 22 west through inland Orange County, merging onto I-405 north. After another mile or so, exit onto Seal Beach Blvd, which crawls 3 miles toward the coast. Turn right onto Hwy 1, also known as the Pacific Coast Hwy (PCH) throughout Orange County, then take a left onto Main St in Seal Beach.

2 Seal Beach

In the SoCal beauty pageant for pint-sized beach towns, Seal Beach is the winner of the crown. It's a refreshingly unhurried alternative to the more crowded Orange County coast further south. Its three-block **Main St** is a stoplight-free zone that bustles with mom-and-pop restaurants and indie shops that are low on 'tude and high on nostalgia. Follow barefoot surfers trotting toward the beach where Main St ends, then walk out onto **Seal Beach Pier**. The 1906 original first fell victim to winter storms in the 1930s, and since then it has been rebuilt three times with a splintery, wooden boardwalk.

Down on the **beach**, you'll find families spread out on blankets, building sandcastles and playing in the water – all of them ignoring that hideous oil derrick offshore. The gentle waves make Seal Beach a great place to learn to surf. **M&M Surfing School** (☎714-846-7873; www.surfingschool.com; 1hr/3hr group lesson $77/85; ⏲ lessons 8am-noon early Sep–mid-Jun and Sat & Sun all year, to 2pm Mon-Fri mid-Jun–early Sep; 👪) parks its van in the lot just north of the pier, off Ocean Ave at 8th St.

The Drive » Past a short bridge south along Hwy 1, drivers drop onto a mile-long spit of land known as Sunset Beach, with its biker bars and harborside kayak and stand-up paddle boarding (SUP) rental shops. Keep cruising Hwy 1 south another 6 miles past Bolsa Chica State Beach and Ecological Reserve to Huntington Beach Pier.

LINK YOUR TRIP

Pacific Coast Highways

Orange County is California's official section of the Pacific Coast Hwy (PCH), running along Hwy 1 between Seal Beach and Dana Point.

Palm Springs & Joshua Tree Oases

Loving the SoCal sunshine? Go 110 miles further inland from Anaheim to find desert hot-springs resorts and all-natural parklands.

TRIP HIGHLIGHT

3 Huntington Beach

In 'Surf City USA,' SoCal's obsession with wave riding hits its frenzied peak. There's a statue of Hawaiian surfer Duke Kahanamoku at the intersection of Main St and PCH, and if you look down, you'll see names of legendary surfers in the sidewalk **Surfers' Hall of Fame** (www.hsssurf.com/shof; 300 Pacific Coast Hwy). A few blocks east, the **International Surfing Museum** (714-960-3483; www.surfingmuseum.org; 411 Olive Ave; adult/child $2/1; noon-5pm Tue-Sun) honors those same legends. Join the crowds on the **Huntington Beach Pier**, where you can catch up-close views of daredevils barreling through tubes. The surf here may not be the ideal place to test your newbie skills, however – locals can be territorial. In summer, the US Open of Surfing draws more than 600 world-class surfers and 500,000 spectators with a minivillage of concerts and more. As for **Huntington City Beach** itself, it's wide and flat – a perfect place to snooze on the sand on a giant beach towel. Snag a fire pit just south of the pier to build an evening bonfire with friends.

The Drive » From the Huntington Beach Pier at the intersection of Main St, drive south on Hwy 1 alongside the ocean for another 4 miles to Newport Beach. Turn right onto W Balboa Blvd, leading onto the Balboa Peninsula, squeezed between the ocean and Balboa Island, off Newport Harbor.

BEACH MEDIA / SHUTTERSTOCK ©

DETOUR: KNOTT'S BERRY FARM

Start: 1 Disneyland

Hear the screams? Got teens? Hello, **Knott's Berry Farm** (714-220-5200; www.knotts.com; 8039 Beach Blvd, Buena Park; adult/child 3-11yr $75/42; from 10am, closing hours vary 5-11pm; P), America's first theme park, which opened in 1940. Today high-scream coasters lure fast-track fanatics. Look up as you enter to see the bare feet of riders who've removed their flip-flops for the Silver Bullet, the suspended coaster careening past overhead, famed for its corkscrew, double spiral and outside loop. In October, Knott's hosts SoCal's scariest after-dark Halloween party. Year-round, the *Peanuts* gang keeps moppets happy in Camp Snoopy, while the next-door water park **Knott's Soak City** (714-220-5200; www.soakcityoc.com; 8039 Beach Blvd, Buena Park; adult/child 3-11yr $43/38; 10am-5pm, 6pm or 7pm mid-May–mid-Sep; P) keeps you cool on blazing-hot summer days. Knott's is a 20-minute drive from Disneyland via I-5 north to Hwy 91 west to Beach Blvd south.

Newport Beach Yachts on the water

TRIP HIGHLIGHT

4 Newport Beach

As seen on Bravo's *Real Housewives of Orange County* and Fox' *The OC* and *Arrested Development*, in glitzy Newport Beach wealthy socialites, glamorous teens and gorgeous beaches all share the spotlight. Beachgoers strut along the sand stretching between the peninsula's twin piers, while boogie boarders brave human-eating waves at the **Wedge** and the ballet of yachts in the harbor makes you dream of being rich and famous. From the harbor, hop aboard a ferry over to old-fashioned **Balboa Island** (http://explorebalboaisland.com; P) or climb aboard the Ferris wheel at the pint-sized **Balboa Fun Zone** (www.thebalboafunzone.com; 600 E Bay Ave; Ferris wheel $4; Ferris wheel 11am-6pm Sun-Thu, to 9pm Fri, to 10pm Sat;), near the landmark 1906 **Balboa Pavilion** (www.balboapavilion.com; 400 Main St). Just inland, visit the cutting-edge contemporary **Orange County Museum of Art** (949-759-1122; www.ocma.net; 850 San Clemente Dr; adult/student & senior/child under 12yr $10/7.50/free; 11am-5pm Wed-Sun, to 8pm Fri; P) to escape SoCal's vainglorious pop culture.

p534

The Drive » South of Newport Beach, prime-time ocean views are just a short detour off Hwy 1. First drive south across the bridge over Newport Channel, then after 3 miles turn right onto Marguerite Ave in Corona del Mar. Once you reach the coast, take another right onto Ocean Blvd.

5 Corona del Mar

Savor some of SoCal's most celebrated ocean views from the bluffs of Corona del Mar, a chichi bedroom community south of Newport Channel. Several postcard beaches, rocky coves and child-friendly tide pools beckon along this idyllic stretch of coast.

One of the best viewpoints is at breezy **Lookout Point** on Ocean Blvd near Heliotrope Ave. Below the rocky cliffs to the east is half-mile-long **Main Beach** (Corona del Mar State Beach; 949-644-3151; www.newportbeachca.gov; off E Shore Ave; 6am-10pm; P), with fire rings and volleyball courts (arrive early on weekends to get a parking spot). Stairs lead down to **Pirates Cove**, which has a great, waveless pocket beach for families – scenes from the classic TV show *Gilligan's Island* were shot here.

Head east on Ocean Blvd to **Inspiration Point**, near the corner of Orchid Ave, for more vistas of surf, sand and sea.

The Drive » Follow Orchid Ave back north to Hwy 1, then turn right and drive southbound. Traffic thins out as ocean views become more wild and uncluttered by housing developments that head up into the hills on your left. It's just a couple of miles to the entrance of Crystal Cove State Park.

6 Crystal Cove State Park

With more than 3 miles of open beach and 2400 acres of undeveloped woodland, **Crystal Cove State Park** (949-494-3539; www.parks.ca.gov; 8471 N Coast Hwy; per car $15; 6am-sunset; P) lets you almost forget that you're in a crowded metro area. That is, once you get past the parking lot and stake out a place on the sand. Many visitors don't know it, but it's also an underwater park where scuba enthusiasts can check out the wreck of a Navy Corsair fighter plane that went down in 1949. Or just go tide pooling, fishing, kayaking and surfing along Crystal Cove's exhilaratingly wild, windy shoreline. On the inland side of Hwy 1, miles of hiking and mountain-biking trails wait for landlubbers.

p534

The Drive » Drive south on Hwy 1 for another 4 miles or so. As shops, restaurants, art galleries, motels and hotels start to crowd the highway once again, you've arrived in Laguna Beach. Downtown is a maze of one-way streets just east of the Laguna Canyon Rd (Hwy 133) intersection.

TRIP HIGHLIGHT

7 Laguna Beach

This early-20th-century artist colony's secluded coves, romantic-looking cliffs and arts-and-crafts bungalows come as a relief after miles of suburban beige-box architecture. With joie de vivre, Laguna celebrates its bohemian roots with summer arts festivals, dozens of galleries and the acclaimed **Laguna Art Museum** (949-494-8971; www.lagunaartmuseum.org; 307 Cliff Dr; adult/student & senior/child under 13yr $7/5/free, 5-9pm 1st Thu of month free; 11am-5pm Fri-Tue, to 9pm Thu). In downtown's village, it's easy to while away an afternoon browsing the chic boutiques.

Down on the shore, **Main Beach** is crowded with volleyball players and sunbathers. Just north atop the bluffs, **Heisler Park** winds past public art, palm trees, picnic tables and grand views of rocky shores and tide pools. Drop down to **Divers Cove**, a deep, protected inlet.

Heading south, dozens of public beaches sprawl along just a few miles of coastline. Keep a sharp eye out for 'beach access' signs off Hwy 1, or pull into locals' favorite **Aliso Beach County Park** (949-923-2280; http://ocparks.com/beaches/aliso; 31131 S Pacific Coast Hwy; parking per hour $1; 6am-10pm; P).

p535

The Drive » Keep driving south of downtown Laguna Beach on Hwy 1 (PCH) for about

3 miles to Aliso Beach County Park, then another 4 miles into the town of Dana Point. Turn right onto Green Lantern St, then left onto Cove Rd, which winds past the state beach and Ocean Institute onto Dana Point Harbor Dr.

DETOUR: PACIFIC MARINE MAMMAL CENTER

Start: 7 Laguna Beach

About 3 miles inland from Laguna Beach is the heart-warming **Pacific Marine Mammal Center** (949-494-3050; www.pacificmmc.org; 20612 Laguna Canyon Rd; donations welcome; 10am-4pm; P), dedicated to rescuing and rehabilitating injured or ill marine mammals. This nonprofit center has a small staff and many volunteers who help nurse rescued pinnipeds (mostly sea lions and seals) back to health before releasing them into the wild. Stop by and take a self-guided facility tour to learn more about these marine mammals and to visit the 'patients' out back.

8 Dana Point

Marina-flanked Dana Point is the namesake of 19th-century adventurer Richard Dana, who famously thought it was the only romantic place on the coast. These days it's more about family fun and sportfishing boats at **Dana Point Harbor**. Designed for kids, the **Ocean Institute** (949-496-2274; www.ocean-institute.org; 24200 Dana Pt Harbor Dr; adult/child 2-12yr $10/7.50; 10am-4pm Mon-Fri, 10am-3pm Sat & Sun, last entry 2:15pm; P) owns replicas of historic tall ships, maritime-related exhibits and a floating research lab. East of the harbor, **Doheny State Beach** (949-496-6171; www.dohenystatebeach.org; 25300 Dana Point Harbor Dr; per car $15; park 6am-10pm, visitor center 10am-4pm Wed-Sun; P) is where you'll find picnic tables, volleyball courts, an oceanfront bike path and a sandy beach for swimming, surfing and tide pooling.

Eating & Sleeping

Disneyland 1

Alpine Inn — Motel $

(714-535-2186; www.alpineinnanaheim.com; 715 W Katella Ave; r $99-149; P) Connoisseurs of kitsch will hug their Hummels over this 42-room, snow-covered chalet facade on an A-frame exterior and icicle-covered roofs – framed by palm trees, of course. Right on the border of Disney California Adventure, the inn also has Ferris-wheel views. It's circa 1958, and air-con rooms are well kept. Simple grab 'n' go breakfast served in the lobby.

Disney's Grand Californian Hotel & Spa — Resort $$$

(info 714-635-2300, reservations 714-956-6425; https://disneyland.disney.go.com/grand-californian-hotel; 1600 S Disneyland Dr; d from $360; P) Soaring timber beams rise above the cathedral-like lobby of the six-story Grand Californian, Disney's homage to the arts-and-crafts architectural movement. Cushy rooms have triple-sheeted beds, down pillows, bathrobes and all-custom furnishings. Outside there's a faux-redwood waterslide into the pool. At night, kids wind down with bedtime stories by the lobby's giant stone hearth.

Newport Beach 4

Bear Flag Fish Company — Seafood $

(949-673-3474; www.bearflagfishco.com; 3421 Via Lido; mains $10-16; 11am-9pm Tue-Sat, to 8pm Sun & Mon;) This is *the* place for generously sized, grilled and *panko*-breaded fish tacos, ahi burritos, spankin' fresh ceviche and oysters. Pick out what you want from the ice-cold display cases, then grab a picnic-table seat. About the only way this seafood could be any fresher is if you caught and hauled it off the boat yourself!

Bay Shores Peninsula Hotel — Hotel $$$

(949-675-3463; www.thebestinn.com; 1800 W Balboa Blvd; r $190-300; P) This three-story, reimagined motel flexes some surf-themed muscle. From *Endless Summer* posters to complimentary fresh-baked cookies and free rental movies, it's beachy, casual and customer-focused; its location at the elbow of the peninsula partially explains the steep rates. Complimentary parking, beach gear and continental breakfast buffet, best enjoyed on the 360-degree-view sun deck. Coin-op laundry available.

Crystal Cove State Park 6

Ruby's Crystal Cove Shake Shack — American $

(949-464-0100; www.rubys.com; 7703 E Coast Hwy; items $3-11; 7am-8pm, until 9pm summer;) Although this been-here-forever wooden snack stand is now owned by the Ruby's Diner chain, the shakes – and the ocean views – are as good as ever. Don't fear the date shake; it's delish. Also serves three squares a day (burgers, fries etc) and a kids menu.

Crystal Cove Beach Cottages — Cabin $$

(reservations 800-444-7275; www.crystalcovealliance.org; 35 Crystal Cove, Crystal Cove State Park Historic District; r with shared bath $35-140, cottages $171-249; check-in 4-9pm; P) Right on the beach, these two dozen preserved cottages (circa 1930s to '50s) now host guests for a one-of-a-kind stay. Each cottage is different, sleeping between two and eight people in a variety of private or dorm-style accommodations. To snag one, book on the first day of the month seven months before your intended stay – or pray for cancellations.

Laguna Beach 7

Stand — Vegetarian, Vegan $

(949-494-8101; www.thestandnaturalfoods.com; 238 Thalia St; mains $6-11; 7am-8pm;) With its friendly, indie-spirited vibe comes this tiny tribute to healthy cuisine. From hummus and guac sandwiches to sunflower sprout salads and black-beans-and-rice burritos, the menu is varied and all of it soul-satisfying. Try a smoothie or an all-natural shake. Order at the counter in the red mini-barn, then cross your fingers for an outdoor patio table.

Laguna Beach House — Hotel $$$

(949-497-6645; www.thelagunabeachhouse.com; 475 N Coast Hwy; r $205-419; P) Be it good feng shui, friendly staff or proximity to the beach, this 36-room courtyard inn feels right. From the surfboards in the lobby to colorful throw pillows and clean white walls and linens, the decor is contemporary, comfy and clean. Settle into the outdoor heated Jacuzzi with a glass of wine as the sun drops over the ocean.

Palm Springs & Joshua Tree Oases

Southern California's deserts can be brutally hot, barren places – escape to Palm Springs and Joshua Tree National Park, where shady fan-palm oases and date gardens await.

TRIP HIGHLIGHTS

60 miles
Keys View
Capture sunset panoramas from summit to sea

50 miles
Hidden Valley
Cool off inside Joshua Tree National Park

Joshua Tree
Twentynine Palms
4
5
Desert Hot Springs
1 START
7
Coachella Valley
Indio
FINISH

Palm Springs
Fabulously hip resort town with mid-century modern style
0 miles

Cottonwood Spring
Where fan-palm trees shade the desert sun
125 miles

2–3 DAYS
170 MILES / 274KM

GREAT FOR...

BEST TIME TO GO

February to April for spring wildflower blooms and cooler temperatures.

Sunset from Keys View.

Hike to the Lost Palms Oasis.

Joshua Tree National Park Whimsical trees and giant boulders dot the landscape

43 Palm Springs & Joshua Tree Oases

Just a short drive from the chic resorts of Palm Springs, the vast Mojave and Sonoran Deserts are serenely spiritual places. You may find that what at first looked like desolate sands transform on foot into perfect beauty: shady palm tree and cactus gardens, tiny wildflowers pushing up from hard-baked soil in spring, natural hot-springs pools for soaking, and uncountable stars overhead in the inky dark.

TRIP HIGHLIGHT

❶ Palm Springs

Hollywood celebs have always counted on Palm Springs as a quick escape from LA. Today, this desert resort town shows off a trove of well-preserved mid-century modern buildings. Stop at the **Palm Springs Official Visitors Center** (☎ 760-778-8418; www.visitpalmsprings.com; 2901 N Palm Canyon Dr; ⏰9am-5pm), inside a 1965 gas station by modernist Albert Frey, to pick up a self-

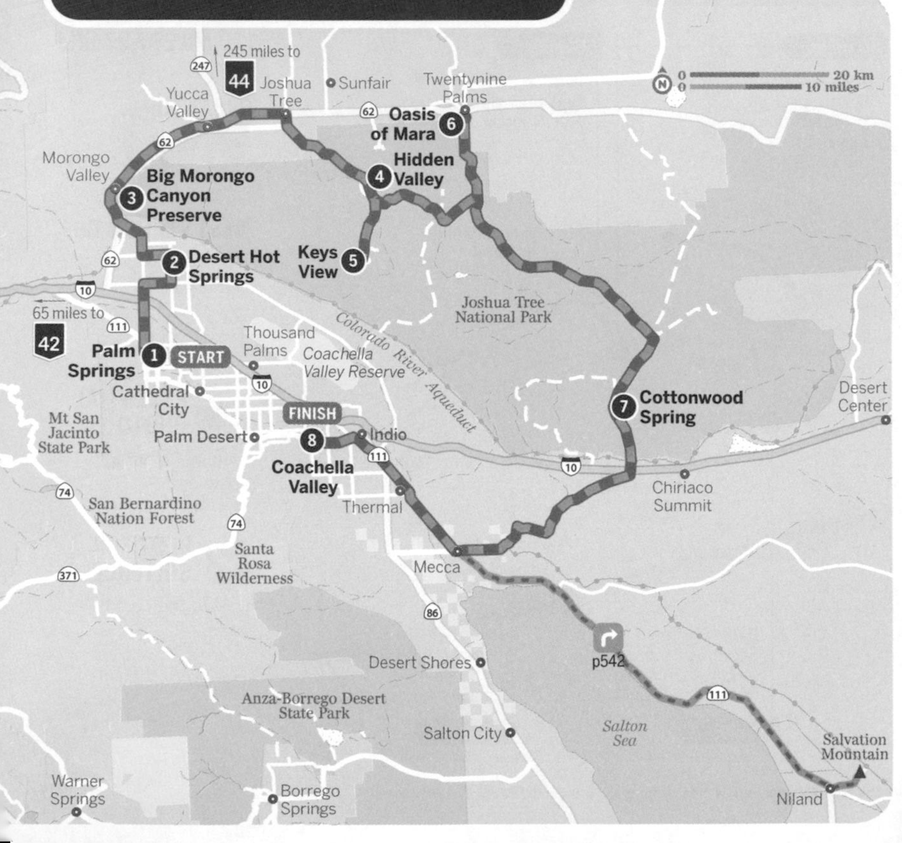

guided architectural tour map. Then drive uphill to clamber aboard the **Palm Springs Aerial Tramway** (☎760-325-1391; www.pstramway.com; 1 Tram Way; adult/child $26/17, parking $5; ⊙1st tram up 10am Mon-Fri, 8am Sat & Sun, last tram down 9:45pm daily, varies seasonally; P ♿), which climbs nearly 6000 vertical feet from the hot Sonoran Desert floor to the cool, even snowy San Jacinto Mountains in less than 15 minutes.

Back down on the ground, drive south on Palm Canyon Dr, where you can hop between art galleries, cafes, cocktail bars, trendy restaurants and chic boutiques. For a dose of culture, check out the latest exhibit at the excellent **Palm Springs Art Museum** (☎760-322-4800; www.psmuseum.org; 101 Museum Dr; adult/student $12.50/free, 4-8pm Thu free; ⊙10am-5pm Sun-Tue & Sat, noon-9pm Thu & Fri; P).

p543

The Drive » Drive north out of downtown Palm Springs along Indian Canyon Dr for 7 miles, passing over I-10. Turn right onto Dillon Rd, then after 2.5 miles turn left onto Palm Dr, which heads north into central Desert Hot Springs.

2 Desert Hot Springs

In 1774 Spanish explorer Juan Bautista de Anza was the first European to encounter the desert Cahuilla tribe. Afterward, the Spanish name Agua Caliente came to refer to both the indigenous people and the natural hot springs, which still flow restoratively today through the town of Desert Hot Springs (www.visitdeserthotsprings.com), where hip boutique hotels have appeared atop healing waters bubbling up from deep below.

Imitate Tim Robbins in Robert Altman's film *The Player* and have a mud bath at **Two Bunch Palms Spa Resort** (☎760-676-5000; www.twobunchpalms.com/spa; 67425 Two Bunch Palms Trail; day-spa package from $195; ⊙by reservation 9am-7pm Tue-Thu, 9am-8:30pm Fri, 8am-8:30pm Sat, 8am-7pm Sun & Mon), which sits atop an actual oasis. Bounce between a variety of pools and sunbathing areas, but maintain the code of silence (actually, whispers only).

p543

The Drive » Head west on Pierson Blvd back to Indian Canyon Dr. Turn right and drive northwest through the dusty outskirts of Desert Hot Springs. Turn right onto Hwy 62 eastbound toward Yucca Valley; after about 4 miles, turn right onto East Dr and look for signs for Big Morongo Canyon Preserve.

3 Big Morongo Canyon Preserve

An oasis hidden in the high desert, **Big Morongo Canyon Preserve** (☎760-363-7190; www.bigmorongo.org; 11055 East Dr, Morongo Valley; ⊙7:30am-sunset; P ♿) is a bird-watching hot spot. Tucked into the Little San Bernardino Mountains, this stream-fed riparian habitat is flush with cottonwood and willow trees. Nearly 250 bird species have been identified here, including over 70 that use the area as breeding grounds. Tramp along wooden boardwalks through marshy woodlands as hummingbirds flutter atop flowers and woodpeckers hammer away.

The Drive » Rejoin Hwy 62 eastbound past Yucca Valley, with its roadside antiques, vintage shops, art galleries and

LINK YOUR TRIP

42 Disneyland & Orange County Beaches

Drive 110 miles west starting on I-10 to Disney's Magic Kingdom, then cruise the OC's bodacious beach towns.

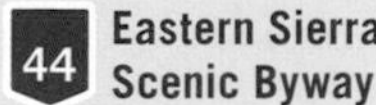

44 Eastern Sierra Scenic Byway

Head northwest via I-10, I-15 and Hwy 395 for 245 miles to Lone Pine, cinematically set beneath the majestic Sierra Nevada.

DANITA DELIMONT / GETTY IMAGES ©

cafes, to the town of Joshua Tree about 16 miles away, which makes a good place to base yourself for the night. At the intersection with Park Blvd, turn right and drive 5 miles to Joshua Tree National Park's west entrance. Make sure you've got a full tank of gas first.

TRIP HIGHLIGHT

4 Hidden Valley

It's time to jump into **Joshua Tree National Park** (☎760-367-5500; www.nps.gov/jotr; 7-day entry per car $25; ⏰24hr; P 👪), a wonderland of jumbo rocks interspersed with sandy forests of Joshua trees. Related to agave plants, Joshua trees were named by Mormon settlers who thought the twisted, spiky arms resembled a prophet's arms stretching toward God.

Revel in the scenery as you drive along the winding park road for about 8 miles to **Hidden Valley** picnic area. Turn left and drive past the campground to the trailhead for **Barker Dam**. Here a kid-friendly nature trail loops for just over a mile past a pretty little artificial lake and a rock incised with Native American petroglyphs.

If you enjoy history and Western lore, check with the national park office if ranger-led walking tours of nearby **Keys Ranch** (☎760-367-5500; www.nps.gov/jotr; tour adult/child $10/5; ⏰tour schedules vary; P 👪) are offered during your stay. Pioneer homesteaders tried their hand at cattle ranching, mining and desert farming here in the 19th century.

The Drive » Backtrack to Park Blvd, turn left and head south again past jumbled rock formations and fields of spiky Joshua trees. Take the well-signed right turn toward Keys View. You'll pass several trailheads and roadside interpretive exhibits over the

Golf course with San Jacinto views

next 5.5 miles leading up to the viewpoint.

TRIP HIGHLIGHT

5 Keys View

Make sure you embark at least an hour before sunset for the drive up to **Keys View** (5185ft), where panoramic views look into the **Coachella Valley** and reach as far south as the shimmering Salton Sea or, on an unusually clear day, Mexico's Signal Mountain.

Looming in front of you are **Mt San Jacinto** (10,800ft) and **Mt San Gorgonio** (11,500ft), two of Southern California's highest peaks, often snow-dusted even in spring. Down below snakes the shaky **San Andreas Fault**.

The Drive » Head back downhill to Park Blvd. Turn right and wind through the park's Wonderland of Rocks (where boulders call out to scampering kids and serious rock jocks alike), passing more campgrounds. After 10 miles, veer left to stay on Park Blvd and drive north for 8 miles toward the town of Twentynine Palms onto Utah Trail.

6 Oasis of Mara

Drop by Joshua Tree National Park's **Oasis Visitor Center** (www.nps.gov/jotr; 74485 National Park Dr, Twentynine Palms; 8:30am-5pm;) for its educational exhibits about Southern California's desert fan palms. These palms are often found growing along fault lines, where cracks in the earth's crust allow subterranean water to surface.

Outside the visitor center, a gentle half-mile nature trail leads around the **Oasis of Mara**, where Serrano peoples once camped. Ask for directions to the trailhead off Hwy 62 for the 3-mile, round-trip hike to **49 Palms Oasis**,

DETOUR: SALTON SEA

Start: 7 Cottonwood Spring

Driving along Hwy 111 southeast of Mecca, it's a most unexpected sight: California's largest lake in the middle of its largest desert. It was created by accident in 1905 when spring flooding breached irrigation canals built to bring water from the Colorado River to the farmland in the Imperial Valley. Marketed to mid-20th-century tourists as the 'California Riviera' with beachfront vacation homes, the **Salton Sea** has been mostly abandoned because agricultural runoff has increased the lake's salinity to the point where few fish species can survive. An even stranger sight is folk-art **Salvation Mountain** (☎760-624-8754; www.salvationmountaininc.org; 603 E Beal Rd, Niland; donations accepted; ⌚dawn-dusk; P), an artificial hill covered in acrylic paint and found objects and inscribed with Christian religious messages. It's outside Niland, about 3 miles east of Hwy 111 en route to Slab City.

where a sun-exposed dirt trail marches you over a ridge, then drops you into a rocky gorge, doggedly heading down past barrel cacti toward a speck of green in the distance.

The Drive » Drive back south on Utah Trail and re-enter the park. Follow Park Blvd south, turning left at the first major junction onto Pinto Basin Rd for a winding 30-mile drive southeast to Cottonwood Spring.

TRIP HIGHLIGHT

7 Cottonwood Spring

On your drive to Cottonwood Spring, you'll pass from the high Mojave Desert into the lower Sonoran Desert. At the **Cholla Cactus Garden**, handily labeled specimens burst into bloom in spring, including unmistakable ocotillo plants, which look like green octopus tentacles adorned with flaming scarlet flowers.

Turn left at the **Cottonwood Visitor Center** (www.nps.gov/jotr; ⌚8:30am-4pm; 🚻) for a short drive east past the campground to **Cottonwood Spring** (☎760-367-5500; www.nps.gov/jotr; P). Once used by the Cahuilla, who left behind archaeological evidence such as mortars and clay pots, the springs became a hotbed for gold mining in the late 19th century. The now-dry springs are the start of the moderately strenuous 7.5-mile round-trip trek out to **Lost Palms Oasis**, a fan-palm oasis blessed with solitude and scenery.

The Drive » Head south from Cottonwood Spring and drive across I-10 to pick up scenic Box Canyon Rd, which burrows a hole through the desert, twisting its way toward the Salton Sea. Take 66th Ave west to Mecca, then turn right onto Hwy 111 and drive northwest ('up valley') toward Indio.

8 Coachella Valley

The hot but fertile Coachella Valley is the ideal place to find the date of your dreams – the kind that grows on trees, that is. Date farms let you sample exotic-sounding varieties like halawy, deglet noor and zahidi for free, but the signature taste of the valley is a rich date shake from certified-organic **Oasis Date Gardens** (☎760-399-5665; www.oasisdate.com; 59-111 Grapefruit Blvd/Hwy 111, Thermal; ⌚9am-4pm; P 🚻) or the 1920s pioneer **Shields Date Garden** (☎760-347-7768; www.shieldsdategarden.com; 80-225 Hwy 111, Indio; ⌚9am-5pm; P 🚻).

Eating & Sleeping

Palm Springs 1

Sherman's Deli & Bakery — Deli $

(☎760-325-1199; www.shermansdeli.com; 401 E Tahquitz Canyon Way; sandwiches $8-18; ⏱7am-9pm;) Every community with a sizeable retired contingent needs a good Jewish deli. Sherman's is it. With a breezy sidewalk patio, it pulls in an all-ages crowd with its 40 sandwich varieties (great hot pastrami!), finger-lickin' rotisserie chicken, lox and bagels and to-die-for pies.

Workshop Kitchen + Bar — American $$$

(☎760-459-3451; www.workshoppalmsprings.com; 800 N Palm Canyon Dr; mains $26-45; ⏱5-10pm Mon-Sun, 10am-2pm Sun;) Hidden away in the back of the ornate 1920s El Paseo building, a large patio with olive trees leads to this starkly beautiful space centered on a lofty concrete tunnel flanked by mood-lit booths. The kitchen crafts market-driven American classics reinterpreted for the 21st century and the bar is among the most happening in town.

Arrive Hotel — Boutique Hotel $$

(☎760-507-1650; www.arrivehotels.com; 1551 N Palm Canyon Dr; studio from $179; P) Ecofriendly rusted steel, wood and concrete are the main design ingredients of this new adult-only lair where the bar doubles as the reception. The 32 rooms (some with patio) tick all the requisite hipster boxes such as rain shower, Apple TV and fancy bath products. The poolside restaurant, coffee shop, ice-cream parlor and craft-beer bar score high among locals.

Desert Hot Springs 2

El Morocco Inn & Spa — Boutique Hotel $$

(☎760-288-2527; http://elmoroccoinn.com; 66810 4th St; r $199-219; P) Heed the call of the casbah at this drop-dead gorgeous hideaway where the scene is set for romance. Twelve exotically furnished rooms wrap around a pool deck where your enthusiastic hosts serve free 'Morocco-tinis' during happy hour. The on-site spa offers such tempting massages as 'Moroccan Rain' using an essential oil to purge the body of toxins.

Spring Resort & Spa — Resort $$

(☎760-251-6700; www.the-spring.com; 12699 Reposo Way; r $189-219, villa $299; P) A humble 1950s motel has been recast as a chic, whisper-quiet spa retreat where natural hot mineral water feeds three pools. The dozen rooms are minimalist in design but not in amenities (rich linens, fluffy robes, small kitchens). Achieve a state of bliss while having a treatment or simply enjoy calming valley and mountain views. Adults only.

Joshua Tree

Pie for the People — Pizza $

(☎760-366-0400; www.pieforthepeople.com; 61740 29 Palms Hwy/Hwy 62; pizza $8-26; ⏱11am-9pm Sun-Thu, to 10pm Fri & Sat;) This neighborhood-adored lair is in the business of thin-crust pizzas ranging from classics to creatives like the David Bowie: white pizza with mozzarella, Guinness caramelized onions, jalapeños, pineapple, bacon and sweet plum sauce.

Spin & Margie's Desert Hide-a-Way — Inn $$

(☎760-366-9124, 760-774-0850; www.deserthideaway.com; 64491 29 Palm Hwy/Hwy 62; d $145-185; P) This handsome hacienda-style inn is perfect for restoring calm after a long day on the road. The five boldly colored suites are an eccentric symphony of corrugated tin, old license plates and cartoon art. Each has its own kitchen and flat-screen TV with DVD and CD player. Knowledgeable, gregarious owners ensure a relaxed visit.

Eastern Sierra Scenic Byway

A straight shot north along California's arched geological backbone, Hwy 395 dazzles with high-altitude vistas, crumbling Old West ghost towns and limitless recreational distractions.

TRIP HIGHLIGHTS

FINISH Reno

Carson City

220 miles

Bodie State Historic Park
A haunting and solitary Wild West ghost town

Bridgeport 10

190 miles 9

Mono Lake
An eerie blue desert basin sprouting towers of tufa

7 6

130 miles

Mammoth Lakes
A snow-sports resort with summertime mountain biking

Bishop

140 miles

Reds Meadow
Shuttle to an ancient volcanic formation and a splendid waterfall

Lone Pine
START

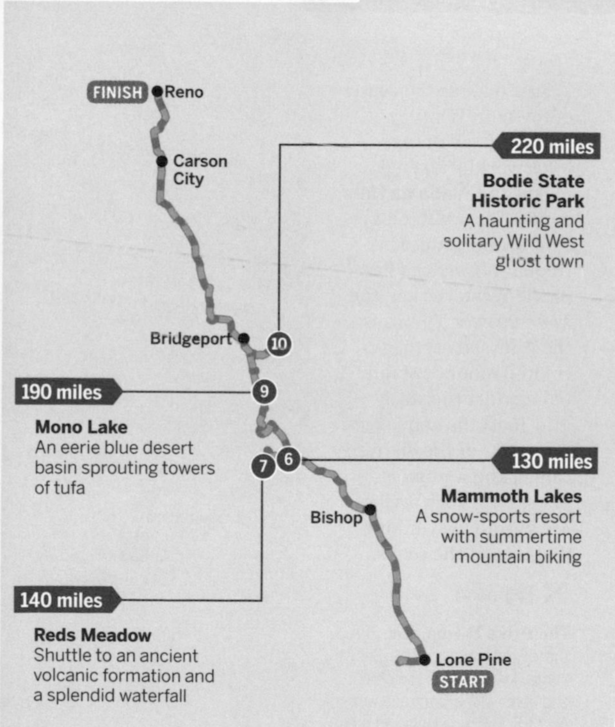

3–5 DAYS
360 MILES / 580KM

GREAT FOR...

BEST TIME TO GO

June to September for warm days and (mostly) snow-free mountain ramblings.

ESSENTIAL PHOTO

Sunrise or sunset at the Alabama Hills, framed by the snowy Sierra Nevada.

BEST FOR OUTDOORS

Hike tranquil mountain trails and camp in Mammoth Lakes.

Alabama Hills A dramatic rock arch

44 Eastern Sierra Scenic Byway

The gateway to California's largest expanse of wilderness, Hwy 395 – also called the Eastern Sierra Scenic Byway – borders towering mountain vistas, glistening blue lakes and the seemingly endless forests of the eastern Sierra Nevada Mountains. A lifetime of outdoor activities beckons beyond the asphalt, and desolate Old West ghost towns, unique geological formations and burbling natural hot springs await exploration.

❶ Lone Pine

The diminutive town of Lone Pine stands as the southern gateway to the craggy jewels of the Eastern Sierra. At the southern end of town, drop by the **Museum of Western Film History** (760-876-9909; www.museumofwesternfilmhistory.org; 701 S Main St; adult/under 12yr $5/free; 10am-6pm Mon-Wed, to 7pm Thu-Sat, to 4pm Sun Apr-Oct, 10am-5pm Mon-Sat, to 4pm Sun Nov-Mar; P), which contains exhibits of paraphernalia from the over 450 movies shot in the area. Don't miss the occasional screenings in its theater or the tricked-out Cadillac convertible in its foyer.

Just outside the center of town on Whitney Portal Rd, an orange otherworldly alpenglow makes the **Alabama Hills** a must for watching a slow-motion sunset. A frequent backdrop for movie Westerns and the *Lone Ranger* TV series, the rounded earthen-colored mounds stand out against the steely gray foothills and jagged pinnacles of the Sierra range, and a number of graceful rock arches are within easy hiking distance of the roads.

p553

The Drive » From Lone Pine, the jagged incisors of the Sierra surge skyward in all their raw and fierce glory. Continue west past the Alabama Hills and then brace yourself for the dizzying ascent to road's end – a total of 13 miles from Hwy 395. The White Mountains soar to the east, and the dramatic Owens Valley spreads below.

2 Whitney Portal

At 14,505ft, the celestial granite giant of **Mt Whitney** (www.fs.usda.gov/inyo) stands as the loftiest peak in the Lower 48 and the obsession of thousands of high-country hikers every summer. Desperately coveted permits (assigned by advance lottery) are your only passport to the summit, though drop-in day-trippers can swan up the mountain as far as Lone Pine Lake – about 6 miles round-trip – to kick up some dust on the iconic Whitney Trail. Ravenous hikers can stop by the **Whitney Portal**

LINK YOUR TRIP

41 Yosemite, Sequoia & Kings Canyon National Parks

In Lee Vining, go west on Hwy 120 to enter Yosemite National Park via the 9945ft Tioga Pass.

43 Palm Springs & Joshua Tree Oases

From Lone Pine, it's a 245-mile drive southeast via Hwy 395, I-15 and I-10 to SoCal's desert playground.

Store (☎760-876-0030; www.whitneyportalstore.com; ⊙hours vary May-Oct; 📶) for enormous burgers and plate-sized pancakes.

As you get a fix on this majestic megalith cradled by scores of smaller pinnacles, remember that the country's lowest point is only 80 miles (as the crow flies) east of here: Badwater in Death Valley.

The Drive » Double back to Lone Pine and drive 9 miles north on divided Hwy 395. Scrub brush and tumbleweed desert occupy the valley between the copper-colored foothills of the Sierra Nevada and the White Mountain range. Well-signed Manzanar sits along the west side of the highway.

3 Manzanar National Historic Site

A monument to one of the darkest chapters in US history, Manzanar unfolds across a barren and windy sweep of land cradled by snow-dipped peaks. During the height of WWII, the federal government interned more than 10,000 people of Japanese ancestry here following the attack on Pearl Harbor. Though little remains of the infamous war concentration camp, the camp's former high-school auditorium houses a superb **interpretive center** (☎760-878-2194; www.nps.gov/manz; 5001 Hwy 395; ⊙9am-5:30pm Apr–mid-Oct, 10am-4:30pm mid-Oct–Mar; P 👪). Watch the 22-minute documentary film, then explore the thought-provoking exhibits chronicling the stories of the families that languished here yet built a vibrant community. Afterwards, take a self-guided 3.2-mile driving tour around the grounds, which include a re-created mess hall and barracks, vestiges of buildings and gardens, and the haunting camp cemetery.

Often mistaken for Mt Whitney, 14,375ft Mt Williamson looms above this flat, dusty plain, a lonely expanse that bursts with yellow wildflowers in spring.

The Drive » Continue north 6 miles on Hwy 395 to the small town of Independence. In the center of town, look for the columned Inyo County Courthouse and turn left onto W Center St. Drive six blocks through a residential area to the end of the road.

4 Independence

This sleepy highway town has been a county seat since 1866 and is home to the **Eastern California Museum** (☎760-878-0364; www.inyocounty.us/ecmsite; 155 N Grant St; donation requested; ⊙10am-5pm; P 👪). An excellent archive of Eastern Sierra history and culture, it contains one of the most complete collections of Paiute and Shoshone baskets in the country, as well as historic photographs of local rock climbers scaling Sierra peaks – including

OLEG BAKHIREV / SHUTTERSTOCK ©

Mt Whitney – with huge packs and no harnesses. Other highlights include artifacts from Manzanar and an exhibit about the fight to keep the region's water supply from being diverted to Los Angeles.

Fans of Mary Austin (1868–1934), renowned author of *The Land of Little Rain* and vocal foe of the desertification of the Owens Valley, can follow signs leading to her former house at **253 Market St**.

The Drive » Depart north along Hwy 395 as civilization again recedes amid a buffer of dreamy granite mountains, midsized foothills and (for most of the year) an expanse of bright

Mammoth Lakes

blue sky. Tuffs of blackened volcanic rock occasionally appear roadside. Pass through the blink-and-you'll-miss-it town of Big Pine, and enter Bishop.

5 Bishop

The second-largest town in the Eastern Sierra and about a third of the way north from Lone Pine to Reno, Bishop is a major hub for hikers, cyclists, anglers and climbers. To see what draws them here, visit the **Mountain Light Gallery** (760-873-7700; www.mountainlight.com; 106 S Main St; 10am-5pm Mon-Sat, 11am-4pm Sun), featuring the stunning outdoor photography of the late Galen Rowell, whose High Sierra images are some of the best in existence.

Where Hwy 395 swings west, continue northeast for 4.5 miles on Hwy 6 to reach the **Laws Railroad Museum & Historic Site** (760-873-5950; www.lawsmuseum.org; Silver Canyon Rd; donation $5; 10am-4pm;), a remnant of the narrow-gauge Carson and Colorado rail line that closed in 1960. Train buffs will hyperventilate over the collection of antique railcars, and kids love exploring the 1883 depot and clanging the brass bell. Dozens of historic buildings from the region have been reassembled with period artifacts to create a time-capsule village.

p553

The Drive » Back on Hwy 395, continue over 40 miles north to Hwy 203, passing Lake Crowley and the southern reaches of the Long Valley Caldera seismic hot spot. On Hwy 203 before the center of town, stop in at the Mammoth Lakes Welcome Center for excellent local and regional information.

TRIP HIGHLIGHT

6 Mammoth Lakes

Splendidly situated at 8000ft, Mammoth Lakes is an active year-round

DETOUR: ANCIENT BRISTLECONE PINE FOREST

Start: 4 Independence

For encounters with some of the earth's oldest living things, plan at least a half-day trip to the **Ancient Bristlecone Pine Forest** (760-873-2500; www.fs.usda.gov/inyo; usually mid-May–Nov; P). These gnarled, otherworldly looking trees thrive above 10,000ft on the slopes of the seemingly inhospitable White Mountains, a parched and stark range that once stood even higher than the Sierra. One of the oldest trees – called Methuselah – is estimated to be over 4700 years old, beating even the Great Sphinx of Giza by about two centuries.

To reach the groves, take Hwy 168 east 12 miles from Big Pine to White Mountain Rd, then turn left (north) and climb the curvy road 10 miles to **Schulman Grove**, named for the scientist who first discovered the trees' biblical age in the 1950s. The entire trip takes about one hour one-way from Independence. There's access to self-guided trails near the solar-powered **Schulman Grove Visitor Center** (760-873-2500; www.fs.usda.gov/inyo; White Mountain Rd; per person/car $3/6; 10am-4pm Fri-Mon mid-May–early Nov). White Mountain Rd is usually closed from November to April.

outdoor-recreation town buffered by alpine wilderness and punctuated by its signature 11,053ft peak, Mammoth Mountain. This ever-burgeoning **resort complex** (760-934-2571, 24hr snow report 888-766-9778; www.mammothmountain.com; adult/13-18yr/7-12yr $125/98/35;) has 3100 vertical feet – enough to whet any snow-sports appetite – and an enviably long season that may last from November to June.

When the snow finally melts, the ski and snowboard resort does a quick costume change and becomes the massive Mammoth Mountain Bike Park, and with a slew of mountain-bikers decked out in body armor, it could be mistaken for the movie set of an apocalyptic *Mad Max* sequel. With more than 80 miles of well-tended single-track trails and a crazy terrain park, it draws those who know their knobby tires.

Year-round, a vertiginous **gondola** (800-626-6684; www.mammothmountain.com; adult/13-18yr/5-12yr $29/24/12; hours vary; P) whisks sightseers to the apex for breathless views of snow-speckled mountaintops.

p553

The Drive » Keep the car parked at Mammoth Mountain and catch the mandatory Reds Meadow shuttle bus from the Gondola Building. However, you may want to drive up 1.5 miles west and back on Hwy 203 as far as Minaret Vista to contemplate eye-popping views of the Ritter Range, the serrated Minarets and the remote reaches of Yosemite National Park.

TRIP HIGHLIGHT

7 Reds Meadow

One of the most beautiful and varied landscapes near Mammoth is the Reds Meadow Valley, west of Mammoth Mountain. The most fascinating attraction in Reds Meadow is the surreal 10,000-year-old volcanic formation of **Devils Postpile National Monument** (760-934-2289; www.nps.gov/depo; shuttle day pass adult/child $7/4; late May-Oct). The 60ft curtains of near-vertical, six-sided basalt columns formed when rivers of molten lava slowed, cooled and cracked with perplexing symmetry. This honeycomb design is best appreciated from atop the columns, reached by a short trail. The columns are an easy, half-mile hike from the **Devils Postpile Ranger Station** (☎760-934-2289; www.nps.gov/depo; ⊙9am-5pm mid-Jun–mid-Oct).

From the monument, a 2.5-mile hike passing through fire-scarred forest leads to the spectacular **Rainbow Falls**, where the San Joaquin River gushes over a 101ft basalt cliff. Chances of actually seeing a rainbow forming in the billowing mist are greatest at noon. The falls can also be reached via an easy 1.5-mile walk from the Reds Meadow shuttle stop.

The Drive » Back on Hwy 395, continue north to Hwy 158 and pull out the camera for the alpine lake and peak vistas of the June Lake Loop.

8 June Lake Loop

Under the shadow of massive Carson Peak (10,909ft), the stunning 16-mile June Lake Loop (Hwy 158) meanders through a picture-perfect horseshoe canyon, past the relaxed resort town of June Lake and four sparkling, fish-rich lakes: Grant, Silver, Gull and June. It's especially scenic in fall when the basin is ablaze with golden aspens. Hardy ice climbers scale its frozen waterfalls in winter.

June Lake is backed by the Ansel Adams Wilderness, which runs into Yosemite National Park. From Silver Lake, Gem and Agnew Lakes make spectacular day hikes, and boat rentals and horseback rides are available.

The Drive » Rejoin Hwy 395 heading north, where the rounded Mono Craters dot the dry and scrubby eastern landscape and the Mono Lake Basin unfolds into view.

TRIP HIGHLIGHT

9 Mono Lake

North America's second-oldest lake is a quiet and mysterious expanse of deep blue water, whose glassy surface reflects jagged Sierra peaks, young volcanic cones and the unearthly tufa (*too*-fah) towers that make the lake so distinctive. Protruding from the water like drip sand castles, tufas form when calcium bubbles up from subterranean springs and combines with carbonate in the alkaline lake waters.

The salinity and alkaline levels are unfortunately too high for a pleasant swim. Instead, paddle a kayak or canoe around the weathered towers of tufa, drink in wide-open views of the Mono Craters volcanic field, and discreetly spy on the water birds that live in this unique habitat.

The **Mono Basin Scenic Area Visitor Center** (☎760-647-3044; www.fs.usda.gov/inyo; 1 Visitor Center Dr; ⊙generally 8am-5pm Apr-Nov; 👪), half a mile north of Lee Vining, has interpretive displays, a bookstore and a 20-minute movie about Mono Lake.

✕ p553

The Drive » About 10 miles north of Lee Vining, Hwy 395 arrives at its highest point, Conway Summit (8148ft). Pull off at the vista point for awe-inspiring panoramas of Mono Lake, backed by the Mono Craters and June and Mammoth Mountains. Continue approximately 8 miles north, and go 13 miles east on Hwy 270 (closed in winter); the last 3 miles are unpaved.

EASTERN SIERRA HOT SPRINGS

Nestled between the White Mountains and the Sierra Nevada near Mammoth is a tantalizing slew of natural pools with snowcapped panoramic views. When the high-altitude summer nights turn chilly and the coyotes cry, you'll never want to towel off. About 9 miles southeast of Mammoth Lakes, Benton Crossing Rd juts east off Hwy 395, accessing a delicious bounty of hot springs. For detailed directions and maps, pick up Matt Bischoff's excellent *Touring Hot Springs California and Nevada: A Guide to the Best Hot Springs in the Far West* or see www.mammothweb.com/recreation/hottubbing.cfm for directions to a few.

DETOUR: VIRGINIA CITY

Start: ⑩ Bodie State Historic Park

During the 1860s gold rush, Virginia City was a high-flying, rip-roaring Wild West boomtown. It was the site of the legendary Comstock Lode, a massive silver bonanza that began in 1859 and stands as one of the world's richest strikes. Some of the silver barons went on to become major players in California history, and much of San Francisco was built with the treasure dug up from the soil beneath the town. Mark Twain spent time in this raucous place during its heyday, and his eyewitness descriptions of mining life were published in *Roughing It*.

The high-elevation town is a National Historic Landmark, with a main street of Victorian buildings, wooden sidewalks, wacky saloons and small museums ranging from hokey to intriguing. On the main drag, C St, you'll find the **visitor center** (775-847-7500; www.visitvirginiacitynv.com; 86 S C St; 9am-5pm Mon-Sat, 10am-4pm Sun). To see how the mining elite lived, stop by the **Mackay Mansion** (775-847-0373; www.uniquitiesmackaymansion.com; 291 S D St; adult/child $5/free; 10am-6pm) and the **Castle** (cnr Taylor & B Sts).

From Carson City on Hwy 395, go east on Hwy 50, and then another 7 miles via Hwy 341 and Hwy 342. Continuing on to Reno, wind through a spectacular 13 miles of high desert along Hwy 341 to rejoin Hwy 395, with another 7 miles to reach Reno.

TRIP HIGHLIGHT

⑩ Bodie State Historic Park

For a time warp back to the gold-rush era, swing by **Bodie** (760-647-6445; www.parks.ca.gov/bodie; Hwy 270; adult/child $8/4; 9am-6pm mid-Mar–Oct, to 4pm Nov–mid-Mar; P), one of the West's most authentic and best-preserved ghost towns. Gold was discovered here in 1859, and the place grew from a bare-bones mining camp to a lawless boomtown of 10,000. The hills disgorged some $35 million worth of gold and silver in the 1870s and '80s, but when production plummeted, Bodie was abandoned, and about 200 weather-beaten buildings now sit frozen in time in this cold, barren and windswept valley. Peering through dusty windows you'll see stocked stores, furnished homes, a schoolhouse with desks and books, the jail and many other buildings. The former Miners' Union Hall now houses a **museum** and **visitor center**, and rangers conduct free tours in summer.

The Drive » Retrace your way back to Hwy 395, where you'll soon come to the settlement of Bridgeport. From here, it's approximately two hours to Reno along a lovely two-lane section of the highway that traces the bank of the snaking Walker River.

⑪ Reno

Nevada's second-largest city has steadily carved a noncasino niche as an all-season outdoor-recreation spot. The Truckee River bisects the heart of the mountain-ringed city, and in the heat of summer, the **Truckee River Whitewater Park** teems with urban kayakers and swimmers bobbing along on inner tubes. Two kayak courses wrap around Wingfield Park, a small river island that hosts free concerts in summertime. **Tahoe Whitewater Tours** (775-787-5000; www.gowhitewater.com; 400 Island Ave; 2hr kayak rental/tour from $48/68) and **Sierra Adventures** (775-323-8928; www.wildsierra.com; Truckee River Lane; kayak rental from $22) offer kayak rentals, tours and lessons.

p553

Eating & Sleeping

Lone Pine 1

Alabama Hills Cafe — Diner $

(760-876-4675; 111 W Post St; mains $8-14; 7am-2pm;) At everyone's favorite breakfast joint, the portions are big, the bread is freshly baked, and the hearty soups, sandwiches and fruit pies make lunch an attractive option too. You can also plan your drive through the Alabama Hills with the help of the map on the menu.

Dow Hotel & Dow Villa Motel — Hotel, Motel $$

(760-876-5521; www.dowvillamotel.com; 310 S Main St; hotel r with/without bath from $89/70, motel r $117-158; P) John Wayne and Errol Flynn are among the stars who have stayed at this venerable hotel. Built in 1922, the place has been restored but retains much of its rustic charm. The rooms in the newer motel section have air-con and are more comfortable and bright, but also more generic.

Bishop 5

Erick Schat's Bakkerÿ — Bakery $

(760-873-7156; www.erickschatsbakery.com; 763 N Main St; sandwiches $6-9; 6am-6pm Sun-Thu, to 7pm Fri;) A deservedly hyped tourist mecca filled to the rafters with racks of fresh bread, Schat's has been making its signature sheepherder bread and other baked goodies since 1938. Some of the desserts, including the crispy cookies and bear claws, are addictive, and call for repeated trips while in town. Also has a popular sandwich bar and outdoor tables.

Mammoth Lakes 6

Toomey's — American $$

(760-924-4408; www.toomeyscatering.com; 6085 Minaret Rd; mains $12-33; 7am-9pm;) Since 2012, Toomey's chef, once of legendary Whoa Nellie Deli in Lee Vining, has been preparing his eclectic menu of wild-buffalo meatloaf, seafood jambalaya and lobster *taquitos* (filled, rolled and fried tortillas) with mango salsa. The central location's perfect for grabbing a to-go breakfast or a sit-down dinner near the Village Gondola.

Mono Lake 9

Whoa Nellie Deli — American $$

(760-647-1088; www.whoanelliedeli.com; Tioga Gas Mart, 22 Vista Point Rd; mains $9-19; 6:30am-8:30pm late Apr-Oct;) Years after its famed chef moved on to Toomey's at Mammoth Lakes, this Mobil-gas-station restaurant off Hwy 120 is still, surprisingly, a damn good place to eat. Stop in for delicious burgers, fish tacos, wild-buffalo meatloaf and other tasty morsels, and live bands some nights.

Reno 11

Old Granite Street Eatery — American $$

(775-622-3222; www.oldgranitestreeteatery.com; 243 S Sierra St; dinner mains $12-29; 11am-10pm Mon-Thu, to 11pm Fri, 10am-11pm Sat, to 3pm Sun;) A lovely well-lit place for organic and local comfort food, old-school artisanal cocktails and craft beers, this antique-strewn hot spot enchants diners with its stately wooden bar, water served in old liquor bottles and lengthy seasonal menu. Forgot to make a reservation? Check out the iconic rooster and pig murals and wait at a communal table fashioned from a barn door.

Whitney Peak — Design Hotel $$

(775-398-5400; www.whitneypeakhotel.com; 255 N Virginia St; d from $129; P) What's not to love about this independent, inventive, funky, friendly, non-smoking, non-gambling downtown hotel? Spacious guest rooms have a youthful, fun vibe celebrating the great outdoors and don't skimp on designer creature comforts. With an executive-level concierge lounge, free use of the external climbing wall (if you're game), a noteworthy on-site restaurant and friendly, professional staff, Whitney Peak is hard to beat.

Highway 49 Through Gold Country

There's plenty to see on winding Hwy 49. A trip through Gold Country shows off California's early days, when hell-raising prospectors and ruffians rushed helter-skelter into the West.

TRIP HIGHLIGHTS

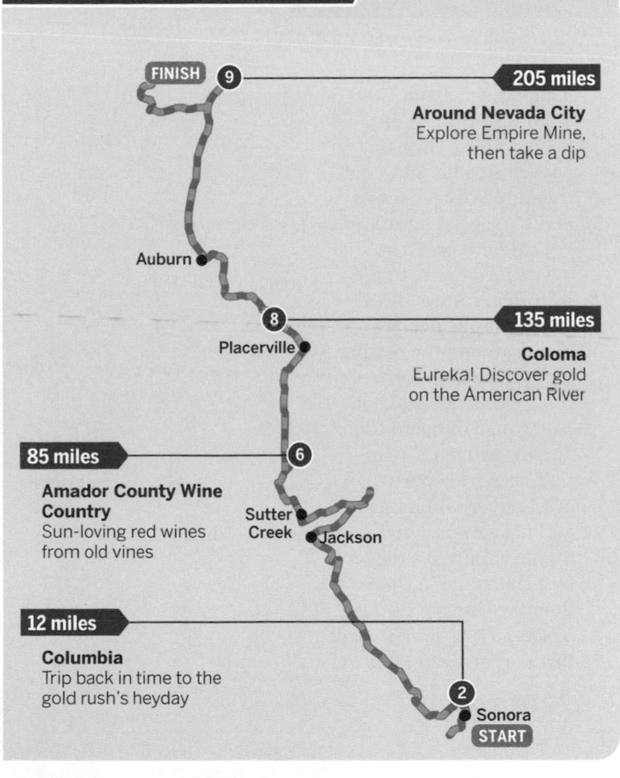

FINISH 9
Auburn
8
Placerville
6
Sutter Creek
Jackson
2
Sonora
START

205 miles
Around Nevada City
Explore Empire Mine, then take a dip

135 miles
Coloma
Eureka! Discover gold on the American River

85 miles
Amador County Wine Country
Sun-loving red wines from old vines

12 miles
Columbia
Trip back in time to the gold rush's heyday

3–4 DAYS
205 MILES / 330KM

GREAT FOR...

BEST TIME TO GO

May to October for sunny skies.

ESSENTIAL PHOTO

Sutter's Mill, California's original gold discovery site.

BEST FOR SWIMMING

South Yuba River State Park.

Columbia State Historic Park Coach ride along Main St

45 Highway 49 Through Gold Country

When you roll into Gold Country on a sunny afternoon, the promise of adventure recalls the days when newspaper headlines screamed about gold discoveries and the Golden State was born. Today this rural region offers different cultural riches: exploring crumbling false-front saloons, rusting machines that once moved mountains and an endless parade of patinaed bronze historical markers along Hwy 49, one of California's most enchantingly scenic byways.

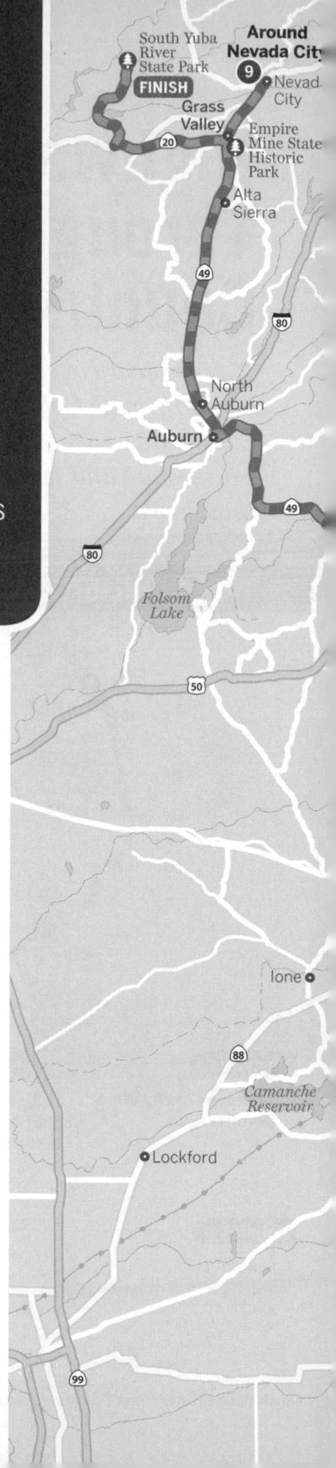

1 Sonora

Settled in 1848 by Mexican miners, Sonora soon became a cosmopolitan center with ornate saloons patronized by gamblers, drunkards and gold diggers. Its downtown district is so well preserved that it's frequently a location for Hollywood films, such as Clint Eastwood's *Unforgiven*. Likewise, **Railtown 1897 State Historic Park** (☎209-984-3953; www.railtown1897.org; 10501 Reservoir Rd, Jamestown; adult/child $5/3, incl train ride $15/10; ⏲9:30am-4:30pm Apr-Oct, 10am-3pm Nov-Mar, train rides 10:30am-3pm Sat & Sun Apr-Oct; P 👪) and the surrounding hills of **Jamestown**, about 4 miles southwest of Sonora along Hwy 49, have been a backdrop for over 200 Western movies and TV shows, including *High Noon*. There's a lyrical romance to the historical railway yard, where orange poppies bloom among the rusting shells of steel goliaths. On some weekends and holidays, you can board the narrow-gauge railroad that once transported ore, lumber and miners. Making a 45-minute, 6-mile circuit, it's the best train ride in Gold Country. The park is five blocks east of Jamestown's pint-sized Main St.

✕ 🛏 p563

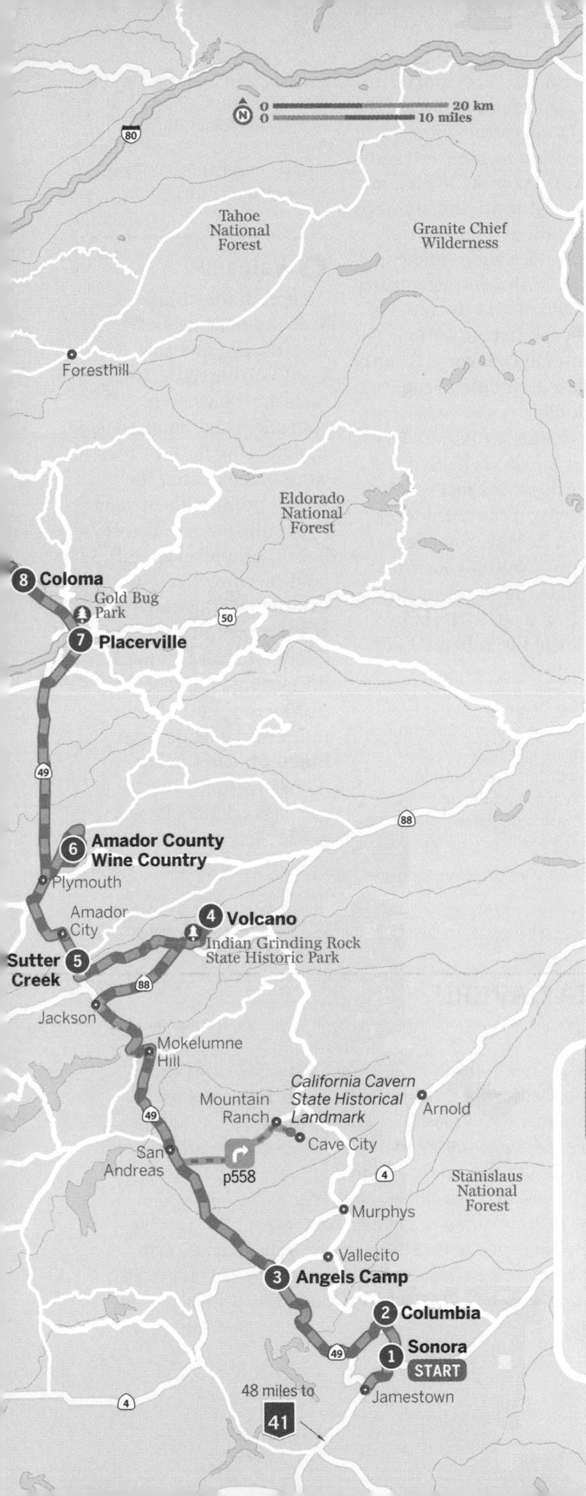

The Drive » Follow Hwy 49 just over 2 miles north of Sonora, then turn right onto Parrots Ferry Rd at the sign for Columbia. The state historic park is 2 miles further along this two-lane country road.

TRIP HIGHLIGHT

2 Columbia

Grab some suspenders and a floppy hat for **Columbia State Historic Park** (209-588-9128; www.parks.ca.gov; Main St; most businesses 10am-5pm; P), near the so-called 'Gem of the Southern Mines.' It's like a miniature gold-rush Disneyland, but with more authenticity and heart.

Four blocks of town have been preserved, where volunteers perambulate in 19th-century dress and demonstrate gold panning. The blacksmith's shop, theater, hotels and saloon are all carefully framed windows into California's past. The yesteryear illusion of Main St is shaken only a bit by fudge shops and the occasional banjo

LINK YOUR TRIP

41 Yosemite, Sequoia & Kings Canyon National Parks

Wind 45 miles southeast to Hwy 49 to Yosemite's Big Oak Flat entrance on Hwy 120.

picker or play-acting forty-niner whose cell phone rings. Stop by the **Columbia Museum** (☎209-532-3184; www.parks.ca.gov; cnr Main & State Sts; ⊙10am-5pm Apr-Sep, to 4pm Oct-Mar) inside Knapp's Store to learn more about historical mining techniques.

The Drive » Backtrack south on Parrots Ferry Rd, veering right and then turning right to stay on Springfield Rd for just over a mile. Rejoin Hwy 49 northbound, which crosses a long bridge over an artificial reservoir. After a dozen miles or so, Hwy 49 becomes Main St through the small town of Angels Camp.

❸ Angels Camp

On the southern stretch of Hwy 49, one literary giant looms over all other Western tall-tale tellers: Samuel Clemens, aka Mark Twain, who got his first big break with the short story *The Celebrated Jumping Frog of Calaveras County,* written in 1865 and set in Angels Camp. With a mix of Victorian and art-deco buildings that shelter antiques shops and cafes, this 19th-century mining town makes the most of its Twain connection. The annual **Calaveras County Fair & Jumping Frog Jubilee** (www.frogtown.org; 2465 Gun Club Rd; from $8; ⊙May; 👪) is held at the fairgrounds just south of town on the third weekend in May. You could win $5000 if your frog beats the world-record jump (over 21ft) set by 'Rosie the Ribeter' back in 1986.

The Drive » Hwy 49 heads north of Angels Camp through rolling hillside farms and ranches. Past San Andreas, make a short detour through Mokelumne ('Moke') Hill, another historic mining town. In Jackson, turn right onto Hwy 88 east. After 9 miles, turn left on Pine Grove-Volcano Rd for 3 miles to reach Volcano, passing Indian Grinding Rock State Historic Park en route.

❹ Volcano

Although the village of Volcano once yielded tons of gold and saw Civil War intrigue, today it slumbers away in solitude. Huge sandstone rocks lining Sutter Creek were blasted from the surrounding hills using a hydraulic process before being scraped clean of gold-bearing dirt. Hydraulic mining had dire environmental consequences, but at its peak, miners raked in nearly $100 a day. Less than a mile southeast of town, **Black Chasm Cavern** (☎888-762-2837; www.caverntours.com; 15701 Pioneer Volcano Rd, Pine Grove; adult/child $17.50/9.50; ⊙9am-5pm

DETOUR: CALIFORNIA CAVERN

Start: ❸ Angels Camp

A 20-minute drive east of San Andreas via Mountain Ranch Rd, off Hwy 49 about 12 miles north of Angels Camp, **California Cavern State Historic Landmark** (☎209-736-2708; www.caverntours.com; 9565 Cave City Rd, Mountain Ranch; adult/child from $17.50/9.50; ⊙10am-5pm, to 4pm early Sep–mid-May; P👪) has the mother lode's most extensive system of natural underground caverns. John Muir described them as 'graceful flowing folds deeply plicated like stiff silken drapery.' The family-friendly walking tours take 60 to 80 minutes, or get a group together and reserve ahead for a three-hour 'Mammoth Expedition' ($99) or a five-hour 'Middle Earth Expedition' ($130), which include some serious spelunking (no children under age 16 allowed). The Trail of Lakes walking tour, available only during the wet season in winter and spring, is magical.

mid-May–early Sep, 10am-4pm early Sep–mid-May; P 🚻) has the whiff of a tourist trap, but one look at the helictite crystals – sparkling white formations in rare horizontal clusters – makes the crowds bearable.

Two miles southwest of town at **Indian Grinding Rock State Historic Park** (Chaw'se; ☎209-296-7488; www.parks.ca.gov; 14881 Pine Grove-Volcano Rd; per car $8; ⊙museum 11am-4pm), a limestone outcrop is covered with petroglyphs and over 1000 *chaw'se* (mortar holes) used for grinding acorns into meal. Learn more about the Sierra Nevada's indigenous tribes inside the park's museum, shaped like a Native American *hun'ge* (roundhouse).

🛏 p563

The Drive » Backtrack along Pine Grove-Volcano Rd, turning right onto Hwy 88 for about half a mile, then turn right onto Ridge Rd, which winds for around 8 miles back to Hwy 49. Turn right and head north about a mile to Sutter Creek.

5 Sutter Creek

Perch on the balcony of one of Main St's gracefully restored buildings and view this gem of a Gold Country town, boasting raised, arcaded sidewalks and high-balconied, false-fronted buildings that exemplify California's 19th-century frontier architecture.

Pick up self-guided walking and driving tour maps at the **visitor center** (☎209-267-1344; www.suttercreek.org; 71a Main St; ⊙10am-6pm).

The nearby **Monteverde General Store** (☎209-267-0493; www.suttercreek.org; 11 Randolph St; entry by donation; ⊙by appointment) is a trip back in time, as is the **Sutter Creek Theatre** (☎916-425-0077; www.suttercreektheater.com; 44 Main St; tickets $15-40), an 1860s saloon and billiards hall, now hosting live-music concerts and occasionally plays, films and cultural events. The rest of the town's four-block-long Main St is crowded with antiques shops, county boutiques, cafes and tasting bars pouring regional wines and craft spirits.

🛏 p563

The Drive » Follow Main St north of Sutter Creek for 3 miles through quaint Amador City. Back at Hwy 49, turn right and continue north toward Plymouth.

TRIP HIGHLIGHT

6 Amador County Wine Country

Amador County might be something of an underdog among California's winemaking regions, but a circuit of welcoming wineries and local characters make for great sipping without any pretension. Planted with California's oldest surviving Zinfandel vines, the countryside has a lot in common with its most celebrated grape varietal – bold, richly colored and earthy.

North of tiny Amador City, **Drytown Cellars** (☎209-245-3500; www.drytowncellars.com; 16030 Hwy 49, Drytown; ⊙11am-5pm; P) has a gregarious host and an array of big red blends and single-varietal wines. Drive further north to the one-horse town of Plymouth, then head east on Shenandoah Rd, where rolling hills are covered with rocky rows of neatly pruned vines, soaking up gallons of sunshine. Pause at modern **Andis Wines** (☎209-245-6177; www.andiswines.com; 11000 Shenandoah Rd, Plymouth; tasting fee $5; ⊙11am-4:30pm; P) for a rich array of reds, particularly Barbera, and picnic tables with vineyard views.

Further along, turn left onto Steiner Rd toward **Renwood Winery** (☎209-245-6979; www.renwood.com; 12225 Steiner Rd, Plymouth; tasting fee $5-10, incl tour $15; ⊙11am-6pm; P), crafting outstanding Zinfandel. Backtrack and continue straight across Shenandoah Rd, bending south toward hilltop estate **Wilderotter Vineyard** (☎209-245-6016; www.wilderottervineyard.com; 19890 Shenandoah School Rd, Plymouth; tasting fee $10; ⊙10:30am-5pm; P), which pours Sauvignon Blanc and smoothly balanced reds.

p563

The Drive » Follow Shenandoah School Rd briefly west until it ends. Turn left back onto Shenandoah Rd for 1.5 miles, then turn right onto Hwy 49 northbound. Less than 20 miles later, after up-and-down roller-coaster stretches, you'll arrive in downtown Placerville, south of Hwy 50.

7 Placerville

Things get livelier in 'Old Hangtown,' a nickname Placerville earned for the vigilante-justice hangings that happened here in 1849. Most buildings along Placerville's Main St date from the 1850s. Poke around antiques shops or ho-hum **Placerville Hardware** (530-622-1151; 441 Main St; 8am-6pm Mon-Sat, 9am-5pm Sun), the oldest continuously operating hardware store west of the Mississippi River. Downtown dive bars get an annual cleaning at Christmas and are great for knocking elbows with odd birds.

For family-friendly shenanigans, head a mile north of town via Bedford Ave to **Hangtown's Gold Bug Park & Mine** (530-642-5207; www.goldbugpark.org; 2635 Gold Bug Lane; adult/child $7/4; 10am-4pm Apr-Oct, from noon Sat & Sun Nov-Mar; P), where hard-hatted visitors can descend into a 19th-century mine shaft, or try gem panning ($2 per hour).

Around Placerville, El Dorado County's mountainous terrain and volcanic soil combine with intense summertime heat and cooling night breezes off the Sierra Nevada to produce some noteworthy wines. Welcoming wineries on Apple Hill north of Hwy 50 include **Lava Cap Winery** (530-621-0175; www.lavacap.com; 2221 Fruit Ridge Rd; tasting fee free-$5; 10am-5pm; P), which sells well-stocked picnic baskets, and **Boeger Winery** (530-622-8094; www.boegerwinery.com; 1709 Carson Rd; tasting $5-15; 10am-5pm; P), whose vineyards were first planted during the gold rush.

STEPHEN SAKS PHOTOGRAPHY / ALAMY STOCK PHOTO ©

The Drive » Back on Hwy 49 northbound, you'll ride along one of the most scenic stretches of the Gold Country's historic route. Patched with shade from oak and pine trees, Hwy 49 drifts beside Sierra Nevada foothills for the next 9 miles to Coloma.

CHASING THE ELEPHANT

Every gold prospector in the Sierra Nevada foothills came to 'see the elephant,' a phrase that captured the adventurous rush for gold, and a colloquialism of the forty-niners. Those on the overland California Trail were 'following the elephant's tracks,' and when they hit it rich, they'd seen the beast from 'trunk to tail.' Like hunting a rare wild animal, rushing Gold Country's hills was a once-in-a-lifetime risk, with potential for a jumbo reward.

Marshall Gold Discovery State Historic Park Old-fashioned doctoring on display

TRIP HIGHLIGHT

8 Coloma

At pastoral, low-key **Marshall Gold Discovery State Historic Park** (☎530-622-3470; www.parks.ca.gov; Hwy 49; per car $8; ⏰8am-8pm late May-early Sep, to 5pm early Sep-late May; P 👪 🐾), a simple dirt path leads to the place along the banks of the American River where James Marshall made his famous discovery of gold flecks below Sutter's Mill on January 24, 1848. Today, several reconstructed and restored historical buildings are all within a short stroll along grassy trails that pass mining artifacts, a blacksmith's shop, pioneer emigrant houses and the **Gold Discovery Museum and Visitor Center** (☎530-622-6198; http://marshallgold.com; 310 Back St; free with park entry, guided tour adult/child $3/2; ⏰10am-4pm, guided tours 11am & 1pm year-round; P 👪). Panning for gold is always popular at **Bekeart's Gun Shop** (329 Hwy 49; per person $7; ⏰10am-3pm Sat & Sun; 👪). Opposite the pioneer cemetery, you can walk or drive up Hwy 153 – the sign says it's California's shortest state highway (but it's not really) – to where the **James Marshall Monument** marks Marshall's final resting place. Ironically, he died bankrupt, penniless and a ward of the state.

The Drive » Rolling northbound, Hwy 49 unfolds more of the region's historical beauty over the next 17 miles. In Auburn, drive across I-80 and stay on Hwy 49 north for another 22 miles, gaining elevation while heading toward Grass Valley. Exit onto Empire St, turning right to follow the signs for Empire Mine State Historic Park's visitor center.

TRIP HIGHLIGHT

9 Around Nevada City

You've hit the biggest bonanza of the mother lode: **Empire Mine State Historic Park** (530-273-8522; www.empiremine.org; 10791 Empire St; adult/child $7/3; 10am-5pm; P), where California's richest hard-rock mine produced 5.8 million ounces of gold between 1850 and 1956. The mine yard is littered with the massive mining equipment and buildings constructed from waste rock.

Backtrack west, then follow the Golden Chain Hwy (Hwy 49) about 5 miles further north to Nevada City. On the town's quaint main drag, hilly Broad St, the **National Hotel** (530-265-4551; www.thenationalhotel.com; 211 Broad St; r $80-140; P) purports to be the oldest continuously operating hotel west of the Rockies. Mosey around the block to **Historic Firehouse No 1 Museum** (530-265-3937; www.nevadacountyhistory.org; 214 Main St; by donation; 1-4pm Tue-Sun May-Oct, by appointment Nov-Apr), where Native American artifacts join displays about Chinese laborers and creepy Donner Party relics.

Last, cool off with a dip at **South Yuba River State Park** (530-432-2546; www.parks.ca.gov; 17660 Pleasant Valley Rd, Penn Valley; park sunrise-sunset, visitor center 11am-4pm May-Sep, to 3pm Thu-Sun Oct-Apr; P), which has popular swimming holes and forest hiking trails near Bridgeport, the USA's longest covered wooden bridge (temporarily closed for restoration at the time of research). It's a 30-minute drive northwest of Nevada City or Grass Valley.

p563

Eating & Sleeping

Sonora 3

Legends Books, Antiques & Old-Fashioned Soda Fountain Cafe $

(209-532-8120; 131 S Washington St; 11am-5pm) The place to sip sarsaparilla, snack on a Polish dog or share a scoop of huckleberry ice cream at a 26ft-long mahogany bar here since 1850. Then browse antiques and books downstairs in the old tunnel miners used to secret their stash directly into the former bank.

Bradford Place Inn B&B $$

(209-536-6075; www.bradfordplaceinn.com; 56 W Bradford St; r $145-265;) Gorgeous gardens and inviting porch seats surround this four-room B&B, which emphasizes green living. With a two-person claw-foot tub, the Bradford Suite is the definitive, romantic B&B experience. Breakfast can be served on the verandah: try the crème brûlée French toast or the filling Mother Lode Skillet.

Volcano 4

Union Inn Historic Hotel $$

(209-296-7711; www.volcanounion.com; 21375 Consolation St; r $130-150; P) The more comfortable of the two historic hotels in Volcano: there are four lovingly updated rooms with crooked floors, two with street-facing balconies. Flat-screen TVs and modern touches are a bit incongruous in the old building, but it's a cozy place to stay. The on-site **Union Pub** (mains $10-30; 5-8pm Mon & Thu, to 9pm Fri, noon-9pm Sat, noon-8pm Sun) has the best food in town and a lovely patio garden.

Sutter Creek 5

Hanford House Inn B&B $$

(209-267-0747; www.hanfordhouse.com; 61 Hanford St; d $145-245; P) Nod off on platform beds in contemporary rooms or fireplace cottage suites. Chef-prepared breakfasts are harvested from the inn's garden, freshly baked goods appear every afternoon and evening brings wine tasting.

Amador County Wine Country 6

Taste Californian $$$

(209-245-3463; www.restauranttaste.com; 9402 Main St, Plymouth; small plates $5-16, dinner mains $24-41; 11:30am-2pm Fri-Sun, 5-9pm Mon, Tue, Thu & Fri, from 4:30pm Sat & Sun) Book a table at Taste, where excellent Amador County wines are paired with a fine menu of California-style cooking (big on meat and game). There's open seating in the wine bar.

Imperial Hotel B&B $$

(209-267-9172; www.imperialamador.com; 14202 Hwy 49, Amador City; r $110-155, ste $125-195;) Built in 1879, this is one of the area's most inventive updates to the typical antique-cluttered hotel, with sleek art-deco touches accenting the warm red brick, a genteel bar and a very good, seasonally minded restaurant (dinner mains $14 to $30). On weekends and holidays, expect a two-night minimum.

Around Nevada City 9

Ike's Quarter Cafe Creole, Breakfast $

(530-265-6138; www.ikesquartercafe.com; 401 Commercial St; mains $11-15; 8am-3pm Thu-Mon;) Right out of New Orleans' Garden District, Ike's serves splendid brunch fare with a sassy charm. Sit outside under the cherry tree or in the cluttered, funky interior. There's eggs Sardou, jambalaya, vegetarian po'boy sandwiches and more. It's an excellent place to get 'Hangtown Fry' – a cornmeal-crusted mess of oysters, bacon, caramelized onions and spinach. Vegan and gluten-free options are available, including gluten-free cornbread.

Outside Inn Inn, Cottage $$

(530-265-2233; http://outsideinn.com; 575 E Broad St; d $79-210; P) The best option for active explorers, this is an unusually friendly and fun inn, with 12 rooms and three cottages maintained by staff who love the outdoors. Some rooms have a patio overlooking a small creek; all have nice quilts and access to BBQ grills. It's a 10-minute walk from downtown and there's a small unheated outdoor pool.

STRETCH YOUR LEGS LOS ANGELES

Start/Finish Union Station

Distance 3.5 miles

Duration Four to six hours

Nobody walks in LA? That's just not true in Downtown's historic core. Sample the jumbled sights, sounds and tastes of the city's Mexican, Asian and European heritage, with iconic architecture and famous TV and film locations, on this half-day ramble.

Take this walk on Trips

Union Station

This iconic 1939 **edifice** (www.amtrak.com; 800 N Alameda St; P) was the last of America's grand railway stations to be built. It's a glamorous exercise in Mission Revival style with art-deco and American Indian accents. The main hall, with cathedral ceilings and 3000-lb chandeliers has been glimpsed in dozens of movies and hit TV shows from *Speed* to *24*.

The Walk » Walk a block up N Alameda St, cross over W Cesar E Chavez Ave and walk west a half block. Turn left down the passageway of Olvera St.

El Pueblo de Los Angeles

Compact, colorful and car-free, this historical monument (p494) sits near the spot where LA's first Spanish colonists plunked down in 1781. Dotted with tiny museums and some of the city's oldest buildings, it's a microcosm of LA's multiethnic immigrant history. Grab a map at the visitor center inside **Avila Adobe** (213-628-1274; www.elpueblo.lacity.org; 10 Olvera St; 9am-4pm), then wander through narrow Olvera St's eclectic Mexican-themed stalls. Free guided tours leave from the **Old Plaza Firehouse** (134 Paseo de la Plaza; 10am-3pm Tue-Sun).

The Walk » Northwest of the open-air bandstand, cross Main St. To your right is 'La Placita,' LA's oldest Catholic church. After peeking inside, walk back down Main St a half block.

La Plaza de Cultura y Artes

This **museum** (213-542-6200; www.lapca.org; 501 N Main St; noon-5pm Mon, Wed & Thu, to 6pm Fri-Sun;) offers snapshots of the Mexican-American experience in Los Angeles, from Spanish colonization in the late 18th century and the Mexican–American War, to the Zoot Suit Riots, activist César Chávez and the Chicana movement. Exhibitions include a re-creation of 1920s Main St as well as rotating showcases of modern and contemporary art by LA-based Latino artists.

The Walk » Continue southwest along Main St, crossing over Hwy 101 toward LA's City Hall (1928). Turn left onto E Temple St, right onto S Los Angeles St and left onto E 1st St, entering Little Tokyo.

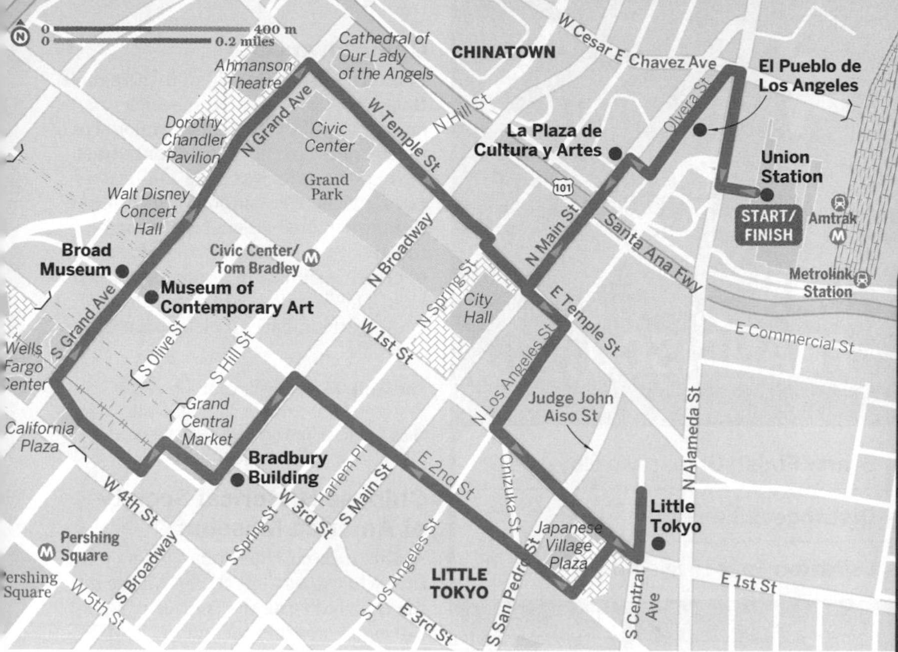

Little Tokyo

Walk past ramen shops to the **Japanese American National Museum** (☎213-625-0414; www.janm.org; 100 N Central Ave; adult/child $10/6, 5-8pm Thu & all day 3rd Thu of month free; ⊙11am-5pm Tue, Wed & Fri-Sun, noon-8pm Thu; 👪). Exhibits include those on WWII internment camps and life for immigrant families. Beside it lies **MOCA Geffen** (☎213-625-4390; www.moca.org; 152 N Central Ave; adult/student/child under 12yr $15/8/free, 5-8pm Thu free; ⊙11am-6pm Mon, Wed & Fri, to 8pm Thu, to 5pm Sat & Sun), dedicated to the Museum of Contemporary Art's more cutting-edge and experimental exhibits.

The Walk » West of Central Ave, turn left to walk through Japanese Village Plaza. Turn right onto E 2nd St, walk five blocks uphill to S Broadway, then turn left and walk a block southwest to W 3rd St.

Bradbury Building

A favorite of movie location scouts since *Blade Runner* was shot here, the 1893 **Bradbury Building** (www.laconservancy.org; 304 S Broadway; ⊙lobby usually 9am-5pm) is one of the city's architectural treasures. Its red-brick facade conceals a glass-roofed atrium with inky filigree grillwork, rickety birdcage elevators and yellow-brick walls.

The Walk » Opposite, walk through LA's Grand Central Market. Walk uphill to California Plaza, veering northwest to Grand Ave. Turn right and walk a block northeast.

Broad Museum

From the instant it opened in September 2015, the Broad (p494; rhymes with 'road') became a must-visit for contemporary art fans. It houses a world-class collection of modern and contemporary art by dozens of heavy hitters, including Cindy Sherman, Jeff Koons, Andy Warhol, Roy Lichtenstein, Robert Rauschenberg and Kara Walker. It's free, though advance ticket reservation is advised.

The Walk » Continue northeast up Grand Ave, passing Walt Disney Concert Hall. Turn right on Temple St and roll downhill to City Hall, retracing your steps north through El Pueblo to Union Station.

STRETCH YOUR LEGS SAN FRANCISCO

Start/Finish Chinatown Gate

Distance 3.3 miles

Duration Four to five hours

Limber up and look sharp: on this walk, you'll pass hidden architectural gems, navigate the winding alleys of Chinatown and catch shimmering views of the bay. Along the way, enjoy controversial art, savory street snacks and a flock of parrots.

Take this walk on Trips

Chinatown Gate

The elaborate threshold of the **Dragon's Gate** (cnr Grant Ave & Bush St), which was donated by Taiwan in 1970, announces the entrance to Chinatown. The street, beyond the gate, was once a notorious red-light district, but forward-thinking Chinatown businessmen reinvented the area in the 1920s, hiring architects to create a signature 'Chinatown Deco' look. The jumble of glittering shops is the perfect place to pick up a cheap souvenir.

The Walk » Huff it uphill from Chinatown Gate, past gilded dragon lamps on Grant Ave to Old St Mary's Square. Two blocks beyond the noble Old St Mary's Church take a left on Clay St.

Chinese Historical Society of America Museum

At this intimate museum, visitors picture what it was like to be Chinese during the gold rush, the transcontinental railroad construction and the Beat heyday. The **Chinese Historical Society of America Museum** (CHSA; 415-391-1188; www.chsa.org; 965 Clay St; adult/student/child $15/10/free; 11am-4pm Wed-Sun;) hosts rotating exhibits across the courtyard in a graceful building, built as Chinatown's YWCA in 1932.

The Walk » Backtrack past Stockton St and turn left down Spofford Alley where mah-jongg tiles click and Sun Yat-sen plotted the 1911 overthrow of China's last dynasty. At Washington St, take a right. Then go left on Ross Alley.

Golden Gate Fortune Cookie Factory

Ross Alley (sometimes marked as Old Chinatown Alley) might seem familiar to movie buffs; it's been the backdrop for flicks like *Karate Kid, Part II* and *Indiana Jones and the Temple of Doom.* The humble little warehouse at No 56 is where to get your fortune while it's hot, folded into warm cookies at the **Golden Gate Fortune Cookie Factory** (415-781-3956; 56 Ross Alley; 9am-6pm). For a small fee you can even write custom fortunes.

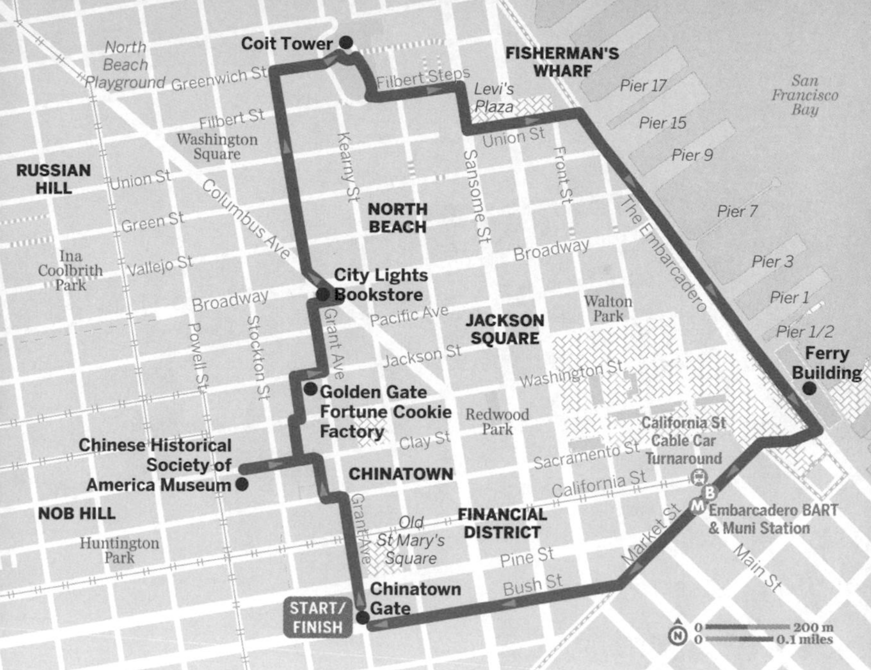

The Walk ❯❯ Go right on Jackson St and left on Grant Ave. You'll pass a number of Chinese bakeries. Take a shortcut through Jack Kerouac Alley, where the poetic vagabond once strolled.

City Lights Bookstore

Ever since manager Shigeyoshi Murao and Beat poet Lawrence Ferlinghetti successfully defended their right to 'willfully and lewdly print' Allen Ginsberg's magnificent *Howl and Other Poems* in 1957, **City Lights Bookstore** (☎415 362-8193; www.citylights.com; 261 Columbus Ave; ⏲10am-midnight; 👪) has been a free-speech landmark. Snuggle into the Poet's Chair upstairs overlooking Jack Kerouac Alley. If reading makes you thirsty, grab a pint at Vesuvio next door.

The Walk ❯❯ Go left on Columbus Ave. Make a slight right on Grant Ave and walk for five blocks, then take a right and hoof it up the Greenwich St steps.

Coit Tower

Adding an exclamation mark to San Francisco's landscape, a visit to **Coit Tower** (☎415-249-0995; www.sfrecpark.org; Telegraph Hill Blvd; nonresident elevator fee adult/child $8/5; ⏲10am-6pm Apr-Oct, to 5pm Nov-Mar) is the high point of the walk atop Telegraph Hill. This peculiar 210ft-projectile is a monument to San Francisco firefighters. When it was completed in 1934, the Diego Rivera-style murals lining the lobby were denounced as Communist. To see more murals hidden inside Coit Tower's stairwell, take a free guided tour at 11am on Wednesday or Saturday.

The Walk ❯❯ Take the Filbert Steps downhill past wild parrots and hidden cottages to Levi's Plaza. Head right on Embarcadero to the Ferry Building.

Ferry Building

The historic Ferry Building (p488) is a transit hub that has transformed itself into a destination for foodies. Artisan food producers, boutique vendors, famous-name restaurants and a thrice-weekly farmers market (p489) make it a mouthwatering stop.

The Walk ❯❯ Walk down Market St. Turn right on Bush St back to Chinatown Gate.

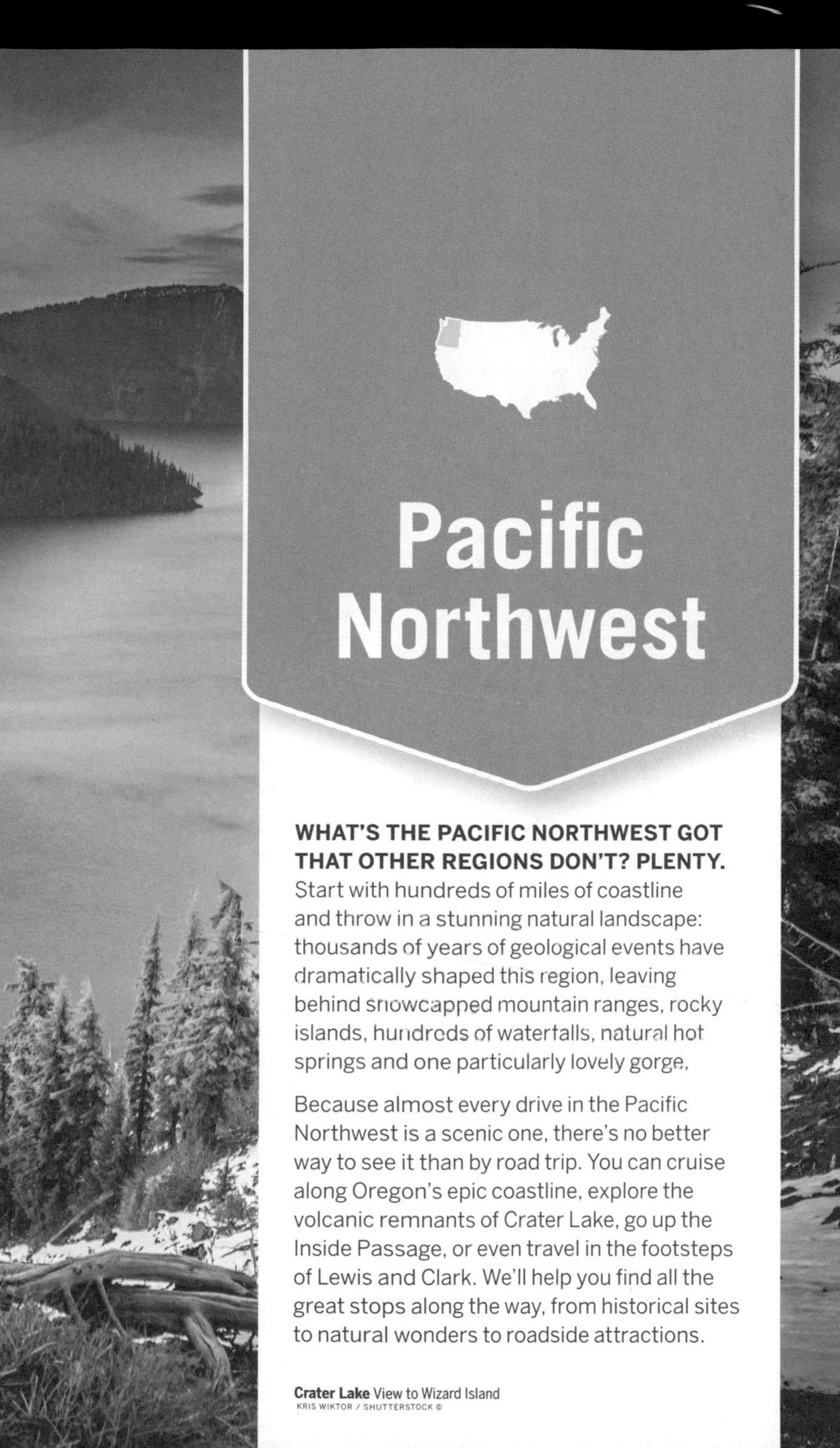

Pacific Northwest

WHAT'S THE PACIFIC NORTHWEST GOT THAT OTHER REGIONS DON'T? PLENTY. Start with hundreds of miles of coastline and throw in a stunning natural landscape: thousands of years of geological events have dramatically shaped this region, leaving behind snowcapped mountain ranges, rocky islands, hundreds of waterfalls, natural hot springs and one particularly lovely gorge.

Because almost every drive in the Pacific Northwest is a scenic one, there's no better way to see it than by road trip. You can cruise along Oregon's epic coastline, explore the volcanic remnants of Crater Lake, go up the Inside Passage, or even travel in the footsteps of Lewis and Clark. We'll help you find all the great stops along the way, from historical sites to natural wonders to roadside attractions.

Crater Lake View to Wizard Island
KRIS WIKTOR / SHUTTERSTOCK ©

Pacific Northwest
0 200 km
0 100 miles
Shuswap Lake
Kamloops
BRITISH COLUMBIA
Fraser River
Merritt
Kelowna
Okanagan Lake
Kootenay Lake
Strait of Georgia
Parksville
Vancouver
Hope
Tofino
Nanaimo
CANADA
USA
Vancouver Island
Mt Baker (10,781ft)
Colville National Forest
Strait of Juan de Fuca
Victoria
San Juan Islands
Bellingham
Okanogan River
Cape Flattery
Cascade Range
Glacier Peak Wilderness
Lake Roosevelt
Lake Pend Oreille
Port Angeles
Everett
Glacier Peak (10,541ft)
46
WASHINGTON
Olympic National Park
Mt Olympus (7965ft)
Chelan
Bremerton
Seattle
Leavenworth
Wenatchee
47
IDAHO
Tacoma
Moses Lake
Ellensburg
Olympia
Aberdeen
Potholes Reservoir
Mt Rainier National Park
Willapa Bay
Mt Rainier (14,411ft)
Columbia River
Snake River
Yakima
Cape Disappointment
Mt St Helens (8363ft)
Toppenish
Tri-Cities
Walla Walla
Astoria
Mt Adams (12,276ft)
Kennewick
Longview
Mt St Helens National Volcanic Monument
Blue Mountains
PACIFIC OCEAN
Hood River
Hells Canyon Wilderness
Vancouver
48
Arlington
Cape Lookout
Portland
The Dalles
Pendleton
Snake River
Tillamook
John Day River
Newberg
Mt Hood (11,240ft)
OREGON
49
Salem
Dale
Mt Jefferson (10,495ft)
Baker City
Willamette River
Newport
Albany
Madras
Mitchell
Lake Billy Chinook
Oregon Dunes National Recreation Area
Three Sisters Wilderness
Sisters
John Day
Florence
Bend
Eugene
Mt Bachelor (9065ft)
Vale
50
La Pine
Riley
Burns
Coos Bay
Cascade Range
Roseburg
Silver Lake
Malheur Lake
Crater Lake National Park
Summer Lake
51
Summer Lake
Albert Lake
Port Orford
Rome
Upper Klamath Lake
Grants Pass
Valley Falls
Medford
Ashland
Klamath Falls
Lakeview
Brookings
Goose Lake
McDermitt
Crescent City
Klamath River
CALIFORNIA
NEVADA

Cape Perpetua, OR

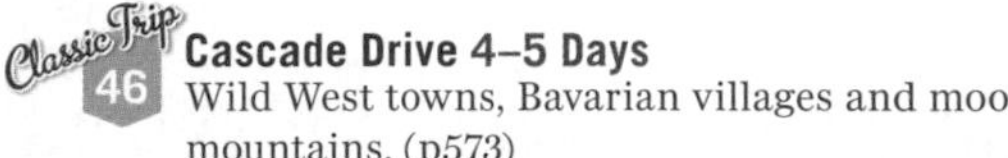

Classic Trip
46 **Cascade Drive 4–5 Days**
Wild West towns, Bavarian villages and moody mountains. (p573)

47 **Olympic Peninsula Loop 4 Days**
Tolkien meets *Twilight* in surreal, wet forest. (p583)

48 **On the Trail of Lewis & Clark 3–4 Days**
American pioneer history etched in stone, wood and interactive state parks. (p591)

Classic Trip
49 **Highway 101 Oregon Coast 7 Days**
Diversions include whale-watching, lighthouses and seafood. (p601)

50 **Oregon Cascades Scenic Byways 4 Days**
A nonstop parade of forests, lakes, waterfalls and mountains. (p615)

51 **Crater Lake Circuit 2–3 Days**
The very best route to get to Oregon's only national park. (p625)

DON'T MISS

Cape Disappointment

Few leave Cape Disappointment disappointed, thanks to its spectacular, end-of-the-world setting. Check it out on Trip 48

Leavenworth

German theme towns rarely work in the US, but Leavenworth's alpine backdrop makes it look like the real deal on Trip 46

Cape Perpetua

The best view of the coast can't be seen from the highway; drive to the top of Cape Perpetua for dizzyingly gorgeous vistas on Trip 49

Ross Lake Resort

No wonder Kerouac loved this region with its cold, almost terrifying, beauty. Find this floating hotel on a wilderness lake with no road access on Trip 46

Proxy Falls

Oregon has waterfalls to spare, but one of the prettiest is Proxy Falls, accessed via an easy hike on Trip 50

Classic Trip

Cascade Drive

Rugged and inaccessible for half the year, this brawny mountain drive is etched with the kind of monumental, Alaskan-style beauty that once inspired Jack Kerouac.

TRIP HIGHLIGHTS

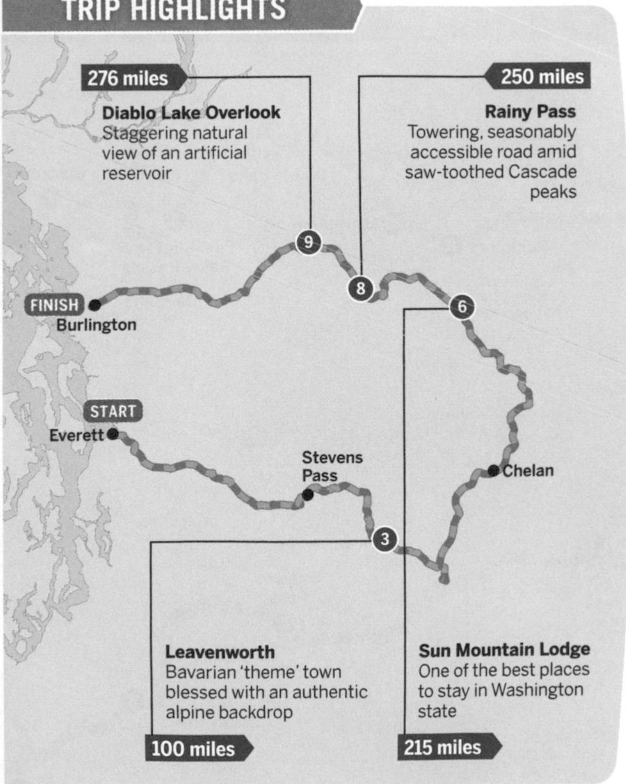

276 miles

Diablo Lake Overlook
Staggering natural view of an artificial reservoir

250 miles

Rainy Pass
Towering, seasonably accessible road amid saw-toothed Cascade peaks

9
8
6

FINISH Burlington

START Everett

Stevens Pass

Chelan

3

Leavenworth
Bavarian 'theme' town blessed with an authentic alpine backdrop

100 miles

Sun Mountain Lodge
One of the best places to stay in Washington state

215 miles

4–5 DAYS
350 MILES / 563KM

GREAT FOR...

BEST TIME TO GO

June to September when roads are snow-free and passable.

ESSENTIAL PHOTO

View from Sun Mountain Lodge.

BEST FOR HIKING

The Maple Pass Loop Trail from Rainy Pass.

North Cascades Hikers on the Maple Pass Loop Trail

Classic Trip

46 Cascade Drive

Nature defies modern engineering in the North Cascades where high-altitude roads succumb to winter snow storms, and the names of the mountains – Mt Terror, Mt Fury, Forbidden Peak – whisper forebodingly. Less scary are the scattered settlements, small towns with esoteric distractions such as Bavarian Leavenworth and 'Wild West' Winthrop. Fill up the tank, put on your favorite Springsteen track and prepare for one of the rides of your life.

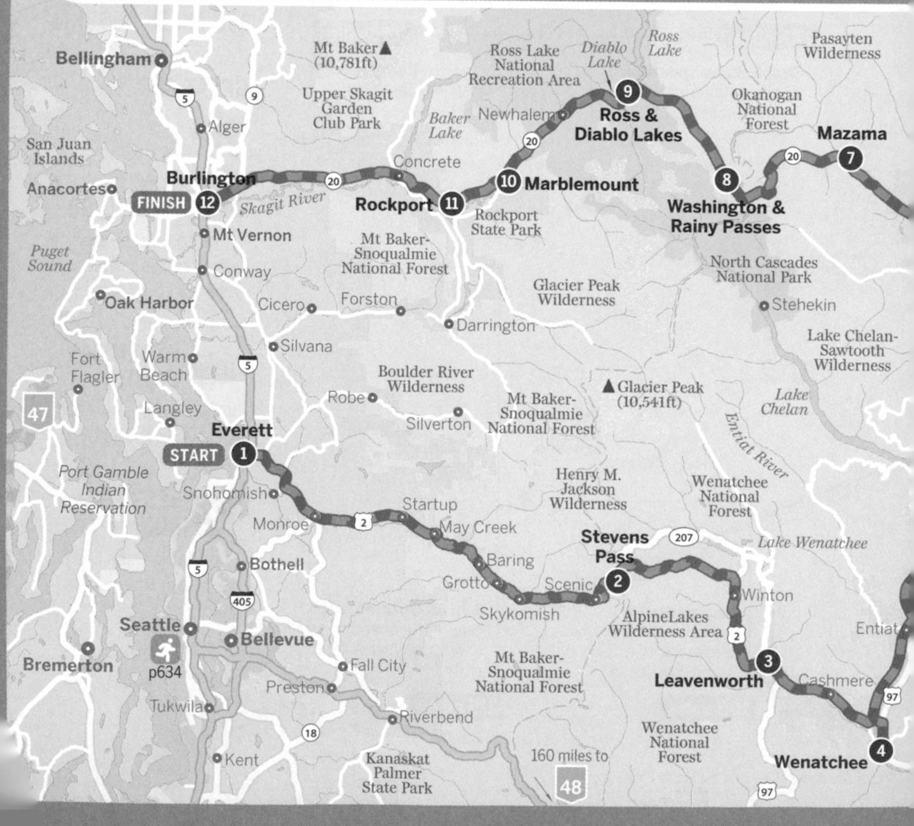

❶ Everett

This drive incorporates four-fifths of the popular 'Cascade Loop.' You can complete the other fifth by taking in the second half of the trip through Whidbey Island. There's not much to detain you in Everett, the route's starting point 30 miles north of Seattle. It's known mainly for its Boeing connections and as the genesis for countless Seattle-region traffic jams. Head directly east and don't stop until Stevens Pass.

The Drive » The starting point of Hwy 2, a 2579-mile cross-continental road that terminates in Maine, is in Everett. Crossing I-5, the route, which parallels the Great Northern Railway and Skykomish River for much of its journey, passes the towns of Startup, Sultan and Index, climbing toward Stevens Pass, 66 miles away. If you're thirsty, stop at one of the drive-through espresso huts en route.

❷ Stevens Pass

Accessible year-round thanks to its day-use **ski area** (www.stevenspass.com; day pass $67-74), Stevens Pass was only 'discovered' by white settlers as recently as 1890. Despite its lofty vantage – at 4045ft it is over 1000ft higher than Snoqualmie Pass – it was chosen for the Great Northern railroad's cross-Cascade route, but you won't see any train tracks here. Instead, the railway burrows underneath the pass via North America's longest rail tunnel (7.8 miles). The long-distance **Pacific Crest Trail** also crosses the highway here. Tempted?

The Drive » From Stevens Pass the descent begins immediately with subtle changes in the vegetation; the cedars and hemlocks of the western slopes are gradually replaced with pine, larch and spruce. The road threads through the steep-sided Tumwater Canyon alongside the turbulent Wenatchee River. Suddenly, German-style houses start to appear against an eerily familiar alpine backdrop.

TRIP HIGHLIGHT

❸ Leavenworth

Blink hard and rub your eyes. This isn't some strange Germanic hallucination. This is Leavenworth, a former lumber town that underwent a Bavarian makeover in the 1960s after the re-routing of the cross-continental railway threatened to put it permanently out of business. Swapping loggers for tourists, Leavenworth today has successfully reinvented itself as a traditional *Romantische Strasse* village, right down to the beer and bratwurst. The *Sound of Music*–style setting helps, as does

LINK YOUR TRIP

47 Olympic Peninsula Loop

Drop down WA 20 and take the ferry over to Port Townsend to pick up the Olympic Peninsula Loop.

48 On the Trail of Lewis & Clark

Head southeast on Hwy 90 and Hwy 82 for 247 miles from Everett to Kennewick.

the fact that Leavenworth serves as the main activity center for sorties into the nearby **Alpine Lakes Wilderness** (permit for certain areas $5) and **Wenatchee National Forest** (www.fs.usda.gov/okawen; 215 Melody Lane; ⏰hours vary).

A surreal stroll through the gabled alpine houses of Leavenworth's Front St with its dirndl-wearing waitstaff, wandering accordionists and European cheesemongers is one of Washington state's oddest, but most endearing experiences. For white-water rafting trips, call by **Osprey Rafting Co** (☎509-548-6800; www.ospreyrafting.com; 4342 Icicle Rd), which offers excursions from $79.

✕ 🛏 p581

The Drive » The 22 miles between Leavenworth and Wenatchee highlight one of the most abrupt scenery changes in the state. One minute you're in quasi-Bavaria surrounded by crenellated alpine peaks, the next you're in a sprawled couldn't-be-anywhere-but-America town amid bald hills and a Nile-like river valley. East of Leavenworth Hwy 2 shares the road briefly with Hwy 97.

4 Wenatchee

Fruit stands start peppering the highway soon after you leave Leavenworth, paving your entry into Wenatchee, the self-proclaimed – and who's arguing? – Apple Capital of the World. Something of an ugly sister after cute Leavenworth, Wenatchee's a place to go local and taste the apples from the nearby orchards before swinging north. The best fruit stands enliven Hwy 2/97 on the way to Chelan. As an overture to your tasting experience, check out the **Washington Apple Commission Visitor Center** (www.bestapples.com; 2900 Euclid Ave; ⏰8am-5pm Mon-Fri) on the way into town, where you can bone up on the relative merits of a Gala versus a Braeburn over a surprisingly interesting video.

The Drive » Hwy 2/97 plies the east side of the Columbia River between Wenatchee and Chelan. This is one of the best places to 'shop' at impromptu seasonal fruit outlets run by enterprising local farmers who haul their freshly plucked produce from the nearby fields and orchards to sell roadside from semi-permanent stores, carts or just plain old boxes.

5 Chelan

Lake Chelan shelters some of the nation's cleanest water and has consequently become one of Washington's premier water recreation areas. Not surprisingly, the place is cheek-to-jowl in summer, with all number of speedboats, Jet Skis and power-craft battling it out for their own private slice of water. To avoid any high-speed collisions, try renting a kayak from **Lake Rider Sports** (www.lakeridersports.com; Lakeshore Waterfront Park; single/double kayak rental per day $70/90; ⏰7am-6:30pm) and paddling up the lake to see some undiluted Cascadian nature firsthand.

There are public beaches at **Lakeside Park**, near the west side

KEROUAC & THE VOID

A turnout at milepost 135 on Hwy 20 offers the drive's only roadside views of **Desolation Peak**. The peak's lookout tower was famously home to Zen-influenced Beat writer Jack Kerouac who, in 1956, spent 63 days here in splendid isolation, honing his evolving Buddhist philosophy, raging at 'the Void' of nearby Hozomeen Mountain (also visible from the turnout) and penning drafts of *Desolation Angels*. It was the last time Kerouac would enjoy such anonymity; the following year saw the publication of *On the Road*, and his propulsion to the status of literary icon.

of Chelan town, and at **Lake Chelan State Park**, 9 miles west on S Lakeshore Rd.

If you have kids, don't even think they'll let you sneak past **Slidewaters Water Park** (www.slidewaters.com; 102 Waterslide Dr; day pass adult/child $23/18; ⌚10am-7pm May-Sep; 👪), located on a hill above the *Lady of the Lake* boat dock.

The Drive » Rejoin Hwy 97 and follow it north through the grand coulees of the Columbia River valley to the small town of Pateros. From here SR 153, aka the Methow Hwy, tracks the younger, faster-flowing Methow River north to Twisp. At a junction with Hwy 20 turn left, and continue on the highway into Winthrop, 61 miles from Chelan.

LOCAL KNOWLEDGE: METHOW VALLEY TRAILS

The Methow's combination of powdery winter snow and abundant summer sunshine has transformed the valley into one of Washington's primary recreation areas. You can bike, hike and fish in the summer, and cross-country ski on the second-biggest snow-trail network in the US in the winter. The 125 miles of trails are maintained by a nonprofit organization, the **Methow Valley Sport Trails Association** (MVSTA; ☎509-996-3287; www.methowtrails.org; 309 Riverside Ave, Winthrop; ⌚9am-3:30pm Mon-Fri), and in the winter it provides the most comprehensive network of hut-to-hut (and hotel-to-hotel) skiing in North America.

TRIP HIGHLIGHT

6 Winthrop

Winthrop is – along with Leavenworth – one of two themed towns on this Cascade Drive. Once a struggling mining community, it avoided ghost town status in the 1960s when it was made over to look like a cowboy settlement out of the Wild West. Although on paper it sounds more like corny Hollywood than *Gun Fight at the OK Corral,* the Gary Cooper touches are surprisingly authentic. Winthrop's *High Noon* shopfronts hide a genuine frontier spirit (the road ends in winter not far beyond here), along with some fantastic accommodations and places to eat.

The facades of downtown Winthrop are so realistic it's easy to miss the collection of homesteader cabins that make up the **Shafer Museum** (285 Castle Ave; admission by donation; ⌚10am-5pm Memorial Day-Labor Day). But best of all is the unmissable **Sun Mountain Lodge** (p581), a sporting and relaxation dreamscape 10 miles out of town overlooking the valley.

✖ 🛏 p581

The Drive » Out of Winthrop, SR 20 enters the most bucolic and endearing stretch of the Methow Valley whose broad valley floor scattered with farms gives little hint of the jagged wilderness that lies beyond. If you thought Winthrop was small, don't blink in Mazama, a small cluster of wooden buildings reminiscent of a gunslinger movie.

7 Mazama

The last outpost before the raw, desolate, occasionally terrifying North Cascades, Mazama's half-dozen wooden abodes sit at the western end of the Methow Valley. Fuel up on brownies at the **Mazama Store** (www.themazamastore.com; 50 Lost River Rd; ⌚7am-6pm), an espresso bar for outdoorsy locals, but also a great place to pick up trail tips.

The Drive » You'll be working through your gears soon after leaving Mazama as the North Cascade Mountains start to close in. This part of Hwy 20 is unlike any other trans-Cascade road. Not only is the scenery more spectacular, but the road itself is a major engineering feat. Only completed in 1972, it still remains closed November to May due to snow blockage.

Classic Trip

CHECUBUS / SHUTTERSTOCK ©

PIERDELUNE / SHUTTERSTOCK ©

WHY THIS IS A CLASSIC TRIP

CELESTE BRASH, WRITER

This route could well be called 'The Heart of the Cascades' because it takes you over, around and deep into the most glorious corners of some of the most astounding mountains in the Americas. It's difficult not to blurt out with 'oohs' as you round corners to vistas of blue lakes framed by sharp, white peaks and shaded by evergreens. Perfect for road-tripping, the highway scenery never falters.

Above: Leavenworth
Left: Winthrop
Right: Alpine scenery around Leavenworth

MARINA POUSHKINA / SHUTTERSTOCK ©

TRIP HIGHLIGHT

8 Washington & Rainy Passes

Venture less than 100yd from your car at the **Washington Pass overlook** (5477ft) and you'll be rewarded with fine views of the towering Liberty Bell and its Early Winter Spires, while the highway drops below you in ribbonlike loops. By the time the highway reaches **Rainy Pass** (5875ft) a couple of miles further west, the air has chilled and you're well into the high country, a hop and a skip from the drive's highest hiking trails. The 6.2-mile **Maple Pass Loop Trail** is a favorite, climbing 2150ft to aerial views over jewel-like Lake Ann.

The epic **Pacific Crest Trail** also crosses Hwy 20 nearby, so keep an eye open for wide-eyed and bushy-bearded through-hikers popping out of the undergrowth. Perhaps the best choice to shake the crowds is the excellent climb up to **Easy Pass** (7.4 miles return), hardly 'easy,' but offering spectacular views of Mt Logan and the Fisher Basin below.

The Drive » Surrounded by Gothic peaks, the North Cascades Scenic Hwy makes a big swing north shadowing Granite Creek and then Ruby Creek, where it swings back west and enters the Ross Lake National Recreation Area near Ruby Arm.

Classic Trip

TRIP HIGHLIGHT

9 Ross & Diablo Lakes

The odd thing about much of the landscape on this trip is that it's unnatural, born from the construction of three huge dams that still supply Seattle with much of its electricity. The wilderness that surrounds it, however, is the rawest you'll get outside Alaska. **Ross Lake** (Hwy 20, Mile 134) was formed in the 1930s after the building of the eponymous dam. It stretches north 23 miles into Canada. Soon after the **Ross Lake overlook**, a path leads from the road to the dam. You'll see the unique Ross Lake Resort (p581) floating on the other side.

A classic photo opportunity comes a couple of miles later at the **Diablo Lake** (supply ferries adult/child 1 way $10/5) overlook. The turquoise lake is the most popular part of the park, offering beaches, gorgeous views and a boat launch at **Colonial Creek Campground** (☎206-386-4495; www.nps.gov; Hwy 20, Mile 130; campsites $16), with nearby hikes to Thunder Knob (3.6 miles return) and Thunder Creek (12 miles return).

p581

The Drive » From Diablo, head west alongside the sinuous Gorge Reservoir on Hwy 20. Pass through Newhalem (where you can stop at the North Cascades National Park Visitor Center). As the valley opens out and the damp West Coast air drifts in from the Pacific, you'll enter Marblemount, 23 miles from Diablo Lake.

10 Marblemount

There's not much to the town of Marblemount, but the thought of buffalo burgers may entice you to pull over at the **Buffalo Run Restaurant** (www.buffaloruninn.com; 60084 Hwy 20; mains $10-34; lunch & dinner;), the first decent restaurant for miles, as long as you don't mind being greeted by the sight of several decoratively draped animal skins and a huge buffalo head mounted on the wall.

p581

The Drive » The Skagit River remains your constant companion as you motor the 8 miles from Marblemount to equally diminutive Rockport. Look out for rafters, floaters and bald eagles.

11 Rockport

As the valley widens further you'll touchdown in Rockport, where the mirage-like appearance of an Indonesian-style Batak hut, aka the **Cascadian Home Farm** (☎360-853-8173; Hwy 20, Mile 100; 10am-6pm May & Oct, 9am-7pm Jun-Sep;), begs you to stop for organic strawberries, delicious fruit shakes and lifesaving espresso, which you can slurp down on a short self-guided tour of the farm.

Nearby, a 10-mile stretch of the Skagit River is a wintering ground for over 600 bald eagles who come here from November to early March to feast on spawning salmon. January is the best time to view them, ideally on a winter float trip with **Skagit River Guide Service** (☎888-675-2448; www.skagitriverfishingguide.com; Mt Vernon), whose boats use propane heat and are equipped with comfy cushioned seats. Three-hour trips run early November to mid-February and cost $75.

The Drive » From Rockport, head west for 37 miles on Hwy 20 through the Cascade Mountain foothills and the ever-broadening Skagit River Valley to the small city of Burlington, which sits just east of busy I-5.

12 Burlington

The drive's end, popularly known as the 'Hub City,' is not a 'sight' in itself (unless you like shopping malls), although the settlement's location in the heart of the Skagit River Valley means it acts as a hub for numerous nearby attractions, including the tulip fields of La Conner, Chuckanut Dr (which officially ends here) and the San Juan Islands.

Eating & Sleeping

Leavenworth 3

München Haus — German $

(☎509-548-1158; www.munchenhaus.com; 709 Front St; brats $5-7; ⏰11am-9pm) The Haus is 100% alfresco, meaning that the hot German sausages and pretzels are essential stomach warmers in winter, while the Bavarian brews will cool you down in summer. The casual beer-garden atmosphere is complemented by an aggressively jaunty accordion soundtrack, laid-back staff, a kettle of cider relish and an epic mustard bar. Hours vary outside summer.

Enzian Inn — Hotel $$

(☎509-548-5269; www.enzianinn.com; 590 Hwy 2; d from $140;) At this Leavenworth classic the day starts with a blast on an alpenhorn before breakfast. If that doesn't send you running for your lederhosen, consider the free putting green (with resident grass-trimming goats), the indoor and outdoor swimming pools, and the nightly pianist pounding out requests in the Bavarian lobby.

Winthrop 6

Duck Brand Cantina — Mexican, Brunch $$

(☎509-996-2408; www.centralreservations.net/lodging/duckbrand; 248 Riverside Ave; mains $7-15; ⏰7am-9pm) No standard Mexican restaurant, the 'Duck' nonetheless serves quesadillas, enchiladas and tacos that could roast the socks off any authentic Monterey diner. The Wild West saloon-style cantina also churns out a mean American breakfast. In the winter the hearty porridge will keep you skiing all day.

Sun Mountain Lodge — Lodge $$$

(☎509-996-2211; www.sunmountainlodge.com; 604 Patterson Lake Rd; r from $205, cabins from $405;) Without a doubt one of the best places to stay in Washington, Sun Mountain Lodge has an incomparable natural setting, perched like an eagle's nest high above the Methow Valley, and its assorted cabins provide luxury without pretension. The 360-degree views from its highly lauded restaurant are awe-inspiring, and people travel from miles around just to enjoy breakfast here.

Ross & Diablo Lakes 9

Ross Lake Resort — Historic Hotel $$

(☎206-386-4437; www.rosslakeresort.com; 503 Diablo St, Rockport; cabins $195-370; ⏰mid-Jun–late Oct;) The floating cabins at this secluded resort, on the lake's west side, were built in the 1930s for loggers working in the valley soon to be flooded by Ross Dam. There's no road in – either hike the 2-mile trail from Hwy 20 or take the resort's supply boat from the parking area near Diablo Dam.

Marblemount 10

Marblemount Diner — Diner $$

(60147 Hwy 20; mains $9-22; ⏰11am-8pm Mon, Thu & Fri, 8am-8pm Sat & Sun) A filling as-much-as-you-can-eat breakfast buffet (served 8am to 11am) at weekends is the highlight of this friendly diner with booths, tables and seating at the bar. Obey 'rule one' of all buffets: arrive early, before all the food is taken and/or dried out.

Buffalo Run Inn — Motel $

(☎360-873-2103; www.buffaloruninn.com; 58179 Hwy 20; s/d from $54/69;) Situated on a sharp bend on Hwy 20, the Buffalo doesn't look much from the outside. But within its wooden walls is a clean motel (kitchenettes, TVs and comfy beds) and backcountry cabin (kitschy bear and buffalo paraphernalia). Five of the 15 rooms share baths and a sitting area. There's an included microwaveable breakfast 'buffet' stuffed in a communal fridge.

Olympic Peninsula Loop

Freakishly wet, fantastically green and chillingly remote, the Olympic Peninsula looks like it has been resurrected from a wilder, pre-civilized era.

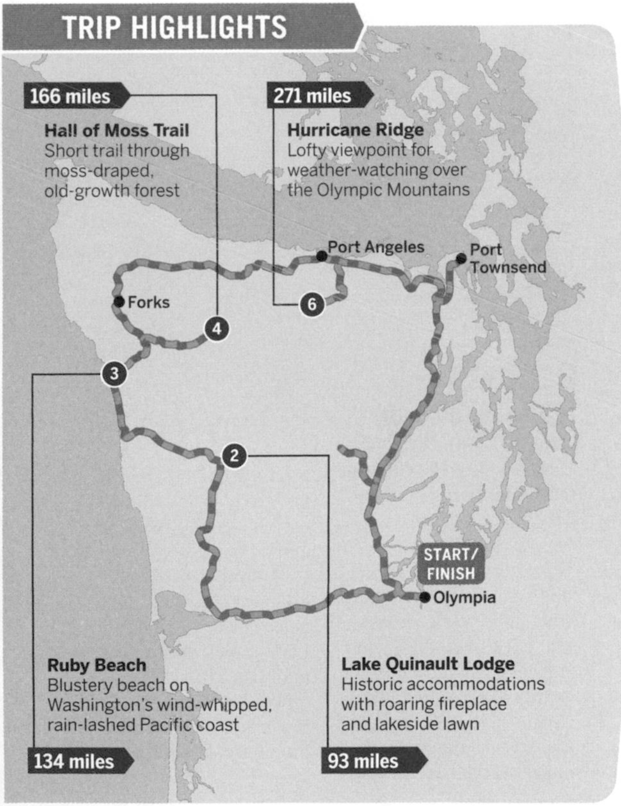

TRIP HIGHLIGHTS

166 miles
Hall of Moss Trail
Short trail through moss-draped, old-growth forest

271 miles
Hurricane Ridge
Lofty viewpoint for weather-watching over the Olympic Mountains

Port Angeles
Port Townsend
Forks
4
6
3
2
START/ FINISH
Olympia

Ruby Beach
Blustery beach on Washington's wind-whipped, rain-lashed Pacific coast
134 miles

Lake Quinault Lodge
Historic accommodations with roaring fireplace and lakeside lawn
93 miles

4 DAYS
435 MILES / 700KM

GREAT FOR...

BEST TIME TO GO
June to September when deluges are slightly less likely.

The Hoh Rainforest to see greens you've never imagined.

Roosevelt elk at the Hoh Rainforest.

Olympic National Park One of the world's few temperate rainforests

47 Olympic Peninsula Loop

Imagine pine-clad beaches fused with an American Mt Olympus, with a slice of Stephenie Meyer's *Twilight* saga thrown in for good measure, and you've got an approximation of what a drive around the Olympic Peninsula looks like. This is wilderness of the highest order, where thick forest collides with an end-of-the-continent coastline that hasn't changed much since Juan de Fuca sailed by in 1592. Bring hiking boots – and rain gear!

❶ Olympia

Welcome to Olympia, city of weird contrasts, where street-side buskers belt out acoustic grunge, and stiff bureaucrats answer their ringtones on the lawns of the expansive state legislature. A quick circuit of the **Washington State Capitol** (☎360-902-8880; 416 Sid Snyder Ave SW; ⏰7am-5:30pm Mon-Fri, 11am-4pm Sat & Sun), a huge Grecian temple of a building, will give you a last taste of civilization before you depart. Then load up the car and head swiftly for the exits.

✕ p589

The Drive » Your basic route is due west, initially on Hwy 101, then (briefly) on SR 8 before joining Hwy 12 in Elma. In Grays Harbor, enter the twin cities of Aberdeen and Hoquiam, famous for producing William Boeing and the grunge group Nirvana. Here, you swing north on Hwy 101 (again!) to leafier climes at Lake Quinault, 88 miles from Olympia.

TRIP HIGHLIGHT

❷ Lake Quinault

Situated in the extreme southwest of the **Olympic National Park** (www.nps.gov/olym; 7-day access per vehicle $25, pedestrian/cyclist $10, 1yr unlimited entry $50), the thickly forested Quinault River Valley is one of the park's least-crowded corners. Clustered on the south shore of deep-blue glacial Lake Quinault is the tiny village of **Quinault**, complete with the luscious Lake Quinault Lodge (p589), a US Forest Service (USFS) office and a couple of stores.

A number of short **hiking trails** begin just below Lake Quinault Lodge; pick up a free map from the USFS office. The shortest of these is the **Quinault Rain Forest Nature**

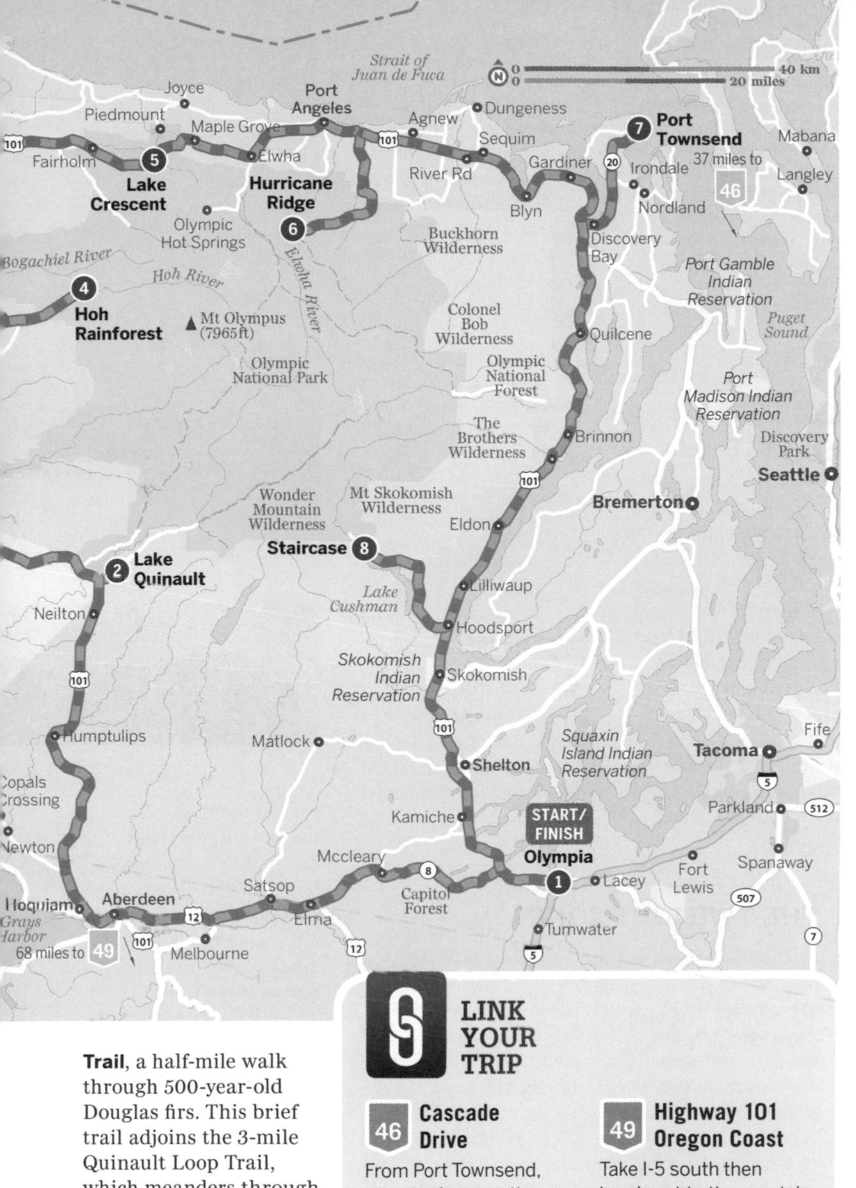

46 Cascade Drive

From Port Townsend, take the ferry north then follow WA 20 to Burlington.

49 Highway 101 Oregon Coast

Take I-5 south then headwest to the coastal town of Astoria, OR.

Trail, a half-mile walk through 500-year-old Douglas firs. This brief trail adjoins the 3-mile Quinault Loop Trail, which meanders through the rainforests before circling back to the lake. The Quinault region is renowned for its huge trees. Close to the village is a 191ft Sitka spruce tree (supposedly over 1000 years old), and nearby are the world's largest red cedar, Douglas fir and mountain hemlock trees.

p589

The Drive ›› West from Lake Quinault, Hwy 101 continues through the Quinault Indian Reservation before entering a thin strip of national park territory that protects the beaches around Kalaloch (klay-lock). This is some of the wildest coastal scenery in the US accessible by road; various pullovers allow beach forays. After a total of 40 miles you'll reach Ruby Beach.

TRIP HIGHLIGHT

3 Ruby Beach

Inhabiting a thin coastal strip that was added to the national park in 1953, Ruby Beach is accessed via a short 0.2-mile path that leads down to a large expanse of windswept coast embellished by polished black stones and wantonly strewn tree trunks. To the south toward Kalaloch, other accessible beaches include unimaginatively named Beach One through to Beach Six, all of which are popular with beachcombers. At low tide, rangers give talks on tidal-pool life at **Beach Four** and on the ecosystems of the Olympic coastal strip.

p589

The Drive ›› North of Ruby Beach, Hwy 101 swings sharply northeast and inland, tracking the Hoh River. Turn right off 101 onto the Hoh River Rd to explore one of the national park's most popular inner sanctums, the Hoh Rainfore st. Suspend your excitement as the trees eerily close in as you (re)enter the park.

TRIP HIGHLIGHT

4 Hoh Rainforest

Count yourself lucky if you arrive on a day when it isn't raining! The most popular detour off Hwy 101 is the 19-mile paved road to the Hoh Valley, the densest, wettest, greenest and most intensely surreal temperate rainforest on planet earth. The essential hike here is the short but fascinating **Hall of Moss Trail**, an easy 0.75-mile loop through the kind of weird, ethereal scenery that even JRR Tolkien couldn't have invented. Old-man's beard drips from branches above you like corduroy fringe, while trailside licorice ferns and lettuce lichens overwhelm the massive fallen trunks of maple and Sitka spruce. Rangers lead interesting free guided walks here twice a day

DIANE FETZNER / SHUTTERSTOCK ©

THE TWILIGHT ZONE

It would have been impossible to envisage 15 years ago: diminutive Forks, a depressed lumber town full of hard-nosed loggers, reborn as a pilgrimage site for 'tweenage' girls following in the ghostly footsteps of two fictional sweethearts named Bella and Edward. The reason for this weird metamorphosis was, of course, the *Twilight* saga, a four-part book series by US author Stephenie Meyer about love and vampires on the foggy Olympic Peninsula that in just a few years has shifted more than 100 million books and spawned five Hollywood movies. With Forks acting as the book's main setting, the town was catapulted to international stardom, and the cachet has yet to wear off. Daily **Twilight Tours** (360-374-5634; www.forkswa.com; 130 S Spartan Ave) visit most of the places mentioned in Meyer's books.

Ruby Beach

during summer and can help you spot some of the park's 5000-strong herd of **Roosevelt elk**.

The Drive » Rejoining Hwy 101, motor north to the small and relatively nondescript but handy settlement of Forks. Press on through as Hwy 101 bends north then east through a large logging area before plunging back into the national park on the shores of wondrous Lake Crescent, which is 66 miles from the Hoh Rainforest.

5 Lake Crescent

Before you've even had time to erase the horror of teenage vampires from your head, the scenery shifts again as the road winds along the glittering pine-scented shores of glacial-carved Lake Crescent. The lake looks best from water level, on a rental kayak, or from high above at its eastern edge on the **Storm King Mountain Trail** (named after the peak's wrathful spirit), accessible via a steep, 1.7-mile ascent that splits off the Barnes Creek Trail. For the less athletic, the **Marymere Falls Trail** is a 2-mile round-trip to a 90ft cascade that drops down over a basalt cliff. Both hikes leave from a parking lot to the right of SR 101 near the **Storm King Ranger Station** (☎360-928-3380; 343 Barnes Point Rd; ⏰May-Sep). The area is also the site of the Lake Crescent Lodge (p589), the oldest of the park's trio of celebrated lodges, which first opened in 1916.

🛏 p589

The Drive » From Lake Crescent take Hwy 101 22 miles east to the town of Port Angeles, a gateway to Victoria, Canada, which is reachable by ferry to the north. Starting in Race St, the 18-mile Hurricane Ridge Rd climbs 5300ft toward extensive wildflower meadows and expansive mountain vistas often visible above the clouds.

TRIP HIGHLIGHT

6 Hurricane Ridge

Up above the clouds, stormy Hurricane Ridge lives up to its name with fickle weather and biting winds made slightly more bearable by the park's best high-altitude views. Its proximity to Port Angeles is another bonus; if you're heading up here be sure to call into the museum-like **Olympic National Park Visitor Center** (☎360-565-3100; www.nps.gov/olym; 3002 Mt Angeles Rd; ⌚8am-6pm Jul & Aug, to 4pm Sep-Jun) first. The smaller **Hurricane Ridge Visitor Center** (⌚9:30am-5pm daily summer, Fri-Sun winter) has a snack bar, gift shop and toilets, and is the starting point of various hikes. **Hurricane Hill Trail** (which begins at the end of the road) and the **Meadow Loop Trails** network are popular and moderately easy. The first half-mile of these trails is wheelchair accessible.

The Drive » Wind back down the Hurricane Ridge Rd, kiss the suburbs of Port Angeles and press east through the retirement community of Sequim (pronounced 'squwim'). Turn north on SR 20 to reach another, more attractive port, that of Port Townsend.

7 Port Townsend

Leaving the park momentarily behind, ease back into civilization with the cultured Victorian comforts of Port Townsend, whose period charm dates from the railroad boom of the 1890s, when the town was earmarked to become the 'New York of the West.' That never happened, but you can pick up a historic walking tour map from the **visitor center** (☎360-385-2722; www.ptchamber.org; 2409 Jefferson St; ⌚9am-5pm Mon-Fri) and wander the waterfront's collection of shops, galleries and antique malls. Don't miss the old-time **Belmont Saloon** (925 Water St; mains lunch $10-14, dinner $15-32; ⌚10:30-2am Mon-Fri, 9am-2am Sat & Sun), the **Rose Theatre** (235 Taylor St), a gorgeously renovated theater that's been showing movies since 1908, and the fine Victorian mansions on the bluff above town, where several charming residences have been turned into B&Bs.

p589

The Drive » From Port Townsend, head back to the junction of Hwy 101, but this time head south passing Quilcene, Brinnon, with its great diner, and the Dosewallips park entrance. You get more unbroken water views here on the park's eastern side courtesy of the Hood Canal. Track the watery beauty to Hoodsport where signs point west off Hwy 101 to Staircase, 67 miles from Port Townsend.

8 Staircase

It's drier on the park's eastern side and the mountains are closer. The Staircase park nexus, accessible via Hoodsport, has a ranger station, a campground and a decent trail system that follows the drainage of the North Fork Skokomish River and is flanked by some of the most rugged peaks in the Olympics. Nearby **Lake Cushman** has a campground and water-sports opportunities.

Eating & Sleeping

Olympia ❶

Traditions Cafe & World Folk Art — Health Food $

(360-705-2819; www.traditionsfairtrade.com; 300 5th Ave SW; mains $6-12; 9am-6pm Mon-Fri, 10am-6pm Sat, 11am-5pm Sun;) This comfortable hippie enclave at the edge of Heritage Park offers fresh salads and tasty, healthy sandwiches (lemon-tahini, smoked salmon etc), coffee drinks, herbal teas, local ice cream, beer and wine. Posters advertise community-action events, and in the corner is a 'Peace and Social Justice Lending Library.' It's attached to an eclectic folk-art store.

Lake Quinault ❷

Lake Quinault Lodge — Historic Hotel $$$

(360-288-2900; www.olympicnationalparks.com; 345 S Shore Rd; r $219- 450;) Everything you could want in a historic national-park lodge and more, the suspended-in-time Quinault, built in 1926, has a massive fireplace, a manicured cricket-pitch-quality lawn, huge, comfy leather sofas, a regal reception area, and a dignified lake-view restaurant serving upscale American cuisine. Trails into primeval forest leave from just outside the door.

Ruby Beach ❸

Kalaloch Lodge — Historic Hotel $$$

(360-962-2271; www.thekalalochlodge.com; 157151 US 101; r from $299;) The Kalaloch (built in 1953) makes up for a relatively unassuming facade with a spectacular setting perched on a bluff overlooking the crashing Pacific. In addition to rooms in the old lodge, there are log cabins and motel-style units. The family-friendly **Creekside Restaurant** (mains $13-33; 8am-8pm Oct-Apr, 7am-9pm May-Sep) offers the best breakfasts on the coast and incomparable ocean views.

Lake Crescent ❺

Lake Crescent Lodge — Lodge $$

(888-896-3818; www.olympicnationalparks.com; 416 Lake Crescent Rd; lodge r from $123, cabins from $292; May-Dec, limited availability winter; P) This turn-of-the-century lodge is handsomely furnished with antiques and surrounded by giant fir trees. There's a wide variety of lodging available, but the most popular (and the only ones open in winter – weekends only) are the cozy cottages. Sumptuous Northwestern-style food is served in the lodge's ecofriendly restaurant.

Port Townsend ❼

Sweet Laurette Cafe & Bistro — French $$

(www.sweetlaurette.com; 1029 Lawrence St; mains $10-20, brunch $9-15; 8am-9pm, closed Tue;) This French shabby-chic cafe serves breakfast, lunch and dinner in the bistro and delicious coffee and pastries between mealtimes. The food is made with sustainable and mostly local ingredients – try a breakfast *croque madame* with honey-baked ham and Gruyère on French bread for breakfast, or Whidbey Island mussels in a white-wine cream sauce or Cape Cleare king salmon for dinner.

Palace Hotel — Historic Hotel $$

(360-385-0773; www.palacehotelpt.com; 1004 Water St; r $109-159, higher on festival weekends;) Built in 1889, this beautiful Victorian building was once a brothel run by the locally notorious Madame Marie, who did business out of the 2nd-floor corner suite. It's been reincarnated as an attractive, character-filled period hotel with antique furnishings (plus all the modern amenities). Pleasant common spaces; kitchenettes available. The cheapest rooms share a bathroom.

On the Trail of Lewis & Clark

Follow the Columbia River on this historic drive that marks the climax of American explorers Lewis and Clark's cross-continental 1805 journey as they stumbled toward the Pacific and instant immortality.

TRIP HIGHLIGHTS

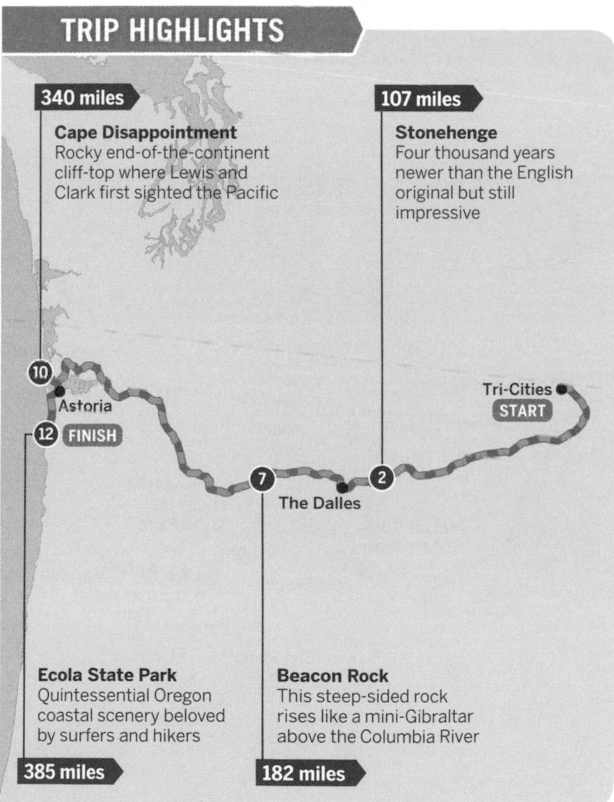

3–4 DAYS
385 MILES / 620KM

GREAT FOR…

BEST TIME TO GO

Year-round – if you don't mind frequent rain, the Columbia River valley is always open.

ESSENTIAL PHOTO

Indian Beach, Ecola State Park – the Oregon coast personified.

BEST FOR HISTORY

The Lewis & Clark Interpretive Center in Cape Disappointment State Park.

Lewis & Clark National Historical Park Log cabins at Fort Clatsop

48 On the Trail of Lewis & Clark

It would take most people their combined annual leave to follow the Lewis and Clark trek in its entirety from St Louis, MO, to Cape Disappointment, WA. Focusing on the final segment, this trip documents the contradictory mix of crippling exhaustion and building excitement that the two explorers felt as they struggled, car-less and weather-beaten, along the Columbia River on their way to completing the greatest overland trek in American history.

❶ Tri-Cities

This trip's start point has a weighty historical significance. The arrival of Lewis and Clark and the Corps of Discovery at the confluence of the Snake and Columbia Rivers on October 16, 1805, marked a milestone achievement on their quest to map a river route to the Pacific. After a greeting by 200 Indians singing and drumming in a half circle, the band camped at this spot for two days, trading clothing for dried salmon. The **Sacajawea**

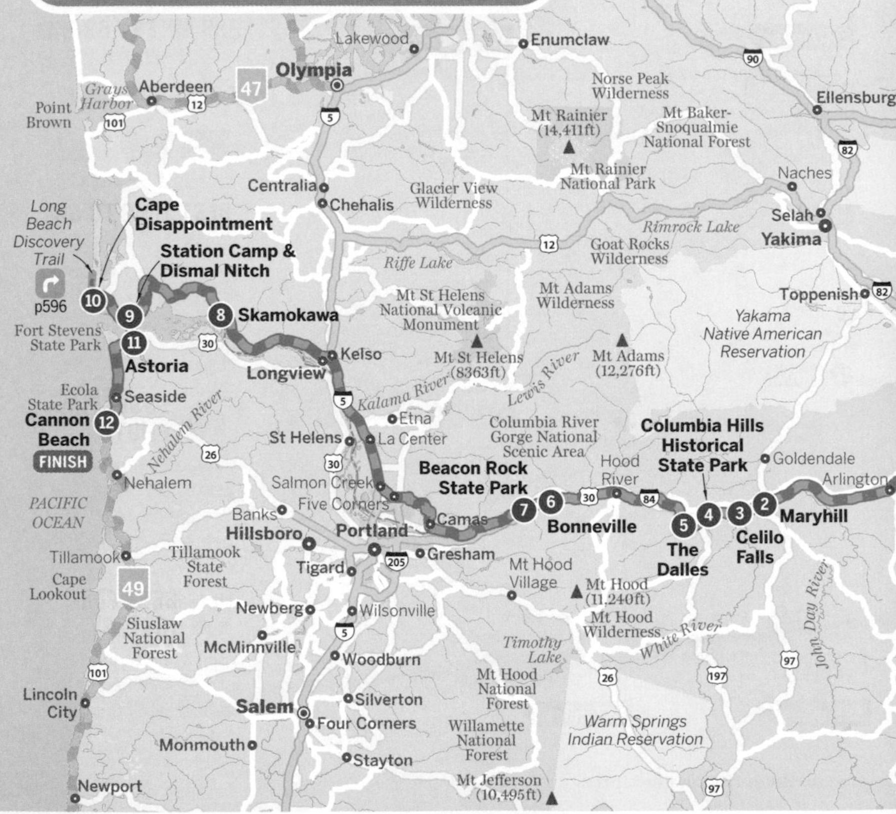

Interpretive Center (509-545-2361; www.parks.state.wa.us/250/sacajawea; 2503 Sacajawea Park Rd, Pasco; suggested donation $1; 10am-5pm late Mar-Nov 1;) situated at the river confluence 5 miles southeast of present-day Pasco, relates the story of the expedition through the eyes of Sacajawea, the Shoshone Native American guide and interpreter the Corps had recruited in North Dakota.

The Drive » Head south on I-82 before switching west at the Columbia River on SR 14, aka the Lewis & Clark Hwy. Here, in dusty sagebrush country, you'll pass a couple of minor sites – Wallula Gap, where the Corps first spotted Mt Hood, and the volcanic bluff of Hat Rock, first named by William Clark. The next stop is 107 miles from Tri-Cities.

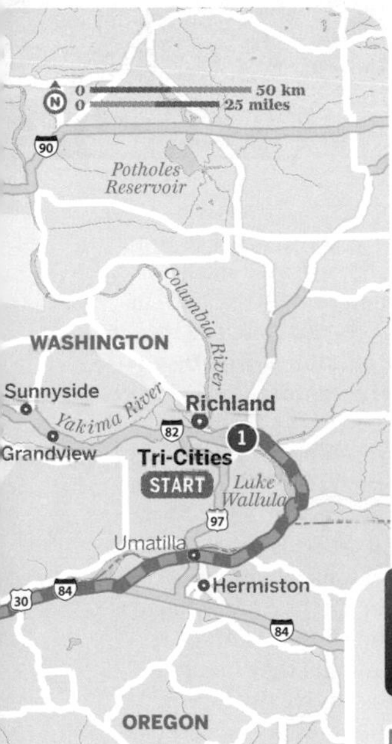

TRIP HIGHLIGHT

2 Maryhill

Conceived by great Northwest entrepreneur and road builder Sam Hill, the **Maryhill Museum of Art** (509-773-3733; www.maryhillmuseum.org; 35 Maryhill Museum Dr; adult/child $9/3; 10am-5pm mid-Mar–mid-Nov) occupies a mansion atop a bluff overlooking the Columbia River. Its eclectic art collection is enhanced by a small Lewis and Clark display, while its peaceful gardens are perfect for a classy picnic punctuated by exotic peacock cries. Interpretive signs point you to fine views down the Columbia Gorge to the riverside spot (now a state park) where Meriwether Lewis and William Clark camped on October 21, 1805. The park is just one of several along this trip where you can pitch a tent within a few hundred yards of the Corps' original camp.

Another of Hill's creations – a life-sized unruined replica of **Stonehenge** (US Hwy 97) – lies 2 miles to the east.

The Drive » Continue west from Maryhill on SR 14 for 5 miles to the site of the now submerged Celilo Falls.

3 Celilo Falls

A vivid imagination can be as important as sunscreen when following the 'Trail.' One example of this is the turnout 5 miles west of Maryhill that overlooks what was once the Indian salmon fishing center of Celilo Falls. The explorers spent two days here in late October 1805, lowering their canoes down the crashing falls on elk-skin ropes. A century and a half later, the rising waters of the dammed Columbia drowned the falls – which were the sixth-most voluminous in the world – destroying a centuries-old Native American fishing site

LINK YOUR TRIP

47 Olympic Peninsula Loop

From Astoria, take Hwy 101 north 78 miles to Aberdeen to join up with this loop.

49 Highway 101 Oregon Coast

At the end of this trip, head south down the coast starting in Astoria.

and rendering much of Clark's description of the region unrecognizable.

The Drive » Head west on SR 14, paralleling the mighty Columbia, for another 15 miles to Columbia Hills Historical State Park.

❹ Columbia Hills Historical State Park

Indian tribes like the Nez Perce, Clatsop and Walla Walla were essential to the success of the Lewis and Clark expedition, supplying them not only with food but also with horses and guides. One of the best places to view tangible traces of the region's Native American heritage is the Temani Pesh-wa (Written on Rocks) Trail at **Columbia Hills Historical State Park** (509-439-9032; Hwy 14, Mile 85; day-use fee $10; Apr-Oct), which highlights the region's best petroglyphs. Reserve a spot in advance on the free guided tours on Friday and Saturday at 10am to view the famous but fragile pictograph of the god Tsagagalal (She Who Watches). The park is also a popular site for rock climbers and windsurfers.

The Drive » Two miles west of Horsethief Lake, turn south onto Hwy 197, which takes you across the Columbia River into the Dalles in Oregon. Two miles upriver sits the Dalles Dam, which completely submerged the once-magnificent Celilo Falls and rapids on its completion in 1957.

❺ The Dalles

Once the urban neighbor of the formidable Celilo Falls, the Dalles' image is more mundane these days. The local economy focuses on cherry-growing, computer technology and outdoor recreation. Notwithstanding, the town hosts one of the best Lewis and Clark–related museums along this stretch of the Columbia, sited in the **Columbia Gorge Discovery Center** (541-296-8600; www.gorgediscovery.org; 5000 Discovery Dr; adult/child $9/5; 9am-5pm) on the western edge of the city. Displays detail the 30 tons of equipment the Corps dragged across the continent and the animals they had to kill to survive (including 190 dogs and a ferret). Kids will get a kick from dressing up in Lewis and Clark period costume.

p599

LEWIS & CLARK HISTORICAL PARK

The so-called **Lewis & Clark National Historical Park** (503-861-2471; www.nps.gov/lewi; 92343 Fort Clatsop Rd; adult/child $5/free; 9am-6pm mid-Jun–Aug, to 5pm Sep–mid-Jun) combines 10 different historical sites clustered around the mouth of the Columbia River, each of which relates to important facts about the Corps of Discovery and its historic mission to map the American West. It was formed through the amalgamation of various state parks and historic sites in 2004, and is run jointly by the National Park Service and the states of Washington and Oregon. Highlights include Cape Disappointment, Fort Clatsop and the 6.5-mile **Fort to Sea Trail** linking Clatsop and the ocean at Sunset Beach.

PHOTOMATZ / SHUTTERSTOCK ©

Beacon Rock State Park

The Drive ›› You can continue west from the Dalles on either side of the Columbia (the expedition traveled straight down the middle by canoe) via SR 14 (Washington), or the slower, more scenic SR 30 (Oregon). En route to Bonneville, 46 miles away, look for the views down to macabre Memaloose Island, once a burial site for Native Americans who left their dead here in canoes of cedar.

6 Bonneville

There are two Bonnevilles: Bonneville, OR, and North Bonneville, WA. At this stage in their trip, Lewis and Clark were flea-infested and half-starved from a diet of dog meat and starchy, potatolike wapato roots. Fortunately, 21st-century Bonneville – which is famous for its Depression-era dam completed in 1938 – has some tastier culinary offerings to contemplate.

🛏 p599

The Drive ›› Just west of North Bonneville on SR 14 lies Beacon Rock State Park.

TRIP HIGHLIGHT

7 Beacon Rock State Park

On November 2, 1805, a day after passing modern Bonneville, Clark wrote about a remarkable 848ft-tall monolith he called Beaten Rock, changing the name on his return to Beacon Rock. Just over a century later, Henry Biddle bought the rock for the bargain price of $1 (!) and you can still hike his snaking 1-mile trail to the top of the former lava plug in **Beacon Rock State Park** (☎509-427-8265; www.parks.state.wa.us/474/Beacon-Rock; Hwy 14, Mile 35; day-use fee $10). As you enjoy the wonderful views, ponder the fact that you have effectively climbed up the *inside* of an ancient volcano. For the Corps, the rock brought a momentous discovery, for it was here that the excited duo first noticed the tide, proving at last that they were finally nearing their goal of crossing the American continent.

The Drive » Your next stop along SR 14 should be the fantastic views of the flood-carved gorge and its impressive cascades from the Cape Horn overview. From here, it's a straight shot on I-5 to Kelso and then over the Lewis and Clark Bridge to parallel the Columbia River westward on SR 4. Skamokawa is 103 miles in total from the state park.

8 Skamokawa

For most of their trip down the Columbia River, Lewis and Clark traveled not on foot but by canoe. There's nowhere better to paddle in the Corps' canoe wake than at **Pillar Rock**, where Clark wrote of his joy at finally being able to camp in view of the ocean. **Columbia River Kayaking** (360-747-1044; www.columbiariverkayaking.com; 957 Steamboat Slough Rd; half-day tours from $65; noon-4pm Fri-Sun) in the town of Skamokawa offers one- and two-day kayak tours to this site, as well as Grays Bay.

The Drive » Continue on SR 4 northwest out of Skamokawa. In Naselle, go southwest on SR 401. From Skamokawa to Dismal Nitch is 35 miles, along the north bank of the Columbia River.

LINCOLN ROGERS / SHUTTERSTOCK ©

DETOUR: LONG BEACH DISCOVERY TRAIL

Start: 10 Cape Disappointment

Soon after arriving in 'Station Camp,' the indefatigable Clark, determined to find a better winter bivouac, set out with several companions to continue the hike west along a broad sandy peninsula, coming to a halt near present-day 26th St in Long Beach, where Clark dipped his toe in the Pacific and carved his name on a cedar tree for posterity. The route of this historic three-day trudge has been re-created in the Long Beach Discovery Trail, a footpath that runs from the small town of Ilwaco, adjacent to Cape Disappointment, to Clark's 26th St turnaround. Officially inaugurated in September 2009, the trail has incorporated some dramatic life-size sculptures along its 8.2-mile length. One depicts a giant gray whale skeleton, another recalls Clark's recorded sighting of a washed-up sea sturgeon, while a third re-creates in bronze the original cedar tree (long since uprooted by a Pacific storm).

9 Station Camp & Dismal Nitch

Just east of the Astoria-Megler Bridge on the north bank of the Columbia River, a turnout marks Dismal Nitch, where the drenched duo were stuck in a pounding week-long storm that Clark described as the most disagreeable time he had ever experienced. The Corps finally managed to make camp at Station Camp, 3 miles further west, now an innocuous highway pullout, where they stayed for 10 days while the two leaders, no doubt

View from Cape Disappointment

sick of each other by now, separately explored the headlands around Cape Disappointment.

The Drive » You're nearly there! Contain your excitement as you breeze the last few miles west along Hwy 101 to Ilwaco and the inappropriately named Cape Disappointment.

TRIP HIGHLIGHT

⑩ Cape Disappointment

Disappointment is probably the last thing you're likely to be feeling as you pull into blustery cliff-top **Cape Disappointment State Park** (360-642-3078; Hwy 100; dawn-dusk). Find time to make the short ascent of Mackenzie Hill in Clark's footprints and catch your first true sight of the Pacific. You can almost hear his protracted sigh of relief over two centuries later.

Located on a high bluff inside the park not far from the Washington town of Ilwaco, the sequentially laid-out **Lewis & Clark Interpretive Center** (http://capedisappointment.org/lewis-clark-interpretive-center; Hwy 100; adult/child $5/2.50; 10am-5pm Wed-Sun Oct-Mar, daily Apr-Sep) faithfully recounts the Corps of Discovery's cross-continental journey using a level of detail the journal-writing explorers would have been proud of. Information includes everything from how to use an octant to what kind of underpants Lewis wore! A succinct 20-minute film backs up the permanent exhibits. Phone ahead and you can also tour the impressive end-of-continent **North Head Lighthouse** (http://northheadlighthouse.com; tours $2.50; 10am-5pm) nearby.

The Drive » From Ilwaco, take Hwy 101 back east to the 4.1-mile-long Astoria-Megler

Bridge, the longest continuous truss bridge in the US. On the other side lies Astoria in Oregon, the oldest US-founded settlement west of the Mississippi.

⓫ Astoria

After the first truly democratic ballot in US history (in which a woman and a black slave both voted), the party elected to make their winter bivouac across the Columbia River in present-day Oregon. A replica of the original **Fort Clatsop** (adult/child $5/free; 9am-6pm Jun-Aug, to 5pm Sep-May), where the Corps spent a miserable winter in 1805–6, lies 5 miles south of Astoria.

Also on site are trails, a visitor center and buckskin-clad rangers who wander the camp between mid-June and Labor Day sewing moccasins (the Corps stockpiled an impressive 340 pairs for their return trip), tanning leather and firing their muskets.

p599

The Drive » From Fort Clatsop, take Hwy 101, aka the Oregon Coast Hwy, south through the town of Seaside to Cannon Beach, 25 miles from Astoria.

TRIP HIGHLIGHT

⓬ Cannon Beach

Mission accomplished – or was it? Curiosity (and hunger) got the better of the Corps in early 1806 when news of a huge beached whale lured Clark and Sacagawea from a salt factory they had set up near the present-day town of Seaside down through what is now Ecola State Park to Cannon Beach.

Ecola State Park (503-436-2844; www.oregonstateparks.org; day use $5) is the Oregon you may have already visited in your dreams: sea stacks, crashing surf, hidden beaches and gorgeous pristine forest. Crisscrossed by paths, it lies 1.5 miles north of Cannon Beach, the high-end 'antiresort' resort so beloved by Portlanders.

Clark found the whale near **Haystack Rock**, a 295ft sea stack that's the most spectacular landmark on the Oregon coast and accessible from the beach. After bartering with the Tillamook tribe, he staggered away with 300lb of whale blubber – a feast for the half-starved Corps of Discovery.

p599, p612

Eating & Sleeping

The Dalles 5

Baldwin Saloon American $

(☎541-296-5666; http://baldwinsaloon.com; 205 Court St; mains $11-20; ⏰11am-10pm Mon-Sat) This 1876 building, with the remnants of a rare cast-iron facade, has been a bar, a brothel and a coffin-storage warehouse. Today it's a casual establishment with a brick interior full of large oil paintings, and a historic dark-wood bar. Food choices include a dozen salads, sandwiches, burgers and pasta dishes.

Celilo Inn Motel $$

(☎541-769-0001; www.celiloinn.com; 3550 E 2nd St; d $119-164;) The beautifully remodeled Celilo Inn was once an old motel, but is now a slick and trendy stay with gorgeous contemporary rooms, many offering views of the Dalles' bridge and dam. Luxurious touches include flat-screen TVs and a cool pool for those guaranteed hot summer days. Weekday discounts.

Bonneville 6

Bonneville Hot Springs Resort & Spa Hotel $$$

(☎866-459-1678; www.bonnevilleresort.com; 1252 E Cascade Dr, North Bonneville; r $129-229, mineral pool per hour $10-15; @) With a grand, five-star lobby and 78 stylish rooms (nearly half with private balcony hot tubs), this resort offers fine dining and full spa services. There's an elegant, 25m indoor pool filled with mineral water, plus Jacuzzis.

Astoria 11

Astoria Coffeehouse & Bistro American $$

(☎503-325-1787; www.astoriacoffeehouse.com; 243 11th St; dinner mains $12-25; ⏰7am-9pm Sun, to 10pm Mon-Thu, to 11pm Fri & Sat) Small, popular cafe with attached bistro offering an eclectic menu – things like Peruvian root-vegetable stew, wasabi wonton prawns, chili-relleno burger, fish tacos and pad Thai. Everything is made in-house There's sidewalk seating and excellent cocktails. Expect a wait at dinner and Sunday brunch.

Commodore Hotel Boutique Hotel $$

(☎503-325-4747; www.commodoreastoria.com; 258 14th St; d with shared/private bath from $79/154;) Hip travelers should make a beeline for this stylish hotel, which offers attractive but small, minimalist rooms. Choose a room with bathroom or go Euro style (sink in room, bathroom down the hall; 'deluxe' rooms have better views). There's a lounge-style lobby with cafe, free samples of local microbrews from 5pm to 7pm, an impressive movie library and record players to borrow.

Cannon Beach 12

Irish Table Irish $$$

(☎503-436-0708; 1235 S Hemlock St; mains $20-30; ⏰5:30-9pm Fri-Tue) Excellent restaurant hidden at the back of the **Sleepy Monk coffee shop** (☎503-436-2796; www.sleepymonkcoffee.com; drinks & snacks $2-7; ⏰8am-3pm Mon, Tue & Thu, to 4pm Fri-Sun), serving a fusion of Irish and Pacific Northwest cuisine made with local and seasonal ingredients. The menu is small and simple, but the choices are tasty; try the vegetarian shepherd's pie, lamb-loin chops or seared Piedmontese flat-iron steak. If the curried mussels are on the menu, don't hesitate.

Waves Motel Motel $$

(☎503-436-2205; www.thewavescannonbeach.com; 188 W 2nd St; d $149-329;) Disregard the word 'motel' here – this place is more like an upscale inn. Furnishings are elegant and the rooms comfortable and bright, and some come with kitchens, two bedrooms and decks overlooking the beach. Also on offer are suites, a two-bedroom townhouse and three-bedroom beach house next door at the Argonauta Inn.

Ocean Lodge Hotel $$$

(☎503-436-2241; www.theoceanlodge.com; 2864 S Pacific St; d $219-369;) This gorgeous place has some of Cannon Beach's most luxurious rooms, most with ocean view and all with fireplace and kitchenette. A complimentary continental breakfast, an 800-DVD library and pleasant sitting areas are available to guests. Located on the beach at the southern end of town.

Classic Trip

Highway 101 Oregon Coast

Routes like Hwy 101 are the reason the road trip was invented. It meanders the length of the Oregon coast past sandy beaches, colorful tide pools and nearly a dozen lighthouses.

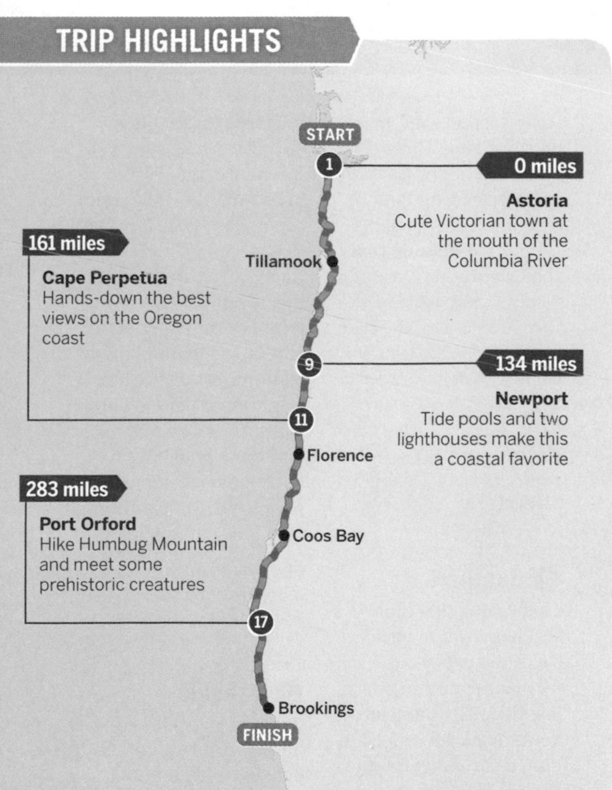

7 DAYS
340 MILES / 547KM

GREAT FOR...

BEST TIME TO GO

July to October, when the weather is more cooperative.

ESSENTIAL PHOTO

Silhouette of Haystack Rock in Cannon Beach.

BEST HIKING

Cape Perpetua offers several breathtaking hikes.

Ecola State Park Secluded beaches

Classic Trip

49 Highway 101 Oregon Coast

Scenic, two-lane Hwy 101 follows hundreds of miles of shoreline punctuated with charming seaside towns, exhilarating hikes and ocean views that remind you you're on the edge of the continent. In this trip, it's not about getting from point A to point B. Instead, the route itself is the destination. And everyone from nature lovers to gourmands to families can find their dream vacation along this exceptional coastal route.

TRIP HIGHLIGHT

1 Astoria

We begin our coastal trek in the northwestern corner of the state, where the Columbia River meets the Pacific Ocean. Ever so slightly inland, Astoria doesn't rely on beach proximity for its character. It has a rich history, including being a stop on the Lewis and Clark trail. Because of its location, it also has a unique maritime history, which you can explore at the **Columbia River Maritime Museum** (503-325-2323; www.crmm.org; 1792 Marine Dr; adult/child $14/5; 9:30am-5pm;).

Astoria has been the location of several Hollywood movies, making it a virtual Hollywood by the sea: it's best known as the setting for cult hit *The Goonies*. Fans can peek at the **Historic Clatsop County Jail** (Oregon Film Museum; www.oregonfilmmuseum.com; 732 Duane St; adult/child $6/2; 11am-4pm Oct-Apr, 10am-5pm May-Sep;).

p599, p612

The Drive » Head south on Hwy 101 for 14.5 miles to Gearhart.

2 Gearhart

Check your tide table and head to the beach; Gearhart is famous for its razor clamming at low tide. All you need are boots, a shovel or a clam gun, a cut-resistant glove, a license (available in Gearhart) and a bucket for your catch. Watch your fingers – the name razor clam is well earned. Boiling up a batch will likely result in the most memorable meal of your trip. For information on where, when and how to clam, visit the Oregon Department of Fish and Wildlife website (www.dfw.state.or.us); it's a maze of a site, so just punch 'ODFW clamming' into the search bar.

The Drive » Don't get too comfortable yet: Seaside is just 2.4 miles further down the coast.

3 Seaside

Oregon's biggest and busiest resort town delivers exactly what

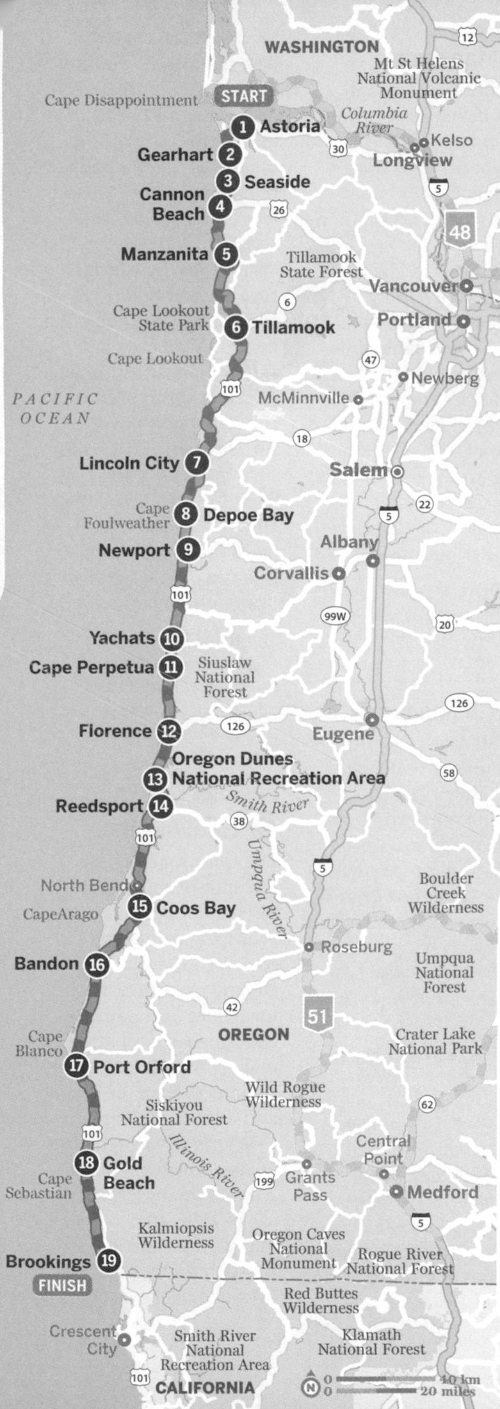

you'd expect from a town called Seaside, which is wholesome, Coney Island–esque fun. The 2-mile boardwalk – known as 'the Prom' – is a kaleidoscope of seaside kitsch, with surrey rentals, video arcades, fudge, elephant ears, caramel apples, saltwater taffy and more. It's also where you'll find the **Seaside Aquarium** (503-738-6211; www.seasideaquarium.com; 200 N Promenade; adult/child $8/4; 9am-7pm, closes earlier winter;). Open since 1937, the privately owned aquarium isn't much more than a few fish tanks, a touch pool and a small indoor seal tank where you can feed the splashy critters, but it's a fun stop for inquisitive kids.

p612

The Drive » Leave the beach behind for a bit as you veer inland for the 8.8-mile drive to Cannon Beach.

LINK YOUR TRIP

48 On the Trail of Lewis & Clark

Do the Hwy 101 trip backwards and you can pick up the trail of Lewis and Clark in Astoria.

51 Crater Lake Circuit

Continue south to Crescent City then take Hwy 199 northeast to Grant's Pass.

❹ Cannon Beach

Charming Cannon Beach is one of the most popular beach resorts on the Oregon coast. The wide sandy beach stretches for miles, and you'll find great photo opportunities and tide-pooling possibilities at glorious **Haystack Rock**, the third-tallest sea stack in the world. (What's a sea stack, you might ask? It's a vertical rock formation – in this case, one that's shaped like a haystack.) For the area's best coastal hiking, head immediately north of town to **Ecola State Park** (☎503-436-2844; www.oregonstateparks.org; day use $5) where you can hike to secluded beaches.

✕ 🛏 p599, p612

The Drive » Follow the coast 14.4 miles through Oswald West State Park to reach your next stop.

❺ Manzanita

One of the more laid-back beach resorts on Oregon's coast is the hamlet of Manzanita – much smaller and far less hyped than Cannon Beach. You can relax on the white-sand beaches, or, if you're feeling more ambitious, hike on nearby **Neahkahnie Mountain**, where high cliffs rise dramatically above the Pacific's pounding waves. It's a 3.8-mile climb to the top, but the views are worth it: on a clear day, you can see 50 miles out to sea.

The Drive » Drive 27 miles from Nehalem Bay to Tillamook Bay to reach inland Tillamook.

❻ Tillamook

Not all coastal towns are built on seafood and sand. Tillamook has an entirely different claim to fame: cheese. Thousands stop annually at the **Tillamook Cheese Factory** (☎800-542-7290; www.tillamookcheese.com; 4175 N US 101; ⏲8am-8pm mid-Jun–Labor Day, to 6pm Labor Day–mid-Jun) for free samples. You might choose to skip the dairy altogether and head to one of two interesting museums: the **Pioneer Museum** (☎503-842-4553; www.tcpm.org; 2106 2nd St; adult/child $4/1; ⏲10am-4pm Tue-Sun) has antique toys, a great taxidermy room (check out the polar bear) and a basement full of pioneer artifacts. And just south of town, the **Tillamook Naval Air Museum** (☎503-842-1130; www.tillamookair.com; 6030 Hangar Rd; adult/child $9.75/6.50; ⏲10am-5pm) has a large collection of fighter planes and a 7-acre blimp hangar.

The Drive » South of Tillamook, Hwy 101 follows the Nestucca River through pastureland and logged-off mountains 44 miles to Lincoln City.

❼ Lincoln City

The sprawling modern beach resort of Lincoln City serves as the region's principal commercial center. In addition to gas and groceries, the town does offer a unique enticement to stop: from mid-October to late May volunteers from the Visitor and Convention Bureau hide brightly colored glass floats – which have been hand-blown by local artisans – along the beaches, making a memorable souvenir for the resourceful and diligent vacationer.

THREE CAPES LOOP

South of the town of Tillamook, Hwy 101 veers inland from the coast. An exhilarating alternative route is the slow, winding and sometimes bumpy Three Capes Loop, which hugs the shoreline for 30 miles and offers the chance to go clamming. En route you'll traverse Cape Meares, Cape Lookout and Cape Kiwanda – three stunning headlands that you'd otherwise miss entirely.

The Drive » It's back to the coast for the 12-mile drive south to Depoe Bay.

8 Depoe Bay

Though edged by modern timeshare condominiums, Depoe Bay still retains some original coastal charm. It lays claim to having the 'world's smallest navigable harbor' and being the 'world's whale-watching capital' – pretty big talk for such a pint-sized town. Whale-watching and charter fishing are the main attractions in the area, though 5 miles south of town there is the **Devil's Punchbowl**, an impressive collapsed sea cave that churns with waves and offers good tide pools nearby.

The Drive » Another 12.8 miles brings you to the lively tourist city of Newport.

TRIP HIGHLIGHT

9 Newport

Don your marine-biologist cap and head to **Yaquina Head Outstanding Natural Area** (☎541-574-3100; 750 NW Lighthouse Dr; vehicle fee $7; ⏰8am-sunset, interpretive center 10am-6pm), a giant spit of land that protrudes nearly a mile into the ocean. This headland is home to some of the best touch pools on the Oregon coast. You'll also get a good look at the tallest lighthouse in Oregon, **Yaquina Head Lighthouse** (not to be confused with **Yaquina Bay Lighthouse**, 3 miles south).

YAQUINA HEAD LIGHTHOUSE

If Yaquina Head Lighthouse in Newport, OR, seems a little creepier than a lighthouse ought, that's because it was featured in the 2002 horror film starring Naomi Watts, *The Ring*. Built in 1873, it was originally called Cape Foulweather Lighthouse, but in the movie it was known as the Moesko Island Lighthouse. (The lighthouse was also in the 1977 masterpiece *Nancy Drew: Pirate's Cove*.)

Also worth a stop: the cutting-edge **Oregon Coast Aquarium** (☎541-867-3474; www.aquarium.org; 2820 SE Ferry Slip Rd; adult/3-12yr/13-17yr $23/15/20; ⏰10am-6pm Jun-Aug, to 5pm Sep-May; 👪). The seals and sea otters are cute as can be, and the jellyfish room is a near psychedelic experience. But what really knocks this place off the charts is the deep-sea exhibit that lets you walk through a Plexiglas tunnel through sharks, rays and other fish.

🍴 🛏 p612

The Drive » Another 24 miles to Yachats along the edge of the Siuslaw National Forest.

10 Yachats

One of the Oregon coast's best-kept secrets is the friendly little town of Yachats (ya-*hots*), which kicks off about 20 miles of spectacular shoreline. This entire area was once a series of volcanic intrusions that resisted the pummeling of the Pacific long enough to rise as oceanside peaks and promontories. Acres of tide pools are home to starfish, sea anemones and sea lions.

Fourteen miles south of town, picturesque **Heceta Head Lighthouse** (☎541-547-3416; Heceta.h.lighthouse@oregon.gov; ⏰11am-3pm, to 2pm winter) is one of the most photographed lighthouses on the Oregon coast. You can't see it from the highway, but you can park at **Heceta Head State Park** (day use $5) for great views from afar, as well as a trail leading past the former **lightkeeper's quarters** (now a bed and breakfast) and up to the lighthouse.

🍴 🛏 p613

The Drive » Just 3 miles down the coast is dramatic Cape Perpetua.

TRIP HIGHLIGHT

11 Cape Perpetua

Whatever you do, don't miss the spectacular scenery of the **Cape Perpetua Scenic Area**

Classic Trip

HEATHSMITH73 / GETTY IMAGES ©

WOLLERTZ / SHUTTERSTOCK ©

WHY THIS IS A CLASSIC TRIP

MARIELLA KRAUSE, WRITER

Meandering your way down Oregon's coastline is the epitome of a carefree vacation. There are no major cities, no hustle, no bustle – just miles of ocean on one side of the road and miles of hiking on the other. My personal favorite part of the trip? Spending the night at Heceta Head Lighthouse and waking up to a seven-course breakfast, followed by hiking at Cape Perpetua.

Above: Heceta Head Lighthouse
Left: Sea lions, Florence
Right: Sandboarding, Oregon Dunes

CSNAFZGER / SHUTTERSTOCK ©

(Hwy 101; day-use fee $5), just 3 miles south of Yachats. You could easily spend a day or two exploring trails that take you through moss-laden, old-growth forests to rocky beaches, tide pools and blasting marine geysers.

At the very least, drive up to the **Cape Perpetua Overlook** for a colossal coastal view from 800ft above sea level – the highest point on the coast. While you're up there, check out the historic **West Shelter** observation point built by the Civilian Conservation Corps in 1933.

If you have more time to spend, stop at the **visitor center** (☎541-547-3289; www.fs.usda.gov/siuslaw; 2400 Hwy 101; vehicle fee $5; ⌚9:30am-4:30pm Jun-Aug, 10am-4pm Sep-May) to plan your day. High points include **Devil's Churn**, where waves shoot up a 30ft inlet to explode against the narrowing sides of the channel, and the **Giant Spruce Trail**, which leads to a 500-year-old Sitka spruce with a 10ft diameter.

The Drive » It's 22 miles to Florence, but only 12 to the Sea Lion Caves.

⓬ Florence

Looking for a good, old-fashioned roadside attraction? North of

Florence is the **Sea Lion Caves** (☎541-547-3111; www.sealioncaves.com; 91560 Hwy 101; adult/child $14/8; ⏰9am-5pm), an enormous sea grotto that's home to hundreds of groaning sea lions. Open to the public since the 1930s, the cave is accessed by an elevator that descends 208ft to the sea lions' stinky lair.

Here's the deal: it can be fascinating, but you might feel a little taken when you realize the view is exactly the same as what was on the monitor up in the gift shop – and there's not even free fudge samples down there. But if money's no object, you'll enjoy watching the sea lions cavort, especially if you have kids in tow.

✕ p613

The Drive » The Oregon Dunes start just south of Florence and continue for the next 50 miles.

⑬ Oregon Dunes National Recreation Area

As you drive south you start to notice something altogether different: sand. Lots of it. Stretching 50 miles, the **Oregon Dunes** are the largest expanse of oceanfront sand dunes in the US. Sometimes topping heights of 500ft, these mountains of sand undulate inland up to 3 miles. Hikers and birdwatchers stick to the peaceful northern half of the dunes, and the southern half is dominated by dune buggies and dirt bikes.

At Mile 200.8, the **Oregon Dunes Overlook** is the easiest place to take a gander if you're just passing through. To learn more about trails and off-road vehicles, visit the **Oregon Dunes NRA Visitors Center** (☎541-271-6000; www.fs.usda.gov/siuslaw; 855 Hwy 101; ⏰8am-4:30pm Mon-Sat Jun-Aug, Mon-Fri Sep-May). For the area's biggest dunes, the 6-mile **John Dellenbeck Trail** (at Mile 222.6) loops through a wilderness of massive sand peaks.

The Drive » Reedsport is about halfway into the dunes area, about 22 miles south of Florence.

⑭ Reedsport

Reedsport's location in the middle of the Oregon Dunes makes it an ideal base for exploring the region. Check out the **Umpqua Lighthouse State Park**, offering summer tours of a local 1894 **lighthouse** (☎541-271-4631; 1020 Lighthouse Rd; adult/child $8/4; ⏰10am-5pm May-Oct, hours vary rest of year). Opposite is a whale-watching platform, and a nearby nature trail rings freshwater **Lake Marie**, which is popular for swimming.

Want to see how Oregon's largest land mammal spends its free time? Three miles east of town on Hwy 38, you can spy a herd of about 120 Roosevelt elk meandering about at the **Dean Creek Elk Viewing Area**.

The Drive » Enjoy the sand for another 27.5 miles, as you reach Coos Bay and the end of the dunes.

⑮ Coos Bay

The no-nonsense city of Coos Bay and its modest neighbor North Bend make up the largest urban area on the Oregon coast. Coos Bay was once the largest timber port

WHALE-WATCHING

Each year, gray whales undertake one of the longest migrations of any animal on earth, swimming from the Bering Strait and Chukchi Sea to Baja California – and back. Look for them migrating south in winter (mid-December through mid-January) and north in spring (March through June).

in the world. The logs are long gone, but tourists are slowly taking their place.

In a historic art-deco building downtown, the **Coos Art Museum** (☎541-267-3901; www.coosart.org; 235 Anderson Ave; adult/child $5/2; ⏲10am-4pm Tue-Fri, from 1pm Sat)provides a hub for the region's art culture with rotating exhibits from the museum's permanent collection.

Cape Arago Hwy leads 14 miles southwest of town to **Cape Arago State Park** (☎800-551-6949; www.oregonstateparks.org), where grassy picnic grounds make for great perches over a pounding sea. The park protects some of the best tide pools on the Oregon coast and is well worth the short detour.

The Drive » Highway 101 heads inland for a bit then gets back to the coast 24 miles later at Bandon.

16 Bandon

Optimistically touted as Bandon-by-the-Sea, this little town sits happily at the bay of the Coquille River, with an Old Town district that's been gentrified into a picturesque harborside shopping location that offers pleasant strolling and window-shopping.

Along the beach, ledges of stone rise out of the surf to provide shelter for seals, sea lions and myriad forms of life in tide pools. One of the coast's most interesting rock formations is the much-photographed **Face Rock**, a huge monolith with some uncanny facial features that does indeed look like a woman with her head thrown back – giving rise to a requisite Native American legend.

The Drive » Follow the coastline another 24 miles south to Port Orford. This part of the drive isn't much to look at, but not to worry: there's more scenery to come.

TRIP HIGHLIGHT

17 Port Orford

Perched on a grassy headland, the hamlet of Port Orford is located in one of the most scenic stretches of coastal highway, and there are stellar views even from the center of town. If you're feeling ambitious, take the 3-mile trail up **Humbug Mountain** (☎541-332-6774), which takes you up, up, up past streams and through prehistoric-looking landscapes to the top, where you'll be treated to dramatic views of Cape Sebastian and the Pacific.

Speaking of prehistoric scenery: your kids may scream at the sight of a Tyrannosaurus rex 12 miles south of town in front of **Prehistoric Gardens** (☎541-332-4463; www.prehistoricgardens.com; 36848 US 101; adult/child $12/8; ⏲9am-6pm summer, 10am-5pm rest of year; 👪). Life-size replicas of the extinct beasties are set in a lush, first-growth temperate rainforest; the huge ferns and trees set the right mood for going back in time.

✕ 🛏 p613

The Drive » The scenery starts to pick up again, with unusual rock formations lining the 28-mile drive to Gold Beach.

18 Gold Beach

Next you'll pass through the tourist hub of Gold Beach, where you can take a jet boat excursion up the scenic **Rogue River**. But the real treat lies 13 miles south of town, when you enter the 12-mile stretch of coastal splendor known as the **Samuel Boardman State Scenic Corridor**, featuring giant stands of Sitka spruce, natural rock bridges, tide pools and loads of hiking trails.

Along the highway are well over a dozen roadside turnouts and picnic areas, with short trails leading to secluded beaches and dramatic viewpoints. A 30-second walk from the parking area to the viewing platform at **Natural Bridge Viewpoint** (Mile 346, Hwy 101) offers a glorious photo op of rock arches – the remnants of collapsed sea caves – after which

you can decide whether you want to commit to the hike down to **China Beach**.

p613

The Drive » It's just 34 miles to the California border, and 28 to Brookings.

19 Brookings

Your last stop on the Oregon coast is Brookings. With some of the warmest temperatures on the coast, Brookings is a leader in Easter lily-bulb production; in July, fields south of town are filled with bright colors and a heavy scent. In May and June you'll also find magnificent displays of flowers at the hilly, 30-acre **Azalea Park** (Azalea Park Rd).

History buffs take note: Brookings has the unique distinction of being the location of the only WWII aerial bombing on the US mainland. In 1942, a Japanese seaplane succeeded in bombing nearby forests with the intent to burn them, but they failed to ignite. The Japanese pilot, Nobuo Fujita, returned to Brookings 20 years later and presented the city with a peace offering: his family's 400-year-old samurai sword, which is now displayed at the **Chetco Community Public Library** (541-469-7738; http://chetcolibrary.org; 405 Alder St; 10am-6pm Mon & Fri, to 7pm Tue & Thu, to 8pm Wed, to 5pm Sat).

p613

VICTORIA DITKOVSKY / SHUTTERSTOCK ©

Natural Bridge Viewpoint
VICTORIA DITKOVSKY / SHUTTERSTOCK ©

Eating & Sleeping

Astoria 1

Wet Dog Café — Pub Food $$

(503-325-6975; www.wetdogcafe.com; 144 11th St; mains $14-22; 11am-9pm;) For casual dining there's this large, family-friendly brewpub, with beers like Poop Deck Porter and Bitter Bitch IPA. The grub is typically pub style (huge burgers, good fish-and-chips), and big windows offer nice views over the water. There's live music on weekends.

Seaside 3

Bell Buoy — Seafood $$

(503-738-6348; www.bellbuoyofseaside.com; 1800 S Roosevelt Dr; mains $8-18; 11:30am-7:30pm, closed Tue & Wed winter) Best known as a seafood store, this down-to-earth, family-run establishment has an attached seafood restaurant serving outstanding fish-and-chips, chowder and more.

Cannon Beach 4

Newman's at 988 — French, Italian $$$

(503-436-1151; www.newmansat988.com; 988 Hemlock St; mains $21-37; 5:30-9pm daily Jul–mid-Oct, Tue-Sun mid-Oct–Jun) Expect a fine-dining experience at this small, quality restaurant on the main drag. Award-winning chef John Newman comes up with a fusion of French and Italian dishes such as marinated rack of lamb and chargrilled portabello mushrooms with spinach and gorgonzola. Desserts are sublime; reserve ahead.

Blue Gull Inn Motel — Motel $$

(800-559-0893; www.bluegullinn.net; 632 S Hemlock Street; d from $160;) These are some of the more affordable rooms in town, with comfortable atmosphere and toned-down decor, except for the colorful Mexican headboards and serapes on the beds. Kitchenette and Jacuzzi units are available. It's run by Haystack Lodgings, which also manages six other properties in town and does vacation rentals. Two-night minimum in summer.

Newport 9

Rogue Ales Public House — Pub $$

(541-265-3188; www.rogue.com; 748 SW Bay Blvd; 11am-11pm Sun-Thu, to midnight Fri & Sat) Don't miss out on tasting some of the state's best-loved craft brews at the source – the Shakespeare stout is an old favorite, but there are dozens of choices. Sit at an outdoor table or inside at the big wooden bar. There's an extensive food menu, too.

Sylvia Beach Hotel — Hotel $$

(541-265-5428; www.sylviabeachhotel.com; 267 NW Cliff St; d $135-235;) This book-themed hotel offers simple and classy rooms, each named after a famous author and decorated accordingly. The best rooms are higher up, and the 3rd-floor common room has a wonderful ocean view and is great for talking to fellow guests. Full breakfast included; reservations required. Note there are no TVs, phones or wi-fi. Prices vary widely depending on day and season.

Newport Belle — B&B $$

(541-867-6290; http://newportbelle.com; 2126 SE Marine Science Dr, South Beach Marina, H Dock; d $165-175; Feb-Oct;) For a unique stay there's no beating this sternwheeler B&B. The five small but lovely and shipshape rooms all have private baths and water views, while the common spaces are wonderful for relaxing. Best for couples; reservations required.

Beverly Beach State Park — Campground $

(541-265-9278; www.oregonstateparks.org; tent/RV sites $21/29, yurts $44) This large campground, 7 miles north of town on Hwy

101, has more than 250 sites, 21 yurts and hookups to cable TV. Also has showers and flush toilets.

Yachats ⑩

Green Salmon Coffee House Cafe $
(541-547-3077; www.thegreensalmon.com; 220 Hwy 101; coffee drinks $2-5; 7:30am-2:30pm;) Organic and fair trade are big words at this eclectic cafe, where locals meet for tasty breakfast items (pastries, lox bagels, homemade oatmeal). The inventive list of hot beverages ranges from regular drip coffee to organic chocolate chai latte to lavendar rosemary cocoa. Vegan menu available, plus a used-book exchange.

Ya'Tel Motel Motel $
(541-547-3225; www.yatelmotel.com; cnr Hwy 101 & 6th St; d $74-119;) This eight-room motel has personality, along with large, clean rooms, some with kitchenette. A large room that sleeps six is also available ($119). Look for the (changeable) sign out front, which might say something like, 'Always clean, usually friendly.'

Florence ⑫

Waterfront Depot Northwestern US $$
(541-902-9100; http://thewaterfrontdepot.com; 1252 Bay St; mains $17-30; 4-10pm) This cozy, atmospheric joint is one of Florence's best restaurants. Come early to snag one of the few waterfront tables, then enjoy your jambalaya pasta or crab-encrusted halibut. There are excellent small plates, a great wine list and spectacular desserts. Reserve ahead – it's well priced and very popular.

Port Orford ⑰

Redfish Seafood $$$
(541-366-2200; www.redfishportorford.com; Hawthorne Gallery, 517 Jefferson St; mains $18-34; 11am-9pm Mon-Fri, 10am-9pm Sat & Sun) At first glance this slick, sea-view restaurant would seem better located in Portland's Pearl District – it's even attached to a highbrow art gallery, owned by glass artist Chris Hawthorne and family. Redfish boasts the freshest seafood in town, so take advantage; the menu changes seasonally. Weekend brunch, too.

Wildspring Guest Habitat Cabin $$$
(866-333-9453; www.wildspring.com; 92978 Cemetery Loop; d $298-328;) A few acres of wooded serenity greet you at this quiet retreat, set in a sheltered grove a half-mile from town. Five luxury cabin suites, all filled with elegant furniture and modern amenities such as radiant-floor heating and slate showers, make for a very comfortable and romantic getaway. An outdoor Jacuzzi with spectacular views is included, as is breakfast.

Gold Beach ⑱

Anna's by the Sea Northwestern US $$
(541-247-2100; www.annasbythesea.com; 29672 Stewart St; mains $24-39; 5-8:30pm Wed-Sat) One of Gold Beach's best restaurants, this homey spot serves up just a few key mains like black rock cod with sweet onions, oven-seared breast of duck and chicken thighs in chanterelle gravy. Great wine list, but don't expect upscale: it's self-proclaimed as 'Rejecting trendy from the start.'

Ireland's Rustic Lodges Lodge $$
(541-247-7718; http://irelandsrusticlodges.com; 29330 Ellensburg Ave; d $109-255;) A wide variety of accommodations awaits you at this woodsy place. There are regular suites with kitchenette, rustic one- and two-bedroom cabins, beach houses or even RV sites. A glorious garden sits in front while beach views are out back. Three communal Jacuzzis with faraway ocean views, too.

Brookings ⑲

Mattie's Pancake & Omelette American $
(541-469-7211; 15975 US 101 S; mains $6-14; 6am-1:45pm Tue-Sat) This casual breakfast and lunch spot offers 18 kinds of omelets (such as crab and Swiss cheese) along with pancakes (yes! chocolate chip!) and waffles. For lunch there are sandwiches and salads.

Oregon Cascades Scenic Byways

Oregon's Central Cascades are a bonanza of natural wonder. Scenic byways pack in lush forests, thundering waterfalls, snowcapped mountains, high desert and lakes galore.

TRIP HIGHLIGHTS

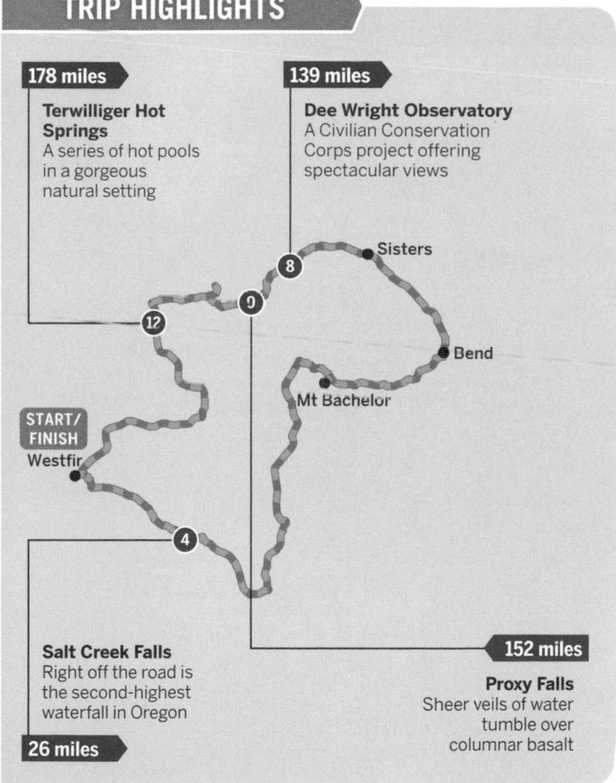

178 miles

Terwilliger Hot Springs
A series of hot pools in a gorgeous natural setting

139 miles

Dee Wright Observatory
A Civilian Conservation Corps project offering spectacular views

Sisters

Bend

Mt Bachelor

START/ FINISH

Westfir

Salt Creek Falls
Right off the road is the second-highest waterfall in Oregon

26 miles

152 miles

Proxy Falls
Sheer veils of water tumble over columnar basalt

4 DAYS
240 MILES / 386KM

GREAT FOR...

BEST TIME TO GO

Go June through September to avoid seasonal road closures.

ESSENTIAL PHOTO

Salt Creek Falls, the second-highest waterfall in Oregon.

BEST HOT SPRINGS

Terwilliger Hot Springs at Cougar Reservoir.

Salt Creek Falls Oregon's second highest waterfall

50 Oregon Cascades Scenic Byways

The region around Oregon's Central Cascades is, without a doubt, some of the most spectacular terrain in the entire state. But one scenic byway just isn't enough to see it all. Here you have our version of an Oregon sampler platter: a loop that brings together several of the best roads to create a majestic route full of the state's best features.

❶ Westfir

Before you spend several days enjoying abundant natural wonders, start with a quick photo op of an entirely constructed one: Oregon's longest covered bridge, the 180ft **Office Bridge**. Built in 1944, the bridge features a covered walkway to enable pedestrians to share the way with logging trucks crossing the Willamette River.

If you plan to do some exploring or mountain biking in the area, pick up a map of the

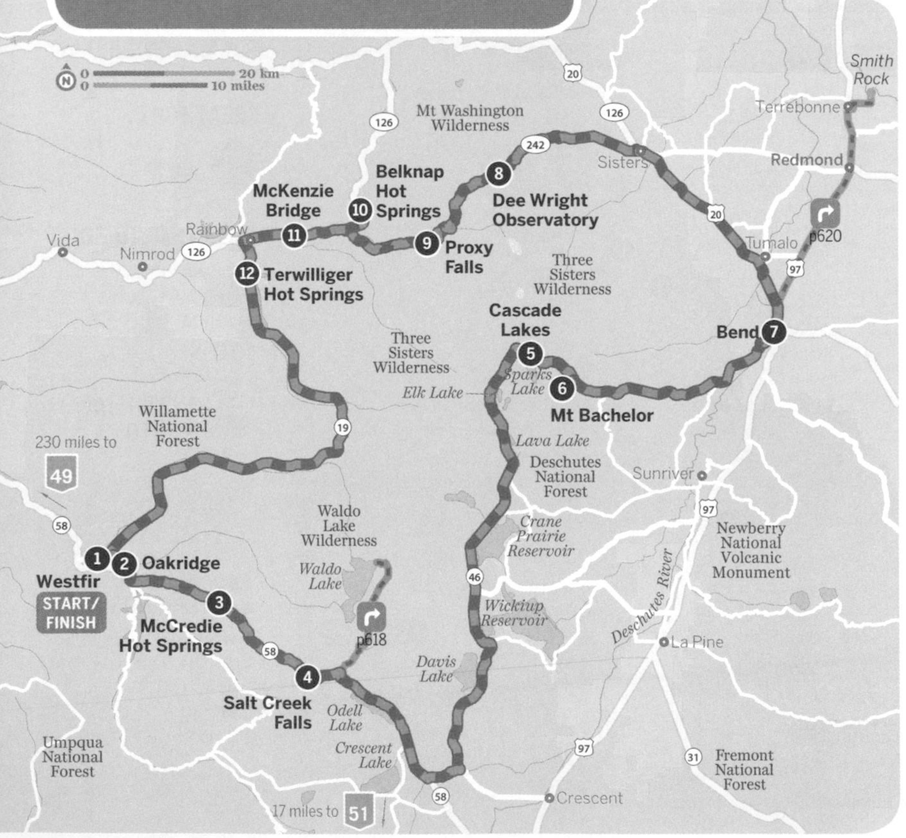

Willamette National Forest at the **Middle Fork Ranger District** (☎541-782-2283; 46375 Hwy 58; ⏲8am-4:30pm Mon-Fri, plus Sat in summer).

🛏 p623

The Drive » Oakridge is just a few miles to the east on either Hwy 58 or Westfir–Oakridge Rd.

2 Oakridge

Oakridge is one of Oregon's mountain-biking hot spots. There are hundreds of miles of trails around town, ranging from short, easy loops to challenging single-track routes. For novice riders, the **Warrior Fitness Trail** is a mostly flat 12-mile loop. The **Larison Creek Trail** is a challenging ride through old-growth forests, and the 16-mile **Alpine Trail** is considered the 'crown jewel' of the local trails for its 7-mile downhill stretch. **Oregon Adventures** (☎541-968-5397; www.oregon-adventures.com; 47921 Hwy 58; day trips from $30, 3-day tours $749; ⏲Jul-Sep) offers shuttles to the top so you can skip the climb; it also offers bike-tour packages.

The Drive » From Oakridge, Hwy 58 climbs steadily up the Cascade Range's densely forested western slope. Your next stop is about 10 miles east of Oakridge; park on the right just past Mile Marker 45.

3 McCredie Hot Springs

Because **McCredie Hot Springs** (☎541-782-2283; Hwy 58, Oakridge; per person $6; ⏲dawn-dusk) lies just off the highway, it's a very popular spot for everyone from mountain bikers fresh off the trails near Oakridge to truckers plying Hwy 58. Despite this, it's worth a stop if only because it's the site of one of the largest – and hottest – thermal pools in Oregon. If you can hit it early in the morning or late in the evening midweek, you could have the place to yourself.

There are five pools in all: two upper pools that are often dangerously hot (as in don't-even-dip-your-foot-in hot), two warm riverside pools and one smaller, murkier but usually perfectly heated pool tucked back into the trees. **Salt Creek** rushes past only steps from the springs and is ideal for splashing down with icy water.

The Drive » Keep heading east another 12 miles and pull off the highway at the signed parking lot.

TRIP HIGHLIGHT

4 Salt Creek Falls

At 286ft, this monster of a waterfall is Oregon's second highest. After a good snowmelt, this aqueous behemoth really roars, making for one of the most spectacular sights on the trip. Walk from the parking lot to the viewpoint and there below, in a massive basalt amphitheater hidden by the towering trees, 50,000 gallons of water pour every minute over a cliff into a giant, dark, tumultuous pool.

Be sure to hike the short trail downhill toward the bottom of the falls. It's lined with rhododendrons that put on a colorful show in springtime, and the views of the falls on the way down are stunning.

Salt Creek Falls is also the starting point for some excellent short hikes, including a 1.5-mile jaunt to **Diamond Creek Falls** and a 4.75-mile hike to **Vivian Lake**.

LINK YOUR TRIP

Highway 101 Oregon Coast

Follow Hwy 58 northwest to I-5 and head north to Portland. From there, follow Hwy 30 along the south side of the Columbia River to Astoria.

Crater Lake Circuit

Crater Lake is a must-see, and it's just south of the Cascades. Take Hwy 97 south from Bend to join this route.

The Drive » Continue 19 miles along Hwy 58 until you reach the Cascade Lakes Scenic Byway (Hwy 46), which winds its way north through numerous tiny lakes and up to Mt Bachelor. This road is closed from November to May; as an alternative, follow Hwy 97 to Bend.

5 Cascade Lakes

We could get all scientific and explain how lava from nearby volcanoes created the lakes around this area, or we could just tell you that Hwy 46 isn't called the Cascade Lakes Scenic Byway for nothing. The road winds past lake after beautiful lake – **Davis Lake**, **Crane Prairie Reservoir**, **Lava Lake**, **Elk Lake** – all worth a stop. Most have outstanding camping, trout fishing, boating and invigorating swimming ('invigorating' being a euphemism for *cold*).

We love **Sparks Lake** for its scenic beauty set against the backdrop of Mt Bachelor, and it's perfect for peaceful paddling. If you find yourself without a boat, **Wanderlust Tours** (☎800-862-2862; www.wanderlusttours.com; 61535 S Hwy 97, Suite 13, Bend; canoe & kayak day tour adult/child $75/55) can hook you up with a guided canoe or kayak tour.

p623

The Drive » Mt Bachelor is just a few miles past Sparks Lake. If Hwy 46 is closed for the season, you can backtrack from Bend to reach Mt Bachelor.

DETOUR: WALDO LAKE

Start: 4 Salt Creek Falls

There's no shortage of lakes in the area, but lovely Waldo Lake stands out for its amazing clarity. Because it's at the crest of the Cascades, water doesn't flow into it from other sources; the only water that enters it is rainfall and snowfall, making it one of the purest bodies of water in the world. In fact, it's so clear that objects in the water are visible 100ft below the surface. You can swim in the summer months (it's too cold in the winter), and if you're feeling ambitious after playing 'I Spy' on the lakebed, you can hike the **Waldo Lake Trail**, a 22-mile loop that circumnavigates the lake.

To get there, head 2 miles east of Salt Creek Falls on Hwy 58, and turn left at the Waldo Lake Sno-Park; follow the signs for 8 more miles to the lake.

6 Mt Bachelor

Glorious Mt Bachelor (9065ft) provides Oregon's best skiing. Here, Central Oregon's cold, continental air meets up with the warm, wet Pacific air. The result is tons of fairly dry snow and plenty of sunshine, and with 370in of snow a year, the season begins in November and can last until May.

At **Mt Bachelor Ski Resort** (☎800-829-2442; www.mtbachelor.com; lift tickets adult/child $92/52, cross-country day pass $19/12; ⏰Nov-May, depending on snowfall; 👪), rentals are available at the base of the lifts. Mt Bachelor grooms about 35 miles of cross-country trails, though the day pass (adult/child $19/12) may prompt skiers to check out the free trails at **Dutchman Flat Sno-Park**, just past the turnoff for Mt Bachelor on Hwy 46.

The Drive » Ready to add a little civilization to your rugged outdoor adventure? Head east to Bend, which is just 22 miles away.

7 Bend

Sporting gear is de rigueur in a town where you can go rock climbing in the morning, hike through lava caves in the afternoon, and stand-up paddleboard yourself into the sunset. Plus, you'll probably be

SVETLANA57 / GETTY IMAGES ©

Mt Bachelor Ski lifts

enjoying all that activity in great weather, as the area gets more than 250 days of sunshine each year (don't forget the sunscreen!).

Explore downtown on foot, and be sure to check out the excellent **High Desert Museum** (541-382-4754; www.highdesertmuseum.org; 59800 Hwy 97; adult/child $12/7; 9am-5pm May-Oct, 10am-4pm Nov-Apr;). It charts the exploration and settlement of the Pacific Northwest, but it's no slog through history. The fascinating Native American exhibit shows off several wigwams' worth of impressive artifacts, and live animal exhibits and living history are sure to be hits with the kids.

 p623

The Drive » Head 22 miles north to Sisters, then drive northwest along Hwy 242. This is part of the McKenzie Pass–Santiam Pass Scenic Byway – closed during the winter months. Your next stop is 15 miles from Sisters.

TRIP HIGHLIGHT

8 Dee Wright Observatory

Perched on a giant mound of lava rock, built entirely of lava rock, in the middle of a field of lava rock, stands the historic Dee Wright Observatory. The structure, built in 1935 by Franklin D Roosevelt's Civilian Conservation Corps, offers spectacular views in all directions. The observatory windows, called 'lava tubes,' were placed to highlight all the prominent Cascade peaks that can be seen from the summit, including Mt Washington, Mt Jefferson, North Sister, Middle Sister and a host of others.

The Drive » Head west on Hwy 242 for 13 miles to Mile Marker 64 and look for the well-signed Proxy Falls trailhead.

TRIP HIGHLIGHT

9 Proxy Falls

With all the waterfalls around the Central Cascades – hundreds of them in Oregon alone – it's easy to feel like 'You've seen one, you've seen 'em all.' Not so fast. Grab your camera and see if you're not at least a little impressed by photogenic Proxy Falls. If there were a beauty contest for waterfalls, Proxy would certainly be in the running, scattering into sheer veils down a mossy wall of columnar basalt. It's not even like the falls

WISANU BOONRAWD / SHUTTERSTOCK ©

DETOUR: SMITH ROCK

Start: 7 Bend

Best known for its glorious rock climbing, **Smith Rock State Park** (800-551-6949; www.oregonstateparks.org; 9241 NE Crooked River Dr; day use $5) boasts rust-colored 800ft cliffs that tower over the pretty Crooked River, just 25 miles north of Bend. Nonclimbers can enjoy miles of hiking trails, some of which involve a little rock scrambling.

Proxy Falls

make you work for it: it's an easy 1.3-mile loop from the parking area. If you want to save the best for last, take the path in the opposite direction from what the sign suggests so you hit Upper Proxy Falls first and you can build up to the even better Lower Proxy Falls.

The Drive » Nine miles from the falls, turn right on Hwy 126 (McKenzie Hwy); Belknap is just 1.4 miles away.

10 Belknap Hot Springs

Although nudity is the norm at most hot springs, Belknap is the sort of hot spring resort that you can take your grandmother to and neither of you will feel out of place.

Two giant swimming pools filled with 103°F (40°C) mineral water provide optimum soaking conditions in a family environment. The McKenzie River rushes by below, trees tower over everything, and everyone still has a good time. An excellent alternative to camping, the resort has rooms for nearly all budgets.

p623

The Drive » Head southwest on Hwy 126 for 6 miles to get to your next stop.

VOLCANO SIGHTS

The Cascades are a region of immense volcanic importance. Lava fields can be seen from McKenzie Pass and along Hwy 46. Road cuts expose gray ash flows. Stratovolcanoes like South Sister and Mt Bachelor and shield volcanoes like Mt Washington tower over the landscape. Although it's not instantly obvious when you drive to the center of **Newberry National Volcanic Monument** (39 miles south of Bend), you're actually inside the caldera of a 500-sq-mile volcano. What could be stranger than that? It's still active.

⓫ McKenzie Bridge

Although from the road it looks like there is nothing but trees, there's actually plenty to do around here, including fishing on the McKenzie River and hiking on the nearby **McKenzie River National Recreation Trail.**

To learn more about all your recreational options, stop at the **McKenzie Ranger Station** (541-822-3381; www.fs.fed.us/r6/willamette; 57600 McKenzie Hwy; 8am-4:30pm Mon-Sat), about 2 miles east of town. The rangers are fonts of information, plus you can find anything you ever wanted to know about the McKenzie River trail, including maps and books.

p623

The Drive » About 6 miles west of McKenzie Bridge, turn left on Hwy 19 (aka Aufderheide Memorial Dr) just past Rainbow. After almost 8 miles, you'll come to the parking lot from which you'll take a 0.25-mile trail through old-growth forest.

TRIP HIGHLIGHT

⓬ Terwilliger Hot Springs

Located in a picturesque canyon in the Willamette National Forest is one of the state's most stunning hot springs. From a fern-shrouded hole, scorching water spills into a pool that maintains a steady minimum temperature of 108°F (42°C). The water then cascades into three successive pools, each one cooler than the one above it. Sitting there staring up at the trees is an utterly sublime experience.

After hiking back to the car, you can even jump into Cougar Reservoir from the rocky shore below the parking lot.

The Drive » From Terwilliger Hot Springs, take Aufderheide/Hwy 19 south 41 miles to return to Westfir.

Eating & Sleeping

Westfir ❶

Westfir Lodge Lodge $

(541-782-3103; http://westfirlodge.com; 47365 1st St; d $90-140;) A stone's throw from Oregon's longest covered bridge is this spacious B&B lodge with eight homey guest rooms. Some rooms share bathrooms down the hall. Check out the central vault, left over from when this building used to be a lumber company office.

Cascade Lakes ❺

Cultus Lake Resort Cabin $$

(541-408-1560; www.cultuslakeresort.com; Hwy 46; cabins $85-175; mid-May–Sep; restaurant closed Mon;) This pleasant lakeside resort offers several homey cabins with a two-night minimum; from July 4 to Labor Day they rent by the week only. There's a restaurant and marina, too.

Sparks Lake Campground Campground $

(Hwy 46; campsites free; Jul-Sep) A scenically situated campground on the Cascade Lakes Scenic Byway, with views of Mt Bachelor and meadows. Pit toilets available; no water.

Bend ❼

Chow American $

(541-728-0256; www.chowbend.com; 1110 NW Newport Ave; mains $8-15; 7am-2pm) The poached-egg dishes here are spectacular and beautifully presented, coming with sides such as crab cakes, house-cured ham and cornmeal-crusted tomatoes (don't miss the house-made hot sauces). Gourmet sandwiches and salads, some with an Asian influence, are served for lunch.

Deschutes Brewery & Public House Cafe $$

(541-382-9242; www.deschutesbrewery.com; 1044 NW Bond St; 11am-11pm) Bend's first microbrewery serves good, hearty food (fish and chips, burgers, salads) at its beautiful two-story restaurant. Noteworthy beers include Mirror Pond Pale Ale, Black Butte Porter and Obsidian Stout, as well as anything on the seasonal or pub-only menu. Deschutes' Red Chair NWPA was voted 'world's best beer' in the 2012 World Beer Awards.

McMenamins Old St Francis School Hotel $$

(541-382-5174; www.mcmenamins.com; 700 NW Bond St; r from $155;) This old schoolhouse has been remodeled into a classy 19-room hotel – two rooms even have side-by-side clawfoot tubs. A recent expansion has added 41 new rooms. The fabulous tiled saltwater Turkish bath alone is worth the stay, though nonguests can soak for $5. A restaurant-pub, three bars, a movie theater and artwork complete the picture.

Oxford Hotel Boutique Hotel $$$

(541-382-8436; www.oxfordhotelbend.com; 10 NW Minnesota Ave; r from $249;) Bend's premier boutique hotel is deservedly popular. The smallest rooms are still huge (470 sq ft) and are decked out with ecofriendly features such as soy-foam mattresses and cork flooring. High-tech aficionados will love the iPod docks and smart-panel desks. Suites are available, and the basement restaurant is slick.

Belknap Hot Springs ❿

Belknap Hot Springs Resort Resort $$

(541-822-3512; www.belknaphotsprings.com; Hwy 126, near Hwy 242; tent/RV sites $30/40, r $110-185, cabins $135-425, day use only $8-15) In addition to soaking, the resort boasts an 18-room lodge, 14 private cabins and 15 tent sites, so it's affordable for nearly all budgets.

McKenzie Bridge ⓫

Cedarwood Lodge Cabin $$

(541-822-3351; www.cedarwoodlodge.com; 56535 McKenzie Hwy; cabins $130-185; closed Nov–Apr;) Ensconce yourself in one of eight rustic, comfortable, fully equipped cabins set above the McKenzie River.

Crater Lake Circuit

Make it a (big) day trip or stay a week – serene, mystical Crater Lake is one of Oregon's most enticing destinations. The best route takes you on a heavily forested, waterfall-studded loop.

TRIP HIGHLIGHTS

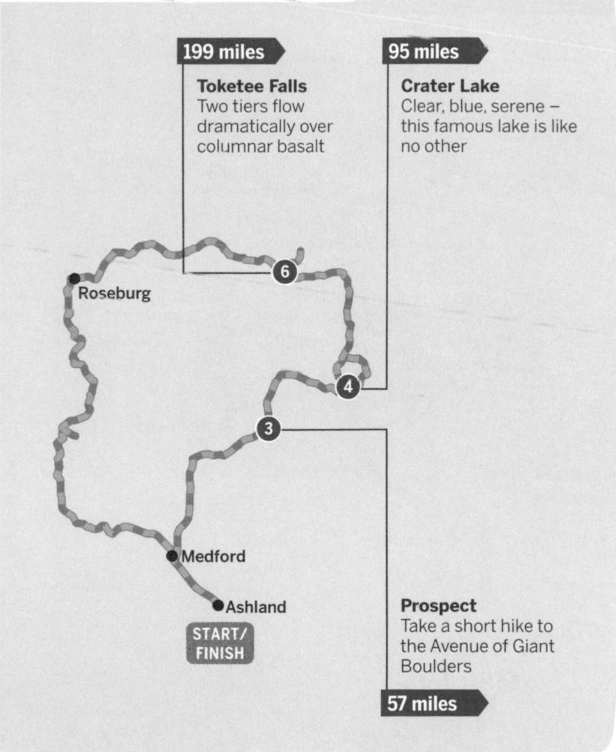

199 miles

Toketee Falls
Two tiers flow dramatically over columnar basalt

95 miles

Crater Lake
Clear, blue, serene – this famous lake is like no other

Roseburg

6

4

3

Medford

Ashland

START/ FINISH

Prospect
Take a short hike to the Avenue of Giant Boulders

57 miles

2–3 DAYS
365 MILES / 587KM

GREAT FOR...

BEST TIME TO GO

Late May to mid-October when all the roads are open.

ESSENTIAL PHOTO

No surprise here: Crater Lake.

BEST WATERFALL

Two-tiered Toketee Falls is our favorite.

Ashland Lithia Park

51 Crater Lake Circuit

The star attraction of this trip is Crater Lake, considered by many to be the most beautiful spot in all of Oregon. The sight of the still, clear and ridiculously blue water that fills an ancient volcanic caldera is worth the trip alone, but the drive there is lined with beautiful hikes, dramatic waterfalls and natural hot springs, all right off the highway.

1 Ashland

A favorite base for day trips to Crater Lake, Ashland is bursting at the seams with lovely places to sleep and eat (though you'll want to book your hotel room far in advance during the busy summer months). Home of the **Oregon Shakespeare Festival** (OSF; ☎541-482-4331; www.osfashland.org; cnr Main & Pioneer Sts; tickets $30-136; ⏰Tue-Sun Feb-Oct), it has more culture than most towns its size, and is just far enough off the

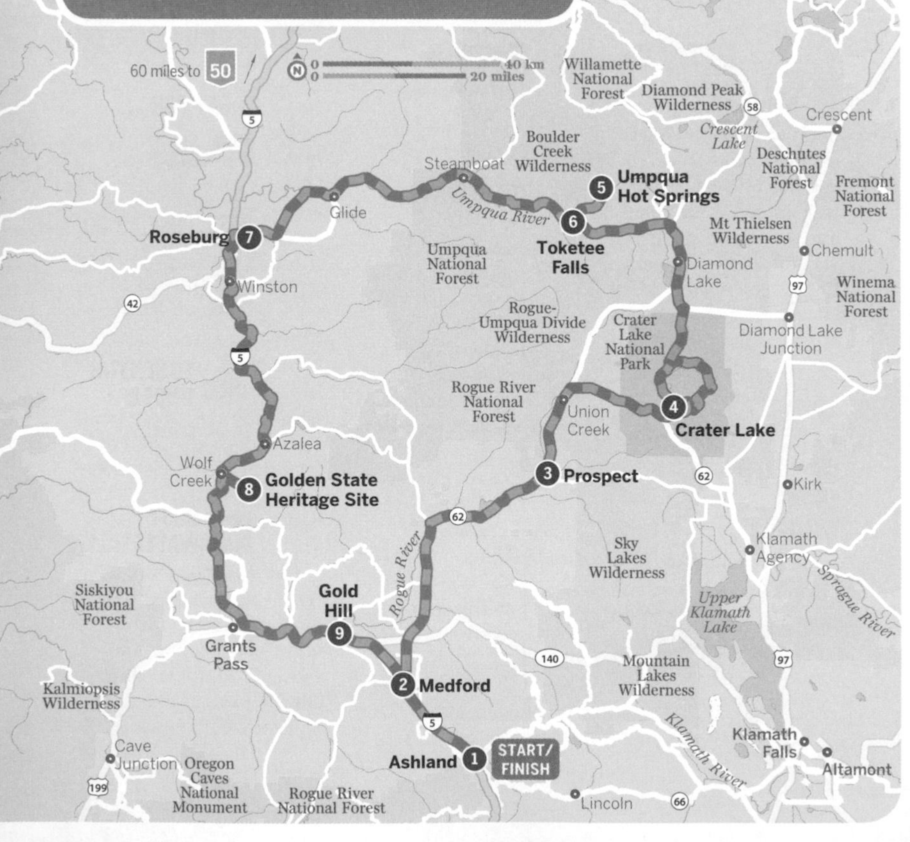

highway to resist becoming a chain-motel mecca.

It's not just Shakespeare that makes Ashland the cultural heart of southern Oregon. If you like contemporary art, check out the **Schneider Museum of Art** (☎541-552-6245; http://sma.sou.edu; 1250 Siskiyou Blvd; suggested donation $5; ⏲10am-4pm Mon-Sat).

Ashland's historic downtown and lovely **Lithia Park** (59 Winburn Way) make it a dandy place to go for a walk before or after your journey to Crater Lake.

 p631

The Drive » Medford is 13 miles north of Ashland on I-5.

❷ Medford

Southern Oregon's largest metropolis is where you hop off I-5 for your trek out to Crater Lake, and it can also serve as a suitable base of operations if you want a cheap, convenient place to bunk down for the night.

LINK YOUR TRIP

50 Oregon Cascades Scenic Byways

From Roseburg head north on I-5 and then southeast towards Westfir on Hwy 58.

On your way out, check out the **Table Rocks**, impressive 800ft mesas that speak of the area's volcanic past and are home to unique plant and animal species. Flowery spring is the best time for hiking to the flat tops, which were revered Native American sites. After **TouVelle State Park** (Table Rock Rd), fork either left to reach the trailhead to Lower Table Rock (3.5-mile round-trip hike) or right for Upper Table Rock (2.5-mile round-trip hike).

p631

The Drive » The drive along Hwy 62 isn't much until after Shady Cove, when urban sprawl stops and forest begins. Your next stop is 45 miles northeast in Prospect.

TRIP HIGHLIGHT

❸ Prospect

No wonder they changed the name of Mill Creek Falls Scenic Area – that implies you're just going to see another waterfall (not that there's anything wrong with that). But the real treat at **Prospect State Scenic Viewpoint** is hiking down to the **Avenue of Giant Boulders**, where the Rogue River crashes dramatically through huge chunks of rock and a little bit of scrambling offers the most rewarding views.

Take the trail from the southernmost of two parking lots on Mill Creek Dr. Keep left to get to the boulders or right for a short hike to two viewpoints for **Mill Creek Falls** and **Barr Creek Falls**. If you've got one more falls-sighting left in you, take the short hike from the upper parking lot to the lovely **Pearsony Falls**.

The Drive » Follow Hwy 62 for another 28 miles to get to the Crater Lake National Park turnoff at Munson Valley Rd.

TRIP HIGHLIGHT

❹ Crater Lake

This is it: the main highlight and reason for being of this entire trip is Oregon's most beautiful body of water, **Crater Lake** (☎541-594-3000; www.nps.gov/crla; 7-day vehicle pass $15). This amazingly blue lake is filled with some of the clearest, purest water you can imagine – you can easily peer 100ft down – and sits inside a 6-mile-wide caldera created when Mt Mazama erupted nearly 8000 years ago. Protruding from the water and adding to the drama of the landscape is **Wizard Island**, a volcanic cinder cone topped by its own mini crater called Witches Cauldron.

Get the overview with the 33-mile **Rim Drive** (⏲Jun–mid-Oct), which offers over 30 viewpoints as it winds around the edge of Crater Lake. The gloriously still waters reflect surrounding mountain peaks like a giant dark-blue mirror, making for spectacular photographs and breathtaking panoramas.

You can also camp, ski or hike in the surrounding old-growth forests. The popular and steep mile-long **Cleetwood Cove Trail**, at the north end of the crater, provides the only water access at the cove. Or get up close with a two-hour **boat tour** (☎888-774-2728; www.craterlakelodges.com/activities/volcano-boat-cruises; Cleetwood Cove boat dock; adult/child $41/27; ⏱late Jun–mid-Aug).

 p631

The Drive » Head north on Hwy 138 for 41 miles and turn right on Rd 34.

5 Umpqua Hot Springs

Set on a mountainside overlooking the North Umpqua River, Umpqua Hot Springs is one of Oregon's most splendid hot springs, with a little bit of height-induced adrenaline thanks to its position atop a rocky bluff. Springs are known for soothing weary muscles, so earn your soak at Umpqua by starting with a hike – it is in a national forest, after all – where you'll be treated to lush, old-growth forest and waterfalls punctuating the landscape. Half a mile from the parking lot is the scenic **North Umpqua Trail**.

The Drive » The turnout for Toketee Falls is right on Hwy 138, 2 miles past the Umpqua turnoff.

TRIP HIGHLIGHT

6 Toketee Falls

More than half a dozen waterfalls line this section of the Rogue-Umpqua Scenic Byway, but the one that truly demands a stop is the stunning, two-tiered **Toketee Falls** (USFS Rd 34). The falls' first tier drops 40ft into an upper pool behind a cliff of columnar basalt, then crashes another 80ft down the rock columns into yet another gorgeous, green-blue pool below. One tiny disclaimer: although the hike is just 0.4 miles, there's a staircase of 200 steps down to the viewpoint, so climbing back up to your car is a bit of a workout.

PUNG / SHUTTERSTOCK ©

The Drive » From here, the scenery tapers back down to only moderately spectacular as you leave the Umpqua National Forest. It's one hour to Roseburg.

7 Roseburg

Sprawling Roseburg lies in a valley near the confluence of the South and

✓ TOP TIP: VISITING CRATER LAKE

Crater Lake's popular south entrance is open year-round. In winter you can only go up to the lake's rim and back down the same way; no other roads are plowed. The north entrance is only open from early June to late October, depending on snowfall.

Crater Lake

North Umpqua Rivers. The city is mostly a cheap, modern sleepover for travelers headed elsewhere (such as Crater Lake), but it does have a cute, historic downtown area and is surrounded by award-winning wineries.

Don't miss the excellent **Douglas County Museum** (☎541-957-7007; www.umpquavalleymuseums.org; 123 Museum Dr, I-5 exit 123; adult/child $8/2; ⏲10am-5pm Tue-Sat; 👪), which displays the area's cultural and natural histories. Especially interesting are the railroad derailment photos and *History of Wine* exhibit. Kids have an interactive area and live snakes to look at.

✕ p631

The Drive » Go south on I-5 for 47 miles and take the Wolf Creek exit. Follow Old State Hwy 99 to curve back under the interstate. Golden is 3.2 miles east on Coyote Creek Rd.

8 Golden State Heritage Site

Not ready to return to civilization quite yet? Stop off in the ghost town of **Golden**, population zero. A former mining town that had over 100 residents in the mid-1800s, Golden was built on the banks of Coyote Creek when gold was discovered there.

A handful of structures remain, as well as some newfangled interpretive signs that tell the tale of a curiously devout community that eschewed drinking and dancing, all giving a fascinating glimpse of what life was like back then.

The weathered wooden buildings include a residence, the general store/post office, and a classic country church. Fun fact: the town was once used as a location for the long-running American Western TV series *Gunsmoke*.

The Drive » Go south another 45 miles on I-5 and take exit 43. The Oregon Vortex is 4.2 miles north of the access road.

9 Gold Hill

Just outside the town of Gold Hill lies the cheesy but fun roadside attraction of **Oregon Vortex** (☎541-855-1543; www.oregonvortex.com; 4303 Sardine Creek L Fork Rd; adult/child $12.75/9; ⏰9am-4pm Mar-Oct, to 5pm Jun-Aug), where the laws of physics don't seem to apply – or is it all just an optical illusion created by skewed buildings on steep hillsides? However you see it, the place is definitely bizarre: objects roll uphill, a person's height changes depending on where they stand, and brooms stand up on their own...or so it seems.

Eating & Sleeping

Ashland ❶

Morning Glory Cafe $

(☎541-488-8636; 1149 Siskiyou Blvd; mains $9.50-15; ⌚8am-1:30pm) This colorful, casual cafe is one of Ashland's best breakfast joints. Creative dishes include the Alaskan-crab omelet, vegetarian hash with roasted chilies, and shrimp cakes with poached eggs. For lunch there's gourmet salad and sandwiches. Go early or late to avoid a long wait.

New Sammy's Cowboy Bistro French, American $$$

(☎541-535-2779; 2210 S Pacific Hwy, Talent; mains $25-28, prix fixe $45; ⌚noon-1:30pm & 5-9pm Wed-Sat) Some consider this cool spot, run by an eclectic couple, Oregon's best restaurant. There are only a handful of tables and the wine selections are spectacular. Mains are few but the flavor combinations can be incredible; many vegetables come from the garden outside. Located in Talent, about 2 miles north of Ashland. Reserve a week in advance for dinner; limited winter hours.

Country Willows B&B $$

(☎541-488-1590; www.countrywillowsinn.com; 1313 Clay St; d $120-210, ste $165-295;) Only minutes from downtown is this luxurious B&B on 5 acres in the 'countryside.' The nine rooms, suites and a cottage sport a mix of antiques and contemporary furniture; some suites are as big as small apartments and have a kitchenette or private deck. The gorgeous breakfast room is next to the swimming pool.

Medford ❷

Organic Natural Café Cafe $

(☎541-773-2500; http://organicnaturalcafe.com; 226 E Main St; mains $6-14; ⌚9am-3pm Mon-Sat;) Step up to the cafeteria here and order a panini-style sandwich or burger (choose from vegetarian/buffalo/organic beef). There's a salad bar, along with fresh juices and fruit smoothies. The theme – in case you haven't guessed yet – is all about local, organic and gluten-free.

Crater Lake ❹

Annie Creek American $$

(www.craterlakelodges.com; Mazama Village; mains $9-18; ⌚8am-8pm late Apr-Sep) Family-friendly Annie Creek is a wings-and-burgers kind of joint; there are also pizzas, pot roast and fried chicken.

Crater Lake Lodge Lodge $$

(☎888-774-2728; www.craterlakelodges.com; r from $220; ⌚late May–mid-Oct;) This grand old lodge has 71 simple but comfortable rooms (no TV or telephone), but it's the common areas that are most impressive. Large stone fireplaces, rustic leather sofas and a spectacular view of Crater Lake from the patio make this place special. There's a fine **dining room** (☎541-594-2255; dinner mains $24-43; ⌚7-10am, 11:30am-2:30pm & 5-9pm mid-May–mid-Oct), too.

Roseburg ❼

McMenamins Roseburg Station Pub American $$

(☎541-672-1934; www.mcmenamins.com/roseburg-station-pub-brewery; 700 SE Sheridan St; mains $11-22; ⌚11am-11pm Mon-Thu, to midnight Fri & Sat, to 10pm Sun) This is a beautiful, cozy pub-restaurant in subdued McMenamins style – dark-wood paneling and lots of antique chandeliers. Typical burgers, sandwiches and salads dominate the menu. It's in an old train depot; sit and order a microbrew on the sunny patio in summer, or cozy up in the little dark bar on a bleak day.

STRETCH YOUR LEGS PORTLAND

Start/Finish Stumptown Coffee Roasters

Distance 2 miles

Duration 3 hours

With green spaces galore, the world's largest independent bookstore, art, handcrafted beer, a vibrant food culture and a livability rating that's off the charts, Portland is made for walking. This route takes you to the highlights of downtown.

Coffee & Doughnuts

Start with coffee at **Stumptown Coffee Roasters** (www.stumptowncoffee.com; 128 SW 3rd Ave; 6am-7pm Mon-Fri, 7am-7pm Sat & Sun;), which has been roasting its own beans since 1999. A minute's walk away is **Voodoo Doughnut** (503-241-4704; www.voodoodoughnut.com; 22 SW 3rd Ave; doughnuts from $2; 24hr), which bakes quirky treats – go for the bacon maple bar or the 'voodoo doll' filled with raspberry jelly 'blood.'

The Walk » Head toward the waterfront on pedestrian-only SW Ankeny St.

Saturday Market & Tom McCall Waterfront Park

Victorian-era architecture and the lovely **Skidmore Fountain** give the area beneath the Burnside Bridge near-European flair. Hit it on a weekend to catch the chaotic **Saturday Market** (503-222-6072; www.portlandsaturdaymarket.com; 2 SW Naito Pkwy; 10am-5pm Sat, 11am-4:30pm Sun Mar-Dec;), an outdoor crafts fair with yummy food carts. From here you can explore the **Tom McCall Waterfront Park** along the Willamette River.

The Walk » Walk north under the Burnside Bridge through the park, then turn left on NW Couch St and right into NW 3rd Ave.

Chinatown

The ornate **Chinatown Gates** (cnr W Burnside St & NW 4th Ave) define the southern edge of Portland's so-called Chinatown – but you'll be lucky to find any Chinese people here at all. The main attraction is the **Lan Su Chinese Garden** (503-228-8131; www.lansugarden.org; 239 NW Everett St; adult/child $10/7; 10am-7pm mid-Apr–mid-Oct, to 5pm mid-Oct–mid-Apr), a one-block haven of tranquillity, ponds and manicured greenery.

The Walk » Make your way west on NW Davis St to NW 8th Ave.

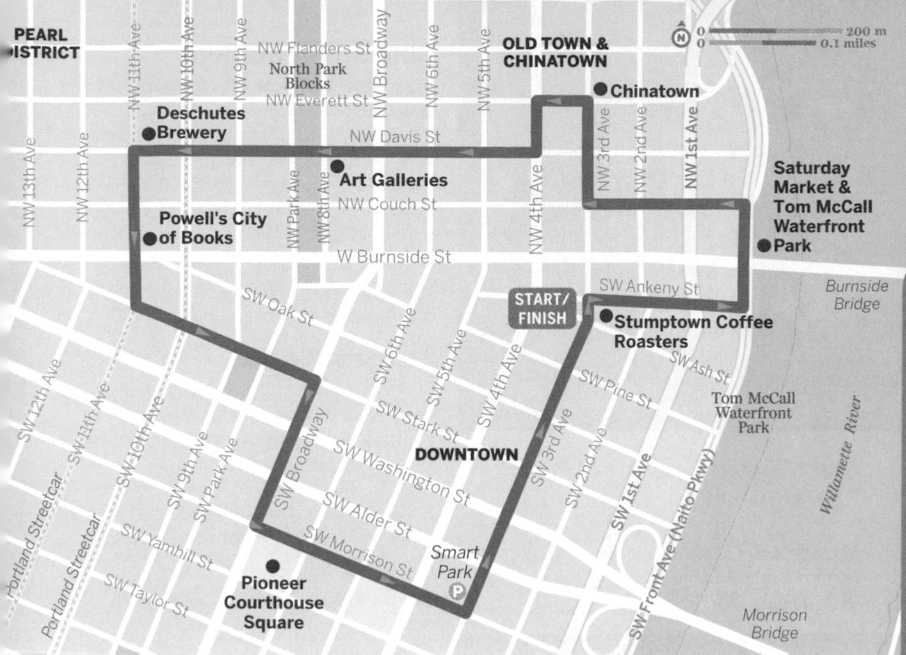

Art Galleries

Several top-notch galleries can be found on this block. They're open late the first Thursday of each month, when new exhibits open and crowds of appreciative gawpers stroll through the area.

The Walk » Continue up NW Davis St to NW 11th Ave.

Deschutes Brewery

Since walking makes you thirsty and you're in Beervana (a group is lobbying to make this Portland's official name), it's time for a pint and/or lunch. Grab a table under the arches framing the restaurant at **Deschutes Brewery** (☎503-296-4906; www.deschutesbrewery.com; 210 NW 11th Ave; ⊙11am-10pm, to midnight Fri & Sat).

The Walk » Walk south on NW 11th Ave one block to find yourself in the Pearl District's upmarket shopping area.

Powell's City of Books

Until someone proves otherwise, **Powell's City of Books** (☎800-878-7323; www.powells.com; 1005 W Burnside St; ⊙9am-11pm) is the world's largest independent bookstore. Find a whole, awe-inspiring city block of new and used titles and prepare to get lost.

The Walk » Cross W Burnside St then turn left on SW Stark St and right on SW Broadway to SW Morrison St.

Pioneer Courthouse Square

End your walk in the heart of downtown Portland. This brick plaza is nicknamed 'Portland's living room' and is the most visited public space in the city. When it isn't full of hacky-sack players, sunbathers or office workers lunching, the square hosts concerts, festivals, rallies, farmers markets – and even summer Friday-night movies, **Flicks on the Bricks** (https://thesquarepdx.org/events; ⊙7pm Fri Jul-Aug). Around the square is an endless array of shopping, restaurants and food carts.

The Walk » Head east three blocks down SW Morrison St, turn left on SW 3rd Ave and in six blocks you'll be back at Stumptown Coffee Roasters.

STRETCH YOUR LEGS SEATTLE

Start/Finish King Street Station/ EMP Museum

Distance 2 miles

Duration 3½ hours

Successive mayors have tried hard to alleviate Seattle's car chaos, and – hills and drizzly rain aside – this is now a good city for walking. Strategically placed coffee bars provide liquid fuel for urban hikers.

Take this walk on Trip

King Street Station

King Street Station (303 S Jackson St) was designed to imitate St Mark's bell tower in Venice. Now dwarfed by loftier towers, it was the tallest structure in Seattle upon its completion in 1906. It lay neglected until the late 2000s when restoration work revealed a once-grandiose interior.

The Walk » From the station entrance, head quite literally around the corner onto S Jackson St.

Zeitgeist Coffee

Start this walk the way Seattleites start each day: with a latte. You'll find chain coffee shops on every corner, but **Zeitgeist Coffee** (206-583-0497; www.zeitgeistcoffee.com; 171 S Jackson St; 6am-7pm Mon-Fri, 7am-7pm Sat, 8am-6pm Sun;), in a converted warehouse, is a great place to hang out.

The Walk » Go west on S Jackson St and right on 1st Ave S, admiring the historic redbrick buildings.

Pioneer Square

Seattle was born in the muddy shores of Elliott Bay and reborn here post the catastrophic 1889 fire. The handsome redbrick buildings remain, built in a style known as Richardson Romanesque in the 1890s. Yesler Way was America's original 'Skid Row,' so named as they used to skid logs down the thoroughfare toward the harbor.

The Walk » Walk north on 1st Ave into the modern downtown core.

Seattle Art Museum

Seattle isn't just a meeting ground for Gore-Tex–wearing adventurers planning sorties into the surrounding mountains. There's culture here too. The **Seattle Art Museum** (SAM; 206-654-3210; www.seattleartmuseum.org; 1300 1st Ave; adult/student $25/15; 10am-5pm Wed & Fri-Sun, to 9pm Thu) is the best place to start. The collections span genres, from Warhol to Northwestern totem poles.

The Walk » Continue north on 1st Ave two blocks to Pike Place Market.

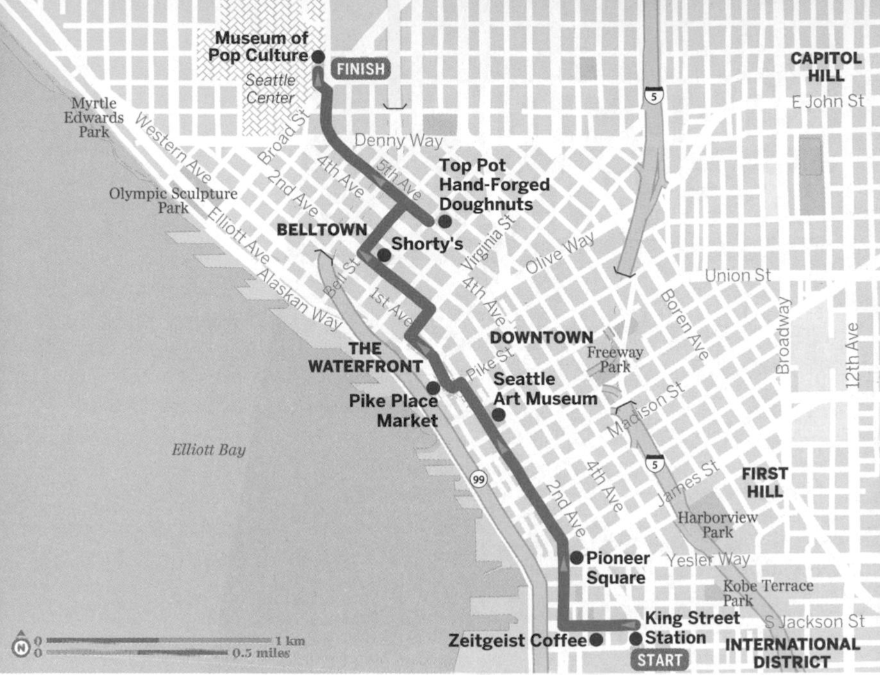

Pike Place Market

The soul of the city is encased in **Pike Place Market** (www.pikeplacemarket.org; 85 Pike St; 9am-6pm Mon-Sat, to 5pm Sun), first launched in 1907. You'll need an early start if you want to spend more time dodging flying fish and less time dodging hordes of people. Locals love it for its fresh flowers, produce and seafood; for visitors, its big neon sign is a quintessential Seattle photo op.

The Walk » Exit the north end of Pike Pl and you're in Belltown.

Shorty's

An early pulpit for grunge music, Belltown, north of downtown, has gone upscale since the 1990s with new condo developments and huddles of restaurants. A relic of old Belltown is **Shorty's** (206-441-5449; www.shortydog.com; 2222 2nd Ave; noon-2am), a cross between a pinball arcade and a dive bar.

The Walk » Turn right on Bell St and right again on 5th Ave.

Top Pot Hand-Forged Doughnuts

Top Pot Hand-Forged Doughnuts (www.toppotdoughnuts.com; 2124 5th Ave; doughnuts from $1.50; 6am-7pm Mon-Fri, 7am-7pm Sat & Sun) has done for doughnuts what Champagne did for wine. The coffee isn't bad either.

The Walk » Walk along 5th Ave to the intersection with Denny Way. Hang a left and you'll see the Seattle Center and Space Needle in front of you.

Museum of Pop Culture

It's hard to miss the huge, crazily colorful building at the foot of the Space Needle. That would be the **Museum of Pop Culture** (206-770-2700; www.mopop.org; 325 5th Ave N; adult/child $25/16; 10am-7pm Jun-Aug, to 5pm Sep-May) and its on-site *Icons of Science Fiction* exhibit, a fun place to immerse yourself in rock and roll and/or sci-fi for one admission price.

The Walk » To get back to the start simply catch bus 131 ($2.75) from Wall St and 3nd Ave, which drops you in S Jackson St near King Street Station.

ROAD TRIP ESSENTIALS

USA Driving Guide

With a network of interstate highways, enthusiastic car culture and jaw-dropping scenery, the USA is an ideal road-tripping destination, even year-round in some spots.

DRIVING LICENSE & DOCUMENTS

All US drivers must carry a valid driving license from their home state, proof of vehicle insurance and their vehicle's registration papers or a copy of their vehicle-rental contract.

Foreign drivers can legally drive in the USA for 12 months using their home driver's license. An International Driving Permit (IDP) isn't required, but will have more credibility with traffic police and will simplify the car-rental process, especially if your home license isn't written in English and/or doesn't have a photo. International automobile associations issue IDPs, valid for one year, for a fee. Always carry your home license with your IDP.

To ride a motorcycle in the USA, you will need either a valid US state motorcycle license or an IDP specially endorsed for motorcycles.

The American Automobile Association (AAA) has reciprocal agreements with some international auto clubs (eg Canada's CAA, AA in the UK). Bring your membership card from home.

Driving Fast Facts

Right or left? Drive on the right

Legal driving age 16

Top speed limit 70mph on some highways

Best bumper sticker 'Where the heck is Wall Drug?'

Best radio station National Public Radio (NPR)

INSURANCE

Liability All driver's are required to obtain a minimum amount of liability insurance, which would cover the damage that you might cause to other people and property in case of an accident. Liability insurance can be purchased from rental-car companies for about $12 per day.

Collision For damage to the rental vehicle, a collision damage waiver (CDW) is available from the rental company for about $18 a day.

Alternative sources Your personal auto insurance may extend to rental cars, so it's worth investigating before purchasing liability or collision from the rental company. Additionally, some credit cards offer reimbursement coverage for collision damages if you rent the car with that credit card; again, check before departing. Most credit-card coverage isn't valid for rentals of more than 15 days or for exotic models, SUVs, vans and 4WD vehicles.

RENTING A VEHICLE

To rent your own wheels, you'll usually need to be at least 25 years old, hold a valid driver's license and have a major credit card, *not* a check or debit card.

Road Trip Websites

AUTO CLUBS

American Automobile Association (www.aaa.com) Roadside assistance, travel discounts, trip planning and maps for members.

Better World Club (www.betterworldclub.com) Ecofriendly alternative to AAA.

MAPS

America's Byways (www.fhwa.dot.gov/byways) Inspiring itineraries, maps and directions for scenic drives.

GasBuddy (www.gasbuddy.com) Website and app that finds the cheapest places to gas up nearby.

Google Maps (www.maps.google.com) Turn-by-turn driving directions with estimated traffic delays.

Waze (www.waze.com) Popular, free crowdsourced traffic and navigation app.

ROAD CONDITIONS & CLOSURES

US Department of Transportation (www.fhwa.dot.gov/trafficinfo) Links to state and local road conditions, traffic and weather.

Cars

Rental car rates generally include unlimited mileage, but expect surcharges for additional drivers and one-way rentals. Airport locations may have cheaper base rates but higher add-on fees. If you get a fly-drive package, local taxes may be extra when you pick up the car. Child and infant safety seats are legally required; reserve them (around $10 per day, or $50 per trip) when booking your car.

Some major car-rental companies offer 'green' fleets of hybrid or alternative-fuel rental cars, but they're in short supply. Make reservations far in advance and expect to pay significantly more for these models. Many companies rent vans with wheelchair lifts and hand-controlled vehicles at no extra cost, but you must also reserve these well in advance.

International car-rental companies with hundreds of branches nationwide include the following:

Alamo (www.alamo.com)

Avis (www.avis.com)

Budget (www.budget.com)

Dollar (www.dollar.com)

Enterprise (www.enterprise.com)

Fox (www.foxrentacar.com)

Hertz (www.hertz.com)

National (www.nationalcar.com)

Thrifty (www.thrifty.com)

To find local and independent car-rental companies, check:

Car Rental Express (www.carrentalexpress.com) Search for independent car-rental companies and specialty cars (eg hybrids).

Rent-a-Wreck (www.rentawreck.com) Often rents to younger drivers (over-18s) and those without credit cards; ask about long-term rentals.

Wheelchair Getaways (www.wheelchairgetaways.com) Rents wheelchair-accessible vans across the country.

Zipcar (www.zipcar.com) Car-sharing club in dozens of cities; some foreign drivers are eligible for membership.

If you don't mind no-cancellation policies or which company you rent from, you may find better deals on car rentals through online travel discounters such as **Priceline** (www.priceline.com) and **Hotwire** (www.hotwire.com).

Motorcycles

Motorcycle rentals and insurance are very expensive, with steep surcharges for one-way rentals. Discounts may be available for three-day and weekly rentals. National rental outfitters include the following:

Eagle Rider (www.eaglerider.com) Motorcycle rentals and tours in more than 25 states.

Harley-Davidson (www.harley-davidson.com) Links to scores of local places that rent Harleys.

RVs & Campervans

Popular with road-trippers, recreational vehicles (RVs, also called motorhomes) are cumbersome to drive and burn fuel at an alarming rate. They do solve transportation, accommodation and self-catering kitchen needs in one fell swoop. Even so, there are many places in national parks and scenic areas (eg narrow mountain roads) that they can't be driven.

Make reservations for RVs and smaller campervans as far in advance as possible. Rental costs vary by size and model; basic rates often don't include mileage, bedding or kitchen kits, vehicle prep and cleaning or additional taxes and fees. If bringing pets is allowed, a surcharge may apply.

National rental agencies include the following:

Cruise America (www.cruiseamerica.com) With 125 RV rental locations nationwide.

El Monte RV (www.elmonterv.com) RV rentals in more than 25 states.

Happy Travel Campers (www.camperusa.com) Rents campervans in Los Angeles, San Francisco, Las Vegas and Denver.

Jucy Rentals (www.jucyusa.com) Campervan rentals in Los Angeles, San Francisco and Las Vegas.

BORDER CROSSING

Citizens of Canada and Mexico who are driving across the border should be sure to bring their vehicle's registration papers, proof of liability insurance valid for driving in the USA and their home driving license. An International Driving Permit (IDP) isn't required, but may be helpful. Only some rental-car companies allow their vehicles to be driven across international borders.

Road Distances (miles)

	Atlanta	Boston	Chicago	Dallas	Denver	El Paso	Houston	Las Vegas	Los Angeles	Miami	New Orleans	New York	Oklahoma City	Phoenix	Portland	Salt Lake City	San Francisco	Seattle	St Louis
Boston	1100																		
Chicago	720	1005																	
Dallas	790	1770	935																
Denver	1405	2005	1010	785															
El Paso	1425	2405	1490	635	700														
Houston	800	1860	1090	240	1030	750													
Las Vegas	1990	2755	1760	1225	750	725	1475												
Los Angeles	2210	3025	2035	1445	1025	815	1560	275											
Miami	660	1510	1380	1320	2070	1940	1190	2545	2750										
New Orleans	475	1530	930	525	1305	1100	350	1740	1915	860									
New York	870	215	800	1565	1800	2200	1655	2550	2820	1290	1310								
Oklahoma City	865	1690	790	210	675	695	450	1125	1345	1500	725	1470							
Phoenix	1860	2690	1800	1070	825	430	1185	285	375	2370	1535	2480	1010						
Portland	2605	3120	2130	2030	1260	1630	2270	1020	965	3265	2555	2925	1925	1335					
Salt Lake City	1880	2395	1405	1265	535	865	1505	420	690	2545	1785	2190	1205	655	765				
San Francisco	2510	3100	2145	1750	1270	1190	1940	570	380	3130	2295	2930	1645	750	635	745			
Seattle	2675	3070	2065	2105	1330	1725	2345	1165	1150	3335	2630	2865	2000	1490	175	840	810		
St Louis	555	1190	295	630	855	1195	840	1615	1840	1215	680	955	500	1505	2050	1325	2065	2120	
Washington DC	635	440	700	1330	1690	1965	1415	2460	2690	1055	1090	230	1345	2350	2820	2095	2835	2770	845

Driving Problem-Buster

What should I do if my car breaks down? Put on your hazard lights (flashers) and carefully pull over to the side of the road. Call the roadside emergency assistance number for your auto club or rental-car company. Otherwise, call information (☎411) for the number of the nearest towing service or auto-repair shop.

What if I have an accident? If you're safely able to do so, move your vehicle out of traffic and onto the road's shoulder. For minor collisions with no major property damage or bodily injuries, be sure to exchange driver's license and auto-insurance information with the other driver, then file a report with your insurance provider or notify your car-rental company as soon as possible. For major accidents, call ☎911 and wait for the police and emergency services to arrive.

What should I do if I'm stopped by the police? Don't get out of the car unless asked. Keep your hands where the officer can see them (ie on the steering wheel). Always be courteous. Most fines for traffic or parking violations can be handled by mail or online within a 30-day period.

What happens if my car gets towed? Call the local non-emergency police number and ask where to pick up your car. Towing and vehicle storage fees accumulate quickly, up to hundreds of dollars for just a few hours or a day, so act promptly.

MAPS

Tourist information offices and visitor centers distribute free but often very basic maps. GPS navigation can't be relied upon everywhere, notably in thick forests and remote mountain, desert and canyon areas. If you're planning on doing a lot of driving, you may want a more detailed fold-out road map or map atlas, such as those published by **Rand McNally** (www.randmcnally.com). Members of the American Automobile Association (AAA) and its international auto-club affiliates (bring your membership card from home) can pick up free maps at AAA branch offices nationwide.

USA Playlist

(Get Your Kicks on) Route 66 Bobby Troup, as recorded by Nat King Cole

I've Been Everywhere Johnny Cash

This Land Is Your Land Woody Guthrie

Born to Be Wild Steppenwolf

Runnin' Down a Dream Tom Petty & the Heartbreakers

Life Is a Highway Tom Cochrane

ROAD CONDITIONS

The USA's highways are not always perfect ribbons of unblemished asphalt. Common road hazards include potholes, rockfalls, mudslides, flooding, fog, free-ranging livestock and wildlife, commuter traffic jams on weekday mornings and afternoons, and drivers distracted by technology, kids and pets or blinded by road rage.

In places where winter driving is an issue, snow tires and tire chains may be necessary, especially in the mountains. Ideally, carry your own chains and learn how to use them before you hit the road. Driving off-road or on dirt roads is often forbidden by rental-car contracts, and it can be very dangerous in wet weather.

Major highways, expressways and bridges in some urban areas require paying tolls. Sometimes tolls can be paid using cash (bills or coins), but occasionally an electronic toll-payment sensor is required. If you don't have one, your vehicle's license plate will likely be photographed and you'll be billed later, usually at a higher rate. Ask about this when picking up your rental vehicle to avoid surprising surcharges on your final bill after you've returned the car.

ROAD RULES

- Drive on the right-hand side of the road.
- Talking or texting on a cell (mobile) phone while driving is illegal in most states.

➡ The use of seat belts and infant and child safety seats is legally required nationwide, although exact regulations vary by state.

➡ Wearing motorcycle helmets is mandatory in many states, and always a good idea.

➡ High-occupancy vehicle (HOV) lanes marked with a diamond symbol are reserved for cars with multiple occupants, but sometimes only during specific signposted hours.

➡ Unless otherwise posted, the speed limit is generally 55mph or 65mph on highways, 25mph to 35mph in cities and towns and as low as 15mph in school zones. It's illegal to pass a school bus when its lights are flashing.

➡ Except where signs prohibit doing so, turning right at a red light after coming to a full stop is usually permitted (one notable exception is New York City). Intersecting cross-traffic still has the right of way, however.

➡ At four-way stop signs, cars proceed in order of arrival. If two cars arrive simultaneously, the one on the right goes first. When in doubt, politely wave the other driver ahead.

➡ At intersections, U-turns may be legal unless otherwise posted, but this varies by state – don't do it in Oregon and Illinois, for example.

➡ When emergency vehicles approach from either direction, carefully pull over to the side of the road.

➡ In many states, it's illegal to carry open containers of alcohol (even if they're empty) inside a vehicle. Unless the containers are full and still sealed, put them in the trunk instead.

➡ Most states have strict anti-littering laws; throwing trash from a vehicle may incur a $1000 fine. Besides, it's bad for the environment.

➡ Hitchhiking is illegal in some states, and restricted in others.

Driving Under the Influence

The maximum legal blood-alcohol concentration for drivers is 0.08%. Penalties for 'DUI' (driving under the influence of alcohol or drugs) are severe, including heavy fines, driver's license suspension, court appearances and/or jail time.

Police may give roadside sobriety checks to assess if you've been drinking or using drugs. If you fail, they'll require you to take a breath, urine or blood test to determine the level of drugs and alcohol in your body. Refusing to be tested is treated the same as if you'd taken the test and failed.

PARKING

Free parking is plentiful in small towns and rural areas, but scarce and often expensive in cities. Municipal parking meters and centralized pay stations usually accept coins and credit or debit cards. Parking at broken meters is often prohibited; where allowed, the posted time limit still applies.

When parking on the street, carefully read all posted regulations and restrictions (eg 30-minute maximum, no parking during scheduled street-cleaning hours) and pay attention to colored curbs, or you may be ticketed and towed. In many towns and cities, overnight street parking is prohibited downtown and in designated areas reserved for local residents with permits.

At city parking garages and lots, expect to pay at least $2 per hour and $10 to $45 for all-day or overnight parking. For valet parking at hotels, restaurants, nightclubs etc, a flat fee of $5 to $40 is typically charged. Tip the valet attendant at least $2 when your keys are handed back to you.

FUEL

Many gas stations in the USA have fuel pumps with automated credit-card pay screens. Some machines ask for your ZIP code after you swipe your card. For foreign travelers, or those with cards issued outside the US, you'll have to pay inside before fueling up. Just indicate how much you'd like to put on the card. If there's still credit left over after you fuel up, pop back inside and the attendant will put the difference back on your card.

SAFETY

Vehicle theft, break-ins and vandalism are a problem mostly in urban areas. Be sure to lock your vehicle's doors, leave the windows rolled up and use any anti-theft devices that have been installed (eg car alarm, steering-wheel lock). Do not leave any valuables visible inside your vehicle; instead, stow them in the trunk before arriving at your destination, or else take them with you once you've parked.

USA Travel Guide

GETTING THERE & AWAY

Every visitor entering the USA from abroad needs a passport. Your passport must be valid for at least six months longer than your intended stay in the USA. Also, if your passport does not meet current US standards, you'll be turned back at the border.

Canadian and Mexican citizens arriving in the USA by air or overland will need to show either a valid passport or another pre-approved identification card for 'trusted travelers' who cross the border frequently. For more information see www.cbp.gov/travel/us-citizens/western-hemisphere-travel-initiative.

Practicalities

Smoking The majority of states prohibit smoking inside all public buildings, including airports, hotels, restaurants and bars.

Time The continental USA has four time zones: Eastern (GMT/UTC -5), Central (GMT/UTC -6), Mountain (GMT/UTC -7) and Pacific (GMT/UTC -8). Daylight Saving Time (DST), when clocks move one hour ahead (except in parts of Indiana and Arizona), applies from the second Sunday in March through to the first Sunday in November.

TV & DVD PBS (Public Broadcasting Service); major cable stations: ESPN (sports), HBO (movies), Weather Channel. DVDs coded region 1 (USA and Canada only).

Weights & Measures Imperial system used, except 1 US gallon = 0.83 imperial gallons.

For visa requirements for entering the USA, see the visa information on p649. Remember that no matter what your visa says, US immigration officers have an absolute authority to refuse admission. They will ask about your travel plans and whether you have sufficient funds. It's a good idea to list an itinerary, produce an onward or round-trip ticket and have at least one major credit card.

AIR

Major international gateway and domestic hub airports across the USA:

Charlotte-Douglas International Airport (CLT; www.cltairport.com) In Charlotte, NC.

Chicago O'Hare International Airport (ORD; www.flychicago.com)

Dallas/Fort Worth International Airport (DFW; www.dfwairport.com)

Denver International Airport (DEN; www.flydenver.com)

Dulles International Airport (IAD; www.metwashairports.com) Near Washington, DC.

George Bush Intercontinental Airport (IAH; www.fly2houston.com) In Houston, TX.

Hartsfield-Jackson Atlanta International Airport (ATL; www.atlanta-airport.com)

John F Kennedy International Airport (JFK; www.panynj.gov/airports) In NYC.

Los Angeles International Airport (LAX; www.lawa.org)

McCarran International Airport (LAS; www.mccarran.com) In Las Vegas, NV.

Miami International Airport (MIA; www.miami-airport.com)

Newark Liberty International Airport (EWR; www.panynj.gov/airports/newark-liberty.html) Near NYC.

Phoenix Sky Harbor International Airport (PHX; www.skyharbor.com)

San Francisco International Airport (SFO; www.flysfo.com)

Seattle-Tacoma International Airport (SEA; www.portseattle.org/Sea-Tac)

If you are flying to the US, the first airport that you land in is where you must go through immigration and customs, even if you are continuing on the flight to another destination. Upon arrival, all international visitors must register with the Department of Homeland Security, which involves having your fingerprints scanned and a digital photo taken.

Most mid-sized and larger US airports have car-rental counters staffed by major international agencies in the arrivals area near baggage claim. Courtesy shuttles usually wait curbside to transport rental-car customers to each company's on- or off-site parking lot.

Always make airport car-rental reservations in advance to ensure a car is available, as well as to lock in the lowest rental rates and minimize wait times. You may also save time and money by signing up in advance for the rental company's rewards program; membership is usually free, and could entitle you to perks such as priority check-in, free upgrades etc.

CAR & MOTORCYCLE

On weekends and holidays, especially during summer, traffic at the main border crossings between the USA and its neighboring countries Canada and Mexico can be heavy and waits long. Check current border-crossing wait times online with US Customs & Border Protection (https://bwt.cbp.gov).

Be sure to bring all necessary documentation with you, including your vehicle's registration papers, proof of liability insurance valid for driving in the USA and your home driving license. Occasionally law-enforcement and customs authorities from the USA, Canada or Mexico will decide to search a car very thoroughly for contraband or undeclared dutiable items.

TRAIN

For Canadians living near the US border, taking the train can be an economical option. It also eliminates the hassle of driving a car across the border, which some rental companies do not allow. Instead, you can just rent a car upon arrival in the USA, then return it before leaving.

The USA's national passenger railway, **Amtrak** (www.amtrak.com), operates cross-border trains, including to and from Toronto, ON; Montréal, QC; and Vancouver, BC. Immigration and customs inspections at the US–Canada border can delay trains by an unpredictable amount of time.

Rental car pick-ups are available at some bigger Amtrak train stations in the USA, but usually only with advance bookings. Expect your choice of rental-car companies to be more limited than at airports.

Book Your Stay Online

For more accommodations reviews by Lonely Planet authors, check out http://hotels.lonelyplanet.com. You'll find independent reviews, as well as recommendations on the best places to stay. Best of all, you can book online.

DIRECTORY A–Z

ACCOMMODATIONS

Budget-conscious options for road-trippers include campgrounds, hostels and motels. Motels are ubiquitous on both highways and byways, while hostels are only common in cities and some popular vacation destinations. A variety of camping options exist, from free, bare-bones wilderness tent sites to full-service RV parks with wi-fi and cable-TV hookups.

At midrange motels and hotels, expect clean, decently sized rooms with a private bathroom, direct-dial telephone, cable TV and perhaps a coffeemaker, mini fridge and microwave. If it's included, breakfast might be just stale doughnuts and weak coffee, or a full hot-and-cold breakfast buffet. Wi-fi (wi-fi icon) is usually free, but sometimes slow or with a weak signal. A shared internet computer (@) for guests to use may be available, usually in the lobby.

Top-end hotels and luxury resorts offer many more amenities (eg swimming pool, fitness room, business center, restaurants and bars) and sometimes a scenic location or edgy contemporary design. Additional parking, internet and 'resort' fees may add $10 to $50 or more per day. Air-conditioning (❄) is standard in most rooms, with the exception of some historical hotels and coastal or mountain resorts.

Smaller and more intimate, B&Bs and inns offer widely varying amenities. Although their idiosyncratic design can be a relief from cookie-cutter chains, B&B rooms may lack phones, TVs, internet and private bathrooms. Breakfast is not always served, regardless of what the name 'bed-and-breakfast' implies. Some properties close during the off-season, many do not allow children or pets, and almost all require advance reservations.

Rates & Reservations

Generally, midweek rates are lower, except at business-oriented hotels in cities, where weekend leisure rates may be cheaper. Rates quoted in this book usually apply for high season, which means summer (June to August) across much of the country. At ski resorts and sunny winter-escape destinations, rates peak from Thanksgiving in late November through spring break in March or April.

Demand and prices also skyrocket around major holidays and special events, when some properties require multi-night stays. Reservations are recommended for holidays, festivals and weekends year-round, and also on weekdays in high season. If you reserve by phone, ask about the cancellation policy up front and get a booking confirmation number.

Sleeping Price Ranges

The following price ranges refer to a private room with bathroom in high season excluding tax, unless otherwise stated.

$	less than $100
$$	$100 to $200
$$$	more than $200

If you plan to arrive late in the evening, you may want to call ahead on the day of your stay to ask the front desk to hold your room. Hotels commonly overbook, but if you've guaranteed your reservation with a credit card, they should accommodate you regardless. At off-peak times, polite bargaining may be possible for walk-in guests without reservations.

Even if motels or hotels advertise that 'children sleep free,' this may be true only if kids use existing bedding in their parents' room. Requesting a rollaway bed or cot may cost extra.

Helpful Resources

Airbnb (www.airbnb.com) Nightly vacation rentals, sublet apartments as well as private rooms of varying quality; use at your own risk.

BedandBreakfast.com (www.bedandbreakfast.com) Online directory of B&Bs and inns with user reviews and professionally inspected 'Diamond Collection.'

Hostelling International USA (www.hiusa.org) Operates more than 50 hostels scattered across the country (nightly surcharge for non-members $3).

Hostelz.com (www.hostelz.com) Search engine, online bookings and reviews for independent hostels nationwide.

Hotel Coupons (www.hotelcoupons.com) Website and mobile app for the same motel and hotel discounts available in free booklets at tourist offices and highway rest areas.

KOA (www.koa.com) Network of nearly 500 private RV parks and campgrounds across the country.

Recreation.gov (www.recreation.gov) Reservations for federal recreation-area campgrounds and cabins, including in national parks and forests.

ReserveAmerica (www.reserveamerica.com) Reservations for public campgrounds and cabins, including at many state parks.

Vacation Rentals by Owner (www.vrbo.com) Vacation rental houses, apartments, condos and more lodging options, most privately owned and operated.

ELECTRICITY

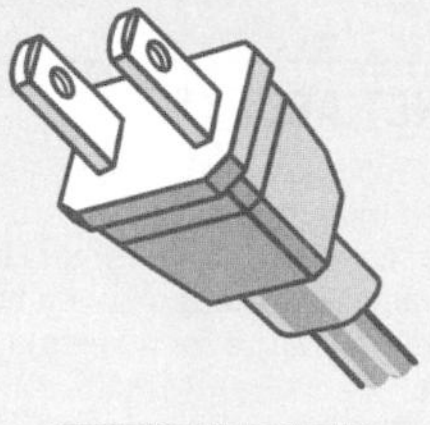

Type A
120V/60Hz

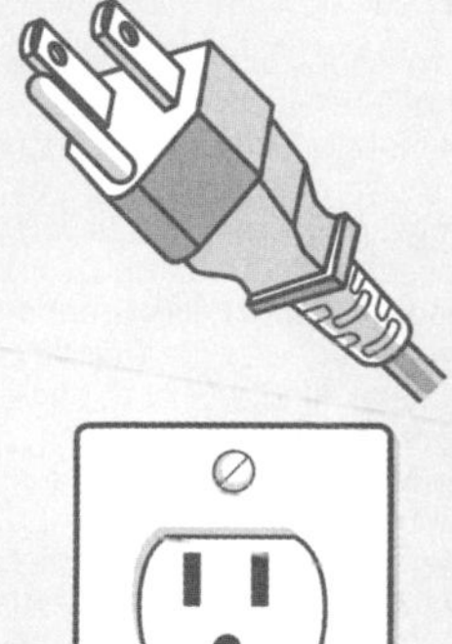

Type B
120V/60Hz

FOOD

At most restaurants, lunch is more casual and generally cheaper, sometimes half the price of dinner. Some diners and cafes serve breakfast all day, and a few stay open 24 hours. Weekend brunch is typically available from mid-morning until early afternoon on Saturdays and Sundays.

Eating Price Ranges

The following price ranges refer to a main course excluding taxes and tip, unless otherwise stated.

$	less than $10
$$	$10 to $20
$$$	more than $20

Dress codes rarely apply except at top-end restaurants, where a collared shirt and possibly a jacket may be required for men. More often than not, smoking is illegal indoors at restaurants; ask first or look around for an ashtray before lighting up on an outdoor patio or at sidewalk tables. Don't expect your neighbors to be happy about inhaling secondhand smoke.

You can bring your own wine (BYOB) at many restaurants, although a 'corkage' fee of $10 to $30 may be charged. If two diners share one main course, there's sometimes a split-plate surcharge. Vegetarians and travelers with food allergies or other dietary restrictions can usually be accommodated, especially in urban areas and at popular vacation destinations.

It's perfectly fine to bring kids along to casual restaurants, where high chairs, booster seats, special kids' menus, crayons and paper placemats for drawing are often available. Look for the family-friendly icon ( ) included with listings throughout this book.

LGBTIQ TRAVELERS

Most US cities have a visible and open LGBTIQ community that is easy to connect with. The level of everyday acceptance varies nationwide. In some places there is no tolerance whatsoever, while in others acceptance is predicated on one's sexual preference and identity being downplayed or hidden. In conservative enclaves, some people follow a 'don't ask, don't tell' policy.

Although anti-hate crime legislation has been enacted across the country and popular attitudes are increasingly tolerant, bigotry still exists. Verbal harassment and occasional violence against lesbians, gay men, bisexuals and transgender people still occurs in both urban and rural areas, but most travelers are unlikely to experience anything seriously threatening.

Helpful Resources

The Queerest Places: A Guide to Gay and Lesbian Historic Sites by Paula Martinac is full of juicy details and history, and covers the country. Visit her blog at www.queerestplaces.com.

Advocate (www.advocate.com) Gay-oriented news website reports on business, politics, arts, entertainment and travel.

Damron (www.damron.com) Publishes the classic gay travel guides, but they're advertiser-driven and sometimes outdated.

Gay & Lesbian National Help Center (www.glnh.org) Counseling, information and referrals.

Gay Travel (www.gaytravel.com) Online guides to dozens of US destinations.

National LGBTQ Task Force (www.thetaskforce.org) National activist group's website covers news, politics and current issues.

Out Traveler (www.outtraveler.com) Gay-oriented travel articles.

Purple Roofs (www.purpleroofs.com) Lists gay-owned and gay-friendly B&Bs and hotels.

HEALTH

Medical treatment in the USA is high-caliber, but the expense could kill you. Many health-care professionals demand payment at the time of service, especially from out-of-towners and international tourists.

Except for medical emergencies (in which case call ☎911 or go to the nearest 24-hour hospital emergency room, or ER), phone around to find an urgent-care or walk-in clinic or doctor's office that will accept your insurance.

Keep all receipts and documentation for billing and insurance claims, and later reimbursement. Some health-insurance (eg HMOs) and travel-insurance policies with medical benefits require you to get pre-authorization for treatment over the phone before seeking help.

Pharmacies are abundantly supplied, but you may find that some medications available over the counter in your home country will require a prescription in the USA, and without US health insurance, prescriptions can be shockingly expensive. Bring a signed, dated letter from your doctor describing all medications (including their generic names) that you regularly take.

INTERNET ACCESS

Travelers will have few problems staying connected in tech-savvy USA. Most hotels, guesthouses, hostels and motels have wi-fi (usually free, though luxury hotels are more likely to charge for access); ask when reserving.

Across the US, most cafes offer free wi-fi. Some cities have wi-fi-connected parks and plazas. If you're not packing a laptop or other web-accessible device, try the public library – most have public terminals (though they have time limits) in addition to wi-fi. Occasionally out-of-state residents are charged a small fee.

If you're not from the US, remember that you will need an AC adapter for your laptop, plus a plug adapter for US sockets; both are available at larger electronics shops, such as Best Buy.

MONEY

Prices in this book are quoted in US dollars and exclude state and local taxes, unless otherwise noted. Most locals don't carry large amounts of cash for everyday use, instead relying on credit cards, ATMs and debit or check cards. Smaller businesses may refuse to accept bills in denominations larger than $20 or traveler's checks.

ATMs are available 24/7 at banks, shopping malls, airports and grocery and convenience stores. Expect a transaction surcharge of at least $2, in addition to any fees charged by your home bank. Withdrawing cash from an ATM using your credit card requires a four-digit PIN and usually incurs a significant fee; check with your credit-card company first.

Credit cards are almost universally accepted, and are typically required for making reservations online or over the phone. Visa, MasterCard and American Express are the most widely accepted issuers. If you use a debit or check card for transactions, large holds may be placed on your account, which will inconveniently freeze some or all available funds.

International exchange rates for withdrawals at ATMs are usually as good as you'll get at major banks, airport moneychangers and currency-exchange offices such as American Express (www.

Tipping Guide

Tipping is *not* optional; only withhold tips in cases of outrageously bad service.

Airport & hotel porters $2 per bag, minimum per cart $5

Bartenders 15% to 20% per round, minimum per drink $1

Hotel maids $2 to $4 per night, left under the card provided

Restaurant servers 15% to 20%, unless a gratuity is already charged on the bill

Taxi drivers 10% to 15%, rounded up to the next dollar

Valet parking attendants At least $2 when handed back the keys

americanexpress.com). Outside cities and larger towns, exchanging foreign currency may be a problem, so make sure you have a credit card and sufficient cash on hand.

Traveler's checks are becoming obsolete, except as a trustworthy back-up. If you do carry them, purchase them in US dollars. Visa or American Express are the most widely accepted issuers.

OPENING HOURS

Typical normal opening times are as follows:

Bars 5pm–midnight Sunday to Thursday, to 2am Friday and Saturday

Banks 8:30am–4:30pm Monday to Thursday, to 5:30pm or 6pm Friday (and possibly 9am–noon Saturday)

Nightclubs 10pm–4am Thursday to Saturday

Post offices 9am–5pm Monday to Friday

Shopping malls 9am–9pm

Stores 10am–6pm Monday to Saturday, noon–5pm Sunday

Supermarkets 8am–8pm, some open 24 hours

PUBLIC HOLIDAYS

On the following national public holidays, banks, schools and government offices (including post offices) are closed, and transportation, museums and other services operate on a Sunday schedule. Holidays falling on a weekend are usually observed the following Monday.

New Year's Day January 1

Martin Luther King Jr Day Third Monday in January

Presidents' Day Third Monday in February

Memorial Day Last Monday in May

Independence Day July 4

Labor Day First Monday in September

Columbus Day Second Monday in October

Veterans' Day November 11

Thanksgiving Fourth Thursday in November

Christmas Day December 25

During spring break, high school and college students get a week off from school so they can overrun beach towns and resorts. This occurs throughout March and April. For students of all ages, summer vacation runs from June to August.

SAFE TRAVEL

Despite its seemingly apocalyptic list of dangers – guns, violent crime, riots, earthquakes, tornadoes, hurricanes, wildfires – the USA is a reasonably safe place to visit. The greatest danger to visitors is traffic accidents (buckle up – it's the law).

For travelers, petty theft is the biggest concern, not violent crime. Wherever possible, withdraw money from ATMs during the day or in well-lit, busy areas at night. When driving, secure valuables in the trunk of your car before arriving at your destination and don't leave valuables in your car overnight. Many hotels provide in-room wall safes, some of which can fit a tablet or laptop computer.

TELEPHONE

The US phone system comprises regional service providers, competing long-distance carriers and several cell-phone and pay-phone companies. Overall, the

Important Numbers

Country code ☎1

Emergency (police, fire, ambulance) ☎911

International access code ☎011

International operator ☎00

Local directory assistance ☎411

Local operator ☎0

Toll-free directory assistance ☎800-555-1212

system is very efficient, but it can be expensive. Avoid making long-distance calls on a hotel phone or on a pay phone. It's usually cheaper to use a regular landline or cell phone. Most hotels allow guests to make free local calls.

Telephone books can be handy resources: some list community services, public transportation and things to see and do as well as phone and business listings. Online phone directories include www.411.com and www.yellowpages.com.

Cell (Mobile) Phones

Tri- or quad-band phones brought from overseas will generally work in the USA. However, you should check with your service provider to see if roaming charges apply, as these will turn even local US calls into pricey international calls.

It's often cheaper to buy a compatible prepaid SIM card for the USA, such as those sold by AT&T, which you can insert into your international cell phone to get a local phone number and voicemail. Telestial (www.telestial.com) offers these services, as well as cell-phone rentals.

If you don't have a compatible phone, you can buy inexpensive, no-contract (prepaid) phones with a local number and a set number of minutes, which can be topped up at will. Virgin Mobile, T-Mobile, AT&T and other providers offer phones starting around $20, with a package of minutes starting around $20 for 400 minutes, or $30 monthly for unlimited minutes. Electronics stores such as Radio Shack and Best Buy sell these phones.

Huge swathes of rural America, including many national parks and recreation areas, don't pick up a signal. Check your provider's coverage map.

Dialing Codes

➡ US phone numbers consist of a three-digit area code followed by a seven-digit local number.

➡ When dialing a number within the same area code, usually you'll need to dial just the seven-digit number. If that doesn't work, try dialing all 10 digits.

➡ If you are making a long-distance call to another area code, dial ☎1 plus the area code, plus the local phone number.

➡ Toll-free numbers beginning with ☎800, 866, 877 and 888 must be preceded by ☎1 when dialing.

➡ To make a direct international call, dial ☎011 then the country code, plus area code, plus local number.

➡ If calling from abroad, the country code for the USA is ☎1 (the same as for Canada, but international rates apply for calls between the two countries).

Phonecards

If you're traveling without a cell phone or in a region with limited cell service, a prepaid phonecard is an alternative solution. Phonecards typically come precharged with a fixed number of minutes that can be used on any phone, including landlines. You'll generally need to dial an ☎800 number and enter a PIN (personal identification number) before placing each call. Phonecards are available from online retailers such as amazon.com and at some convenience stores. Be sure to read the fine print, as many cards contain hidden charges such as 'activation fees' or per-call 'connection fees' in addition to the per-minute rates.

TOURIST INFORMATION

For links to the official tourism websites of every US state and most major cities, see www.visit-usa.com. The similarly named www.visittheusa.com is jam-packed with itinerary planning ideas and other useful info.

Any tourist office worth contacting has a website, where you can download free travel e-guides. They also field phone calls; some local offices maintain daily lists of hotel-room availability, but few offer reservation services. All tourist offices have self-service racks of brochures and discount coupons; some also sell maps and books.

State-run 'welcome centers,' usually placed along interstate highways, tend to have free state road maps, brochures and other travel planning materials. These offices are usually open longer hours, including weekends and holidays.

Many cities have an official convention and visitors bureau (CVB). These sometimes double as tourist bureaus, but since their main focus is drawing the business trade, CVBs can be less useful for independent travelers.

Keep in mind that in smaller towns where the local chamber of commerce runs the tourist bureau, its lists of hotels, restaurants and services usually mention only chamber members; the town's cheapest options may be missing.

Similarly in prime tourist destinations, some private 'tourist bureaus' are really agents that book hotel rooms and tours on commission. They may offer excellent service and deals, but you'll get what they're selling and nothing else.

TRAVELERS WITH DISABILITIES

The USA is reasonably well-equipped for travelers with mobility issues or other physical disabilities, although this varies by region. Some local tourist offices and visitor centers helpfully publish detailed accessibility guides. At national parks, US citizens or permanent residents with permanent disabilities are entitled to a free 'America the Beautiful' Access Pass (visit http://store.usgs.gov/pass for more information).

The Americans with Disabilities Act (ADA) requires all public transit and public buildings built after 1993 to be wheelchair-accessible, including restrooms. However, it's a good idea to call ahead and check, especially at historical or private buildings, for which there are no accessibility guarantees. Most intersections in cities have dropped curbs and audible crossing signals.

All major airlines, Greyhound buses and Amtrak trains and buses can accommodate people with disabilities with at least 48 hours of advance notice. Local buses, trains and subways are usually equipped with wheelchair lifts and ramps. City taxi companies typically have at least one wheelchair-accessible van, but you'll have to call for one and probably wait a while. For hand-controlled car and wheelchair-accessible van rentals, see p638.

Service animals (ie guide dogs) are allowed to accompany passengers on public transit and in public buildings; bring documentation and make sure your animal wears its identifying vest. Most banks offer ATMs with instructions in Braille and earphone jacks. Telephone companies provide relay operators (dial ☎711) for hearing-impaired customers.

VISAS

Warning: All of the following information is highly subject to change. US entry requirements keep evolving as national security regulations change. Double-check visa and passport requirements *before* coming to the USA.

The US Department of State (https://travel.state.gov) provides the most comprehensive visa information, with downloadable application forms, lists of US consulates abroad and visa wait times by country.

Currently, under the US Visa Waiver Program (VWP), visas are not required for stays of up to 90 days (no extensions) for citizens of 38 countries, as long as your passport meets current US standards. Citizens of VWP countries must still register with the Electronic System for Travel Authorization (https://esta.cbp.dhs.gov/esta) at least 72 hours before traveling. Once approved, ESTA registration ($14) is usually valid for up to two years or until your passport expires, whichever comes first.

Most Canadian citizens with passports that meet current US standards do not need a visa for short-term visits to the USA. Citizens of Mexico usually need to get a non-immigrant or border-crossing 'laser' visa in advance. For more information see www.cbp.gov/travel/us-citizens/western-hemisphere-travel-initiative.

Citizens of all other countries or whose passports don't meet current US requirements will need to apply for a temporary visitor visa. Best done in your home country, the process costs a nonrefundable fee (minimum $160), involves a personal interview and can take several weeks, so apply early.

BEHIND THE SCENES

SEND US YOUR FEEDBACK

We love to hear from travelers – your comments help make our books better. We read every word, and we guarantee that your feedback goes straight to the authors. Visit **lonelyplanet.com/contact** to submit your updates and suggestions.

Note: We may edit, reproduce and incorporate your comments in Lonely Planet products such as guidebooks, websites and digital products, so let us know if you don't want your comments reproduced or your name acknowledged. For a copy of our privacy policy visit lonelyplanet.com/privacy.

WRITER THANKS

SIMON RICHMOND

Many thanks to Van Vahle, Tonny Wong and Curtis Maxwell Perrin for insights, assistance and hospitality along the way.

KATE ARMSTRONG

La'Vell Brown: thank you for your magic wand, plus your passion, knowledge and insights into Disney World, and for transforming me from the Beastess into Cinderella herself. Thanks to Cory O'Born, Visit Orlando; Nathalia Romano and Ashlynn Webb, Universal Orlando; Jessica Savage, Greater Fort Lauderdale Convention & Visitors Bureau; and to Chris, for your flexibility, patience and everything (except holding my hand on the Hogwarts Express). Finally, thank you to Lauren Keith and Trisha Ping for their understanding and helping to put out a few nothing-but-Disney fireworks.

CAROLYN BAIN

My warmest thanks to all the chatty innkeepers, bartenders and barflies I had the good fortune to spend time with – who else would you ask for tips on the region's best beach/trail/lobster roll/craft brew etc? Sincerest thanks to the people of Nantucket for welcoming me back into your fold and embracing my nostalgia – especially to Roselyne Hatch and Tania Jones. Special mention goes to Emily Golin, Carla Tracy, Thomas Masters, and Kimberly and Barry Hunter for their kindnesses.

AMY C BALFOUR

I had a blast checking out my regional neighborhood. Special thanks to the following folks who shared their favorite places: Dave Dekema, Sketchy, Barbra Byington, Ed & Melissa Reid, Lynn Neumann, Lori Jarvis,

THIS BOOK

This 3rd edition of Lonely Planet's *USA's Best Trips* guidebook was curated by Simon Richmond and researched and written by Simon, Kate Armstrong, Carolyn Bain, Amy C Balfour, Ray Bartlett, Loren Bell, Sara Benson, Celeste Brash, Gregor Clark, Michael Grosberg, Ashley Harrell, Mark Johanson, Adam Karlin, Brian Kluepfel, Stephen Lioy, Carolyn McCarthy, Hugh McNaughtan, Becky Ohlsen, Christopher Pitts, Kevin Raub, Brendan Sainsbury, Regis St Louis, Ryan Ver Berkmoes, Mara Vorhees, Benedict Walker and Karla Zimmerman.

Updates were also provided by Andrew Bender, Jade Bremner, Cristian Bonetto, Josephine Quintero, Andrea Schulte-Peevers and Helena Smith.

This guidebook was produced by the following:

Destination Editors Alexander Howard, Evan Godt, Lauren Keith, Trisha Ping, Clifton Wilkinson

Product Editors Carolyn Boicos, Hannah Cartmel, Kate Mathews

Senior Cartographer Alison Lyall

Book Designer Virginia Moreno

Assisting Cartographers Julie Dodkins, Corey Hutchison, Julie Sheridan

Assisting Editors Janet Austin, James Bainbridge, Judith Bamber, Imogen Bannister, Michelle Bennett, Janice Bird, Kate Chapman, Nigel Chin, Melanie Dankel, Andrea Dobbin, Carly Hall, Paul Harding, Jennifer Hattam, Gabrielle Innes, Anita Isalska, Kellie Langdon, Ali Lemer, Anne Mason, Jodie Martire, Anne Mulvaney, Rosie Nicholson, Kristin Odijk, Susan Paterson, Gabrielle Stefanos, Saralinda Turner, Sarah Reid, Simon Williamson

Assisting Book Designers Nicholas Colicchia, Lauren Egan, Katherine Marsh, Jessica Rose

Cover Researcher Naomi Parker

Thanks to Sasha Drew, Kate James, Indra Kilfoyle, Claire Naylor, Karyn Noble, Lauren O'Connell, Donna Watson, Tony Wheeler, Susanne Zimmermann

Andrew McRoberts, Tom Fleming, Melissa & Mary Peeler, Erin Stolle, Alicia Hay Matthai, Liz Smith Robinson, Alice Merchant Dearing, Severn Miller, James Foley, John Park, Suzie Lublin Tiplitz, Sharon Nicely, Eone Moore Beck, Kendall Sims Hunt, Lee Bagby Ceperich, Justin Shephard, Tim Stinson, Trish Mullen and Steve Bruce.

RAY BARTLETT

This project couldn't have happened without the awesome love and support of my family, including my extended family out in Pennsylvania, who offered to put me up and show me around as I was researching. Many thanks too to the numerous guides, hotel receptionists, waiters and waitresses, and museum curators who took time to share their info and views. A lovely part of the planet, and one I hope to visit again soon. Readers, you're in for a treat.

LOREN BELL

To all of my family and friends on the way who provided hot tips, cold beer, and warm support: thank you; your friendships make this all worthwhile. To Kari: I don't know how you put up with me during these projects, but your patience must be deeper than Grand Prismatic Spring – your beauty certainly is. Finally, to Hawkeye: I know you can't read, but having you by my side was the highlight of the trip. You're a good boy.

SARA BENSON

Thank you to editors Cliff Wilkinson and Alex Howard for guidance and long-distance support. A big thank you to Jonathan Hayes for driving thousands of miles with me through Gold Country, Wine Country, the Sierra Nevada and all around the Bay Area. PS Hi, Beth!

CELESTE BRASH

Thanks to my husband Josh and kids Jasmine and Tevai, to the Irwins in Spokane, Jackie Caplan-Auerbach and family in Bellingham, the Joneses in Olympia, the Pilot/Forsters in Port Angeles, Iain on Orcas, park rangers, tourist info people, random people met along the ways and so many more!

GREGOR CLARK

Thanks to all the generous New Englanders who helped with this project, especially Katherine Quinn, Sarah Pope and Margo Whitcomb. Love and special thanks to Gaen, Meigan and Chloe, for helping me explore this beautiful region and always sharing my excitement for the road less traveled.

ASHLEY HARRELL

Thanks to: editors Lauren and Trisha, and my co-authors for your support. Josie, Nora and Ashley Guttuso for having me at the fort. Tiffany Grandstaff for the upgrade. Alex Pickett for existing. Trevor, Malissa and Soraya Aaronson for being my surrogate family. Tom Francis for finally coming. Alanna Bjork for dog-sitting and the cozy shack. Beanie Guez for destroying me in shuffleboard and Elodie Guez for bringing wine (and glasses). Andy Lavender for showing up in Sarasota, and in general.

MARK JOHANSON

A big thanks to my parents for dragging me across America on road trips as a kid and inspiring me to appreciate different landscapes and cultures. Thanks to my partner Felipe for allowing me to spend so much time away from my current home in South America to explore the bowels of my native country. I'm grateful for the help, warm meals and inspiration along the way from JP Bumby, Jamie Thomas and all the welcoming Great Plains folks.

ADAM KARLIN

Thanks y'all: to Lauren Keith and Trisha Ping, editors extraordinaire; to my brother in arms on Southern road trips, Kevin Raub; to the parks workers and bartenders and baristas and service-industry folks who showed me how much there is to discover in my own backyard; to Mom and Dad, for their constant support; to Karen Shacham and Michelle Putnam (and Lior!), the best hosts Atlanta could provide; and Rachel and Sanda, both for joining me on the road and tolerating my absences.

BRIAN KLUEPFEL

Paula Zorrilla, my guiding light and co-pilot – I couldn't have done it without you. Trisha Ping, Greg Benchwick, Jane Grisman and Dianne Schallmeiner at LP for moral and technical support.Tom Kluepfel, honorary mayor of Hoboken and 'mutz' maven. Laura Collins, Rebecca Rozen and her dog Gizmo for Hamptons knowledge and good cheer. Stacey Borelli and Peggy Watson at Siemens for holding the fort. The Ocean Grove cop who didn't give me a ticket. June McPartland for selling me that car.

STEPHEN LIOY

Many thanks to many people, but specifically to these: Aileen for the thousand tips, Anthony for the co-pilot miles and company, Jess and Kevin for always being there, Kalli and Tonie for helping me enjoy inefficiency, Shane for tips and time and sometimes beer, Cindy/Payton/Pres for being so bad at Catan, Dav and Nan and UpChuck for the very many nights and meals and help, and Jack.

CAROLYN MCCARTHY

My many thanks go out to the Utah tourism office and friends Drew and Zinnia, Francisco Kjolseth and Meg and Dave. Thanks also to my co-writers, especially Chris Pitts. Utah worked its magic once more. It is a privilege to go back year after year.

HUGH MCNAUGHTAN

My sincere thanks to everyone who helped me through an epic research trip through Arizona – Tas and my girls, editor Alex, the ever-helpful support crew at LP, and the kind people of the Grand Canyon State. And Matt for the mescal.

BECKY OHLSEN

Becky thanks her dad for being the greatest research assistant thus far, all the various park rangers and campground officials who talked about the weather and gave reassurances about road conditions, Paul Bracke for over-the-top intel on Spokane, the previous authors of this content, and ace editor Alex Howard.

CHRISTOPHER PITTS

Thanks to the inordinately kind people of New Mexico, in particular Michael Benanav in Dixon, John Feins and Cynthia Delgado in Santa Fe, and all the rangers at the national parks – especially the guy who led the incredible Carlsbad Cave tour – keep up the great work! At the writing desk, thanks to co-authors Carolyn McCarthy, Benedict Walker and Hugh McNaughtan for suggestions and Alex Howard for keeping the whole project on track.

KEVIN RAUB

Thanks to my wife, Adriana Schmidt Raub, who shockingly sticks around despite my travels! Lauren Keith, Trisha Ping, MaSovaida Morgan and all my partners in crime at Lonely Planet. On the road: Jana Clauser, Kristi Amburgey, Susan Dallas, Dawn Przystal, Niki Heichelbech-Goldey, Erin Hilton, Courtney McKinney, Brian Mansfield, Alison Duke, Erin Donovan, Liz Beck, Eleanor Talley, Dodie Stephens, Sarah Lowery, Anne Fitten Glenn, Kaitlin Sheppard, Heather Darnell, Scott Peacock, Doug Warner, Halsey Perrin, Charlie Clark, Kim Jamieson and Jeff Hulett.

BRENDAN SAINSBURY

Thanks to all the untold bus drivers, chefs, hotel receptionists, tour guides, and innocent bystanders who helped me during this research. Special thanks to my wife Liz and son Kieran for their company on the road.

REGIS ST LOUIS

Countless people helped along the way, and I'm grateful to national park guides, lodging hosts, restaurant servers, barkeeps and baristas who shared tips and insight throughout South Florida. Big thanks also to Adam Karlin. I'd also like to thank Cassandra and our daughters, Magdalena and Genevieve, who made the Miami trip all the more worthwhile.

RYAN VER BERKMOES

Fond thanks to those many people who were so helpful in Texas two decades ago and again this time. And fond love to Alexis Ver Berkmoes, who is proof that as some things fade away, other things just get better.

MARA VORHEES

Thanks to friends and neighbors who have taught me so much about New England over the years. I am grateful to my faithful travel companions, Shay and Van: it's always more fun to travel – though more difficult to write – when you're along for the ride. And thank you, Jerz, for going along with the sunrise thing, all 19 times (and counting).

BENEDICT WALKER

A huge thank you to Alex Howard from LP for granting me this amazing opportunity and sticking by me until I got 'er done. I dedicate this update to Mr and Mrs Bruce and Cheryl Cowie, my self-adopted Canadian parents and the original high rollers of my world. Thanks to Mum for giving Nanna's prayer-chair a workout; to Kirk, Alex and friends for showing me their Vegas; to Justin and the burners in Reno; my birthday buddy Nicole in Carson City; and my favorite American, Brad, for speaking my language and keeping me sane. You all rock.

KARLA ZIMMERMAN
Deep appreciation to all of the locals who spilled the beans on their favorite places. Thanks most to Eric Markowitz, the world's best partner-for-life, who kindly indulges my Abe Lincoln fixation. You top my Best List.

ACKNOWLEDGEMENTS

Climate map data adapted from Peel MC, Finlayson BL & McMahon TA (2007) 'Updated World Map of the Köppen-Geiger Climate Classification', *Hydrology and Earth System Sciences*, 11, 163344.

Front cover photographs: (top) Barn in Grand Teton National Park, Christian Hütter/Alamy ©; (bottom left) Truck crossing covered bridge, New England, Radius Images/Alamy ©; (bottom right) Sign at Classical Gas Museum, Embudo, New Mexico, Mark Sykes/AWL ©

Back cover photograph: Bodega Bay, Bildagentur Zoonar GmbH/Shutterstock ©

INDEX

C

D

E

F

G

H

I

J

K

L

M

N

O

P

Q

R

S

T

U

V

W

Y

Z

BRENDAN SAINSBURY

Originally from Hampshire (the 'old' one in England), Brendan has been covering Seattle and the Pacific Northwest for Lonely Planet for over a decade. He is currently based in White Rock, BC, 45 minutes south of Vancouver and just 2km from the US border. Researching for this book, he enjoyed trying copious new beers, getting drunk on coffee and doughnuts, and taking his son (yet again!) to Seattle's legendary pinball museum.

REGIS ST LOUIS

Regis grew up in a small town in the American Midwest – the kind of place that fuels big dreams of travel – and he developed an early fascination with foreign dialects and world cultures. He spent his formative years learning Russian and a handful of Romance languages, which served him well on journeys across much of the globe. Regis has contributed to more than 50 Lonely Planet titles, covering destinations across six continents. Follow him on www.instagram.com/regisstlouis.

RYAN VER BERKMOES

Ryan has written more than 110 guidebooks for Lonely Planet. He grew up in Santa Cruz, California, which he left at age 17 for college in the Midwest, where he first discovered snow. All joy of this novelty soon wore off. Since then he has been traveling the world, both for pleasure and for work – which are often indistinguishable. Read more at ryanverberkmoes.com and at @ryanvb.

MARA VORHEES

Born and raised in St Clair Shores, Michigan, Mara traveled the world (if not the universe) before settling in the Hub. The pen-wielding traveler covers destinations as diverse as Belize and Russia, as well as her home of New England. She lives in a pink house in Somerville, Massachusetts with her husband, two kiddies and two kitties.

BENEDICT WALKER

Ben was born in Newcastle, Australia, and grew up in the 'burbs, spending weekends and long summers by the beach whenever possible. Japan was the first gig he got for Lonely Planet, in 2008, and he's been blessed to have been asked back often since then. He really is someone who is living his dreams, though life on the road can have its ups and downs. He's also written and directed a play, toured Australia managing the travel logistics for music festivals and is playing around with photography and film-making. Join him on his journeys on Instagram: @wordsandjourneys.

KARLA ZIMMERMAN

Karla lives in Chicago where she eat doughnuts, yells at the Cubs and writes stuff for books, magazines, and websites when she's not doing the first two things. She has contributed to 40-plus guidebooks and travel anthologies covering destinations in Europe, Asia, Africa, North America and the Caribbean – all of which are a long way from the early days, when she wrote about gravel for a construction magazine and got to trek to places like Fredonia, Kansas. To learn more, follow her on Instagram and Twitter (@karlazimmerman).

STEPHEN LIOY

Stephen is a photographer, writer, hiker, and travel blogger. A 'once in a lifetime' Euro trip and post-university move to China set the stage for what would eventually become a semi-nomadic lifestyle, based on sharing his experiences and helping provide that initial push out of comfort zones and into all that the planet has to offer. Follow Stephen's travels at www.monkboughtlunch.com or on Instagram, Twitter, Facebook, Pinterest, YouTube, or Google+ for regular photos and occasional witticisms.

CAROLYN MCCARTHY

Carolyn specializes in travel, culture and adventure in the Americas. She has written for *National Geographic*, *Outside*, *BBC Magazine*, *Boston Globe* and other publications. A former Fulbright fellow and Banff Mountain Grant recipient, she has documented life in the most remote corners of Latin America. Carolyn gained her expertise by researching guidebooks in diverse destinations. She has contributed to over 30 guidebooks for Lonely Planet. For more information, visit www.carolynmccarthy.org or follow her Instagram travels at @masmerquen.

HUGH MCNAUGHTAN

A former English lecturer, Hugh decided visa applications beat grant applications, and turned his love of travel into a full-time thing. Having also done a bit of restaurant reviewing in his home town (Melbourne, Australia), he's now eaten his way across Europe and North America, and found the best way to work up an appetite for the USA's great, gut-busting food is spending all day cycling through its stunning landscapes.

BECKY OHLSEN

Becky is a freelance writer, editor and critic based in Portland, Oregon. She writes guidebooks and travel stories about Scandinavia, Portland and elsewhere for Lonely Planet.

CHRISTOPHER PITTS

Chris's first expedition in life ended in failure when he tried to dig from Pennsylvania to China at the age of six. Hardened by reality but still infinitely curious about the other side of the world, he went on to study Chinese in university, living for several years in China and Taiwan. A chance encounter in an elevator led to a relocation to Paris, where he lived with his wife and two children for over a decade before the lure of Colorado's sunny skies and outdoor adventure proved too great to resist. His website is www.christopherpitts.net.

KEVIN RAUB

Atlanta native Kevin Raub started his career as a music journalist in New York, working for *Men's Journal* and *Rolling Stone* magazines. He ditched the rock 'n' roll lifestyle for travel writing and has written nearly 50 Lonely Planet guides, focused mainly on Brazil, Chile, Colombia, USA, India, the Caribbean and Portugal. Kevin also contributes to a variety of travel magazines in both the USA and UK. Follow him on Twitter and Instagram (@RaubOnTheRoad).

GREGOR CLARK

Gregor has been exploring New England's back roads since childhood, when he rode bikes through Cape Cod's dunes, skated on frozen ponds in northwestern Connecticut and saw his first shooting star in Vermont's Green Mountains. A lifelong polyglot with an insatiable curiosity for what lies around the next bend, Gregor has contributed to over three dozen Lonely Planet guides, with an emphasis on North America, Latin America and Europe. He lives with his wife and daughters in Middlebury, VT.

MICHAEL GROSBERG

Michael has worked on over 45 Lonely Planet guidebooks. Whether covering Myanmar or New Jersey, each project has added to his rich and complicated psyche and taken years from his (still?) relatively young life. Prior to his freelance writing career, other international work included development on the island of Rota in the western Pacific; South Africa, where he investigated and wrote about political violence and helped train newly elected government representatives; and Quito, Ecuador, as a teacher.

ASHLEY HARRELL

After a brief stint selling day spa coupons door-to-door in South Florida, Ashley decided she'd rather be a writer. She went to journalism grad school, convinced a newspaper to hire her, and started covering wildlife, crime and tourism, sometimes all in the same story. Fueling her zest for storytelling and the unknown, she traveled widely and moved often, from a tiny NYC apartment to a vast California ranch to a jungle cabin in Costa Rica, where she started writing for Lonely Planet.

MARK JOHANSON

Mark grew up in Virginia and has called five different countries home over the last decade. His travel-writing career began as something of a quarter-life crisis, and he's happily spent the past eight years circling the globe reporting for Australian travel magazines, British newspapers, American lifestyles and global media outlets. When not on the road, you'll find him gazing at the Andes from his home in Santiago, Chile. Follow the adventure at www.markjohanson.com.

ADAM KARLIN

Adam is a Lonely Planet author based out of wherever he happens to be. Born in Washington, DC and raised in the rural Maryland tidewater, he's been exploring the world and writing about it since he was 17. For him, it's a blessedly interesting way to live life. Also, it's good fun. He just read two good quotes, so with thanks to Italy, ancient and modern: '*Tutto il mondo e paese*' and '*Ambulare pro deus*'. If you ever meet Adam on the road, be sure to share a drink and a story.

BRIAN KLUEPFEL

Brian has worked for Lonely Planet across the Americas since 2006. He's been the editor of the *Bolivian Times* in La Paz, a correspondent for Major League Soccer, and a contributor to Frontier Airlines inflight magazine. His Lonely Planet adventures have taken him to Venezuela, Bolivia and even the pine barrens of New Jersey. His stories on Sleepy Hollow Cemetery and the mines of Potosi, Bolivia, feature in Lonely Planet's *Secret Marvels of the World*.

CAROLYN BAIN

Australian-born Carolyn worked a glorious season on Nantucket a decade or so back, and fell in love with Cape Cod at first sight. Sand dunes and salt spray, history and wholesomeness, cozy inns and seafood feasts: this was (and still is) the USA at its most charming. On this trip, Maine made an awesome adjunct, and she relished the chance to go beyond lighthouses and lobsters to uncover craft brews, moose trails and road-tripping nirvana.

AMY C BALFOUR

After a stint as a writer's assistant on *Law & Order*, Amy jumped into freelance writing, focusing on travel, food, and the outdoors. She has hiked, biked, and paddled across Southern California and the Southwest. She recently criss-crossed the Great Plains in search of the region's best burgers and barbecue. Her top picks for US adventure include the cables of Half Dome, the South Kaibab Trail to Phantom Ranch, the road to the Racetrack Playa in Death Valley, and the doorbell at LA's Museum of Jurassic Technology.

RAY BARTLETT

Ray is a travel writer specializing in Japan, Korea, Mexico and the United States. He has worked on numerous Lonely Planet titles, starting with *Japan* in 2004.

LOREN BELL

When Loren first backpacked through Europe, he was in the backpack. That memorable experience corrupted his six-month-old brain, ensuring he would never be happy sitting still. His penchant for peregrination has taken him from training dogsled teams in the Tetons to chasing gibbons in the jungles of Borneo – with only brief pauses for silly 'responsible' things like earning degrees. When he's not demystifying destinations for Lonely Planet, Loren writes about science and conservation news.

SARA BENSON

After graduating from college, Sara jumped on a plane to California with just one suitcase and $100 in her pocket. She has bounced around the Golden State ever since, including all over the San Francisco Bay Area, Los Angeles and the Sierra Nevada, where she worked as a seasonal national park ranger. Sara is the author of over 70 travel and nonfiction books.

CELESTE BRASH

The beauty of the Pacific Northwest coaxed Celeste back to the US after 15 years in Tahiti. For the last few years she's revelled in exploring her new back yard, its mountains, coasts, wineries and fantastic restaurants, while getting back in touch with her cowboy and Indian roots. Her award-winning writing has appeared in publications from BBC Travel to Afar and Islands Magazine and she's contributed to about 60 Lonely Planet titles.

OUR WRITERS

OUR STORY

A beat-up old car, a few dollars in the pocket and a sense of adventure. In 1972 that's all Tony and Maureen Wheeler needed for the trip of a lifetime – across Europe and Asia overland to Australia. It took several months, and at the end – broke but inspired – they sat at their kitchen table writing and stapling together their first travel guide, *Across Asia on the Cheap*. Within a week they'd sold 1500 copies. Lonely Planet was born.

Today, Lonely Planet has offices in Franklin, London, Melbourne, Oakland, Dublin, Beijing, and Delhi, with more than 600 staff and writers. We share Tony's belief that 'a great guidebook should do three things: inform, educate and amuse'.

SIMON RICHMOND

Journalist and photographer Simon Richmond has specialized as a travel writer since the early 1990s and first worked for Lonely Planet in 1999 on the *Central Asia* guide. He's long since stopped counting the number of guidebooks he's researched and written for the company, but countries covered include Australia, China, India, Iran, Japan, Korea, Malaysia, Mongolia, Myanmar (Burma), Russia, Singapore, South Africa and Turkey. For Lonely Planet's website he's penned features on topics from the world's best swimming pools to the joys of Urban Sketching. Follow him on Instagram to see some of his photos and sketches.

KATE ARMSTRONG

Kate has spent much of her adult life traveling and living around the world. A full-time freelance travel journalist, she has contributed to around 40 Lonely Planet guides and trade publications and is regularly published in Australian and worldwide publications. She is the author of several books and children's educational titles. You can read more about her on www.katearmstrongtravelwriter.com and @nomaditis.

 MORE WRITERS

Published by Lonely Planet Global Limited

CRN 554153

3rd edition – Mar 2018

ISBN 978 1 7865 735 99

© Lonely Planet 2018 Photographs © as indicated 2018

10 9 8 7 6 5 4 3 2 1

Printed in China

All rights reserved. No part of this publication may be copied, stored in a retrieval system, or transmitted in any form by any means, electronic, mechanical, recording or otherwise, except brief extracts for the purpose of review, and no part of this publication may be sold or hired, without the written permission of the publisher. Lonely Planet and the Lonely Planet logo are trademarks of Lonely Planet and are registered in the US Patent and Trademark Office and in other countries. Lonely Planet does not allow its name or logo to be appropriated by commercial establishments, such as retailers, restaurants or hotels. Please let us know of any misuses: lonelyplanet.com/ip.

Although the authors and Lonely Planet have taken all reasonable care in preparing this book, we make no warranty about the accuracy or completeness of its content and, to the maximum extent permitted, disclaim all liability arising from its use.